J. Rees

Singing with Understanding

SINGING

with

UNDERSTANDING

By

Edward E. White

B.A. (Hons.), M.Sc., Ph.D., Dip.Ed

A COMMENTARY ON EACH HYMN AND TUNE IN "CHURCH HYMNAL," THE OFFICIAL HYMN-BOOK OF THE SEVENTH-DAY ADVENTIST CHURCH.

"I will sing with the spirit,
and I will sing with the understanding also."
1 Corinthians 14: 15.

SIGNS PUBLISHING COMPANY
(Australasian Conference Association Limited, Proprietors)
Warburton, Victoria, Australia

Dedication

To

Joseph Harker

Of Reading, Berkshire, England

composer and choir conductor
organist and music editor
musician and poet
youth leader and gospel minister
Christian gentleman

who made earth happy with his
songs of heaven.

National Library of Australia card number and ISBN
0 949809 05 5

Introduction

MANY years ago the author of this book and I were associated in the compilation of "The New Advent Hymnal" in England, and I then became more intimately aware of his interest and competence in hymnology. During the intervening years I have known that Dr. White was making a historical study of our "Church Hymnal." To chronicle the origin and evolution of these 703 hymns into their present form was no small task, but the persistence and wide research of the author in England, Australia, the United States and elsewhere, have produced a book which is very rewarding.

The Scriptural Index and the biographical section will be of great assistance to ministers in co-ordinating worship in song with sermon topics, thus contributing to the impact of Biblical preaching. The author has exercised good judgment and restraint in avoiding the exaggerations and inaccuracies that surround certain hymn stories, but he has provided vital and interesting facts that will add to our interest in both the lyrics and poetry of our "Church Hymnal."

The story of these hymns is condensed with great skill, and the combination of conciseness and ample coverage will be unusually gratifying to busy preachers. It will also add immensely to the worshippers' intelligent enjoyment of hymn singing as a vital part of Christian worship.

Viewed in true perspective, this commentary gives us a reassurance of the guiding Spirit of God through Christian poets and musicians across the years. The same Spirit has surely guided in the preparation of these pages, and will henceforth direct in its perusal and use to the glory of God.

H. W. LOWE.

Preface

FOR a large majority of church worshippers, hymn-singing is but a filling of time or an introduction to the sermon, and unfortunately to a lesser number this exercise is an expendable item. Even to those who sing, the pleasure of making a joyful noise often detracts from the real meaning of the hymn, and this valuable act of worship thereby loses its full significance. Although in another context, the words of the Apostle Paul are most appropriate: "I will sing," he wrote, "with the spirit, and I will sing with the understanding also." 1 Corinthians 14: 15. It is with this purpose in mind that this commentary on the "Church Hymnal" has been compiled, namely that congregations singing hymns may sing with understanding, appreciating that they are entering into a most intimate form of worship. Not only is the repetition of words in song a most effective means of fixing them in the memory, but it must be admitted that "as a part of religious service, singing is as much an act of worship as is prayer."—*"Education,"* page 168.

Hymns vary in quality, some tunes are more worthy than others, some words are not great poetry, and it would indeed be strange to find one person by whom all 703 selections in "Church Hymnal" are considered good. However, the background of the writing of the words or the composing of the tune will make more interesting and therefore more singable a less worthy hynm. It is regretted that there still remain many anonymous hymns and tunes, and further information regarding these would be most gratefully received and incorporated in any future edition.

Thanks are due to the following individuals who have provided information, in many cases personal, concerning Seventh-day Adventist writers and composers, either by correspondence or by interview, namely: Mrs. A. W. Anderson, Dr. D. A. R. Aufranc, Miss L. Belden*, Mark Bovee, E. R. Colson, Roy F. Cottrell, Henry de Fluiter, L. E. Froom, Edgar Halstead, A. N. Harker, J. Harker, D. F. Haynes, S. Ledington, Ernest Lloyd, L. C. Metcalfe, Mrs. G. Barnes Miller, Professor* and Mrs. H. A. Miller, Mrs. R. Santee Parrett, F. O. Rathbun*, Mrs. H. Steinel Hare, Edgar Warren, A. L. White. We regret to state that in the interim those marked with an asterisk (*) have passed to their rest.

Thanks are also given to Mrs. Dorothy H. Jones of the Washington Cathedral Library for access to various special musical collections, to Mrs. Hedwig Jemison of Andrews University, Michigan, for making available sources in the vaults of Adventist early church history, to ministers who have encouraged me in the preparation of this book, and most of all to Mr. Ron Cable of Brisbane who has carefully, assiduously, and critically read every word of the manuscript and made many helpful suggestions.

In a work of this kind which contains many details it is difficult to avoid error, and no infallibility is claimed. Every effort has been made to be accurate, and it may be worth noting that sometimes dates of composition are not necessarily the dates of publication. Any error that is pointed out will be gladly corrected as soon as possible. "Singing with Understanding" is sent forth as a labour of love which, it is hoped, will bring new meaning and new purpose to those who sing, and which will lift those of downcast spirit to higher ground, where perchance they may catch the echoes from the heavenly choir around the throne of God.

Wahroonga, March, 1968.

Preface to the Second Edition

In this welcome reprint opportunity has been taken to correct several type-setting errors, but the prohibitive expense of resetting the whole book precludes the possibility of adding additional material.

Since 1967, when the original manuscript was sent to the printers, the following contributors to "Church Hymnal" have passed away, with the result that there are now no survivors listed in the indexes of authors and composers whose hymns and tunes found a place in this hymn-book of the church. Fortunately their words and music live on in the voices of those who delight to sing with understanding. Douglas Albert Raoul Aufranc (1892-1980), Ellis Richard Colson (1898-1967), Henry de Fluiter (1872-1970), LeRoy Edwin Froom (1890-1974), Edgar Halstead (1885-1969), Alfred Norman Knightly Harker (1879-1973), Joseph Harker (1880-1970), Donald Frederick Haynes (1907-1975), Pearl Waggoner Howard (1885-1969), Stanley Ledington (1889-1974), Lon Clyde Metcalfe (1880-1970)

Bracknell, Berks., May, 1981 Edward E. White.

Table of Contents

SINGING
with Understanding

1. BEFORE JEHOVAH'S AWFUL THRONE

Psalm 100

Isaac Watts (1674-1748), see appendix, broke away from the metrical version of the psalms, which adhered very strictly to the wording of the Old Testament, and consequently in many instances produced awkward, clumsy lines. He made paraphrases, skilfully using the main thought of the psalm and omitting local references that became inapplicable in Christian times. These words are his paraphrase of Psalm 100, and could profitably be compared with the metrical version of the same psalm given in hymn No. 13. His original first stanza was:—

> 1. Sing to the Lord with joyful voice;
> Let every land His name adore;
> The British Isles shall send the noise
> Across the ocean to the shore.

This patriotic stanza was omitted by John Wesley (1703-91), who also changed the first two lines of Watts's second stanza from:—

> Nations attend before His throne,
> With solemn fear, with sacred joy,

to the present opening lines of the hymn. The other omitted stanza is:—

> 4. We are His people, we His care,
> Our souls, and all our mortal frame:
> What lasting honours shall we rear,
> Almighty Maker, to Thy name?

The tune was composed by John Hatton (?-1793) who, like Watts, was a dissenter, and was first set to Addison's 19th psalm (see No. 91). Note the almost complete ascending octave with which the melody begins. It is named *Duke Street* after the street in St. Helens, Lancashire, where Hatton lived. The same tune is used also for No. 507, "O God, Beneath Thy Guiding Hand."

2. FROM ALL THAT DWELL BELOW THE SKIES

Psalm 117

The shortest chapter of the Bible, Psalm 117, contains only two verses: "O praise the Lord, all ye nations: praise Him, all ye people. For His merciful kindness is great toward us: and the truth of the Lord endureth for ever. Praise ye the Lord." It was paraphrased by Isaac Watts (1674-1748), see appendix, and appears in his "Psalms of David," 1719. The second line of his original reads "Redeemer's" where we have "Creator's," and the first stanzas alone are his. The third and fourth stanzas appeared in John Wesley's (1703-91) "Pocket Hymnbook," 1786.

The tune *Angels* is by Orlando Gibbons (1583-1625), who at the early age of twenty-one became organist of the Chapel Royal, and later of Westminster Abbey in 1623. He was a composer of church music, and the finest organist of his time. He composed music for the wedding of Charles I at Canterbury, but died suddenly while waiting to officiate at the service.

3. COME, THOU ALMIGHTY KING

Daniel 7: 22

These words are sometimes attributed to Charles Wesley (1707-88), see appendix, because the hymn appeared in 1757 with one by him on a tract published by George Whitefield. However, it is not claimed by him, nor does it appear in the older Methodist hymnals. The metre is unusual and identical with that of the English national anthem (No. 506). One of the many different titles used for the Godhead—Ancient of days—is taken from Daniel 7: 22, "Until the Ancient of days came." The omitted second stanza, which is an invitation to the Son, shows the real Trinitarian structure of the hymn:—

> 2. Come, Thou incarnate Word,
> Gird on Thy mighty sword,
> Our prayer attend;
> Come and Thy people bless,
> And give Thy word success;
> Spirit of holiness,
> On us descend.

This fits very appropriately between the stanza addressed to the Father and the one to the Holy Ghost. The first part of the last stanza has been altered from its original summary of the Trinity, which was:—

4. To the great One in Three,
Eternal praises be
Hence. evermore.
His sovereign majesty
. . .

The tune *Italian Hymn* is by Felice de Giardini (1716-96) of Turin, Italy, and is sometimes named *Moscow* after the city where he died. A violinist and composer for strings who spent thirty-six years of his life in England, he composed the tune in 1769 specially for these words at the request of the Countess of Huntingdon (see No. 190); hence the tune is also called *Hymn to the Trinity,* one of its many other names. In the sixth line the original retains the same note G for the three notes corresponding to the words "Come and reign." The same tune is also used for No. 452, "Christ for the World."

4. WITH REVERENCE LET THE SAINTS APPEAR

Psalm 89: 7-14

This hymn is a selection from Part II of the paraphrase of Psalm 89 by Isaac Watts (1764-1748), see appendix, and appears in his "Psalms of David," 1719. It consisted of six stanzas covering verses seven to fourteen, the omitted stanzas being:—

3. The northern pole and southern rest
On Thy supporting hand;
Darkness and day, from east to west,
Move round at Thy command.

4. Thy words the raging winds control,
And rule the boisterous deep;
Thou mak'st the sleeping billows roll,
The rolling billows sleep.

5. Heaven, earth, and air, and sea are Thine,
And the dark world of hell;
How did Thine arm in vengeance shine,
When Egypt durst rebel!

6. Justice and judgment are Thy throne,
Yet wondrous is Thy grace;
While truth and mercy, joined in one,
Invite us near Thy face.

Stanzas three and four of "Church Hymnal" are not found in Watts's paraphrase.

The tune *Harvey's Chant* is by William Batchelder Bradbury (1816-68), see appendix. Its frequent repetition of similar chords, five times in each of the first three lines, is virtually a chant written out in full, for a chant is essentially a series of chords each having several words or syllables corresponding to each chord. Similar examples are: Nos. 24 *Burton,* and 35 tune of "God Be with You."

5. GOD'S FREE MERCY STREAMETH

Ecclesiastes 11: 7

William Walsham How (1823-97), see appendix, wrote a special seasonal hymn entitled "Summer," beginning "Summer suns are glowing." This is the second stanza in "Church Hymnal," and has been transposed with the first stanza. The poem was based on Ecclesiastes 11: 7, "Truly the light is sweet, and a pleasant thing it is for the eyes to behold the sun." Notice the spiritual lesson in the words, which liken the sun's cheering rays to the rays of mercy and love and kindness of God, which in the same way reach every corner of earth, dispelling the clouds of doubt.

The tune *Ruth* was composed in 1865 by Samuel Smith (1821-1917), an organist at Windsor, England, and set to these words in 1874.

6. O WORSHIP THE LORD

1 Chronicles 16: 29

John Samuel Bewley Monsell (1811-75), one-time chaplain of the Chapel of Ease, Derby, and later vicar of Egham, Surrey, believed that hymns should not be dull and dreary, and that they were too often sung formally and without enthusiasm. The words of this hymn for Epiphany, the commemoration of the visit of the wise men to our Lord Jesus Christ, were written in the summer of 1861 under the title of "For the Fourth Sunday after Easter," and catch the happy spirit of the psalmist. The first line has an extra syllable, for it is an exact word-for-word rendering of Psalm 96: 9, but the parallel scripture, used by Monsell and lacking this "O," is found in 1 Chronicles 16: 29, "Worship the Lord in the beauty of holiness." In the hymn, the gifts of the wise men—gold, frankincense and myrrh—are shown to have their counterparts in the Christian's offering of "gold of obedience, and incense of lowliness" and "burden of carefulness," which last is also expressed as sorrows and represented by the bitter myrrh. Such gifts will be accepted as treasure indeed, just as precious as were the gifts of the magi in their worship of the Lord. There were five stanzas in the original, the fifth being a repetition of the first. Monsell also wrote No. 264, "To Thee, O Dear, Dear Saviour."

The tune *Southampton* was composed by Edwin Barnes (1864-1930), see appendix.

7. THE LORD IN ZION REIGNETH

Revelation 19: 6, 7

Most of the hymns of Fanny Crosby (1820-1915), see appendix, are very simple and very earnest, many being subjective, and most of them of the gospel-hymn type. The great hymnic authority Dr. J. Julian says that her poems are weak and poor, but have become popular because of the melodies associated with them. The strong words of this hymn, however, are very appropriate to the majestic title, and are based on the vivid description of the final triumphant chorus of myriads of voices at the adoration of the Lamb, recorded in Relevation 19: 6, 7. "Alleluia: for the Lord God omnipotent reigneth. Let us be glad and rejoice, and give honour to Him."

The tune was composed by Hart Pease Danks (1834-1903) of New Haven, Connecticut, later of Chicago. Although a carpenter, he showed a keen interest in music, and wrote over 1,000 songs appealing to popular taste. He also composed No. 558, *No Night There.*

8. WE GATHER TOGETHER

Hebrews 13: 6

This old Dutch song is reminiscent of the struggles between the Protestant Netherlands and the Catholic Spanish oppressors at the time of the supremacy of Philip II in Europe. At his death in 1598, the United Provinces of the northern section of the Netherlands continued their struggle for independence and gained a truce for eleven years. Although this did not recognize their independence, and an attempt at reconquest was renewed, the Dutch Republic became a sovereign state at that time under Maurice of Nassau. Religious warfare and divine guidance and deliverance are noted through all these stanzas, which enlarge upon Hebrews 13: 6, "The Lord is my helper, and I will not fear what man shall do unto me." The lines were first published in 1626 to celebrate the liberation of the Netherlands from Spain, and were later translated into English by Dr. Theodore Baker in 1917.

The tune *Kremser* is named after Eduard Kremser (1838-1914), a Viennese director of a singing society, who rediscovered the tune, originally written in 1625 by Adrianus Valerius (1575-1625) of Veere on the island of Walcheren. Valerius is noted as a compiler of tunes, and he wrote commentaries on their origin in "The Collections," published in Haarlem in 1621 and 1626.

9. PRAISE YE THE FATHER

Psalm 148: 1, 2, 12, 13

Elizabeth Rundle (1828-96) of Tavistock, Devonshire, was the daughter of a member of Parliament, and wife in 1851 of a London barrister, Andrew Paton Charles. She wrote books on the history of Christian life, and was the authoress of these three stanzas. They are written in rhythm not rhyme, one to the Father, one to the Son, and one to the Holy Ghost, choosing the characteristics mentioned in the Pauline benediction of 2 Corinthians 13: 14, namely, grace, love, and communion: the Father for His loving-kindness; the Saviour for His compassion, graciously; the Spirit, or Comforter, for His blessing. The last half of the third stanza sums up the preceding lines with an ascription of praise to the Trinity, the Three in One. Parts of the hymn use the words of Psalm 148: 1, 2, 12, 13, "Praise ye the Lord from the heavens. . . . Praise ye Him, all His angels. . . . Both young men, and maidens; old men, and children: let them praise the name of the Lord."

The tune *Flemming* was composed in 1811 for a male voice chorus by a German physician, Dr. Friedrich Ferdinand Flemming (1778-1813). The same tune is used for No. 55, and is called there *Integer Vitae,* and written in crotchets in 4/4 time instead of in quavers in 2/4 time as here.

10. PRAISE, O PRAISE OUR GOD AND KING

Psalm 136

John Milton (1608-74), while still a schoolboy of fifteen, wrote a metrical version of Psalm 136 in twenty-four stanzas each of two lines, beginning:—

> Let us with a gladsome mind
> Praise the Lord for He is kind

with the refrain,

> For His mercies aye endure
> Ever faithful, ever sure.

This psalm is the one in which each one of the twenty-six verses close with the words, "for His mercy endureth for ever." Sir Henry Williams Baker (1821-77), an Anglican clergyman, used Milton's version as the basis of this hymn, whose stanzas cover verses 2, 8, 9, and 25 of the psalm. Compare stanza two with Milton's:—

8. He the golden tresséd sun
Caused all day his course to run:

9. And the hornéd moon at night
Mid her spangled sisters bright.

Some of Milton's other couplets are:—

Praise Him that He gave the rain
To mature the swelling grain.

And hath bid the fruitful field
Crops of precious increase yield.

Glory to our bounteous King;
Glory let creation sing;

Glory to the Father, Son,
And blest Spirit, Three in One.

Baker, who edited "Hymns Ancient and Modern," also wrote No. 86, "The King of Love My Shepherd Is," and composed the melody of No. 341, *Stephanos*.

The tune *Monkland* was taken from "Hymn Tunes of the United Brethren," 1824, and arranged in 1861 by John Bernard Wilkes (1785-1869). He named it after the town of Monkland near Leominster, Herefordshire, where he was organist at the same time that Baker was vicar. The first line of the melody with its ascending arpeggio and scale passage gives the atmosphere of joy and lifting up of the spirit appropriate to the words.

11. THE LORD JEHOVAH REIGNS

Psalm 148: 5

This hymn was first thought to be a very free rendering by Isaac Watts (1674-1748), see appendix, of some verses of Psalm 148, orginally given in four stanzas of eight lines each. "Let them praise the name of the Lord: for He commanded, and they were created." Psalm 148: 5. A paraphrase is recognizable with some difficulty, but it is now reckoned an original hymn not related to any particular psalm. It is listed in Watts's collection as Hymn 169, "The Divine Perfections," based on the 148th Psalm, one of three on the same topic.

The tune *Millennium* possibly originated in England and was taken by early settlers to Kentucky and Tennessee. It appears in Henry Ward Beecher's "Plymouth Collection" of 1855, but is of much earlier date than that. Notice the descending scale passage in line 4, and the nearly complete ascending octave in line 6 of the melody.

12. PRAISE TO THE LORD

Psalm 103: 2-5

Joachim Neander (1650-80?)—the name is a Greek form of the German Neumann, or English Newman—was a great nature-lover, and took long walks in the valleys of the Dussel near Dusseldorf, leaving his name to one of them, Neanderthal, later made famous by discoveries there of fossil human bones. The German words of his hymn were written in 1680 while he was a serious-minded assistant preacher at St. Martin's, Bremen, and many translations have been made of them. The present one was made in 1863 by Miss Catherine Winkworth (1827-78), see appendix, and constitutes a very free paraphase of Psalm 103: 2-5 "Bless the Lord, O my soul: . . . who forgiveth all thine iniquities; who healeth all thy diseases; who redeemeth thy life from destruction; who crowneth thee with loving-kindness and tender mercies; who satisfieth thy mouth with good things." There are two other stanzas:—

3. Praise thou the Lord, who with marvellous wisdom hath made thee,
Decked thee with health and with loving hand guided and stayed thee.
How oft in grief
Hath not He brought thee relief,
Spreading His wings to o'er-shade thee.

4. Praise to the Lord! O let all that is in me adore Him!
All that hath life and breath, come now with praises before Him!
Let the Amen
Sound from His people again;
Gladly for aye we adore Him.

The tune probably came from an older melody appearing in 1665, and it was adapted and varied by Neander in 1680 for his words, which began in German *Lobe Den Herren*—Praise the Lord—and this title has since been attached to the tune. Harmony was added by the musical editors of the "Chorale Book for England," 1863, William Sterndale Bennett and Otto Goldschmidt.

13. ALL PEOPLE THAT ON EARTH DO DWELL

Psalm 100

This hymn is an old metrical version by William Kethe (c. 1510-c. 1594) of Psalm 100 as distinct from later paraphrase (see No. 1). Such versions keep very, very close to the original scriptures as will be noted by the following complete expressions taken from hymn and psalm:—

Hymn 13	Psalm 100
1. All people . . . on earth . . . to the Lord	Make a joyful noise unto the Lord, all the earth (margin) Verse 1.
Come ye before Him and rejoice.	come before His presence with singing. Verse 2.
2. The Lord ye know is God indeed;	know ye that the Lord He is God:
Without our aid He did us make;	it is He that hath made us, and not we ourselves;
We are His folk,	we are His people,
And for His sheep	the sheep of His pasture. Verse 3.
3. Enter . . . His gates with praise,	Enter into His gates . . . with praise
Approach . . . His courts	Into His courts
Bless His name	bless His name. Verse 4.
4. For . . . the Lord . . . is good,	For the Lord is good;
His mercy is for ever	His mercy is everlasting;
His truth . . . shall from age to age endure.	His truth endureth to all generations. Verse 5.

Kethe is thought to have been a native of Scotland, who became a Presbyterian minister, fleeing his country during the persecution of Queen Mary of England, and finding refuge with John Huss and John Knox at Geneva. He was one of the scholars who prepared the English translation of the Geneva Bible 1560, and he wrote this paraphrase in 1561.

The tune *Old Hundredth,* used also for No. 683, "Praise God, from Whom All Blessings Flow," has been associated with Psalm 100 for nearly four centuries, and is probably by Louis Bourgeois (1510-c. 1561). He was appointed by John Calvin in Geneva to provide musical settings for the metrical psalms. He added harmonies, to Calvin's disapproval, altered secular melodies, and adapted German psalm tunes, and his work resulted in a tremendous stimulation of congregational singing in Geneva. The earliest known version of the tune is in a Huguenot Psalter compiled by

Guillaume Franc of Rouen (died 1570), and published in Geneva in 1551, where it is set to Psalm 134. The prefix "Old" refers to the version of 1562 by Sternhold and Hopkins of metrical psalms, this particular tune being set, of course, to Psalm 100. The "New" version was by Tate and Brady in 1696.

14. PRAISE YE THE LORD

Psalm 147: 1-11

These words are a very close paraphrase by Isaac Watts (1674-1748), see appendix, of the first half of Psalm 147, and were published in 1719 under the title "The Divine Nature, Providence and Grace." There were eight stanzas originally, the three omitted being:—

2. The Lord builds up Jerusalem,
And gathers nations to His name;
His mercy melts the stubborn soul,
And makes the broken spirit whole.

4. Great is our Lord and great His might;
And all His glories infinite:
He crowns the meek, rewards the just,
And treads the wicked to the dust.

7. What is the creature's skill or force,
The sprightly man, the warlike horse,
The nimble wit, the active limb?
All are too mean delights for Him.

The tune *Rimington,* was published in 1904, although written many years earlier by Francis Duckworth (1862-1941), organist of the Methodist Church in Colne, Lancashire. It is named after the small Yorkshire village of Riming, Ribblesdale, near Blackburn, Lancashire, where he was born.

15. ALL GLORY, LAUD, AND HONOR

Matthew 21: 1-16

Theodulph (750-821), an Italian who became bishop of Orleans by 785, was imprisoned in 818 in the cloisters of the church in Angers by the Emperor Louis the Pious, because it was alleged that the bishop had taken part in a plot to depose him. While a prisoner he wrote this hymn (in Latin), describing the children waving palm branches and singing hosannas at our Lord's triumphal entry into Jerusalem. He sang his own hymn while the Palm Sunday procession, which included the Emperor, passed by his prison on the way into the church. Louis heard the voice chanting, ordered the procession to be stopped, and sent for the singer. One story says that Theodulph was pardoned on the spot and liberated, but other historians say that he died in prison three years later. Others cast doubt on the whole story in view of the fact that its first appearance is in the year 1516, but there is no doubt about the historicity of Theodulph and his imprisonment. Many translations from this Latin hymn have been made, this one by John Mason Neale (1818-66), see appendix. There are nine stanzas of four lines each, the first six being grouped in "Church Hymnal" as three eight-line stanzas. Those omitted are:—

7. Be Thou, O Lord, the rider
And we the little ass,
That to God's holy city
Together we may pass.

8. Receive, instead of palm-boughs,
Our victory o'er the foe,
That is the Conqueror's triumph
This strain may ever flow.

9. is a repetition of the first four lines of the hymn.

The scriptures on which the hymn is based are Matthew 21: 1-16 with parallel stories in Mark 11: 1-11 and Luke 19: 29-38.

The tune *St. Theodulph* was composed by the German Lutheran, Melchior Teschner (1584-1635), in 1613, for a funeral hymn by Valerius Herberger (1562-1627), a faithful pastor of his congregation in Poland during the great pestilence of 1613-30. It is a very bright tune, however, and more suitable as here set for words of praise, for the melody begins with a low note, middle C, and rises continually to top E, more than an octave higher.

16. PRAISE THE LORD, HIS GLORIES SHOW

Psalm 150

Henry Francis Lyte (1793-1847), Anglican vicar of Brixham, Devon, is best known as the author of "Abide With Me," but in this hymn, written in 1834 in his "Spirit of the Psalms," he has further shown his poetic gift in a paraphrase of the 150th Psalm. This psalm has six verses, each containing the word "praise" twice, with the exception of the first verse which has this word three times. Three of the verses named musical instruments, and Lyte has caught the spirit of elation of the psalmist with his words "in the concert bear your parts; all that breathe, your Lord adore." This unity of praise is the climax leading to the last triumphant Hallelujah, a word which is simply the Hebrew for "Praise ye Jehovah." Lyte also wrote Nos. 50, "Abide with Me"; 252, "My Spirit on Thy Care"; 267, "Jesus, I My Cross Have Taken"; 399, "There Is a Safe and Secret Place," and possibly 394, "Saviour, Like a Shepherd."

The tune *Thanksgiving* was published in 1862 by Dr. Walter Bond Gilbert (1829-1910) especially for the hymn "Come, Ye Thankful People, Come" (see No. 496), hence its name. Gilbert was an organist in Devonshire, in Kent, and in Lincolnshire, and later in New York, U.S.A. Another tune very suitable for these words is *Worgan* (No. 134) with the Hallelujahs, making it a four stanza hymn with sixteen Hallelujahs, an appropriate epitome of Psalm 150.

17. REJOICE, YE PURE IN HEART

Psalm 20: 5

These words were written by Edward Hayes Plumptre (1821-91) especially for the choir festival at Peterborough Cathedral in 1865, and they were first sung there to a tune by Dr. William Henry Monk (see Nos. 50, 196, 357). The theme is taken from Psalm 20: 5 "We will rejoice in Thy salvation, and in the name of our God we will set up our banners." The length of time occupied in a choir festival processional in a large cathedral demands a long hymn, and consequently there were originally eleven stanzas, those omitted being:—

3. Yes onward, onward still,
With hymn, and chant, and song,
Through gate and porch, and column'd aisle
The hallowed pathways throng.

5. Your clear Hosannas raise
And Alleluias loud;
Whilst answering echoes upward float
Like wreaths of incense cloud.

6. With voice, as full and strong
As ocean's surging praise,
Send forth the hymns our fathers loved,
The psalms of ancient days.

8. Still lift your standard high,
Still march in firm array,
As warriors through the darkness toil
Till dawns the golden day.

9. At last the march shall end,
The wearied ones shall rest,
The pilgrims find their Father's house,
Jerusalem the blest.

11. Praise Him who reigns on high,
The Lord whom we adore,
The Father, Son and Holy Ghost,
One God for evermore.

The complete text of the hymn shows that from the processional march for the choir festival, the author has drawn the likeness to the pilgrim's spiritual march to the New Jerusalem, singing all the way. Plumptre was a noted scholar and poet, and became dean of Wells Cathedral and bishop of Gloucester.

The tune *Marion* was composed in 1883 by Arthur Henry Messiter (1834-1916), and named for his mother Marion. It is unusual in that it undergoes several changes of key in a short hymn, those of C, D, and E, being easily recognizable, apart from its main key of G. major. Messiter was an organist and choirmaster who emigrated from Frome, Somerset, to the United States in 1859. From 1866 to 1898 he was organist and choirmaster at Trinity Church, New York City.

18. O FOR A HEART TO PRAISE MY GOD

Psalm 51: 10

Charles Wesley (1707-88), see appendix, wrote eight stanzas of this hymn in his "Hymns and Sacred Poems," 1742, under the title, "Create in Me a Clean Heart, O God; and Renew a Right Spirit Within Me," Psalm 51: 10. It is further summarized by its shorter title of "Holiness Desired." The omitted stanzas are:—

3. A humble, lowly, contrite heart,
Believing, true, and clean,
Which neither life nor death can part
From Him that dwells within.

5. Thy tender heart is still the same,
And melts at human woe:
Jesu, for Thee distress'd I am,
I want Thy love to know.

6. My heart Thou know'st can never rest.
Till Thou create my peace,
Till of mine Eden repossess'd,
From self and sin I cease.

7. Fruit of Thy gracious lips, on me
Bestow the peace unknown,
The hidden manna, and the tree
Of life, and the white stone.

The tune *Beatitudo* was composed in 1875 for Isaac Watts's hymn "How Bright These Glorious Spirits Shine," by John Bacchus Dykes (1823-76), see appendix. The name, meaning blessedness, is an apt description of the glories of the new earth depicted in that hymn. The same tune is used for No. 166, "Jesus, These Eyes Have Never Seen."

19. ANGEL VOICES EVER SINGING

Revelation 4: 8, 11

The Rev. Francis Pott (1832-1909), an Anglican rector of Northill, Bedfordshire, wrote this hymn in 1861 under the title, "For the Dedication of an Organ, or for a Meeting of Choirs." His friend, who was later to become Bishop Macrorie of Maritzburg, was then in charge of the Church of St. John the Evangelist in Wingate, Lancashire, and a new organ was to be dedicated, hence Pott's reference in the third stanza to "ears and hands and voices . . . craftsman's art and music's measure." There is one omitted stanza, which refers, as was often the custom, to the Trinity:—

5. Honour, glory, might, and merit
Thine shall ever be,
Father, Son, and Holy Spirit,
Blessed Trinity.
Of the best that Thou hast given
Earth and heaven
Render Thee.

The scripture basis suggested is Rev. 4: 8, 11, "They rest not day and night, saying . . . . Thou art worthy, O Lord, to receive glory and honour and power: for Thou hast created all things."

The tune *Angel Voices* was composed especially for this hymn in 1872 by Arthur Seymour Sullivan (1842-1900), see appendix, hence the name.

20. LORD OF ALL BEING, THRONED AFAR

1 Chronicles 29: 11

Oliver Wendell Holmes (1809-94), man of letters and professor of anatomy and physiology at Harvard, wrote this hymn in 1848 and published it as a Sunday hymn in the *Atlantic Monthly* of

1859. It occurs at the end of his essays on "The Professor at the Breakfast Table," and is preceded by the following introduction:—

> "Thanks to all those friends who from time to time have sent their messages of kindly recognition and fellow-feeling. Peace to all such as may have been vexed in spirit by any utterance the pages have repeated. They will doubtless forget for the moment the difference in the lines of truth we look at through our human prisms, and join in singing (inwardly) this hymn to the Source of the light we all need to lead us, and the warmth which can make us all brothers."

Holmes was a Unitarian, though his words are acceptable to any devout Christian desiring to render praise to God. While not based on any particular text of scripture, one giving a similar thought is found in 1 Chronicles 29: 11 "Thine, O Lord, is the greatness, and the power, and the glory, and the victory, and the majesty: for all that is in the heaven and in the earth is Thine; Thine is the kingdom, O Lord, and Thou art exalted as head above all." Holmes also wrote No. 144, "O Love Divine, That Stooped to Share."

The tune *Park Street* probably obtains its name from the Congregational Church in Park Street, Boston, which was an old Puritan meeting-house and a stronghold of orthodoxy. The tune is an arrangement of a composition in 1810 by Frederick Marco Antonio Venua (1788-1872), a member of the Royal Society of Musicians. It was introduced into the church in 1820 in a Hymnal compiled by the Handel and Haydn society of Boston. It is also used for No. 455, "Lord of the Sabbath."

21. MY GRACIOUS LORD, I OWN THY RIGHT

Philippians 1: 22

Philip Doddridge (1702-51), see appendix, wrote these words, which were published posthumously in 1755, under the title "Christ's Service, the Fruit of Our Labours on Earth," basing them on Philippians 1: 22 "But if I live in the flesh, this is the fruit of my labour." It is one of his didactic hymns contrasting the things of earth—pleasure, wealth, fame, and honour—with the lasting joy and delight of service for Christ. Some slight alterations have been made, for example in lines 3 and 4 of stanza four, which were originally as follows:—

> Nor could untainted Eden give
> Such bliss as blossoms at His side.

The last line of the hymn was originally a contrast with the lack of youthful vigour mentioned in the preceding lines, and read:—

> His love hath animating power.

The tune *Lebanon* was composed by Chester G. Allen (1812-77), a teacher of singing in New York, and a conductor of singing at conventions; he also composed No. 645, "Praise Him! Praise Him!"

22. FOR THE BEAUTY OF THE EARTH

Hebrews 13:15

This hymn was written by Folliott Sandford Pierpoint (1835-1917), especially for the communion service, and consisted of eight stanzas, but slight alterations, approved by him, give the words much wider use. They were inspired by a view from a hilltop of his native city of Bath, Somerset, in the year 1864. It was the time of late spring with violets and primroses in full bloom, and as he rested and meditated at the top of the hill, his thoughts were filled with the manifold gifts of God. The omitted stanzas are:—

2. For the beauty of each hour,
Of the day and of the night;
Hill and vale, and tree and flower,
Sun and moon, and stars of light;

3. For the joy of ear and eye,
For the heart and mind's delight,
For the mystic harmony
Linking sense to sound and sight,

5. For each perfect gift of Thine
To our race so freely given,
Graces human and divine,
Flowers of earth and buds of heaven,

6. For Thy Bride that evermore
Lifteth holy hands above,
Offering up on every shore
This pure sacrifice of love:

7. For Thy martyrs' crown of light,
For Thy prophets' eagle eye,
For Thy bold confessors' might,
For the lips of infancy:

8. For Thy virgins' robes of snow,
For Thy maiden mother mild,
For Thyself, with hearts aglow,
Jesu, Victim undefiled,
Offer we at Thine own shrine
Thyself, Sacrament Divine.

Each stanza, except the last, is followed by two additional lines, forming a kind of refrain, namely:—

Christ, our God, to Thee we raise
This our sacrifice of praise.

These words are a direct quotation from Hebrews 13: 15 "Let us offer the sacrifice of praise to God continually."

The tune *Dix* is so called because it was used for Dix's hymn "As with Gladness Men of Old" (No. 112). It was published in 1838 in a collection of hymns by Conrad Kocher (1786-1872), an organist and composer of Stuttgart, Germany, who did much to popularize four-part singing in the churches. The original tune had seven lines, now reduced to six by the omission of the fifth line.

23. LORD, WITH GLOWING HEART I'D PRAISE THEE

1 Peter 2: 9

Francis Scott Key (1779-1843) of Frederick County, Maryland, a member and strong supporter of the Episcopal Church, was a lawyer and Bible class teacher who is best remembered as the author of "The Star Spangled Banner." His hymn of four stanzas, written in 1817, is a song of thanksgiving for the joy of salvation, and appeared under the title, "Praise for Pardon and Peace," and recalls the text 1 Peter 2: 9, "Ye should show forth the praises of Him who hath called you out of darkness into His marvellous light." The omitted stanza is:—

3. Praise thy Saviour God that drew thee
To that cross, new life to give,
Held a blood-sealed pardon to thee,
Bade thee look to Him and live.
Praise the grace whose threats alarmed thee,
Roused thee from thy fatal ease,
Praise the grace whose promise warmed thee,
Praise the grace that whispered peace.

The tune *Preston* is by Harold Amadeus Miller (1891-1966), see appendix, and is named in memory of Elder B. M. Preston, a departmental secretary of the Southern Union of Seventh-day Adventists. In 1939 he was preaching at Southern Missionary College, Collegedale, Tennessee, and Miller was the pianist for the church service. Instead of opening a door and going down several steps to take his seat in the congregation, Miller went into the music studio and picked up an old copy of "Hymns and Tunes." He thumbed through this book looking for words for a new hymn, and came across No. 96 by Francis Scott Key. Immediately he began to compose, using the studio blackboard, and completed this tune by the time he had to return to the piano to acompany the closing hymn. The sermon is doubtless forgotten, but the tune remains as a memorial to the preacher.

24. HOW PLEASANT, HOW DIVINELY FAIR

Psalm 84: 1-7

This hymn is a paraphrase of certain verses of Psalm 84 under the title of "The Pleasure of Public Worship," made by Isaac Watts (1674-1748), see appendix, and appearing in his "Psalms of David," 1719. The ommitted stanzas, corresponding to verses 2 to 4 of the psalm are:—

2. My flesh would rest in Thine abode,
My panting heart cries out for God;
My God! my King! why should I be
So far from all my joys and Thee?

3. The sparrow chooses where to rest,
And for her young provides her nest;
But will my God to sparrows grant
That pleasure which His children want?

4. Bless'd are the saints who sit on high
Around Thy throne of majesty;
Thy brightest glories shine above,
And all their work is praise and love.

The tune *Burton* is by Isaac Baker Woodbury (1819-58), see appendix. The repetition of the same chord in each line gives the tune a chant-like character, as in Nos. 4, *Harvey's Chant,* and 35 the tune of "God Be With You."

25. AGAIN OUR EARTHLY CARES WE LEAVE

Psalm 122: 7

John Newton (1725-1807), see appendix, wrote a hymn under the title "On Opening a Place for Social Prayer," but Thomas Cotterill (1779-1823), an Anglican clergyman of Sheffield (see No. 195), rewrote this in 1810 in the present form, and entitled it "For the Blessing of God in Public Worship." Two only of Newton's original stanzas as in No. XLIII, Book II of the "Olney Hymns," 1779, remain virtually unchanged, namely, our present stanzas two and four. Those omitted are as follows:—

1. O Lord, our languid souls inspire,
For here we trust Thou art!
Send down a coal of heavenly fire,
To warm each waiting heart.

3. Show us some token of Thy love,
Our fainting hope to raise,
And pour Thy blessings from above,
That we may render praise.

4. Within these walls let holy peace,
And love and concord, dwell:
Here give the troubled conscience ease,
The wounded spirit heal.

6. May we in faith receive Thy word,
In faith present our prayers;
And in the presence of our Lord,
Unbosom all our cares!

7. And may the gospel's joyful sound,
Enforced by mighty grace,
Awaken many sinners round,
To come and fill the place!

An appropriate text summarizing the hymn is Psalm 122: 7, "Peace be within thy walls, and prosperity within thy palaces."

The tune *Manoah* is an arrangement by Henry Wellington Greatorex (1813-58) in his "Church Music," 1851, but the name—the father of Samson—has no special significance. It is also used for one of Cowper's hymns in No. 383, "O, for a Closer Walk!" Greatorex also composed Nos. 174, *Leighton,* 689, *Gloria Patri,* and arranged Nos. 48 and 318, *Seymour.* He was born in Burton-on-Trent, Derbyshire, and emigrated to the United States in 1838, to become organist at the Centre Congregational Church, Hartford, Connecticut. Then he served in New York as organist in the Protestant Episcopal churches.

26. AGAIN WE MEET

Luke 15: 11-24

These words were written in 1824, by Lady Lucy Elizabeth Georgiana Whitmore (1792-1840), daughter of the Earl of Bradford. They appeared with thirteen of her other hymns in her "Family Prayers for Every Day in the Week," and are based on one of the parables of Luke 15, which describes the Father's loving and merciful reception of the returning penitent, prodigal son: "I have sinned against heaven, and in thy sight, and am no more worthy to be called thy son." Luke 15: 21.

The tune *Pax Dei* (= peace of God) was composed in 1868 by John Bacchus Dykes (1823-76), see appendix, for another hymn, namely, Ellerton's one for closing of worship (No. 34), and is so named because this hymn mentions the peace of God four times in three stanzas. Dykes submitted his tune to his children first for approval, and they considered it one of his best compositions.

27. BLESSED JESUS, AT THY WORD

Psalm 119: 18

In Germany in the 17th century it was customary for the congregation to sing a "sermon-hymn," part immediately before the sermon, and part just after the sermon had ended. Tobias Clausnitzer (1619-84), a German Lutheran pastor, published these words in 1663 for use as a hymn of this type. Hence the direct statement in the first two lines and throughout the hymn of the desire of the congregation to hear the Word of God, thus making it very appropriate to sing preceding a sermon. Such expressions as "we are gathered all to hear Thee," "By Thy teachings sweet and holy," "Open Thou our ears and heart," reflect the main purpose of the hymn: "Open Thou mine eyes, that I may behold wondrous things out of Thy law." Psalm 119: 18. The translation is one of many from German hymnody by Catherine Winkworth (1827-78), see appendix, and it adheres to the original metre.

The tune *Liebster Jesu* (= dearest Jesus) was published in 1664 by Johann Rudolph Ahle (1625-73) of Mulhausen, Thuringia; but for the words of another hymn. He was an accomplished organist who copied the Italian school of rhythm and ornate melody in an attempt to break away from the dull and stodgy German church music. His so-called sacred arias, however, were subjected to much criticism and were considered as introducing too lively a secular influence into sacred singing. Another of Ahle's tunes is No. 68, *Nuremberg* which is a variant of *Liebster Jesu,* written in a different key and metre, transposed a tone higher, and with lines 3 and 4, which repeat lines 1 and 2, omitted.

28. BLEST HOUR WHEN MORTAL MAN RETIRES

Genesis 28: 17

This hymn by Thomas Raffles (1788-1863), a Congregational minister, was written in 1823 under the title "The Hour of Prayer." While three of the stanzas are suitable for any time of worship, the closing line of the second stanza "the holy day of rest," marks it as a Sabbath hymn. The true worshipper will echo Jacob's experience when he said, "This is none other but the house of God, and this is the gate of heaven." Genesis 28: 17. Raffles ministered first in London, but then was for forty-nine years the pastor of the Great George Street chapel in Liverpool, during which time he wrote a hymn for each New Year's day.

The tune *Rogers* was composed in 1939 by Harold Amadeus Miller (1891-1966), see appendix, and commemorates some students of this name who learned music from this well-known Seventh-day Adventist musician.

29. WE WOULD SEE JESUS

John 12: 21

Anna Bartlett Warner (1820-1915), a Sunday school teacher at West Point, New York, wrote seven stanzas of this hymn in 1852, and they appeared in her novel, *"Dollars and Cents,"* under her pen-name of Amy Lothrop. She based her poem on the incident of the Greeks who had come to the temple at Jerusalem to worship, and who, after our Lord's triumphal entry, came to Philip with the request, "Sir, we would see Jesus." John 12: 21. The omitted stanzas are:—

2. We would see Jesus: for life's hand hath rested,
With its dark touch, upon both heart and brow;
And though our souls have many a billow breasted,
Others are rising in the distance now.

4. We would see Jesus: yet the spirit lingers
Round the dear objects it has loved so long,
And earth from earth can scarce unclasp its fingers;
Our love to Thee makes not this love less strong.

5. We would see Jesus: sense is all too blinding:
And heaven appears too dim, too far away:
We would see Thee, Thyself our hearts reminding
What Thou hast suffered our great debt to pay.

Miss Warner also wrote the popular children's hymn, "Jesus Loves Me! This I Know," and No. 622, "One More Day's Work for Jesus."

The tune is by Franklin Edson Belden (1858-1945), see appendix.

30. LORD, WE COME BEFORE THEE NOW

Psalm 73: 28

These earnest words entitled "A Hymn to be Sung at Public Worship," were written by a Calvinistic Methodist and later Moravian minister, William Hammond (1719-83), being one of his "Psalms, Hymns and Spiritual Songs" which were published in 1745. Though an eminently learned man (he wrote his autobiography in Greek), he here expresses his simple Christian faith in God much as did the psalmist: 'But it is good for me to draw near to God." Psalm 73: 28. The hymn, consisting of eight stanzas each of eight lines, was abridged by Martin Madan in 1760. Some of the original lines are:—

1. . . .
In Thy temple, lo, we wait,
Knocking at Thy mercy's gate;
Now let all Thy chosen race
See with joy Thy blessed face.

2. Oh! that we might lift our eyes,
Oh! that our poor hearts would rise
To the throne of grace above,
And enjoy the sweets of love.
. . .

4. In Thine own appointed way
Now we seek Thee; here we stay;
Lord, we know not how to go
Till a blessing Thou bestow.
. . .

7. Son of man, in this Thy day
Thine abundant grace, display;
Preach the acceptable year,
Bring the gospel tidings near;
Sin and Satan, Lord, dethrone,
Rule and reign in us alone;
Save us all from sin and wrath
Make us heirs of God through faith.

8. Stablish, Lord, our hearts with grace,
Give us an abiding peace;
Then though floods around us flow,
Though winds from all quarters blow,
Built upon Thyself the rock,
We endure the mighty shock;
We are over and above
Conqu'rors through Thy matchless love.

The tune *Hendon* was composed in 1827 by Henri Abraham Cesar Malan (1787-1864), a brilliant preacher of Geneva, and its name is a reminder that he spent some time in England, for Hendon is a suburb of London. It is also used for Nos. 192, "Hark! That Shout," and 273, "Take My Life, and Let It Be." Malan also composed No. 408, *Rosefield.*

31. ETERNAL FATHER, GOD OF LOVE

Psalm 141:3

Both words and music were written in 1886 by Franklin Edson Belden (1858-1945), see appendix. The prayer, one very suitable for a closing hymn, asks that the words that we hear in divine service may find some fruit in our daily lives, and that we have a constant sense of the abiding presence of God. "Set a watch, O Lord, before my mouth; keep the door of my lips." Psalm 141: 3.

The name of the tune *Mason* commemorates Lowell Mason, the American composer, see appendix.

32. LORD, AT THIS CLOSING HOUR

Isaiah 27: 12

Eleazar Thompson Fitch (1791-1871), professor of divinity at Yale, wrote these words under the title of "Close of Divine Service." Four Christian virtues are mentioned—peace, love, faith, and patience—all designed to be exemplified in the kingdom of grace in anticipation of the kingdom of glory. A fitting scripture reference is Isaiah 27: 12, "Lord, Thou wilt ordain peace for us: for Thou also hast wrought all our works in us."

The tune *Nares* commemorates the composer James Nares (1715-83), Mus. Doc., who was organist at St. George's Chapel, Windsor, and later at York Minster; returning in 1756 to the Chapel Royal, London, where he had been a chorister years before. He published treatises on singing and on the playing of the organ and the harpsichord, and also composed No. 668, *Amsterdam.* The bass part of *Nares* moves more than is usual in a hymn tune, and carries an interesting tune in its last two lines.

33. LORD, DISMISS US WITH THY BLESSING

Numbers 6: 24-26

John Fawcett (1740-1817), one of Whitefield's converts, who later became a Baptist minister, is credited with this hymn of parting. Although it is not included in his published works, the editors of the "York Collections" of 1786 and 1791 attribute the hymn to him. It was written in 1773 in three stanzas, the omitted one being:—

3. So whene'er the signal's given
Us from earth to call away,
Borne on angels' wings to heaven,
Glad the summons to obey,
May we ever
Reign with Christ in endless day.

The parallel is drawn between the conclusion of a meeting and the conclusion of our earthly life, each being blessed by the presence of the Lord. The hymn recalls the blessing to be used by the high priest Aaron, "The Lord bless thee, and keep thee: . . . and give thee peace." Numbers 6: 24-26. Fawcett also wrote No. 432, "Blest Be the Tie That Binds."

The tune *Sicilian Mariners* is unknown today in Sicily, but does resemble some folk-tunes of the south of France.

34. SAVIOUR, AGAIN TO THY DEAR NAME

Psalm 29: 11

These words are a Sunday hymn written by John Ellerton (1826-93), then vicar of Crewe Green, specially for the festival of the Nantwich choral association (see also No. 58). They were written in 1866 in six stanzas on the back of his previous Sunday sermon notes in a metre to fit James Langran's tune *St. Agnes* (or *Langran,* No. 289). The thought of peace dominates the whole hymn and is mentioned four times in the three stanzas, as well as seven times in three omitted stanzas as follow:—

2. Grant us Thy peace, Lord, through the coming night,
Turn Thou for us its darkness into light;
From harm and danger keep Thy children free,
For dark and light are both alike to Thee.

4. Grant us Thy peace—the peace Thou didst bestow
On Thine apostles in Thine hour of woe;
The peace Thou broughtest, when at eventide
They saw Thy piercéd hands, Thy wounded side.

6. Thy peace in life, the balm of every pain,
Thy peace in death, the hope to rise again;
In that dread hour speak Thou the soul's release,
And call it, Lord, to Thine eternal peace.

The hymn was revised in 1868 to a four-stanza one, the final stanza being:—

Grant us Thy peace throughout our earthly life;
Peace to Thy church from error and from strife;
Peace to our land, the fruit of truth and love,
Peace in our heart, Thy Spirit from above.

The whole hymn enlarges upon the text: "The Lord will bless His people with peace." Psalm 29: 11. Ellerton also wrote Nos. 37, "The Lord Be with Us"; 57, "The Day Thou Gavest"; 58, "Our Day of Praise Is Done"; 461, "This Is the Day of Rest," and had a part in No. 78, "God the Omnipotent."

The tune *Ellers* is by Edward John Hopkins (1818-1901) and was composed specially for these words, its name being coined from the first part of the author's name, Ellerton. It is noteworthy that the words of the first stanza speak of raising a song in the first half and then of kneeling in the last line, this rise and fall being closely followed by a rise and fall in the melody. Hopkins was organist in the Temple Church, London, for fifty-five years, devoting his life to the improvement of church music. In 1882 he received the Mus. D. Lambeth from the archbishop of Canterbury. Of his many other hymn tunes we have Nos. 61, *Pascal,* and 229, *St. Athanasius.*

35. GOD BE WITH YOU

2 Corinthians 13: 11

Jeremiah Eames Rankin (1828-1904), was pastor of the First Congregational Church at 10th and G streets in Washington, D.C. In his congregation were several government officials who were changed to other positions, and consequently many good-byes had to be said. Rankin wrote the first stanza in 1880 as a etymological composition on the word "good-bye" which is an abbreviation of the blessing, "God be with you." The Apostle Paul uses a similar parting greeting to close his epistles; for example: "The God of love and peace shall be with you." 2 Corinthians 13: 11. In order to obtain a suitable tune, the poem was sent to two friends, one a well-known composer, and the other, William Gould Tomer (1833-96), a schoolmaster and amateur musician. The latter's tune was preferred, and stimulated Rankin to write more stanzas. The tune, later revised by the organist of the church, Dr. John W. Bischoff (1849-1909), was, in Rankin's opinion, the main reason for the popularity of the hymn. It is written somewhat in the form of a chant, the same chord being used for several successive syllables, as in Nos. 4, *Harvey's Chant,* and 24, *Burton.* Bischoff, who was blind, was choir director of the church for thirty-five years, and composed the unnamed tune for No. 577, "The Lord is My Light."

36. THY VOICE HATH SPOKEN

John 16: 8

Mary Hamlin Maxwell (1814-53), an American hymn-writer, here gives a brief summary of the steps leading a sinner to become a saint. In the first stanza she writes of conviction: "He will reprove [margin, convince] the world of sin, and of righteousness," John 16: 8; in stanza two, of the next step, repentance from sin, even those sins unknown to our fellows: "Cleanse Thou me from secret faults," Psalm 19: 12; then in stanza three, of salvation from the power that brings men "into captivity to the law of sin." Romans 7: 23. The fourth stanza tells of complete forgiveness, likening the life of sin to the experience of the Gadarene demoniac, who was "often bound with fetters and chains." Mark 5: 4. The last stanza sings of the victory which God gives, and draws from Matthew, chapter 8, which is the parallel story of the demoniac. In this chapter, in verses 3 and 23-27, we find the Lord's strong "I will," and the account of the stilling of the storm, which was symbolic of His power over the waves of doubt and sorrow. The final thought closely paraphrases Acts 1: 8, "Ye shall be witnesses unto Me," and Isaiah 26: 3, "Thou wilt keep him in perfect peace." The hymn is placed in the section for "closing of worship," but can well be used on other occasions.

The tune *Pembroke* was composed in 1842 by John Foster (1807-85), a self-taught musician who was organist of the Bristol Tabernacle, England. He was musical editor of the Rev. John Waite's "The Hallelujah, or Devotional Psalmody," and contributed this tune, knowing the editor's desire for tunes that congregations could not only sing, but for tunes that could be sung in parts. It will be noticed that each one of the four parts of this tune is interesting, the bass part particularly showing movement, and avoiding the monotonous repetitions of dohs and sohs with occasional fahs, which dominate many gospel songs. *Pembroke* is also used for No. 148, "O Love Divine, How Sweet Thou Art."

37. THE LORD BE WITH US

Ruth 2: 4

A friend requested the Rev. John Ellerton (1826-93) in 1870 to write a hymn suitable for the close of an afternoon service when an evening hymn would be inappropriate. This beautiful Sunday afternoon prayer requesting the Lord to be present in His house, on the way to the worshipper's home, and with him in the home continually, was the result. The omitted stanza is:—

4. The Lord be with us through the hours
Of slumber calm and deep;
Protect our homes, renew our powers,
And guard His people's sleep.

The thought throughout the hymn is reminiscent of the old Jewish greeting used by Boaz: "The Lord be with you." Ruth 2:4. Ellerton also wrote Nos. 34, "Saviour, Again to Thy Dear Name"; 57, "The Day Thou Gavest"; 58, "Our Day of Praise Is Done"; 461, "This Is the Day of Rest," and had a part in No. 78, "God the Omnipotent."

The tune *Sawley* was composed in 1857 by James Walch (1837-1901), a Bolton organist, and commemorates the Lancashire town near his birthplace. The Amen added is a reminder that the hymn throughout is a communal prayer. Walch also composed Nos. 449, *Tidings,* and 467, *St. George's, Bolton.*

38. GOD BLESS AND KEEP THEE

Genesis 31:49

Henry de Fluiter, born in Holland on August 29, 1872, is a Seventh-day Adventist retired minister who served as a singing evangelist in the United States for forty-six years. He composed many songs while meditating in the night season, this one both words and music, as a result of thinking over Jacob's experience when he made a covenant of friendship with his father-in-law Laban. He was trying to find a hymn for closing of worship, which would include the idea of the fellowship of God's people and His presence with each one as they separated after meeting together. The basis of the words is Genesis 31:49, "And Mizpah; for he said, The Lord watch between me and thee, when we are absent one from another." Henry de Fluiter died in 1970.

Mizpah, meaning watch-tower, is therefore a fitting name for the tune, this Hebrew word being used twice in the first stanza. The metre is given as 9.9.12.10, but there is an additional rhyme immediately evident in the last half of the hymn, so the tune would be better classified as 9.9.6.6.6.4., the concluding four-syllable line rhyming with the first two lines. Another hymn and tune by the same composer is No. 543, "Tell It to Every Kindred and Nation," to *Hail Him the King of Glory.*

39. LORD, IN THE MORNING

Psalm 5

This paraphrase of the fifth Psalm by Isaac Watts (1674-1748), see appendix, was entitled "For the Lord's Day, Morning," and appeared in his "Psalms of David," 1719. It consisted of eight stanzas, those omitted being:—

3. Thou art a God, before whose sight
The wicked shall not stand;
Sinners shall ne'er be Thy delight,
Nor dwell at Thy right hand.

4. But to Thy house will I resort,
To taste Thy mercies there;
I will frequent Thy holy court,
And worship in Thy fear.

6. My watchful enemies combine
To tempt my feet astray;
They flatter with a base design
To make my soul their prey.

7. Lord, crush the serpent in the dust,
And all his plots destroy;
While those that in Thy mercy trust,
For ever shout for joy.

The tune *Mear* is probably by the music engraver Aaron Williams (1731-76), of Welsh descent and a member of the Scots Church in London, and editor of "Williams's Psalmody," 1770. *Mear* does appear in an early New England collection of hymn-tunes appended to a copy of an edition of Tate and Brady's New Version published in Boston in 1757. It is certainly a shortened form of the tune *Holborn* which first appeared in 1763, in Williams's "The Universal Psalmist." For congregational singing the minims at the end of the second line are better extended by three whole beats or one complete bar of music. Another Watts-Williams combination is No. 442, "How Beauteous Are Their Feet," to *St. Thomas*.

40. SWEETLY THE HOLY HYMN

Psalm 5: 3

This is probably the most well-known of the score of hymns written by the famous Baptist preacher, Charles Haddon Spurgeon (1854-92). It was written in 1866 under the title "Early Morning Prayer Meeting," and throughout emphasizes the importance of prayer at the outset of the day. It is based on Psalm 5: 3, "My voice shalt thou hear in the morning." The omitted stanza is:—

4. Ere yet our vessel sails
Upon the stream of day,
We plead, O Lord, for heavenly gales
To speed us on our way.

The tune *Greenwood,* also used for No. 315, "Still with Thee," was composed in 1849 by Joseph Emerson Sweetzer (1825-73), an organist who emigrated from England to the United States. He joined George Frederick Root (see No. 93) in publishing a collection of church music in 1849, from which this tune is taken.

41. O CHRIST, WITH EACH RETURNING MORN

Hebrews 1:3

These words are a translation made in 1837 for his "Hymns of the Primitive Church" by John Chandler (1806-76), vicar of Witley, Surrey, an Anglo-Catholic and translator of several hymns from the French and Latin. The original Latin hymn was written by St. Ambrose (340-97), the bishop of Milan, who had been formerly a lawyer, and who was a stout defender of the doctrine of the Trinity. The hymn was dedicated to Christ the Light of the world, and was entitled "Splendor paternae gloriae" (= brightness of the Father's glory), an obvious reference to the description of the Son of God in Hebrews 1: 3, "Who being the brightness of His glory." It is a prayer for Christ's guidance throughout the day, as expressed in stanza 2 from "morning ray" through "noontide light" until "calm sunset." There were eight stanzas, our selection being Nos. 8, 7, and 5, and the omitted ones being:—

1. O Jesu, Lord of heavenly grace,
Thou brightness of Thy Father's face,
Thou fountain of eternal light,
Whose beams disperse the shades of night!

2. Come, holy Son of heavenly love,
Shower down Thy radiance from above;
And to our inward hearts convey
The Holy Spirit's cloudless ray.

3. And we the Father's help will claim,
And sing the Father's glorious name;
His powerful succour we implore,
That we may stand, to fall no more.

4. May He our actions deign to bless,
And loose the bonds of wickedness;
From sudden falls our feet defend,
And bring us to a prosperous end.

6. And Christ shall be our daily food,
Our daily drink His precious blood;
And thus, the Spirit's calm excess
Shall fill our souls with holiness.

The tune *Zephyr,* also used for No. 253, "The Tempter to My Soul," was composed in 1844 by William Batchelder Bradbury (1816-68), see appendix.

42. NEW EVERY MORNING

Lamentations 3: 22, 23

The first stanza in "Church Hymnal" is number six of a sixteen-stanza poem written in 1822 by John Keble (1792-1866), beginning "Hues of the rich unfolding morn." In many hymnals it begins with the fifth stanza, namely:—

5. O timely happy, timely wise,
Hearts that with rising morn arise,
Eyes that the beam celestial view
Which evermore makes all things new.

Our selection is stanzas 6, 7, 8, 14, 16, some of the others being:—

13. We need not bid, for cloister'd cell,
Our neighbour and our work farewell,
Nor strive to wind ourselves too high
For sinful man beneath the sky:

15. Seek we no more; content with these,
Let present rapture, comfort, ease,
As heaven shall bid them, come and go:
The secret this of rest below.

The poem was published in 1827 as the opening one in Keble's phenomenally successful "Christian Year," which contained thoughts in verse for the Sundays and Holy Days throughout the year. The Scriptural basis is Lamentations 3: 22, 23, "It is of the Lord's mercies that we are not consumed, because His compassions fail not. They are new every morning: great is Thy faithfulness." Keble, commemorated by Keble College, Oxford, also wrote Nos. 92, "There Is a Book," and 321, "Sun of My Soul."

The tune *Melcombe* was composed in 1782 by Samuel Webbe (1740-1816) of London, a Roman Catholic organist and composer. It has a flowing melody which progresses in short intervals generally speaking between successive notes, thus being easy to sing. It also has a bass part which is by no means stationary, but of interest in itself. The name is perhaps taken from Melcombe Regis, the northern part of Weymouth, Dorset, which was made famous by the frequent visits of King George III. *Melcombe* is used also for No. 312, "Weeping Endures But for a Night." Webbe also composed No. 223, *Consolation* and probably No. 87, *Dulce Carmen.*

43. WHEN MORNING GILDS THE SKIES

Psalm 150: 6

From a hymn in a German collection published in 1828 in fourteen stanzas each of four lines, the Rev. Edward Caswell (1814-78) translated six stanzas in 1854 and then added eight more by another four years' time. Some of the omitted stanzas, each separated into couplets as are the others by the words "May Jesus Christ be praised!" are:—

When sleep her balm denies,
My silent spirit sighs,
When evil thoughts molest,
With this I shield my breast,

Does sadness fill my mind,
A solace here I find,
Or fades my earthly bliss,
My comfort still is this,

When you begin the day,
O never fail to say;
And at your work rejoice
To sing with heart and voice,

Be this at meals your grace,
In every time and place;
Be this, when day is past,
Of all your thoughts the last,

My tongue shall never tire
Of chanting with the choir:
This song of sacred joy,
It never seems to cloy,

To God, the Word, on high,
The hosts of angels cry,
Let mortals too upraise
Their voice in hymns of praise:

The hymn re-echoes at length the last verse of the Psalms: "Let every thing that hath breath praise the Lord. Praise ye the Lord." Psalm 150: 6. Caswall was a well-known translator of Latin hymns, e.g., No. 158, "Jesus, the Very Thought of Thee." He seceded from the Anglicans to the Roman Catholics in 1847, and wrote this hymn while at the Oratory, Edgbaston, Birmingham.

The tune *Laudes Domini* (= praises of the Lord) was composed by Sir Joseph Barnby (1838-96), see appendix, especially for these words, though he himself did not give names to any of the tunes he composed. The upward lift in this bright melody is very fitting with the joyous, exultant words.

44. AWAKE, MY SOUL

Psalm 143: 8

Thomas Ken (1637-1711) was born at Berkhamsted, Hertfordshire, and educated at Winchester and Oxford, where he wrote hymns for his own use. He was exceptionally honest and was not afraid to rebuke King Charles II for his immoral habits. In spite of his frankness, he was appointed Bishop of Bath and Wells in 1685, but was later deposed for refusing to read the Declaration of Indulgence. Bishop Ken was noted for his early rising, and he had hymns hung on the walls of the dormitory at Winchester. He wrote, "A Manual of Prayers for the Use of the Scholars of Winchester College" in 1674, and added hymns to the 1695 edition. Three hymns were specifically for morning, for evening, and for midnight, and were accompanied by the admonition to remember the psalmist's injunction, "Cause me to hear Thy lovingkindness in the morning; for in Thee do I trust: cause me to know the way wherein I should walk; for I lift up my soul unto Thee." Psalm 143: 8. A further edition in 1709 included revisions by Ken himself of the original fourteen stanzas. Our present selection is Nos. 1, 13, 14, our second being an addition. The word "joyful" has been substituted for "early" in the third line of the opening stanza, which originally marked it as a hymn for the early morning. Two of the omitted stanzas are:—

5. Wake, and lift up thyself, my heart,
And with the angels bear thy part,
Who all night long unwearied sing
Glory to the eternal King.

12. Lord, I my vows to Thee renew,
Scatter my sins as morning dew,
Guard my first springs of thought and will,
And with Thyself my spirit fill.

Ken also wrote Nos. 53, "All Praise to Thee," and 683, "Praise God From Whom All Blessings Flow." which is really part of No. 53.

The tune *The Morning Watch* was composed in 1913 by Carl Fowler Price (1881-1948) of New Brunswick, New Jersey, a great hymnologist who wrote more than two hundred hymn tunes. This was especially written for the words, "Lord, in the morning let me hear Thy voice," by William Brattle Oliver, and first published by the World's Morning Watch, a religious organization. The composer made slight alterations in the tune so as to adjust it to these words in long metre. Price, an active member of the Methodist Church, was the founder in 1922 of the Hymn Society of America and its first president, and lectured frequently on hymnology.

45. THE SUN IS ON THE LAND

Lamentations 3: 23

Louis Fitzgerald Benson (1855-1930), born in Philadelphia, Pennsylvania, was an editor of hymnals, who had spent seven years as a lawyer and six years as a Presbyterian minister, being ordained in 1888. He resigned in order to edit hymnals of the church. These words were written by him in 1897 at the seaside resort of Bar Harbour, Maine, and describe the all-sufficiency of God. The length of the day is the length of our praise to God, the vast extent of the heavens is the measure of His love and mercy, and the cares of the day will not cause the servant of God to cease to sing. The hymn closes with a beautiful doxology to the Trinity. An appropriate scripture text is Lamentations 3: 23, "They are new every morning."

The tune *Wentworth* was composed in 1876 by Frederick Charles Maker (1844-1927), a Congregational organist of three different churches in Bristol, Gloucestershire. It was written specially for another hymn, namely, "My God I Thank Thee, Who Hast Made the Earth So Bright." An unusual feature of the tune is the first line where all four parts are in unison. The melody in each pair of lines follows the same musical pattern of initial rise, steady fall, and final rise and fall. Maker also composed Nos. 116 and 314, *Whittier* or *Rest,* and 280, *St. Christopher.*

46. SWEET IS THE WORK, MY GOD

Psalm 92

Isaac Watts (1674-1748), see appendix, paraphrased Psalm 92 in 1719 under the title "A Psalm for the Lord's Day." There were originally seven stanzas in Part I, those omitted being:—

4. Fools never raise their thoughts so high,
   Like brutes they live, like brutes they die;
   Like grass they flourish, till Thy breath
   Blast them in everlasting death.

5. But I shall share a glorious part
   When grace hath well refined my heart;
   And fresh supplies of joy are shed,
   Like holy oil, to cheer my head.

6. Sin, my worst enemy, before,
   Shall vex my eyes and ears no more;
   My inward foes shall all be slain,
   Nor Satan break my peace again.

The tune *For the Sabbath* was written in 1938 especially for these words by Stanley Ledington (1889-) of Durham, England, who emigrated to the United States. He was a composer and organist and spent forty years as a music teacher in various Seventh-day Adventist schools and colleges. He also composed Nos. 98, *Rose of Sharon;* 476, *Communion,* and 700, *Benediction.* He died in 1974.

47. FORTH IN THY NAME

Matthew 11:30

The title that Charles Wesley (1707-88), see appendix, gave to this hymn was "For Believers Before Work," and it appeared in 1749 in his "Hymns and Sacred Poems" in six stanzas of four lines each. The omitted ones are:—

3. Preserve me from my calling's snare,
And hide my simple heart above,
Above the thorns of choking care,
The gilded baits of worldly love.

4. Thee may I set at my right hand,
Whose eyes mine inmost substance see,
And labour on at Thy command,
And offer all my works to Thee.

For the last line of the second stanza, Wesley wrote "And prove Thy acceptable will," which throws an unusual accent on the word acceptable. He evidently had in mind the verse, "That ye may prove what is that good, and acceptable, and perfect, will of God." Romans 12: 2. The present change to "Thy good and perfect will" is therefore an excellent one, keeping to the exact words of the text. While many other texts are used in the hymn, for Wesley was a diligent student and user of the Scriptures, an effective summary would be "For My yoke is easy." Matthew 11: 30.

The tune *Pixham* was composed in 1901 by Horatio William Parker (1863-1919), who also wrote Nos. 58 and 177, *Garden City;* 110, *Stella (Parker);* 133, *Jubilate,* and 198, *Pro Patria.* He was professor of music at Yale from 1894, and wrote tunes to less well-known hymn texts. He was church organist in New York and in Boston at Holy Trinity, and a composer of cantatas, oratorios, and opera, receiving the degree of Mus. Doc. in 1902 from Cambridge University, England.

48. SOFTLY NOW THE LIGHT OF DAY

Psalm 141: 2

George Washington Doane (1799-1859), later bishop of New Jersey, wrote these words in 1824 in "Songs of the Way," when he was professor of rhetoric at Trinity College, Hartford. There were four stanzas originally, based on the thought in Psalm 141: 2, "Let my prayer be set forth before Thee as incense; and the lifting up of my hands as the evening sacrifice." The omitted stanza is:—

4. Thou who, sinless, yet hast known
All of man's infirmity;
Then, from Thine eternal throne,
Jesus, look with pitying eye.

The students of St. Mary's Hall, Burlington, New Jersey, a school for girls which Doane founded in 1837, sang this hymn for Wednesday vesper services. Another of his hymns is No. 450, "Fling Out the Banner!"

The tune *Seymour,* also used for No. 318, "Come My Soul," is an arrangement of the opening chorus of "Oberon," written 1824-26, the last opera of Carl Maria Friedrich Ernst von Weber (1786-1826), which he had been commissioned to write by the London Covent Garden Theatre. The arrangement was made in 1851 by Henry Wellington Greatorex (1813-58), who was an organist at the Centre Church, Hartford, Connecticut. He named it *Seymour* to commemorate the name of a bass singer there. He also arranged Nos. 25 and 383, *Manoah,* and composed Nos. 174, *Leighton,* and 689, *Gloria Patri.* Another tune by von Weber is No. 404, *Jewett.*

49. SAVIOUR, BREATHE AN EVENING BLESSING

Psalm 139: 12

James Edmeston (1791-1867) was an architect by profession who used to write a hymn every Sunday to be read for family worship. This one was inspired in 1820 by the reading of Salte's "Travels in Abyssinia," where he noted particularly the Ethiopian evening hymn. Over his two eight-line stanzas he wrote the quotation, "At night their short evening hymn, 'Jesus, forgive us,' stole through the camp." While some lines are almost direct quotations from the 91st Psalm, a summary is better expressed in "Yea, the darkness hideth not from Thee." Psalm 139: 12. The last line but one has been changed from "May the morn in heaven awake us," in order better to accord with the doctrine of death being a sleep until the resurrection at the second advent of Christ. Edmeston also wrote Nos. 87, "Lead Us, Heavenly Father," and 460, "How Sweet the Light."

The tune *Evening Prayer,* or *Sunset,* was composed in 1876 by George Coles Stebbins (1846-1945), see appendix, especially as a response to be sung after prayer by his choir at the Boston Tremont Temple. It is most suitable for a group of trained singers, for each one of the four parts is quite tuneful. In 1878 the tune was used for the words of the present hymn.

50. ABIDE WITH ME

Luke 24:29

This hymn by Henry Francis Lyte (1793-1847) has come into common use as an evening hymn, whereas it is in reality more appropriate for funerals, as the eventide of life is meant rather than the sunset of a natural day. It is based on the words of the two disciples at Emmaus to our Lord, "Abide with us: for it is toward evening, and the day is far spent," Luke 24: 29, but these words are used metaphorically, as shown by the expressions "life's little day" (stanza 2), "where is death's sting? where grave, thy victory?" (stanza 4), and "Heaven's morning breaks" (stanza 8 omitted). Lyte was born near Kelso, Scotland, and became an Anglican minister at the age of 22. Five years later, in 1820, he was visiting a dying friend who constantly repeated the words "Abide with me." He composed the stanzas, it is said, and handed a copy to the dying man's brother. Later he ministered at Brixham, Devon, for twenty-five years, but was a victim of consumption and planned to go to the Riviera to restore his failing health. After preaching his farewell sermon, he returned to his room and later produced this hymn, which may have been in his mind for a long time. His grandson leans to the year 1847 for the origin of the hymn rather than the 1820 date. On the morrow he sailed for Italy, but died at Nice, this hymn now fulfilling a desire expressed in one of his last poems entitled "Declining Days":—

> Might my poor lyre but give
> Some simple strain, some spirit-moving lay,
> Some sparklet of the soul, that still might live
> When I was passed to clay!
>
> O Thou whose touch can lend
> Life to the dead, Thy quickening grace supply;
> And grant me, swan-like, my last breath to spend
> In songs that may not die.

Other stanzas of this famous hymn are:—

3. Not a brief glance I beg, a passing word;
   But as Thou dwell'st with Thy disciples, Lord,
   Familiar, condescending, patient, free,
   Come, not to sojourn, but abide with me.

4. Come not in terrors as the King of kings,
   But kind and good, with healing in Thy wings,
   Tears for all woes, a heart for every plea;
   Come, Friend of sinners, and abide with me!

5. Thou on my head in early youth didst smile;
And though rebellious and perverse meanwhile,
Thou hast not left me, oft as I left Thee:
On to the close, O Lord, abide with me.

8. Hold Thou Thy cross before my closing eyes,
Shine through the gloom, and point me to the skies;
Heaven's morning breaks, and earth's vain shadows flee:
In life, in death, O Lord, abide with me.

Lyte also wrote Nos. 16, "Praise the Lord, His Glories Show"; 252, "My Spirit on Thy Care"; 267, "Jesus, I My Cross Have Taken"; 399, "There Is a Safe and Secret Place," and possibly 394, "Saviour, Like a Shepherd."

Lyte wrote his own tune for these majestic words, but the hymn is now sung to *Eventide,* composed in 1861 especially for these words by Dr. William Henry Monk (1823-89), the musical editor of "Hymns Ancient and Modern," and organist and professor of vocal music at King's College, London. One story says that he composed it in ten minutes at the close of a committee meeting, in spite of a piano lesson given in a nearby room, but his widow said that at a time of great sorrow they were standing together watching the glories of the setting sun. Dr. Monk was so inspired by the sight that, as the twilight descended, he took up paper and pen and wrote the tune, which is noteworthy as the melody is limited to a range of only six notes. He wrote only one tune to secular words, and placed a very high value on church music, the organ being, in his opinion, an instrument for reaching souls and not for showing skill. Monk also wrote Nos. 196, *Beverley,* and 357, *Vigilate,* and harmonized 341, *Stephanos.*

51. DAY IS DYING IN THE WEST

Isaiah 6:3

Bishop John H. Vincent was the founder in 1874 of the Chautauqua Literary and Scientific Circle, which gave ten-week summer lectures on Sunday school methods, together with concerts and high class entertainment at an old Methodist camp-meeting ground on the shores of Lake Chautauqua in the Finger Lakes district of New York state. He requested Miss Mary Artemisia Lathbury (1841-1913) to write a study hymn for the group, and these words were first used on August 5, 1876, at evening worship outdoors. The chorus quotes Isaiah 6: 3, "Holy, holy, holy, is the Lord of hosts: the whole earth is full of His glory." The hymn was first introduced to the public by the assistant director of music, George Coles Stebbins (1846-1945), see appendix, who played the tune as a cornet duet with his brother. Then the composer of the tune *Chautauqua,* otherwise *Sennens,* and *Evening Praise,* William Fisk

Sherwin (1826-88), see appendix, sang it as a solo, and then conducted the choir, all in boats a little distance from the shore. The exclamatory "O" in the refrain comes most appropriately on the single highest note of the melody. The last two stanzas were written a week after the first two, as Miss Lathbury considered the hymn unfinished. She was engaged in editorial work, and was also a teacher of art and gave great assistance to the Chautauqua movement, which spread throughout the United States. She was the daughter of a Methodist local preacher, and had two brothers who were Methodist ministers. She also wrote No. 218, "Break Thou the Bread of Life," in similar circumstances to the present hymn.

52. NOW THE DAY IS OVER

Proverbs 3:24

These words with five other stanzas were written in 1865 by the Rev. Sabine Baring-Gould (1834-1924), noted novelist, poet and historian, who also wrote No. 360, "Onward, Christian Soldiers." The omitted stanzas are:—

2. Now the darkness gathers,
Stars begin to peep,
Birds and beasts and flowers
Soon will be asleep.

4. Grant to little children
Visions bright of Thee;
Guard the sailors tossing
On the deep blue sea.

5. Comfort every sufferer
Watching late in pain;
Those who plan some evil
From their sin restrain.

7. When the morning wakens,
Then may I arise
Pure and fresh and sinless
In Thy holy eyes.

8. Glory to the Father,
Glory to the Son,
And to Thee, blest Spirit,
Whilst all ages run.

The words are based on the verse: "When thou liest down, thou shalt not be afraid: yea, thou shalt lie down, and thy sleep shall be sweet." Prov. 3: 24.

Baring-Gould composed his own tune *Eudoxia* for the words, but in most American hymnals it has been displaced by *Merrial,* composed in 1868 by Joseph Barnby (1838-96), see appendix. *Merrial* was named by Dr. Charles S. Robinson, an American who used this then unnamed tune in his collection of "Spiritual Songs for Social Worship," 1878. It commemorates his daughter's name, Mary L. Robinson, his first arrangement being the initials M. L. R., i.e., *Emmelar,* and his final one Mary L., or *Merrial.* The tune is noteworthy for the fact that of the twenty-three notes in the melody, more than half are confined to E, a series of six starting the tune, and a succession of seven E's ending it. However, it is nevertheless a good tune because of the harmony provided by both tenor and bass parts.

53. ALL PRAISE TO THEE

Psalm 42:8

Thomas Ken (1637-1711) was born at Berkhamsted, Hertfordshire, and educated at Winchester and Oxford. He was appointed bishop of Bath and Wells in 1685, but forfeited this high office because of his adherence to principle. He wrote "A Manual of Prayers for the Use of the Scholars of Winchester College" in 1674, and to the 1695 edition added some original hymns. A group of three, for morning, for evening, and for midnight, all concluded with the doxology (No. 683). This hymn consisting of twelve stanzas, written about 1672, accompanied the exhortation: "Be sure to sing the morning and evening hymn in your chamber devoutedly, remembering that the psalmist, upon happy experience, assures you that it is a good thing to tell of the lovingkindness of the Lord early in the morning and of His truth in the night season." This is evidently a reference to Psalm 42:8: "Yet the Lord will command His lovingkindness in the daytime, and in the night His song shall be with me, and my prayer unto the God of my life." Our selection of the original hymn is stanzas 1, 2, 4, 12, three of the omitted ones being:—

3. Teach me to live that I may dread
The grave as little as my bed;
Teach me to die, that so I may
Triumphing rise at the last day.

5. When in the night I sleepless lie,
My soul with heavenly thoughts supply,
Let no ill dreams disturb my rest,
No powers of darkness me molest.

9. O when shall I in endless day
For ever chase dark sleep away,
And hymns with the supernal choir
Incessant sing, and never tire.

Ken's morning hymn is No. 44, "Awake, My Soul," and the doxology, identical with the last stanza, is No. 683, "Praise God, From Whom All Blessings Flow."

The tune *Tallis' Canon* was chosen by Bishop Ken for the words of his three hymns, and appears in a psalter issued about the year 1560 by Matthew Parker, archbishop of Canterbury. It was composed by Thomas Tallis (c. 1510-85), who is known as the father of English cathedral music, and who was organist at Waltham Abbey and the Chapel Royal. He was royal organist to Henry VIII, Edward VI, Mary, and Elizabeth, of the house of Tudor. A canon (or fugue) is a piece of music in which one part, after a few beats, repeats another part exactly. In this particular tune, the tenor part copies exactly the soprano part, but is four beats behind. In other words, if the tenor part is played separately it will appear to sound unfinished, being four notes short, these four notes being found, of course, at the beginning of the part. Alto and bass parts are added later to complete the four-part harmony. Tallis also composed Nos. 92 and 332, *Tallis' Ordinal.*

54. THE SHADOWS OF THE EVENING HOURS

Psalm 27:7

These words were written for a festival at St. Mary's Church, Hulme, Manchester, by Adelaide Anne Procter (1825-64), the author of the popular song, "The Lost Chord." She first wrote under the pen-name of Mary Berwick, and was converted to the Roman Catholic faith in 1851. This hymn likens the evening shadows to the sorrows of life, and prays for the peace of God, like the quiet of the night, to enter the soul. The omitted stanza is:—

3. Slowly the rays of daylight fade;
So fade within our heart
The hopes in earthly love and joy,
That one by one depart:
Slowly the bright stars, one by one,
Within the heavens shine;
Give us, O Lord, fresh hopes in heaven,
And trust in things divine.

An appropriate text is "Hear, O Lord, when I cry with my voice: have mercy also upon me, and answer me." Psalm 27: 7.

The tune *St. Leonard,* composed in 1867 by Henry Hiles (1826-1904), a lecturer in music at Manchester University, is named arbitrarily, although it was written specially for the words. The melody is noteworthy for the steady climb in lines 5 and 6 from middle C to the octave above, and then a further rise to E flat. Leonard, who died about A.D. 500, was the patron saint of prisoners, because those he visited in Limosin, France, were later released by King Clodeveus.

55. NOW GOD BE WITH US

Matthew 6:9-13

Petrus Herbert (1510-71) was one of the Bohemian Brethren who were the precursors of the Moravians and who suffered much persecution for their faith. He was an accomplished hymn-writer and hymnologist, and a co-editor of the Moravian hymnbook "Kirchengesang," 1566. He included this hymn, which was translated a second time by Catherine Winkworth (1827-78), see appendix, in 1863, retaining the original metre. It is a prayer for protection in oppression during the unknown night and throughout the whole day, and closes in the last stanza with a paraphrase of the Lord's prayer: "Our Father . . . Hallowed be Thy name. Thy kingdom come. Thy will be done in earth, as it is in heaven. Give us this day our daily bread. And forgive us our debts, . . . deliver us from evil . . . for ever." Matthew 6: 9-13. The omitted stanzas are:—

3. Let pious thoughts be ours when sleep o'ertakes us;
   Our earliest thoughts be Thine when morning wakes us;
   All day serve Thee, in all that we are doing
   Thy praise pursuing.

4. As Thy belovéd, soothe the sick and weeping;
   And bid the sufferer lose his griefs in sleeping;
   Widows and orphans, we to Thee commend them,
   Do Thou befriend them.

The tune, here called *Integer Vitae* is the same as No. 9, *Flemming,* but written in crotchets in 4/4 time instead of quavers in 2/4 time. Friedrich Ferdinand Flemming (1778-1813) was a German physician who wrote this tune in 1811 for Horace's Latin Ode XXII Integer Vitae (= He who is upright).

56. AGAIN AS EVENING'S SHADOW FALLS

Psalm 18:28

Samuel Longfellow (1819-92), younger brother of the poet Henry Wadsworth Longfellow, wrote these words in 1859 at Brooklyn, New York, where he was the pastor of the Unitarian church. An apposite text would be, "The Lord my God will enlighten my darkness." Psalm 18: 28. The omitted stanza is:—

4. Life's tumult we must meet again,
We cannot at the shrine remain,
But in the spirit's secret cell
May hymn and prayer for ever dwell.

Longfellow disdained all hymns that attributed supernatural qualities to Jesus, but this one can be sung equally well by those believing in His divinity. Longfellow also adapted Andrew Reed's hymn, No. 213, "Spirit Divine."

The tune *Abends* was composed in 1874 by Herbert Stanley Oakeley (1830-1903) within the short space of half an hour, and is so named (abends = at evening) because it was written especially for the evening hymn No. 321, "Sun of My Soul," in order to replace the tune *Hursley* which he felt inappropriate for such fine words, as the tune is very similar to a drinking song. Each one of the four parts of *Abends* is interesting, carrying a melody of its own. Oakeley, who also composed No. 287, *Edina,* was knighted in 1876 for his outstanding services to church music, and was professor of music at Edinburgh University from 1865-91.

57. THE DAY THOU GAVEST

Daniel 7:14

John Ellerton (1826-93) wrote hymns for special occasions, this one of five stanzas he entitled "Evening." While most often used for the evening of the Sabbath, it is appropriate for any evening worship, reminding us of the extent of the church and kingdom of God. "And there was given Him dominion, and glory, and a kingdom, that all people, nations, and languages should serve Him: His dominion is an everlasting dominion, which shall not pass away." Daniel 7: 14. It was written in 1870 for "A Liturgy for Missionary Meetings" when Ellerton was chaplain to Lord Crewe and vicar of Crewe Green. The first line was borrowed from an anonymous hymn in "Church Poetry," 1855, and Ellerton's omitted stanza is:—

4. The sun that bids us rest is waking
Our brethren 'neath the western sky,
And hour by hour fresh lips are making
Thy wondrous doings heard on high.

Ellerton also wrote Nos. 34, "Saviour, Again to Thy Dear Name"; 37, "The Lord Be With Us"; 58, "Our Day of Praise Is Done"; 461, "This Is the Day of Rest," and had a part in No. 78, "God the Omnipotent."

The tune *St. Clement* was composed especially for these words in 1874 by Clement Cotterill Scholefield (1839-1904), a self-taught musician, who was one time chaplain of Eton College and vicar of Holy Trinity Church of England, Knightsbridge, London. He was curate of St. Paul's South Kensington, where Arthur Seymour Sullivan (1842-1900), see appendix, was organist. Sullivan published the tune in "Church Hymns with Tunes," 1874, of which he was musical editor, and named the tune by "canonizing" his friend.

58. OUR DAY OF PRAISE IS DONE

John 1:9

John Ellerton (1826-93) in 1868 added three stanzas of his own and a doxology to four stanzas of William John Blew's (1808-94) six-stanza hymn which he had translated in 1850 from the Latin. The occasion was for the Nantwich Festival of Choirs when he was vicar of Crewe Green. (See also No. 34.) In 1869 Ellerton revised these eight stanzas, and again in 1871, and now there remains nothing of Blew's original except the thought of the contrast of limited daily praise on earth with the angelic eternal praise in heaven. Some phrases recall the text: "That was the true Light, which lighteth every man that cometh into the world," John 1: 9. An omitted stanza from the 1871 edition is:—

4. Yet, Lord, to Thy dear will
If Thou attune the heart,
We in Thine angel's music still
May bear our lower part.

Ellerton also wrote Nos. 34, "Saviour, Again to Thy Dear Name"; 37, "The Lord Be With Us"; 57, "The Day Thou Gavest"; 461, "This Is the Day of Rest," and had a part in No. 78, "God the Omnipotent."

The tune *Garden City,* also used for No. 177, "The Church Has Waited Long," was composed in 1893 by Horatio William Parker (1863-1919) for the dedication of a new church building at Garden City, Long Island. The name commemorates his period as professor of music at the Cathedral School of St. Paul, Garden City, from 1885-87. At the time of composition he was organist at the Holy Trinity Church, New York, and in the next year he became professor of music at Yale. He also composed Nos. 47, *Pixham;* 110, *Stella (Parker);* 133, *Jubilate,* and 198, *Pro Patria.* Parker disliked his tune *Garden City* so much that he would have recalled it had it been possible.

59. THE SUN ROLLS DOWN

Leviticus 23:32

These words were written by Caroline Matilda Cory (1838-1913) of Pinkney, Michigan, who married Martin W. Rathbun in 1857. She became an Adventist in her early youth in Michigan, where the message of the second advent began to be preached prior to 1855. Her gift of poetic expression was seen in a few unpublished poems, and also in this one which was sent to the *Review and Herald,* then but a newly established church paper of the Sabbath-keeping Adventists. The hymn was first published in 1861 in a hymnal compiled by James White entitled "Hymns for Those Who Keep the Commandments of God and the Faith of Jesus," but no credit was there given for authorship. Consequently, "Hymns and Tunes" and later "Church Hymnal" followed this lead and assumed that the authorship was unknown. However, Mrs. Rathbun told the origin of the words to her sons, and one of them, Floyd Otto Rathbun (1874-1963), a missionary to Jamaica who later served on the staff of Southern Missionary College, Emmanuel Missionary College, and Pacific Union College, passed on the story to Harold Amadeus Miller. The last two stanzas indicate the time of origin of the hymn, when Sabbath-keepers were not as numerous as now, and when Sabbath-keeping according to God's commandment was not an easy matter. The hymn appropriately calls the worshipper to begin Sabbath observance at the setting of the sun, for "from even unto even, shall ye celebrate your Sabbath" (Leviticus 23: 32), and to introduce the sacred hours by songs of praise. The original fourth stanza, omitted in "Hymns and Tunes," was:—

4. For God in great creation's week
Did rest upon this day.
Now let us for His mercy seek,
He'll turn us not away.

A different fourth stanza composed by the editorial staff appeared in the 1886 edition and has persisted to the present.

The tune *Vesper,* named for the sentiment of the poem, was composed in 1939 by Harold Amadeus Miller (1891-1966), see appendix, who was on the staff of Southern Missionary College, Tennessee, at the same time as Floyd Rathbun.

60. O BLESSED HOUR

Colossians 2: 10

These words by N. J. Squires describe the evening as a time of prayer and fellowship when we can seek God's blessing of faith and power. They lead to a climax which states that God fills all our need: "Ye are complete in Him." Colossians 2: 10.

The tune *Ernan,* also used for No. 471, "Thy Broken Body, Gracious Lord," was composed for his compilation "Cantica Laudis" in 1850 by Lowell Mason (1792-1872), see appendix, but is a name of random choice from the Old Testament having no associated significance.

61. THE SABBATH DAY HAS REACHED ITS CLOSE

Psalm 63:6

Charlotte Elliott (1789-1871) of Brighton, England, wrote these words in 1839 as a Sunday evening hymn. The quiet restful words seek the peace and forgiveness of the Spirit of God at the close of the day, and lead to the same prayer for the final evening of life. "When I remember Thee upon my bed, and meditate on Thee in the night watches." Psalm 63: 6. Miss Elliott was a life-long invalid, but fought against her weakness and depression with Christian fortitude. She also wrote Nos. 222, "Just As I Am"; 325, "My God, Is Any Hour So Sweet," and 357, "Christian, Seek Not Yet Repose." All of these hymns are in the same form, having their fourth line different either in rhyme or metre from the three preceding lines.

The tune *Pascal* was composed by Edward John Hopkins (1818-1901) who was organist at the Temple Church, London, for fifty-five years, devoting his life to the improvement of church music. He also composed Nos. 34, *Ellers,* and 229, *St. Athanasius.*

62. ETERNAL DEPTH OF LOVE DIVINE

Ephesians 3:18, 19

Count Nicholas Ludwig von Zinzendorf (1700-60), Moravian bishop and hymn writer, wrote this hymn of praise and gratitude to God for His grace in deigning to dwell in the hearts of sinful men. It was written for the birthday, September 21, 1726, of his friend Count Henkel of Oderberg. Published in 1730, it was freely translated from the German in 1739 by his friend John Wesley (1703-91), in four stanzas, each of eight lines. The omitted stanzas are:—

3. O King of glory, Thy rich grace
Our feeble thought surpasses far;
Yea, even our sins, though numberless,
Less numerous than Thy mercies are.
Still on Thee, Father, may we rest!
Still may we pant Thy Son to know!
Thy Spirit still breathe in our breast,
Fountain of peace and joy below!

4. Oft have we seen Thy mighty power
Since from the world Thou mad'st us free:
Still may we praise Thee more and more,
Our hearts more firmly knit to Thee!
Still, Lord, Thy saving health display,
And arm our souls with heavenly zeal;
So fearless shall we urge our way
Through all the powers of earth and hell.

The hymn recalls Ephesians 3: 18, 19: ". . . the breadth, and the length, and depth, and height; and to know the love of Christ, which passeth knowledge." Zinzendorf also wrote Nos. 330, "O Thou to Whose All-Searching Sight," and 676, "Jesus, Still Lead On." John Wesley also translated No. 330, "O Thou to Whose All-Searching Sight," from Zinzendorf, and No. 146, "Jesus, Thy Boundless Love to Me," from Gerhardt.

The tune *Rothwell* was composed by William Tansur (1706-83), a teacher of psalmody classes and a music teacher of St. Neots, Huntingdonshire.

63. THY MIGHTY LOVE, O GOD

2 Corinthians 5:14

Emily May Grimes (1864-1927) was a victim of constant pain and suffering, but wrote many sacred poems expressing trust in God. In 1893 she went to Pondoland, South Africa, and in 1904 married Dr. T. W. W. Crawford, who was a missionary to the Kikuyu, continuing her service in Africa. In this hymn based on 1 Corinthians 5: 14: "The love of Christ constraineth us," she describes the love of God as a strong tide whose force cuts its own channel through any opposition. The power of love is not explosive, but steady and persistent, gaining by gentleness rather than by violence. The simile is maintained throughout the hymn in expressions such as "sweep away," "break through," "clear every avenue," "flood," "stream," until the tide of God's love, flowing freely into the life, will eventually flow from the life, bearing with it a love for others. Miss Grimes also wrote No. 329, "Speak, Lord, In the Stillness."

64. HOW GENTLE GOD'S COMMANDS

1 Peter 5:7

Philip Doddridge (1702-51), see appendix, based his hymns on the sermons he preached, this one of four stanzas being under the title "God's Care a Remedy for Ours." It is an exposition of Psalm 55: 22: "Cast thy burden upon the Lord, and He shall sustain thee," although his text for this sermon was the similar one in 1 Peter 5: 7: "Casting all your care upon Him; for He careth for you."

65. THERE'S A WIDENESS

Psalm 89:14

Frederick William Faber (1814-63) wrote 150 hymns, a total equal in number to the Psalms, with the object of having them read as devotions by Roman Catholics, just as Protestants had a wealth of hymns to sing. This was originally a poem of eight stanzas, first published in 1854 under the title of "Come to Jesus," and increased in 1862 to thirteen stanzas. The omitted stanzas are:—

1. Souls of men! why will ye scatter
Like a crowd of frightened sheep?
Foolish hearts! why will ye wander
From a love so true and deep?

2. Was there ever kindest shepherd
Half so gentle, half so sweet
As the Saviour who would have us
Come and gather round His feet?

3. It is God: His love looks mighty,
But is mightier than it seems!
'Tis our Father: and His fondness
Goes far out beyond our dreams.

5. There's no place where earthly sorrows
Are more felt than up in heaven;
There's no place where earthly failings,
Have such kindly judgment given.

7. There is grace enough for thousands
Of new worlds as great as this;
There is room for fresh creations
In that upper home of bliss.

9. But we make His love too narrow
By false limits of our own;
And we magnify His strictness
With a zeal He will not own.

10. There is plentiful redemption
In the blood that has been shed,
There is joy for all the members
In the sorrows of the Head.

11. 'Tis not all we owe to Jesus;
It is something more than all;
Greater good because of evil,
Larger mercy through the fall.

12. Pining souls! come nearer Jesus,
And oh, come, not doubting thus,
But with faith that trusts more bravely
His vast tenderness for us.

A fitting summary would be "Justice and judgment are the habitation of Thy throne: mercy and truth shall go before Thy face." Psalm 89: 14. Faber also wrote Nos. 349, "Faith of Our Fathers"; 375 and 376, "Hark! Hark, My Soul!" and 443, "Workman of God."

The tune *Wellesley* was composed as a graduation song by Lizzie Shone Tourjée, later Estabrook (1858-1913), in 1877 while she was still a pupil in Newton High School, Massachusetts. Later she attended Wellesley College, Massachusetts, and her tune was used there. In 1900 Hamilton C. MacDougal became professor of music at the college and it came to his notice. He included the tune when he compiled a song book for the college and named it to commemorate the place where it was first used. Miss Tourjée was the oldest daughter of Dr. Eben Tourjée, a Methodist musical director of Huguenot ancestry.

66. LIKE AS A FATHER

Psalm 103:13

These words were written in 1878 by Franklin Edson Belden (1858-1945), see appendix, and appear in "Hymns and Tunes," 1886. They are based on Psalm 103: 13, "Like as a father pitieth his children, so the Lord pitieth them that fear Him."

The tune was composed in 1878 by D. S. Hakes who wrote "Pearly Portals for the Sabbath School" published by the Pacific Press in 1882, and containing 146 tunes, ninety of them by Hakes. He also, with Belden and James Edson White (see Nos. 230, 235), brought out the "Song Anchor" in 1878, the first Sabbath school song book of Seventh-day Adventists. The present tune was originally written and published without a soprano part in the first line, the tenor carrying the melody. Hakes also composed Nos. 493, 500, *Standard;* 520, 613, *My Song,* and 629, all except No. 520 to Belden's words.

67. O LOVE OF GOD

Jeremiah 31:3

In 1861 Horatius Bonar (1808-89), see appendix, wrote these majestic words on the love and power of God, expounding and enlarging the message of the whole of the Scriptures, but particularly the thought of Jeremiah 31: 3, "I have loved thee with an everlasting love; therefore with lovingkindness have I drawn thee." This eternal love is manifested in God's creation, but chiefly in the death and resurrection of our Lord. There were originally ten stanzas, the omitted ones being:—

1. O love of God, how deep and great!
Far deeper than man's deepest hate;
Self-fed, self-kindled like the light,
Changeless, eternal, infinite.

2. O heavenly love, how precious still,
In days of weariness and ill!
In nights of pain and helplessness,
To heal, to comfort, and to bless.

5. We read Thee in the flowers, the trees,
The freshness of the fragrant breeze,
The songs of birds upon the wing,
The joy of summer and of spring.

7. We read Thee in the manger-bed
On which His infancy was laid;
And Nazareth that love reveals,
Nestling amid its lonely hills.

8. We read Thee in the tears once shed
Over doomed Salem's guilty head,
In the cold tomb of Bethany,
And blood-drops of Gethsemane.

The tune *Ombersley* was composed in 1872 by William Henry Gladstone (1840-91), a classical scholar and musician, and eldest son of William Ewart Gladstone, the Grand Old Man of English politics. It is named after a village near Worcester, England. Gladstone was a member of Parliament for Chester, for Whitby, and for East Worcestershire.

68. JESUS, LORD, WE LOOK TO THEE

Galatians 6:2

Charles Wesley (1707-88), see appendix, wrote this plea for harmony among the new believers in 1749 in his "Hymns and Sacred Poems," and headed it "For a family." He combines the thought of "the Prince of Peace" (Isaiah 9: 6) with the practical instruction of the Apostle Paul to "bear ye one another's burdens, and so fulfil the law of Christ." Galatians 6: 2. The hymn really belongs to the section on Christian life rather than to that on God's majesty and power.

The tune *Nuremberg* was composed in 1664 by Johann Rudolph Ahle (1625-73) of Mulhausen, Thuringia, director of the Erfurt music school, and a radical reformer of church music, who endeavoured to introduce the more lively Italian style in place of the dull German church music. Ahle also composed No. 27, *Liebster Jesu,* which is a variant of *Nuremberg* in different key and metre, transposed down one tone, and containing two extra lines, a repetition of lines one and two.

69. HIGH IN THE HEAVENS

Psalm 36:5-8

Isaac Watts (1674-1748), see appendix, here paraphrases four of the verses of Psalm 36, the actual words duplicated in hymn and psalm being doubly underlined, and the general thought being shown by single underlining. The hymn appears in his "Psalms of David," 1719. Psalm 36: 5-8, "Thy mercy, O Lord, is in the heavens; and Thy faithfulness reacheth unto the clouds. Thy righteousness is like the great mountains; Thy judgments are a great deep: O Lord, Thou preservest man and beast. How excellent is Thy lovingkindness, O God! therefore the children of men put their trust under the shadow of Thy wings. They shall be abundantly satisfied with the fatness of Thy house; and Thou shalt make them drink of the river of Thy pleasures." The two omitted stanzas are:—

3. Thy providence is kind and large
Both man and beast Thy bounty share;
The whole creation is Thy charge,
But saints are Thy peculiar care.

6. Life, like a fountain, rich and free,
Springs from the presence of my Lord;
And in Thy light our souls shall see
The glories promised in Thy Word.

The tune *St. Alban* comes from "St. Alban's Tune Book" (about 1866) edited by Thomas Morley, organist of St. Albans, Holborn, London. Alban was the first British Christian martyr, losing his life at the Roman town of Verulamium, now known as St. Albans.

70. HOLY, RIGHTEOUS, HEAVENLY KING

John 16:13

Both words and music are by Lon Clyde Metcalfe (1889-) who was an evangelistic singer for the Seventh-day Adventist Church for thirty-three years, and also a teacher of voice in Walla Walla

College, Broadview Academy, Battle Creek Academy, and Oakland Academy, and for three years teacher and coach for the Voice of Prophecy quartet. The words, written in 1916, are based on John 14: 26, "The Holy Ghost . . . shall teach you all things, and bring all things to your remembrance," and on John 16: 7, 13, "If I go not away, the Comforter will not come unto you; but if I depart, I will send Him unto you." "Howbeit when He, the Spirit of truth, is come, He will guide you into all truth."

The tune *Metcalfe* was written in 1925 when the composer was asked to supply a hymn for the book "Gospel in Song." He died in 1970.

71. MY MAKER AND MY KING

1 Chronicles 29:14

Anne Steele (1717-78), daughter of a Baptist pastor of Broughton, near Salisbury, Hampshire, England, wrote six stanzas of this hymn in 1769 under the title of "God My Creator and Benefactor." Omitted stanzas are:—

2. Thou ever good and kind,
A thousand reasons move,
A thousand obligations bind
My heart to grateful love.

5. Shall I withhold Thy due?
And shall my passions rove?
Lord, form this wretched heart anew,
And fill it with Thy love.

Note the emphasis on the word "all" and "each" indicating a complete consecration to God, thus "my all I owe," "all my blessings," "all is Thine," "every word," "each desire," "all my days." Due to an accident in childhood Miss Steele was an invalid all her life and on the eve of her wedding her fiancé was drowned. The hymn echoes David's words: "For all things come of Thee, and of Thine own have we given Thee." 1 Chronicles 29: 14. She also wrote Nos. 224, "O Could Our Thoughts," and 333, "Father, Whate'er of Earthly Bliss," all under her pen-name of Theodosia.

The tune *El Kader* is also used for No. 351, "Ye Servants of the Lord." ~~He died in 1970.~~

72. EARLY, MY GOD, WITHOUT DELAY

Psalm 63:1-3

David wrote Psalm 63 when he was hunted for his life by King Saul and took refuge in the wilderness of Judah. He longed for the peaceful atmosphere of the sanctuary, and Isaac Watts (1674-1748), see appendix, in paraphrasing the first three verses in his "Psalms of David," 1719, has applied this longing to the experience of the Christian generally, entitling it "For Sunday Morning." The words duplicated are doubly underlined and the thought singly, so as to show his skilful arrangement of the Old Testament prose into a metrical psalm. Psalm 63: 1-3: "O God Thou art my God; early will I seek Thee: my soul thirsteth for Thee, my flesh longeth for Thee in a dry and thirsty land, where no water is; to see Thy power and Thy glory, so as I have seen Thee in the sanctuary. Because Thy lovingkindness is better than life, my lips shall praise Thee." The two stanzas omitted from part 1 are:—

4. Not all the blessings of a feast
Can please my soul so well,
As when Thy richer grace I taste,
And in Thy presence dwell.

6. Thus till my last expiring day
I'll bless my God and King;
Thus will I lift up hands to pray,
And tune my lips to sing.

73. HOLY, HOLY, HOLY

Revelation 4:8-11

In the early part of the nineteenth century most members of the Church of England despised the Methodist and Independent churches, and looked with disfavour on their practice of hymn-singing which had received such tremendous impetus under Charles Wesley and Isaac Watts. However, Reginald Heber (1783-1826), a natural poet, noted the effect of hymn-singing on the people and was determined to introduce the same enthusiasm into the Anglican Church, which then confined itself only to psalm singing or chanting. He was vicar of Hodnet, Salop, from 1807-23 and then bishop of Calcutta until his sudden death at Trichinopoli. He had won the Newdigate prize for an English poem while at Oxford in 1803, so combining his talent and his culture he wrote several hymns, all at Hodnet, each based on some phase of the church year. He was very careful to use reverent language and choice phrases so as to avoid the criticism of cheapening religion. This hymn was specially written for Trinity Sunday and is a metrical paraphrase of Revelation 4: 8-11, being designed to be sung between the recitation of the Nicene Creed and the sermon. The omitted stanza is:—

4. Holy, holy, holy, Lord God Almighty!
All Thy works shall praise Thy name, in earth and sky and sea;
Holy, holy, holy, merciful and mighty!
God in three persons, blessed Trinity!

Heber also wrote Nos. 178, "In the Sun, and Moon, and Stars"; 340, "By Cool Siloam's Shady Rill"; 361, "The Son of God Goes Forth to War"; 445, "From Greenland's Icy Mountains," and 467, "Bread of the World."

The tune, interesting in all its four parts, was composed especially for these words in 1861 by John Bacchus Dykes (1823-76), see appendix, and is named *Nicaea* in memory of the famous council of 300 bishops which convened there in A.D. 325. They had met to decide the controversy concerning the relationship of Christ and the Holy Spirit to the Godhead. Arius denied the divinity of Jesus, but the then comparatively unknown Athanasius defended the doctrine of the Trinity with such success that it has been an article of faith ever since.

74. ROUND THE LORD IN GLORY SEATED

Isaiah 6:1-3

In 1837, Richard Mant (1776-1848), then bishop of Down and Connor, Northern Ireland, wrote a paraphrase of the first three verses of Isaiah chapter six, beginning:—

1. Bright the vision that delighted
Once the sight of Judah's seer;
Sweet the countless tongues united
To entrance the prophet's ear.

Then follow the first lines of this hymn ascribing holiness to the Lord, and entitled "Hymn Commemorative of the Thrice Holy." "And one cried unto another, and said, Holy, holy, holy, is the Lord of hosts: the whole earth is full of His glory." Isaiah 6: 3. Other omitted lines are:—

3. Ever thus in God's high praises,
Brethren, let our tongues unite;
Chief the heart when duty raises
God-ward at this mystic rite:
. . .

Mant was born in Southampton, England, and educated at Winchester and Oxford.

The tune *Faben* was composed in 1849 by John Henry Willcox (1827-75), Mus. Doc., an American organist and composer.

75. O WORSHIP THE KING

Psalm 104: 1-3, 10, 13

Robert Grant (1779-1838), later knighted and appointed the governor of Bombay, was impressed to write these words in 1833 after reading William Kethe's (see No. 13) quaint rendering of the 104th Psalm. It is not strictly a paraphrase but several verses are used quite closely, for example: "Who covereth Thyself with light as with a garment: who stretchest out the heavens like a curtain: . . . who maketh the clouds His chariot: who walketh upon the wings of the wind. . . . He sendeth the springs into the valleys, which run among the hills. . . . He watereth the hills from his chambers." Psalm 104: 2, 3, 10, 13. There were originally three stanzas each of eight lines entitled "Glory and goodness of God." Omitted lines are:—

2. The earth with its stores of wonder untold,
   Almighty! Thy power hath founded of old,
   Hath stablished it fast by a changeless decree,
   And round it hath cast like a mantle, the sea.
   . . .

3. . . .
   O measureless might—ineffable love,
   While angels delight to hymn Thee above,
   The humble creation, though feeble their lays,
   With true adoration shall lisp to Thy praise.

The tune *Lyons* was composed in 1770 by Johann Michael Haydn (1737-1806), organist for the archbishop of Salzburg, and composer, who was overshadowed by his older brother Franz Joseph. (See Nos. 91, 304.) All his works were initialled O.a,M.D.Gl., an abbreviation from *Omnia ad majorem Dei Gloriam* (= all for the greater glory of God). Another of his tunes is No. 164, *Greenland.* This arrangement is by William Gardiner (1770-1853) in his "Sacred Melodies II," 1815, who also arranged Nos. 295, *Belmont,* and 519, *Gardiner.* He was a stocking manufacturer of Leicester who used to take instrumental classics and use them as hymn tunes.

76. THE GOD OF ABRAHAM PRAISE

Exodus 3:14, 15

The Hebrew, *Yigdal* (= magnify), embodies the thirteen articles of the Jewish faith and is sung at synagogues on the eves of festivals and of the Sabbath, and also in the home at family worship on Friday evening. The first article is "Extolled and praised be the living God, who exists unbounded by time," and this was taken as a basis and freely translated with a Christian bent by Thomas Olivers (1725-99), one of Whitefield's converts and for forty-six years one of Wesley's preachers. It was entitled "A Hymn to the God of Abraham," and nearly every line echoes a Scripture text. The one chosen for the summary of the hymn is Exodus 3: 14, "I AM THAT I AM," and the next verse identifies the I AM, or Jehovah, as "the Lord God of your fathers, the God of Abraham." There are actually twelve stanzas altogether, arranged in three equal parts. The omitted stanzas are:—

3. The God of Abraham praise,
Whose all-sufficient grace
Shall guide me all my happy days,
In all my ways:
He calls a worm His friend!
He calls Himself my God!
And He shall save me to the end
Through Jesu's blood.

4. He by Himself hath sworn,
I on His oath depend,
I shall on eagle's wings upborne.
To heaven ascend;
I shall behold His face,
I shall His name adore,
And sing the wonders of His grace
For evermore.

PART II

5. Tho' nature's strength decay,
And earth and hell withstand,
To Canaan's bounds I urge my way,
At His command:
The wat'ry deep I pass,
With Jesus in my view;
And thro' the howling wilderness
My way pursue.

6. The goodly land I see,
With peace and plenty bless'd;
A land of sacred liberty,
And endless rest.
There milk and honey flow;
And oil and wine abound,
And trees of life for ever grow,
With mercy crown'd.

7. There dwells the Lord, our King,
The Lord our Righteousness,
Triumphant o'er the world and sin,
The Prince of Peace;
On Sion's sacred height
His kingdom He maintains,
And, glorious with His saints in light,
For ever reigns.

8. He keeps His own secure,
He guards them by His side,
Arrays in garments, white and pure,
His spotless bride:
With streams of sacred bliss,
With groves of living joys—
With all the fruits of Paradise
He still supplies.

PART III

9. Before the great THREE-ONE
They all exulting stand;
And tell the wonders He hath done
Thro' all their land:
The list'ning spheres attend,
And swell the growing fame;
And sing the songs which never end,
The wond'rous name.

10. The God who reigns on high
The great archangels sing,
And "Holy, holy, holy," cry
"Almighty King!
Who was, and is, the same
And evermore shall be:
Eternal Father, Great I AM,
We worship Thee."

11. Before the Saviour's face
The ransom'd nations bow;
O'erwhelm'd at His almighty grace,
For ever new:
He shows His prints of love—
They kindle—to a flame!
And sound thro' all the world above,
The slaughter'd Lamb.

12. This is the third stanza of "Church Hymnal."

The melody governed the metre and was given to Olivers by the noted public singer, Rabbi Leoni, after whom it is named. He was a chorister of the Aldgate Great Synagogue and perpetuated this melody which, according to tradition, was sung at the dedication of Solomon's temple. Leoni is an Italian form of Leon (Chazzan) his real name. Another writer has pointed out a close likeness to the melody in a secular song, "Why, Soldiers, Why," sung in 1729 at the Haymarket Theatre. The hymn is one of the few written in a minor key.

77. YE WATCHERS AND YE HOLY ONES

Revelation 19:6

The tune of this hymn in unusual metre came long before the words, and was in extensive use in southern Germany before 1700. The musical structure is very simple, consisting mainly of a four note descending phrase with its balancing five note ascending phrase, climaxing with a descending octave. The tune derives its name, *Lasst uns Erfreuen,* from the German words to which it was first published in 1623, namely an Easter hymn, "Lasst uns Erfreuen Herzlich Sehr" ("Let Us Most Heartily Rejoice"). Then it seems to have been neglected until its revival as a setting to these words written in 1906 by John Athelstan Laurie Riley (1858-1945). He wrote four stanzas, the omitted ones being:—

2. O higher than the cherubim,
More glorious than the seraphim,
Lead their praises, Alleluia!
Thou Bearer of the eternal word,
Most gracious, magnify the Lord,
Alleluia!

3. Respond, ye souls in endless rest,
Ye patriarchs and prophets blest.
Alleluia! Alleluia!
Ye holy twelve, ye martyrs strong
All saints triumphant, raise the song
Alleluia!

The appropriate Scripture reference is Revelation 19: 6, "The voice of a great multitude, and as the voice of many waters, and as the voice of mighty thunderings, saying, Alleluia: for the Lord God omnipotent reigneth."

78. GOD THE OMNIPOTENT

Psalm 29:11

The tune *Russian Hymn,* the former Russian national anthem, was composed late one night in 1833 by the violinist Alexis Feodorovich Lvoff (1799-1870), who had been requested by the Tsar to find a new one to replace the English tune of which he had become tired. This tune was played to the Tsar the next morning in the Court Chapel, approved, and adopted.

The words which began "God the all terrible! King who ordainest," were freely paraphrased in 1842 by Henry Fothergill Chorley (1808-72), a Lancashire journalist, song publisher and musical and literary critic. The first two stanzas were imitated and altered in 1870 and three more stanzas added by John Ellerton (1826-93). Chorley's second stanza, not used at all in our version, was as follows:—

2. God the Omnipotent! mighty avenger,
Watching invisible, judging unheard,
Doom us not now in the day of our danger:
Grant to us peace, O most merciful Lord.

There are other variants, for example:

God the all-wise! by the fire of Thy chastening
Earth shall to freedom and truth be restored;
Through the thick darkness Thy kingdom is hastening:
Thou wilt give peace in Thy time, O Lord.

In its present form the hymn is a prayer for peace from a penitent people, an assurance that God will prosper the side of right, and a glorious ascription of praise and thanksgiving to the all-powerful God. It is well summarized in Psalm 29: 11, "The Lord will give strength unto His people; the Lord will bless His people with peace." Ellerton also wrote Nos. 34, "Saviour, Again to Thy Dear Name"; 37, "The Lord With Us"; 57, "The Day Thou Gavest"; 58, "Our Day of Praise Is Done," and 461, "This Is the Day of Rest."

79. ERE MOUNTAINS REARED THEIR FORMS SUBLIME

Psalm 90

These words were written in 1829 by Harriet (Henrietta) Auber (1773-1862), who was the great-granddaughter of a Huguenot refugee, and who possessed a deeply devotional spirit. It is a paraphrase of the Ninetieth Psalm in which Moses contrasts the eternity of God with the frailty of man. Miss Auber also wrote No. 214, "Our Blest Redeemer."

The tune *Schroeder* was composed in 1939 by Harold Amadeus Miller (1891-1966), see appendix, and was so named to commemorate a fellow faculty member at Southern Missionary College, Tennessee, who was an assistant in the science department. The melody ascends a complete octave in the first line and makes an almost complete descent in the last line.

80. HOLY AS THOU, O LORD

Psalm 99:9

Charles Wesley (1707-88), see appendix, wrote these words in "Short Hymns," 1762, and here describes the unique holiness, purity, majesty, power, and love of God, qualities which must be given to the believer, and which will cause him to worship his Saviour with heartfelt adoration. A fitting summary is: "Exalt the Lord our God, and worship at His holy hill; for the Lord our God is holy." Psalm 99: 9.

The tune *Massachusetts* was composed in 1939 by Harold Amadeus Miller (1891-1966), see appendix, and was so named in memory of one of his talented students who moved to that state.

81. O GOD, OUR HELP

Psalm 90:1-5

Isaac Watts (1674-1748), see appendix, wrote nine stanzas, now usually reduced to six, of this hymn in 1719, at a time of national perplexity. It is a very close paraphrase of the first part of the psalm attributed to Moses, and Watts's title was "Man Frail and God Eternal." His opening word "Our" was changed to "O" by John Wesley. The omitted stanzas are:—

4. Thy word commands our flesh to dust
"Return, ye sons of men,"
All nations rose from earth at first,
And turn to earth again.

6. The busy tribes of flesh and blood
With all their lives and cares,
Are carried downwards by the flood,
And lost in following years.

7. Time, like an ever rolling stream
Bears all its sons away;
They fly, forgotten, as a dream
Dies at the opening day.

8. Like flowery fields the nations stand
Pleased with the morning's light;
The flowers beneath the mower's hand
Lie withering ere 'tis night.

Watts was a master of simplicity, for in our five stanzas there is a total of 140 syllables, ninety-one of which are separate words. The last stanza has twenty-three monosyllabic words and only two others, namely, ages and eternal.

The tune *St. Anne* was probably composed in 1708 by William Croft (1678-1727), organist at St. Anne's, Soho, and at the Chapel Royal, and later at Westminster Abbey where he is now buried. It appears, however, in Barber's "Psalm Tunes," 1687, where it is credited to a Mrs. Denby. It is pealed daily by the bells of St. Clements, Strand, London. The same tune is also used for No. 435, "O Where Are Kings." Croft also composed No. 342, *Hanover*.

82. BENEATH THY WING

Psalm 61:4

Anna Laetitia Waring (1823-1910) was a Welsh Quaker who joined the Anglican Church in order to be able to participate in the sacramental service. She learned Hebrew in order to study Old Testament poetry in the original, and it was her daily practice to read the Hebrew Psalter. Here she has given a hymn of five stanzas written in 1850, based on a sentence from Psalm 61: 4, "I will trust in the covert of Thy wings." The omitted stanza is:—

4. I would not rise this rest above,
I do not mourn my low estate,
Sure of my riches in His love,
I feel it good to trust and wait.

Miss Waring also wrote Nos. 332, "My Heart Is Resting," and 674, "In Heavenly Love Abiding."

The tune *Blackburn* was composed by William Hay Macdowall Hunter Aitken (1841-?), an Anglican minister of Liverpool, England, who composed twenty-four tunes in a collection "Hymns for a Parochial Mission" which he edited in 1873 and 1877.

83. GOD OF MY LIFE

Psalm 3:3

Charles Wesley (1707-1788), see appendix, and his brother John often met with fierce opposition in their itinerant preaching. Frequently they were compelled to hide in the hedgerows from a furious mob, but through all these "varied scenes" they kept firm their trust in God's over-ruling providence. The hymn was written in 1740 and is entitled "At the Approach of Temptation," originally consisting of fifteen stanzas, which do not include the present third and fourth in "Church Hymnal" which came from another hymn entitled "At Lying Down." Some of the omitted stanzas are:—

3. On Thee my helpless soul is cast,
And looks again Thy grace to prove;
I call to mind the wonders past,
The countless wonders of Thy love.

Then the next three stanzas speak of deliverance from death, the sea, the grave.

7. But, O! the mightier work of grace,
That still the life of faith I live,
That still I pant to sing Thy praise,
That still my all I gasp to give.

The next seven stanzas tell of deliverance from the lion, of safety under God's wings, of trials, snares, weakness, helplessness, and blindness, the closing stanza being:—

> 15. Enlarge my heart to make Thee room;
> Enter, and in me ever stay:
> The crooked then shall straight become,
> The darkness shall be lost in day!

A suitable text for the hymn is, "But Thou, O Lord, art a shield for me; my glory, and the lifter up of mine head." Psalm 3: 3.

The tune *Uxbridge,* used also for No. 338, "One Precious Boon, O Lord, I Seek," was composed in 1830 by Lowell Mason (1792-1872), see appendix.

84. GOD MOVES IN A MYSTERIOUS WAY

John 13:7

William Cowper (1731-1800), see appendix, was subject to fits of extreme melancholy, and on more than one occasion attempted to commit suicide, by knife, by poison, by drowning, by hanging. At Olney in Buckinghamshire in the first few months of the year 1773 he suffered anguish because, in his Calvinistic beliefs, he feared he was eternally lost. He felt that he should make some great sacrifice for God and was willing, like Isaac, to lay down his life. One story says that in his extreme depression he hired a chaise to take him to the river Ouse to an unfrequented spot where he planned to drown himself. By mistake the driver took him to a popular riverside place where there were many people. Consequently Cowper's mind changed, and walking back home across the fields, his depression faded and he composed these words under the title "Light Shining Out of Darkness." The "Olney Hymns," 1779, No. XV of Book III, has this footnote to the last stanza—John 13: 7, "Thou shalt know hereafter." The omitted stanza is:

> 2. Deep in unfathomable mines
> Of never-failing skill,
> He treasures up His bright designs
> And works His sovereign will.

The tune *Dundee,* also known by its older name *French,* appears in the "Scottish Psalter," 1615. It was named *Dundee* to commemorate the Scottish town which strongly propagated the Protestant doctrines and which was a haven of refuge and religious liberty, as Geneva had been in Switzerland. It is also used for Nos. 88, "O God of Bethel," and 392, "Unshaken as the Sacred Hills."

85. ETERNAL LIGHT

1 John 1:5

In or about 1826, Thomas Binney (1798-1874), then a Congregational minister in Newport, Isle of Wight, was sitting at his open window meditating on the peaceful scene before him. The sun sank in the west and the moon appeared, then the stars, one by one lighting up the clear sky. Noticing the gradual mingling of the light of the orb which ruled the day with the softer light of those which ruled the night, he thought "Light is eternal." He continued to sit there in silence, contemplating this theme, and gradually the words of this hymn formed in his mind. It is summarized in 1 John 1: 5, "God is light, and in Him is no darkness at all." Binney was a well-known preacher and twice was chosen to be chairman of the Congregational Union.

The tune *Newcastle,* commemorating the birthplace of Dr. Binney, was composed in 1875 at the request of Mr. Edwin Moss for inclusion in the "London Tune Book" of which he was one of the editors. The composer was Henry Litchfield Morley (1830-1916), one-time organist of St. Paul's, Herne Hill, London, who later emigrated to the United States. The fourth line is noteworthy for the contrary motion of soprano and bass parts, the former rising one octave, and the latter falling one note more than an octave.

86. THE KING OF LOVE MY SHEPHERD IS

Psalm 23

Sir Henry Williams Baker (1821-77), Anglican clergyman and editor of "Hymns Ancient and Modern," wrote this paraphrase of the Shepherd Psalm in 1868. It is actually more than a paraphrase for he also used Luke 15: 5, "And when he hath found it, he layeth it on his shoulders, rejoicing," in the third stanza, thus giving an additional thought. The omitted stanzas are:—

4. In death's dark vale I fear no ill,
With Thee, dear Lord, beside me;
Thy rod and staff my comfort still,
Thy cross before to guide me.

5. Thou spread'st a table in my sight;
Thy unction grace bestoweth;
And O what transport of delight
From Thy pure chalice floweth.

Baker also wrote No. 10, "Praise, O Praise Our God and King!" and composed the melody of No. 341, *Stephanos.*

He also composed a tune in 1868 for his paraphrase but it was not successful so he asked his friend John Bacchus Dykes (1823-76), see appendix, for one. The resultant tune was named *Dominus Regit Me* (*The Lord Rules Me*), these words being taken from the first three words of Psalm 23 in the Latin Vulgate.

87. LEAD US, HEAVENLY FATHER

Psalm 27:10-11

James Edmeston (1791-1867) was a successful London architect and surveyor, and a prolific writer of hymns, writing one every Sunday and reading it for family worship. He was an ardent lover of children and a special benefactor of the London Orphan Asylum. This hymn is a special prayer written in 1821 after an annual speech day at that institution, committing to God those fatherless and motherless ones who were leaving and going out to new homes. An appropriate Scripture reference is, "When my father and my mother forsake me, then the Lord will take me up. Teach me Thy way, O Lord, and lead me in a plain path." Psalm 27: 10, 11. The three stanzas form a neat prayer to the Trinity, the first to the Father, the second to the Son, the Saviour, and the last to the Spirit. Edmeston also wrote Nos. 49, "Saviour, Breathe an Evening Blessing," and 460, "How Sweet the Light."

The tune *Dulce Carmen* (*Sweet Song*) is so named because it was used in 1782 for the hymn "Alleluia, Dulce Carmen," translated later by John Mason Neale (1818-66), see appendix, as "Alleluia, Song of Sweetness." It was first published anonymously in "An Essay on the Church Plain Chant" in 1782 and was arranged and probably composed by Samuel Webbe (1740-1816) of London, a Roman Catholic organist and composer. He also wrote Nos. 42 and 312, *Melcombe,* and 223, *Consolation*, and probably 105 and 255, *Portuguese Hymn* or *Adeste Fideles.*

88. O GOD OF BETHEL

Genesis 28:20-22

This hymn entitled "Jacob's Vow" was written in 1736 by Philip Doddridge (1702-51), see appendix, and is based on that patriarch's experience at Bethel as recorded in Genesis 28: 20-22. It was altered in 1781 by John Logan (1748-88) (see commentary on No. 137 in this book), the conditional "if" of Jacob's vow in the original being changed to a direct request for God's guidance. The second stanza was changed considerably, the original being:—

2. To Thee our humble vows we raise,
To Thee address our prayer,
And in Thy kind and faithful breast
Deposit all our care.

The omitted stanza is:—

5. To Thee as to our covenant God
We'll our whole selves resign
And count that not our tenth alone
But all we have is Thine.

This stanza not only introduces tithe-paying, but the very fundamental principle of this doctrine.

The tune *Dundee,* known also by its older name *French,* appears in the "Scottish Psalter," 1615. It was so named to commemorate the Scottish town which strongly propagated the Protestant doctrines and which was a haven of refuge and religious liberty as Geneva had been in Switzerland. It is also used for Nos. 84, "God Moves in a Mysterious Way," and 392, "Unshaken As the Sacred Hills."

89. GOD IS THE REFUGE

Psalm 46:1-5

Isaac Watts (1674-1748), see appendix, wrote this paraphrase of the first part of Psalm 46 in six stanzas and entitled it, "The Church's Safety and Triumph Among National Desolations." It appears in his "Psalms of David," 1719, and the omitted stanza is:

2. Let mountains from their seats be hurled
Down to the deep and buried there;
Convulsions shake the solid world,
Our faith shall never yield to fear.

The tune *Rockingham Old* was published in 1790 by Dr. Edward Miller (1731-1807) in his "Psalm Tunes." He commented that a tune in triple time called *Tunbridge* would make a good long metre tune and probably derived this tune from it. Miller was the organist of the Doncaster parish church from 1756 until his death fifty-one years later. The tune is named to commemorate the Marquis of Rockingham, the friend and patron of Miller. It is also used for No. 118, "When I Survey the Wondrous Cross."

90. NOW THANK WE ALL OUR GOD

Psalm 126:2, 3

Martin Rinkart (1586-1649), a Lutheran pastor, wrote the first two stanzas of this hymn in 1630 for use as a grace after meals, and to be sung by his household to a tune also composed by the author. Later, about 1636, the third stanza was added as a doxology, a typical one which ascribes praise to the Trinity, although the word "Spirit" is not actually named. The whole hymn is based on some verses in the Apocrypha, Ecclesiasticus 1: 22-24: "Now bless ye the God of all, who everywhere doeth great things. May He grant us joyful hearts, and may peace be in our days for ever." The corresponding thought in Sacred Scripture is found in Psalm 126: 2, 3, "Then was our mouth filled with laughter, and our tongue with singing. . . . The Lord hath done great things for us: whereof we are glad." The hymn was sung at the close of the Thirty Years War (1618-48), virtually a Catholic-Protestant conflict, but it appears to be a coincidence that the Elector of Saxony should have selected the above text from the Apocrypha for preachers to use at the thanksgiving services in every church after the peace of Westphalia in 1648. The words were translated into English in 1858 by Catherine Winkworth (1827-78), see appendix, and the hymn, known as the "Te Deum" of Germany, has been further popularized by Mendelssohn by his use of it in his oratorio "Hymn of Praise," 1840.

The tune *Nun Danket* (*Now Thank*) was written in 1647 by Johann Cruger (1598-1662), one of Germany's leading composers and compilers of hymns, and a strong promoter of congregational singing.

91. THE SPACIOUS FIRMAMENT ON HIGH

Psalm 19:1-3

In *The Spectator* of August 23, 1712, the noted essayist Joseph Addison (1672-1719) wrote on the strengthening of faith, recommending that this be done best by retiring from the bustle of life so that one could quietly meditate on the wonderful works of God. He then referred to the first verse of the nineteenth psalm, saying that David had some "very beautiful strokes of poetry to this purpose in that exalted strain." "The heavens declare the glory of God; and the firmament sheweth His handiwork. Day unto day uttereth speech, and night unto night sheweth knowledge. There is no speech nor language, where their voice is not heard." Psalm 19: 1-3. Then followed this poem consisting of the words of this hymn.

The tune *Creation* is an arrangement from the oratorio (1798) of this name by Franz Joseph Haydn (1732-1809), the famous Austrian composer. It is an adaptation of the first part of "The Heavens Are Telling," a work on which Haydn daily asked God's special blessing while composing. All his compositions were prefaced with the words "In nomine Domini" (in the name of the Lord) and concluded with "Laus Deo" (praise to God). Haydn also composed No. 304, *Austria.*

92. THERE IS A BOOK

Romans 1:20

This original poem was written in 1819 for John Keble's (1792-1866) "Christian Year." For Septuagesima Sunday, the third Sunday before Lent, the first lesson appointed is Genesis, chapter 1. This scripture together with the related verse in Romans 1: 20, "For the invisible things of Him from the creation of the world are clearly seen, being understood by the things that are made," form the basis of the hymn, which has twelve stanzas altogether. Those omitted are as follows:—

4. The moon above, the church below,
A wondrous race they run;
But all their radiance, all their glow,
Each borrows of its sun.

5. The Saviour lends the light and heat
That crown His holy hill;
The saints, like stars, around His seat
Perform their courses still.

6. The saints above are stars in heaven—
What are the saints on earth?
Like trees they stand whom God has given
Our Eden's happy birth.

7. Faith is their fix'd unswerving root,
Hope their unfading flower,
Fair deeds of charity their fruit,
The glory of their bower.

9. One name, above all glorious names,
With its ten thousand tongues,
The everlasting sea proclaims
Echoing angelic songs.

10. The raging fire, the roaring wind,
Thy boundless power display;
But in the gentler breeze we find
Thy Spirit's viewless way.

11. Two worlds are ours: 'tis only sin
Forbids us to descry
The mystic heaven and earth within,
Plain as the sea and sky.

The book written of by Keble is, of course, the book of nature, but the opening line, "There is a book, who runs may read," has been altered because this is a common misquotation of Habakkuk 2: 2, which states the exact opposite, namely, that he who reads may run—"that he may run that readeth it." Keble, who is commemorated by Keble College, Oxford, also wrote Nos. 42, "New Every Morning," and 321, "Sun of My Soul."

The tune was composed in 1567 by Thomas Tallis (c. 1510-85) for the prayer "Veni, Creator" of the ordination service. It is named *Tallis' Ordinal* after the name of the book used in the Anglican Church which contains instructions for the ordination of bishops. The same tune is also used for No. 332, "My Heart Is Resting." A notable feature of this tune is that the third line is a repetition of the first, and the melody of the fourth line is exactly an interval of the fifth below the second line. Tallis, known as the father of English cathedral music, was organist at Waltham Abbey till 1540 and later at the Chapel Royal. He was the royal organist for Henry VIII, Edward VI, Mary, and Elizabeth, of the house of Tudor. He also wrote No. 53, *Tallis' Canon.*

The Choir Tune was composed by Dr. Geoffrey Turton Shaw (1879-1943), an inspector of music in schools who specialized in the writing of descants. This is a typical fa-burden with Tallis' melody in the tenor part. Fa-burden or *faux bourdon* (= false bass) is a fourteenth century method of inverting a triad (that is, a chord of three notes, root, third, and fifth, or doh, me, soh) so that the third, or middle note, remains in the lower part. The term is now used to signify a main melody in the tenor part and a secondary melody in the soprano.

93. I SING THE MIGHTY POWER

Genesis 1

These words were written in 1715 in "Divine Songs for Children" by Isaac Watts (1674-1748), see appendix, in eight stanzas under the title "Praise for Creation and Providence," and was a paraphrase specially for children. His thoughts come from the creation story of Genesis 1 and from the creation psalm, Psalm 104, as the following quotations indicate:—

Stanza 1

"And God said . . . let the dry land appear." Genesis 1: 9.

"And God said, Let there be a firmament." Verse 6.

"And God made two great lights; the greater light to rule the day, and the lesser light to rule the night: He made the stars also." Verse 16.

Stanza 2

"And God said, Behold, I have given you every herb . . . and every tree . . . to you it shall be for meat." Verse 29.

"That He may bring forth food out of the earth." Psalm 104: 14.

"And God said, Let the earth bring forth the living creature after his kind, cattle, and creeping thing, and beast of the earth after his kind: and it was so." Genesis 1: 24.

"And God saw that it was good." Verse 25.

"O Lord, how manifold are Thy works! in wisdom hast Thou made them all: the earth is full of Thy riches." Psalm 104: 24.

Stanza 3

"For He commandeth, and raiseth the stormy wind, which lifteth up the waves thereof." Psalm 107: 25.

"These wait all upon Thee." Psalm 104: 27.

"Even there shall Thy hand lead me, and Thy right hand shall hold me." Psalm 139: 10.

"Whither shall I go from Thy Spirit? or whither shall I flee from Thy presence?" Psalm 139: 7.

The tune *Varina,* also used for No. 299, "There Is a Land of Pure Delight," was published in 1856 by George Frederick Root (1820-95), an American choir conductor, music teacher, and music publisher. He was associated with Lowell Mason, see appendix, in the Boston Academy of Music, and composed many sentimental ballads and Civil War songs. He also composed Nos. 418, *Jewels;* 620, unnamed, and 690, *Quam Dilecta.*

94. ALL BEAUTIFUL THE MARCH OF DAYS

Psalm 147:16, 17

Dr. William Channing Gannett (1840-1923), a Unitarian minister at Rochester, New York, was compiling a hymn-book and found himself in need of a hymn to be sung in the winter season. He therefore wrote and asked one of his parishioners with a poetic gift to write one. Mrs. Frances Whitmarsh Wile (1878-1939), who lived in a secluded home in Bristol Valley, New York, accepted this invitation, taking portions of time spread over two years before completing the hymn in 1912. It is a beautiful poem expressing the power of God in snow, frost, ice and clear skies, and the changing wonders of the seasons. Mrs. Wile, who later became a theosophist, quotes several scriptures, two examples being: Psalm 19: 2, "Day unto day uttereth speech, and night unto night showeth knowledge," and Job 38: 29, "the hoary frost of heaven," and also paraphrases Psalm 147: 16, 17, "He giveth snow like wool: He scattereth the hoarfrost like ashes. He casteth forth His ice like morsels: who can stand before His cold?" The original third stanza, here omitted, runs:—

3. Oh, glory of the winter land!
The peace of nature's rest,
And sweet the dream of coming spring
That stirs within the breast.
On move the resurrection hours,
The Easter heralds throng—
Till sudden bursts the miracle
Of blossom and of song.

The tune *Shackelford* was composed in 1889 by Frederick Henry Cheeswright.

95. THE GLORY OF THE SPRING

Psalm 104:30

Thomas Hornblower Gill (1819-1906) was impressed to write these words on Whitsunday, 1867, "a day of singular loveliness." There were nine stanzas originally, the omitted ones being:—

2. The blessed vernal airs to hail
In their renewing power,
The new song of the nightingale,
The new birth of each flower.

5. These sinful souls Thou hallowest,
These hearts Thou makest new,
These mourning souls by Thee made blest,
These faithless hearts made true:

8. Grant me the grace of the new birth,
The joy of the new song!
The vernal bloom, the vernal mirth
In my new heart prolong!

Gill considered hymns to be utterances of a soul. They are made to be sung, not as doctrinal expositions, but as divine love songs. His title for this hymn was "The Divine Renewer," and from the new growth in the spring he has drawn the lesson of the new birth of the Christian, basing his thoughts on Psalm 104: 30, "Thou renewest the face of the earth," with the lesson drawn from Ephesians 4: 23: "Be renewed in the spirit of your mind." Notice how many times he uses the idea of renewal:

Stanza 1. Newborn life, new raiment, Divine Renewer, renewed earth.

Stanza 2. New births, newborn glow of faith, newborn ecstasy of song.

Stanza 3. Divine Renewer, renew this heart, new life and strength, new joy, new song, new earth and heaven.

Gill wrote over 200 hymns, including No. 386, "Lord, In the Fullness."

The tune *Noel* was arranged by Arthur Seymour Sullivan (1842-1900), see appendix, from an English folk song, "Dives and Lazarus." He was given the melody of only four lines in 1874 and modified it slightly, adding four other lines of his own composition, and then the harmony. It was first set to the Christmas hymn, "It Came Upon the Midnight Clear" (No. 99), hence its name.

96. GLORIOUS ARE THE LOFTY MOUNTAINS

Psalm 125:1, 2

Arthur Warren (1883-1947) of Darwen, Lancashire, was for many years the circulation manager of the Stanborough Press, Watford, England. He was an ardent admirer of the beauties of nature, the Pennines of his native Lancashire and the rugged mountains of Norway where he had once worked, being his great delight. In the words of his hymn we find a paraphase of Psalm 125: 1, 2, "They that trust in the Lord will be as Mount Zion, which cannot be removed, but abideth for ever. As the mountains are round about Jerusalem, so the Lord is round about His people from henceforth even for ever."

The words were first sung in 1930 by a student of Stanborough College (now Newbold College), England, in the college chapel, to a tune composed especially by another student. They were later set to *Snowdon,* by Edgar Halstead, A.R.C.O. (1885-), an organist in Manchester and district for over fifty years. The words reminded him of an occasion when he climbed Snowdon, the highest peak in England and Wales. Halstead also composed No. 696, *Vesper Hymn.* He died in 1969.

97. LORD OF THE OCEAN

Matthew 6:13

Alfred Norman Harker was born in Weymouth, England, in January, 1879, and emigrated to New Zealand as a small boy of about six years of age. In 1895 he came into contact with Pastor J. E. Fulton and other Seventh-day Adventists and became a baptized member of the church. He attended the Australasian Missionary College at Avondale, New South Wales, and later spent ten years as a colporteur-evangelist, and became a resident of Australia. These stanzas, under the title, "O Lord Omnipotent," appear in a collection, "Time's Grand Finale," which is a selection of twenty-one of the author's many poems. The poem of five stanzas, with some minor alterations, appeared on the front page of the *Review and Herald* of May 11, 1933. The omitted stanza is:—

3. Lord of the realms beyond the sky,
Restrain the demons with Thine eye,
So may Thy glorious love be known,
The love of Him who shares Thy throne.

The words were not based on any particular scripture, but part of Matthew 6: 13, "Thine is the kingdom, and the power, and the glory," was given as a sub-title after the poem was written.

The tune *Omnipotent* was composed by Pastor Albert William Anderson (1868-1949), well-known editor of the Australian *Signs of the Times,* vigorous preacher, author, musician, sturdy religious liberty secretary, and a pioneer Seventh-day Adventist, who was largely instrumental in opening up the Warburton district in Victoria. The tune was originally written a semi-tone higher in A flat, with different harmony in the third line particularly. The name was chosen because of the author's title for the poem, "O Lord Omnipotent." Harker died in 1973.

98. ON HILLS AND VALES OF HEAVEN

Song of Solomon 2:1

This hymn is part of a cantata written in 1929 at Broadview College, Illinois, by two Seventh-day Adventist faculty members. The words were by Eugene Clark Rowell (1875-1956), a ministerial graduate of Union College, Nebraska, and later a faculty member there. Then he taught in Bermuda, and in 1921 was appointed head of the English department at Broadview. His words are based on Song of Solomon 2: 1, "I am the Rose of Sharon, and the Lily of the valleys," words which conclude each stanza.

The music was composed by Stanley Ledington (1889-), organist and composer, who was born in Durham, England, and emigrated to the United States, where he received the Mus. Bac. degree from the Sherwood Music School, Chicago, specializing in composition. He spent forty years teaching music in various Seventh-day Adventist academies and colleges. The tune is named *Rose of Sharon* because it was written for these particular words. Ledington also composed Nos. 46, *For the Sabbath;* 476, *Communion,* and 700, *Benediction.* He died in 1974.

99. IT CAME UPON THE MIDNIGHT CLEAR

Luke 2:13, 14

These words were written in 1849 by an American Unitarian minister, Edmund Hamilton Sears (1810-76). In his boyhood he was an adept versifier, on one occasion writing a third verse of poetry on the spot to prove that he was the author of two other verses which he had chalked on his hat while at play earlier in the day. He believed and preached the divinity of Christ at a time when Unitarians emphasized the social gospel, and he wrote hymns for the special purpose of summarizing his sermons so that their message would be retained. This principle is shown well in this hymn, which draws a modern lesson from the song of the angels to the shepherds on the first Christmas day—"And suddenly there was with the angel a multitude of the heavenly host praising God, and saying, Glory to God in the highest, and on earth peace, good will toward men." Luke 2: 13, 14. The omitted stanzas from the original five are:—

3. But with the woes of sin and strife
The world has suffered long:
Beneath the angel strain have rolled
Two thousand years of wrong,
And man, at war with man, hears not
The love-song which they bring:
Oh, hush the noise, ye men of strife,
And hear the angels sing!

5. For lo! the days are hastening on,
By prophet-bards foretold,
When with the ever circling years,
Comes round the age of gold;
When peace shall over all the earth
Its ancient splendours fling,
And the whole world give back the song
Which now the angels sing.

The tune *Carol,* which means to dance in a ring, suitably named for this Christmas hymn, was composed in 1850 by Richard Storrs Willis (1819-1900) of Detroit, one of Mendelssohn's American friends. He was a graduate of Yale University, possessing both musical and literary talents. He also harmonized No. 165, *Crusader's Hymn. Carol* is Willis's Study No. 23, rearranged by Uzziah Christopher Burnap (1834-1900), a Brooklyn organist who also arranged No. 141, *Serenity.*

100. TO US A CHILD OF HOPE IS BORN

Isaiah 9:6, 7

This hymn is an extract from a longer hymn which is a paraphrase of Isaiah 9: 2-8. It was written in 1781 by John Morison (1749-98), who was a member of a committee appointed to revise the 1745 "Translations and Paraphrases" of the Scriptures. The omitted stanzas are:—

1. The race that long in darkness pin'd
Have seen a glorious light;
The people dwell in day who dwelt
In death's surrounding night.

2. To hail Thy rise, thou better Sun!
The gathering nations come,
Joyous, as when the reapers bear
The harvest-treasures home.

3. For Thou our burden hast remov'd,
And quell'd th' oppressor's sway;
Quick as the slaughter'd squadrons fell
In Midian's evil day.

4. Through shrieks of woe, and scenes of
blood,
The warrior urges on;
The lightning's speed, great Saviour! marks
The conquest Thou hast won.

The present stanzas are the fifth and an extended sixth, and closely paraphrase Isaiah 9: 6, 7, "For unto us a Child is born, unto us a Son is given: and the government shall be upon His shoulder: and His name shall be called Wonderful, Counsellor, The mighty God, The everlasting Father, The Prince of Peace. Of the increase of His government and peace there shall be no end, upon the throne of David . . . to establish it with judgment and with justice from henceforth even for ever." Morison was ordained in 1780 and settled in Caithness, writing poetry and historical studies of the shire, in addition to his church duties.

The tune is an arrangement from the opera "Siroe" (= Cyrus) written in 1728 by George Frederick Handel (1685-1759), the famous German composer of opera and oratorio, who became a naturalized Englishman in 1726, having resided there from 1712. It is named *Christmas* because of the words, and because it is often set to another Christmas hymn, No. 101, "While Shepherds Watched." Handel also had a part in No. 189, *Antioch,* and wrote No. 484, *Samson.*

101. WHILE SHEPHERDS WATCHED THEIR FLOCKS

Luke 2:8-14

This poem-story of the birth of Jesus in Bethlehem was written in 1700 by Nahum Tate (1652-1715), who was then Poet Laureate. It is virtually a metrical version of Luke 2: 8-14, "And there were in the same country shepherds abiding in the fields, keeping watch over their flocks by night. And, lo, the angel of the Lord came upon them, and the glory of the Lord shone round about them: and they were sore afraid. And the angel said unto them, Fear not: for, behold, I bring you good tidings of great joy, which shall be to all people. For unto you is born this day in the city of David a Saviour, which is Christ the Lord. And this shall be a sign unto you; Ye shall find the Babe wrapped in swaddling clothes, lying in a manger. And suddenly there was with the angel a multitude of the heavenly host praising God, and saying, Glory to God in the highest, and on earth peace, good will toward men."

The tune *Winchester Old* is one of the common metre tunes to which psalms were sung, and appeared in the sixteenth century. It was named by Thomas Ravenscroft in 1621, and is one of the earliest tunes to be given a specific name, although it is not named in Este's Psalter 1592, where we find names first given to three other tunes. Thomas Este (1535-1608) or East, was a music publisher who issued works of Elizabethan madrigals as well as metrical psalm tunes.

102. SILENT NIGHT, HOLY NIGHT

Luke 2:11

On December 24, 1818, in Oberndorf, near Salzburg, Austria, the organ of St. Nicola church failed to function. Joseph Mohr (1792-1848), the assistant priest, thereupon decided to write a new hymn for the Christmas Eve service and to accompany it on his guitar. He wrote the words and took them to the organist, Franz Xavier Grüber (1787-1863), at the neighbouring village of Arnsdorf, asking him to write a tune for it. A few days previously, the two men had been discussing music, and they concluded that a perfect Christmas song had never been written. With only a short time remaining, the task was completed. In the church that evening, Mohr sang the tenor and played the guitar accompaniment, and Grüber sang the bass. When the organ was repaired by an organ builder from Zillertal, he heard the story, and taught the carol to the four Strasser sisters, who used it in their programme of Tyrolean mountain songs. The words recall the night in Bethlehem when Jesus was born: "Unto you is born this day in the city of David a Saviour, which is Christ the Lord." Luke 2: 11. An alternative translation of the second stanza is:—

2. Silent night, holy night,
   Shepherds quake at the sight,
   Glories stream from heaven afar,
   Heavenly hosts sing alleluia,
   Christ the Saviour is born.

The tune *Stille Nacht* (= silent night) receives its name from the words.

103. THOU DIDST LEAVE THY THRONE

Luke 2:7

Miss Emily Elizabeth Steele Elliott (1836-97) was the daughter of the rector of St. Mark's, Brighton, England, and the niece of Charlotte Elliott (see Nos. 61, 222, 325, 357). She wrote these words in 1864 for the choir and the children of the parish school, basing them on Luke 2: 7: "There was no room for them in the inn."

The tune *Margaret* was composed in 1876 by Timothy Richard Matthews (1826-1910), an Anglican minister, who also composed Nos. 290, *Chenies,* and 460, *Saxby.*

104. O LITTLE TOWN OF BETHLEHEM

Luke 2:13, 14

Phillips Brooks (1835-93), while rector of Holy Trinity, Philadelphia, made a special visit in 1866 to the Holy Land, and was in Bethlehem on Sunday, December 24. In the evening he visited the field of the shepherds where, according to tradition, the angel host appeared. Then from 10 p.m. to 3 a.m. on Christmas morning he attended the service in the Church of the Nativity. The music and the scenes so impressed him that a new carol was born in his mind. He did not commit it to paper, however, until two years later in 1868, and he then wrote five stanzas, based on Luke 2: 13, 14: "And suddenly there was with the angel a multitude of the heavenly host praising God, and saying, Glory to God in the highest, and on earth peace, good will toward men." The omitted stanza is:—

4. Where children pure and happy
Pray to the blessed Child,
Where misery cries out to Thee,
Son of the mother mild,
Where Charity stands watching
And Faith holds wide the door,
The dark night wakes, the glory breaks,
And Christmas comes once more.

The two halves of the second stanza have been interchanged from the original.

Brooks gave the words to his organist, Lewis Henry Redner (1831-1908), who was also the Sunday school superintendent, promising to name the anticipated tune after him. In vain the latter waited for an inspirational melody, but not until Christmas Eve was he satisfied. He fell asleep, and woke after a few hours with this melody ringing in his ears. He jotted it down quickly on paper at his bedside, and harmonized it in the morning, ready to be first sung on December 27, 1868. The tune was later named *St. Louis,* the different spelling of his Christian name being to avoid embarrassment. Redner was a talented real-estate agent and became a wealthy man in this profession, but always kept his interest in Sunday school and church and music.

105. O COME, ALL YE FAITHFUL

Matthew 2:11

This hymn was in use in France about 1700 and manuscript copies of it in Latin are known dated about 1750. The translation, published in 1852, was the revision of an 1841 effort of Canon Frederick Oakeley (1802-80) who was ordained an Anglican minister in 1826 and became a Roman Catholic in 1845. The words are based on the incident of the wise men who adored the babe Jesus. "When they were come into the house, they saw the young child with Mary His mother, and fell down, and worshipped Him." Matthew 2: 11. Other stanzas are:—

> God of God, Light of Light,
> Lo, He abhors not the virgin's womb;
> Very God, begotten not created:

and additions by W. T. Brooke:—

> See how the shepherds, summoned to His cradle,
> Leaving their flocks, draw nigh in holy fear;
> We too will thither bend our joyful footsteps:
>
> Lo, star-led chieftains, Magi, Christ adoring,
> Offer Him incense, gold, and myrrh;
> We to the Christ child bring our heart's oblations:
>
> Child, for us sinners, poor and in a manger,
> Fain would we embrace Thee, with awe and love;
> Who would not love Thee, loving us so dearly?

The tune has been attributed to John Reading, the organist of Westminster College in 1680, and also to Samuel Webbe senior (1740-1816). It is known as *Portuguese Hymn* because it was used in England in 1785 at the Portuguese embassy and received this name from the Duke of Leeds who heard it used in the chapel there. He used it later at concerts under this name, supposing it to come from Portugal. However, the tune was commonly used in Catholic chapels as their regular Christmas hymn and sung to the Latin words "Adeste Fideles" ("Come Near, Faithful Ones"). John Francis Wade (c. 1711-86), a Roman Catholic writer and copyist, transcribed the tune in 1751. The same tune, transposed down one tone to the key of G, is used for No. 255, "How Firm a Foundation." In his "Cantus Diversi," 1751, there also appeared his other tune, No. 176, *Holywood.*

106. THERE'S A SONG IN THE AIR

Matthew 2:2

The words were written in 1872 by Josiah Gilbert Holland (1819-81) of Belchertown, Massachusetts, a lecturer and author, but then editor of *Scribner's Magazine,* and they appear in his "The Marble Prophecy and Other Poems." The hymn emphasizes the thought echoed in the question which the wise men asked King Herod, "Saying, Where is He that is born King of the Jews? for we have seen His star in the east, and are come to worship Him." Matthew 2: 2.

The tune *Christmas Song* was composed in July, 1904, by Karl Pomeroy Harrington (1861-1953) while on vacation at his summer cottage in New Hampshire. He was an organist and choir director of the Methodist Church and a musical editor of his church's hymnal. The tune is so named because of the words of the first line and the general Christmas sentiment of the hymn. No. 703, *Invocation Sentence,* is also by the same composer.

107. WE THREE KINGS OF ORIENT

Matthew 2:1, 2, 11

Both words and music of this Christmas carol were written in 1857 and published in 1863 by an American, John Henry Hopkins (1820-91), a Protestant Episcopal minister of Williamsport, Pennsylvania, and appear in his "Carols, Hymns, and Songs." The Scripture basis is: "When Jesus was born in Bethlehem . . . there came wise men from the east . . . saying, . . . We have seen His star in the east." "And when they had opened their treasures, they presented unto Him gifts; gold, and frankincense, and myrrh." Matthew 2: 1, 2, 11. Objection has been raised in that the wise men are not called kings, neither is the number of them given in the Bible. However, the hymn details the three gifts with the probable significance of each in the life of our Lord, namely: gold for kingship, frankincense for worship and adoration, myrrh for sacrifice, representing His office as King, Priest, and Lamb.

The tune *Kings of Orient* recalls in its name the seventh century tradition which says that the gold was brought by the old man Melchior, the frankincense by the ruddy youth Kaspar, and the myrrh by the swarthy, dark-skinned Balthasar. The tune for the stanzas is written in a minor key, modulating to the major for the refrain.

108. THE FIRST NOEL

Luke 2:11

In the Middle Ages all the singing inside the church was done by the priests. However, outside the church the people gave vent to their emotions and sang their semi-sacred songs based mainly on Bible stories and characters, this one based on Luke 2: 11: "For unto you is born this day in the city of David a Saviour, which is Christ the Lord." From this practice there grew up the carol or ring dance (see No. 99) which was less formal than a solemn religious chant and performed in a freer atmosphere. The words were made up spontaneously and fitted to the rhythm of the music. This explains the irregular metre of this hymn and also the slight inaccuracies, for it describes the shepherds as seeing a star shining in the east. The wise men were in the east and saw the star obviously is a westerly direction, whereas the shepherds saw only the angels overhead. Furthermore the star was not visible continuously, for the wise men "rejoiced with exceeding great joy" (Matthew 2: 10) when they saw it again standing over the house where Mary and the Babe were. Again the specific direction of "to the north-west" sounds like a manufactured on-the-spot rhyme for a typical carol. There were nine stanzas, the omitted ones being:—

5. Then did they know assuredly
Within that house the King did lie;
One entered in then for to see,
And found the Babe in poverty.

7. Between an ox stall and an ass,
This Child truly there born He was;
For want of clothing they did Him lay
All in the manger, among the hay.

8. Then let us all with one accord
Sing praises to our heavenly Lord
That hath made heaven and earth of nought,
And with His blood mankind hath bought.

9. If we in our time shall do well,
We shall be free from death and hell,
For God hath prepared for us all
A resting place in general.

The tune *The First Noel* was first published in William Sandy's (1792-1874) collection of "Christmas Carols," 1833, but it is obviously of much older origin, at least seventeenth century. "Noel" may be from the French "nouvelle" or news, that is good tidings of great joy. Another interesting derivation suggested is that it is the echo of the last two syllables of the word Emmanuel, the prophetic name reserved for the child Jesus. (Matthew 1: 23.) Yet another traces the word from "nadal" or "natalis"—"birthday." It is noteworthy that the melody is very easy to sing, being mainly a succession of notes separated by a single interval, or in other words, a series of scale passages or portions thereof.

109. O COME, O COME, IMMANUEL

Isaiah 7:14

In the monasteries of the twelfth century it was the regular practice to sing the antiphon at vespers. During the season of Advent this consisted of a long drawn out "O," a wail of sorrow and desire, expressing an earnest longing for the advent of our Lord. Subsequently another word or two was added to this great "O" of Advent, one of our Lord's titles being chosen, namely: Immanuel, Wisdom, Desire, Root of Jesse, Key of David, Lord, Daystar. Three of the last four are in the omitted stanzas:—

O come, Thou Rod of Jesse, free
Thine own from Satan's tyranny;
From depths of hell Thy people save,
And give them victory o'er the grave.

O come, Thou Key of David, come
And open wide our heav'nly home,
Make safe the way that leads on high,
And close the path to misery.

O come, Adonai, Lord of might,
Who to Thy tribes, on Sinai's height,
In ancient times didst give the law
In cloud and majesty and awe.

The seven were incorporated into one hymn presumably in the twelfth century, and the words have been translated from the Latin by John Mason Neale (1818-66), see appendix. The second and third stanzas are translations in 1916 by Henry Sloane Coffin (1877-1954) of New York, a Presbyterian minister and president of Union Theological Seminary for many years. One of the many texts referred to is Isaiah 7: 14, "Shall call His name Immanuel."

Plain song was the customary form of singing in the early Christian church and the music had no accents and no bars, the rhythm being determined by the words. It was in unison, all singing the melody, and not intended to be harmonized, nor to be accompanied by a musical instrument. This tune *Veni Immanuel* (= Come, Immanuel) is ascribed to the thirteenth century and could be a rearrangement of several phrases which are reconstituted to fit the hymn. It resembles a Kyrie (= O Lord) in the "Missa Regia" of Henri Dumont (1610-84).

110. ALL MY HEART THIS NIGHT REJOICES

Luke 2-11

Paul Gerhardt (1607-76) was, next to Martin Luther, the greatest German hymn-writer, and all of his more than 100 hymns stress the love of God to man, and are of a comforting, devotional nature. They mark the change from the formal ecclesiastical type to the personal subjective one. These words were written in 1651 as a German Christmas hymn, and the unusual metre and lilt of the lines have been retained perfectly in this translation of 1858 by Catherine Winkworth (1827-78), see appendix. There were originally fifteen eight-line stanzas, later reduced to ten stanzas, some of those omitted being:—

2. For it dawns—the promised morrow
Of His birth
Who the earth
Rescues from her sorrow.
God to wear our form descendeth,
Of His grace
To our race
Here His Son He lendeth.

3. Yea, so truly for us careth,
That His Son
All we've done
As our offering beareth;
As our Lamb who, dying for us,
Bears our load,
And to God
Doth in peace restore us.

9. Blessed Saviour, let me find Thee!
Keep Thou me
Close to Thee,
Cast me not behind Thee!
Life of life, my heart Thou stillest;
Calm I rest
On Thy breast,
All this void Thou fillest.

10. Thee, dear Lord, with heed I'll cherish
Live to Thee,
And with Thee
Dying, shall not perish;
But shall dwell with Thee for ever,
Far on high,
In the joy
That can alter never.

The Scripture basis is Luke 2: 11: "For unto you is born this day in the city of David a Saviour, which is Christ the Lord." Gerhardt also wrote No. 146, "Jesus, Thy Boundless Love to Me," and translated No. 130, "O Sacred Head, Now Wounded."

The tune *Stella* was composed in 1894 by Horatio William Parker (1836-1919), who was an organist, composer of cantatas and oratorios, and from 1894 professor of music at Yale. In 1902 he received the degree of Mus. Doc. from Cambridge University, England. He named the tune *Stella* (= *Star*), because of the mention of the star of Bethlehem in the hymn, and added his own name Parker to distinguish it from the other tune *Stella* (English), No. 151. Parker also composed Nos. 47, *Pixham;* 58 and 177, *Garden City;* 133, *Jubilate,* and 198, *Pro Patria.*

111. HARK! THE HERALD ANGELS SING

Luke 2-14

Charles Wesley (1707-88), see appendix, wrote in 1739 a hymn of ten stanzas, each of four lines, beginning:—

1. Hark, how all the welkin rings
Glory to the King of kings.

In 1753 the first two lines of the hymn were changed to the present form, and since then other alterations have been made. The omitted stanzas are:—

7. Come, Desire of nations, come,
Fix in us Thy humble home;
Rise, the woman's conquering Seed,
Bruise in us the serpent's head.

8. Now display Thy saving power,
Ruin'd nature now restore;
Now in mystic union join
Thine to ours, and ours to Thine.

9. Adam's likeness, Lord, efface;
Stamp Thy image in its place;
Second Adam from above
Re-instate us in Thy love.

10. Let us Thee, though lost, regain,
Thee the life, the inner man;
O! to all Thyself impart,
Form'd in each believing heart.

While many scriptures are quoted in the hymn, a summary would be Luke 2: 14, "Glory to God in the highest, and on earth peace, good will toward men."

In 1840 the words were set to music by the famous composer Jakob Ludwig Felix Mendelssohn-Bartholdy (1809-47), who wrongly prophesied that although singers and hearers would like the tune, it would never be appropriate to sacred words. The present tune *Mendelssohn* is an arrangement in 1856 by the organist William Hayman Cummings (1831-1915), a singer in Mendelssohn's "Elijah" in 1847 conducted by the composer, and who had his own choir sing this successful arrangement. Mendelssohn, son of a Jewish banker of Hamburg, Germany, also composed Nos. 257, *Trust;* 674, *Abiding;* 687, unnamed, and 692 *Birmingham,* and arranged No. 217, *Munich.*

112. AS WITH GLADNESS MEN OF OLD

Matthew 2:1-11

William Chatterton Dix (1837-98) was an insurance agent of Bristol, England, who in 1860 was slowly recovering from a serious illness. On Epiphany Sunday, January 6, he was reading the story of the wise men given in Matthew 2: 1-11, and realized that there were lessons there for our own Christian witness. Later in the day he wrote five stanzas pointing out the present-day application in that we, too, should be led to Jesus to offer our treasures to Him, and willingly to adore Him. The omitted stanza is:—

5. In the heav'nly country bright
Need they no created light;
Thou its Light, its Joy, its Crown,
Thou its Sun which goes not down;
There for ever may we sing
Alleluias to our King.

The tune *Dix* was composed in 1838 by Conrad Kocher (1786-1872), who popularized choral singing in Germany. Although Dix actually disliked the tune, he finally accepted the very popular combination of his words with this German chorale. *Dix* is also used for No. 22, "For the Beauty of the Earth."

113. ANGELS FROM THE REALMS OF GLORY

Philippians 2:10

This poem was written in 1816 by James Montgomery (1771-1854), see appendix, and printed in the December 24 issue of the newspaper *Sheffield Iris,* where he was a member of the staff. Its title was "Nativity" and its other stanza was:—

5. Sinners, wrung with true repentance,
Doomed for guilt to endless pains,
Justice now repeals the sentence;
Mercy calls you—break your chains:
Come and worship,
Worship Christ, the new-born King.

Another later addition is:—

Though an infant now we view Him,
He shall fill His Father's throne,
Gather all the nations to Him;
Every knee shall then bow down:
Come and worship,
Worship Christ, the new-born King.

There are many Scriptural allusions, e.g., "there were in the same country shepherds abiding in the field, keeping watch over their flocks by night" (Luke 2: 8); "the Word was made flesh, and dwelt among us" (John 1: 14); "the Desire of all nations shall come" (Haggai 2: 7); "the Lord, whom we seek, shall suddenly come to His temple" (Malachi 3: 1); but all of them lead to the same conclusion, namely, "that at the name of Jesus every knee should bow." Philippians 2: 10.

The tune *Regent Square,* also used for No. 487, "Christ Is Made the Sure Foundation," but there transposed to the key of B flat, was composed in 1867 by Henry Thomas Smart (1813-79), an organist and organ builder. He had been afflicted by blindness for about three years. It was specially written for a Presbyterian hymnbook and named *Regent Square* in 1867 by the editor, Dr. James Hamilton, who was the Presbyterian minister of St. Philip's church, Regent Square, London, where Smart had been organist for two years also. Other tunes by Smart are Nos. 135 and 362, *Lancashire;* 363, *Chebar,* and 376, *Pilgrims.*

114. THE HIDDEN YEARS AT NAZARETH

Matthew 2:23

Very little is revealed in the Bible concerning the life of Jesus as a boy and as a young man. We know that after Joseph and Mary returned from their refuge in Egypt they "came and dwelt in a city called Nazareth." Matthew 2: 23. This was "their own city Nazareth" (Luke 2: 39), and here "the Child grew, and waxed strong in spirit, filled with wisdom: and the grace of God was upon Him." Luke 2: 40. A brief visit to the Passover at Jerusalem at the age of twelve is recorded, after which Jesus "went down with them, and came to Nazareth, and was subject unto them." Luke 2: 51. The environment was most unpropitious for the city's reputation was very low—"Can there any good thing come out of

Nazareth?" John 1: 46. Nevertheless, as the author of this hymn, Allen Eastman Cross (1864-1943), says, those years were full of deeds of kindness and were days of decision. Cross had been urged to write a new hymn on the youth of our Lord. Thinking of these hidden years, he recalled his earlier visit to the Holy Land, where he had been most impressed by the countryside of Galilee, especially the town and environs of Nazareth, rather than by the shrines and churches that abound in disputed spots. As he continued to meditate on the boyhood of our Lord, the words came to him effortlessly. The two references to Syria (stars and sky) remind us of the early origin of God's chosen people—"a Syrian ready to perish was my father," (Deuteronomy 26: 5)—although Jesus Himself made only a brief visit to Syria, and that long after His boyhood. (Mark 8: 24-31.) Most of the hymn deals with the hidden years, but the last four lines make a grand appeal for the youth to follow in the footsteps of Jesus, placing truth above death, and God above fate. Cross was a Congregational minister at Boston from 1901-1911, made a world trip in 1911-12, and was then transferred to Milford, Massachusetts, where he retired from active ministry in 1925. He then moved to Manchester, New Hampshire, and concentrated on writing.

The tune *Nazareth,* named because of the words for which it was written, was composed in 1927 by Harry L. Harts.

115. WHEN THE LORD OF LOVE WAS HERE

Matthew 13:34

Stopford Augustus Brooke (1832-1916), a noted Irish preacher and Anglican minister, wrote these words in 1881, the year after he seceded from the Church of England and became an Independent minister, inclining to Unitarianism. He deliberately wrote long hymns on the grounds that congregations liked to sing and to hear singing, hence some of his hymns have fifty lines. This one tells of Christ's healing ministry, of His personal interest in individuals, and of His teaching in parables: "All these things spake Jesus unto the multitude in parables; and without a parable spake He not unto them." Matthew 13: 34. The hymn also speaks of His power to help in our present-day problems and perplexities. The original had six stanzas, the omitted one being:—

6. And when in the fields and woods,
We are filled with nature's moods,
May the grace be given
With Thy faithful heart to say,
All I see and feel today,
Is my Father's heaven.

The tune *Armstrong* was composed in 1893 for the "Plymouth Hymnal" by George Whitefield Chadwick (1854-1931), an American organist and composer. He became director of the New England Conservatorium of Music in 1897, and composed overtures, symphonies, choral works, and string quartettes.

116. DEAR LORD AND FATHER

1 Kings 19:11, 12

After reading the "Sama Veda," one of the sacred books of the Hindus, John Greenleaf Whittier (1807-92), the Quaker poet, contrasted the ceremonies surrounding the preparation of their intoxicating drink "soma" with the Christian Communion service. He expressed his thoughts in a long religious poem of seventeen stanzas, written in 1872 entitled "The Brewing of Soma," and described the pagan Indian who imbibes the soma in order to attain union with his gods, comparing him with the superficial Christian who partakes of the Communion wine for the same purpose. The latter, argues Whittier, is just as pagan, for

"In sensual transports wild and vain
We brew in many a Christian fane
The heathen soma still."

Then follow the words of this hymn, which consists of stanzas 12, 13, 14, 16, 17. The one omitted from this succession of stanzas is:—

15. With that deep hush subduing all
Our words and works that drown
The tender whisper of Thy call,
As noiseless let Thy blessing fall
As fell Thy manna down.

The poem pleads for the quiet, inward spiritual communion of the soul with God, an experience fittingly described by a Quaker, which is far better than any outward excitement. It can well be summarized in the last few lines of his poem which draws a lesson from the experience of Elijah as recorded in 1 Kings 19: 11, 12: "After the wind an earthquake . . . after the earthquake a fire . . . after the fire a still small voice." Whittier also wrote Nos. 141, "We May Not Climb," and 483, "All Things Are Thine."

The tune *Whittier* (*Rest*) was composed specially for these words in 1887 by Frederick Charles Maker (1844-1927), a Congregational organist of three different churches in Bristol, England. It is known also as *Elton* and used for No. 314, "When Darkness Gathers." Maker also composed Nos. 45, *Wentworth,* and 280, *St. Christopher.*

117. PRINCE OF PEACE, CONTROL MY WILL

Ephesians 2:14

Mary Ann Serrett Barber (1801-64), of Huguenot ancestry, was an enthusiastic supporter of the Anglican Church. She contributed verse to the church magazine and edited a children's magazine also. In 1838 she sent in a poem of four stanzas each of eight lines, entitled "He Is Our Peace" (Ephesians 2: 14), from which the present hymn is a modified selection. Its theme is a desire for peace from the Prince of Peace, the word "peace" being mentioned five times in three stanzas.

The tune *Flower* was composed by James Henry Fillmore (1849-?) of Cincinnati, one of three brothers in a musical family, who learned printing and also wrote hymns, and then combined the two and formed a music publishing firm (see also No. 417). The two halves of this tune are almost identical musically.

118. WHEN I SURVEY THE WONDROUS CROSS

Galatians 6:14

Isaac Watts (1674-1748), see appendix, based this hymn written in 1707 on Galatians 6: 14, "But God forbid that I should glory, save in the cross of our Lord Jesus Christ, by whom the world is crucified unto me, and I unto the world." He entitled it "Crucifixion to the World, by the Cross of Calvary," and intended it to be sung on Good Friday. It has been altered somewhat, the original second stanza reading:—

2. Forbid it Lord, that I should boast
Save in the death of Christ my God; (compare stanza 3)
All the vain things that charm me most,
I sacrifice them to His blood.

Then follows our second stanza, and then Watts's fourth, generally omitted:—

4. His dying crimson, like a robe
Spread o'er His body on the tree
Then am I dead to all the globe,
And all the globe is dead to me.

The greatest praise for this hymn came from Charles Wesley who said that he would gladly exchange all the hymns he had ever written in return for this matchless one. Strangely enough, a similar compliment was paid in reverse by Watts to Wesley regarding the latter's "Come, O Thou Traveller Unknown" (No. 243).

The tune *Rockingham Old,* sometimes called *Communion,* was published in 1790 by the Doncaster Parish Church organist, Dr. Edward Miller (1731-1807), a position which he held for over fifty years. He published "Psalm Tunes" in which he set this tune to these words, probably deriving it from a triple-time tune called *Tunbridge* appearing in "Psalmody in Miniature," 1778, by Aaron Williams (1731-76). Miller commented that this tune would make a good long metre, and said that "part of the melody [was] taken from a hymn tune." *Rockingham Old* is also used for No. 89, "God Is the Refuge of His Saints," and was so named to commemorate Miller's friend and patron, the Marquis of Rockingham.

119. WHEN I SURVEY THE WONDROUS CROSS

Galatians 6: 14

For the words, see No. 118.

The melody is identical with that of No. 118, *Rockingham Old,* but it is found in the tenor part. The harmony differs and the tune is a typical fa-burden by Dr. Geoffrey Turton Shaw (1879-1943), an inspector of music in schools who specialized in the writing of descants. Fa-burden is a corruption of the French *faux-bourdon* or false bass, which was a first inversion of a triad (or chord of three notes consisting of root, third, and fifth, or doh, me, soh) leaving the third or middle note as the lower or bass part. This fourteenth century meaning no longer applies today, as a fa-burden now consists of a main melody in the tenor part with a secondary melody in the soprano. Another illustration of Shaw's fa-burdens is written to No. 92, *Tallis' Ordinal.*

120. WHEN I SURVEY THE WONDROUS CROSS

Galatians 6: 14

For the words see No. 118.

The tune *McCabe* was composed by E. S. Widdemer.

121. 'TIS MIDNIGHT; AND ON OLIVES' BROW

Luke 22: 41-44

This hymn was written in 1822 by William Bingham Tappan (1794-1849), an American Congregational minister and promoter of Sunday schools. It describes our Lord's agony in the Garden of

Gethsemane on the lower slopes of the Mount of Olives. "And He was withdrawn from them about a stone's cast, and kneeled down, and prayed." Luke 22: 41. "And being in agony He prayed more earnestly: and His sweat was as it were great drops of blood falling down to the ground." Verse 44. "And there appeared an angel unto Him from heaven, strengthening Him." Verse 43. One slight alteration has been made in the substitution in the last stanza of the word "ether" for the original "heavenly."

The tune *Olives' Brow* was composed especially for these words in 1853 by William Batchelder Bradbury (1816-68), see appendix.

122. GO TO DARK GETHSEMANE

John 19: 30

These words were written in 1820 by James Montgomery (1771-1854), see appendix, but considerably revised by him in 1825. The first and third stanzas are from the later version, the second from the original. A fourth and last stanza of the 1820 text, now omitted, is:—

4. Early to the tomb repair,
Where they laid His breathless clay;
Angels kept their vigil there:
Who hath taken Him away?
"Christ is risen!" He seeks the skies;
Saviour, teach us so to rise.

The culmination of the hymn is found in the Scripture verse, "Jesus . . . said, It is finished: and He bowed His head, and gave up the ghost." John 19: 30.

The tune appeared in 1853 in the collection "Church Hymn Tunes, Ancient and Modern," by Richard Redhead (1820-1901), an English organist and director of boys' choirs. It is No. 76 in that book, and is therefore sometimes named *Redhead No. 76.* It has also been named *Ajalon, Petra* (= rock), because it is so often associated with the hymn, "Rock of Ages," No. 474, and because of its association with the words of No. 122, *Gethsemane.*

123. THERE WAS ONE WHO WAS WILLING

Colossians 2: 13, 14

These words were written in 1899 by Mrs. Frank A. (Carrie Ellis) Breck (1855-?) who married in 1884 and then lived in Portland, Oregon, raising a family of five daughters. She had written verse for religious periodicals, and altogether wrote about 2,000 hymns and poems, composing many of them while doing her housework. She tried to use the exact language of Scripture (see stanza 2, line 2 for Romans 8: 1) because of the promise that God's Word "shall not return unto Me void" (Isaiah 55: 11), and based this hymn on Colossians 2: 13, 14, "Being dead in your sins . . . hath He quickened together with Him, having forgiven you all trespasses . . . nailing it to His cross." Mrs. Breck also wrote No. 545, "Face to Face With Christ My Saviour."

The tune *Nailed to the Cross* was composed in 1898 by Grant Colfax Tullar (1869-19?) of Bolton, Connecticut, to a nature poem by Laura Newell entitled "By the Murmuring Brook." Mrs. Breck liked the tune and thought it could well be used as a hymn tune, and asked permission of the composer to write a gospel song to it. Tullar was named after the president and vice-president of the United States (Ulysses S. Grant and Schuyler Colfax), and became a minister of the Methodist Episcopal Church as well as the musical director and main speaker of evangelistic campaigns. He founded a music publishing business with Isaac Meredith in 1893, and was its president for over thirty years. He also composed Nos. 425, *Peek,* and 545, *Face to Face.*

124. ALAS! AND DID MY SAVIOUR BLEED?

1 Timothy 1: 15

Isaac Watts (1674-1748), see appendix, wrote six stanzas of this hymn in 1707 under the title "Godly Sorrow Arising From the Sufferings of Christ." The second stanza now omitted is:—

2. Thy body slain, sweet Jesus, Thine,
And bathed in its own blood,
While all exposed to wrath divine
The glorious Sufferer stood!

The hymn is fitly summarized in the Apostle Paul's statement: "Christ Jesus came into the world to save sinners." 1 Timothy 1: 15. Watts's membership of the Independent Church gave rise to the mistaken impression that he was a Unitarian. However, he shows his clear belief on this point in the third line of the third stanza which was originally, "When God the mighty Maker died," thus identifying Jesus as very God. The refrain is not found in Watts's works.

The tune *Avon,* which is sometimes called *Martyrdom* as in No. 378, and formerly *Fenwick,* was composed in 1800 by Hugh Wilson (1766-1824), a shoemaker of Fenwick in Ayrshire, Scotland. It was first written in 4/4 time, but changed in 1825 to 3/4 time.

125. IN THE CROSS OF CHRIST I GLORY

Galatians 6: 14

The title of this hymn is, appropriately enough, engraved on the tombstone of the author, Sir John Bowring (1792-1872). The words were published in his "Poems" in 1825, and are based on Galatians 6: 14: "But God forbid that I should glory, save in the cross of our Lord Jesus Christ." The original has a fifth stanza identical with the first. The story that Bowring wrote the hymn at Macao is fictional, as he was not appointed as British consul to China until 1849, twenty-four years after the hymn was written.

The tune *Rathbun* was composed in 1849 by Ithamar Conkey (1815-67) in Norwich, Connecticut. It was inspired by a series of seven sermons preached on the words of Christ on the cross, and also by Bowring's words. Conkey was the organist and choir director of the Central Baptist church in Norwich, and named the tune in honour of his leading soprano, Mrs. Beriah S. Rathbun. It is also used for No. 511, "Gentle Peace, From Heaven Descended."

126. THERE IS A GREEN HILL FAR AWAY

Hebrews 13: 12, 13

Miss Cecil Frances Humphreys (1818-95), who married the Rev. William Alexander in 1850, used to drive into Londonderry by a grass-covered hill which reminded her of the hill of Calvary, which was probably a small hillock outside old Jerusalem. She had a desire to make the Apostles' Creed comprehensible to children, and with a picture of this hill in mind she wrote this children's hymn in 1848 to amplify the fourth section of the creed, which is: "Suffered under Pontius Pilate, was crucified, dead, and buried." The second line of the hymn, "without a city wall," is based on Hebrews 13: 12, "suffered without the gate," but it caused confusion to a little child, who took "without" to mean "not having." Mrs. Alexander then changed it to the unambiguous "outside." "Wherefore Jesus also, that He might sanctify the people with His own blood, suffered without the gate. Let us go forth therefore unto Him without the camp, bearing His reproach." Hebrews 13: 12, 13. Mrs. Alexander, whose husband became the bishop of Derry and Raphoe in 1867, wrote about 200 poems and 200 hymns, among them being Nos. 421, "All Things Bright and Beautiful"; 424, "Once in Royal David's City," and 521, "Jesus Calls Us."

The tune *Horsley* was composed in 1844 by the organist William Horsley (1774-1858), an intimate friend of the composer Mendelssohn, and one of the founders in 1813 of the London Philharmonic Society. At the time, he was organist and singing teacher at the Royal Female Orphan Asylum in Lambeth, London, and this tune was composed specially for the girls there.

127. RIDE ON IN MAJESTY

Matthew 21: 7-9

Henry Hart Milman (1791-1868), later dean of St. Paul's Cathedral, London, was a talented poet who won many verse prizes at Oxford, where later he became professor of poetry in 1821. His friend Reginald Heber (see Nos. 73, 178, 340, 361, 445, 476) suggested that he turn his gift to hymn writing, and as a result these words were written in 1821, to be sung especially on Palm Sunday, the week before Easter. There were originally five stanzas, the one omitted being:—

> 4. Ride on! ride on in majesty!
> Thy last and fiercest strife is nigh;
> The Father on His sapphire throne
> Expects His own anointed Son.

The third line of the first stanza was changed in 1852 from "Thine humble beast pursues his road" to the present wording. The Scripture basis is, ". . . brought the ass, and the colt, . . . and set Him thereon. And a very great multitude spread their garments in the way; others cut down branches from the trees, and strawed them in the way . . . and . . . cried, saying, Hosanna." Matthew 21: 7-9. The hymn was first printed in 1827 in Heber's "Hymns for Weekly Church Services of the Year."

The tune *St. Drostane* was composed in 1862 by John Bacchus Dykes (1823-76), see appendix, especially for these words. The name commemorates an Irish monk, nephew of Columba, who founded churches in Ireland and in eastern Scotland.

128. INTO THE WOODS MY MASTER WENT

1 Peter 2: 24

Sidney Lanier (1842-81) of Macon, Georgia, a Presbyterian who departed gradually from orthodox Christianity, wrote this unusual poem in November, 1880. Its title is "A Ballad of the Trees and the Master" and it is more of a carol than a hymn. Lanier was a lecturer in English Literature at Johns Hopkins University, and at home in Baltimore he dashed off the poem in twenty minutes while his wife was changing into warmer clothes. She was planning to visit a sick friend, and he handed the poem to her to pass on. It was possibly in his mind before, as he often loved to walk alone in Druid Hill Park, where he found communion with the trees. He was often very sick because of tuberculosis, and went there to find peace and relief. The theme of the poem is the woods, first the olives in the Garden of Gethsemane, and then the wood of the cross, which the Apostle Peter refers to also as a tree: "Who His own self bare our sins in His own body on the tree." 1 Peter 2: 24.

The tune was composed in 1904 by Peter Christian Lutkin (1858-1931), organist at various Episcopal churches in America, musical editor of the "Methodist Hymnal" of 1905, and founder and dean of the school of music at North-western University in 1896, where Lutkin Hall of Music perpetuates his memory. The tune is named *Lanier* to commemorate the author, as it was composed especially for the words. It is written in a minor key, giving it a haunting quality, and fitting very aptly with the sad words. Lutkin also wrote No. 695, *Choral Blessing*.

129. BEHOLD THE LAMB OF GOD

John 1: 29

Matthew Bridges (1800-94) wrote seven stanzas of this hymn in 1848 under the title "Ecce Agnus Dei" = "Behold the Lamb of God." His first line had only four syllables, "Behold the Lamb" for each stanza, and not six as in our version. The three omitted stanzas are:—

3. Behold the Lamb!
Archangels—fold your wings—
Seraphs—hush all the strings
Of million lyres:
The Victim, veil'd on earth, in love—
Unveil'd—enthron'd—ador'd above,
All heaven admires!

4. Behold the Lamb!
Drop down, ye glorious skies—
He dies—He dies—He dies—
For man once lost!
Yet lo! He lives—He lives—He lives—
And to His church Himself He gives—
Incarnate Host!

6. Behold the Lamb!
Saints, wrapt in blissful rest—
Souls—awaiting to be blest—
Oh! Lord—how long!
Thou church on earth o'erwhelm'd with fears,
Still in this vale of woe and tears,
Swell the full song.

The latter part of the third stanza (Bridges's fifth) was:—

. . . Purge out our leaven;
Clothe us with godliness and good,
Feed us with Thy celestial food—
Manna from heaven!

The last three lines of the hymn are notable as a typical conclusion to a hymn, namely, an expression of the doctrine of the Trinity, but the metaphors here are unusual, namely: Ancient of days, Lamb, Comforter. Bridges wrote a polemic against the Roman Catholic Church in 1828, but twenty years later joined this communion. He also wrote No. 162, "Crown Him With Many Crowns."

The tune *St. John* was composed in 1864 by John Bacchus Dykes (1823-76), see appendix, especially for these words, and is so named because of John the Baptist's words recorded in John 1: 29: "Behold the Lamb of God, which taketh away the sin of the world." The first part is written in a minor key, modulating to a major key in the second part, a not unusual device by this composer, for example: Nos. 225, *Vox Dilecti,* and 367, *St. Andrew of Crete.*

130. O SACRED HEAD NOW WOUNDED

Matthew 27: 29

Bernard of Clairvaux (1091-1153), a Cistercian monk, persuaded Louis VII to attempt the second crusade, and after its tragic failure, retired to a solitary life. While contemplating a crucifix, he had a vision in which the figure of Christ came down from the cross and embraced him. After the vision, he composed a long poem in seven parts, one for each day of the week, each addressed to a different member of the body of Christ. Each part consisted of five stanzas each of ten lines, and was addressed to the feet, knees, hands, side, breast, heart, and face respectively. Paul Gerhardt (1607-76) made a free translation of the last section of the hymn in 1656 from Latin to German. Incidentally, the Latin original has also been attributed to Arnulf von Loewen (1200-51). The English version is part of a 10-stanza hymn translated in 1830 from Gerhardt's version by Dr. James Waddell Alexander (1804-59), a Presbyterian minister in New York, editor, and professor, who entitled it "To the Suffering Face of Jesus Christ." Some omitted lines are:—

1. Once reigning in the highest
In light and majesty,
Dishonoured now Thou diest,
Yet here I worship Thee.

This follows the first half of the first stanza.

> 3. Receive me, my Redeemer;
> My Shepherd, make me Thine,
> Of every good the Fountain,
> Thou art the Spring of mine!

This follows the second stanza in "Church Hymnal." An appropriate Scripture reference, is, "When they had plaited a crown of thorns, they put it upon His head, and a reed in His right hand: and they bowed the knee before Him, and mocked Him." Matthew 27: 29. Bernard also wrote the original of Nos. 154, "Jesus, Thou Joy of Loving Hearts," and 158, "Jesus, the Very Thought of Thee." Gerhardt, a noted hymn-writer, also wrote Nos. 110, "All My Heart This Night Rejoices," and 146, "Jesus, Thy Boundless Love to Me."

The tune was originally an air of a German love song, composed in 1601 by the German organist Hans Leo Hassler (1564-1612), who for the last four years of his life was organist at Dresden to the Elector of Saxony. It was set to words of a hymn in 1613, and later to the German words of this hymn and harmonized by Johann Sebastian Bach (1685-1750) for his St. Matthew's Passion, which was first performed at Leipzig on Good Friday, 1729. Its name is *Passion Chorale* because it is a sacred choral song telling of the sufferings of our Lord. Bach played many instruments, especially the organ, of which he was the most outstanding exponent of his day. He also harmonized the melodies of Nos. 197, *Wachet Auf*, or *Sleepers, Wake*, and 201, *Yule*.

131. HAIL THE DAY THAT SEES HIM RISE

Psalm 24: 7

Charles Wesley (1707-88), see appendix, wrote ten stanzas of this ascension-day hymn in 1739. Slight changes have been made; for example, the first stanza was originally:—

> 1. Hail the day that sees Him rise,
> Ravished from our wishful eyes!
> Christ, awhile to mortals given,
> Reascends His native heaven.

Note the skilful use in the second stanza of most of the words of Psalm 24: 7: "Lift up your heads, O ye gates . . . ye everlasting doors; and the King of glory shall come in." The omitted stanzas are:—

> 3. Circled round with angel powers,
> Their triumphant Lord, and ours,
> Conqueror over death and sin,
> Take the King of glory in!

6. Still for us His death He pleads;
Prevalent, He intercedes;
Near Himself prepares our place,
Harbinger of human race.

7. Master (will we ever say),
Taken from our head today:
See Thy faithful servants, see!
Ever gazing up to Thee.

9. Ever upward let us move,
Wafted on the wings of love;
Looking when our Lord shall come,
Longing, gasping after home.

10. There we shall with Thee remain,
Partners of Thy endless reign;
There Thy face unclouded see,
Find our heaven of heavens in Thee!

The tune *Vienna* was composed in 1797 by Justin Heinrich Knecht (1752-1817), who also wrote Nos. 231 and 278, *St. Hilda*. He was a famous organist of Wurttemberg in southern Germany, although he started his career as a professor of literature.

132. OUR LORD IS RISEN

Psalm 24: 7, 8

Charles Wesley (1707-88), see appendix, wrote this second ascension hymn in 1741, and published it in his "Collection of Psalms and Hymns." This is the second part of the hymn, which began: "The earth with all her fulness owns," and was a three-stanza hymn of eight lines each. The total of twenty-four lines is accounted for by the fact that the second stanza of "Church Hymnal" is repeated between stanzas four and five. An earlier ascension hymn was written two years previously. See No. 131. This one is a paraphrase of Psalm 68: 18: "Thou hast ascended on high, Thou hast led captivity captive" and also of Psalm 24: 7, 8, "Lift up your heads, O ye gates; and be ye lift up, ye everlasting doors; and the King of glory shall come in. Who is this King of glory? The Lord strong and mighty, the Lord mighty in battle."

The tune *Brockham* or *Confidence* was composed in 1707 by Jeremiah Clarke (c. 1669-1707), organist of St. Paul's Cathedral, London, from 1695, and of the Chapel Royal in 1704. He composed many songs, hymns, odes, and anthems, but came to an untimely end when he shot himself in the churchyard because of a love affair. A short time before this he tossed a coin in the air to decide whether to commit suicide by drowning or by shooting, but the coin came down in the mud and landed on edge!

133. ON WINGS OF LIVING LIGHT

Matthew 28: 1-6

William Walsham How (1823-97), see appendix, wrote these words in 1872 to tell the simple story of the resurrection in language that children could understand. It appeared with three other of his hymns in a special compilation for children. The first three stanzas are really a paraphrase of the following verses of Scripture: "As it began to dawn toward the first day of the week . . . the angel of the Lord descended from heaven, and came and rolled back the stone. . . . His countenance was like lightning, and his raiment white as snow: and for fear of him the keepers did shake, and became as dead men. And the angel . . . said . . . Ye seek Jesus, which was crucified. He is not here: for He is risen." Matthew 28: 1-6. The two omitted stanzas are:—

5. Leave in the grave beneath
The old things passed away:
Buried with Him in death,
Oh, live with Him today!
Your voices raise with one accord
To bless and praise your risen Lord.

6. We sing Thee, Lord divine,
With all our hearts and powers;
For we are ever Thine,
And Thou art ever ours!
Your voices raise with one accord
To bless and praise your risen Lord.

The hymn was written to the tune of Darwall's 148th (No. 485, *Darwall*) which has six lines only. In order to fit the present tune, the first two lines of the refrain have been added.

The tune *Jubilate* was composed in 1894 by Horatio William Parker (1863-1919), and is so named because it was first set to Charles Wesley's hymn, "Rejoice, the Lord is King" (jubilate = rejoice). Parker was a noted professor of music at Yale University, organist at Holy Trinity church, Boston, and also New York, and a composer of cantatas, oratorios, and operas. He also composed Nos. 47, *Pixham,* 58 and 177, *Garden City,* 110, *Stella (Parker)*, and 198, *Pro Patria.*

134. CHRIST THE LORD IS RISEN TODAY

Revelation 19: 1

This triumphant hymn of resurrection was written by Charles Wesley (1707-88), see appendix, in 1739. It had eleven stanzas and appeared in Church of England collections in 1780, although up to that time his brother John Wesley did not include it in the Wesleyan hymnbook. The victorious repetition of the Alleluias conjures up the picture given by the Apostle John, "I heard a great voice of much people in heaven, saying, Alleluia; Salvation, and glory, and honour, and power, unto the Lord our God." Revelation 19: 1. The present third stanza is really the first half of one, and the last half of a succeeding stanza, the omitted lines being:—

2. . . .
Lo! our Sun's eclipse is o'er!
Lo! He sets in blood no more!

3. Vain the stone, the watch, the seal,
Christ hath burst the gates of hell;
Death in vain. . . .

Some other omitted lines are:—

6. What though once we perished all,
Partners in our parents' fall?
Second life we all receive,
In our heavenly Adam live.

7. Risen with Him, we upward move;
Still we seek the things above;
Still pursue, and kiss the Son
Seated on His Father's throne:

11. King of glory, soul of bliss,
Everlasting life is this,
Thee to know, Thy power to prove,
Thus to sing, and thus to love!

The tune *Worgan,* or *Easter Hymn,* first appeared in "Lyra Davidica," a collection of divine songs and hymns made by John Walsh (?-1736) in 1708. He was a music publisher from Ireland who had established himself in London by 1695, publishing among others, the works of George Frederick Handel. (See Nos. 100, 189, 484.)

135. THE DAY OF RESURRECTION

1 Corinthians 5: 7

John of Damascus (700-780) was born in that city and held high office there until he decided to become a monk. He entered the monastery of Mar Saba overlooking the Kidron Valley and the Dead Sea, and specialized in hymn writing and singing. He died in the monastery at the age of about eighty years, having acquired the reputation of being the greatest of the Greek hymn-writers.

This hymn is one ode of the Golden Canon written for Easter Sunday, each ode describing how the resurrection fulfilled certain types prophesied in the Old Testament. The first ode as seen in lines three and four of the first stanza likens the resurrection to a new passover, "For even Christ our Passover is sacrificed for us." 1 Corinthians 5: 7. The hymn was translated from the Greek in 1862 by John Mason Neale (1818-66), see appendix, who added a note that John was "the last but one of the fathers of the Eastern Church, and the greatest of her poets." The quotation "All hail!" in line seven of the second stanza is from Matthew 28: 9: "Jesus met them, saying, All hail!" Another hymn by John of Damascus, also translated by Dr. Neale, is No. 136, "Come, Ye Faithful."

The tune *Lancashire,* also used for No. 362, "Lead on, O King Eternal," was composed in 1836 by Henry Thomas Smart (1813-79), for the occasion of the Reformation tercentenary celebrations in Blackburn, Lancashire, and was written for Heber's hymn, "From Greenland's Icy Mountains" (No. 445). Smart, who was organist at Blackburn and four London churches, and also an organ builder, wrote Nos. 113 and 487, *Regent Square;* 363, *Chebar,* and 376, *Pilgrims.*

136. COME, YE FAITHFUL

Exodus 15: 13

John of Damascus (700-780), a monk and choir leader at the monastery of Mar Saba near the Dead Sea, wrote a canon for the Sunday after Easter, St. Thomas' day, or Low Sunday. The first ode of this canon was based on the deliverance of the people of God at the Red Sea as recorded in the song of Moses: "Thou in Thy mercy hast led forth the people which Thou hast redeemed: Thou has guided them in Thy strength unto Thy holy habitation." Exodus 15: 13. The ode was written in the middle of the eighth century and translated from the Greek in 1859 by John Mason Neale (1818-66), see appendix. The third stanza, which is in the nature of the doxology to the Trinity, was added by the compilers of "Hymns Ancient and Modern," according to the current custom. Neale's last stanza was: —

4. Neither might the gates of death,
Nor the tomb's dark portal,
Nor the watchers, nor the seal,
Hold Thee as a mortal;
But today amidst the twelve
Thou didst stand, bestowing
That Thy peace, which evermore
Passeth human knowing.

A variant on the last half is:—

Who, though never door unclose,
In th' assembly standing,
Breathest on Thy friends the peace
Past all understanding.

Other omissions are:—

1\. . . .
Loosed from Pharaoh's bitter yoke
Jacob's sons and daughters
Led them with unmoisten'd foot
Through the Red Sea waters.

3\. Now the queen of seasons bright
With the day of splendour,
With the royal feast of feasts,
Comes its joy to render;

which is followed by the second half of the first stanza in "Church Hymnal." John of Damascus also wrote No. 135, "The Day of Resurrection," also translated by Neale.

The tune was composed especially for these words in 1872 by Arthur Seymour Sullivan (1842-1900), see appendix. Its name *St. Kevin,* so designated in the composer's "Hymn Tunes," 1902, commemorates a hermit who established a monastery in the vale of Glendalough, Ireland, where he died about A.D. 618 at the reputed age of 120.

137. WHERE HIGH THE HEAVENLY TEMPLE STANDS

Hebrews 4: 14-16

John Logan (1748-88) (See No. 88), borrowed a manuscript book of hymns written by his friend Michael Bruce (1746-67), a student for the ministry of the Church of Scotland, and when asked to return it, alleged that it had been burned by the servants. In 1781 he published this hymn in a book of poems purporting to be his own, but the members of the singing class at Kinneswood, Scotland, recognized the hymn as one written by Bruce about 1764 and sung in the class. It is a paraphrase of Hebrews 4: 14-16, "Seeing then that we have a great High Priest, that is passed into the heavens, Jesus the Son of God, let us hold fast our profession. For we have not an High Priest which cannot be touched with the feeling of our infirmities; but was in all points tempted like as we are, yet without sin. Let us therefore come boldly unto the throne of grace, that we may obtain mercy, and find grace to help in time of need." Two stanzas are omitted, namely:—

3. Though now ascended up on high,
He bends on earth a brother's eye;
Partaker of the human name,
He knows the frailty of our frame.

4. Our Fellow-Sufferer yet retains
A fellow-feeling of our pains,
And still remembers in the skies,
His tears, His agonies and cries.

The tune *Ward,* is an old Scottish melody, harmonized in 1830 by Lowell Mason (1792-1872), see appendix. Its two halves are almost identical.

138. WITHIN THE VEIL

Hebrews 6: 19

Mrs. Freda Hanbury Allen of Tunbridge Wells, Kent, has taken the last three words of Hebrews 6: 19 and used them as the basis of this poem written in 1900 and entitled "Within the Veil." "Which hope we have as an anchor of the soul, both sure and steadfast, and which entereth into that within the veil." This phrase is used six times in four stanzas, each time to introduce a description of the effect upon the Christian of communion with God. One of these, the second stanza, recalls the Apostle Paul's reference to another vail (Exodus 34: 33), the one which Moses wore to cover God's reflected glory. "But we all, with open face beholding as in a glass the glory of the Lord, are changed into the same image from glory to glory." 2 Corinthians 3: 18. Two words from this text in the Revised Version are also placed by Mrs. Allen in her sub-title—"reflecting and transformed." There is one marked contrast in stanza three reminding us that the Christian life is not wholly communion within the veil, but that it is also a manifestation of the Spirit in our lives to others without the veil. There are ten stanzas, those omitted being:—

3. Within the veil—there only in its fullness
The loveliness of Christ our King is seen;
There may thy spirit fall in adoration
Without a cloud, without a shade between.

4. Within the veil—O place of sweetest refuge,
The storm may beat, the tempest rage without,
The enemy assail with fierce temptation,
Or seek to snare thee with some subtle doubt.

5. Within—all, all is peace and quiet stillness,
For there the cruel tempter may not come,
And on the bosom of thy Saviour folded,
Thy soul hath found her everlasting home.

6. There drinking evermore of life's pure river,
In fullness flowing from the Fountain head,
Thou shalt the "earthen vessel" be this treasure,
The life and love of Christ, abroad to spread.

9. Within the veil—tongue cannot tell the glories
Of Him, the "altogether lovely" One,
Yet shalt thou know the mystery of glory,
That Christ and His belov'd for aye are one.

10. Within the veil—there tarry, O beloved,
To go no more for ever from His face,
There take the uttermost His bounty giveth
To magnify on earth His boundless grace.

139. SINCE TO THE HOLIEST

Hebrews 10: 19

C. Butler Stoney has written this hymn describing the uniqueness and the sufficiency of the Lord Jesus Christ for the sinner, not only in life, but also in the hour of death, and further, beyond the tomb in the day of resurrection. Several scriptures are used, as follows: Hebrews 10: 19, "Having therefore, brethren, boldness to enter into the holiest by the blood of Jesus"; 1 John 1: 7, "the blood of Jesus Christ His Son cleanseth us from all sin"; Deuteronomy 12: 23, "for the blood is the life"; Colossians 3: 4, "Christ, who is our life"; Revelation 1: 18, "I am He that liveth, and was dead; and, behold, I am alive for evermore"; Mark 16: 19, ". . . the Lord . . . sat on the right hand of God"; John 17: 24, "I will that they . . . be with Me where I am"; John 14: 6, "Jesus saith unto him, I am the way, the truth, and the life."

140. MY BLEST REDEEMER

Revelation 14: 4

Isaac Watts (1674-1748), see appendix, wrote this hymn in 1707 under the title "The Example of Christ," and began it with the words "My Dear Redeemer." The second stanza has been changed, the original being:—

2. Such was Thy truth and such Thy zeal,
Such deference to Thy Father's will,
Such love and meekness so divine,
I would transcribe, and make them mine.

The hymn states that our duty to God is best exemplified by the life of Christ, which manifested truth, and love, and zeal, and victory over temptation. It closes with a prayer that we may more closely follow this pattern on earth, so as to follow Christ in heaven, thus fulfilling the words of Revelation 14: 4, "These are they which follow the Lamb whithersoever He goeth."

The tune *Rockingham New,* was composed in 1830 by Lowell Mason (1792-1872), see appendix, but the name is not associated in any way with the words.

141. WE MAY NOT CLIMB

Romans 10: 6-8

The Quaker poet, John Greenleaf Whittier (1807-92), wrote in 1866 a long poem of thirty-eight stanzas entitled, "Our Master." He denied being a hymn writer or having any knowledge of music, but selections from this poem appear in many hymnals, the present choice being stanzas 5, 13, 14, and 16. Some of the omitted stanzas are:—

1. Immortal love, for ever full,
For ever flowing free,
For ever shared, for ever whole,
A never-ebbing sea!

2. Our outward lips confess the name
All other names above;
Love only knoweth whence it came
And comprehendeth love.

11. In joy of inward peace, or sense
Of sorrow over sin,
He is His own best evidence,
His witness is within.

33. Not Thine the bigot's partial plea,
Nor Thine the zealot's ban;
Thou well canst spare a love of Thee
Which ends in hate of man.

35. We bring no ghastly holocaust,
We pile no graven stone;
He serves Thee best who lovest most
His brothers and Thy own.

36. Thy litanies, sweet offices
Of love and gratitude;
Thy sacramental liturgies
The joy of doing good.

37. In vain shall waves of incense drift
The vaulted naves around,
In vain the minster turret lift
Its brazen weights of sound:

38. The heart must ring Thy Christmas bells,
Thy inward altars raise;
Its faith and hope Thy canticles,
And its obedience praise!

Throughout the poem, Whittier emphasizes the inward experience of the spiritual omnipresence of God, as in Romans 10: 6-8, "Who shall ascend into heaven? (that is, to bring Christ down from above:) or, Who shall descend into the deep? . . . But what saith it? The word is nigh thee, even in thy mouth, and in thy heart." Whittier also wrote Nos. 116, "Dear Lord and Father," and 483, "All Things Are Thine."

The tune *Serenity* composed in 1856, is so named because it was later used for these serene words. The composer was William Vincent Wallace (1812-65), an Irish violinist who is remembered by one of his operas, "Maritana." The tune was re-arranged by a Brooklyn organist, Uzziah Christopher Burnap, Mus. D. (1834-1900), from Wallace's "Ye Winds that Waft." Burnap also arranged No. 99, *Carol.*

142. LOVE DIVINE

Psalm 106: 4

Charles Wesley (1707-88), see appendix, wrote these four stanzas in 1747 under the title, "Jesus, Show Thy Salvation." At the time there was a popular tune set by Purcell to the "Song of Venus" in Dryden's play, "King Arthur." The words begin:—

Fairest isle, all isles excelling,
Seat of pleasures and of loves,
Venus here will choose her dwelling
And forsake her Cyprian groves.

Wesley capitalized on the tune and wrote this hymn in the same metre, using two of Dryden's rhymes also. The words show how Wesley used actual Scripture phrases, in addition to Psalm 106: 4, "Visit me with Thy salvation," which is the basis of the hymn. For example stanza one uses Isaiah 57: 15 and Matthew 9: 36; stanza two uses John 20: 22, Hebrews 4: 9, Revelation 22: 13, and Hebrews 12: 2; stanza three uses Malachi 3: 1, Revelation 4: 8 and Revelation 5: 11, 12; stanza four uses 2 Corinthians 5: 17, Ephesians 5: 27, Psalm 51: 12, 2 Corinthians 3: 18, and Revelation 4: 10.

The tune *Beecher* was composed especially for these words and first appeared in "Christian Heart Songs," 1870, by John Zundel (1815-82), a German organist who spent over thirty years in the United States of America. It was named to commemorate the famous preacher Henry Ward Beecher at whose church in Brooklyn, New York, Zundel was organist for twenty-eight years. Zundel was the assistant musical editor for the "Plymouth Collection," and wrote twenty-eight tunes, including this one, for this hymn book prepared for Beecher's congregation.

143. THE WONDERS OF REDEEMING LOVE

Hebrews 4: 14-16

Roswell Fenner Cottrell (1814-92) wrote these words in 1886 when he was a minister of the Seventh-day Adventist Church. He was formerly a Seventh-day Baptist, but joined the Seventh-day Adventists in 1851 after coming into contact with their church paper. Then he became a pioneer in tent-meeting evangelism and a regular contributor in poetry and prose to the church paper, the *Review and Herald,* of which his great-grandson is now an associate editor. The hymn describes the great love of God for man, shown in sending His Son to die for us. Now He pleads on our behalf, for He knows our weaknesses, and will not be satisfied until He restores us, faithful ones in sinless glory. A Scripture summary is: "Seeing then that we have a great High Priest, that is passed into the heavens, Jesus the Son of God, let us hold fast our profession. For we have not an High Priest which cannot be touched with the feeling of our infirmities; but was in all points tempted like as we are, yet without sin. Let us therefore come boldly unto the throne of grace." Hebrews 4: 14-16. Cottrell also wrote Nos. 307, "The Time Is Near," and 481, "O Solemn Thought!"

The tune *Woodland* was composed in 1832 by Nathaniel Duren Gould (1731-1864), and has been slightly changed from a 3/2 time to the present 4/4 time. He wrote a *"History of Church Music in America,"* 1853.

144. O LOVE DIVINE, THAT STOOPED TO SHARE

Acts 17: 27

Oliver Wendell Holmes (1809-94) wrote this poem in 1849 while he was professor of anatomy at Harvard University. It was printed in 1859 in his book, *"The Professor at the Breakfast Table."* Its title is "Trust" and its theme is emphasized in the last three words of each stanza—"Thou art near," an idea used in the Apostle Paul's sermon at Athens: "Though He be not far from every one of us." Acts 17: 27. Dr. Holmes also wrote No. 20, "Lord of All Being, Throned Afar."

The tune *York* was composed by Edwin Barnes (1864-1930), see appendix.

145. O LOVE THAT WILL NOT LET ME GO

Psalm 69: 17

George Matheson (1842-1906) began to lose his sight before he was a year old and at seventeen years of age he was almost completely blind. He was a brilliant student in spite of this, both at school and university, and became a noted preacher. In the manse at Innellan, Argyllshire, on the evening of June 6, 1882, he was "suffering from extreme mental distress and the hymn was the fruit of pain." This pain was not caused by a broken engagement, as that had happened about twenty years earlier, but it might have been a bereavement or his worry over the inroads that Darwinism was making in the church. This hymn was written very quickly, as though it were dictated by an inward voice, and not revised or retouched, with the one exception that was later suggested and agreed to, this being in the third stanza which was originally "I climb the rainbow" and now reads "I trace." In spite of the author's statement that it was written in June, 1882, it was already in print in January of that year, so June, 1881, is most probably the date of its origin. The words, as in most of Matheson's poems, are not easy to understand on first reading, and need much thought and meditation. They reflect discouragement, darkness, and pain, but these disappointments are not overwhelming, for the brighter side is shown in a yielded life which sees a purpose in life's frustations. In view of the circumstances in which the hymn was written, a fitting text would be, "Hide not Thy face from Thy servant; for I am in trouble: hear me speedily." Psalm 69: 17. Matheson also wrote No. 284, "Make Me a Captive, Lord."

The tune *St. Margaret* was likewise composed very rapidly in 1884 by Dr. Albert Lister Peace (1844-1912), the organist of Glasgow Cathedral, and one of England's greatest. He was requested to supply a tune for this uncommon metre 8.8.8.8.6, and in accordance with his usual practice, carried with him the words of hymns for which tunes were required, ready to jot down the melody as it came to him. He was sitting down on the sand on the isle of Arran reading Matheson's words when inspiration came, and he said, "The ink of the first note was hardly dry when I had finished the tune." The name *St. Margaret* commemorates the doubly Scottish origin of the hymn, for it is the name of a queen of Scotland who was a benefactress of the church.

146. JESUS, THY BOUNDLESS LOVE TO ME

Jeremiah 31: 3

Paul Gerhardt (1607-76) was the most well-known of the German hymn writers, and, living through the whole of the Thirty Years' War, his thoughts were directed to a better world, free from suffering, sorrow, and pain. This long hymn, published in 1653, consisted originally of sixteen nine-line stanzas, as it was intended to be sung on the way to church. It began "O Jesu Christ, mein schönstes Licht" (= O Jesus Christ, my dearest light). John Wesley (1703-91) translated it from the German in 1739 under the title "Living by Christ," and as with his other excellent translations, made it appear as if it were originally written in English. In the previous year, on his return from his unsuccessful mission to Georgia, he had been greatly impressed by this hymn, and he expressed the cry of his own heart in the first two lines of the second stanza. Note that the word "love" is used in every stanza, and eight times altogether, recalling God's everlasting love: "Yea, I have loved thee with an everlasting love: therefore with lovingkindness have I drawn thee." Jeremiah 31: 3. Two of the omitted stanzas are:—

4. Unwearied may I this pursue,
Dauntless to the high prize aspire;
Hourly within my breast renew
This holy flame, this heavenly fire;
And day and night be all my care,
To guard this sacred treasure there.

15. Still let Thy love point out my way,
(How wondrous things Thy love hath wrought!)
Still lead me, lest I go astray,
Direct my work, inspire my thought;
And when I fall, soon may I hear
Thy voice, and know that Love is near.

Then follows the fourth stanza of "Church Hymnal." Gerhardt also wrote No. 110, "All My Heart This Night Rejoices," and translated No. 130, "O Sacred Head Now Wounded." John Wesley also translated Nos. 62; "Eternal Depth of Love Divine," and 330, "O Thou to Whose All-Searching Sight," both from Zinzendorf.

The tune *Pater Omnium* (= Father of all), also used for No. 169, "Thou Hidden Source," was composed in 1875 by Henry James Ernest Holmes (1852-1938), a London violinist and composer, and later a solicitor, who emigrated to the United States. He also composed No. 353, *Eventide (Holmes)*.

147. DEAR SAVIOUR, WE WOULD KNOW

Ephesians 3: 19

These words by an anonymous author deal with two topics, salvation by grace in a world of woe, and the desire for ultimate salvation into glory at the coming of the Lord Jesus Christ. It is a recognition that Christians have no permanent part in this sinful world, but are rather strangers bound for the heavenly city, trusting in the immeasurable "love of Christ, which passeth knowledge." Eph. 3: 19.

The tune *Collegedale* was composed in 1939 by Harold Amadeus Miller (1891-1966), see appendix, and named after the village where Southern Missionary College, Tennessee, is situated. Miller was professor of music here on two occasions, and loved this place very much, composing many of his tunes there.

148. O LOVE DIVINE, HOW SWEET THOU ART!

Ephesians 3: 18, 19

Charles Wesley (1707-88), see appendix, wrote these words in 1749 in his "Hymns and Sacred Poems" as a seven-stanza hymn. Its title was "Desiring to Love," under which title he wrote another hymn in 1742, No. 151, "O Love Divine, What Hast Thou Done!" It was one of three of his hymns which George Frederick Handel set to music. The word "love" occurs in each of the first three stanzas and seven times altogether. Several scriptures are used, as is common in Wesley's hymns, but one sufficing as a summary could be: "To comprehend with all saints what is the breadth, and length, and depth, and height; and to know the love of Christ, which passeth knowledge." Eph. 3: 18, 19. The omitted stanzas are:—

5. O that with humbled Peter I
Could weep, believe, and thrice reply
My faithfulness to prove,
Thou knowest (for all to Thee is known)
Thou knowest, O Lord, and Thou alone,
Thou knowest that Thee I love.

6. O that I could with favour'd John
Recline my weary head upon
The dear Redeemer's breast!
From care, and sin, and sorrow free
Give me, O Lord, to find in Thee
My everlasting rest.

7. Thy only love do I require,
Nothing in earth beneath desire,
Nothing in heaven above,
Let earth and heaven, and all things go,
Give me Thy only love to know,
Give me Thy only love.

These illustrations of the apostles Peter and John emphasize the other illustration taken from Luke 10: 39-42, which tells of Mary choosing the better part and sitting at the feet of Jesus.

The tune *Pembroke* was composed in 1842 by John Foster (1807-85), a self-taught musician who was organist of the tabernacle in Bristol, England. He contributed the tune to the Rev. John Waite's "The Hallelujah, or Devotional Psalmody," of which he was musical editor. He gave each part an interesting melody because he knew of Waite's desire to have his congregations sing, and if possible, to sing in parts. The tune is also used for No. 36, "Thy Voice Hath Spoken."

149. O GIFT OF GOD, WE PRAISE THEE

2 Corinthians 9: 15

Grace Elma Uhler has paraphrased some Scripture texts and given a new name to the Lord Jesus Christ—the Gift of God. This is in harmony with the Apostle Paul's statements: "Thanks be unto God for His unspeakable gift" (2 Corinthians 9: 15), and "The gift of God is eternal life through Jesus Christ our Lord." Rom. 6: 23. The three stanzas show a neat progression,

1. thanking God for His gift,
2. accepting the gift of Christ who is all and in all,
3. offering ourselves as a gift to God.

The tune *Donum Dei* (= gift of God), so named because of the words, was composed by Latham True, who flourished in the 1920s.

150. HOW SWEET THE NAME!

Song of Solomon 1: 3

This hymn, No. LVII in the "Olney Hymns," 1779, is one of the 280 contributed by John Newton (1725-1807), see appendix; its title being "The Name of Jesus." It had seven stanzas originally, those omitted being:—

4. By Thee my prayers acceptance gain,
   Although with sin defiled:
   Satan accuses me in vain,
   And I am owned a child.

7. Till then I would Thy love proclaim
   With every fleeting breath;
   And may the music of Thy name
   Refresh my soul in death.

The hymn is based on Song of Solomon 1: 3: "Thy name is as ointment poured forth," and the term *husband* was first used in the fourth stanza, but it now altered to *guardian*.

NAH = New Advent Hymnal
SU = Singing With Understanding
wm = words and music
w = words only
m = music only

NAH	SUwm	SUw	SUm
2	13		
3	14		
4	76		
6	12		
7	90		
8	23		
10	71		
11		19	
12	9		
16		75	342
17			2
18	1		
19		2	77
20	20		
22	73		
24			304
30	11		
31	85		
32	84		
34		69	
37			325
40		16	
41	5		
42			261
44			125
47		65	
48		62	
49	67		
50	86		
51	91		
52	93		
54			18
57		22	
58		92	193
59			45
60	646		
61		155	
63	171		
64			328
66	43		
69			485
70	166		
71			11
72	15		
73		164	
74	150		
76	154		
77	158		
79		141	
80	160		
82		667	
83		342	
84	106		
85	105		
86	111		
87	112		
88	109		
89	104		
90		100	
91	101		
92	102		
94			194
95		110	
96	95		
98		113	
101	103		
103		140	
107		474	
108		127	
109	296		
110	151		
111	124		
112	125		
113	118		
120	130		
123	135		
124	134		
125	136		
126	131		
127	132		
129		188	
130			221
131	69		
134		143	
135			485
136		176	
137			237
139	196		
141	188		
144	187		
145	192		
147	306		
148	191		
149		359	
152			349
153		353	
154			135
156	185		
157		184	
158	178		
159	541		
160	549		

NAH	SUwm	SUw	SUm
161		174	
166	195		
169	481		
171			337
172		190	384
173		157	
174	157		
176	194		
179			496
180	162		
181		189	
186		193	
187			113
188		198	
189		179	
190			187
191	213		
192	214		
193	206		
194	207		
195	211		
196	679		
197	216		
198	208		
199	205		
200	210		
202		204	
203			22
211	219		
212	220		
213		217	290
216	218		
220	329		
224			132
228	7		
229	27		
230	26		
233	6		
234		24	
235			349
237		291	33
239			509
242		262	
248			221
250			378
251	89		
253	81		
256			84
259		88	
263	433		
264	304		
265			195
266	515		
267	516		
268	25		
271	432		
273	64		
274	36		
275		451	3
276		351	
278		627	
281		175	
286			496
287		437	
288	445		
289	454		
294		364	
296	440		
297	293		
298	261		
299	360		
300	262		
301			304
302	442		
303	441		
305	456		
306		462	
307	466		
308	468		
309	455		
311		46	
313		459	131
314			67
316			56
319			295
320	461		
321	470		
322	463		
323	57		
324		58	
325	34		
326			217
327	39		
328	40		
330			442
331	45		
332	41		
333	42		
334			187
335		47	
336	315		
337			193
338		44	
342			54
344	49		
347	53		
349	321		
350	48		
351		52	
353	50		
355			296
356	51		
357	241		
358	60		
359		317	
362		325	
363	357		
367	694		
371	683		
372		477	
373			42
378	438		
379	439		

NAH	SUwm	SUw	SUm
382	471		
383	472		
386			89
387			238
388		475	
390			378
393			150
395			42
396	362		
397			289
398	676		
400			336
403	341		
404	66		
405	223		
406		231	
407		401	
408	280		
409	225		
410		278	235
413	222		
414	581		
415			217
416	254		
417	245		
418		251	
419	246		
421	255		
423	311		
426	256		
428	252		
429	253		
431			402
432	283		
433		169	
434		146	
435			350
436	298		
437	145		
438		148	
439	276		

NAH	SUwm	SUw	SUm
440	238		
441		339	18
444			328
445	382		
446	248		
448	310		
450	265		
451			153
452		17	
454	640		
456	116		
458			36
459	142		
460	336		
461	383		
462			40
463			279
464	284		
465		18	
467		273	
469			350
470	271		
471	603		
472		682	
473		333	
474	322		
475	272		
476	519		
479		250	
480		407	
482	346		
483	21		
485	447		
486	446		
487	478		
488	274		
489		345	
494			509
495			10
496		152	
499	521		

NAH	SUwm	SUw	SUm
502	243		
504		361	
505	354		
506	349		
508		366	
509	355		
510			484
511			1
512			438
513		674	
514	399		
515	391		
517	403		
519	393		
520		257	304
522	395		
524	397		
525		87	
528		409	
529	376		
534	300		
535	372		
536			605
537	371		
539		377	
542			407
543	373		
544	201		
545	202		
546	309		
547		299	
548			132
550			193
553		95	
554	496		
558			135
559			279
560	416		
562	410		
563	411		
564	412		
566			235

NAH	SUwm	SUw	SUm	NAH	SUwm	SUw	SUm	NAH	SUwm	SUw	SUm
568			81	644	344			727	655		
569			296	654			193	728	630		
570		489		659	423			729	545		
572	379			661			427	731	539		
573	380			664	417			732	652		
574			164	669			516	735	525		
575	485			671	126						
576	486			672	301						
577	487			673		421					
581	35			675	497						
582	506			676	418						
583		512	506	678		427					
591		287		679	419						
593			365	680	420						
~~595~~				686	424						
596	645			690	574						
597	613			691	563						
500	290			692	637						
601	266			694	534						
604		264		696	635						
605			208	697	608						
606	385			699	594						
607		386		700	582						
610	428			703	313						
614		389		705	609						
615	282			706	610						
616	288			707	588						
618			430	708	631						
619	390			709	258						
620	267			710	681						
623	332			713	584						
624	348			714	595						
625	578			716	593						
631	576			717	224						
633			265	718	523						
634		363		719	586						
637	259			720	569						
639	629			721	598						
640			254	722	320						
641	229			723	599						
643		56	648	726	316						

The tune *St. Peter* was composed about 1836 by Alexander Robert Reinagle (1799-1877), and commemorates the church of St. Peter-in-the-East, Oxford, where he was organist from 1822 to 1853. He was born in Brighton, England, of Austrian descent, and published two books of hymn tunes. *St. Peter,* originally written as a tune for Psalm 118, is also used for Nos. 309, "Jerusalem, My Happy Home," and 436, "In Christ There Is No East or West." The soprano part is noteworthy for a descent of one octave with some repeated notes, in the first two lines.

151. O LOVE DIVINE, WHAT HAST THOU DONE!

1 Peter 2: 24

Charles Wesley (1707-88), see appendix, wrote a hymn of nine stanzas in 1742 under the title of "Desiring to Love" (see also No. 148). It was divided into two parts, and these stanzas come from Part II, being stanzas 6, 8, 7, respectively, the omitted one being:—

9. Then let us sit beneath His cross,
And gladly catch the healing stream,
All things for Him account but loss,
And give up all our hearts for Him.
Of nothing speak or think beside,
My Lord, My Love, is crucified.

The last line of each stanza "My Lord, My Love, is crucified" has been traced back to the first century, and was in common use throughout the Middle Ages. A scripture summary is: "Who His own self bare our sins in His own body on the tree." 1 Peter 2: 24.

The tune *Stella* is named after a small village near Newcastle-on-Tyne, England, where Henri Frederick Hemy (1818-88), the editor of the Catholic Sunday School Book, heard it used by children at play. He adapted it for use as a hymn tune, and published it in "Easy Music for Church Chorus," 1851, where it is set to the words, "Stella Maris, Queen of Heaven," which is translated as "Hail, Queen of Heaven, the Ocean Star." Hemy, who was a professor of music at Tynemouth, composed No. 349, *St. Catherine.*

152. JESUS, AND SHALL IT EVER BE

Mark 8: 38

Joseph Grigg (c. 1720-68), see also No. 227, was a Presbyterian minister for four years at the Silver Street church, London, but in 1747 married a wealthy widow and retired to the city of St. Albans, Hertfordshire, where he continued to preach and to write. He published this hymn in 1765, but it is said to have been re-published in 1774 under the title of "Shame of Jesus, Conquered by Love, by a Youth of Ten Years," with the note, "Composed when the author was ten years of age, and first altered from the original by the Rev. Benjamin Francis." It was extensively revised in 1787 by Francis (1734-99), a Welsh Baptist minister, who also wrote No. 485, "Great King of Glory." Grigg's hymn is based on Mark 8: 38: "Whosoever therefore shall be ashamed of Me and of My words in this adulterous and sinful generation; of him also shall the Son of man be ashamed, when He cometh in the glory of His Father with the holy angels." The omitted stanza is:—

4. Ashamed of Jesus! shall yon field
Blush when it thinks who bids it yield?
Yet blush I must, while I adore,
I blush to think I yield no more.

The tune *Federal Street,* was composed in 1832 by Henry Kemble Oliver (1800-85) of Salem, Massachusetts, who loved music as a child. His wife was born, courted, and married in Federal Street, Salem, and this tune, commemorating the name, was specially written for Anne Steele's hymn: "So Fades the Lovely Blooming Flower." It was nearly called Sally, after Oliver's wife's Christian name.

153. COME, LET US SING

Revelation 5: 9-13

James Montgomery (1771-1854), see appendix, wrote seven stanzas of this hymn in 1841, and published them twelve years later under the title "The Song of Songs." It is virtually a paraphrase of Revelation 5: 9-13: "And they sung a new song, saying, Thou art worthy . . . for Thou wast slain, and has redeemed us to God by Thy blood. . . . And hast made us unto our God kings and priests. . . . Worthy is the Lamb that was slain to receive power, and riches, and wisdom, and strength, and honour, and glory, and blessing. . . . Power be unto Him that sitteth upon the throne, and unto the Lamb for ever and ever." The two omitted stanzas are:—

2. Youth in its prime, and failing age,
With hearts and voices swell the strain,
To cheer their steps in pilgrimage,
Worthy the Lamb, for He was slain.

6. Come, Holy Spirit, from on high,
Our faith, our hope, our love sustain,
Living to sing, and dying cry,
Worthy the Lamb, for He was slain.

The seventh stanza has been altered somewhat to become the fifth in "Church Hymnal," and was:—

7. Yea, in eternity of bliss,
If called through grace with Him to reign,
Our song—our song of songs be this:
Worthy the Lamb, for He was slain.

The tune *Russia* was composed in 1825 by Dimitri Stepanovitch Bortniansky (1752-1825), and commemorates the country of his birth. He wrote church music for Russian words, and was director of the Empress Catherine's choir.

154. JESUS, THOU JOY OF LOVING HEARTS

Psalm 130: 5, 6

Bernard of Clairvaux (1091-1153) is credited with a hymn of about forty-eight stanzas entitled "Jesu Dulcis Memoria" (= Jesus, sweet memory), and known as the "Jubilee Rhythm of the Name of Jesus." Several translations of this hymn have been made from the Latin (See No. 158), this one being made in 1858 by Ray Palmer (1808-87), then a Congregational minister in Albany, New York. He has used several Scriptural similes, but a summary could well be Psalm 130: 5, 6, "I wait for the Lord, my soul doth wait, and in His word do I hope. My soul waiteth for the Lord more than they that watch for the morning." Bernard also wrote Nos. 130, "O Sacred Head Now Wounded," and 158, "Jesus, the Very Thought of Thee." Palmer also wrote Nos. 166, "Jesus, These Eyes Have Never Seen"; 235, "We Stand in Deep Repentance"; 246, "My Faith Looks Up to Thee," and 285, "I Give My Heart to Thee."

The tune *Migdol* was composed in 1840 by Lowell Mason (1792-1872), see appendix. It is one of his many Old Testament names, having no association with the words or music.

155. O FOR A THOUSAND TONGUES

Psalm 47: 6

Charles Wesley (1707-88), see appendix, underwent a great spiritual change on May 21, 1738, and dated his real conversion from this date. On the first anniversary in 1739, inspired by his Moravian friend Peter Böhler's remark: "Had I a thousand tongues, I would praise Jesus Christ with them all," Wesley burst forth in this rapturous poem of eighteen stanzas. His title was "For the Anniversary Day of One's Conversion" and an appropriate scripture is Psalm 47: 6: "Sing praises to God, sing praises: sing praises unto our King, sing praises." The first six stanzas, now omitted, show that this was Wesley's own experience:—

1. Glory to God, and praises, and love
Be ever, ever given,
By saints below, and saints above,
The church in earth and heaven.

2. On this glad day the glorious Sun
Of righteousness arose;
On my benighted soul He shone,
And fill'd it with repose.

3. Sudden expired the legal strife;
'Twas then I ceased to grieve;
My second, real, living life
I then began to live.

4. Then with my heart I first believed,
Believed with faith divine:
Power with the Holy Ghost received
To call the Saviour mine.

5. I felt my Lord's atoning blood
Close to my soul applied;
Me, me He loved—the Son of God
For me, for me He died!

6. I found, and owned His promise true,
Ascertain'd of my part;
My pardon passed in heaven I knew,
When written on my heart.

Then follow the six stanzas in "Church Hymnal," followed by five others addressed to nations, harlots, thieves, and murderers, and concluding with:—

18. With me, your chief, you then shall know,
Shall feel your sins forgiven;
Anticipate your heaven below,
And own that love is heaven.

The tune *Howard* was composed by Elizabeth Howard Cuthbert (1800-57) of Dublin, Ireland, and arranged by Lowell Mason (1792-1872), see appendix.

156. ALL HAIL THE POWER OF JESUS' NAME!

Revelation 19: 12

Edward Perronet (1726-92) was an associate of the Wesley brothers, and in the "Journal" he is mentioned as having been rolled in the mud after preaching at Bolton, Lancashire. He wrote these words anonymously in 1779, but they were later published in 1785 under his name. They were revised by Dr. Rippon (1751-1836), see No. 255, a Baptist pastor of New Park Street, London, and the last two stanzas are entirely his. Omitted stanzas are:—

2. Let high-born seraphs tune the lyre,
And as they tune it, fall
Before His face who tunes their choir,
And crown Him Lord of all!

3. Crown Him, ye morning stars of light,
Who fixed this floating ball;
Now hail the Strength of Israel's might,
And crown Him Lord of all!

4. Crown Him, ye martyrs of your God,
Who from His altar call;
Extol the Stem of Jesse's rod,
And crown Him Lord of all!

6. Hail Him, ye heirs of David's line,
Whom David Lord did call,
The God incarnate, Man divine
And crown Him Lord of all!

7. Sinners, whose love can ne'er forget
The wormwood and the gall,
Go—spread your trophies at His feet,
And crown Him Lord of all!

9. Let every tribe and every tongue
That bound creation's call,
Now shout in universal song,
The crownéd Lord of all.

The repetitive last line recalls the description of our Lord in Revelation 19: 12: "And on His head were many crowns."

The tune *Coronation,* so named because of these words emphasizing "Crown Him," for which it was specially written, was composed in 1792 and published in 1793 by the Baptist Oliver Holden (1765-1844), a carpenter and self-taught musician of Charlestown, Massachusetts, who later became a music teacher and composer of sacred music, and also a member of the United States Congress. The third line of music reverts really to two-part harmony, for sopranos and tenors are in unison, and so are altos and basses.

157. ALL HAIL THE POWER OF JESUS' NAME

Revelation 19: 12

For the words, see the previous hymn No. 156.

The tune *Miles Lane* was composed in 1780 especially for these words by William Shrubsole (1760-1806), who was a friend of Edward Perronet, the author of the words, and with him joined the Countess of Huntingdon's Connexion (see No. 190). He was the organist of St. Michael's church, which was until 1831 in St. Michael's Lane, corrupted to Miles Lane. This is near Upper Thames Street and Crooked Lane in the City of London. The tune was used by the Rev. Stephen Addington, the minister of the Miles Lane meeting house, in his "Collection of Psalm Tunes."

158. JESUS, THE VERY THOUGHT OF THEE

Matthew 1: 21

These words are another portion of the hymn attributed to Bernard of Clairvaux (1091-1153) entitled, "Jesu, Dulcis Memoria" (= Jesus, sweet memory) (see No. 154), a hymn which exalts the name and work of Jesus: "And thou shalt call His name JESUS: for He shall save His people from their sins." Matthew 1: 21. Edward Caswell (1814-78) translated some of Bernard's early stanzas from the German translation in 1849, two years after he had forsaken the Anglican faith to join the Roman Catholic Church. He translated many hymns from the German, one of them being No. 43, "When Morning Gilds the Skies." Bernard also wrote Nos. 130, "O Sacred Head Now Wounded," and 154, "Jesus, Thou Joy of Loving Hearts."

The tune *St. Agnes,* also used for Nos. 209, "Come, Holy Spirit," and 413, "Happy the Home," was composed especially for these words in 1866 by John Bacchus Dykes (1823-76), see appendix. The name commemorates a young Roman girl, Agnes, who at the tender age of thirteen was martyred for her faith in A.D. 304 under the persecution of Diocletian. She had refused to marry a Roman nobleman because she had given her heart to the Lord Jesus, and her dying words could well have been the language of this hymn.

159. MAJESTIC SWEETNESS SITS ENTHRONED

Song of Solomon 5: 10

This hymn was written in 1787 by Dr. Samuel Stennett (1727-95) for one of his sermons entitled "The chiefest among ten thousand; or the excellencies of Christ," based on Song of Solomon 5: 10: "My beloved is white and ruddy, the chiefest among ten thousand." Stennett was a grandson of Joseph Stennett and like him, a Seventh-day Baptist. He was a personal friend of King George III, and not only preached regularly on Sabbaths, but also for the other Baptists on Sundays. This hymn had nine stanzas originally, those omitted being:—

1. To Christ, the Lord, let every tongue
   Its noblest tribute bring,
   When He's the subject of the song,
   Who can refuse to sing.

2. Survey the beauties of His face,
   And on His glories dwell,
   Think of the wonders of His grace,
   And all His triumphs tell.

6. His hand a thousand blessings pours
   Upon my guilty head;
   His presence gilds my darkest hours,
   And guards my sleeping bed.

Stennett also wrote Nos. 535, " 'Tis Finished," and 553, "On Jordan's Stormy Banks."

The tune *Ortonville,* also used for No. 656, "A Glory in the Word," was composed in 1837 by Thomas Hastings (1784-1872), see appendix.

160. O THOU IN WHOSE PRESENCE

Song of Solomon 7: 10

These words of explicit adoration to God were written by the Baptist pastor, Joseph Swain (1761-96) of Birmingham, England, who was baptized in 1783 by Dr. John Rippon (see No. 255), and ordained to the ministry in 1792. The hymn specifies the presence, the voice, the breath, the lips, the smiles, the looks, and the words of the Lord, singling each out for the ascription of praise, reminiscent of many expressions in the Song of Solomon, particularly Song of Solomon 7: 10: "I am my beloved's and his desire is toward me." Stanzas two and three are not in Swain's poem, but there are four other stanzas now omitted, namely:—

2. Where dost Thou, dear Shepherd, resort with Thy sheep,
   To feed them in pastures of love?
   Say, why in the valley of death should I weep,
   Or alone in this wilderness rove?

3. O why should I wander an alien from Thee,
Or cry in the desert for bread?
Thy foes will rejoice when my sorrows they see
And smile at the tears I have shed.

4. Ye daughters of Zion, declare, have you seen
The Star that on Israel shone?
Say, if in your tents my Beloved has been,
And where with His flocks He is gone.

6. Dear Shepherd, I hear, and will follow Thy call;
I know the sweet sound of Thy voice.
Restore and defend me, for Thou art my all,
And in Thee I will ever rejoice.

Swain also wrote No. 431, "How Sweet, How Heavenly."

The tune *Beloved,* or *Dulcimer,* was composed in 1813 by Freeman Lewis (1780-1859) a surveyor of Uniontown, Pennsylvania, and a musician, and appears to be derived from an old folk song. The melody of the first line is almost identical with that used by Haydn in his Drum Roll Symphony No. 103 in E flat major, 2nd movement Andante. It was arranged in 1869 by Hubert Platt Main (1839-1925), composer of over 1,000 songs, hymn tunes, and anthems, and editor of collections for use in church and Sunday school. Main also arranged Nos. 267 and 663, *Ellesdie,* and composed No. 532, *My Lord and I.*

161. O COULD I SPEAK THE MATCHLESS WORTH

1 Peter 2: 9

Samuel Medley (1738-99) had been a sailor, but after being converted was first a school teacher, then became a minister of the gospel, first in Watford, and then in Liverpool, for the Baptist Church. These words of praise and personal testimony were written in 1789, and fulfil the text "that ye should show forth the praises of Him who hath called you out of darkness into His marvellous light." 1 Peter 2: 9. Medley also wrote No. 667, "Awake, My Soul, in Joyful Lays."

The tune *Ariel* was an arrangement made in 1836 by Lowell Mason (1792-1872), see appendix, but its name, meaning lion of God, has no associated significance. It is also used for No. 190, "When Thou, My Righteous Judge." Mason took the tune from a composition by Wolfgang Amadeus Mozart (1756-91) of Salzburg, Austria, the infant musical prodigy who composed much church music before he was fifteen years old. Another arrangement from Mozart is Nos. 267 and 663, *Ellesdie.*

162. CROWN HIM WITH MANY CROWNS

Revelation 19: 12

Matthew Bridges (1800-94) in his youth was a very ardent Protestant but in 1848 he became a member of the Roman Catholic Church. Three years later he wrote this hymn of six stanzas amplifying the text, "And on His head were many crowns." Revelation 19: 12. All but the first stanza have been quite largely revised by Godfrey Thring (1823-1903), author of No. 287, "Saviour, Blessed Saviour."

Omitted lines are as follows:—

2. Crown Him the virgin's Son,
The God incarnate born,
Whose arm those crimson trophies won
Which now His brow adorn:
Fruit of the mystic Rose
As of that Rose the Stem;
The Root whence mercy ever flows,
The Babe of Bethlehem.

5. . . .
Glass'd in a sea of light,
Where everlasting waves
Reflect His throne—the Infinite!
Who lives—and loves—and saves.

6. Crown Him the Lord of heaven!
One with the Father known—
And the blest Spirit, through Him given
From yonder triune throne!
. . .

Bridges also wrote No. 129, "Behold the Lamb of God."

The tune, *Diademata* (= crowns), also used for No. 366, "Soldiers of Christ, Arise," was composed especially for these words in 1868 by Sir George Job Elvey (1816-93), who was organist at St. George's Chapel, Windsor, from 1835 to 1882. He also wrote Nos. 496, *St. George's, Windsor,* and 686, a response.

163. THERE IS A FOUNTAIN

Zechariah 13: 1

William Cowper (1731-1800), see appendix, based these words on Zechariah 13: 1: "There shall be a fountain opened . . . for sin and for uncleanness." They were written in 1770 after an attack of temporary madness, and the original words of the last line of stanza 2, show his rapture and confidence in God's saving power. They were in the past tense and describe his own spiritual experience:—

And there *have* I, as vile as he,
Wash'd all my sins away.

The very last line of all has been altered from "lies silent in the grave" to "is ransomed from the grave," so as to accord with the doctrine of the unconscious sleep of the dead. Stanzas 6 and 5 of "Church Hymnal" have been interchanged and the omitted stanza referring to the golden harp of the last line of stanza 5 is:—

7. 'Tis strung, and tun'd, for endless years,
And form'd by power divine;
To sound in God the Father's ears
No other name but Thine.

The hymn appears as No. LXXIX in "Olney Hymns," 1779.

The tune *Fountain,* also named *Cleansing Fountain,* was arranged by Lowell Mason (1792-1872), see appendix, from an early American melody. It is a pentatonic tune (see No. 181) and can be played on the black notes of the piano exclusively, by transposing it to the key of G flat, i.e., up a minor fifth.

164. O SAVIOUR, PRECIOUS SAVIOUR

Psalm 45: 11

This hymn was written at Leamington, Warwickshire, in November, 1870, by Frances Ridley Havergal (1836-79), see appendix, and illustrates her sister Maria's comment that "My sister Fanny's books are not about religion, but about the Lord Jesus as a personal, living Saviour." To her the gospel was not simply "good news," but a living Person, it was Him, not it. Miss Havergal was very familiar with the Scriptures and used their language almost subconsciously as shown in all her hymns. This one was inspired by Psalm 45: 11: "He is thy Lord; and worship thou Him," a theme which makes almost a refrain in the second part of the hymn. The title of the poem was "Our King, Worship Thou Him," and another Scripture basis was 1 Peter 1: 8: "Whom having not seen, ye love."

The tune *Greenland* is by Johann Michael Haydn (1737-1806), organist for the archbishop of Salzburg, and composer, and a younger brother of the more famous Franz Joseph Haydn. It is so named because it was used with Heber's hymn, "From Greenland's Icy Mountains" (No. 445). Haydn also composed No. 75, *Lyons.* He initialled all his works with the initial letters of the words "Omnia ad majorem dei gloriam" = all for the greater glory of God.

165. FAIRIEST LORD JESUS

Philippians 2: 9

A Roman Catholic hymnal of 1677 calls this a new hymn and it is now entitled *Crusader's Hymn,* because it was supposed to be traditionally sung in the twelfth century by German pilgrims on their way to Jerusalem. The meadows, woodland, sun, moon, and stars, and other objects of nature, beautiful as they were, turn the pilgrims' thoughts to the outstanding excellence of their Lord. The same idea is conveyed in Philippians 2: 9, "Wherefore God also has highly exalted Him, and given Him a name which is above every name."

The tune is a Silesian folk song, discovered in 1836 by Heinrich Hoffman von Fallersleben (1798-1874). With his friend Richter he listened to peasants singing in the fields, and together they compiled a collection of folk-songs, the "Schlesische Volkslieder," 1842. It was harmonized in 1850 by Richard Storrs Willis (1819-1900) of Detroit, a friend of the composer Mendelssohn and a graduate of Yale University. The melody was used by Franz Liszt in his "Legend of St. Elizabeth" as a march tune for crusader knights, thus giving rise to the name *Crusader's Hymn.* Willis also wrote No. 99, *Carol.*

166. JESUS, THESE EYES HAVE NEVER SEEN

John 20: 29

In 1858, Dr. Ray Palmer (1808-87), then a Congregational minister in Albany, New York, was preparing a sermon with Christ as its special theme. He thought of a book which would help him in his study, and opening the bookcase, his eyes fell on the required volume immediately. He thought of how in a similar way the face of Jesus would be suddenly unveiled to him one day, and this idea so impressed him that he set aside his sermon and wrote the words of this hymn. They are based on John 20: 29: "Blessed are they that have not seen, and yet have believed," and on the similar statement in 1 Peter 1: 8: "Whom having not seen, ye love; in whom, though now ye see Him not, yet believing, ye rejoice with joy unspeakable and full of glory." Palmer's last words on the day before his death were the words of the fifth stanza of this his favourite hymn:—

5. When death these mortal eyes shall seal,
And still this throbbing heart,
The rending veil shall Thee reveal
All-glorious as Thou art.

Palmer also wrote Nos. 154, "Jesus, Thou Joy of Loving Hearts," 235, "We Stand in Deep Repentance," 246, "My Faith Looks Up to Thee," and 285, "I Give My Heart to Thee."

The tune *Beatitudo,* also used for No. 18, "O For a Heart to Praise My God," was composed in 1875 by John Bacchus Dykes (1823-76), see appendix. It has this name meaning blessedness, because it was specially written for Isaac Watts's hymn "How Bright Those Glorious Spirits Shine," words which aptly describe the blessedness of the heavenly kingdom.

167. SHEPHERD OF TENDER YOUTH

Deuteronomy 32:7

This is the first known Christian hymn and it appeared at the end of a Greek book, "The Tutor," written by Titus Flavius Clemens (c. 170-c. 220). After studying the writings of the early Christian fathers he left Athens, renounced paganism, and became a teacher in the Christian school in Alexandria. The object of his book was to present Christ as the perfect tutor and to erect a bulwark against the inroads of paganism. The complete hymn presents many types of Christ, some of them not from the Scriptures, e.g.:—

Bridle of colts untamed,
Wing of unwandering birds,
Rudder of youth unbending,
Shepherd with wisdom tending,
Curb of the stubborn steed,
Helm for the ships.

The four stanzas given present Him as King, Lord, Word, High Priest, Guide, and Shepherd. The hymn was freely translated from the Greek in 1846 by Henry Martyn Dexter (1821-90) of Manchester, New Hampshire, a Congregational minister, for use in a sermon on Deuteronomy 32:7: "Remember the days of old," when he preached on some prominent characteristics of early Christians. His fifth stanza was:—

5. So now, and till we die,
Sound we Thy praises high,
And joyful sing;
Let all the holy throng,
Who to Thy church belong,
Unite and swell the song
To Christ our King.

The tune *Kirby Bedon,* which means the church near Bedon, a village three miles south-east of Norwich, Norfolk, was composed in 1887 by Dr. Edward Bunnett (1834-1923), who was born in Norfolk and was the organist at Norwich Cathedral.

168. WORTHY, WORTHY, IS THE LAMB

Revelation 5: 12

This anonymous hymn recalls three scriptures from the Book of Revelation:—

Stanza 1—Revelation 5: 12: "Worthy is the Lamb that was slain to receive . . . glory."

2—Revelation 20: 3: "That he should deceive the nations no more, till the thousand years [= millennium] should be fulfilled."

3—Revelation 14: 1: "Lo, a Lamb stood on the Mount Sion, and with Him an hundred forty and four thousand."

The bass part of the tune *Worthy* has a noteworthy ascending octave passage in its first and third lines, and there is an interesting unison passage in the second line of the refrain.

169. THOU HIDDEN SOURCE

Proverbs 18: 10

Charles Wesley (1707-88), see appendix, wrote these words of trust and confidence in Jesus in 1749 under the title "For the Morning." The first two stanzas speak of His name, reminding us of the statement in Proverbs 18: 10: "The name of the Lord is a strong tower: the righteous runneth into it, and is safe." The last two stanzas are notable for their many contrasts, six in each stanza, namely: rest and toil, ease and pain, war and peace, loss and gain, smile and frown, shame and glory; want and supply, weakness and power, bonds and liberty, light and dark, grief and joy, life and death.

The tune *Pater Omnium* (= Father of all), also used for No. 146, "Jesus, Thy Boundless Love to Me," was composed in 1875 by Henry James Ernest Holmes (1852-1938), a London violinist and composer, and later solicitor, who emigrated to the United States. He also composed No. 353, *Eventide (Holmes).*

170. BEYOND THE STARRY SKIES

1 Timothy 3: 16

James Fanch (1704-67), a Baptist minister of Romsey, Hampshire, wrote a seven stanza hymn in common metre (8.6.8.6.) which was published in "The Gospel Magazine" in 1776 and began "Beyond the glittering, starry globes." In 1794 he and his brother-in-law, Daniel Turner (1710-98), a Baptist minister of Abingdon,

Berkshire, for fifty years, adapted and expanded this hymn into twenty-eight stanzas of a short metre hymn (6.6.8.6.). The present version is a selection of both of these, mainly by Turner, and retained in short metre. It is based on 1 Timothy 3: 16: "God was manifest in the flesh . . . seen of angels," for it describes the angels' adoration of Christ in heaven, their ministry to Him on earth, their presence at the resurrection, and their triumphant ascension with Him to glory. Turner also wrote No. 237, "Jesus, Full of All Compassion."

The tune *Jenkins* was composed in 1939 by Harold Amadeus Miller (1891-1966), see appendix, and is named after a boyhood friend in New York State. Herald (named after the *Review and Herald,* the general church paper of Seventh-day Adventists) Jenkins later became a member in Washington of Miller's Mellotone chorus.

171. THERE IS A NAME I LOVE

Acts 4: 12

Frederick Whitfield (1829-1904), an Anglican clergyman of Kirkby-Ravensworth, Yorkshire, wrote these words in 1855 under the title of "The Name of Jesus." It appeared with twenty-five other original hymns in "Sacred Poems and Prose" 1861. There were nine stanzas, the omitted ones being:—

4. It tells me what my Father hath
In store for every day;
And though I tread a darksome path,
Yields sunshine all the way.

5. It tells of One whose loving heart
Can feel my deepest woe;
Who in my sorrow bears a part
That none can bear below!

6. It bids my trembling soul rejoice,
It dries each rising tear;
It tells me, in a "still small voice,"
To trust and never fear.

9. And there, with all the blood-bought throng,
From sin and sorrow free,
I'll sing the new eternal song
Of Jesu's love to me.

A fitting Scripture text is, "There is none other name under heaven given among men, whereby we must be saved." Acts 4: 12. Whitfield also wrote No. 605, "I Need Thee, Precious Jesus."

172. COME, SOUND HIS PRAISE

Psalm 95

Isaac Watts (1674-1748), see appendix, wrote this paraphrase of the ninety-fifth psalm in 1719 with the instruction—To be sung before the sermon. It had originally six stanzas, the omitted ones being:—

5. But if your ears refuse
The language of His grace,
And hearts grow hard, like stubborn Jews,
That unbelieving race;

6. The Lord, in vengeance dress'd,
Will lift His hand and swear,
"You that despise My promised rest
Shall have no portion there."

The portions paraphrased in the four stanzas in "Church Hymnal" are:—

Psalm 95: 2: "Let us come before His presence with thanksgiving, and . . . psalms."
3: "For the Lord is a great God, and a great King above all gods."
4: "In His hand are the deep places."
5: "The sea is His, and He made it: and His hands formed the dry land."
6: "O come, let us worship and bow down: let us kneel before the Lord our maker."
7: "We are the people of His pasture, and the sheep of His hand. . . . Today if ye will hear His voice."
8: "As in the provocation."

The tune *Waugh* was composed by Ralph Harrison (1748-1810), a Presbyterian minister at Shrewsbury and then at Manchester, who compiled tunes for use in the latter district. One of these tunes is No. 187, *Warrington.* Harrison also arranged Nos. 355 and 356, *Arlington,* as a hymn tune.

173. O BROTHER, BE FAITHFUL

Matthew 25: 21

Uriah Smith (1832-1903), brother of Annie Rebekah Smith, see appendix, was a Millerite in his boyhood. After the disappointment of October, 1844, he lost interest in religion, but was re-converted in 1852. He joined the *Review and Herald* staff the next year and completed a half century of service there, for a large part of the time as editor. He was an inventor of a school desk and patented an artificial leg, and was a deep student, an accomplished writer, and a pillar of the church throughout his denominational service. He was secretary of the General Conference of Seventh-day Adventists for four periods totalling twenty-one years, and treasurer for one year, 1876-77. He is probably best known as the author of "Thoughts on Daniel and the Revelation." The words of this hymn are a fit epitome of his own life which was remarkable for its faithfulness to duty. The sentiments are derived from the words of commendation given by the lord of the three servants, "Well done, thou good and faithful servant." Matthew 25: 21. The poem entitled "Be Faithful" appeared on the front page of the *Review and Herald* of September 27, 1853, with instructions to be sung to the tune of "Be Kind to the Loved Ones at Home." Uriah Smith also wrote No. 492, "Dark Is the Hour."

The tune suggested by Smith was to a secular song beginning "Be Kind to Thy Father, for When Thou Wert Young," which was written in 1847 by Jacob E. Hosmer to a tune by Isaac Baker Woodbury (1819-58), see appendix. The tune is here named *Faithful* because of its association with this hymn which mentions this word ten times in its four stanzas.

174. COME, LORD, AND TARRY NOT

Hebrews 10: 37

Horatius Bonar (1808-89), see appendix, wrote these words in 1846 under the heading "Come, Lord," and a motto taken from St. Augustine, *Senuit mundus* = "the world grows old." Bonar was a deep student of the Scriptures, and was well acquainted with texts dealing with the second advent of Christ, as shown by quotations throughout the hymn. A summary is found in Hebrews 10: 37, "He that shall come will come, and will not tarry." There are fourteen stanzas in the complete hymn, some of the omitted ones being:—

2. Come for Thy saints still wait,
   Daily ascends their sigh;
   The Spirit and the Bride say, Come;
   Dost Thou not hear their cry?

5. Come, for Thy foes are strong;
   With taunting lip they say,
   "Where is the promised Advent now,
   And where the dreaded day?"

6. Come, for the good are few;
   They lift their voice in vain;
   Faith waxes fainter on the earth,
   And love is on the wane.

7. Come, for the truth is weak,
And error pours abroad
Its subtle poison o'er the earth—
An earth that hates her God.

8. Come, for love waxes cold,
Its steps are faint and slow;
Faith now is lost in unbelief,
Hope's lamp burns dim and low.

11. Come, in Thy glorious might,
Come with the iron rod,
Scattering Thy foes before Thy face,
Most mighty Son of God.

13. Come, and make all things new,
Build up this ruined earth,
Restore our faded Paradise,
Creation's second birth.

Stanzas 4 and 9, not quoted here, make up the complete hymn.

The tune *Leighton* was composed in 1849 by Henry Wellington Greatorex (1813-58), organist at the Centre church, Hartford, Connecticut, and was published in 1851 in his "Collection of Sacred Music." He was born in Burton-on-Trent, Derbyshire, and emigrated to the United States in 1838, serving as organist also in New York Protestant Episcopal churches. He also composed No. 689, *Gloria Patri,* and arranged Nos. 25 and 383, *Manoah,* and 48, *Seymour. Leighton* is unusual in that the first half is written mainly in quavers, and the second half entirely in crotchets or longer notes. This does correspond at least in the first stanza with words of a rapid sense of urgency succeeded by words denoting slowness and waiting.

175. AWAKE, YE SAINTS

Romans 13: 11

Philip Doddridge (1702-51), see appendix, entitled this hymn, which was published posthumously in 1755, "The Near Approach of Salvation, an Engagement to Diligence and Love." He based it on the text "And that, knowing the time, that now it is high time to awake out of sleep: for now is our salvation nearer than when we believed." Rom. 13: 11. The last two lines have been altered from the original:

Fast as ye bring the night of death
Ye bring eternal day.

The tune *Zerah* was composed by Lowell Mason (1792-1872), see appendix.

176. LO! HE COMES

Revelation 1: 7

This is a composite hymn by three authors, the first two stanzas and most of the fourth by Charles Wesley (1707-88), see appendix. He wrote in 1758 from an original in 1752 by John Cennick (1718-55), one of Wesley and Whitefield's converts, who later became a Moravian preacher. This version began, "Lo! He cometh, countless trumpets." The first two stanzas are based on Revelation 1: 7: "Behold, He cometh with clouds; and every eye shall see Him, and they also which pierced Him: and all kindreds of the earth shall wail because of Him. Even so, Amen," and the last stanza on Revelation 22: 12: "And, behold, I come quickly; and My reward is with Me, to give every man according as his work shall be." The hymn was further edited by Martin Madan in 1760. Wesley's third stanza was:—

3. The dear tokens of His passion
Still His dazzling body bears,
Cause of endless exultation
To His ransom'd worshippers;
With what rapture
Gaze we on those glorious scars.

The tune *Holywood* is from a compilation in 1751, "Cantus Diversi" (= various songs) by John Francis Wade (c. 1711-86), who lived in Lancashire, and spent his time making copies of musical manuscripts so that they could be used in wealthy Roman Catholic homes and in institutions. This collection also contains No. 105, *Adeste Fideles* which is the same as No. 255, *Portuguese Hymn*.

177. THE CHURCH HAS WAITED LONG

Revelation 6: 9-11

These words were written in 1844 by Horatius Bonar (1808-89), see appendix, with a refrain, "Come then, Lord Jesus, come." They were published in 1856 and are virtually a paraphrase of some verses in the Book of Revelation, particularly: "I saw . . . the souls of them that were slain for the word of God, and for the testimony which they held: and they cried with a loud voice, saying, How long, O Lord, holy and true, dost Thou not judge and avenge our blood. . . . And it was said unto them, that they should rest yet for a little season." Revelation 6: 9-11. There were five stanzas, each of eight lines, those omitted being:—

1. . . .
Age after age has gone,
Sun after sun has set,
And still, in weeds of widowhood,
She weeps a mourner yet.

3. The serpent's brood increase,
The powers of hell grow bold,
The conflict thickens, faith is low,
And love is waxing cold.
. . .

4. . . .
Should not the loving Bride
The absent Bridegroom mourn?
Should she not wear the weeds of grief
Until her Lord return?

5. The whole creation groans,
And waits to hear that voice,
That shall restore her comeliness,
And make her wastes rejoice.
. . .

The tune *Garden City,* also used for No. 58, "Our Day of Praise Is Done," was composed in 1890 for the dedication of a new church building at Garden City, Long Island, by the American Episcopal organist and composer, Horatio William Parker (1863-1919). He disliked congregational singing, and his own tune *Garden City* was offensive to him, and had it been possible he would have recalled it. He was professor of music in Garden City, Long Island, at the Cathedral School of St. Paul from 1885-87, then organist at Holy Trinity Church, New York, and in 1894 professor of music at Yale. He also wrote Nos. 47, *Pixham;* 110, *Stella (Parker);* 133, *Jubilate,* and 198, *Pro Patria.*

178. IN THE SUN, AND MOON, AND STARS

Luke 21:25-28

Reginald Heber (1783-1826) wrote hymns for specific events of the Anglican church year, this one published in 1811 being for the second Sunday in Advent. It is a close paraphrase of our Lord's prophecy, the words and ideas used being underlined. "And there shall be signs in the sun, and in the moon, and in the stars; and upon the earth distress of nations, with perplexity; the sea and the waves roaring; men's hearts failing them for fear, and for looking after those things which are coming on the earth: for the powers of heaven shall be shaken. And then shall they see the Son of man coming in a cloud with power and great glory. And when these things begin to come to pass, then look up, and lift up your heads; for your redemption draweth nigh." Luke 21: 25-28. Heber was vicar of Hodnet, Salop, from 1807-23, and then bishop of Calcutta until his sudden death at Trichinopoli. He had won the Newdigate prize for an English poem while at Oxford in 1803. He also wrote Nos. 73, "Holy, Holy, Holy"; 340, "By Cool Siloam's Shady Rill"; 361, "The Son of God Goes Forth to War"; 445, "From Greenland's Icy Mountains," and 476, "Bread of the World."

The tune *Lubeck* was composed in 1704 by Johann Anastasius Freylinghausen (1670-1739), the hymn-writer of the German Pietists. He wrote forty-four hymns and twenty-two tunes, and his "Gesangbuch" (= song book) of 1704 used less ponderous tunes than the common chorales of his day. The fourth line of this melody is exactly a fifth lower than the second line, making it an easier tune to learn to sing (see also No. 92). One stanza of one of his hymns was used by John Wesley in his translation of a Zinzendorf hymn, No. 330, "O Thou, to Whose All-Searching Sight."

179. HE REIGNS! THE LORD, THE SAVIOUR, REIGNS

Psalm 97: 1-5

These words are a paraphrase appearing in the "Psalms of David," 1719, by Isaac Watts (1674-1748), see appendix, of the first part of the 97th Psalm, the following verses being used: "The Lord reigneth; let the earth rejoice. . . . Clouds and darkness are round about Him: righteousness . . . the habitation of His throne. A fire goeth before Him, and burneth up His enemies. . . . The earth saw, and trembled. The hills melted like wax." Psalm 97: 1-5. Watts's original words of the latter part of the first stanza are closer to the psalm than the present words, for he wrote:—

Let the whole earth in songs rejoice,
And distant islands join the voice.

The last part of the last stanza shows Watts's predilection for making the Psalms teach New Testament doctrine, for he practically quotes Luke 21: 28: "Lift up your heads; for your redemption draweth nigh."

The tune *Sessions,* "the tune with a slur," was composed by Luther Orlando Emerson (1820-1915), a composer born at Parsonfield, Maine. He had returned from church one summer in 1847, and idly picking up his hymnbook, noted the words: "Sinner, O

Why So Thoughtless Grown?" He read the hymn through several times and was impressed to convey his feelings in music. He prayed, then went to the piano, and took only one minute to compose this tune. It is a very difficult one to sing, because although strictly in 2/2 time, the change in note values and in accent is much too varied for a hymn-tune. Emerson was a teacher and choirmaster for eight years at Salem, Massachusetts, and organist and musical director for another four years at Boston. He composed songs, quartets, piano pieces, and choral anthems, and in 1891 received the degree of Mus. D. from Findlay College, Ohio.

180. WATCHMAN, TELL ME

Isaiah 21: 11, 12

Sidney S. Brewer was a believer in William Miller's preaching of the second advent of Jesus, and passed through the disappointment of 1843 and 1844. However, he did not give up hope, and became a prominent preacher of the soon coming of the Lord, setting a new date around 1853-54. He did not become a Sabbath-keeper, but differed from other Sunday-keeping Adventists in believing as did the Seventh-day Adventists in the "sleep of death." This doctrine is included in the second half of the second stanza:—

When the Jubal trumpet, sounding
Shall awake from earth and sea
All the saints of God, now sleeping.

Brewer helped in the formation of the Adventist Christian Church in 1861. The illustration of the watchman is taken from Isaiah 21: 11, 12: "Watchman, what of the night? The watchman said, The morning cometh." However, more than half of the hymn is occupied with descriptions of the eternal glories, given not by the watchman, but by the pilgrim to the watchman.

The tune *Dawning,* an appropriate title for a watchman's hymn, was composed by William Batchelder Bradbury (1816-68), see appendix. It does not have much variety, as lines 1, 3, 7 are identical, so are lines 2, 4, 8, and line 6 is a repetition of line 5.

181. YE WHO ROSE TO MEET THE LORD

Revelation 22: 20

This anonymous hymn is a composite of many scriptures. For example:—

Stanza 1. "We shall reap, if we faint not," Galatians 6: 9; "I come quickly; and My reward is with Me," Revelation 22: 12; "Take ye heed, watch and pray," Mark 13: 33.

Stanza 2: "He that shall endure unto the end," Matthew 24: 13; "A man which had not on a wedding garment," Matthew 22: 11; "He is faithful that promised," Hebrews 10: 23; "Those virgins arose, and trimmed their lamps," Matthew 25: 7; "Thy Word is a lamp . . . and a light," Psalm 119: 105; "For we walk by faith, and not by sight," 2 Corinthians 5: 7; "Henceforth there is laid up for me a crown," 2 Timothy 4: 8.

Stanza 3: "Surely I come quickly. Amen. Even so, come, Lord Jesus," Revelation 22: 20; "Priests of God and of Christ, and shall reign with Him," Revelation 20: 6.

Stanza 4: "Blessed are they which are called unto the marriage supper of the Lamb," Revelation 19: 9; "She should be arrayed in fine linen, clean and white: for the fine linen is the righteousness of saints," Revelation 19: 8; "The voice of a great multitude . . . and as the voice of mighty thunderings, saying, Alleluia." Revelation 19: 6.

It appears in the 1861 edition of "Hymns for Those Who Keep the Commandments of God and the Faith of Jesus." An omitted stanza is:—

3. Mid the darts of angry foe,
Onward, fearless, onward go,
The good soldier's courage show,
On to victory!
Let thine eyes be turned to Me,
Jesus says, "I'll rescue thee,
Overcome and faithful be,
Thou shalt glory see!

The tune *Caledonia* is an old Scottish bagpipe air dating back at least to the fifteenth century. It is an interesting example of the pentatonic scale of five notes only, the 4th and 7th notes of the usual octave being absent. If the note F sharp or G flat be taken as the tonic or lowest note of the scale, the pentatonic scale is then identical with the black notes of the piano. *Caledonia* can be played thus if transposed down three semitones to the key of G flat, with three minor exceptions, namely, the 6th note of lines 2 and 5, and the 7th note of line 6, all of which could be lowered one note without affecting the melody seriously. Many Scottish airs, e.g., *"Loch Lomond,"* are in the pentatonic scale, and can therefore be played entirely on the black keys if the right key is selected. Chinese, Japanese, and Indian hill-tribe tunes, as well as African and consequently American Negro tunes are often in the pentatonic scale, e.g., *"Nobody knows the trouble I've seen."* Other tunes in the pentatonic scale are Nos. 163, *Fountain;* 221, *Balerma,* 268, *Autumn;* 301, *World to Come;* 343, *I Love Thee,* 473, *Alida;* 561, unnamed, and 567, *Only Trust Him.*

182. 'TIS ALMOST TIME FOR THE LORD TO COME

Genesis 32: 24

Both words and music were composed by G. W. Sederquist, who flourished around 1902, and the theme and the title of the tune come from an expression found in Genesis 32: 24, "the breaking of the day," which describes the wrestling of Jacob with the angel. This dawn is taken metaphorically as the end of earth's long night which precedes the "breaking of the day" of Christ's second coming. There are five stanzas, the omitted one being:—

4. There must be those in the field of sin,
Far from the fold away;
Who once were happy in Jesus' love,
And look for the breaking of the day.

183. LET EVERY LAMP BE BURNING

Matthew 25: 7

Both words and music are by Franklin Edson Belden (1858-1945), see appendix, and appear in "Hymns and Tunes," 1886. The hymn is based on the parable of the wise and foolish virgins who, after slumbering while awaiting the bridegroom, awoke at the midnight cry. "Then all those virgins arose, and trimmed their lamps." Matthew 25: 7.

The tune *Diligence* is named for the sentiment expressed in the last stanza, which associates faith and works.

184. WATCHMEN, ON THE WALLS OF ZION

Isaiah 21: 11, 12

These four stanzas fall into two simple divisions, the first two asking questions and the last two giving the response. The question asked in the first stanza is found in Isaiah 21: 11, "Watchman what of the night?" The figure then changes from anxious enquiries in a city, to travellers on a ship making for the heavenly haven, who are eagerly watching for the shore. The answers then come from the watchmen in the language of Isaiah 21: 12: "The watchman said, The morning cometh." The ship metaphor is retained to the end by the mention of "chart and compass," and much of the language in the questions is repeated in the replies. The two middle stanzas are omitted, the originals being:—

3. They are silent—what's the meaning?
Are the watchmen all asleep?
Have they lost their chart and compass?
Do they now no vigil keep?
Have they left us
In our sad despair to weep?

4. Blessed be the God of heaven
He can from our fears release;
If we listen to His mandate
From all trust in man to cease,
He will guide us
To the port of endless peace.

The tune *Zion* was composed in 1830 in Washington, Connecticut, by Thomas Hastings (1784-1872), see appendix, especially for Thomas Kelly's hymn, "On the Mountain Top Appearing," which tells of a herald carrying good news to Zion.

185. HEIR OF THE KINGDOM

Romans 13: 11, 12

The expression which gives the title of the hymn and which occurs in each stanza is taken from James 2: 5, "Heirs of the kingdom which He hath promised to them that love Him," but a summary of the theme could well be Romans 13: 11, 12, "And that, knowing the time, that now it is high time to awake out of sleep: for now is our salvation nearer than when we believed. The night is far spent, the day is at hand: let us therefore cast off the works of darkness, and let us put on the armour of light." The hymn pictures a pilgrim who is on his way to meet the chariot of the king, but who falls asleep, unarmed, and unprepared. The challenge comes to look beyond the abounding fears to the portents that show that the king is near, and to remember that earthly attractions are but transient.

The tune *Rodman* was composed by Lowell Mason (1792-1872), see appendix.

186. LONG FOR MY SAVIOUR I'VE BEEN WAITING

Hebrews 10: 37

The words reflect the feelings of the Millerites as they waited for the expected coming of the Lord in 1844. They endured scoffing and ridicule from unbelievers, and even from members of the popular churches who did not accept the premillennial view of the second advent. The words are by an anonymous Advent believer prior to 1844, and tell of the hope of the second advent which cheered the heart through the darkness of temptation and opposition, with faith fixed firmly in the promises of God. "For yet a little while, and He that shall come will come, and will not tarry." Hebrews 10: 37.

The tune *Expectation* is named for the thought of hope throughout the hymn.

187. THE LORD IS COMING

1 Corinthians 16: 22

It is said that the greeting of the early Christian believers was "Maranatha," 1 Corinthians 16: 22 (= The Lord is coming). This salutation from the heart is the theme of this second advent hymn by an anonymous believer. There are four other stanzas, namely:

5. The Lord is coming, seas retire!
Ye mountains, melt to liquid fire!
Ye oceans, cease to ebb and flow!
His stately steppings ye should know.

6. The Lord is coming! who shall stand?
Who shall be found at His right hand?
He that hath the white garments on
That Christ our righteous King hath won

7. The Lord is coming; watch and pray!
Watch ye, and haste unto the day;
So shalt thou then escape the snare,
And Christ's eternal glory share.

8. is almost identical with the first. The hymn appears in the 1861 edition of "Hymns for Those Who Keep the Commandments of God and the Faith of Jesus."

The tune *Warrington* was composed in 1784 by Ralph Harrison (1748-1810), a Presbyterian minister and teacher of ancient languages at Manchester. It appeared in a collection of psalm tunes for use in the Manchester district, and its name commemorates the Lancashire town where he was educated. It is noteworthy for the descending succession of nine notes in the melody of lines three and four. Harrison also wrote No. 172, *Waugh,* and arranged Nos. 355 and 356, *Arlington,* as a hymn tune.

188. STAR OF OUR HOPE

1 Thessalonians 4: 16, 17

These words by an anonymous writer depict the resurrection of the righteous dead to glorious immortality at the coming of the Saviour, when He is crowned King of kings and Lord of lords. "For the Lord Himself shall descend from heaven with a shout, with the voice of the archangel, and with the trump of God: and the dead in Christ shall rise first: then we which are alive and remain shall be caught up together with them in the clouds, to meet the Lord in the air: and so shall we ever be with the Lord." 1 Thessalonians 4: 16, 17.

The tune *Wareham,* also used for No. 294, where it is set a semitone higher in B flat, was composed in 1738 by William Knapp (1698-1768). It was first written for Psalm 36: 5-10, and commemorates the town of Wareham in Dorset, England, where Knapp was born and where he was later organist. The melody is noteworthy in that it proceeds by successive notes of the scale, with one exception only in the first line.

189. JOY TO THE WORLD

Psalm 98: 4-9

This hymn is a paraphrase by Isaac Watts (1674-1748), see appendix, of the second part of the 98th psalm, and was published in 1719 in his "Psalm of David Imitated." He wrote in the first line, "the Lord *is* come," and Seventh-day Adventists who have changed these words to "*will* come" and other tenses from present to future, have been accused of distorting Scripture to suit their doctrine of the second advent. However, it is quite obvious that the psalmist is describing a future event as though he were witnessing it in the present, for he speaks of the Lord coming to judge the earth, an event which has not yet taken place. Furthermore, the psalmist reverts to the future tense in the very last sentence, saying, "with righteousness shall He judge the world." Psalm 98: 9.

The tune is said to be arranged from George Frederick Handel (1685-1759), the world-famous German composer, naturalized an Englishman in 1726, and who is buried in Westminster Abbey. It only slightly resembles any of his airs, though the first four notes are identical with the first four notes of "Lift up your heads" from the "Messiah," a musical phrase common in Handel. There is a resemblance also in lines 3 and 4 to the introduction to "Comfort ye," also from the "Messiah." The tune was named *Antioch* by Lowell Mason (1792-1872), see appendix, one of comparatively few New Testament names chosen by him. It commemorates the first Christian church in Antioch in Syria (Acts 11: 26), where tradition says that antiphonal singing was first introduced by Ignatius after his dream of a choir of angels singing in this way. Handel also wrote Nos. 100, *Christmas,* and 484, *Samson.*

190. WHEN THOU, MY RIGHTEOUS JUDGE

Malachi 3: 2

These words are the second part of a nine-stanza poem on the judgment day, the first part being the following five stanzas:—

1. We soon shall hear the midnight cry,
   And Gabriel's trump shall shake the sky,
   And cleave the starry plain;
   The angel-herald shall proclaim
   Redemption through the slaughtered Lamb,
   And break death's powerful chain.

2. Then shall the Judge descend in clouds
   Circled around with countless crowds
   Of the celestial choir;
   Before whose rapid glorious ray
   The frightened heavens shall flee away,
   And hide themselves in fire.

3. How, how shall sinners venture nigh
   Before the Lamb in yonder sky?
   Yet, oh, they must draw near
   To hear the dreadful word—Depart!
   Which, like some deadly-pointed dart,
   Their hearts will wound and tear;

4. While vengeful, fiery tempests hurled
   Shall chase them downward to the world
   Of everlasting pain:
   Then they their helpless grief shall mourn
   Who to the Lamb would never turn—
   The Lamb for sinners slain.

5. Dear Lord, I sink at Thy pierced feet;
   O let me by experience sweet
   Taste Thy forgiving love;
   And when Thou dost to judgment come,
   Take me with Thee to Thy blest home
   In Salem's land above.

It was written in 1772 by Selina Shirley, Countess of Huntingdon (1707-91), who was converted by and then became a patroness of George Whitefield. She visited the poor and the sick on her husband's estates, and was scorned by her titled friends, who did not consider that the gospel was for the underprivileged. As a result, she formed a separate Countess of Huntingdon's Connexion of God-fearing people who had been impressed by the Wesleyan evangelistic revival but who were still members of the Church of England. Among them were Perronet and Shrubsole (see Nos. 156, 157). The hymn is fittingly summarized by the questions asked in the last book of the Old Testament—"But who may abide the day of His coming? and who shall stand when He appeareth?" Malachi 3: 2.

The tune *Ariel,* also used for No. 161, "O Could I Speak the Matchless Worth," is an arrangement from a Mozart tune by Lowell Mason (1792-1872), see appendix. The name means "Lion of God," and is taken from Isaiah 29: 1, but is one of Mason's many Old Testament names which have no meaning associated with the words of the hymn. Wolfgang Amadeus Mozart (1756-91) of Salzburg, Austria, was an infant musical prodigy, composing much church music before he was fifteen years old. Another arrangement from his music is Nos. 267 and 633, *Ellesdie.*

191. HE'S COMING ONCE AGAIN

Revelation 6: 14-17

Both words and music are by Franklin Edson Belden (1858-1945), see appendix, and appear in "Hymns and Tunes," 1886. While the hymn has no specific title or Scripture reference, it is evidently based mainly on Revelation 6: 12, 14-17: "There was a great earthquake. . . . And the heaven departed as a scroll when it is rolled together; and every mountain and island were moved out of their places. And the kings of the earth, and the great men . . . hid themselves in the dens and in the rocks of the mountains; and said . . . Hide us from . . . the wrath of the Lamb: for the great day of His wrath is come; and who shall be able to stand?"

192. HARK! THAT SHOUT

1 Thessalonians 4:16, 17

Thomas Kelly (1769-1855) actually wrote "Hark! that shout of rapt'rous joy," and here shows his knowledge of the second advent of Jesus. While still a minister in the Episcopal Church he held strong evangelical views, and later from his own private means built four Independent churches in Ireland to propagate these doctrines. He based this hymn on 1 Thessalonians 4: 16, 17: "The Lord Himself shall descend from heaven with a shout, with the voice of the archangel, and with the trump of God . . . then we which are alive and remain shall be caught up . . . to meet the Lord in the air: and so shall we ever be with the Lord." Kelly also wrote Nos. 220, "I Love the Sacred Book"; 296, "We Sing the Praise," and 308, "We've No Abiding City Here," as well as over seven hundred and fifty others.

The tune *Hendon,* also used for Nos. 30, "Lord, We Come Before Thee Now," and 273, "Take My Life, and Let It Be," was composed in 1827 by Henri Abraham Cesar Malan (1787-1864). He was a brilliant preacher from Geneva, who spent some time in London, England, which has a suburb Hendon. He also composed No. 408, *Rosefield.*

193. THY KINGDOM COME

Isaiah 11: 9

Frederick Lucian Hosmer (1840-1929) a Unitarian minister ordained in 1869, wrote two hymns on the same theme of the coming kingdom of God. This one was especially for the graduation service of the Meadville, Pennsylvania, theological school on June 12, 1891. While the coming of God's glorious kingdom seems to be delayed, yet it will come as surely as dawn follows a long night. Then justice, knowledge, peace, and righteousness will mark the reign of God on earth, as prophesied in Isaiah 11: 9, "They shall not hurt nor destroy in all My holy mountain: for the earth shall be full of the knowledge of the Lord, as the waters cover the sea."

The tune *St. Flavian* is the first half of a hymn tune from the English psalter of 1562. This psalter contained forty-six tunes known as proper or church tunes to which the Psalms could be sung, and it was published by John Day (1522-84), a music printer. These tunes are now distinguished by prefixing the adjective "old" to the number of the psalm to which they were written, *St. Flavian* being the Old 132nd. Flavian was a bishop of Constantinople who died in A.D. 449.

194. THE KING SHALL COME

Matthew 24: 30

John Brownlie (1859-1925) a minister of the Free Church of Scotland, translated many Latin and Greek hymns. This one is from a Greek source and appeared in his "Hymns from the East," 1907, with two additional stanzas, namely:—

6. And let the endless bliss begin,
   By weary saints foretold,
   When right shall triumph over wrong,
   And truth shall be extolled.

7. The King shall come when morning dawns
And light and beauty brings:
Hail, Christ the Lord! Thy people pray,
Come quickly, King of kings.

The hymn contrasts 1. the second coming of Christ as King with His first coming as a babe,
2. the glory of the second advent with the glory of the resurrection day, and
3. the glorious heavenly day that never ends with a night which symbolizes the total history of the earth.

Many texts speak of the glorious appearing of our Lord, for example, Matthew 24: 30, "They shall see the Son of man coming in the clouds of heaven with power and great glory."

The tune *St. Stephen* was composed in 1789 as a setting for the 23rd Psalm, by William Jones (1726-1800), Anglican vicar of Nayland, Suffolk, a student of music, theology, and science, who had also ministered in Kent and Northamptonshire. It was named after the first Christian martyr because Jones admired him above other Bible characters.

195. GREAT GOD, WHAT DO I SEE

Amos 4: 12

The idea behind these words was put into verse in 1586 by a village pastor, Bartholomäus Ringwaldt (1532-97), who virtually translated the Dies Irae (= day of wrath). In 1812, Dr. William Bengo Collyer (1782-1854) an eloquent Congregational preacher and a hymn-writer, was impressed by the first stanza, and added three of his own composition, following the same idea. Later in 1820 Thomas Cotterill (1779-1823), an Anglican clergyman of Sheffield, who introduced Watts's and Wesley's hymns to his congregation in spite of fierce opposition and litigation, altered the last three stanzas, mainly in the first halves, but still retaining the essential idea. Note the climax of each stanza: "Prepare to meet thy God." Amos 4: 12. Another stanza is:—

4. Great Judge, to Thee our prayers we pour,
In deep abasement bending;
O shield us through that last dread hour,
Thy wondrous love extending:
May we, in this our trial day,
With faithful hearts Thy Word obey,
And thus prepare to meet Thee.

Collyer also wrote No. 221, "Return, O Wanderer."

The tune *Luther* was introduced by Martin Luther (1483-1546) (see No. 261) and was first published in 1535, although he probably arranged it from the melody of a popular song in common use by travelling artisans at that time. It appeared in the Gesangbuch (= song book) of Johann Klug, who flourished in the 16th century.

196. THOU ART COMING, O MY SAVIOUR

Revelation 1:7

Frances Ridley Havergal (1836-79), see appendix, wrote this hymn at Winterdyne, near Bewdley, Worcestershire, on November 16, 1873, under the title "Advent Song—Behold He Cometh." It is based on Revelation 1: 7, "Behold, He cometh with clouds," and it consisted of seven stanzas, those omitted being:—

3. Thou art coming! Rays of glory,
Through the veil Thy death hath rent,
Touch the mountain and the river
With a golden glowing quiver,
Thrill of light and music bent.
Earth is brightened when this gleam
Falls on flower and rock and stream;
Life is brightened when this ray
Falls upon its darkest day.

4. Not a cloud and not a shadow,
Not a mist and not a tear,
Not a sin and not a sorrow,
Not a dim and veiled tomorrow,
For that sunrise grand and clear!
Jesus, Saviour, once with Thee,
Nothing else seems worth a thought!
O how marvellous will be
All the bliss Thy pain hath brought!

5. Thou art coming; at Thy table
We are witnesses for this;
While remembering hearts Thou meetest
In communion clearest, sweetest,
Earnest of our coming bliss,
Knowing not Thy death alone,
And Thy love exceeding great,
But Thy coming and Thy throne,
All for which we long and wait.

Neither Miss Havergal nor her father were pre-millennialists as were many of their evangelical friends. In spite of the excellent sentiments of this hymn, these do not apply to an imminent second advent in her thinking, but to a coming in glory at some time in the future.

She composed a tune for these words named *St. Paul,* but preferred Dr. William Henry Monk's (1823-89) tune *Beverley,* which was composed especially for it in 1875. Monk, the musical editor of "Hymns Ancient and Modern," also composed Nos. 50, *Eventide,* and 357, *Vigilate,* and harmonized 341, *Stephanos.*

197. WAKE, AWAKE, FOR NIGHT IS FLYING

Matthew 25: 6, 7

Both words and music are by Philip Nicolai (1556-1608), a most eloquent Lutheran preacher. In 1597 he was the pastor of the small town of Unna in Westphalia, at a time when the bubonic plague was sweeping through Europe. In his own town over 1,400 died, and occasionally he officiated at thirty burials in one day. The rectory was right opposite the cemetery, and the continual funeral processions caused him to meditate deeply concerning death. His thoughts transcended the gloom, however, for he looked beyond death to God in heaven, and to an eternal life in His presence. Two years later, in 1599, he published a hymnbook as a testimony to the blessed hope of eternal life and to his own peace of mind whether living or dying, endeavouring by his words to give comfort to others. In the book he included this poem entitled "Of the Voice at Midnight," basing it on the parable of the ten virgins: "And at midnight there was a cry made, Behold, the bridegroom cometh; go ye out to meet him. Then all those virgins arose, and trimmed their lamps." Matt. 25: 6, 7. The present translation in the original metre was made in 1858 by Catherine Winkworth (1827-78), see appendix. The hymn has been used by Mendelssohn in the overture to his oratorio "St. Paul," and also to the words "Sleepers, wake, a voice is calling."

The tune *Wachet Auf* (= wake up) is also in Nicolai's hymnbook. The melody was harmonized by Johann Sebastian Bach (1685-1750), the famous composer of religous music and the outstanding organist of his day. He also harmonized the melodies of Nos. 130, *Passion Chorale,* and 201, *Yule.*

198. O LORD OF LIFE

Romans 13: 12

Marion Franklin Ham (1867-1956) was a Unitarian minister at Reading, Massachusetts, when he wrote these words in 1912, likening Christians on earth as pilgrims in a dark night. The morning star, a herald of the day, appears, indicating the soon return of our Lord, a time when He shall rule the world. The last stanza borrows the illustration of the children of Israel who marched forward with the pillar of fire and cloud. The whole hymn looks forward to the imminent end of the reign of sin, or, as expressed by the Apostle Paul, "The night is far spent, the day is at hand." Romans 13: 12. Ham, the author of many poems and stories collected in "The Golden Shuttle," 1896, began to write hymns in 1910. He was ordained in 1898, and served in Chattanooga, in Dallas, in Reading, and in Waverley, Massachusetts, retiring from full-time ministry in 1942.

The tune *Pro Patria* was composed in 1894 by Horatio William Parker (1863-1919), a member of the American Episcopal Church. He was organist at Holy Trinity in Boston and New York, and professor of music at Yale University, and received the degree of Mus. Doc. from Cambridge, England, in 1902. He also composed Nos. 47, *Pixham;* 58 and 177, *Garden City;* 110, *Stella (Parker),* and 133, *Jubilate.*

199. WE SPEAK OF THE REALMS

Psalm 119: 44

Mrs. Elizabeth Mills, née King (1805-29), of Stoke Newington, London, was reading a commentary on the 119th psalm by Bridges. On verse 44: "So shall I keep Thy law continually for ever and ever," he had made the note, "We speak of heaven, but oh, to be there!" This gave her the inspiration to write this hymn on the glories of the New Jerusalem. The words in the fourth stanza: "And shortly I also shall know and feel what it is to be there," were to her friends unwittingly prophetic, for she died three weeks after writing the hymn. (See also refrain of No. 662.)

The tune *Contrast,* also used for Nos. 200, "I Long to Behold Him," and 660, "How Tedious and Tasteless the Hours," is attributed to Lewis Edson (1784-1820), and derives its name from its use for No. 660, which has several contrasts in it. It is taken from an early American melody attached to a secular song of about 1772 entitled: "Farewell, Ye Green Fields and Sweet Groves." Edson, a blacksmith of Massachusetts and Connecticut, conducted singing schools, and was himself a well-known singer.

200. I LONG TO BEHOLD HIM

Isaiah 33: 17

Charles Wesley (1707-88), see appendix, wrote this hymn in 1762 under the title of "Heaven Desired." It is based on Isaiah 33: 17: "Thine eyes shall see the King in His beauty." The third stanza in the 1841 edition is slightly altered, and reads:—

3. How happy the people that dwell
Secure in the city above!
No pain the inhabitants feel,
No sickness or sorrow shall prove;
Physician of souls, unto me
Forgiveness and holiness give;
And then from the body set free,
And then to the city receive.

The tune *Contrast* used also for Nos. 199, "We Speak of the Realms," and 660, "How Tedious and Tasteless the Hours," is discussed in the previous hymn, No. 199.

201. SOON MAY THE LAST GLAD SONG ARISE

Psalm 24: 1

The words of this hymn are thought to have been written by a Mrs. Vokes or Voke, because its sentiments deal with the everlasting reign of our Lord, a topic on which she loved to write. Some of her hymns were published at Portsea, England, in 1797, and others in 1806. When sin and sinners have been exterminated, then as the first stanza says, the statement in Psalm 24: 1 will be true: "The earth is the Lord's, and the fullness thereof; the world, and they that dwell therein." The second stanza looks forward to the fulfilment of the prophecy of Daniel 7: 27: "The most High, whose kingdom is an everlasting kingdom, and all dominions shall serve and obey Him." The last stanza anticipates the final conquest over sin, as depicted in Revelation 19: 6: "Alleluia: for the Lord God omnipotent reigneth."

The tune *Yule* is a mediæval melody to which lower parts were added in 1734 by Johann Sebastian Bach (1685-1750), the famous composer of religious music and the outstanding organist of his day. He also harmonized Nos. 130, *Passion Chorale,* and 197, *Wachet Auf.*

202. O WHAT THEIR JOY MUST BE

Isaiah 66: 23

These words are a translation made in 1854 by John Mason Neale (1818-66), see appendix, of a Latin hymn beginning *"O quanta qualia sunt illa sabbata"* = O how great their Sabbaths are. This was originally written as a hymn for Saturday evening worship by the philosopher and theologian Pierre Abelard (1079-1142), to be sung in the abbey of Nogent-sur-Seine. This was also known as the abbey of the Paraclete where Heloise was the abbess. Note the usual ending to an old hymn with its final ascription of praise to the Trinity. There were seven stanzas, those omitted being:—

2. What are the monarch, his court, and his throne?
What are the peace and the joy that they own?
Tell us, ye blest ones, that in it have share,
If what ye feel ye can fully declare.

5. There dawns no Sabbath—no Sabbath is o'er;
Those Sabbath-keepers have one, and no more;
One and unending is that triumph-song
Which to the angels and us shall belong.

The hymn looks forward to the time when the saints will worship on an endless Sabbath in eternity, a conception not quite in harmony with the gospel prophet's prediction: "And it shall come to pass, that . . . from one Sabbath to another, shall all flesh come to worship before Me, saith the Lord." Isaiah 66: 23. The succession of sabbaths will be endless, but not the sabbaths themselves. Certainly there will be endless rest from care, from sin, from fatigue, of which the Sabbath is a symbol.

The tune *Regnator Orbis* is found in Francois de la Feillée's *"Méthode du Plain-Chant et de la Psalmodie"* of 1808 where it is set to the hymn of this name, viz.: "Ruler of the World." This book was the eighth edition of a work first published in 1745, and comprised tunes said to be derived from plainsong. The composer flourished around 1750, and was a priest in the choir of Chartres Cathedral.

203. THE WORD CAN MAKE ME WHOLE

John 15: 4

This poem by William J. Govan (18 ?-1901) of Glasgow, written after 1893, was entitled "The Palace of the Soul," and based on John 15: 4, "Abide in Me, and I in you. As the branch cannot bear fruit of itself, except it abide in the vine; no more can ye, except ye abide in Me." It traces the transition from an individual in whose soul palace the Lord dwells to the submissive state where the individual dwells in the Lord's palace which He has transferred to the soul. There are fifteen stanzas, the omitted ones being: Nos. 6-14, some of which are:—

6. I quit the outward courts of sense,
Of feeling, reasoning, choice,
To dwell with Him, to go not hence,
But humbly wait His voice.

7. And thus, I leave myself behind,
In stillness enter in;
Abiding in His love, I find
The hiding-place from sin.

9. I serve Him best when I abide
Within His secret place,
The beauty of the Lord who died
Irradiant on my face:

11. I find the blessed holy place
Of prayer, and calm, and rest,
Is where I gaze into His face
And lean upon His breast:

13. But hush! "The Son of God is come!"
Before His feet I fall
Who died for me! my lips are dumb,
And Christ is all in all.

14. How holy, holy, is the Lord!
How evil was my sin!
Yet He, by hosts of heaven adored,
Through faith, abides within.

204. COME, GRACIOUS SPIRIT

John 16: 13

Simon Browne (1680-1732) an Independent minister of Old Jewry, London, wrote in 1720 a hymn of seven stanzas in the first person. Its title was: "The Soul Giving Itself up to the Conduct and Influence of the Holy Spirit" and it began:—

Come, Holy Spirit, heavenly Dove,
My sinful maladies remove,

the first line of which is identical with Isaac Watts's hymn No. 209. It is based on John 16: 13, "When He, the Spirit of truth, is come, He will guide you into all truth." The hymn has since been extensively revised, and the present version follows a change made in 1769, but using parts of the stanzas in a different order. The word "gracious" was substituted for "heavenly" in 1787. Our fourth stanza is a further revision made in 1836. Omitted lines from Browne's original are:—

3. Conduct me safe, conduct me far
From every sin and hurtful snare:
. . .

4. . . .
Lead me to heaven, the seat of bliss,
Where pleasure in perfection is.

5. . . .
Lead to Thy word that rules must give,
And some directions how to live.

6. Lead me to means of grace, where I
May own my wants, and seek supply:
Lead to Thyself, the spring from whence
To fetch all quick'ning influence.

7. Thus I conducted still by Thee,
Of God, a child, belov'd shall be:
Here to His family pertain,
Hereafter with Him ever reign.

Browne also wrote Nos. 236, "Lord, at Thy Feet," and 464, "Hail, Happy Day."

The tune *Ware,* used also for No. 483, "All Things Are Thine," was composed by George Kingsley (1811-84) of Northampton, Massachusetts. He was a music teacher and organist in Boston, a compiler of music for young people, and later became professor of music in Philadelphia. He also composed No. 458, *Elizabethtown*, and arranged No. 381, *Valentia*. Both *Ware* and *Elizabethtown* with their unusual mixture of crotchets and quavers make a difficult rhythm for singing.

205. COME, HOLY SPIRIT, COME

John 16: 8

Joseph Hart (1712-68) was converted at Whitsuntide, 1757, after a period of alternate exaltation and depression. He had listened to a sermon in the Moravian Chapel in Fetter Lane, London, on Whitsunday, May 29, based on Revelation 3: 10, "I also will keep thee." At home he gave his life to the Saviour, and was prompted to write three Whitsunday hymns of which this is one. It appeared in his book of 119 hymns published in July, 1759, and consisted of nine stanzas entitled "To the Holy Ghost." Hart became a Calvinistic preacher and here outlines the work of the Holy Spirit in convincing of sin, in sanctifying the soul, in effecting the new birth, and in leading to a knowledge of Father, Son, and Spirit. The last lines of the first stanza were: "Dispel the darkness from our minds, And open all our eyes," and slight changes have been made in stanzas two and five. The omitted stanzas are:—

2. Cheer our desponding hearts,
Thou heavenly Paraclete;
Give us to lie with humble hope
At our Redeemer's feet.

5. Show us that loving man,
That rules the courts of bliss,
The Lord of hosts, the mighty God,
Th' eternal Prince of Peace.

7. If Thou celestial Dove,
Thine influence withdraw,
What easy victims soon we fall
To conscience, wrath, and law.

8. No longer burns our love;
Our faith and patience fail;
Our sin revives; and death and hell
Our feeble souls assail.

9. Dwell therefore in our hearts,

followed by the rest of our fifth stanza. The first work of the Holy Spirit is told us in John 16: 8, "And when He is come, He will reprove the world of sin." As is not uncommon in the older hymns, the ending, this time one line only, refers to the Trinity.

The tune *Boylston,* named after a main street in Boston, Massachusetts, was composed by Lowell Mason (1792-1872), see appendix. It is also used for No. 502, "Mourn for the Thousands Slain."

206 HOLY SPIRIT, LIGHT DIVINE

1 Corinthians 3: 16

Dr. Andrew Reed (1787-1862) an English Congregational minister and philanthropist who founded six benevolent institutions, wrote this prayer in 1817 while he was in charge of the New Road Chapel, St. George's-in-the-East, London, where he had attended as a boy. The hymn was repeated at his dying bed and brought forth this remark, "That hymn has helped others in time of need, now it helps me." It is an invitation to the Spirit of God first as a light to dispel the darkness of the human heart, second as a power to control the dominion of sin in the heart, third as joy to cheer the sadness in the heart, and finally as the supreme ruler to take full possession of the heart. These different functions of the Spirit are summarized in 1 Corinthians 3: 16: "Ye are the temple of God, and . . . the Spirit of God dwelleth in you." A similar hymn by Reed is No. 213, "Spirit Divine."

The tune *Mercy* has a cosmopolitan flavour for it was composed in 1854 as a piano piece—"Last Hope"—by Louis Moreau Gottschalk (1829-69), who was born in America with a German name of an English father and a French mother. It is named *Mercy* because it was first associated with Charles Wesley's hymn No. 234, "Depth of Mercy." It was arranged as a hymn tune in 1888 by Edwin Pond Parker (1836-1925), a Congregational minister at the Center church, Hartford, Connecticut, for over fifty years. Parker also wrote No. 478, "Master, No Offering," to his own tune, No. 478, *Love's Offering.*

207. LET THY SPIRIT, BLESSED SAVIOUR

Galatians 5: 22

This hymn by an anonymous author requests the fruits and power of the Spirit in the Christian warfare, expresses confidence in the written Word and in the incarnate Word, and anticipates a victorious and joyful experience even amid disheartening surroundings. In the first stanza some of the fruits of the Spirit are named as in Galatians 5: 22, "But the fruit of the Spirit is love, joy, peace."

The tune *Stockwell* was composed in 1847 by Darius Eliot Jones (1815-81) of New York, and is also used for No. 627, "He That Goeth Forth." Jones was editor of a hymnbook, church music conductor, and later studied for the Congregational ministry, being ordained in 1858.

208. LORD, I HEAR OF SHOWERS OF BLESSING

Genesis 27: 34

Ireland was swept by a great religious revival in 1860, and news of it that summer reached Mrs. Elizabeth Codner, née Harris (1824-1919), wife of an Anglican clergyman in Weston-super-Mare, Somerset. She wished to participate in its blessings and desired them also for some of her young friends. So, basing the chorus on the heart cry of Esau, "Bless me, even me also, O my father" (Genesis 27: 34), she wrote these words for private circulation among the group. They received such a favourable reception that Mrs. Codner had the words printed in 1861 as a leaflet under the title "Divine Blessing Desired." Omitted stanzas are:—

3. Pass me not, O tender Saviour,
Let me love and cling to Thee;
I am longing for Thy favour,
When Thou comest, call for me.

6. Love of God, so pure and changeless;
Blood of Christ, so rich and free;
Grace of God, so strong and boundless,
Magnify it all in me.

7. Pass me not! Thy lost one bringing,
Bind my heart, O Lord, to Thee!
While the streams of life are springing,
Blessing others, oh, bless me!

The words have been edited and altered somewhat by the Rev. Vernon J. Charlesworth (1839-?), headmaster of Charles Haddon Spurgeon's (see No. 40) orphanage. He also wrote No. 585, "The Lord's Our Rock."

The tune *Even Me* was composed in 1862 by William Batchelder Bradbury (1816-68), see appendix.

209. COME, HOLY SPIRIT

Matthew 3: 16

Isaac Watts's (1674-1748), see appendix, full title for this hymn was "Breathing After the Holy Spirit; or Fervency of Devotion Desired." Many changes have been made from the doleful original, three stanzas of which are given for comparison with the present version, which retains little more than the rhyme:—

2. Lord, how we grovel here below,
Fond of these trifling toys:
Our souls can neither fly nor go
To reach eternal joys.

3. In vain we tune our formal songs,
In vain we strive to rise,
Hosannas languish on our tongues
And our devotion dies.

4. Dear Lord! and shall we ever live
At this poor, dying rate,
Our love so faint, so cold to Thee,
And Thine to us so great?

The figure of a dove is taken from Matt. 3: 16: "The Spirit of God descending like a dove, and lighting upon Him."

The tune *St. Agnes,* also used for Nos. 158, "Jesus, the Very Thought of Thee," and 413, "Happy the Home," was composed in

1866 by John Bacchus Dykes (1823-76), see appendix. The name commemorates a young Roman girl who was martyred at the age of thirteen in A.D. 304 under the persecution of Diocletian. She refused to deny her faith in the Lord Jesus and be married to a Roman nobleman who was a pagan.

210. O FOR THAT FLAME OF LIVING FIRE

2 Peter 1: 21

On the day of Pentecost the Holy Ghost filled the disciples and "appeared unto them cloven tongues like as of fire, and it sat upon each of them." Acts 2: 3. The Holy Spirit also filled the Old Testament prophets—though not necessarily with this outward manifestation—for "holy men of God spake as they were moved by the Holy Ghost." 2 Peter 1: 21. William Hiley Bathurst (1796-1877), rector of Barwick-in-Elmet, near Leeds, Yorkshire, combined these two thoughts of fire and the Spirit's presence in 1831, and in this hymn picks out by name some of the worthy "saints of old," Abram, Paul, Isaiah, David, Elijah, Moses, and Job. He also wrote No. 245, "O for a Faith that Will Not Shrink."

The tune *Mendon* was arranged from a German melody in 1824 by Samuel Dyer (1785-1835), an Englishman who emigrated to the United States in 1811 and there became a choirmaster and music teacher. He organized sacred concerts in Philadelphia and in 1814 moved to Baltimore. The name, which is the name of a town in Massachusetts, was given by the compilers of the "Methodist Harmonist," 1821. Note that the second and fourth lines are almost identical.

211. HOLY SPIRIT, FAITHFUL GUIDE

John 16: 13

Marcus Morris Wells (1815-95) of Otsego, New York, was a farmer and maker of farm implements. While working in the field in October, 1858, the idea of this hymn formed in his mind. The following day, a stormy Sunday, confined him to the house, and he then committed both words and music to paper, sending them to Isaac Baker Woodbury (1819-58), see appendix, who published the hymn in the New York "Musical Pioneer." The words develop the promise made by Jesus to His disciples just before His betrayal: "Howbeit when He, the Spirit of truth, is come, He will guide you into all truth" (John 16: 13), and this sentiment gives the tune its name.

The tune *Guide* also by Wells, is very repetitive, lines 1 and 2 being identical to lines 3 and 4 and lines 7 and 8. In fact the complete tune consists of two chords only, tonic and dominant, with occasional inversions.

212. HOVER O'ER ME, HOLY SPIRIT

John 14: 16-18

Before our Lord left this earth, He promised His disciples that they would not be left orphans, but that "the Father . . . shall give you another Comforter, that He may abide with you for ever; even the Spirit of truth. . . . He dwelleth with you, and shall be in you. I will not leave you comfortless: I will come to you." John 14: 16-18. Here is the mystery of the Trinity where Jesus identifies Himself with the Spirit, as in the words of the chorus of this hymn, and as shown in Romans 8: 9, 10, "That the Spirit of God dwell in you. Now if any man have not the Spirit of Christ, he is none of His. And if Christ be in you. . . ." Elwood Haines Stokes, D.D., derives the picture of hovering with which his hymn commences from the dovelike appearance of the Spirit at our Lord's baptism, "The Spirit of God descending like a dove." Matthew 3: 16.

The tune *Sweney* commemorates the composer John Robson Sweney (1837-99), see appendix.

213. SPIRIT DIVINE

Acts 2: 2, 3

In 1829 a group of Congregational ministers, resident in and near London, were gathered together for study and council. One of their recommendations was to set aside Good Friday as a day of humiliation and prayer, in order that by the grace and blessing of God a revival of religion might be promoted in the churches of Great Britain. One of their number, Dr. Andrew Reed (1787-1862), a great philantropist who founded six benevolent institutions, wrote these words as a prayer for himself and his fellow ministers. After the first stanza emphasizing the power of the Spirit, he uses four metaphors, (1) light to reveal, (2) fire to cleanse, (3) dew to refresh, (4) wind to convert. Two of these are found in the story of Pentecost: "There came a sound from heaven as of a rushing mighty wind, . . . and there appeared unto them cloven tongues like as of fire." Acts 2: 2, 3. There are two omitted stanzas:—

5. Come as the dove, and spread Thy wings,
The wings of peaceful love;
And let Thy church on earth become
Blest as the church above.

7. Spirit divine, attend our prayers,
Make a lost world Thy home;
Descend with all Thy gracious powers,
O come, Great Spirit, come.

Reed also wrote No. 206, "Holy Spirit, Light Divine." The hymn was adapted by Samuel Longfellow (1819-92), a Unitarian pastor of Brooklyn, New York, and younger brother of the poet Henry Wadsworth Longfellow. He also wrote No. 56, "Again as Evening's Shadow Falls."

The tune *Lambeth* was composed in 1871 by Wilhelm A. F. Schulthes (1816-79), a German who came to England and became a choir director and music teacher at a convent in Roehampton, London. The same tune with slightly different harmony is used for No. 334, "Calm Me, My God."

214. OUR BLEST REDEEMER

John 20: 22

Miss Harriet (Henrietta) Auber (1773-1862) was the great-granddaughter of a Huguenot refugee and lived with another spinster lady, Miss Mary Jane Mackenzie, in the village of Hoddesdon, Hertfordshire. On a Whitsunday she was sitting alone in her bedroom thinking over the sermon she had heard, and the words of this hymn came to her mind. Unable to find pencil or paper quickly, she took a diamond ring from her finger and scratched the stanzas on the window-pane. After her death a dealer tried unsuccessfully to purchase the pane, and not long afterward it was cut out and stolen. Dr. James Moffatt says this story is "no more than a pleasant myth," but gives no grounds for his dismissal of the story, such as, say, the size of the panes in those days. The hymn was first published in 1829 in her "Spirit of the Psalms." The scripture on which it is based is, "He breathed on them, and saith . . . Receive ye the Holy Ghost." John 20: 22. There are two other stanzas, now omitted, and a typical doxology has been added to conclude.

2. He came in semblance of a dove,
With sheltering wings outspread,
The holy balm of peace and love
On earth to shed.

3. He came in tongues of living flame
To teach, convince, subdue;
All powerful as the wind He came,
As viewless, too.

8. O praise the Father; praise the Son;
Blest Spirit, praise to Thee:
All praise to God, the Three in One,
The One in Three.

Miss Auber also wrote No. 79, "Ere Mountains Reared Their Forms Sublime."

The tune *St. Cuthbert* was composed especially for these words in 1861 by John Bacchus Dykes (1823-76), see appendix. The third line of the soprano part copies almost exactly the first line of the tenor part. There is a shrine in Durham Cathedral dedicated to the Scottish monk Cuthbert who converted the north-eastern part of England to Christianity. He died at Lindisfarne in A.D. 687.

215. GRACIOUS SPIRIT, LOVE DIVINE

John 15: 26

John Stocker wrote six stanzas of this hymn in July, 1777, and entitled it, "To God the Holy Ghost," writing "Dove divine" in the original first line instead of our "Love divine." The two omitted stanzas are:—

5. Guard me round on ev'ry side;
Save me from self-righteous pride.
Me with Jesu's mind inspire;
Melt me with celestial fire.

6. Thou my dross and tin consume,
Let Thy inward kingdom come:
All my prayer and praise suggest;
Dwell and reign within my breast.

Stocker expresses a fundamental truth in saying that the Spirit is given to effect salvation through Jesus, as He Himself said, "When the Comforter is come . . . He shall testify of Me." John 15: 26. The hymn appears in 1861 where the publisher regrets that he knows only the name of the author and that he came from Honiton, Devonshire.

The tune *Wirak* was composed in 1939 by Harold Amadeus Miller (1891-1966), see appendix, and is named to commemorate Miss Theodora Wirak who was one-time treasurer and registrar at Southern Missionary College, Tennessee, while Miller was professor of music there.

216. HOLY, SPIRIT, LAMP OF LIGHT

Romans 8: 15, 16

The author George Rawson (1807-89), a lawyer of Leeds, was a member of the Congregational Church who wrote many hymns using the pen-name of "A Leeds Layman." Dr. Julian the noted hymnologist says that "his hymns are noted for refinement of thought, and delicacy and propriety of language." Though of a retiring nature, Rawson assisted the Congregationalists in the preparation of their "Leeds Hymnbook," 1853, and the Baptists in their "Psalms and Hymns," 1858. He also wrote No. 475, "By

Christ Redeemed," a communion hymn on a similar pattern, namely three rhyming lines followed by a fourth line common to all the stanzas. There were nine stanzas in the "Leeds Hymn-book," 1853, not including our first stanza, those omitted being—

1. Come to our poor nature's night
With Thy blessed inward light,
Holy Ghost the Infinite,
Comforter divine.

3. Orphan are our souls and poor
Give us from Thy heavenly store
Faith, love, joy for evermore
Comforter divine.

5. Gentle, awful, holy Guest,
Make Thy temple in each breast;
There Thy presence be confessed,
Comforter divine.

6. With us, for us, intercede,
And, with voiceless groanings, plead
Our unutterable need,
Comforter divine.

A suitable Scripture basis is: "Ye have received the Spirit of adoption, whereby we cry, Abba, Father. The Spirit itself beareth witness with our spirit, that we are the children of God." Romans 8: 15, 16.

The tune *Salisbury* was composed by Edwin Barnes (1864-1930), see appendix, and commemorates the cathedral city about twenty miles north-west of his birthplace Southampton, England.

217. O WORD OF GOD INCARNATE

Proverbs 6: 23

William Walsham How (1823-97), see appendix, wrote these words in 1867 under the title "Holy Scripture," and based them on the first part of Proverbs 6: 23, "For the commandment is a lamp; and the law is light." Throughout the hymn the emphasis is on light as opposed to darkness as seen by the following words:
stanza 1. light, dark, radiance, lantern, shines,
2. light, shine,
3. shineth, darkling,
4. lamp, light, clouds, darkness.

The tune *Munich* was published in 1693 in a book of chorales containing melodies found in certain psalm settings published in 1675. They were for the most part composed by Hieronymus

Kradenthaller, organist at Regensburg. This tune adapted from the Konigsberg Chorale, was used by the eminent composer Jakob Ludwig Felix Mendelssohn-Bartholdy (1809-47) in 1847, and later revised in 1863. Mendelssohn also composed Nos. 111, *Mendelssohn;* 257, *Trust;* 674, *Abiding;* 687, unnamed; and 692, *Birmingham,* a modification of this tune *Munich.*

218. BREAK THOU THE BREAD OF LIFE

Matthew 14: 19

Bishop John H. Vincent was one of the co-founders of the Chautauqua Literary and Scientific Circle where students gathered in conference in a summer retreat at an old Methodist camp-meeting site at Lake Chautauqua in the Finger Lakes region of New York state. Their purpose was for self-improvement, not only academically but spiritually, and to assist in this function in 1877 Vincent asked Miss Mary Artemisia Lathbury (1841-1913) to write a study hymn for the group. She accordingly wrote two stanzas which derived a spiritual lesson from the feeding of the multitude with physical bread: "And looking up to heaven, He blessed, and brake, and gave the loaves to His disciples, and the disciples to the multitude." Matthew 14: 19. The two original stanzas are similar in structure, (1) Break the bread as Thou didst break the loaves, and (2) Bless the truth as Thou didst bless the bread, and make a complete hymn and prayer as such. There have been many additions, such as:—

O send Thy Spirit, Lord, Now unto me,
That He may touch my eyes, And make me see:
Show me the truth concealed Within Thy word
And in Thy Book revealed I see the Lord.

Thou art the bread of life O Lord to me,
Thy holy Word the truth That saveth me;
Give me to eat and live With Thee above;
Teach me to love Thy truth, For Thou art love.

This comes from Alexander Groves (1842-1909). Miss Lathbury also wrote No. 51, "Day Is Dying in the West."

The tune *Bread of Life* was composed by William Fisk Sherwin (1826-88), see appendix, in the same summer of 1877.

219. HOLY BIBLE, BOOK DIVINE

Psalm 119: 9

This intensively personal hymn appeared in his "Youth's Monitor in Verse," 1803, by John Burton senior (1773-1822), a Baptist Sunday school teacher of Nottingham who wrote several other hymns for children. The words in stanza 4, line 2 were originally

"And the rebel sinner's doom." Burton's title for the hymn was "Incentives to Early Piety" and it was published in a Sunday school hymn book in 1805 signed J. B. He exalts the Holy Scriptures as showing his origin and his destiny, as guiding, chiding, and comforting in this life, and as promising eternal joys in the life to come. Notice the frequent use of the possessive pronoun "mine," eleven times in four stanzas. To follow the instruction of the Bible is the Christian's safeguard, "Wherewithal shall a young man cleanse his way? by taking heed thereto according to Thy Word." Psalm 119: 9.

The tune *Horton* was composed in 1826 by Franz Xavier Schnyder von Wartensee (1786-1868), a pianist of Lucerne, Switzerland, who taught piano from 1817 at a ladies' institute at Frankfurt-on-Main, Germany. He founded a choral society and composed operettas, songs, choral works, and pianoforte pieces.

220. I LOVE THE SACRED BOOK OF GOD

Psalm 119: 105

Thomas Kelly (1769-1854) was an Irishman who was ordained in 1792, but was dissatisfied with the doctrines of the Episcopal Church. He had strong evangelical views and was a firm believer in the second advent of Christ. This hymn was written in 1804 at a time when the British and Foreign Bible Society was being formed, and the last stanza summarizes the intentions of this worthy group: "Thy Word is a lamp unto my feet, and a light unto my path." Psalm 119: 105. There were originally seven stanzas, the two omitted being:—

Let all the heathen writers join
To form one perfect work:
Great God, if once compared with Thine,
How mean their writings look!

Not the most perfect rules they gave
Could show one sin forgiven,
Nor lead a step beyond the grave;
But Thine conducts to heaven.

Kelly was a firm believer in the Scriptures, as these words indicate, and from his own private means he built four Independent churches in Ireland for the promulgation of evangelical views. He also wrote Nos. 192, "Hark! that Shout"; 296, "We Sing the Praise"; and 308, "We've No Abiding City Here," as well as more than 750 others.

The tune *Hamburg* was arranged in 1824 by Lowell Mason (1792-1872), see appendix, in the spirit of a Gregorian chant, but the name has no associated significance.

221. RETURN, O WANDERER

Jeremiah 31: 20

William Bengo Collyer (1782-1854) was an eloquent preacher who wrote over fifty hymns, most of them short didactic poems stressing a particular Biblical truth. This one, originally of six stanzas, was written in 1806 and was inspired by Jeremiah 31: 20, "My dear son . . . I do earnestly remember him still: therefore My bowels are troubled for him; I will surely have mercy upon him." One of the omitted stanzas, in long metre, is:—

2. Return, O wanderer, return,
And seek a Father's melting heart;
His pitying eyes thy grief discern,
His hand shall reach thy inward smart.

Collyer also wrote most of No. 195, "Great God, What Do I See!"

The tune *Belerma* slightly resembles an earlier tune, or the first half of it, by Francois Hippolyte Barthelemon (1741-1808), a violinist and a composer of secular music. It was composed as a song for the poem about the death of Durandarte and his love Belerma, found in "The Monk" by Matthew Gregory Lewis (1775-1818), an English dramatist. This melody was adapted and harmonized into its present form by Robert Simpson (1790-1832), a Glasgow weaver and self-taught musician. It is an example of a melody in the pentatonic scale. (See No. 181.) Barthelemon also arranged the tune of No. 268, *Autumn,* another melody which is practically in the pentatonic scale.

222. JUST AS I AM

John 6: 37

In 1822 the Swiss preacher, Dr. Henri Abraham Cesar Malan (1787-1864), visited Brighton, England, and called on Miss Charlotte Elliott (1789-1871). In the course of the conversation she told him that she did not know how to find Christ, to which his reply was "Come to Him just as you are." To this statement she owed her conversion, and although these words were not the immediate cause of her writing the hymn which does repeat in every stanza the words, "Just as I am, O Lamb of God, I come," they seem to have lingered long in her mind. Miss Elliott was a lifelong invalid, and years later, in 1834, she was unable to attend a church bazaar conducted by her brother who was a clergyman. Sitting at home she pondered on religious themes and wrote this hymn, originally of these six stanzas, for her own private comfort and hope. Its title was "Him that Cometh to Me I Will in No Wise Cast Out"—John 6: 37. Her sister-in-law presuaded her to have the hymn printed, and it appeared in "The Invalid's Hymn Book," 1838. There is now an additional stanza:—

7. Just as I am, of that free love,
The breadth, length, depth, and height to prove,
Here for a season, then above,
O Lamb of God, I come.

Miss Elliott also wrote Nos. 61, "The Sabbath Day Has Reached Its Close"; 325, "My God, Is Any Hour So Sweet?" and 357, "Christian, Seek Not Yet Repose." Each of these four poems has the same structure, namely, the last line is different in either rhyme or metre from the preceding three lines.

The tune *Woodworth* was composed in 1849 by William Batchelder Bradbury (1816-68), see appendix, but for another hymn originally. Its interest lies only in the two upper parts which for the most part are separated by an interval of a third. The harmony is completed by the addition of two very simple lower parts.

223. COME, YE DISCONSOLATE

John 14: 18

Thomas Moore (1779-1852), the Irish poet, author of "The Last Rose of Summer" and "Believe Me If All Those Endearing Young Charms," wrote many songs to popular airs of various nations. These words were written in 1816 to a German air which appealed to him, and they give comfort to the sorrowing ones of earth, no matter what their affliction might be. "I will not leave you comfortless: I will come to you." John 14: 18. The original words of the second line of the first stanza were, "Come, at the shrine of God, fervently kneel," but they were altered in 1832 to the present version by Thomas Hastings (1784-1872), see appendix. He also wrote the third stanza completely different from the original, which was:—

3. Come, ask the infidel what boon he brings us,
What charm for aching hearts he can reveal,
Sweet is that heavenly promise hope sings us—
"Earth hath no sorrow that God cannot heal."

The tune *Consolation,* an apt title for this hymn, is a German melody harmonized in 1792 by Samuel Webbe (1740-1816), a Roman Catholic organist at the Sardinian and Portuguese embassy chapels in London. He also composed Nos. 42 and 312, *Melcombe,* and probably 87, *Dulce Carmen,* and 105 and 255, *Portuguese Hymn.*

224. I HEAR THY WELCOME VOICE

Revelation 1: 5

Both words and music of this hymn were written in 1872 by Lewis Hartsough (1828-1919), an American Methodist Episcopal minister, and were published in the same year in "Guide to Holiness" under the title of "The Divine Invitation." They reiterate the saving work of our Lord, who "loved us, and washed us from our sins in His own blood." Revelation 1: 5. Two other stanzas are extant:—

4. 'Tis Jesus who confirms
The blessed work within,
By adding grace to welcomed grace,
Where reigned the power of sin.

5. And He the witness gives
To loyal hearts and free,
That every promise is fulfilled,
If faith but brings the plea.

The name of the tune *Welcome Voice* is taken from the first line of the hymn, but it is also known as *Calvary* because of its description of the event associated with this sacred place.

225. I HEARD THE VOICE OF JESUS SAY

John 1: 16

Horatius Bonar (1808-1889), see appendix, wrote this hymn at Kelso especially for the children of his Sunday school in 1846, and it appeared in 1857 in "Hymns of Faith and Hope" under the title, "Of His Fullness Have All We Received, and Grace for Grace," the second part of each stanza showing the response to the different invitations of Jesus and the profound and satisfying result. The three different metaphors describing the Saviour are a resting-place, a well of water, and a light, providing in turn for the weary, the thirsty, and the benighted pilgrim.

The tune *Vox Dilecti* (= The Voice of the Beloved) was specially composed in 1868 for these words, by John Bacchus Dykes (1823-1876), see appendix. It is noteworthy that the first half is written in a minor key corresponding to the weariness, misery, and gloom expressed in the words. Then the second half modulates to a major key, and its brightness accords well with the words which speak of gladness, life, and light. The minor-major modulation is also used by Dykes in Nos. 129, *St. John,* and 367, *St. Andrew of Crete.*

226. I HEARD THE VOICE OF JESUS SAY

John 1: 16

For the words see the previous hymn No. 225, but note that the very last clause has been changed from Bonar's original, now to read "Till all my journey's done."

The tune *Jerusalem,* or *Invitation,* was composed in 1834 by Louis Spohr (1784-1859) of Brunswick, Germany, and comes from his oratorio "Calvary," which was first performed at Cassel in 1835, and then in London in 1837, and at the Norwich festival, England, in 1839. Spohr was a musical prodigy as a child, and later achieved a high reputation as a composer of operas, oratorios, violin concertos, and string quartets. He became court musical director at Cassel, Germany, in 1822, continuing as such until pensioned off in 1857. The tune is also sometimes named *Gerald,* after Geraldine Sherrill, the secretary to the editor of the American Methodist hymnbook committee 1935. It is an easy tune to sing as lines 1, 3 and 7 are identical, as are also lines 4 and 8, both the latter being very similiar to line 2.

227. BEHOLD THE SAVIOUR AT THE DOOR

Revelation 3: 14-22

The first stanza of this hymn by an anonymous writer is almost identical with the first stanza of one written in 1765 by Joseph Grigg (c. 1720-1768), see No. 152, beginning "Behold a Stranger at the door," but the succeeding stanzas are completely different. They paraphrase fairly closely the message to the seventh church of Laodicea, with the order slightly reversed, and also use an illustration from the Song of Solomon 5: 2, 5, "My heart waketh: it is the voice of my beloved that knocketh, saying, Open to me . . . my head is filled with dew, and my locks with the drops of the night." "I rose up to open to my beloved." Revelation 3: 14-20: "These things saith . . . the Faithful and True Witness. . . . Because thou art lukewarm . . . I will spue thee out of My mouth. . . . I counsel thee to buy of Me gold tried in the fire . . . and white raiment . . . and anoint thine eyes with eyesalve, that thou mayest see. . . . Be zealous therefore, and repent. Behold, I stand at the door, and knock: if any man hear My voice, and open the door, I will come in to him, and will sup with him, and he with Me." One other stanza is quoted from Revelation 22: 11, "He which is filthy, let him be filthy still . . . and he that is holy, let him be holy still." The hymn appears in the 1861 edition of "Hymns for Those Who Keep the Commandments of God and the Faith of Jesus."

The tune *Hartel* was composed by Lowell Mason (1792-1872), see appendix, and the melody is confined, with one exception, to a range of five notes, the last two lines indeed to four notes only.

228. ALMOST PERSUADED

Acts 26: 28

This hymn owes its origin not immediately to King Agrippa's reply, "Almost thou persuadest me to be a Christian" (Acts 26: 28), to Paul's earnest question, but to a sermon preached on this text by the Rev. W. Brundage concluding with the words, "He who is almost persuaded is almost saved, but to be almost saved is to be entirely lost." In a back seat in the congregation was Philipp P. Bliss (1838-76), see appendix, who had sat there because he was waiting for a train. Being impressed with the preacher's theme he immediately began the composition of this hymn, both words and music, while the strong impact of the concluding words was still in his mind.

229. LORD, WE COME WITH HEARTS AFLAME

Isaiah 6: 8

Berton Braley (1882-) echoes the desire of eager youth to devote their strength and energy to the service of God, much as did the youthful Isaiah who responded, "Here am I; send me." Isaiah 6: 8. The first line, which is identical with the last line, recalls the statement of the two travellers to Emmaus who said, "Did not our heart burn within us?" Luke 24: 32. Braley was born at Madison, Wisconsin, January 29, 1882, and became a newspaper reporter in Montana, later transferring to New York. He was a free-lance writer for newspapers and magazines, over 100 short stories and about 10,000 verse contributions coming from his pen.

The tune *St. Athanasius* was composed in 1872 by Edward John Hopkins (1818-1910), organist for over fifty years at the Temple church, London, composer of church music and anthems, and editor of church hymnbooks of several denominations. It is so named because it was composed specially for Christopher Wordsworth's hymn, "Holy, Holy, Holy, Lord," each stanza of which ends with the words, "To the blessed Trinity." The doctrine of the Trinity is emphasized in the Athanasian creed, which was laid down by Athanasius, archbishop of Alexandria during the fourth century. Hopkins also wrote Nos. 34, *Ellers,* and 61, *Pascal.*

230. I GAVE MY LIFE FOR THEE

Galatians 2: 20

Frances Ridley Havergal (1836-1879), see appendix, was staying in Dusseldorf, Germany, and, coming in weary on January 10, 1858, sat down before a picture of the Saviour. Beneath was the motto, "I did this for thee; what hast thou done for Me?" The lines of this hymn flashed into her mind, and she hastily scribbled them in pencil on a scrap of paper. Reading the words later she thought it a poor effort and threw the paper into the fire. However it fell out and she decided to keep it. Later she read the words to an old lady who was so pleased with the sentiments expressing Christ's desire for complete devotion of His servants, that Miss Havergal showed the hymn to her father who composed a tune *Baca* for it. There were six stanzas in the original, those omitted being:—

2. I spent long years for thee
In weariness and woe,
That an eternity
Of joy thou mightest know.
I spent long years for thee;
Hast thou spent one for Me?

5. And I have brought to thee,
Down from My home above,
Salvation full and free,
My pardon and My love,
Great gifts I brought to thee;
Give thou thyself to Me!

6. Oh, let thy life be given,
Thy years for Me be spent,
World-fetters all be riven,
And joy with suffering blent;
I gave Myself for thee:
Give thou thyself to Me!

The first parts of each stanza recall the text, "The Son of God, who loved me, and gave Himself for me." Galatians 2: 20.

The tune *White* commemorates the composer James Edson White (1849-1928), second son of Ellen Gould White. He produced the "Song Anchor," a Sabbath school hymnal, in 1878, and also composed No. 235, *Marietta.* White was a Seventh-day Adventist minister who worked particularly in the southern states and on the Mississippi River. He also assisted in the selection of hymns for the official hymnbook of the Seventh-day Adventist Church, "Hymns and Tunes," 1886.

231. O JESUS, THOU ART STANDING

Revelation 3: 20

This hymn written in 1867 by William Walsham How (1823-1897), see appendix, was not directly inspired by Holman Hunt's painting, "The Light of the World," but both hymn and picture were based on the text, "Behold, I stand at the door, and knock:

if any man hear My voice, and open the door, I will come in to him." Revelation 3: 20. After reading a moving poem by Jean Ingelow (1820-1879) entitled "Brothers and a Sermon," How scribbled on an odd scrap of paper his first draft of this hymn, entitled "Jesus at the Door," and subsequently revised it slightly. In the poem these words occur:—

"Behold!" said He, "I stand at the door and knock!
Open the door with shame, if ye have sinned."

The tune *St. Hilda* was adapted by the famous German organist Justin Heinrich Knecht (1752-1817) of Wurttemberg, from a collection published in Stuttgart in 1799. It was further altered in 1871 and named *St. Hilda* by Edward Husband (1843-1908), an amateur organist and composer, and vicar of Folkestone, Kent. Knecht, who was a professor of literature before making full use of his musical talent, also composed No. 131, *Vienna*. Hilda was a person of royal blood who established a monastery near Whitby, Yorkshire, in the seventh century, and there revived the standards of the early Christian church. The same tune is used for No. 278, "I Lay My Sins on Jesus."

232. FLEE AS A BIRD

Psalm 11: 1, 2

Mary Stanley Bunce Shindler Dana (1810-1883) was the daughter of a Congregational minister at Beaufort, South Carolina, and married Charles E. Dana in 1835, but he died in 1839. In 1848 she married Professor Robert D. Shindler of Shelby College, Kentucky, and later they moved to Texas. She joined several different denominations in her search for truth and was successively a Presbyterian, Unitarian, Protestant Episcopal, and Millerite. In this hymn she has written a very free paraphrase of Psalm 11: 1, 2, "Flee as a bird to your mountain? For, lo, the wicked bend their bow, they make ready their arrow upon the string, that they may privily [margin, in darkness] shoot at the upright in heart." Mrs. Dana also wrote No. 666, "I'm a Pilgrim."

The tune *Spain* is an old Spanish air, its plaintiveness being due to the fact that it is written in a minor key, with only a brief modulation to a major key.

233. JESUS, TO THEE I NOW CAN FLY

Psalm 51: 9, 10

Charles Wesley (1707-1788), see appendix, wrote ten stanzas each of four lines, in 1742, of this hymn entitled "After a Relapse Into Sin." (See also No. 234.) The hymn begins "Long have I laboured in the fire," and the present four stanzas come from the latter half of the hymn, the omitted stanza from this half being:—

2. Soon as I find myself forsook,
The grace again is given:
A sigh can reach Thy heart, a look
Can bring Thee down from heaven.

The doctrine of repentance and forgiveness expressed in the hymn recalls the experience of David when he wrote, "Hide Thy face from my sins, and blot out all my iniquities. Create in me a clean heart, O God; and renew a right spirit within me." Psalm 51: 9, 10.

The tune *Downs* was composed in 1832 by Lowell Mason (1792-1872), see appendix.

234. DEPTH OF MERCY

1 Timothy 1: 15

Charles Wesley (1707-1788), see appendix, wrote two hymns entitled "After a Relapse Into Sin," this one in 1740 and the other (No. 233) in 1742. It is a deep plea for the mercy of God where Wesley identifies himself with the Apostle Paul's description of himself, "Christ Jesus came into the world to save sinners; of whom I am chief." 1 Timothy 1: 15. There were originally thirteen stanzas each of four lines, later revised to six stanzas each of eight lines. Some of the omitted stanzas are:—

4. Whence to me this waste of love?
Ask my Advocate above;
See the cause in Jesus' face,
Now before the throne of grace.

7. Kindled His relentings are;
Me He now delights to spare;
Cries, "How shall I give thee up?"
Lets the lifted thunder drop.

10. Jesus, answer from above:
Is not all Thy nature love?
Wilt Thou not the wrong forget?
Suffer me to kiss Thy feet?

11. If I rightly read Thy heart,
If Thou all compassion art,
Bow Thine ear, in mercy bow!
Pardon and accept me now.

12. Pity from Thine eye let fall;
By a look, my soul recall:
Now the stone to flesh convert!
Cast a look and break my heart.

The tune *Aletta* was composed in 1857 by William Batchelder Bradbury (1816-1868), see appendix, and appears in "The Jubilee" set to a six-line hymn with the last two lines repeating. Aletta was the name of the mother of St. Bernard of Clairvaux (1091-1153), see Nos. 130, 154, 158. She was a very pious woman. The first, second, and fourth lines of the tune are very similar musically.

235. WE STAND IN DEEP REPENTANCE

Hebrews 4: 16

These words were written in 1834 for the season of Lent by Ray Palmer (1808-1887), then a young Congregational minister. They picture the scene described in Hebrews 4: 16, "Let us therefore come boldly unto the throne of grace, that we may obtain mercy, and find grace to help in time of need." They also remind us that the message of Jesus was, "Repent ye, and believe the gospel." Mark 1: 15. Palmer also wrote Nos. 154, "Jesus Thou Joy of Loving Hearts"; 166, "Jesus, These Eyes Have Never Seen"; 246, "My Faith Looks Up to Thee," and 285, "I Give My Heart to Thee."

The tune *Marietta* was composed in 1878 by James Edson White (1849-1928), second son of Ellen Gould White, and composer also of No. 230, *White*. He was a Seventh-day Adventist minister who worked particularly in the southern states and on the Mississippi. He had musical ability and assisted in selecting hymns for "Hymns and Tunes," 1886, and in compiling the first Sabbath school song book for Seventh-day Adventists, "The Song Anchor," in 1878.

236. LORD, AT THY FEET

Ephesians 2: 7

Simon Browne (1680-1732) was a minister of the Independent church in Old Jewry, London, and a contemporary of Isaac Watts. In a struggle with a highwayman he unintentionally killed his assailant, and this preyed on his mind constantly. Shortly afterwards his wife and son both died, and he thought that God was visiting judgment upon him and would remove his reasoning powers. Grace, mercy, and pardon, is the theme of his prayer in this hymn, and it could well be taken from Ephesians 2: 7, "The exceeding riches of His grace in His kindness toward us through Christ Jesus." The original first line written in 1720 was "Lord, at Thy feet a sinner lies," changed in 1787 to "we sinners lie." Two of the omitted stanzas are:—

2. On me the vast extent display
Of Thy forgiving love;
Take all mine heinous guilt away:
This heavy load remove.

6. Thus melt me down, thus make me bend,
And Thy dominion own;
Nor let a rival more pretend
To repossess Thy throne.

Browne also wrote Nos. 204, "Come, Gracious Spirit," and 464, "Hail, Happy Day."

The tune *Branson* was composed in 1939 by Harold Amadeus Miller (1891-1966), see appendix, and is so named to honour William Henry Branson (1887-1961) and his wife, who both expressed great interest in Miller's compositions. Branson was president of the General Conference of Seventh-day Adventists from 1950 to 1954, after having been president of the China Division and also of the Southern African (now Trans-Africa) Division.

237. JESUS, FULL OF ALL COMPASSION

Mark 10: 47

While a Baptist minister at Abingdon, near Reading, Berkshire, Daniel Turner (1710-98) wrote a hymn of ten stanzas each of four lines, in 1769. They were headed "The Supplication" and signed "D.T." and were based on Mark 10: 47, "Jesus, Thou Son of David, have mercy on me." The omitted stanzas are:—

6. Without Thee, the world possessing,
I should be a wretch undone;
Search through heaven, the land of blessing,
Seeking good, and finding none.

7. Hear then, blessed Saviour, hear me,
My soul cleaveth to the dust;
Send the Comforter to cheer me,
Lo, in Thee I put my trust.

8. On the word, Thy blood hath sealed,
Hangs my everlasting all;
Let Thine arm be now revealed,
Stay, O stay me, lest I fall!

9. In the world of endless ruin,
Let it never, Lord, be said,
"Here's a soul that perish'd, suing
For the boasted Saviour's aid!"

Turner also wrote No. 170, "Beyond the Starry Skies."

The tune *Deerhurst,* also used for No. 437, "Lord, Her Watch Thy Church Is Keeping," was composed in 1862 by James Langran (1835-1909), a London organist and music master. Deerhurst is a small town near Tewkesbury, Gloucestershire, and this name was given to the tune in a hymnbook, the "Mitre Hymnal" compiled by an editor whose father had once been a curate there. Langran also composed No. 289, *Langran.* The pattern of the tune *Deerhurst* is consistent in that line 3 copies line 1, and line 7 copies line 5.

238. CHIEF OF SINNERS

Colossians 3: 11

These words were written by an Irish bookseller, William M'Comb (1738-18?) under the title "Christ All and In All," which words he uses in the second line of the last stanza. They are a quotation from Colossians 3: 11, "But Christ is all and in all." He has also used the figure of the vine and the branches as illustrated in John 15: 5, and also the Apostle Paul's statements in Ephesians 3: 19 on the dimensions of the love of Christ, and his own estimate of himself in 1 Timothy 1: 15 as chief of sinners.

The tune *Spanish Hymn* is an arrangement published in 1826 by Benjamin Carr (1769-1831), an Englishman who emigrated to the United States and there became a music dealer and music printer. He was an organist in Philadelphia and helped to introduce both operatic and classical music to America. The last two lines of the tune are an exact repetition of the first two lines.

239. LOW AT THY PIERCED FEET

1 Peter 2: 24

The crucifixion of Jesus on the cross of Calvary was not merely the death of a religious martyr, but it was the freewill offering of the life of the Son of God, having world-wide significance for people of all time. It was a sin offering, bringing forgiveness to all those who repent of their sins. James Stephens (1847-?), an Anglican clergyman, has emphasized this thought throughout this hymn showing that Jesus "His own self bare our sins in His own body on the tree, that we, being dead to sins, should live unto righteousness: by whose stripes ye were healed." 1 Peter 2: 24.

240. SHOW PITY, LORD

Psalm 51: 1-4

The closeness of this paraphrase by Isaac Watts (1674-1748), see appendix, of the first part of the 51st Psalm will be seen by comparing the parallel passages set out below. It is a penitential confession by David after his adultery with Bathsheba, and his consequent condemnation by Nathan the prophet. Its title is "A Penitent Pleading for Pardon," and there are six stanzas in the original.

Stanza 1:	Show pity, Lord	"Have mercy upon me, O God"
	Thy mercies large and free	"the multitude of Thy tender mercies." Verse 1.
2:	Wash my soul from every sin	"wash me throughly from mine iniquity"
	My guilty conscience clean	"Cleanse me from my sin." Verse 2.
3:	My lips my sins confess	"I acknowledge my transgressions." Verse 3.
	Against Thy law, against Thy grace	"Against Thee, Thee only"
	Thou art clear	"be clear"
	Thy judgment	"when Thou judgest." Verse 4.

The omitted lines of this first part of the paraphrase are:—

2. . . .
Great God, Thy nature hath no bound,
So let Thy pard'ning love be found.

3. . . .
Here on my heart the burden lies,
And past offences pain my eyes.

5. Should sudden vengeance seize my breath,
I must pronounce Thee just in death;
And if my soul were sent to hell,
Thy righteous law approves it well.

The tune *Woods* was composed in 1939 by Harold Amadeus Miller (1891-1966), see appendix, and is named after Dr. Robert W. Woods, who was professor of physics and mathematics at Southern Missionary College, Tennessee, and on the same faculty with Miller at the time. An unusual feature of the tune is the ascending octave in the third line of the melody, a vivid contrast to the first line, which uses the same note five times in succession.

241. FROM EVERY STORMY WIND

Exodus 25: 22

Hugh Stowell (1799-1865), rector of Christ Church, Salford, Lancashire, and canon of Chester, had this hymn printed in 1828 in "The Winter's Wreath" under the title "Peace at the Mercy Seat." He was a powerful orator and a lover of children and Sunday schools. In these stanzas, originally six in number, he describes the function of the mercy seat as the meeting-place of God with His children in all their earthly afflictions: "And there I will meet with thee, and I will commune with thee from above the mercy seat, from between the two cherubims." Exodus 25: 22. The omitted stanza reads:—

6. Oh, let my hand forget her skill,
My tongue be silent, cold, and still,
This throbbing heart forget to beat,
If I forget the mercy seat.

The tune *Retreat,* also used for No. 488, "I Know That My Redeemer Lives," was composed in 1840 by Thomas Hastings (1784-1872), see appendix, and published in 1842 in his "Sacred Songs." It is so named because it was specially written for this hymn describing the retreat that can be found from life's cares at the mercy seat.

242. 'TIS BY THE FAITH OF JOYS

2 Corinthians 5: 7

Isaac Watts (1674-1748), see appendix, wrote this hymn in 1709 and entitled it "Faith Our Guide." It consisted of four stanzas, the omitted one being:—

4. So Abram by divine command,
Left his own house to walk with God.
His faith beheld the promised land,
And fired his zeal along the road.

The whole hymn is an apt commentary on 2 Corinthians 5: 7, "(For we walk by faith, not by sight:)."

The tune *Louvan* was published in his "The Sacred Minstrel" in 1846 by Virgil Corydon Taylor (1817-91), an organist, conductor, and singing teacher of Barkhamstead, Connecticut, who later was organist in Brooklyn, in Niagara Falls, and in Des Moines, Iowa.

243. COME, O THOU TRAVELLER

Genesis 32: 24-32

These words were written by Charles Wesley (1707-88), see appendix, in 1742 in two parts, each having seven stanzas each of six lines. They describe the experience of Jacob at the brook Jabbok related in Genesis 32: 24-32, a favourite topic for Wesley's sermons. Though Wesley envied Isaac Watts the authorship of his hymn, "When I Survey the Wondrous Cross" (No. 118), the latter acknowledged that he would rather have been the author of this one of Wesley's than of all the hundreds he had written. The omitted stanzas are:—

Part I. 4. Wilt Thou not yet to me reveal
Thy new, unutterable name?
Tell me, I still beseech Thee, tell;
To know it now resolved I am;
Wrestling, I will not let Thee go,
Till I Thy name, Thy nature know.

5. 'Tis all in vain to hold Thy tongue,
Or touch the hollow of my thigh;
Though every sinew be unstrung,
Out of my arms Thou shalt not fly;
Wrestling, I will not let Thee go,
Till I Thy name, Thy nature know.

6. What though my shrinking flesh complain,
And murmur to contend so long?
I rise superior to my pain,
When I am weak, then am I strong;
And when my all of strength shall fail,
I shall with the God-Man prevail.

7. My strength is gone, my nature dies,
I sink beneath Thy weighty hand,
Faint to revive, and fall to rise;
I fall, and yet by faith I stand,
I stand, and will not let Thee go,
Till I Thy name, Thy nature know.

Part II. 8. Yield to me now, for I am weak,
But confident in self-despair;
Speak to my heart, in blessings speak;
Be conquered by my instant prayer.
Speak, or Thou never hence shalt move,
And tell me if Thy name is Love.

9. 'Tis Love! 'tis Love! Thou diedst for me;
I hear Thy whisper in my heart;
The morning breaks, the shadows flee;
Pure universal Love Thou art;
To me, to all, Thy bowels move,
Thy nature and Thy name is Love.

10. My prayer hath power with God; the grace
Unspeakable, I now receive;
Through faith I see Thee face to face;
I see Thee face to face and live.
In vain I have not wept and strove;
Thy nature and Thy name is Love.

11. I know Thee, Saviour, who Thou art,
Jesus, the feeble sinner's Friend;
Nor wilt Thou with the night depart,
But stay and love me to the end:
Thy mercies never shall remove:
Thy nature and Thy name is Love.

12. The Sun of Righteousness on me,
Hath rose with healing in His wings;
Withered by nature's strength; from Thee
My soul its life and succour brings.
My help is all laid up above:
Thy nature and Thy name is Love.

13. Contented now, upon my thigh
I halt, till life's short journey end;
All helplessness, all weakness, I
On Thee alone for strength depend;
Nor have I power from Thee to move:
Thy nature and Thy name is Love.

14. Lame as I am, I take the prey;
Hell, earth, and sin, with ease o'ercome;
I leap for joy, pursue my way
And as a bounding hart fly home.
Through all eternity to prove,
Thy nature and Thy name is Love.

Our third stanza has unfortunately substituted "Clinging" for the original "Wrestling" for the title of the hymn is "Wrestling Jacob." "There wrestled a man with him until the breaking of the day." Genesis 32: 24.

The tune *Selena* was composed by Isaac Baker Woodbury (1819-58), see appendix, and appeared in his "Anthem Dulcimer," 1850, set to the words "Asleep in Jesus."

244. O COULD OUR THOUGHTS

2 Corinthians 4: 18

These words by Anne Steele (1717-78), daughter of a Baptist minister of Broughton, Hampshire, are part of a seven-stanza poem under the title "Longing After Unseen Pleasures." She was a life-long invalid and had a very sad life, her fiancé being drowned on the eve of her wedding. This hymn calls upon the eye of faith to look beyond the present gloominess of earth to the immortal glories of heaven, and is based on 2 Corinthians 4: 18, "While we look not at the things which are seen, but at the things which are not seen: for the things which are seen are temporal; but the things which are not seen are eternal." The omitted stanzas are:—

1. How long shall earth's alluring toys
Detain our hearts and eyes;
Regardless of immortal joys
And strangers to the skies?

2. These transient scenes will soon decay,
They fade upon the sight;
And quickly will the brightest day
Be lost in endless night.

3. Their brightest day, alas, how vain!
With conscious sighs we own;
While clouds of sorrow, care, and pain,
O'ershade the smiling noon.

Miss Steele also wrote Nos. 71, "My Maker and My King," and 333, "Father, Whate'er of Earthly Bliss," both under her pen-name of Theodosia.

245. O FOR A FAITH

Luke 17:5

William Hiley Bathurst (1796-1877) wrote these words in 1830 while rector of Barwick-in-Elmet, near Leeds, Yorkshire. They were entitled, "The Power of Faith," and based on the request made by the apostles to our Lord, "Increase our faith." Luke 17: 5. The omitted stanza is:—

5. A faith that keeps the narrow way
Till life's last spark is fled,
And with a pure and heavenly ray
Lights up a dying bed.

Bathurst also wrote No. 210, "O for That Flame of Living Fire."

The tune *Northfield* was composed in the town of that name in Massachusetts by Jeremiah Ingalls (1764-1828), a singing-school teacher. He had stopped in a tavern and ordered his dinner, and while waiting for it, wondered how long he would have to wait. This started a train of thought which led to his recalling the hymn of Isaac Watts (1674-1748) beginning, "Lo, what a glorious sight appears," and ending with the stanza:—

How long, dear Saviour, O how long
Shall this bright hour delay?
Fly swifter round ye wheels of time,
And bring the welcome day.

This theme, "How long," occupied his mind, and parodying the words, he composed the tune *Northfield.* Ingalls also preserved No. 343, "I Love Thee," in his "Christian Harmony," which contained several secular and lively tunes set to sacred words. He was a deacon in the Congregational Church, and also a choir leader.

246. MY FAITH LOOKS UP TO THEE

Psalm 61: 1, 2, 4

Ray Palmer (1808-87) wrote these words in 1830 just after his graduation from Yale. They were for his own personal benefit as an expression of his own faith. He said of this, his first hymn, "I gave form to what I felt, by writing with little effort the stanzas. I recollect I wrote them with very tender emotion, and ended the last line with tears." An omitted stanza is:—

4. When ends life's transient dream,
When death's cold sullen stream
Shall o'er me roll;
Blest Saviour, then in love,
Fear and distrust remove,
O bear me safe above,
A ransomed soul.

In brief the four stanzas are: hear me, strengthen me, guide me, save me. While the hymn is not intended to be a paraphrase of any psalm, some of the words recall Psalm 61: 1, 2, 4: "Hear my cry, O God; attend unto my prayer. . . . My heart is overwhelmed: lead me. . . . I will abide in Thy tabernacle for ever." Palmer later became a Congregational minister and wrote many more hymns—thirty-eight are listed as in common use—but this first hymn is his most famous, fulfilling Lowell Mason's prediction that Palmer might live long and do many good things, but would be best remembered as the author of "My Faith Looks Up to Thee." His other hymns in "Church Hymnal" are Nos. 154, "Jesus, Thou Joy of Loving Hearts"; 166, "Jesus, These Eyes Have Never Seen"; 235, "We Stand in Deep Repentance," and 285, "I Give My Heart to Thee."

Palmer carried the poem about with him in his pocket-book for some time, and when asked by Lowell Mason (1792-1872), see appendix, if he had anything to contribute to a new compilation, he produced these lines of the hymn. Mason soon composed the tune *Olivet,* which has been associated with the words ever since, and is also known as *Harlan.* It was first published in 1833 in Mason's "Spiritual Songs for Social Worship."

247. TOIL ON A LITTLE LONGER

Psalm 126: 5

This hymn by Annie Rebekah Smith (1828-55), see appendix, written on February 7, 1854, under the title "Toil On," contrasts the sorrows and trials of earth's pilgrimage with the glories of everlasting life. She has quoted almost word for word in stanza 4, line 5, the well-known verse, Psalm 126: 5: "They that sow in tears shall reap in joy."

The tune *Rest* (or *Magdalen*) was composed for the London Church Choir Association in 1873 by John Stainer (1840-1901) while he was organist of St. Paul's Cathedral, and is named *Rest* because it was written specially for John Wesley's translation of Gerhardt Tersteegen's hymn, "Thou Hidden Love of God." This hymn has for the last two lines of the first stanza:—

My heart is pained, nor can it be
At rest till it finds rest in Thee.

Stainer obtained his Doctor of Music degree from Oxford in 1865, was knighted in 1888, and in 1889 became professor of music at the University of Oxford. He insisted that his tunes be used only with the words for which they were written, although he did permit this tune to be used for another hymn, "The Saints of God, Their Conflict Past," because the theme was still appropriate. The spirit therefore, though not the letter of his desire, is carried out by fitting this tune *Rest* to words which speak of the eternal rest of the saints in heaven.

248. 'TIS MY HAPPINESS BELOW

Hebrews 12: 6-8

William Cowper (1731-1800), see appendix, the poet, was very introspective, and often plunged himself into deep gloom because he felt he had committed the unpardonable sin. This hymn, written by him in 1774, is entitled "In Afflictions," and was written at about the same time as, and in similar circumstances to hymn No. 84, "God Moves in a Mysterious Way." He mentions trials once each in our second and third stanzas and three times in our last stanza, but accepts them now in the spirit of Hebrews 12: 6-8, "For whom the Lord loveth He chasteneth. . . . But if ye be without chastisement, whereof all are partakers, then are ye bastards, and not sons." The original poem had twenty-four lines in three eight-line stanzas, the omitted portion being:—

2. God in Israel sows the seeds
Of affliction, pain, and toil;
These spring up and choke the weeds
Which would else o'erspread the soil:
. . .

3. . . .
Bastards may escape the rod,
Sunk in earthly vain delight;
But the true-born child of God
Must not—would not, if he might.

The tune *Scudamore* was composed in 1862 specially for the Congregational "Hymn and Tune Book," by an Anglican minister, Richard Robert Chope (1830-1928). It was written a semitone higher in three sharps, and in 8.7.8.7. metre to the words "Praise the Lord! ye heavens adore Him." Chope was curate at Stapleton, and in 1875 became vicar of St. Augustine's, South Kensington, London.

249. IF THROUGH UNRUFFLED SEAS

Philippians 4: 11

Augustus Montague Toplady (1740-78) wrote in 1772 a poem of eight stanzas each of eight lines entitled "Weak Believers Encouraged." Our selection is from stanzas 2, with considerable alteration, 3, 4 and 5. Some omitted lines are:—

1. Your harps ye trembling saints
Down from the willows take:
Loud to the praise of love divine,
Bid every string awake.
Though in a foreign land,
We are not far from home:
And nearer to our house above
We every moment come.

2. His grace will to the end
Stronger and brighter shine;
Nor present things, nor things to come,
Shall quench the spark divine.
Fastened within the veil
Hope be your anchor strong,
His loving Spirit the sweet gale
That wafts you smooth along.

3. . . .
The people of His choice
He will not cast away;
Yet do not always here expect
On Tabor's Mount to stay.

5. No wonder, when His love
Pervades your kindling breast,
You wish for ever to retain
The heart-transporting Guest.
. . .

8. . . .
Blest is the man, O God,
That stays himself on Thee!
Who waits for Thy salvation, Lord,
Shall Thy salvation see.

He has enlarged on the attitude adopted by the Apostle Paul—"I have learned, in whatsoever state I am, therewith to be content" (Philippians 4: 11)—an attitude exemplified by our Lord in Gethsemane when He said, "Nevertheless not as I will, but as Thou wilt." Matthew 26: 39. So we should thank God certainly for an untroubled existence, but at the same time realize that sorrow, too, can be a blessing, and that the fearful midnight experience can bring the light of God's mercy. Toplady was a clergyman of the Church of England with strong Calvinistic leanings, was ordained in 1762 and held pastorates in Somerset and Devon. He is better known for his later hymn, No. 474, "Rock of Ages."

The tune *Selvin* was arranged by Lowell Mason (1792-1872), see appendix, but the name has no associated significance. It was first published in his "New Carmina Sacra," 1850. The last two lines 5 and 6, though having a different melody are composed of precisely the same chords as lines 3 and 4, the soprano and tenor parts being interchanged, and alto and bass parts repeated.

250. WHEN, MY SAVIOUR, SHALL I BE

Psalm 51: 17

Charles Wesley (1707-88), see appendix, wrote these words in 1742 in five stanzas each of eight lines. The title was "Submission," and in it he expresses his own humility and desire for holiness. The sentiments are those of the repentant David, who said, "The sacrifices of God are a broken spirit: a broken and a contrite heart, O God, Thou wilt not despise." Psalm 51: 17. The hymn has since been abbreviated to a four-stanza one, each of four lines only, the one omitted stanza being:—

3. So I may Thy Spirit know,
Let Him as He listeth blow:
Let the manner be unknown,
So I may with Thee be one.

The tune *Holley* was composed in 1835 for the hymn "Softly Now the Light of Day" (No. 48) by George Hews (1806-73), an organist, music teacher, and piano manufacturer of Boston, Massachusetts. Holley is the name of a village in Orleans County, New York.

251. I ASK NOT, LORD, FOR LESS

Matthew 26: 39

Annie Rebekah Smith (1828-55), see appendix, expresses her own consecration and devotion in this hymn of perfect confidence in God. It was written at Rochester, New York, on May 2, 1854, under the title "Resignation." Originally it was in long metre, eight syllables to the line, as is shown in stanza 3, line 4, where the words "the truth" have been omitted. Miss Smith shows her familiarity with the Scriptures, for in every stanza except the fourth a part of a verse is quoted. The one which summarizes the whole hymn is Matthew 26: 39: "Nevertheless not as I will, but as Thou wilt."

The tune *Herbert* was composed by Lowell Mason (1792-1872), see appendix. Note the ascending scale passage immediately after the first two notes of the melody which give a joyful lift, not quite in accord with the somewhat sombre words.

252. MY SPIRIT ON THY CARE

Psalm 31: 1, 5

These words of calm trust were written in 1834 by Henry Francis Lyte (1793-1847), then an Anglican minister at Brixham, Devon. They were inspired by meditation on the 31st Psalm, and are a free paraphrase of some of the verses, particularly verse 5, "Into Thine hand I commit my spirit," and verse 1, "In Thee, O Lord, do I put my trust." Lyte also wrote Nos. 16, "Praise the Lord, His Glories Show"; 50, "Abide With Me"; 267, "Jesus, I My Cross Have Taken"; 399, "There Is a Safe and Secret Place," and possibly 394, "Saviour, Like a Shepherd."

The tune *Day* was composed by H. Abbott, who also wrote No. 490, *Protection.*

253. THE TEMPTER TO MY SOUL

Psalm 3

This paraphrase of the 3rd Psalm by James Montgomery (1771-1854), see appendix, appeared in 1822 in "Song of Zion." Its closeness to the original is shown by comparison of the stanzas with the verses of the psalm, the words duplicated being underlined.

Stanza 1. "There is no help for him in God. But Thou, O Lord, art a shield for me; my glory, and the lifter up of mine head." Verses 2, 3.

2. "I cried unto the Lord . . . and He heard me out of His holy hill." Verse 4.
3. "I laid me down and slept; I awaked; for the Lord sustained me." Verse 5.
4. "I will not be afraid . . . Salvation belongeth unto the Lord: Thy blessing is upon Thy people." Verses 6, 8.

The tune *Zephyr,* also used for No. 41, "O Christ, With Each Returning Morn," was written in 1844 by William Batchelder Bradbury (1816-68), see appendix.

254. SOMETIMES A LIGHT SURPRISES

Habakkuk 3: 17, 18

William Cowper (1731-1800), see appendix, wrote this hymn in 1779 under the title "Joy and Peace in Believing," and it was included in the "Olney Hymns" written by him and his associate John Newton, see appendix. Here we see the often depressed poet in a cheerful exultant mood, absorbing the lesson on ceasing to worry that our Lord taught by referring to the ravens and the lilies (Matthew 6: 28-30; Luke 12: 24), and concluding with the triumphant words of the prophet Habakkuk, as in chapter 3: 17, 18, "Although the fig tree shall not blossom, neither shall fruit be in the vines; . . . the fields shall yield no meat; the flock shall be cut off from the fold, and there shall be no herd in the stalls: yet I will rejoice in the Lord." The first two lines of the third stanza were originally:—

It can bring with it nothing,
But He will bear us through.

The tune *Ellacombe* is from a Roman Catholic hymnal published in 1784, made for use in the private chapel of the duchy of Wurttemberg, but containing a majority of Protestant compositions. It is used for No. 434, "O Golden Day." It is an easy tune to sing, for lines 1, 3 and 7 are identical; so are lines 4 and 8, these closely resembling line 2; and line 6 imitates line 5.

255. HOW FIRM A FOUNDATION

2 Peter 1: 4

This hymn of seven stanzas appeared in John Rippon's "Selections," 1787, under the title "Exceeding Great and Precious Promises," and was there attributed to K, who was probably R. Keene, precentor of Rippon's Baptist church in New Park Street, formerly in Carter Lane, Tooley Street, London, and composer of the tune *Geard,* which was the first setting to the words. Rippon (1751-

1836) remained in this church as pastor for a continuous period of sixty-three years, and was an authority on the hymns of Isaac Watts. His "Selections," from the best authors, was a most popular work running into twenty-seven editions. The words of this hymn, as the title indicates, are based on several Scripture promises, for example, 2 Timothy 2: 19; Isaiah 41: 10; 43: 2; Hebrews 13: 5. All of these assurances are included in the Scripture heading given to the hymn, 2 Peter 1: 4, "Whereby are given unto us exceeding great and precious promises." The two omitted stanzas are:—

2. In every condition, in sickness, in health,
In poverty's vale, or abounding in wealth;
At home and abroad, on the land, on the sea,
As thy days may demand, shall thy strength ever be.

6. E'en down to old age, all My people shall prove
My sovereign, eternal, unchangeable love;
And when hoary hairs shall their temples adorn,
Like lambs they shall still in My bosom be borne.

Rippon also wrote part of No. 156, "All Hail the Power of Jesus' Name."

The tune *Portuguese Hymn* has been attributed to John Reading, the organist of Westminster College, 1680, and also to Samuel Webbe senior (1740-1816). It is so named because it was used in England in 1785 at the Portuguese embassy, and heard in the chapel there by the Duke of Leeds, who used it later at concerts under this name, supposing it to have come from Portugal. However, it was commonly used in Catholic chapels as their regular Christmas hymn, and sung to the words "Adeste fideles." This is indeed the same tune as No. 105, which is there raised one tone to the key A. John Francis Wade (c. 1711-86), a Roman Catholic writer and copyist, transcribed the tune in 1751, and it appeared in his "Cantus Diversi" (= various songs), 1751, together with No. 176, *Holywood.* Webbe was also the composer of Nos. 42 and 312, *Melcombe,* and 223, *Consolation,* and probably No. 87, *Dulce Carmen.*

256. I AM TRUSTING THEE

Psalm 62: 8

This hymn was the favourite one of the authoress Frances Ridley Havergal (1836-79), see appendix, and was found in her pocket Bible after her death. It was written at Ormont Dessous, Switzerland, in September, 1874, under the title "Trusting Jesus." The two omitted stanzas are:—

3. I am trusting Thee for cleansing
 In the crimson flood;
 Trusting Thee to make me holy
 By Thy blood.

5. I am trusting Thee for power,
 Thine can never fail;
 Words which Thou Thyself shalt give me
 Must prevail.

A fitting summary for the hymn is Psalm 62: 8, "Trust in Him at all times; ye people, pour out your heart before Him: God is a refuge for us."

She composed her own tune, *Urbane,* for the words, but we now sing them to *Bullinger,* composed in 1874 by Dr. Ethelbert William Bullinger (1837-1913), secretary of the Trinitarian Bible Society, and a London clergyman.

257. CALL JEHOVAH THY SALVATION

Psalm 91: 1, 4, 15, 16

James Montgomery (1771-1854), see appendix, wrote this paraphrase of the 91st Psalm in 1822 in five stanzas, each of eight lines, under the title, "God's Merciful Guardianship of His People." Here we have an abbreviated version, which corresponds thus:—

Stanza 1. "He that dwelleth in the secret place of the Most High shall abide under the shadow of the Almighty." Verse 1.

2. "He shall cover thee with His feathers, and under His wings shalt thou trust; His truth shall be thy shield." Verse 4.

3. "He shall call upon Me, and I will answer him: I will be with him in trouble; I will deliver him. . . . With long life will I satisfy him, and show him My salvation." Verses 15, 16.

The omitted stanzas are:—

1. . . .
 There no tumult shall alarm thee,
 Thou shalt dread no hidden snare;
 Guile nor violence can harm thee;
 In eternal safeguard there.

2. From the sword at noonday wasting,
 From the noisome pestilence,
 In the depth of midnight blasting,
 God shall be thy sure defence:
 Fear thou not the deadly quiver,
 When a thousand feel the blow,
 Mercy shall thy soul deliver,
 Though ten thousand be laid low.

3. Only with thine eye the anguish
Of the wicked thou shalt see,
When by slow disease they languish,
When they perish suddenly:
Thee, though winds and waves be swelling,
God, thine hope, shall bear through all;
Plague shall not come nigh thy dwelling
Thee no evil shall befall.

4. He shall charge His angel legions,
Watch and ward o'er thee to keep;
Though thou walk through hostile regions,
Though in desert wilds thou sleep:
On the lion vainly roaring,
On his young, thy foot shall tread,
And, the dragon's den exploring,
Thou shalt bruise the serpent's head.

The tune *Trust* is an arrangement from the eminent composer Jakob Ludwig Felix Mendelssohn-Bartholdy (1809-47), and is so named because it is usually associated with these words of trust and confidence. He wrote a 16-bar hymn tune called *Contemplation* for Charles Bayles Broadley's metrical version of Psalm 13 in 1840, and *Trust* is bars 1-6 and 15, 16 from this tune. Mendelssohn also composed Nos. 111, *Mendelssohn;* 674, *Abiding;* 687, unnamed; 692, *Birmingham;* and arranged No. 217, *Munich.*

258. I NEED THEE EVERY HOUR

2 Corinthians 3: 5

Mrs. Annie Sherwood Hawks (1835-1918) was a member of a Baptist church at Brooklyn, New York, during the pastorate of Robert Lowry (1826-99), see appendix. He encouraged her to write hymns, and this—one of her almost four hundred Sunday school hymns—was written especially in June, 1872, for his collection of original songs for the Baptist Sunday School Association. The words came to her in an atmosphere of love and joy while she was engaged in routine household duties, and they were first sung at a Sunday school convention in Cinncinnati in the same year. The emphasis on "every hour" led Major D. W. Whittle to write No. 583, "Moment By Moment." The utmost reliance described in Mrs. Hawks's words recall the Apostle Paul's humble statement: "Not that we are sufficient of ourselves to think any thing as of ourselves; but our sufficiency is of God." 2 Corinthians 3: 5.

The tune *Need* was composed in 1872 and published the next year, and a refrain added by Robert Lowry (1826-99), see appendix, and the complete hymn appeared in his "The Royal Diadem" of 1873.

259. ALL THE WAY

Deuteronomy 32: 12

Fanny Crosby (1820-1915), see appendix, while meditating on the leading of providence, was unexpectedly given five dollars by a friend who called at the door. She was short of money at the time, and needed this amount before she was able to draw on her publishers. This experience awakened a train of thought which culminated in the writing of these words in 1874. They are a reminder that she wrote many of her hymns after a day's jostling through the city streets, led by loving hands away from danger: "So the Lord alone did lead him." Deuteronomy 32: 12.

The tune *Lowry* was composed in 1874 by Robert Lowry (1826-99), see appendix, with whom Miss Crosby had become acquainted nine years earlier, and with whom she often consulted regarding the phrasing of a hymn.

260. THE LORD'S MY SHEPHERD

Psalm 23

This paraphrase is a metrical psalm, and follows as closely as possible the language of the Authorized Version of Psalm 23. Compare Nos. 86, 391, 393, 405 and 674, which are free paraphrases. The words are based on the version of 1641 by Frances Rous (1579-1659). He borrowed the text of William Whittingham (1524-79), who married the sister of John Calvin, and who in 1556 wrote fifty-one of the Psalms of David in metrical form. The divines of the Westminster Assembly made a further revision, and it was altered again before appearing in the Scottish Psalter of 1650.

The tune *Walden* was composed in 1906, but one semitone higher in the key of D flat, by James Edmund Jones (1866-?) of Toronto, who was the convenor of the committee for the "Book of Common Praise" for the Church of England in Canada. He conducted an athletic club consisting of young men from his Bible class, named the Aura Lee Club, and this tune first appeared in their "Song and Hymn Book," 1906. It was fitted to Marie Corelli's (see No. 419) paraphrase of the Shepherd Psalm, and the name *Walden* comes from this novelist's story, "God's Good Man," in which the hero is the Rev. John Walden.

261. A MIGHTY FORTRESS

Psalm 46: 1

Martin Luther (1483-1546) became a monk at Erfurt in 1505, published his ninety-five theses at Wittenberg in 1517, and burnt the papal bull, these last two steps leading ultimately to the formation of the Protestant church. In 1529 this name Protestant was earned by the German princes who opposed the Papacy at the Diet of Spires, and furnished Luther the occasion for writing this hymn based on the words, "God is our refuge and strength." Psalm 46: 1. It became the battle-hymn of the Reformation, and entered a protest before the German people against the endeavour to obstruct the promulgation of the gospel, although the words are very positive, manifesting firm faith in God, and not merely expressing a protest in the sense of an objection. The hymn is now Germany's national hymn, and as well as having been sung at Luther's funeral, the first line "Ein feste Burg ist unser Gott," is carved on his tombstone at Eisleben. More than one hundred translations have been made of the hymn, the present one in 1852 by Dr. Frederick Henry Hedge (1805-90), a Unitarian minister who was professor of Ecclesiastical History at Harvard, and then professor of German there.

The tune *Ein' Feste Burg* was also composed by Martin Luther and has been used by Mendelssohn in the 5th movement of his Reformation Symphony, as well as by Meyerbeer in his prelude to the opera, "The Huguenots," and by Wagner in his "Kaisermarsch," 1871. It is so named because these are the first three words of the German text (= a mighty fortress). Luther made a great contribution musically to church life by encouraging the congregations to sing, and hence requiring words in German instead of in Latin.

262. LORD OF OUR LIFE

Psalm 79: 9

These words were written in 1644 by Matthäus Apelles von Löwenstern (1594-1648), a man of both musical and business aptitude, who received a knighthood for the latter from the Emperor Ferdinand III. They reflect the conditions obtaining during the Thirty Years War which was mainly between Catholics and Protestants between the years 1618 and 1648, and the words are a prayer for help from God to send peace on earth. They are based on Psalm 79: 9: "Help us, O God of our salvation, for the glory of Thy name," and they were translated from the German in 1834 by Philip Pusey (1799-1855), brother of the more famous Dr. E. Bouverie Pusey. They were very freely paraphrased and made to refer to the Church of England, which was enfeebled within and assailed from without, but on the verge, nevertheless, of a great awakening. An omitted stanza is:—

2. See round Thine ark the hungry billows curling;
See how Thy foes their banners are unfurling,
Lord, while their darts envenom'd they are hurling,
Thou canst preserve us.

Philip Pusey was an art connoisseur, a member of Parliament, and one of the founders of the Royal Agriculture Society, as well as being interested in hymnology.

The tune *Cloisters* was specially written for these words in 1868 by Joseph Barnby (1838-96), see appendix.

263. COURAGE, BROTHER!

Psalm 37:3

Norman MacLeod (1812-72), chaplain to Queen Victoria and minister of the Church of Scotland, was a most influential orator. He was lecturing to a group of young men in London and describing the life of one of his college friends by way of illustrating his talk on "A life story." To conclude his lecture he read this poem of his own composition, and later it was published in the January, 1857, issue of the *Edinburgh Christian* magazine. The constant refrain is an echo of David's trust in God, "Trust in the Lord, and do good." Psalm 37: 3.

The tune *Courage, Brother* was composed in 1872 by Arthur Seymour Sullivan (1842-1900), see appendix, and named after the opening words of this hymn for which it was specially written.

264. TO THEE, O DEAR, DEAR SAVIOUR

Luke 1:47

These words were written in 1863 by John Samuel Bewley Monsell (1811-75) as five stanzas for the 23rd Sunday after Trinity, and based on the Virgin Mary's statement: "My spirit hath rejoiced in God my Saviour." Luke 1: 47. The omitted stanza is:

3. My grief is in the dullness
With which this sluggish heart
Doth open to the fullness
Of all Thou wouldst impart:
My joy is in Thy beauty
Of holiness divine,
My comfort in the duty
That binds my life in Thine.

Monsell was chaplain of the Chapel of Ease, Derby, and later vicar of Egham, Surrey. He also wrote No. 6, "O Worship the Lord."

The tune *Savoy Chapel* was composed in 1887 by John Baptiste Calkin (1827-1905), organist at the Savoy chapel in London. He also composed No. 450, *Waltham.*

265. MY LIFE FLOWS ON

Psalm 13: 6

These exultant, happy words were written in 1869 by Robert Lowry (1826-99), see appendix, and copy the psalmist's joy, "I will sing unto the Lord, because He hath dealt bountifully with me." Psalm 13: 6.

The tune *Materna* was composed in 1882 by Samuel Augustus Ward (1847-1903) of Newark, New Jersey, and is used also for No. 503, "O Beautiful for Spacious Skies," except that there the last note in the 4th and 8th lines is not required, as it is in the feminine ending of the present tune. Ward, a music store proprietor, was also organist and choirmaster of the Episcopal church. He was seeking a better tune for the hymn, "O Mother Dear, Jerusalem," which was David Dickson's (1583-1663) translation of the hymn written by F. B. P. (see No. 309). He decided at length to write one himself, and to safeguard it from being used for other words, as he thought, he named it *Materna* = mother. It was composed to honour his eldest daughter Clara, who died as a young girl.

266. I WILL FOLLOW THEE

Hebrews 4: 15

Both words and music of this hymn were written by James Lawson Elginburg and appear in "Hymns and Tunes," 1886. The words are a sincere avowal of a Christian to follow his Lord whatever trials and afflictions may beset him. The last four stanzas all begin with the qualifying word "though," and the last half of each emphasizes the encouraging thought that the Saviour endured exactly the same difficulties. "For we have not an high priest which cannot be touched with the feeling of our infirmities; but was in all points tempted like as we are, yet without sin." Hebrews 4: 15. The third stanza, now omitted, reads:—

> 3. Though 'tis lone, and dark, and dreary,
> Cheerless though my path may be;
> If Thy voice I hear before me,
> Fearlessly I'll follow Thee.

267. JESUS, I MY CROSS HAVE TAKEN

Mark 10: 28

Henry Francis Lyte (1793-1847) wrote these words in 1833 as a six-stanza poem, basing it on Peter's words, "Lo, we have left all, and have followed Thee." Mark 10: 28. It stands as a memorial to his wife Anne Maxwell, an Anglican clergyman's daughter who joined the Methodists and was therefore forced to leave her home. Later she married Lyte, then a curate in the Church of England. The sixteen lines omitted are:—

2. . . .
And, while Thou shalt smile upon me,
God of wisdom, love, and might,
Foes may hate, and friends may shun me;
Show Thy face, and all is bright.

3. Go then, earthly fame and treasure!
Come, disaster, scorn and pain!
In Thy service, pain is pleasure,
With Thy favour, loss is gain!
I have called Thee, Abba, Father!
I have stay'd my heart on Thee!
Storms may howl, and clouds may gather,
All must work for good to me.

4. Man may trouble and distress me,
'Twill but drive me to Thy breast;
Life with trials hard may press me,
Heaven will bring me sweeter rest!
. . .

Lyte also wrote Nos. 16, "Praise the Lord, His Glories Show"; 50, "Abide With Me"; 252, "My Spirit on Thy Care"; possibly 394, "Saviour, Like a Shepherd," and 399, "There Is a Safe and Secret Place."

The tune *Ellesdie* is said to come from Wolfgang Amadeus Mozart (1756-91), the famous Viennese composer and infant musical prodigy, and it has at least sixteen other names. It was published in 1831 in two parts only, a melody and a bass, and Hubert Platt Main (1839-1926), composer and musical editor, completed the harmony in 1873. *Ellesdie* is also used for No. 663, "Gracious Father, Guard Thy Children," and Mozart also composed the tune *Ariel* from which Nos. 161 and 190 were arranged. Main also arranged No. 160, *Beloved,* or *Dulcimer,* and composed No. 532, *My Lord and I.*

268. BLESSED JESUS, MEEK AND LOWLY

Luke 24: 29

These words by Annie Rebekah Smith (1828-55), see appendix, indicate some of the trials and scorn suffered by the early Sabbath-keeping Adventists, and also their trust in Jesus for salvation and not in their own good works. The poem was written in July, 1854, at Rochester, New York, in the first person singular. For example, in stanza 2, line 5 ("me") rhymed with line 7 ("glory"), as do these lines in the other stanzas. The hymn is based on the words of the disciples of Emmaus to our Lord, "But they constrained Him, saying, Abide with us: for it is toward evening, and the day is far spent. And He went in to tarry with them." Luke 24: 29.

The tune *Autumn* is an old one dating back to the 16th century, and later arranged by François Hippolyte Barthélémon (1741-1808), a violinist and composer of secular songs. If the passing notes in the melody in the sixth line are ignored, i.e., C and F sharp, we have an example of a tune in the pentatonic scale (See No. 181), which can therefore be played entirely on the black keys of a piano if dropped one semitone. Barthélémon's other tune, No. 221, *Balerma,* is also in the pentatonic scale.

269. TAKE MY HEART, O FATHER

Ezekiel 36: 26

This hymn appeared anonymously in five stanzas in a collection by Cyrus Augustus Bartol (1813-90) of Unitarian "Hymns for the Sanctuary," 1849. It is a quiet prayer for the infilling of the Holy Spirit into a dedicated heart, and a request for the fulfilment of God's promise: "A new heart also will I give you, and a new spirit will I put within you: and I will take away the stony heart out of your flesh, and I will give you an heart of flesh." Ezekiel 36: 26. Barton was pastor of the West church, Boston, an Independent Congregational, for over fifty years from 1837.

The tune *Mount Vernon* was composed by Lowell Mason (1792-1872), see appendix.

270. GIVE THOU THY YOUTH TO GOD

Proverbs 23: 26

These appealing words to children and youth were written by Horatius Bonar (1808-89), see appendix. They amplify the invitation, "My son, give Me thine heart, and let thine eyes observe My ways." Proverbs 23: 26.

The tune *St. Michael* is an adaptation from *Old 134th,* the latter so named because it was the tune set to Psalm 134 in the Old Version of the Psalms in 1562 by Sternhold and Hopkins as opposed to Tate and Brady's New Version of 1696. The Old Version was almost identical to the Anglo-Genevan Psalter of 1561, which perpetuated John Calvin's idea of singing only the actual words of Scripture. This obstinate insistence on an exact rendering from the Hebrew led to some very crude versification in order to harmonize the number of syllables with the nature of the hymn tune. The tune is named *St. Michael* in honour of the college of this name in Tenbury, England, which was founded as a boys' school for general education and cultivation of church music. Tenbury, Worcestershire, is a centre of cathedral tradition, and a daily choral service is held there. The name was given by William Crotch (1775-1847), a child musical prodigy, who later wrote on the history and theory of music, and became principal of the Royal Academy of Music, in 1822, and professor of music at the University of Oxford. *St. Michael* is also used for No. 285, "I Give My Heart to Thee," but it is there transposed up a semitone to the key of A flat.

271. NOT I, BUT CHRIST

Galatians 2: 20

The theme of this hymn is the Apostle Paul's statement: "Yet not I, but Christ." Galatians 2: 20. Only as He dwells within us can we reveal Him in word, thought, and action (stanza 1); can we truly sympathize with others (stanza 2); can we be really humble (stanza 3); can we do all things (stanza 4). The words were written by one A. A. F. and arranged by Frances (or Fannie) Eugenia Bolton (18?-1926) in 1900.

Another stanza is:—

5. Christ, only Christ, ere long will fill my vision,
Glory excelling soon, full soon I'll see—
Christ, only Christ, my every wish fulfilling,
Christ, only Christ, my all in all to be.

Fannie Bolton was a Seventh-day Adventist, who wrote several poems for the *Review and Herald*. She died at Battle Creek, Michigan, on June 28, 1926, and was buried at Eureka, Michigan.

Miss Bolton also wrote the tune, named *Bolton* after her, in 1900.

272. HAVE THINE OWN WAY, LORD

Isaiah 64: 8

Although these words remind us of Isaiah's illustrations, "But now, O Lord . . . we are the clay, and Thou our potter," Isaiah 64: 8, they were inspired by a simple sentence sincerely prayed by an elderly woman in 1907 at a prayer meeting. Instead of asking blessings from the Lord, she gave herself as a living sacrifice in the words, "It doesn't matter what You bring into our lives, Lord, just have Your own way with us." Adelaide Pollard (1862-1934) was present in the meeting, and the clause "have Thine own way" rang in her ears so intensely that before she reached home she had shaped some stanzas mentally. Before retiring that night she had completed the hymn. Sarah Addison Pollard was born in Bloomfield, Iowa, and was nicknamed Addie from her second name. This decided her, at the age of seventeen, to adopt the name Adelaide, and from then on she was known as Adelaide A. Pollard. She was a teacher in private schools, but unfortunately a diabetic, which hindered her desire to be a missionary to Africa. After promising but frustrating visits to faith healers, she accepted her handicap and turned to hymn-writing. She did ultimately serve for a short period in South Africa during World War I, so that the hymn is almost an autobiographical one.

The tune, *Stebbins,* commemorates the composer George Coles Stebbins (1846-1945), see appendix, who set the words to music in the same year, 1907.

273. TAKE MY LIFE AND LET IT BE

2 Samuel 19: 30

In February, 1874, Frances Ridley Havergal (1836-79), see appendix, paid a five-day visit to Areley House, London, where ten other persons were staying. They were all either unconverted or unhappy, and Miss Havergal was impressed to pray for them so that they might all have the joy of conversion. Her prayer was, "Lord, give me ALL in this house." The night before her departure, there were only two young ladies who had not surrendered to the Lord, but after a personal visit from Miss Havergal, they, too, trusted and rejoiced. By that time it was nearly midnight, but the answer to her prayer made her so happy that she could not sleep. Then these couplets, twelve of them, now arranged as four line stanzas, formed in her mind. The two omitted are:—

2. Take my moments and my days;
   Let them flow in ceaseless praise.

8. Take my intellect, and use
   Every power as Thou shalt choose.

Her own title for the hymn was "Self-consecration to Christ," and it was based on the statement by the humble Mephibosheth, "Yea, let him take all." 2 Samuel 19: 30. Later, Miss Havergal wrote concerning the hymn: "That couplet, 'Take my silver and my gold, Not a mite would I withhold,' does not mean that because we have ten shillings in our purse, we are pledged to put it all into the next collecting plate, else we should have none for the next call! But it does mean that every shilling is to be, and I think I may say is, held at my Lord's disposal, and is distinctly not my own."

The hymn was invariably sung by her family to her father's tune *Patmos.* The present tune, *Hendon,* was composed in 1827 by Henri Abraham Cesar Malan (1787-1864), a brilliant preacher of Geneva as well as a composer of over 100 hymn tunes and texts. He lived for some time in London, of which Hendon is a northern suburb. *Hendon* is also used for Nos. 30, "Lord, We Come Before Thee Now," and 192, "Hark! That Shout." Malan also composed No. 408, *Rosefield.*

274. MUST JESUS BEAR THE CROSS ALONE?

Matthew 16: 24

These words appeared in 1693 in "Penitential Cries" by Thomas Shepherd (1665-1739), a minister of the Church of England, who followed his father into the Congregational Church in 1698, and ministered in Northampton and Essex. The full poem is entitled "For Universal Obedience," and consists of five stanzas, the last of only four lines.

1. Lord, Thou hast planted me a vine
In fertile soil and air,
Now, tend and water me as Thine,
Make me Thy daily care.
My Christ I'm wholly Thine, direct
Me wandering in the dark,
O may my constant aims be strait,
Thine honour be my mark.

2. I have observed Thy sacred laws
To be exceeding wide,
Let me not from the least of them
Turn wilfully aside.
Lord, let Thy Word and Spirit guide
Thy servant in Thy way,
May I walk closely with my God
And run no more astray.

3. Shall Simon bear Thy cross alone
And other saints be free?
Each saint of Thine shall find his own
And there is one for me.
Whene'er it falls into my lot
Let it not drive me from
My God, let me be ne'er forgot
Till Thou hast loved me home.

4. O happy Christian, be not loth
To have a coarser fare:
Saints that have had no table-cloth
Had Christ at dinner there.
To do or suffer I am pleased,
So long as Christ stands by,
Support me with Thy constant aid,
Lest all Thy graces die.

5. Thy way is to the upright strength,
Lord make it so to me,
That never tiring with the length,
My soul may reach to Thee.

It is quite obvious that the present hymn is an extensive and almost complete alteration of Shepherd's original, except the first half of stanza 3. It was made by George Nelson Allen (1812-77) of Mansfield, Massachusetts, an instructor in music at Oberlin College, who wrote several other hymns and tunes. Authorship has also been attributed to Charles Beecher (1815-1900), a Congregational minister of Litchfield, Connecticut, and brother of Henry Ward Beecher, the famous preacher. There are several scriptures referred to in the hymn, but an essential summary is: "If any man will come after Me, let him deny himself, and take up his cross." Matthew 16: 24.

The tune *Maitland,* an arbitrary choice of name, was also composed by George Nelson Allen. The tune was composed especially for the words, in the 1840's.

275. IN THE BLOOD FROM THE CROSS

Philippians 3: 12

These words were written by Johnson Oatman, Junior (1856-1930), a Methodist minister of Lumberton, New Jersey, who wrote about 5,000 gospel songs. In this hymn he amplifies the ideal of the Apostle Paul for higher standards: "Not as though I had already attained, either were already perfect: but I follow after, if that I may apprehend that for which also I am apprehended of Christ Jesus." Philippians 3: 12. He has been forgiven, but he desires to be free from sin; he has received blessing, yet desires more power; he has peace, but desires complete purity. The theme is more, higher progress, deeper, and increasing experience in the things of God. Oatman also wrote No. 631, "I'm Pressing On the Upward Way."

The tune *Deeper Yet,* named for the words of the chorus, was composed by William James Kirkpatrick (1838-1921), see appendix.

276. MY JESUS, I LOVE THEE

John 21: 17

These words are the outpourings of a consecrated youthful heart, for they were written in 1858 by a Canadian lad, William Ralf Featherstone (1842-78), then only sixteen years of age. He sent the words to his aunt, who was a poetess, for criticism and an opinion. She felt that they were worthy of publication, and they were first printed in 1862. They amplify Peter's confession after the Lord's resurrection: "Lord, Thou knowest all things; Thou knowest that I love Thee." John 21: 17.

The tune *Gordon* commemorates the composer, Dr. Adoniram Judson Gordon (1836-95) of New Hampton, New Hampshire, who was pastor in the Clarendon Street Baptist church, Boston, when George Coles Stebbins (see appendix) became director of music there. He found an anonymous hymn and tune in "The London Hymnbook," 1864, which appealed to him, but later felt that the tune was unsuitable, and after prayer and meditation, composed this one. Lines 1 and 2 are identical, and differ only in the last few chords from line 4.

277. FADE, FADE EACH EARTHLY JOY

Song of Solomon 2: 16

This hymn was written in 1844 by Mrs. Catherine Jane Bonar, nee Lundie (1821-84), wife of Horatius Bonar, see appendix. Its title was "Jesus, All In All," and it began "Pass Away, Earthly Joy," but the present words suit the accent much better. The possessive theme recalls Mary's "Rabboni," John 20: 16, and the confession of the doubting Thomas, "My Lord and my God," John 20 28. The words are adapted, however, from Song of Solomon 2: 16: "My beloved is mine." Mrs. Bonar's sister, Mrs. Duncan, wrote No. 430, "Jesus, Tender Shepherd, Hear Me."

The tune *Perkins* is named after the composer Theodore Edson Perkins (1831-1912), an American editor of song books and a composer of Sunday school songs. He also composed No. 479, *Freely Give.*

278. I LAY MY SINS ON JESUS

John 1: 29

Horatius Bonar (1808-89), see appendix, was a great lover of children, and wrote these words in order to provide something for them to sing, and also to understand, during divine service. It was written about 1834 in four-line stanzas, and revised in 1843 to four eight-line stanzas. It was entitled "The Fullness of Jesus," and was to be sung by his Sunday school class at South Leith where he was the assistant minister. It was his second hymn, and one of those he wrote each week for his Sunday school. It is based on John 1: 29: "Behold the Lamb of God, which taketh away the sin of the world." Bonar said it was good gospel, but not good poetry, and he was surprised that it became so popular. The following lines from the original are now omitted:—

I lay my griefs on Jesus,
He takes them all from me;
I cast my cares on Jesus,
My shield and tower is He.

I give myself to Jesus,
This weary soul of mine;
His right hand me embraces
I on His breast recline.

I love the name of Jesus,
Immanuel, Christ the Lord;
Like fragrance on the breezes,
His name is poured abroad.

The tune *St. Hilda* was adapted by Justin Heinrich Knecht (1752-1817) the famous German organist of Wurttemberg who started his career as a professor of literature. He took it from a collection published in Stuttgart in 1799, and it was further altered in 1871 by Edward Husband (1843-1908), vicar of Folkestone, Kent, who was also an amateur organist and composer. He named it *St. Hilda* to commemorate a devout lady of royal blood who established a monastery near Whitby, Yorkshire, in the seventh century, and there revived the standards of the early Christian church. *St. Hilda* is also used for No. 231, "O Jesus, Thou Art Standing." Knecht also composed No. 131, *Vienna.*

279. LIVE OUT THY LIFE WITHIN ME

1 Corinthians 6: 19, 20

This hymn by Frances Ridley Havergal (1836-79), see appendix, reflects the experience of the doctrine of the indwelling Christ: "What? know ye not that your body is the temple of the Holy Ghost which is in you, which ye have of God, and ye are not your own? For ye are bought with a price: therefore glorify God in your body, and in your spirit, which are God's." 1 Corinthians 6: 19, 20.

The tune *Aurelia* is by Samuel Sebastian Wesley (1810-76) grandson of Charles Wesley, see appendix, and one of the finest cathedral organists of his time, serving at Hereford, Exeter, Leeds parish church, Winchester, and Gloucester. He received the Mus. Doc. degree from Oxford in 1839 and became professor of organ at the London Royal Academy of Music in 1850. The tune was used in 1864 for the words of the hymn "Jerusalem the Golden" (No. 300), hence the name *Aurelia* = golden. It is also used for No. 433, "The Church Has One Foundation." Samuel Wesley also harmonized No. 676, *Seelenbrautigam.*

280. BENEATH THE CROSS OF JESUS

Proverbs 14: 26

Miss Elizabeth Cecilia Douglas Clephane (1830-69) was asked to write a poem for a children's magazine and was sitting in her room at Melrose, Scotland, seeking inspiration. She overlooked a bridge over the river, and in her imagination she saw the monks of the old abbey nearby, passing over it in bygone days. She visualized a constant procession of these men, now dead and gone, and had a premonition that she, too, would soon depart this life. Her mind was full of her own experience with the hopes and longings of a young Christian, and she decided that the topic of her poem should be the way of the cross of Christ. The text at the heading of her poem was Proverbs 14: 26, "His children shall have a place of refuge." The poem appeared posthumously in 1872 in "Family Treasury," which in 1874 contained another of her poems, No. 673, "There Were Ninety and Nine," both under the general title of "Breathings on the Border." The two omitted stanzas were:—

2. O safe and happy shelter,
O refuge tried and sweet,
O trysting-place where Heaven's love
And Heaven's justice meet!
As to the holy patriarch
That wondrous dream was given,
So seems my Saviour's cross to me,
A ladder up to heaven.

3. There lies beneath its shadow,
But on the further side,
The darkness of an awful grave
That gapes both deep and wide;
And there between us stands the cross,
Two arms outstretched to save,
Like a watchman set to guard the way
From that eternal grave.

The tune *St. Christopher,* named after the patron saint of travellers, was composed expressly for these words in 1881 by Frederick Charles Maker (1844-1927), a Congregational organist of three different churches in Bristol, England. He also composed Nos. 45, *Wentworth,* and 116 and 314, *Whittier,* or *Rest.*

281. THERE LIVES A VOICE WITHIN ME

John 13: 34

Gerald Massey (1828-1907) was born near Tring, Hertfordshire, the son of a canal boatman, and had little of this world's goods. He was an avid reader, a nature lover, and was largely self-taught.

He became a journalist, and considered himself the poet of the working class. He joined the Chartists, then the Christian Socialists, and later became a Spiritualist, and is said to be the original of George Eliot's "Felix Holt, the radical." In 1854 he wrote a long poem entitled "The World Is Full of Beauty," which consisted of seven stanzas each of six lines, the last two of which were a kind of refrain. The first and last of these seven stanzas were altered a little, reduced one syllable from 14.14.14.14. to become 7.6.7.6 doubled, and a new third stanza added to make this hymn. The omitted stanzas, with one original "refrain" are:—

2. Night's starry tendernesses dower with glory evermore,
Morn's budding, bright, melodious hour comes sweetly as of yore;
But there be million hearts accurst, where no sweet sun-bursts shine,
And there be million hearts athirst for Love's immortal wine.
The world is full of beauty as other worlds above,
And if we did our duty it might be full of love.

3. If faith, and hope, and kindness pass'd, as coin, twixt heart and heart,
How thro' the eye's tear-blindness should the slidden soul upstart!
The dreary, dim, and desolate, should wear a sunny bloom,
And Love should spring from buried Hate, like flowers o'er winter's tomb.

4. Were truth our uttered language, angels might talk with men.
And God-illumined earth should see the Golden Age again;
The burthen'd heart should soar in mirth like Morn's young prophet-lark,
And Misery's last tear wept on earth, quench Hell's last cunning spark.

5. Lo! plenty ripens round us, yet awakes the cry for bread,
The millions still are toiling, crusht, and clad in rags, unfed!
While sunny hills and valleys richly blush with fruit and grain,
But the paupers in the palace rob their toiling fellow-men.

6. Dear God! what hosts are trampled 'mid this killing crush for gold!
What noble hearts are sapp'd of love! what spirits lose life's hold!
Yet a merry world it might be, opulent for all, and aye,
With its lands that ask for labour, and its wealth that wastes away.

The thought in the mind of the poet is that the beauty of the earth should be an incentive to us to live a beautiful life, namely one of unselfishness and of love: "A new commandment I give unto you, That ye love one another." John 13: 34.

The tune *Berthold* is named for the composer Berthold Tours (1838-97) of Rotterdam, a violinist, teacher, and composer. It was written in 1872 and appeared in "the Hymnary" that same year, but written in the key of F, a tone higher. The music of the refrain is a direct repetition of the second half of the hymn. Tours settled in London in 1861, and became musical adviser to Novello and Company in 1875.

282. THINE FOREVER

Malachi 3: 17

Mrs. Mary Fowler Maude, née Hooper (1819-1913), the wife of the rector of St. Thomas church, Newport, Isle of Wight, regularly taught a Sunday school class of girls. In 1847 she had a sudden illness and was unable to teach her class, but she kept in touch with them by writing a weekly letter. At the end of one of these she added a poem of seven stanzas spontaneously written, five of which constitute this hymn. The omitted ones are:—

6. Thine forever, in that day
   When the world shall pass away:
   When the trumpet-note shall sound,
   And the nations underground

7. Shall the awful summons hear,
   Which proclaim the judgment near,
   Thine forever. "Neath Thy wings
   Hide and save us, King of kings."

The thought throughout is one of consecration to the Lord with the definite aim of preparing the girls in the class for confirmation in the church as full communicants. The repeated phrase "Thine forever" is the human response to the Lord's promise, "They shall be Mine, saith the Lord of hosts." Malachi 3: 17. Mrs. Maude's memory is honoured by a brass memorial plate with her name and the first two lines on the third stanza placed over the pew she used to occupy at Overton church, Flintshire, Wales.

The tune *Newington* was composed in 1875 by William Dalrymple Maclagan (1826-1910), bishop of Lichfield, who in 1891 became archbishop of York. It commemorates his time as rector at St. Mary's, Newington, London, 1869-75, where he used to hold rehearsals every Sunday evening after service for the congregation, so that they could practise the hymns for the following Sunday.

283. SAVIOUR! THY DYING LOVE

Acts 9: 6

Dr. Sylvanus Dryden Phelps (1816-95), a Baptist minister of New Haven, Connecticut, wrote these words in 1862 under the heading of Paul's question to the Lord Jesus on the road to Damascus, "Lord, what wilt Thou have me to do?" Acts 9: 6. He gave the hymn to another Baptist minister, Robert Lowry (1826-99), see appendix, at the latter's request, as with William Howard Doane, see appendix, he was compiling a hymn book.

Lowry composed the tune *Something for Jesus* in 1871 especially for these words, and included it in the collection "Pure Gold," which was a song book for Sunday schools.

284. MAKE ME A CAPTIVE, LORD

Ephesians 3: 1

Dr. George Matheson (1842-1906), a blind Scottish minister, wrote these words in 1890 at Row, Dumbartonshire, basing them on the expression of the Apostle Paul, "For this cause I Paul, the prisoner of Jesus Christ for you Gentiles." Ephesians 3: 1. It is a hymn of continual contrasts, for example: captive—free; render up sword—conqueror: sink—stand; imprison—strong; weak—master; freely—chain; enslave—reign; my own—Thine; monarch's throne —crown resign; stands—leant; these contrasts show that of the spiritual freedom of the Christian when he has become the bondslave of Jesus Christ. An omitted stanza is:—

3. My power is faint and low
Till I have learned to serve;
It wants the needed fire to glow,
It wants the breeze to nerve;
It cannot drive the world,
Until itself be driven;
Its flag can only be unfurled
When Thou shalt breathe from heaven.

Matheson also wrote No. 145, "O Love That Will Not Let Me Go."

The tune *Leominster* comes from "The Pilgrim Song" composed in 1862 by George Walter Martin (1828-81) of Battersea, London, who popularized good music and trained children's choirs, and was the conductor of the National Choral Society. The tune was arranged by Arthur Seymour Sullivan (1842-1900), see appendix.

285. I GIVE MY HEART TO THEE

Luke 24: 32

Dr. Ray Palmer (1808-87), a Congregational minister and graduate of Yale University, freely translated these words from the Latin hymn entitled "Ad Jesum" (= to Jesus) on August 20, 1868. Note that the word "heart" or "hearts" is mentioned eight times, and the word "love" or "lovest" nine times. The sentiment is the overflowing of a consecrated life in close contact with the Saviour, just as the example of the two disciples of Emmaus who "said one to another, Did not our heart burn within us, while He talked with us." Luke 24: 32. The unusual rhyming pattern is due to a selection of lines from four six-line stanzas, each followed by a two-line refrain. This refrain is actually lines three and four of our stanzas two and five, and the omitted lines are:—

2. . . .
"Give Me thine heart, My son:"
Lord, Thou my heart hast won:

4. Here finds my heart its rest,
Repose that knows no shock;
The strength of love that keeps it blest
In Thee, the riven Rock:
My soul, as girt around,
Her citadel hath found.

Palmer is also the author of Nos. 154, "Jesus, Thou Joy of Loving Hearts"; 166, "Jesus, These Eyes Have Never Seen"; 235, "We Stand in Deep Repentance," and 246, "My Faith Looks Up to Thee."

The tune *St. Michael,* also used for No. 270, "Give Thy Youth to God," where it is written a semitone lower in the key of G, was so named in 1836 by William Crotch (1775-1847), and commemorates the college of that name in Tenbury, Worcestershire, which was founded as a boys' school for general education and cultivation of church music. Crotch was a child musical prodigy who later wrote on the history and theory of music. He was principal of the Royal Academy of Music in 1822 and professor of music at the University of Oxford. *St. Michael* is an adaptation from *Old 134th,* the latter being so named because it was set to Psalm 134 in Sternhold's and Hopkins's version of the Psalms of 1562. This became known as the Old Version after the appearance of Tate and Brady's Psalm Version in 1696. In these psalters the tune is set in a still lower key, namely F major, with a minor ending.

286. I COME TO THEE, O FATHER

1 John 1:9

The authoress of this hymn was Jessie Fremont Waggoner Moser (1860-1944), who accepted the Seventh-day Adventist faith in 1869 in Iowa, and later attended Battle Creek College, Michigan, in 1876-77. When the Seventh-day Adventist Church started a children's paper, "Our Little Friend," she became the assistant editor at its inception. She took a prominent part in Sabbath school work in London, England, in Takoma Park, Washington, and in Glendale, California. She published three song books—"In His Service Songs," "Happy Songs," and "Sing and Praise"—of which she wrote the words, using well-known tunes by various composers. This hymn is a simple exposition of the words, "If we confess our sins, He is faithful and just to forgive us our sins, and to cleanse us from all unrighteousness." 1 John 1: 9.

The composer of the tune *Consecration Hymn,* Irving Arthur Steinel (1884-1945), was also a Seventh-day Adventist. He attended Battle Creek College, Michigan, and became a teacher and a church organist, teaching many years in California. No. 469, *Evans,* is also one of his compositions.

287. SAVIOUR, BLESSED SAVIOUR

Philippians 3: 14

Godfrey Thring (1823-1903), brother of the famous headmaster of Uppingham, was the editor of the "Church of England Hymn Book," 1880. He was first stimulated to write hymns when his mother could not find words to an old tune she loved. This hymn was written in 1861 and based on Philippians 3: 14, "I press toward the mark for the prize of the high calling of God in Christ Jesus," the title being "The Goal." There were eight stanzas, each following the pattern of beginning with a comparative adjective or adverb, the omitted ones being:—

4. Dark and ever darker
Was the wintry past,
Now a ray of gladness
O'er our path is cast;
Every day that passeth,
Every hour that flies,
Tells of love unfeignéd,
Love that never dies.

6. Brighter still, and brighter,
Glows the western sun,
Shedding all its gladness
O'er our work that's done;
Time will soon be over,
Toil and sorrow past,
May we, blessed Saviour,
Find a rest at last.

8. Higher then and higher,
Soars the ransomed soul,
Earthly toils forgetting,
Hastening to its goal;
Where in joys unheard of,
Saints with angels sing,
Never weary raising
Praises to their King.

Thring was also responsible for the revision of No. 162, "Crown Him With Many Crowns."

The tune *Edina* was specially composed for these words in 1868 by Herbert Stanley Oakeley (1830-1903), who also wrote No. 56, *Abends.* He was knighted in 1876 for his outstanding services to church music, and was professor of music at Edinburgh University from 1865 to 1891.

288. O JESUS, I HAVE PROMISED

John 12: 26

John E. Bode (1816-74), an Oxford don, was rector of Castle Camps, Cambridgeshire, at the time when his three children were confirmed in the Church of England. He wrote these words in 1866 especially for his daughter and two sons, the original being, "O Jesus, We Have Promised." It was published in 1868 in six stanzas as a leaflet entitled "Hymn For the Newly Confirmed." The omitted stanzas are:—

3. O! let me hear Thee speaking
In accents clear and still,
Above the storms of passion,
The murmurs of self-will:
O! speak to re-assure me,
To hasten, or control:
O! speak, and make me listen,
Thou guardian of my soul.

4. O! let me see Thy features,
The look that once could make
So many a true disciple
Leave all things for Thy sake;
The look that beamed on Peter
When he Thy name denied;
The look that draws Thy lovers
Close to Thy piercéd side.

6. O! let me see Thy footmarks,
And in them plant mine own;
My hope to follow duly
Is in Thy strength alone;
O guide me, call me, draw me,
Uphold me to the end:
And then in heaven receive me,
My Saviour and my Friend.

An appropriate text is John 12: 26: "If any man serves Me, let him follow Me; and where I am, there shall also My servant be: if any man serve Me, him will My Father honour."

The tune *Angel's Story* takes this name because it was written in 1881 by the organist Arthur Henry Mann (1850-1929) of Norwich, Norfolk, England, for the words of the hymn, "I Love to Hear the Story Which Angel Voices Tell." Mann was appointed organist and choirmaster at Kings College Chapel, Cambridge, in 1876, and as editor of the Church of England "Hymnal" in 1895. He took the Mus. Doc. degree at Oxford in 1882.

289. WEARY OF EARTH

Mark 2: 10

Samuel John Stone (1839-1900) succeeded his father as the vicar of a slum parish in London, St. Paul's, Haggerston. While there in 1866 he wrote an eight-stanza hymn based on Article 10 of the Apostles' Creed, "I believe in . . . the forgiveness of sins." His experience as described in this selection from his hymn was that of the Apostle Paul who said that "when I would do good, evil is present with me." Romans 7: 21. Stone follows on, however, to describe the forgiveness that Jesus offers: "But that ye may know that the Son of man hath power on earth to forgive sins." Mark 2: 10. Our third stanza is an addition to Stone's original, the six omitted stanzas being:—

2. So vile I am, how dare I hope to stand
In the pure glory of that holy land?
Before the whiteness of that throne appear?
Yet there are hands stretched out to draw me near.

4. It is the voice of Jesus that I hear,
His are the hands stretched out to draw me near,
And His the blood that can for all atone,
And set me faultless before the throne.

5. 'Twas He who found me on the deathly wild,
And made me heir of heaven, the Father's child,
And day by day, whereby my soul may live,
Gives me His grace of pardon, and will give.

6. O great Absolver! grant my soul may wear
The lowliest garb of penitence and prayer,
That in the Father's courts my glorious dress
May be the garment of Thy righteousness.

7. Yes, Thou wilt answer for me, righteous Lord;
Thine all the merits, mine the great reward;
Thine the sharp thorns, and mine the golden crown;
Mine the life won, and Thine the life laid down!

8. Naught can I bring, dear Lord, for all I owe,
Yet let my full heart what it can bestow;
Like that sweet nard, let my devotion prove,
Greatly forgiven, how I greatly love.

Stone's other hymn, No. 433, "The Church Has One Foundation," also combined dogma, praise, and prayer, and was based on Article 9 of the creed.

The tune *Langran* or *St. Agnes* (see words of No. 34), written in 1861, commemorates its composer, James Langran (1835-1909), a London organist and music master, who also composed Nos. 237 and 437, *Deerhurst*.

290. O LAMB OF GOD! STILL KEEP ME

Colossians 3: 3

These words were written in 1842 by James George Deck (1802-84) a minister of the Plymouth Brethren Church who after service as a soldier settled in New Zealand. An appropriate Scripture text is "For ye are dead, and your life is hid with Christ in God." Colossians 3: 3.

The tune *Chenies* was composed in 1855 for the words "From Greenland's Icy Mountains" (No. 445) by Timothy Richard Matthews (1826-1910), who was then a curate at St. Mary's, Nottingham. He had been a tutor in the family of the Rev. Lord Wriothesley Russell, canon of Windsor and rector of Chenies, Buckinghamshire, hence the name. Other tunes by Matthews are Nos. 103, *Margaret,* and 460, *Saxby.*

291. COME, THOU FOUNT OF EVERY BLESSING

1 Samuel 7: 12

Robert Robinson (1735-90) wrote these words in 1758 while a Calvinistic minister of the Methodist church in Norfolk, expressing his own feelings after his recent conversion. Omitted lines are:—

Teach me some melodious sonnet
Sung by flaming tongues above.
Praise the mount: I'm fixed upon it,
Mount of God's unchanging love.

4. Oh, that day when, freed from sinning,
I shall see Thy lovely face;
Robéd then in blood-washed linen,
Now I'll sing Thy sovereign grace.
Come, dear Lord, no longer tarry,
Take my raptured soul away;
Send Thine angels down to carry
Me to realms of endless day.

The reference in the second stanza is to 1 Samuel 7: 12, which commemorates a notable victory by the Israelites over the Philistines, "Then Samuel took a stone . . . and called the name of it Ebenezer, saying, Hitherto hath the Lord helped us." The third stanza "prone to wander" proved to be a gloomy prophecy of his own later experience, for he became successively Congregational, Baptist, and Unitarian minister, and then ceased to be a Christian altogether. On a later occasion, his companion in a stage coach was a lady who had been reading this very poem with much pleasure and profit, whereupon Robinson admitted his authorship, and said that he longed to recover the experience he had enjoyed when the words were first written.

The tune *Nettleton* is named for Asahel Nettleton (1783-1844) of Connecticut, who was an itinerant evangelist rather than a composer. He was a Yale graduate of 1809 and became a preacher for the Congregational church. He compiled "Village Hymns," published in 1824, which contained no tunes, and also edited No. 317, "I Love to Steal Awhile Away." This tune *Nettleton* had appeared in 1813 in John Wyeth's (1770-1858) Supplement, and could possibly have been his own composition, as he was a printer, music publisher, and musician. The Supplement was to his "Repository of Sacred Music," 1810. The tune is very simple, for lines 1 and 2 are repeated to give lines 3 and 4, and again to give lines 7 and 8.

292. O HOW HAPPY ARE THEY

Matthew 6: 20

Charles Wesley (1707-88), see appendix, wrote this hymn for "one fallen from grace." It had seven stanzas in Part 1, the omitted ones being:—

6. I rode on the sky
(Freely justified I!)
Nor envied Elijah his seat;
My soul mounted higher
In a chariot of fire,
And the moon it was under my feet.

7. O the rapturous height
Of that holy delight
Which I felt in the life-giving blood!
Of my Saviour possessed,
I was perfectly blessed,
As if fill'd with the fullness of God.

Then follows Part II of nine stanzas, in which he seeks to regain this former experience of peace and power. Seeing that our selection of stanzas comes from Part I only, Wesley's title is hardly appropriate, for these words describe the joyous experience of a Christian in his first love. An appropriate scripture among many that could be chosen is: "Lay up for yourselves treasures in heaven." Matthew 6: 20.

293. AWAKE! JERUSALEM, AWAKE!

Isaiah 52: 1, 2

Charles Wesley (1707-88), see appendix, wrote thirty-two stanzas, each of four lines, in 1741 as a paraphrase of the 52nd chapter of Isaiah. The present selection covers the verses: "Awake, awake; put on thy strength, O Zion; put on thy beautiful garments, O Jerusalem, the holy city. . . . Shake thyself from the dust; arise, and sit down, O Jerusalem: loose thyself from the bands of thy neck, O captive daughter of Zion." Isaiah 52: 1, 2. Wesley divided his paraphrase into three parts having ten, nine, and thirteen stanzas respectively, with a different metre for Part I. Some of the omitted stanzas are:—

Part II. 2. By impious feet no longer trod,
Thy God shall cleanse thy every stain;
O holy city of thy God,
Thou shalt not bear His name in vain.

Then follow our second and third stanzas.

5. For thus the Lord your God hath said—
Ye all have sold yourselves for nought;
A ransom (not by you) is paid,
Receive your liberty unbought.

. . . .

Part III. 1. Depart, ye ransomed souls, depart,
The house of bondage quit, be clean:
Call'd to be saints, be pure in heart,
Abhor the loathsome touch of sin.

Then follows our fourth stanza.

3. For not as fugitives, that try
By hasty flight to escape the foe,
Ye from the power of sin shall fly,
But calmly in full triumph go.

The tune *Heber* was composed in 1886 by Edwin Barnes (1864-1930), see appendix.

294. LIFT UP YOUR HEADS

Psalm 24: 7

George Weissel (1590-1635), pastor at Konigsberg, and one of Prussia's important hymn-writers, wrote five eight-line stanzas of this hymn, which was published in 1642. It is based on the well-known psalm describing the return to heaven of the ascended Christ: "Lift up your heads, O ye gates . . . and the King of glory shall come in." Psalm 24: 7. The words were translated from the German in 1855 by Catherine Winkworth (1827-78), see appendix, and each stanza was abbreviated to four lines written in long metre, i.e., 8.8.8.8., whereas the original was in 8.8.8.8.8.8.6.8. Omitted lines are the latter halves of each stanza:—

1. Life and salvation doth He bring,
Wherefore rejoice, and gladly sing
Praise, O my God, to Thee!
Creator, wise is Thy decree!

2. The end of all our woe He brings,
Wherefore the earth is glad and sings
Praise, O my God, to Thee!
O Saviour, great Thy deeds shall be!

3. The cloudless Sun of joy He is,
Who bringeth pure delight and bliss,
Praise, O my God, to Thee!
Comforter, for Thy comfort free!

4. So shall your Sovereign enter in,
And new and nobler life begin.
Praise, O my God, be Thine,
For word, and deed, and grace divine.

5. Thy Holy Spirit guide us on
Until our glorious goal is won!
Eternal praise and fame
Be offer'd, Saviour, to Thy name!

The tune *Wareham* was composed in 1738 for Psalm 36: 5-10 by William Knapp (1698-1768), and named in honour of his birthplace in Wareham, Dorsetshire, where he was also organist at one time. The same tune, dropped a semitone to the key of A, is used for No. 188, "Star of Our Hope." It is noteworthy that the melody, with one exception in line one, proceeds by successive notes of the scale.

295. AMAZING GRACE!

1 Chronicles 17: 16, 17

John Newton (1725-1807), see appendix, never ceased to thank God for His saving grace in transforming him from a slave and slave-captain to a gospel minister. In this hymn, originally of six stanzas appearing in the "Olney Hymns," 1779, and entitled "Faith's Review and Expectation," he mentions "grace" six times in our present three stanzas. It is a hymn of his own experience and is based on David's humble remarks in 1 Chronicles 17: 16, 17, "Who am I, O Lord God, and what is mine house . . . Thou hast . . . regarded me according to the estate of a man of high degree, O Lord God." The three omitted stanzas are:—

4. The Lord has promised good to me,
His word my hope secures;
He will my shield and portion be,
As long as life endures.

5. Yea, when this flesh and heart shall fail,
And mortal life shall cease;
I shall possess, within the veil,
A life of joy and peace.

6. The earth shall soon dissolve like snow,
The sun forbear to shine;
But God, who called me here below,
Will be for ever mine.

The tune *Belmont* was originally a popular song, but was one of the many adapted by William Gardiner (1770-1853), a stocking manufacturer of Leicester, who used to take instrumental classics and use them as hymn tunes. This one appeared in his "Sacred Melodies I," of 1812. The name Belmont is a corruption of Bellemont or Beaumont, a family whose residence was Beau manor in Leicestershire, England. Gardiner also arranged No. 519, *Gardiner.*

296. WE SING THE PRAISE

Galatians 6: 14

Thomas Kelly (1769-1855) wrote these words in 1815, on the theme of the cross, expanding the thought expressed in Galatians 6: 14: "God forbid that I should glory, save in the cross of our Lord Jesus Christ." The first two stanzas mention the cross and the sacrifice made there by the Lord Jesus; the last three describe its many functions, using eight sentences and five phrases all in apposition to the opening words of the third stanza, "the cross." Stanza five originally ended: " 'Tis all that sinners want below; 'Tis all that angels know above." Kelly was ordained to the Church of England ministry but finally left this communion because of his strong evangelical views. He built four Independent churches in Ireland from his own private means for the promulgation of his beliefs. He also wrote Nos. 192, "Hark! That Shout"; 220, "I Love the Sacred Book," and 308, "We've No Abiding City Here," as well as over 750 others.

The tune *Angelus,* in its first half is an arrangement from Georg Joseph, a German court musician who flourished about 1657, and who adapted secular tunes to make them suitable for hymn tunes. He also composed tunes for a number of hymns written by Johann Scheffler (1624-77), who adopted the name of Angelus Silesius, hence the name given to this tune.

297. LET HEAVEN HIGHEST PRAISES BRING

Revelation 5: 9

This is probably an Italian hymn written in the 13th century by Giovanni de Fidenza, otherwise Saint Bonaventura (1221-74). The story goes that he was only four years old and was stricken with a serious illness and expected to die. However, his mother vowed to dedicate him to the Franciscan order of monks if he recovered, and noticing an immediate change for the better, she exclaimed, "O bonaventura" (= O what good fortune, or happy event). Fidenza became bishop of Albano, and ultimately General of the Order of Franciscans, and a writer on theology and philosophy. The church canonized him in 1482. The words, which were translated by Heloise Soule, remind us of the song of the twenty-four elders who "sung a new song, saying, Thou art worthy . . . for Thou wast slain, and hast redeemed us to God by Thy blood out of every kindred, and tongue, and people, and nation." Revelation 5: 9. Notice the unusual rhyming pattern which is aaabcccb.

The tune *Bonaventura,* named after the author of the words, is by John Henry Gower (1855-1922), Mus. D., a noted organist both in Nottingham, England, and also in Denver, Colorado.

298. HARK, MY SOUL! IT IS THE LORD

John 21: 16

William Cowper (1731-1800), see appendix, suffered several times from mental ailments and was often grievously perplexed concerning his relationship to God. These periods were followed by ones of calm and serenity, and this hymn, entitled "Divine Love," was written at Huntingdon about the year 1765, when the poet was rejoicing in the knowledge of sins forgiven. He likens himself to the repentant Apostle Peter, for this hymn is based on our Lord's repeated question to that disciple, "Simon, son of Jonas, lovest thou Me?" John 21: 16. There were originally six stanzas in No. CXVIII of "Olney Hymns," 1779, those omitted being:—

2. I deliver'd thee when bound,
And, when wounded, heal'd thy wound;
Sought thee wand'ring, set thee right,
Turn'd thy darkness into light.

3. Can a woman's tender care
Cease toward the child she bare!
Yea, she may forgetful be,
Yet will I remember thee.

The tune *St. Bees* was composed in 1862 by John Bacchus Dykes (1823-76), see appendix, while practising with the choir boys at Durham cathedral. He would often drift into some new composition, and this melody kept being repeated. He named it *St. Bees* after the small coastal village in Cumberland where he spent many happy hours. It was originally intended for the hymn "Jesus, Name of Wondrous Love" by Bishop William Walsham How (1823-97), see appendix.

299. THERE IS A LAND OF PURE DELIGHT

Revelation 21: 1

Isaac Watts (1674-1748), see appendix, was sitting at his window in Southampton in 1706, gazing across Southampton Water towards Netley. The pleasant meadows set out before him suggested to him the beauties of the heavenly land, and inspired him to write six stanzas of this hymn, each of four lines. The title he gave was, "A Prospect of Heaven Makes Death Easy," and he uses the figure of the Jordan River as a symbol of death, to be crossed before we reach the promised land. The other two stanzas are:—

3. Sweet fields beyond the swelling flood
Stand dressed in living green;
So to the Jews old Canaan stood,
While Jordan rolled between.

4. But timorous mortals start and shrink
To cross this narrow sea,
And linger shivering on the brink,
And fear to launch away.

The original last two lines of the hymn were

Not Jordan's stream, nor death's cold flood
Should fright us from our shore.

The perfect, restored Eden is described in the last two chapters of the Bible, introduced by the words, "And I saw a new heaven and a new earth." Revelation 21: 1.

The tune *Varina,* used also for No. 93, "I Sing the Mighty Power," was published in 1856 by George Frederick Root (1820-95), an American choir conductor, music teacher and music publisher who was associated with Lowell Mason in the Boston Academy of Music, and who composed many sentimental ballads. He also composed Nos. 418, *Jewels;* 620, unnamed, and 690, *Quam Dilecta.*

300. JERUSALEM THE GOLDEN

Revelation 21: 2

Bernard of Cluny was born of English parents at Morlas in France early in the 12th century, and entered the monastery of Cluny as a monk. This was a very luxurious living and in strong contrast to the prevailing misery in the world. The corruptions and evil of the world, compared with the glories of the New Jerusalem described in the last two chapters of the Bible, led Bernard in 1145 to write a satire on the state of the world. This was a long poem of about 3,000 lines entitled "De Contemptu Mundi" (= on disdain of the world), and sometimes known by its first two words,

Hora novissima (= most recent times). Bernard said that he believed that only the inspiration of the Spirit of God enabled him to write the poem, especially in view of its unusual metre, namely: Hora novissima, tempora péssima sunt; vigilémus. Various translators have retained this metre; for example, Samuel W. Duffield in 1867: These are the latter times, These are not better times; Let us stand waiting.

Or Jackson Mason in 1880:

> Earth very evil is;
> Time through the last of his
> Journeys is hasting.

Or Gerald Moultrie in 1865:

> Here we have many fears,
> This is a vale of tears,
> The land of sorrow;
> Tears are there none at all
> In that celestial hall,
> In life's bright morrow.

The same metre and lilt occur in some of Tennyson's lines in his "Charge of the Light Brigade":

> Their's not to reason why,
> Their's but to do or die,
> Noble six hundred.

Dr. John Mason Neale (1818-66), see appendix, translated in 1849 about 200 lines from the Latin of Bernard's poem, and called it "The Rhythm of the Heavenly Country." From this are taken this hymn and also the fairly well-known hymns, "Brief Life Is Here Our Portion"; "For Thee, O Dear, Dear Country," and "The World Is Very Evil." From one section of twenty-eight successive lines come the first three stanzas of this hymn together with the omitted lines:—

> And when I fain would sing them,
> My spirit fails and faints—
> And vainly would it image
> The assembly of the saints.

These lines appear between stanzas one and two. The description is part of that given in the closing chapters of the Scriptures, in which a vision is given of "the Holy City, New Jerusalem, coming down from God out of heaven, prepared as a bride adorned for her husband." Revelation 21: 2.

The tune *Ewing* is named after its composer, Alexander Ewing (1830-95) of Aberdeen, a lawyer who became a musician. He composed it in 1853 for the words, "For thee, O dear, dear country" and handed it to William Carnie, the conductor of an Aberdeen choir of which Ewing was a member, to try out, and it was immediately successful. It was originally written in triple time, but changed in

"Hymns Ancient and Modern" to the present common time. The range for the soprano part is unusually great, namely an octave and a third, from D flat to F an octave above.

301. THERE IS A HAPPY LAND

Numbers 10: 29

In this hymn the music came first and stimulated the writing of the words. Andrew Young (1807-89), F.R.S., F.R.G.S., headmaster of the Niddry Street school, Edinburgh, was spending a holiday in 1838 at Rothesay on the Isle of Bute. While there he heard the Indian air called *Happy Land* and it appealed to him very much. This is found in "Selected Melodies with Appropriate Words," 1827, and has the words, "I have come from a happy land where care is unknown." Young thought it would be very popular among his Sunday school children if only there were some suitable words to sing to it. So using the theme of *Happy Land,* the title of the tune, he wrote the words of this hymn, which as he had anticipated, proved very popular with the children who sang it in the day school also. The words are based on the words of Moses, "We are journeying unto the place of which the Lord said, I will give it you: come thou with us." Numbers 10: 29.

The melody *World to Come* was harmonized by the Rev. James Gall (1808-95) and appeared in the "Sacred Song Book," 1843. It will be noted that the melody is in the pentatonic scale (see No. 181), and has now been named because of the associated words telling of the world to come.

302. HAIL TO THE BRIGHTNESS

Isaiah 60: 1-3

Thomas Hastings (1784-1872), see appendix, in this hymn written in 1830 describes the triumph of the church much after the fashion of the prophet Isaiah's picture—"Arise, shine; for thy light is come, and the glory of the Lord is risen upon thee. For, behold, the darkness shall cover the earth, and gross darkness the people. . . . And the Gentiles shall come to thy light, and kings to the brightness of thy rising." Isa. 60: 1-3. The omitted stanza is:—

Hail to the brightness of Zion's glad morning!
Long by the prophets of Israel foretold!
Hail to the millions from bondage returning!
Gentiles and Jews the blest vision behold.

The tune *Wesley* was composed in 1830 by Lowell Mason (1792-1872), see appendix, especially for these words, and the complete hymn was first published by Hastings and Mason in their collection, "Spiritual Songs," 1831. The tune was first called *Hail to the Brightness,* and so known till 1850.

303. DAUGHTER OF ZION

Isaiah 52: 1, 2

This anonymous hymn is stated in Mason's and Greene's "Church Psalmody," 1831, to be an anthem from "Fitzgerald's Collection," 1830, and describes the victory of the church in language borrowed from both Isaiah and the Psalms. "Awake, awake; put on strength, O Zion; put on thy beautiful garments, O Jerusalem, the holy city. . . . Shake thyself from the dust . . . O captive daughter of Zion." "The Assyrian oppressed them without cause." "Break forth into joy, sing together." Isaiah 52: 1, 2, 4, 9. "Let the children of Zion be joyful in their King. . . . Let them sing praises unto Him with the timbrel and harp." Psalm 149: 2, 3.

The tune *Daughter of Zion* in six lines is really only a four line tune with the other two lines repeating lines 1 and 2, words as well as music.

304. GLORIOUS THINGS OF THEE ARE SPOKEN

Isaiah 33: 20, 21

John Newton (1725-1807), see appendix, wrote this hymn of five stanzas at Olney, Buckinghamshire, in 1779, especially for one of his weekly prayer meetings, and it appears as No. LX in "Olney Hymns." Its title was "Zion or the City of God" and it opens with an almost exact quotation from Psalm 87: 3, "Glorious things are spoken of thee, O city of God." Then as well as referring to several other scriptures it paraphrases somewhat Isaiah 33: 20, 21, "Look upon Zion, the city of our solemnities: thine eyes shall see Jerusalem a quiet habitation. . . . There the glorious Lord will be unto us a place of broad rivers and streams." The eight lines omitted are the last halves of the original third and fourth stanzas:

3. . . .
Thus deriving from their banner
Light by night and shade by day;
Safe they feed upon the manna
Which He gives them when they pray.

4. . . .
'Tis His love His people raises
Over self to reign as kings
And as priests, His solemn praises
Each for a thank-off'ring brings.

The first halves are our third stanza, and Newton's fifth is our fourth.

The tune *Austrian Hymn* was composed in 1797 by Franz Joseph Haydn (1732-1809) at the suggestion of the prime minister of Austria. He wanted a "Hymn to the Emperor" to counteract the successful campaigns of Napoleon, and this tune was played in Vienna on the birthday of the Emperor Francis I, February 12, 1797, to the words "God save the Emperor Francis." The composer on his visits to London had envied the English their national anthem, and this stimulated him to write this stirring tune to the words by L. L. Haschka, "Gott erhalte Franz den Kaiser." Haydn also composed No. 91, *Creation.* This famous Austrian composer prefaced all his compositions with the words "In nomine Domini" (= in the name of the Lord) and concluded them with the words "Laus Deo" (= praise to God). *Austria* is a theme in his Emperor Quartet, Opus 76, No. 3.

305. WE HAVE HEARD

Revelation 22: 1, 2, 4

William H. Hyde was an early Seventh-day Adventist who had been influenced by a group of fanatics. He was very sick with dysentery, and the doctor had given him no hope of recovery. Pastor James and Mrs. Ellen G. White (then Miss Harmon) visited him in Maine early in 1845 and persuaded him to leave those who were teaching error. They prayed for his restoration to health and he was immediately and permanently healed. (See *"Life Sketches,"* pages 75, 76.) Later he saw Ellen Harmon in vision, and the words of this hymn make a summary of her first vision given in December, 1844, but not published until 1846. The hymn appeared in the *Review and Herald* of July, 1850, and was the first published poem of a Seventh-day Adventist. Phrases and sentences from the vision (see *"Early Writings,"* pages 10-15) are extracted below in order to show how the author received his stimulus from Ellen G. White's description of the heavenly land.

Stanza 1: "A glorious light—far above the dark world—on this path the Advent people were travelling—I saw most glorious houses—to be inhabited by the saints—a pure river of water."

Stanza 2: "A field of tall grass—living green—it waved proudly—field full of all kinds of flowers—mountains, on which grew roses—the angels struck a note higher and sung again."

Stanza 3: "He gave us harps of gold and palms of victory—they were all clothed with a glorious white mantle—the gate of the city—the pearly gate—we all cried out, Alleluia —the fruit of the tree of life."

Stanza 4: "King Jesus—upon His head were many crowns—His eyes were as a flame of fire—in a little while—clean hands and pure hearts—and be at rest."

The last two chapters of the Bible give a description of this better land: "And he showed me a pure river of water of life. . . . And on either side of the river, was there the tree of life, which bare twelve manner of fruits, and . . . the leaves of the tree were for the healing of the nations." "And they shall see His face." Revelation 22: 1, 2, 4. Reminding Mrs. Ellen Gould White of her first vision, it is not surprising that it was one of her favourite hymns, and was sung by her just before her death in 1915.

The tune *We Have Heard* is also called *Better Land.* Of its eight lines, the first, third, and seventh are identical.

306. TEN THOUSAND TIMES TEN THOUSAND

Revelation 21: 4

Henry Alford (1810-71), dean of Canterbury from 1857, wrote three stanzas of this hymn in 1866 and added the fourth in 1870. It was intended as a funeral hymn which depicted the future glories of the deceased, thus providing an antidote to the gloom and sadness that perforce accompanies a bereavement. Alford was a great scholar of the Greek New Testament and there are many Scriptural thoughts and phrases contained in this hymn, the main one being the comforting promise, "And God shall wipe away all tears from their eyes; and there shall be no more death." Rev. 21: 4. Dean Alford also wrote No. 496, "Come, Ye Thankful People."

The tune *Alford,* commemorating the author of the words, was composed especially for these words in 1875 by John Bacchus Dykes (1823-76), see appendix.

307. THE TIME IS NEAR

Isaiah 26: 1, 2

Roswell Fenner Cottrell (1814-92) was brought up as a Seventh-day Baptist, but after contact with the church paper *Review and Herald* he joined the Seventh-day Adventist Church in 1851 and began preaching in 1855. He was one of the pioneers in tent-meeting evangelism, and a regular contributor both in poetry and prose to the *Review and Herald,* of which his great-grandson became an associate editor in 1957. The hymn paraphrases Isaiah 26: 1, 2: "In that day shall this song be sung in the land of Judah; We have a strong city; salvation will God appoint for walls and bulwarks. Open ye the gates, that the righteous nation which keepeth the truth may enter in." Cottrell also wrote Nos. 143, "The Wonders of Redeeming Love," and 481, "O Solemn Thought!"

The tune *Anvern* was composed by Lowell Mason (1792-1872), see appendix. The soprano part has an unusually wide range, from middle C to F an octave above, a compass of eleven notes.

308. WE'VE NO ABIDING CITY HERE

Hebrews 13: 14

Thomas Kelly (1769-1855) was an evangelical preacher who finally left the Church of England because of his emphasis on the doctrine of the second advent of Christ. From his own private means he built four Independent churches in Ireland to propagate his views. This hymn, one of 765 that he wrote, was written in 1802, and entitled "Seeking Heaven." It is based on Hebrews 13: 14: "For here have we no continuing city, but we seek one to come." His own belief in an imminent second advent is shown by his reply to an old school friend who said, "You will live to a great age." The reply was, "Yes, I am confident I shall, as I expect never to die." He also wrote Nos. 192, "Hark! That Shout"; 220, "I Love the Sacred Book," and 296, "We Sing the Praise."

The tune *Andre* is unusual in that its first two lines consist of one chord only and its inversion, with some passing notes.

309. JERUSALEM, MY HAPPY HOME

Revelation 21: 10-12, 21

Joseph Bromehead (1747-1826) published in 1795 the "Eckington Psalms and Hymns," in which this particular hymn appears. In the preface he regrets his inability to give the authors of many of the selections and this one is identified simply by the initials F. B. P. This could be F. B. Price, or Francis Baker, priest (or pater), who was a Roman Catholic imprisoned for his faith in the Tower of London during the sixteenth century. Roman Catholic authorities state that the author was Father Laurence Anderton of the period of King Charles I. There are twenty-six stanzas altogether and they are based on a passage from Augustine which describes the glories of the New Jerusalem, this itself being taken from John's apocalyptic vision given in the last two chapters of the Bible: "That great city, the holy Jerusalem, descending out of heaven from God, having the glory of God: and her light was like unto a stone most precious, even like a jasper stone, clear as crystal; and had a wall great and high, and had twelve gates." "Every several gate was of one pearl: and the street of the city was pure gold." Revelation 21: 10-12, 21. Seven other stanzas, with spelling modernized, are:—

Thy saints are crowned with glory great,
They see God face to face;
They triumph still, they still rejoice;
Most happy is their case.

There David stands with harp in hand
As master of the choir;
Ten thousand times that man were blest
That might this music hear.

10. Within thy gates no thing doth come
That is not passing clean,
No spider's web, no dirt, no dust,
No filth may there be seen.

16. Thy vineyards and thy orchards are
Most beautiful and fair,
Full furnishéd with trees and fruits,
Exceeding rich and rare.

20. Quite through the street with silver sound,
The flood of life doth flow,
Upon those banks on every side,
The wood of life doth grow.

21. There trees for evermore bear fruit,
And evermore do spring;
And evermore the angels sit,
And evermore do sing.

26. Jerusalem! my happy home!
Would God I were in thee!
Would God my woes were at an end,
Thy joys that I might see!

The present selection is stanzas 1 (similar to 26), 7, 17 with alterations, and our fourth stanza in "Church Hymnal" is from some other source.

The tune *St. Peter,* also used for Nos. 150, "How Sweet the Name," and 436, "In Christ There Is No East or West," was composed about 1836 by Alexander Robert Reinagle (1799-1877). Of Austrian descent, he was organist at St. Peter's-in-the-East, Oxford, for over thirty years, and commemorated this church by his hymn tune. The soprano part is noteworthy in the first two lines for a descending scale passage of a complete octave, some notes being repeated.

310. O HAPPY DAY! THAT FIXED MY CHOICE

2 Chronicles 15: 15

Philip Doddridge (1702-51), see appendix, wrote these words without a refrain in 1735 and entitled them, "Rejoicing in Our Covenant Engagements with God." The hymn is based on the story recorded in 2 Chronicles 15: 15: "And all Judah rejoiced at the oath: for they had sworn with all their heart, and sought Him with their whole desire; and He was found of them: and the Lord gave them rest round about." Another stanza, now omitted, reads:—

2. O happy bond, that seals my vows
   To Him who merits all my love!
   Let cheerful anthems fill His house,
   While to that sacred shrine I move.

The present fifth stanza and refrain are additions to the hymn as found in the posthumous 1755 edition, and another change appears in the last half of our third stanza from the original:—

With ashes who would grudge to part
When call'd on angels' food to feast?

The tune is named *Happy Day* because of the opening words and the repetition of this phrase in the refrain. It was an adaptation made in 1854 of a tune *Happy Land,* composed by Edward Francis Rimbault (1816-76) of Soho, London, who also arranged No. 605, *Rutherford.* He began his career as an organist and then, with others, founded in 1840 the Music Antiquarian Society, taking a great interest in editing old church music. The tune does not show much variety, for lines 1 and 3 are identical, as also are lines 5 and 9, lines 7 and 8, and lines 2, 4, 6, 10.

311. PEACE, PERFECT PEACE

Isaiah 26: 3

Edward Henry Bickersteth (1825-1906), later bishop of Exeter, was staying in Harrogate, Yorkshire, in 1875, and heard a sermon based on the words: "Thou wilt keep him in perfect peace." Isaiah 26: 3. That same afternoon he visited a dying relative and cheered his despondency by reminding him of this text. Within a few minutes he had composed the hymn of seven stanzas which is a series of questions and answers. The omitted stanzas are:—

6. Peace, perfect peace, death shadowing us and ours?
   Jesus has vanquished death and all its powers.

7 It is enough; earth's struggles soon shall cease,
   And Jesus call us to heaven's perfect peace.

It was the custom for each member of his family to repeat a hymn at tea-time on Sundays, and he read this newly written one as his contribution. It received wide circulation through the years and an invalid wrote to Bickersteth pointing out that sickness had not been mentioned as one of the disturbing experiences of life, whereupon he wrote the following additional couplet but did not include it officially as part of the hymn:—

Peace, perfect peace—mid suffering's sharpest throes?
The sympathy of Jesus breathes repose.

The tune *Pax Tecum* (= peace be with thee) was composed specially for these words by George Thomas Caldbeck (1852-1918) when he was a student at the Islington theological college, London. Later he became a seller of tracts and text-cards, and when arrested for not having a licence, was dismissed by the magistrate when it was learned that he had written this tune. Harmonization was supplied in 1877 by Charles John Vincent, Mus. Doc. (1852-1934), an organ builder and piano manufacturer, and a noted composer, organist, and examiner in music for the Trinity College of Music, London.

312. WEEPING ENDURES BUT FOR A NIGHT

Psalm 30:5

This hymn was written in 1853 by Annie Rebekah Smith (1828-55), see appendix, and contrasts the darkness of earth's night of weeping with the glory of heaven's light and eternal joy. It appears on the first page of the *Review and Herald* for November 1, 1853, under the title, "Joy Cometh! Psalm 30: 5." The hymn opens with a quotation from this verse, "Weeping may endure for a night, but joy cometh in the morning." There were seven stanzas, the omitted one being:—

5. Let hope thy bosom cheer, forlorn,
To boldly breast each rising storm;
For whatsoe'er thy grief may be,
The morning bringeth joy to thee.

The tune *Melcombe* was composed in 1782 by Samuel Webbe (1740-1816) of London, a Roman Catholic organist and composer, and it is also used for No. 42, "New Every Morning." It has an interesting bass part which most unusually moves successively (with one exception) to different notes; the soprano part moves steadily, too, with no large intervals between successive notes, producing a pleasant, flowing melody. The tune derives its name probably from Melcombe Regis, the northern part of Weymouth, Dorset, which was made famous by the frequent visits there of King George III. Webbe also composed No. 223, *Consolation,* and probably Nos. 87, *Dulce Carmen,* and 105 and 255, *Portuguese Hymn.*

313. WHEN PEACE, LIKE A RIVER

2 Kings 4: 26

Horatio Gates Spafford (1829-88) was a Chicago lawyer who in 1874 sent his wife Anna Lawson Spafford and four daughters, Maggie, Tanetta, Annie and Bessie, aged from eighteen months to twelve years, on a holiday trip to Europe. They were travelling on the ship *Ville de Havre* which collided off Newfoundland with another vessel, the *Loch Earn,* and sank within half an hour. Mrs. Spafford was rescued but all her children were drowned, her youngest being washed from her grasp, and ten days after when she landed at Cardiff she sent a cable to her anxious husband, "Saved alone." He sailed across the Atlantic to meet his wife and they both met the evangelist Dwight Lyman Moody in Liverpool. He comforted them in their sad bereavement and noted their expression of trust and confidence in God in spite of their personal sorrow. "It is well," they said, "the will of God be done." Spafford, who was the elder of a Presbyterian church in Chicago, had the cabled message framed and hung in his office, and on the occasion of Ira David Sankey's visit in 1876 again expressed his resignation to God's will. It was then that he was inspired to put his thoughts into verse, and two years after the tragedy the hymn was written. The theme recalls the question put by the prophet Elisha to the Shunammite woman, "Is it well with thee? is it well with thy husband? is it well with the child? and she answered, It is well." 2 Kings 4: 26.

The tune *It Is Well* was composed by Phillip P. Bliss (1838-76), see appendix, especially for these words.

314. WHEN DARKNESS GATHERS

2 Corinthians 4: 17, 18

In these words Annie Rebekah Smith (1828-55), see appendix, adopts the thought of the Apostle Paul who wrote, "For our light affliction, which is but for a moment, worketh for us a far more exceeding and eternal weight of glory; while we look not at the things which are seen, but at the things which are not seen."

2 Corinthians 4: 17, 18. So she contrasts the darkness, the persecution, and the sorrow of this earthly pilgrimage with the sweetness of the promised heaven, with its light, its smiles, its joy, and its eternal home. The hymn was originally a very personal one, for where we now have "our" and "our wayward" in the fourth lines of the first two stanzas, Miss Smith wrote "thy" and "thy youthful," as well as "thy" for "the" in the second line of the third stanza.

The tune *Rest,* which was specially written for and is used for No. 116, "Dear Lord and Father," was composed in 1887 by Frederick Charles Maker (1844-1927), a Bristol organist in three Congregational churches there. It is sometimes known as *Elton.* Maker also composed Nos. 45, *Wentworth,* and 280, *St. Christopher.*

315. STILL WITH THEE

John 17: 24

James Drummond Burns (1823-64) was a minister of the Free Church of Scotland, and wrote this hymn of six stanzas in 1857 while he was in charge of the Hampstead Presbyterian church, London. It is one of his thirty-one original hymns written for every evening of the month, as also is his other hymn, No. 428, "Hushed Was the Evening Hymn." The omitted stanzas are:—

3. With Thee amid the crowd
That throngs the busy mart,
To hear Thy voice, where time's is loud,
Speak softly to my heart.

5. With Thee when darkness brings
The signal of repose,
Calm in the shadow of Thy wings
Mine eyelids I would close.

The constantly recurring expression, "with Thee," appearing twice in each stanza, recalls the prayer of Jesus, "I will that they also, whom Thou hast given Me, be with Me where I am." John 17: 24.

The tune *Greenwood* was composed in 1849 by Joseph Emerson Sweetser (1825-75) and is used also for No. 40, "Sweetly the Holy Hymn." He was an organist who emigrated from England to the United States, and who joined George Frederick Root (1820-95) (see No. 93) in publication of a collection of church music in 1849, from which this tune is taken.

316. SWEET HOUR OF PRAYER

Psalm 55: 17

William W. Walford, a blind English minister, recited this poem in or about the year 1842 to his acquaintance Thomas Salmon, who was a Congregational minister at Coleshill, Warwickshire, from 1838-42. The latter wrote it down and took it across the Atlantic with him where it was published in the *New York Observer* in 1849 as four stanzas each of eight lines. The omitted stanza is:—

2. Sweet hour of prayer, sweet hour of prayer
The joy I feel, the bliss I share,
Of those whose anxious spirits burn
With strong desire for thy return;
With such I hasten to the place
Where God, my Saviour, shows His face,
And gladly take my station there,
To wait for thee, sweet hour of prayer.

As the psalmist says, any time is appropriate for prayer, "Evening, and morning, and at noon, will I pray, and cry aloud: and He shall hear my voice." Psalm 55: 17.

The tune *Sweet Hour* was specially composed for these words in 1859 by William Batchelder Bradbury (1816-68), see appendix, and is so named because of the opening and closing phrases of each stanza. It shows very little variation, for lines 1, 3 and 7 are identical; so are lines 4 and 8, these resembling line 2 quite closely; and lines 5 and 6 are almost the same.

317. I LOVE TO STEAL AWHILE AWAY

Psalm 104: 34

Mrs. Phoebe Hinsdale Brown (1783-1861), lived in poverty after her marriage in Ellington, Connecticut, and found life extremely difficult. She had four little children, a sick sister, and lived in a small, unfinished house where there was no place for quiet relaxation and private devotion. So at dusk she made a practice of walking along to a wealthy mansion near by which had a large garden. She enjoyed the aroma of the flowers and the quiet communion with God after the taxing duties of the day. However, her motives were misconstrued, for one evening she was rudely rebuked by the owner of the garden, whereupon Mrs. Brown returned home and poured out her soul in the words of this hymn. It carried the title "An Apology for My Twilight Rambles, Addressed to a Lady, August, 1818." It had nine stanzas, the omitted ones being:—

1. Yes, when the toilsome day is gone,
And night, with banners grey,
Steals silently the glade along
In twilight's soft array,

2. This is our first stanza with a change from the original "little ones and care" to "every cumbering care."

3. I love to feast on nature's scenes
When falls the evening dew,
And dwell upon her silent themes,
For ever rich and new.

6. I love to meditate on death!
When shall his message come
With friendly smiles to steal my breath
And take an exile home?

8. I love this silent twilight hour
Far better than the rest;
It is, of all the twenty-four,
The happiest and the best.

9. Thus, when life's toilsome day is o'er
May its departing ray
Be calm as this impressive hour,
And lead to endless day.

A suitable Scripture summary could be, "My meditation of Him shall be sweet: I will be glad in the Lord." Psalm 104: 34. The nine stanzas were compressed to five by the itinerant evangelist Asahel Nettleton (1783-1844) and published in his "Village Hymns," 1824, and slight changes were made by Mrs. Brown. Nettleton was a Yale graduate who became a Congregational preacher and hymn compiler. He could have been the composer of No. 291, *Nettleton,* which carries his name.

The tune *Brown,* named in honour of the authoress of the words, was composed in 1844 by William Batchelder Bradbury (1816-68), see appendix.

318. COME, MY SOUL

1 Kings 3: 5

This is one of the "Olney Hymns" written in 1779 by John Newton (1725-1807), see appendix, and is based on the Lord's gracious offer to King Solomon, "Ask what I shall give thee." 1 Kings 3: 5. The original had seven stanzas and shows that Newton's urgent request was for forgiveness of sin and power to live a holy life. The omitted stanzas are:—

2. Thou art coming to a King,
Large petitions with thee bring;
For His grace and power are such,
None can ever ask too much.

5. As the image in the glass
Answers the beholder's face;
Thus unto my heart appear,
Print Thine own resemblance there.

6. While I am a pilgrim here,
Let Thy love my spirit cheer;
Be my guide, my guard, my friend,
Lead me to my journey's end.

7. Show me what I have to do;
Every hour my strength renew;
Let me live a life of faith;
Let me die Thy people's death.

The tune *Seymour,* also used for No. 48, "Softly Now the Light of Day," is an arrangement made in 1851 by Henry Wellington Greatorex (1813-58), an organist at the Center church, Hartford, Connecticut. The name commemorates a bass singer in the choir in that church. The original tune was composed by Carl Maria Friedrich Ernst von Weber (1786-1826) as an opening chorus of the opera "Oberon," written 1824-26, which he had been commissioned to write for the Covent Garden Theatre, London. He also composed No. 404, *Jewett.* Greatorex also arranged Nos. 25 and 383, *Manoah,* and composed Nos. 174, *Leighton,* and 689, *Gloria Patri.*

319. PRAYER IS THE SOUL'S SINCERE DESIRE

Luke 11: 1

This expanded definition of prayer was written in 1818 by James Montgomery (1771-1854), see appendix, at the request of the Rev. Edward Bickersteth (father of the author of hymn No. 311) who was writing a treatise on prayer. The words were certainly written from the heart, for not until he was forty-three years of age, that is, four years earlier, did he learn to know God as One who answers prayer. The original poem had eight stanzas but no refrain and was entitled, "What Is Prayer?" The omitted stanzas are:—

5. Prayer is the contrite sinner's voice
Returning from his ways,
While angels in their songs rejoice,
And cry, "Behold, he prays!"

6. In prayer on earth the saints are one,
In word, and deed, and mind;
When with the Father and His Son
Sweet fellowship they find.

7. Nor prayer is made on earth alone,
The Holy Spirit pleads,
And Jesus, on the eternal throne,
For sinners intercedes.

The eighth and last stanza is the last four lines of the last stanza in "Church Hymnal," and the very last words, nearly an exact quotation of Scripture, summarize the hymn—"Lord, teach us to pray." Luke 11: 1. The first six words of the hymn are written on the monument over the poet's grave in Sheffield, Yorkshire. The refrain is taken from "The Rime of the Ancient Mariner," by Samuel Taylor Coleridge (1772-1834).

The tune *Audite Audientes Me* (= Hear me, ye who listen) was composed in 1875 by Arthur Seymour Sullivan (1842-1900), see appendix. Note that it begins in a minor key and ends in a major key.

320. WHAT A FRIEND WE HAVE IN JESUS

1 Peter 5: 7

Joseph Medlicott Scriven (1820-86), an Irishman who emigrated to Canada at the age of 25, wrote these words in 1855 at Port Hope, Ontario, Canada. They were never intended as a hymn for public use but were specially written to comfort his mother at a time of sorrow. It was not generally known in his neighbourhood that he was the author of the hymn, and when questioned about it, he replied, "The Lord and I did it between us." The words are an apt commentary on Psalm 55: 22, "Cast thy burden upon the Lord," and on 1 Peter 5: 7, "Casting all your care upon Him; for He careth for you."

The tune *Converse* was composed in 1868 and published in 1870 by Charles Crozat Converse (1832-1918), a lawyer and musician of Erie, Pennsylvania, and is named to commemorate him. As well as church music he also composed overtures and symphonies. He had studied music in Leipzig, but took up a law practice. Lines 1, 3 and 7 of this tune are identical, as are also lines 4 and 8.

321. SUN OF MY SOUL

Luke 24: 29

This hymn is part of a fourteen-stanza poem written on November 25, 1820, by John Keble (1792-1866) while he was a tutor at the University of Oxford, and curate of East Leach and Burthorpe. The first four words are a metaphor referring to a preceding stanza which refers to the setting of the literal sun. This and other omitted stanzas are:—

1. 'Tis gone, that bright and orbéd blaze,
Fast fading from our wistful gaze;
Yon mantling cloud has hid from sight
The last faint pulse of quivering light.

2. In darkness and in weariness
The traveller on his way must press,
No gleam to watch on tree or tower,
Whiling away the lonesome hour.

6. When with dear friends sweet talk I hold,
And all the flowers of life unfold;
Let not my heart within me burn,
Except in all I Thee discern.

9. Thou framer of the light and dark,
Steer through the tempest Thine own ark;
Amid the howling wintry sea
We are in port if we have Thee.

13. Watch by the sick; enrich the poor
With blessings from Thy boundless store:
Be every mourner's sleep tonight
Like infant's slumbers, pure and light.

The hymn is based on Luke 24: 29, "Abide with us: for it is toward evening, and the day is far spent," and it was first published in his *"Christian Year"* in 1827, a book which probably brought the author as much fame as did the naming after him of Keble College, Oxford, in 1869. He also wrote Nos. 42, "New Every Morning," and 92, "There Is a Book."

The tune *Hursley,* also used for No. 414, "My God, How Endless Is Thy Love!" is a German melody closely resembling a drinking song from Mozart's "Nozze di Figaro," and its similarity stimulated Sir Herbert Oakeley to write the tune *Abends* (see No. 56) to replace it. It is named after the parish of Hursley, near Winchester, Hampshire, where Keble was vicar from 1835 to 1865. The church was restored from funds provided by profits from the sale of his *"Christian Year,"* and he is buried there.

322. O, COULD I FIND FROM DAY TO DAY

Psalm 145: 18

Benjamin Cleveland (1733-1811), an American Baptist, wrote these words in 1792, expressing his earnest desire to live as a true Christian. He puts his confidence in David's statement, "The Lord is nigh unto all them that call upon Him, to all that call upon Him in truth." Psalm 145: 18. There were six stanzas originally, those omitted being:—

4. Thus, till my last expiring breath,
Thy goodness I'll adore;
And when my flesh dissolves in death
My soul shall love Thee more.

5. Through boundless grace I then shall spend
An everlasting day
In the embraces of my Friend
Who took my guilt away.

6. That worthy name shall have the praise
To whom all praise is due;
While angels and archangels gaze
On scenes for ever new.

The tune *Naomi,* also used for No. 333, "Father, Whate'er of Earthly Bliss," is an arrangement made in 1836 by Lowell Mason (1792-1872), see appendix, of a tune by Johann George Nägeli (1773-1836) of Zurich, Switzerland. The latter was a composer, teacher, and music publisher, and reformed the teaching of music in schools. He also composed the original of Nos. 379, 432, and 439, *Dennis. Naomi,* here a semitone lower than in No. 333, almost repeats the music of its first part for its second half.

323. COME UNTO ME WHEN SHADOWS DARKLY GATHER

Matthew 11: 28

These words were written in 1839 by Catherine Harbison Watterman (1812-97), who married Captain G. J. Esling in 1840. She was an American Protestant Episcopal church member of Philadelphia and based her thought on the words of Jesus, "Come unto Me, all ye that labour and are heavy laden, and I will give you rest." Matthew 11: 28. There are nine stanzas beginning:—

1. Come unto Me, ye who are heavy-laden,
Come unto Me, ye who are sore oppressed,
The white-haired sire, the young and tender maiden,
Come unto Me, and I will give you rest.

2. Ye who have seen the clouds of tempests cover
All that the earth had promised fair and bright,
Ye who have seen death's pinions darkly hover
Quenching the life that was a joy and light.

Then the remaining stanzas all deal with death, of the young and infants in stanzas 4 and 5, of the old in stanza 6, and of contemporaries in stanza 7. The present selection in "Church Hymnal" is stanzas 3, 8 and 9, all with slight alterations from the original.

The tune *Henley* was composed in 1854 by Lowell Mason (1792-1872), see appendix, but the name has no associated significance. Essentially there are only two chords and their inversions used throughout the whole hymn.

324. 'TIS THE BLESSED HOUR OF PRAYER

1 Peter 5:6, 7

This hymn is one of many, nine in this hymnal, in which the words are by Fanny Crosby (1820-1915) and the music by William Howard Doane (1832-1916)—for both see appendix. It appeared in 1880 and reflects Fanny Crosby's own devotional spirit and experience with Christ. Notice that He is referred to as Saviour in each of the first three stanzas. The hymn first speaks of coming to God in faith, then of His coming in compassion to us, of telling Him our troubles, and finally of faith again in accepting His blessing. An appropriate scripture would be, "Humble yourselves therefore under the mighty hand of God. . . . Casting all your care upon Him; for He careth for you." 1 Peter 5: 6, 7.

325. MY GOD, IS ANY HOUR SO SWEET?

Luke 10:39

These words were written in 1836 by Charlotte Elliott (1789-1871), of Brighton, England, as a hymn in long metre, viz., eight syllables to each line, now abbreviated to four syllables in the last line of each stanza. Two other stanzas of the hymn are:—

3. Blest is the tranquil break of morn,
And blest the solemn hush of eve,
When on the wings of prayer upborne,
This fair, but transient, world I leave.

4. Then is my strength by Thee renewed;
Then are my sins by Thee forgiven:
Then dost Thou cheer my solitude
With clean and beauteous hopes of heaven.

The original second stanza was omitted in the 1837 revision. Miss Elliott imitates the example of the "sister called Mary, which also sat at Jesus' feet, and heard His word." Luke 10: 39. She was a life-long invalid and of herself she wrote, "My heavenly Father knows and He alone, what it is, day after day, and hour after hour, to fight against bodily feelings of almost overpowering weakness and languor and exhaustion, to resolve, as He enables me to do, not to yield to the slothfulness, the depression, the irritability, such a body causes me to long to indulge, but to rise every morning determined on taking this for my motto, 'If any man will come after Me, let him deny himself, take up his cross daily, and follow Me.'" Miss Elliot also wrote Nos. 61, "The Sabbath Day Has Reached Its Close"; 222, "Just As I Am," and 357, "Christian, Seek Not Yet Repose." These four hymns are of similar structure, each having their last line different in rhyme or metre from the preceding three lines.

The tune *Almsgiving* was composed in 1865 by John Bacchus Dykes (1823-76), see appendix, and is so named because it was specially written for Christopher Wordsworth's (see No. 463) hymn, "O Lord of Heaven and Earth and Sea." The title of this hymn was "Giver of All," and each stanza ends with the words, "Who givest all."

326. STILL, STILL WITH THEE

Psalm 139: 18

Mrs. Harriet Elizabeth Beecher Stowe (1811-96), sister of the famous preacher Henry Ward Beecher, and better known as the authoress of "*Uncle Tom's Cabin,*" wrote this hymn in the summer of 1853. She was on a visit to a friend and often arose at 4.30 in the morning so that she could go and enjoy the beauty of the dawn and the early singing of the birds. The thought running through the whole hymn is that of the psalmist, "When I awake, I am still with Thee" (Psalm 139: 18), and this is applied to the sleep of death and the glorious awakening to eternal life in the presence of God. The hymn was first published in 1855 in the "Plymouth Collection" edited by her brother, and had also the following stanza, now omitted:—

4. Still, still with Thee! as to each new-born morning
A fresh and solemn splendour still is given;
So does this blessed consciousness awaking,
Breathe each day nearness unto Thee and heaven.

327. IN THE HOUR OF TRIAL

Luke 22:31, 32

James Montgomery (1771-1854), see appendix, wrote this hymn of four stanzas on October 13, 1834, basing it on the words of Jesus to Peter, just before His agony in Gethsemane, "And the Lord said, Simon, Simon, behold, Satan hath desired to have you, that he may sift you as wheat: but I have prayed for thee, that thy faith fail not." Luke 22: 31, 32. The original manuscript had in the second line, "Jesus, stand by me," but it was altered later to "pray for me," in spite of mistaken protestations that this was unscriptural. Our third stanza was written by Mrs. Frances Annie Hutton (1841-?) of Lincoln and added to a revision of Montgomery's original hymn. There are therefore two omitted stanzas, namely:—

3. If with sore affliction
Thou in love chastise,
Pour Thy benediction
On the sacrifice;
Then upon Thine altar
Freely offered up
Though the flesh may falter
Faith shall drink the cup.

4. When in dust and ashes,
To the grave I sink,
While heaven's glory flashes
O'er the shelving brink,
On Thy truth relying
Through that mortal strife,
Lord, receive me, dying,
To eternal life.

The tune *Penitence* was composed in 1879 by the American, Spencer Lane (1843-1903), a maker of musical instruments. One of the evening hymns for the service at St. James' church, Woonsocket, Rhode Island, had a tune not to his liking, so in the interval between the close of a morning service and dinner, he composed this tune while his wife was making preparation for the meal. It is named *Penitence* because of the sentiment of the words of the hymn.

328. AT FIRST I PRAYED FOR LIGHT

1 John 4:7

This progressive poem was written by Mrs. Edna Dow Cheney, née Littlehale (1824-1904), a social worker of Boston and Jamaica Plains, Massachusetts. It speaks of a suppliant asking first for light for the Christian's pathway, then for strength to walk this road, and then for faith to be serene even amid the current conflicts. The larger prayer which embraces these gifts of light, strength, and faith, is the prayer for love, both to God and to man. "Beloved, let us love one another: for love is of God." 1 John 4: 7.

The tune *Woolwich,* also used for No. 347, "Work, While It Is Today," was composed by Charles Edward Kettle (1833-95), an organist in Woolwich, London, and also in Brighton, England. He was the publisher of "Kettle's Tune Book" which included chants, tunes, and pianoforte pieces.

329. SPEAK, LORD, IN THE STILLNESS

1 Samuel 3: 9

The words of this prayer by Emily May Grimes (1864-1927) were written in Pondoland, South Africa, where she served as a missionary. Three portions of Scripture are given in her title, namely: 1 Samuel 3: 9, "Speak, Lord; for thy servant heareth"; Psalm 62: 1, "My soul waiteth upon God"; and Job 4: 16, "There was silence and I heard a voice" (margin, a still voice). Miss Grimes, who later married Dr. T. W. W. Crawford, a Church Missionary Society missionary to the Kikuyu, wrote eight stanzas originally, the omitted one being:—

4. Satiate my being,
   With Thy fullness fill;
   As the dew descending,
   Let Thy speech distil.

Miss Grimes also wrote No. 63, "Thy Mighty Love, O God."

The tune, aptly named *The Quiet Hour,* or *Quietude,* was composed by Harold Green (1871-1931).

330. O THOU, TO WHOSE ALL-SEARCHING SIGHT

Psalm 139: 1, 12

These words are a free translation from the German, made in 1738 by John Wesley (1703-91) of Nicolaus Ludwig von Zinzendorf's (1700-60) hymn written in September, 1721, and entitled "Seelen Braütigam" (= souls of the bridegroom, See No. 676). There were six stanzas originally, the omitted ones being:—

2. Wash out its stains, refine its dross,
   Nail my affections to the cross;
   Hallow each thought; let all within
   Be clean, as Thou, my Lord, art clean!

6. If rough and thorny be the way,
My strength proportion to my day;
Till toil and grief and pain shall cease,
Where all is calm, and joy, and peace.

Furthermore, our third stanza is not based on Zinzendorf, but is a translation of a hymn of Johann Anastasius Freylinghausen (1670-1739), the noted hymn-writer of the Pietists of Germany, who composed No. 178, *Lubeck*. Zinzendorf, a Moravian bishop and hymn-writer, also wrote Nos. 62, "Eternal Depth of Love Divine," again translated by John Wesley, and 676, "Jesus, Still Lead On." Wesley also translated No. 146, "Jesus, Thy Boundless Love to Me," from Gerhardt. The present hymn is a simple prayer to the God of Light to be present in darkness, in danger, and in despair. "O Lord, Thou hast searched me, and known me. . . . Yea, the darkness hideth not from Thee; but the night shineth as the day: the darkness and the light are both alike to Thee." Psalm 139: 1, 12.

The tune *Bera* was composed in 1849 by John Edgar Gould (1822-75), an American conductor, composer, and song publisher. By the age of thirty he had a music shop on Broadway, New York City, and later he entered into partnership in a retail piano busi-business in Philadelphia with William G. Fischer (see Nos. 518, 592, 600, 633). The name Bera, meaning gift, is also the name of the king of Sodom, but is a random choice of no associated significance. Gould also composed No. 398, *Pilot*.

331. FATHER, LEAD ME DAY BY DAY

Psalm 25: 5

John Page Hopps (1834-1912), first a Baptist and then a Unitarian minister of Leicester, England, wrote these words in 1876 under the title, "A Child Pilgrim's Prayer." Originally it had seven stanzas, the two omitted being:—

4. When my heart is full of glee,
Help me to remember Thee,
Happy most of all to know
That my Father loves me so.

6. May I see the good and bright,
When they pass before my sight:
May I hear the heavenly voice,
When the pure and wise rejoice.

A fitting scripture reference is "Lead me in Thy truth, and teach me." Psalm 25: 5.

The tune *Posen* was composed by George Christoph Strattner (1650-1704), choirmaster at Frankfurt-on-Main, Germany, and appeared in Neander's "Bundes-Lieder," 1691.

332. MY HEART IS RESTING

Lamentations 3: 24

Miss Anna Laetitia Waring (1823-1910), a Welsh Quaker who later became an Anglican in order to partake of the sacrament, wrote this hymn of eleven stanzas, each of eight lines, in 1852, basing her thought on Jeremiah's comforting statement: "The Lord is my portion, saith my soul; therefore will I hope in Him." Lamentations 3: 24. Some of the omitted lines are:—

1. . . .
Now the frail vessel Thou hast made,
No hand but Thine shall fill;
The waters of the earth have failed,
And I am thirsty still.

2. . . .
And a new song is in my mouth
To long loved music set—
Glory to Thee for all the grace
I have not tasted yet.

3. Glory to Thee for strength withheld,
For wants and weakness known,
The fear that sends me to Thy breast,
For what is most my own.
. . .

11. My heart is resting, O my God,
My heart is in Thy care—
I hear the voice of joy and health
Resounding everywhere.
"Thou art my portion," saith my soul,
Ten thousand voices say,
And the music of their glad Amen,
Will never die away.

Miss Waring also wrote Nos. 82, "Beneath Thy Wing," and 674, "In Heavenly Love Abiding."

The tune *Tallis' Ordinal* was composed in 1567 by Thomas Tallis (1510-85), who has been called the father of English cathedral music. He was organist at Waltham Abbey until 1540, and later at the Chapel Royal. He was royal organist for Henry VIII, Edward VI, Mary, and Elizabeth, of the house of Tudor. He also composed No. 53, *Tallis' Canon.* This tune *Ordinal* is also used for No. 92, "There Is a Book," and an unusual feature is the repetition of the first line in line three in all parts, and the similarity of line four to line two, where the melody is transposed down a fifth.

333. FATHER, WHATE'ER OF EARTHLY BLISS

1 Timothy 6: 6-8

Anne Steele (1717-78) of Broughton, near Salisbury, Hampshire, was a member of the Baptist Church and had a very sad life. Due to an accident in childhood she was a life-long invalid, and at the age of twenty-one on the eve of her wedding, her fiancé was accidentally drowned. In 1760 she wrote a ten-stanza hymn entitled "Desiring Resignation and Thankfulness," of which this selection is the last part. The omitted stanzas are:—

1. When I survey life's varied scene,
Amid the darkest hours,
Sweet rays of comfort shine between,
And thorns are mix'd with flowers.

2. Lord, teach me to adore Thy hand
From whence my comforts flow;
And let me in this desert land
A glimpse of Canaan know.

3. Is health and ease my happy share?
O may I bless my God;
Thy kindness let my songs declare,
And spread Thy praise abroad.

4. While such delightful gifts as these,
Are kindly dealt to me,
Be all my hours of health and ease
Devoted, Lord, to Thee.

5. In griefs and pains Thy sacred Word,
(Dear solace of my soul!)
Celestial comforts can afford,
And all their power control.

6. When present sufferings pain my heart,
Or future terrors rise,
And light and hope almost depart
From these dejected eyes:

7. Thy powerful word supports my hope,
Sweet cordial of the mind!
And bears my fainting spirit up,
And bids me wait resign'd.

The hymn is based on 1 Timothy 6: 6-8: "But godliness with contentment is great gain. For we brought nothing into this world, and it is certain we can carry nothing out. And having food and raiment let us therewith be content." Miss Steele's life of suffering did not embitter her, but perfected in her the Christian graces of patience and cheerfulness. She also wrote Nos. 71, "My Maker and My King," and 244, "O Could Our Thoughts," all under her pen-name of Theodosia.

The tune *Naomi* is an arrangement made in 1836 by Lowell Mason (1792-1872), see appendix, from Johann George Nägeli (1773-1836) of Zurich, Switzerland. It is used also, but a semi-tone lower, for No. 322, "O, Could I Find From Day to Day." While the name *Naomi* was given apart from these present words, it is very appropriate considering Naomi's own sorrowful experience in the land of Moab (Ruth 1: 20). Nägeli was a Swiss composer, teacher, and music publisher, who did much to reform the teaching of music in schools. He also composed Nos. 379, 432, and 439, *Dennis*. *Naomi* has its first and second halves almost identical.

334. CALM ME, MY GOD

Psalm 46: 10

The theme of this hymn by Horatius Bonar (1808-89), see appendix, is the quality of Christian calm, for this characteristic is mentioned no less than thirteen times in five stanzas. It appeared in 1857 as eight stanzas under the title "The Inner Calm," and is a fitting commentary on Psalm 46: 10: "Be still." The omitted stanzas are:—

1. Calm me, my God, and keep me calm,
While these hot breezes blow,
Be like the night-dew's cooling balm
Upon earth's fevered brow.

3. Calm me, my God, and keep me calm,
Let Thine outstretchéd wing
Be like the shade of Elim's palm,
Beside her desert spring.

7. Calm me when the world's news with power
My listening spirit stir;
Let not the tidings of the hour
E'er find too fond an ear.

The tune *Lambeth* was composed in 1871 by Wilhelm A. F. Schulthes (1816-79), and is used with slightly different harmony for No. 213, "Spirit Divine." Schulthes was born in Germany, but came to England and became a choir director and music teacher at a convent in Roehampton, London.

335. ALONE WITH THEE

Matthew 14: 23

Both words and music of this meditation were written by Dr. Douglas Albert Raoul Aufranc (1892-), a Seventh-day Adventist physician and dentist living in north London, and a grandson of one of the first converts of J. N. Andrews in Switzerland. During a very happy holiday spent on the Norfolk Broads, the peaceful evening inspired the thought of separation from the bustle of the world, and communion with the God of peace, just as did the Saviour in His earthly ministry; "He went up into a mountain apart to pray: and when the evening was come, He was there alone." Matthew 14: 23. Notice the progression of thought from the second stanza onwards, dealing with the three ages of man. First the morn of youth, then the prime of manhood's noon, and finally the night of old age and death and darkness. Throughout life's little span there can always be the companionship of our Friend and Guardian.

The tune *Windy Ridge* takes its name from the name of the bungalow where the holiday was spent. Dr. Aufranc also wrote the words of Nos. 374, "There Is a Road"; 468, "Far from All Care," and 682, "Father, I Yield to Thee My Life," and the tunes associated with the first two of these, Nos. 374, *Thetford,* and 468, *Pevensey.*

336. COME IN, O COME!

Revelation 3: 20

These words, appearing in "Hymns of Consecration and Faith," 1890, were written by Handley Carr Glyn Moule (1841-1920), and describe the sinful heart as an untidy, disordered room, which can be transformed by the entry of the Lord Jesus. They use the figure of Revelation 3: 20 where the Lord says, "Behold, I stand at the door, and knock: if any man hear My voice, and open the door, I will come in to him." In the author's "Songs in the House of Pilgrimage," 1896, there are seven stanzas, the omitted ones being:—

2. Come, even now. But think not here to find
A lodging, Lord, and converse to Thy mind:
The lamp burns low: the hearth is chill and pale;
Wet through the broken casement pours the gale.

6. Then, as Thou art, all holiness and bliss,
Come in, and see my chamber as it is;
I bid Thee welcome boldly, in the name
Of Thy great glory, and my want and shame.

Dr. Moule became bishop of Durham in 1901, and also wrote No. 648, "My Glorious Victor," another subjective hymn of submission to the Saviour, which likewise appeared in "Hymns of Consecration and Faith."

The tune *Morecambe* was published in 1870 by Frederic Cook Atkinson (1841-96) as a setting for the hymn "Abide With Me" (No. 50). He was born at Norwich, England, and later became assistant organist at the cathedral there, and afterwards organist at Bradford, Yorkshire. Morecambe is an English town in Lancashire, noted for the music festival held there. The same tune, dropped a tone to the key of B flat, is used for No. 684, "O Thou Who Hearest Every Heartfelt Prayer."

337. STAND STILL AND SEE

Exodus 14: 13

These words appearing in the 1902 edition of "Hymns of Consecration and Faith," were written by Charles Armstrong Fox (18?-1902), and are a combination of several scriptures, both quoted and paraphrased, all emphasizing the quiet work of the Spirit of God. Notice how this idea is repeated in the word "still" in the first line of each of the first three stanzas; "silence" in stanza two, line three; "hush" and "stillness" in stanza four, lines one and two. The quoted scriptures are: "Stand still, and see the salvation of the Lord," Exodus 14: 13; "Commune with your own heart upon your bed, and be still," Psalm 4: 4; and "Be still, and know that I am God," Psalm 46: 10. Reference is also made to the three thousand souls who were baptized on the day of Pentecost. (Acts 2: 41.)

The tune *Carey* first appeared in 1723 in "Introduction to Psalmody," set to a paraphrase of the twenty-third psalm. Is is also named *Surrey* or *Yarmouth,* and was composed by Henry Carey (c. 1687-1743), who is better known as a composer of secular, lighter melodies. He is credited, however, with the composition of the British National Anthem, which is used for Nos. 506 and 510, *America.*

338. ONE PRECIOUS BOON, O LORD, I SEEK

Matthew 19: 29

Charles Fitch (1805-44), was the minister of the First Free Congregational Church in Boston when he heard of William Miller's teaching on the second advent. He was much interested and wrote to Miller in 1838 saying that he planned to discuss this doctrine at the ministerial association. The latter, however, would have nothing to do with it and Fitch's ardour was temporarily cooled. He continued to study, and developed the doctrine of holiness, which he presented in many churches. This lost him some adherents, and on his return from an evangelistic preaching tour he encountered much opposition. At this time, in 1841, he met Josiah Litch, who told him that he needed to preach his doctrine of holiness in the setting of the Millerite doctrine of the second coming and the Advent awakening. Fitch's kindly nature recoiled at first, as he thought that he would lose even more friends by embracing this unpopular doctrine. He was particularly afraid of losing the friendship of Dr. W. C. and Mrs. Phoebe Palmer (authoress of Nos. 549 and 598), but to his great delight they followed him into the ranks of Adventist believers. He now entered wholeheartedly and aggressively into the preaching of the imminent return of Christ, and spurned the loss of former associates and their scorn as indicated in the words of this hymn in stanzas 2, 3, and 4. Fitch could well be described as one who "hath forsaken houses, or brethren, or sisters, or father, or mother, or wife, or children, or lands, for My name's sake, shall receive an hundredfold, and shall inherit everlasting life." Matthew 19: 29. He was spared the bitterness of the disappointment of October 22, 1844, for he died of a fever eleven days earlier, having caught a severe chill after baptizing a group of believers in Lake Erie. Returning home, he met a second group who desired baptism, and after acceding to their request and turning again homewards a second time in cold, wet clothes, he met a third group who pleaded for baptism before the anticipated coming of the Lord. Faithful to the last, he set out on horseback the next day to visit other believers, but the chill he developed worsened rapidly and turned in a few days to a fatal fever. Fitch made a great contribution to the Adventist cause by his literal heeding of Habakkuk's instruction, "Write the vision, and make it plain upon tables." Habakkuk 2: 2. He was the first to produce charts of the prophecies of Daniel and Revelation and their application to the second advent of Christ. He is referred to in *"Early Writings,"* page 17, 1945 edition, in Ellen Harmon's first vision (see No. 305) as one "whom God had laid in the grave to save him."

The tune *Uxbridge,* used also for No. 83, "God of My Life," was composed in 1830 by Lowell Mason (1792-1872), see appendix.

339. WALK IN THE LIGHT

1 John 1: 7

These words were written in 1826 by a Quaker poet, Bernard Barton (1784-1849), a bank clerk of Woodbridge, Suffolk, and appeared in his "Devotional Verses" as six stanzas each of four lines. Those omitted are:—

2. Walk in the light: and sin, abhorred,
Shall ne'er defile again;
The blood of Jesus Christ thy Lord
Shall cleanse from every stain.

3. Walk in the light: and thou shalt find
Thy heart made truly His
Who dwells in cloudless light enshrined,
In Whom no darkness is.

The hymn is based on the words, "If we walk in the light, as He is in the light, we have fellowship one with another." 1 John 1: 7. All Barton's poems are pervaded with pious sentiment and religious fervour, and this one in particular emphasizes the Quaker doctrine of the inner light. Barton was admired by the poet Byron and gained the friendship of Charles Lamb.

The tune *Chopin* was composed by Isaac Baker Woodbury (1819-58), see appendix.

340. BY COOL SILOAM'S SHADY RILL

Luke 2: 40

Reginald Heber (1783-1826) wrote a six-stanza hymn in 1812, later revised it, and then it was published posthumously in 1827 under the title "Christ a Pattern for Children." It was especially for the first Sunday after Epiphany and took its theme from the verse describing the early days of Jesus: "And the child grew, and waxed strong in spirit, filled with wisdom: and the grace of God was upon Him." Luke 2: 40. The child's development into manhood and old age is likened to the growth and development of a flower. The omitted stanzas are:—

3. By cool Siloam's shady rill
The lily must decay;
The rose that blooms beneath the hill
Must shortly pass away.

4. And soon, too soon, the wintry hour
Of man's maturer age
Will shake the soul with sorrow's power,
And stormy passion's rage!

5. O Thou, whose infant feet were found
Within Thy Father's shrine!
Whose years with changeless virtue crown'd
Were all alike divine.

Heber was vicar of Crewe Green and later bishop of Calcutta, and used to write hymns especially for the weekly services of the church year. He also wrote Nos. 73, "Holy, Holy, Holy"; 178, "In the

Sun, Moon, and Stars"; 361, "The Son of God Goes Forth to War"; 445, "From Greenland's Icy Mountains," and 476, "Bread of the World."

The tune *Siloam,* also used for No. 431, "How Sweet, How Heavenly," was composed in 1842 by Isaac Baker Woodbury (1819-58), see appendix, while on shipboard during a fierce storm.

341. ART THOU WEARY?

Matthew 11: 28

Stephen (725-794), nephew of John of Damascus (see Nos. 135, 136), entered the monastery of Mar Saba at the early age of ten. This monastery is carved out of the rocks of the Kidron valley and gives a glimpse of the Dead Sea. Stephen later showed poetic talent and became choirmaster of the monks, and composed this hymn which recalls the dreary surroundings of the isolated monastery. The cloudless sky and the white glare of the cliffs give a feeling of langour, desolation, and loneliness. The hymn was very freely translated from the Latin in 1862, and is virtually an original hymn (as No. 377) by John Mason Neale (1818-66), see appendix. Its theme is taken from Matthew 11: 28, "Come unto Me, all ye that labour and are heavy laden, and I will give you rest." Note that each stanza is divided into two parts, the first half asking a question, the second half providing the answer, thus making it very suitable for singing by two groups.

The melody *Stephanos* was composed in 1868 by Henry Williams Baker (1821-77), the editor of "Hymns Ancient and Modern." He had no ear for harmony, so his musical editor William Henry Monk (1823-89) added the other three parts and named the tune to commemorate the original author of the words. Baker also wrote Nos. 10, "Praise, O Praise Our God and King," and 86, "The King of Love My Shepherd Is," and Monk composed Nos. 50, *Eventide;* 196, *Beverley,* and 357, *Vigilate.*

342. YE SERVANTS OF GOD

Revelation 7: 9-12

The year 1744 was a time of great political unrest in England because of the war with France and the effort to re-establish the House of Stuart on the throne. Many Roman Catholic Jacobites and sympathizers with the Young Pretender were at work throughout the country, and the new groups of Methodists formed by the Wesley brothers were often falsely accused of being Papists in disguise. Their meetings were often broken up by hooligans, and both preachers and congregation were pelted with eggs, cabbages, and bricks. Many were brought before magistrates as disturbers of the peace, but this persecution did not daunt them. For their encouragement Charles Wesley (1707-88) wrote several hymns under the title "Hymns for Times of Trouble and Persecution," this particular one having the instruction "To be sung in a tumult." It is based on Psalm 93 and the present stanzas paraphrase Revelation 7: 9-12, "A great multitude . . . stood . . . before the Lamb . . . and cried . . . Salvation to our God which sitteth upon the throne, and unto the Lamb. And all the angels . . . fell before the throne on their faces, and worshipped God, saying, Amen: Blessing, and glory, and wisdom, and thanksgiving, and honour, and power, and might, be unto our God for ever and ever." Omitted stanzas are:—

2. The waves of the sea have lift up their voice,
Sore troubled that we in Jesus rejoice;
The floods they are roaring, but Jesus is here,
While we are adoring, He always is near.
When devils engage, the billows arise,
And horribly rage, and threaten the skies:
Their fury shall never our steadfastness shock,
The weakest believer is built on a rock.
Come, Lord, and display Thy sign in the sky,
And bear us away to mansions on high;
The kingdom be given, the purchase divine,
And crown us in heaven eternally Thine.

The tune *Hanover* was composed in 1708 by William Croft (1678-1727), organist at Westminster Abbey where his tomb now is. It was one of the early departures from the common 4/4 style of singing to a triple time. Its original title in Tate and Brady's New Version of the Psalm was "A New Tune to the 149th Psalm of the New Version and the 104th of the Old." It was called *Bromswick* by John Wesley in 1742, but is now known as *Hanover* in honour of the accession of George III of Hanover to the throne of England. Croft also composed Nos. 81 and 435, *St. Anne.*

343. I LOVE THEE

John 21:15

These words were probably written by John Alexander Grande (17 ?-1807), an American Methodist revivalist preacher of the early 1800's, known as "the wild man of the woods," and who composed many widely sung hymns. Here his sentiments recall the Apostle Peter's triple confession, "Yea, Lord; Thou knowest that I love Thee." John 21: 15, 16, 17. The three omitted stanzas are:

5. O Jesus, my Saviour! I know Thou art mine;
For Thee all the pleasures of sin I resign:
Of objects most pleasing I love Thee the best;
Without Thee I'm wretched, but with Thee I'm blessed.

6. Tho' weak and despiséd, by faith I now stand,
Preserv'd and defended by Heaven's kind hand:
By Jesus supported, I'll praise His dear name,
Regardless of danger, of praise, or of blame.

7. I find Him in singing, I find Him in prayer;
In sweet meditation He always is near:
My constant companion, oh, may we ne'er part!
All glory to Jesus who dwells in my heart!

The tune *I Love Thee* appeared with these words in 1805 in a collection of sacred songs known as "Christian Harmony, or Songster's Companion." Jeremiah Ingalls (1764-1828), a Vermont compiler, edited this book in New Hampshire, using several secular and lively tunes for sacred words. The tune is much older than this, however, and was an early American folk-song which was brought over from Europe by the early settlers. The tune is in the pentatonic scale (see No. 181) and can be played entirely on the black notes by raising it a minor third into the key of G flat. The time, a mixture of 3/4 and 4/4, can be easily modified to either one of these. Ingalls, a deacon, and choir leader of the Congregational Church, and also a singing teacher, also composed No. 245, *Northfield.*

344. ANYWHERE, DEAR SAVIOUR

Matthew 8: 19

Both words and music were written by William Augustine Ogden (1841-97), see appendix, the subject of the hymn being based on the parable of the labourers in the vineyard. "For the kingdom of heaven is like unto a man that is an householder, which went out early in the morning to hire labourers into his vineyard. . . . Go ye also into the vineyard." Matthew 20: 1, 4. The closing line of each stanza is virtually a paraphrase of the statement of "a certain scribe" who "came, and said unto Him, Master, I will follow Thee whithersoever Thou goest." Matthew 8: 19.

345. WORKING, O CHRIST, WITH THEE

2 Corinthians 6: 1

These words by William Augustine Ogden (1841-97), see appendix, emphasize the thought that the gospel worker is not alone, but rather that he is in partnership with the Lord Jesus Christ. Using the Apostle Paul's expression, "We then, as workers together with Him" (2 Corinthians 6: 1), the poet employs the phrase "working with Thee" nine times in four stanzas. The words in quotation marks in the third stanza are not verbatim, but simply re-state 2 Corinthians 12: 9: "My grace is sufficient for thee."

The tune *St. Edmund* was composed in 1872 by Arthur Seymour Sullivan (1842-1900), see appendix, originally for the hymn "We Are But Strangers Here, Heaven Is Our Home" (No. 659). The name commemorates an East Anglican king who was martyred by the invading Danes A.D. 870 when he refused to renounce Christianity. The town Bury St. Edmunds in Suffolk, England, is named after him.

346. O MASTER, LET ME WALK WITH THEE

Genesis 5: 24

Dr. Washington Gladden (1836-1918), an American Congregational pastor at Springfield, Massachussets, wrote a poem of three stanzas (each of eight lines) in March, 1879, entitled, "Walking with God," which appeared in the magazine *Sunday Afternoon.* It was his expression of the human need of divine guidance and companionship in life's varied experiences, and to some extent it depicted his own experience. He was an outstanding preacher of his day, being ordained to the Congregational ministry in 1860. He promoted the social gospel and attacked political corruption and economic evils. The second stanza now omitted was not suited for devotional purposes, and the remaining sixteen lines were rearranged to make four stanzas. His original was:—

2. O Master, let me walk with Thee
Before the taunting Pharisee;
Help me to bear the sting of spite,
The hate of men who hide Thy light,
The sore distrust of souls sincere
Who cannot read Thy judgments clear,
The dullness of the multitude,
Who dimly guess that Thou art good.

The theme progresses from "walking with God" to "closer company with Him," and finally to "living with God," an experience epitomized by Enoch of whom, among others, it is recorded, "And Enoch walked with God." Genesis 5: 24.

The tune *Maryton,* which Gladden preferred to any other for his words, was composed in 1874 by Canon Henry Percy Smith (1825-98), a Church of England clergyman. He actually composed the tune for other words, namely "Sun of My Soul" (No. 321), while he was vicar of Great Barnton in Suffolk, England. Later he ministered in France, and for his last three years he was canon of Gibraltar Cathedral.

347. WORK WHILE IT IS TODAY

John 9: 4

These words were written in 1853 by James Montgomery (1771-1854), see appendix, as a nine-stanza hymn under the title "Working the Works of God." He has used the words of our Lord from John 9: 4: "I must work the works of Him that sent Me, while it is day," using this theme as the opening and closing admonition of the poem. The omitted stanzas are:—

2. We, as He did, should do,
Who practised what He taught;
By precept and example, too
Our Master spake and wrought.

3. To work the works of God,
Was His divine employ,
And we must tread the path He trod,
Or enter not His joy.

4. The night will come full soon,
Life's day with morn may end;
While many a sun goes down ere noon,
Few to their west descend.

6. Our own salvation be
Our first and constant aim,
Then far and wide, o'er land and sea,
Glad tidings to proclaim.

9. For Thee our all to spend,
Still may we watch and pray,
And persevering to the end,
Work while it is today.

The tune *Woolwich,* also used for No. 328, "At First I Prayed for Light," was composed by Charles Edward Kettle (1833-95), an organist in Woolwich, London, and also in Brighton, Sussex. He was the publisher of "Kettle's Tune Book," which included chants, tunes, and pianoforte pieces.

348. IN THE HEART OF JESUS

John 13: 1

Each stanza of this hymn is built on the same structure, the first half telling of some phase of the ministry of Jesus, and the second half asking what our reaction as His servants should be. For example, the first two stanzas tell of the heart and mind of Jesus which is full of warm, pure love and thoughtfulness for us. John 13: 1: "Having loved His own which were in the world, He loved them unto the end." Then the latter portion of these stanzas point out the logical consequence of this love, namely, that there need be no loneliness nor anxiety. "Take no thought for your life" (Matthew 6: 25), "For ye are bought with a price." 1 Corinthians 6: 20. Similarly with stanza 3, having viewed the harvest field which demands labourers, the question comes, "Why stand ye here all the day idle?" Matthew 20: 6. So with the last stanza, which describes the home, "In My Father's house are many mansions" (John 14: 2), and then asks an almost rhetorical question for wanderers who are homeless.

The composer of the tune, *Heart of Jesus,* was C. H. Forrest, who flourished around 1897.

349. FAITH OF OUR FATHERS

Hebrews 11: 33-39

Frederick William Faber (1814-63) wrote a strong polemic against the Roman Catholic Church in 1838, but in 1846 he seceded from the Church of England and joined the church he had attacked, becoming Father Wilfrid. Noting the success of the "Olney Hymns" written by Newton and Cowper (Nos. 84, 150, etc.), he decided to do a similar thing for his new-found faith, and wrote 150 hymns limiting the number to the number of the Psalms. This particular hymn, written in 1849 after three years in the Catholic Church, is an ardent and unashamed propagation of this form of faith, though some of the original words have been changed so that it can apply to any communion. The third line of the first stanza was at first, "Oh! Ireland's heart beats high with joy," but is now changed to "O how our hearts beat high with joy." The third stanza now omitted for obvious reasons, was:—

> 3. Faith of our fathers! Mary's prayers
> Shall win our country back to Thee;
> And through the truth that comes from God,
> England shall then indeed be free.

There was also an Irish version of the same hymn, which had three additional stanzas. The opening stanzas recall the closing verses of the great chapter on faith, where the worthies of old "quenched the violence of fire, escaped the edge of the sword. . . . had trial of . . . bonds and imprisonment." Hebrews 11: 34, 36. Faber also wrote Nos. 65, "There's a Wideness," 375 and 376, "Hark! Hark, My Soul!" and 443, "Workman of God."

The tune *St. Catherine* was composed in 1864 by Henri Frederick Hemy (1818-88), a Roman Catholic organist and professor of music at Tynemouth, and is so named because it was for a hymn entitled "St. Catherine, Virgin and Martyr." Catherine, a "maid most pure," resisted the advances of Maxentius of Alexandria, and for this she was imprisoned. The tune was adapted in 1874 by taking the first four lines and adding two new lines to suit the metre of "Faith of Our Fathers," by James George Walton (1821-1905). Henry, who edited a Catholic Sunday school book, adapted the tune *Stella,* No. 151.

350. WE HAVE NOT KNOWN THEE

Revelation 2: 4

Each one of the first four stanzas of this hymn is a confession of a particular sin of omission, followed in the last two lines of each stanza by a prayer to God to give (1) light for ignorance, (2) faith to generate godly fear, (3) love to appreciate God's love, and (4) zeal for fervent service. The fifth stanza summarizes the preceding four, and emphasizes the desire (1) to know, (2) to fear, (3) to love, and (4) to serve the Lord. The hymn was written in 1889 by Thomas Benson Pollock (1836-96) under the title, "Seeking God," and recalls the rebuke addressed to the church of Ephesus, "Nevertheless I have somewhat against thee, because thou hast left thy first love." Revelation 2: 4. Pollock was at the time curate to his brother, the vicar of St. Albans, Bordesley, Birmingham, and both were subjected to mob violence and severe opposition because of their very definite High Church leanings.

The tune *St. Chrysostom* was composed in 1871 by Joseph Barnby (1838-96), see appendix, for a hymn in a similar metre, "Jesus, My Lord, My God, My All." Chrysostom, whose Greek name means golden-mouthed, lived from 347 to 407 and earned this title because he was a most eloquent theologian and orator.

351. YE SERVANTS OF THE LORD

Luke 12: 35-37

This is a hymn by Philip Doddridge (1702-51), see appendix, published posthumously in 1755 and entitled, "The Active Christian." In his day, hymns were read out line by line and the congregation sang them this way. Often they were composed to fit the sermon as was this one based on the verses, "Let your loins be girded about, and your lights burning; and ye yourselves like unto men that wait for their lord . . . that when He cometh and knocketh, they may open unto Him immediately. Blessed are those servants, whom the Lord . . . shall find watching: verily . . . He shall gird Himself, and make them to sit down to meat, and will come forth and serve them." Luke 12: 35-37. The omitted stanza is:—

5. Christ shall the banquet spread
   With His own royal hand,
   And raise that favourite servant's head
   Amid the angelic band.

The tune *El Kader* is also used for No. 71, "My Maker and My King."

352. ONE SWEETLY SOLEMN THOUGHT

Romans 13: 11

Miss Phoebe Cary (1824-71), of Cincinnati, returned from church one Sunday morning in 1852 after hearing a sermon on the brevity of life, and retired to her little back room on the third floor of a friend's home. Still deeply impressed by the sermon, she wrote the words of this hymn, but did not intend them for publication. Its metre varies somewhat and the words have been modified to suit a short metre tune. Omitted stanzas are:—

5. Closer and closer my steps
   Come to the dread abysm,
   Closer death to my lips
   Presses the awful chrism.

6. But the waves of the silent sea,
   Roll dark before my sight,
   That brightly on the other side,
   Break on a shore of light.

7. Oh, if my mortal feet,
   Have almost gained the brink,
   If it be I am nearer home
   Even today than I think.

8. Father, perfect my trust;
   Let my spirit feel in death
   That her feet are firmly set
   On the rock of living faith.

This last stanza, much altered, is the fifth stanza in "Church Hymnal." The tune of the poem is evidently "Nearer Home," and is an echo of the Apostle Paul's words, "Now is our salvation nearer than when we believed." Romans 13: 11.

The tune *Ambrose* commemorates the composer Robert Steele Ambrose (1824-1908), who wrote it in 1876. It has since been called *"Dulce Domum"* (= sweet home) because of the theme of the hymn. Although the melody begins with six identical notes, all the parts move and comprise an interesting tune. Ambrose was born in England, emigrated with his parents to Canada as a child, and became an organist in Kingston and in Hamilton, Ontario.

353. FORWARD, CHRISTIAN, FORWARD!

Luke 21: 31

The words of this hymn of seven stanzas, entitled, "Song of Victory," were written by a London merchant, Samuel Trevor Francis (1834-1925). Except for stanza two, they speak of the second coming of our Lord—"Know ye that the kingdom of God is nigh at hand." Luke 21: 31. This theme is further emphasized in each of the three omitted stanzas which read:—

4. See the first faint glimmer of the coming dawn
Creeping down the mountains, waking up the morn,
Flushing all the cloudless, tingeing all the sky,
Making all the shadows of the night-hours fly.

6. Then the conflict over; and the rest, how sweet!
Gathered home around Him, at His piercéd feet;
Gazing at His beauty, sitting by His side,
All our hearts' strange yearnings fully satisfied.

7. Saviour, Thou art waiting Thy loved bride to see,
And Thy saints are waiting, Lord, to be with Thee!
For the word we listen, bidding us come home;
Bound we upward, singing: "Jesus, Lord, we come!"

Francis scribbled rhymes as a boy and later wrote numerous songs. He joined the Brethren, and took part in open-air preaching and assisted Ira David Sankey in his musical direction in the London evangelistic campaigns.

The tune *Eventide (Holmes)* was composed by Henry James Ernest Holmes (1852-1938) of London, a violinist and composer who later was a solicitor in Burnley, Lancashire. The second and fourth lines are virtually identical, musically. He also wrote Nos. 146 and 169, *Pater Omnium*.

354. STAND UP! STAND UP FOR JESUS!

Ephesians 6: 14

The Rev. Dudley Atkins Tyng was an ardent opponent of slavery, but the majority of his congregation in Philadelphia were slave owners and forced his resignation. However, he was induced to continue his revivalist preaching in Jaynes Hall, and had great success, one Sunday in 1854 over 1,000 people, a fifth of his audience, signing a pledge of conversion. The following Wednesday he was in the country looking at a piece of farm machinery when his sleeve caught accidentally in the cogs. His arm was dragged into the machine and torn off, the serious injuries proving fatal. He sent a last message to the Young Men's Christian Association in Philadelphia, "Tell them to stand up for Jesus," thinking possibly of Psalm 94: 16, "Who will stand up for Me against the workers of iniquity?" His friend George Duffield (1818-88), a Presbyterian minister, was inspired by these dying words, and wrote this hymn as an exhortation, using it in the funeral sermon, preached on Sunday, April 25, on Ephesians 6: 14, "Stand therefore." He read the poem at the close of the sermon, which also used the verse, "Go now ye that are men, and serve the Lord" (Exodus 10: 11), hence the allusion in stanza 2, line 3, "Ye that are men now serve Him." The two other stanzas are:—

2. Stand up, stand up for Jesus,
The solemn watchword hear;
If, while ye sleep, He suffers,
Away with shame and fear;
Where'er ye meet with evil,
Within you or without,
Charge for the God of battles,
And put the foe to rout.

5. Stand up, stand up for Jesus,
Each soldier to his post:
Close up the broken column,
And shout through all the host:
Make good the loss so heavy,
In those that still remain,
And prove to all around you,
That death itself is gain.

The tune *Webb* commemorates George James Webb (1803-87) who composed it in 1837 while on a voyage from England to America, as a setting for a secular song beginning, "'Tis dawn, the lark is singing." He was an organist and music teacher who, having emigrated from England in 1830, associated with Lowell Mason (see appendix) in founding the Boston Academy of Music. The tune is called *Goodwin* in the "Cantica Laudis" of 1850 by Mason and Webb. It is also used for No. 454, "The Morning Light."

355. AWAKE, MY SOUL!

Philippians 3: 12-14

This hymn by Philip Doddridge (1702-51), see appendix, was published posthumously in 1755 under the title "Pressing On In the Christian Race." It was inspired by Philippians 3: 14, "I press toward the mark for the prize," and also Hebrews 12: 1, 2, "Wherefore seeing we also are compassed about with so great a cloud of witnesses, let us . . . run with patience the race that is set before us, looking unto Jesus," and likewise on 1 Corinthians 9: 25, "And every man that striveth for the mastery is temperate in all things. Now they do it to obtain a corruptible crown; but we an incorruptible." The hymn was used for those who had been newly confirmed, though it is applicable to any stage of the Christian's walk. Stanzas two and three have been interchanged, and the omitted stanza is:—

4. That prize, with peerless glories bright,
Which shall new lustre boast
When victor's wreaths and monarchs' gems
Shall blend in common dust.

The air from which the tune *Arlington* is derived, was composed by Thomas Augustine Arne (1710-78) of London, the principal English composer of his time who wrote songs for all the London theatres. It occurs in a minuet in the overture in his opera "Artaxerxes," which was produced at the Covent Garden theatre, London in 1762. *Arlington,* which is also used for the next hymn, No. 356, "Am I a Soldier of the Cross?" was first arranged as a hymn-tune by Ralph Harrison (1748-1810), a Presbyterian minister who collected several hymn tunes for the use of his Manchester congregation in the compilation "Sacred Harmony," 1784. Two others of his tunes are Nos. 172, *Waugh,* and 187, *Warrington.* Arne is probably better known as the composer of the tune "Rule, Britannia," although he wrote many other operas and music for plays.

356. AM I A SOLDIER OF THE CROSS?

1 Corinthians 16: 13

This hymn by Isaac Watts (1674-1748), see appendix, was written in 1709 and revised in 1721 under the title of "Zeal and Fortitude." (Matthew 5: 16.) It was to conclude a sermon on 1 Corinthians 16: 13, "Watch ye, stand fast in the faith, quit you like men, be strong," but it could well apply also to the apostle's exhortation to his partner Timothy, "Thou therefore endure hardness, as a good soldier of Jesus Christ." 2 Timothy 2: 3. The hymn was a very suitable one for Independent congregations who suffered much persecution in Watts's day for their Nonconformist faith.

The tune *Arlington* is also used for the previous hymn, No. 355, "Awake, My Soul," and is there commented on.

357. CHRISTIAN, SEEK NOT YET REPOSE

Matthew 26: 41

These words were written in 1839 by Miss Charlotte Elliott (1789-1871) and appear in her "Morning and Evening Hymns for a Week," this one being for Wednesday morning. The omitted stanza is:—

2. Principalities and powers,
   Mustering their unseen array;
   Wait for thine unguarded hours:
   Watch and pray!

The hymn is based on the words, "Watch and pray, that ye enter not into temptation." Matthew 26: 41. Miss Elliott was a life-long invalid, but after her conversion in 1822 fought against weakness and depression as a determined Christian. She also wrote Nos. 61, "The Sabbath Day Has Reached Its Close"; 222, "Just As I Am," and 325, "My God, Is Any Hour So Sweet." These four hymns are all of similar structure, each having their last line different in rhyme or in metre from the preceding three lines.

The tune *Vigilate* (= watch ye!) was composed in 1868 especially for the words of Dr. William Henry Monk (1823-89) the musical editor of "Hymns Ancient and Modern," for the appendix to the first edition of this work. He also composed Nos. 50, *Eventide,* and 196, *Beverley,* and harmonized 341, *Stephanos.*

358. MY SOUL, BE ON THY GUARD

Ecclesiastes 8: 8

These words, written in 1781 by George Heath (1745-1822), an English Presbyterian pastor of Honiton, Devonshire, who later became a Unitarian, were unfortunately not heeded by the author, for he fell into unworthy ways and succumbed to "the hosts of sin" who evidently "pressed him hard." An omitted stanza is:—

4. Fight on, my soul, till death
   Shall bring thee to thy God;
   He'll take thee at thy parting breath
   To His divine abode.

These words reflect the common theology of the time regarding the state of those who sleep in death. The constant battle against sin and its wages, death, emphasized throughout the hymn, is a re-statement of the words of Solomon, "There is no discharge in that war." Ecclesiastes 8: 8.

The tune *Laban* was composed in 1830 by Lowell Mason (1792-1872), see appendix, but it is not an associative name.

359. WE ARE LIVING, WE ARE DWELLING

Revelation 20: 7, 8

Arthur Cleveland Coxe (1818-96), later a bishop of New York, wrote these words in 1840 at a time when the slavery question was very much to the fore, and when the war with Mexico was impending. He gave it the title, "Watchwords. A Hymn for the Times." The poem was in stanzas of four lines each, some of the omitted ones being:—

Will ye play, then, will ye dally
With your music and your wine?
Up! it is Jehovah's rally!
God's own arm hath need of thine.

Hark! the onset! will ye fold your
Faith-clad arms in lazy lock?
Up, oh, up, thou drowsy soldier!
Worlds are charging to the shock.

Worlds are charging—heaven beholding:
Thou hast but an hour to fight;
Now the blazoned cross unfolding,
On!—right onward, for the right!

On! let all the soul within you
For the truth's sake go abroad!
Strike! let every nerve and sinew
Tell on ages—tell for God.

The hymn uses the words of scripture that depict the final post-millenial conflict, "Satan shall be loosed. . . . And shall go out to deceive the nations which are in the four quarters of the earth, Gog and Magog, to gather them together to battle." Revelation 20: 7, 8. However, many other scriptures are also skilfully used, for example: Romans 8: 22; Ephesians 6: 12-17; Revelation 12: 12; Matthew 25: 21; Matthew 24: 13. Coxe also wrote No. 435, "O Where Are Kings and Empires Now."

360. ONWARD, CHRISTIAN SOLDIERS!

Matthew 16: 18

In 1865 Sabine Baring-Gould (1834-1924) was the new curate at Horbury Bridge, Yorkshire, and to him was extended the courtesy of selecting the hymns for the annual Whit Monday procession of Sunday school children. They carried banners on this particular occasion and Baring-Gould could find nothing that appeared to him as suitable. So taking one of the hymns with music by Haydn, he sat up far into the night and wrote these stirring martial words. One stanza never sung as a hymn was as follows:—

4. What the saints established
That I hold for true,
What the saints believéd
That believe I, too.
Long as earth endureth
Men that faith will hold—
Kingdoms, nations, empires
In destruction rolled.

The words amplify the Lord's promise concerning the indestructibility of His church, when He said, "Upon this rock I will build My church; and the gates of hell shall not prevail against it." Matthew 16: 18. Baring-Gould, famous as a novelist, also wrote No. 52, "Now the Day Is Over."

The hymn was made extremely popular by the marching tune *St. Gertrude,* composed in 1871 especially for these words by Arthur Seymour Sullivan (1842-1899), see appendix. At the time he was a guest in the home of Mrs. Gertrude Clay-Ker-Seymour in Hanford, Dorset, and he commemorated her name by making her a "saint" and affixing this title to the tune.

361. THE SON OF GOD GOES FORTH TO WAR

Acts 7: 55-60

Reginald Heber (1783-1826), vicar of Crewe Green, Cheshire, and later bishop of Calcutta, wrote hymns especially for the weekly church services of the year, this one being based on the martyrdom of the deacon Stephen, for St. Stephen's day, December 26. This first Christian martyr's experience is described in the second 8-line stanza, although the original hymn published posthumously in 1827 was in eight stanzas each of four lines. "But he . . . looked up stedfastly into heaven, and saw the glory of God, and Jesus standing on the right hand of God, And said, Behold, I see the heavens opened, and the Son of man standing on the right hand of God. . . . And they stoned Stephen, calling upon God, and saying, Lord Jesus, receive my spirit. . . . Lord, lay not this sin to their charge." Acts 7: 55, 56, 59, 60. Heber also wrote Nos. 73, "Holy, Holy, Holy"; 178, "In the Sun, and Moon, and Stars"; 340, "By Cool Siloam's Shady Rill"; 445, "From Greenland's Icy Mountains," and 476, "Bread of the World."

The tune *All Saints New* was specially composed for these words in 1872 by Henry Stephen Cutler (1824-1902) of Boston, an organist and a choirmaster who is remembered for his inception of robing of choirs in 1856. He was also a prominent organist at Trinity church, New York, and later received the degree of Doctor of Music from Columbia University.

362. LEAD ON, O KING ETERNAL

Luke 17: 20, 21

Ernest Warburton Shurtleff (1862-1917), later a Congregational minister, was a student of the Andover Theological Seminary, Massachusetts, and wrote these words for his own graduation class of 1888. The tune was already known very well and the poem was therefore written in this metre. In the first stanza we have reference to his future pastoral work, "Henceforth . . . Thy tents shall be our home"; and to the end of their student days in "The day of march has come," and "Through days of preparation." While the words breathe a martial spirit there is a recognition in stanza two of the fact that "the kingdom of God cometh not with observation . . . for, behold, the kingdom of God is within you." Luke 17: 20, 21. Shurtleff was ordained in 1889 and occupied pastorates in California, in Massachusetts, and in Minnesota.

The tune *Lancashire* was composed in 1835 by Henry Smart (1813-79) for the 300th anniversary of the Reformation in England, and was sung to the words "From Greenland's Icy Mountains" (No. 445) at the musical festival on October 4, 1835, at Blackburn, Lancashire, hence its name. It is used also for No. 135, "The Day of Resurrection." Smart was church organist at Blackburn from 1831-36, and later at Regent's Square Presbyterian church, London, as well as being an organ-builder. Others of his hymn tunes are Nos. 113 and 487, *Regent Square;* 363, *Chebar,* and 376, *Pilgrims.*

363. O MASTER! WHEN THOU CALLEST

Isaiah 6: 8

These words were written by Miss Sarah Geraldine Stock (1838-98) of Islington, London, and were first sung on October 2, 1888, at the valedictory meeting of the Church of England Zenana Society. Miss Stock was particularly interested in Sunday schools and in missionary work, and her words were a specific reference to missionaries who were leaving their homeland for service overseas. They express a willing response to the call of God as did the gospel prophet of old, "Also I heard the voice of the Lord, saying, Whom shall I send, and who will go for Us? Then said I, Here am I; send me." Isaiah 6: 8. Miss Stock also edited a hymnbook for the Church Missionary Society.

The tune *Chebar* was composed in 1876 by Henry Smart (1813-79) who also wrote Nos. 113 and 487, *Regent Square,* 135 and 362, *Lancashire,* and 376, *Pilgrims.* He was an organist and organ builder, serving in Lancashire and also in Regent's Square Presbyterian church, London.

364. FOR ALL THE SAINTS

John 17: 10

William Walsham How (1823-97), see appendix, wrote eleven stanzas each of three lines with Alleluias, in honour of the Christians of bygone ages. His title was "Saint's Days," and it was based on the verse, "I am glorified in them." John 17: 10. The hymn was published in 1864, the six omitted stanzas being:—

3. For the apostles' glorious company
Who, bearing forth the cross o'er land and sea,
Shook all the mighty world, we sing to Thee,
Alleluia!

4. For the evangelists—by whose pure word
Like fourfold stream, the garden of the Lord
Is fair and fruitful, by Thy name adored.
Alleluia!

5. For martyrs—who with rapture-kindled eye
Saw the bright crown descending from the sky
And dying, grasped it—Thee we glorify.
Alleluia!

7. O blest communion! fellowship divine!
We fight, as they did, 'neath the holy sign;
And all are one in Thee, for all are Thine,
Alleluia!

9. The golden evening brightens in the west;
Soon, soon to faithful warriors comes their rest;
Sweet is the calm of Paradise the blest.
Alleluia!

10. But lo! there breaks a yet more glorious day.
The saints triumphant rise in bright array:
The King of glory passes on His way,
Alleluia!

The tune *Sine Nomine* (= without a name) was composed in 1906 by Ralph Vaughan Williams (1872-1958) especially for these words, and given this Latin name by him. He received his Mus. Doc. from Cambridge University in 1901 and took a great interest in studying English country folk-songs. He was awarded the Order of Merit in 1935 for his services to music. He also harmonized No. 685, *Picardy*, and No. 430, *Shipston*.

365. FOR ALL THE SAINTS

John 17: 10

For the words by William Walsham How (1823-97), see appendix, see the previous hymn No. 364.

The tune *Sarum* was composed expressly for these words in 1869 by Joseph Barnby (1838-96), see appendix. It was published in the Sarum hymnal as *Sarum No. 299*, and the name abbreviated is now attached to this tune. Sarum is the old site of the cathedral city of Salisbury, Wiltshire, situated two miles north of the present cathedral.

366. SOLDIERS OF CHRIST, ARISE

Ephesians 6: 11-18

These words are a small selection, namely, stanzas 1, 2, and 16, from the original hymn of sixteen stanzas written in 1749 by Charles Wesley (1707-88), see appendix. They were entitled "The Whole Armour of God"—note the Greek word panoply (= all the arms, armour) in stanza 2—and were based on the Apostle Paul's description in detail of the Christian's weapons of warfare against sin. "Wherefore take unto you the whole armour of God, that ye may be able to withstand in the evil day, and having done all, to stand. . . . For we wrestle . . . against powers, against the rulers of the darkness of this world." Ephesians 6: 13, 12. Some of the omitted stanzas are:—

3. Stand then against your foes,
In close and firm array:
Legions of wily fiends oppose
Throughout the evil day;
But meet the sons of night,
But mock their vain design,
Arm'd in the arms of heavenly light,
Of righteousness divine.

5. Let truth the girdle be,
That binds your armour on,
In faithful, firm sincerity
To Jesus cleave alone.
Let faith and love combine,
To guard your valiant breast;
The plate be righteousness divine,
Imputed, and impress'd.

6. Still let your feet be shod,
Ready His will to do,
Ready in all the ways of God
His glory to pursue.
Ruin is spread beneath,
The gospel greaves put on,
And safe through all the snares of death
To life eternal run.

10. Brandish in faith till then
The Spirit's two-edged sword,
Hew all the snares of fiends and men
In pieces with the Word;
'Tis written; this applied
Baffles their strength and art;
Spirit and soul with this divide,
And joints and marrow part.

11. To keep your armour bright,
Attend with constant care,
Still walking in your Captain's sight,
And watching unto prayer;
Ready for all alarms
Steadfastly set your face,
And always exercise your arms
And use your every grace.

12. Pray, without ceasing pray,
(Your Captain gives the word)
His summons cheerfully obey,
And call upon the Lord;
To God your every want
In instant prayer display,
Pray, always; pray, and never faint,
Pray, without ceasing pray.

The tune *Diademata* (= crowns) was composed in 1868 by Sir George Job Elvey (1816-93) organist of St. George's Chapel, Windsor, for forty-seven years. It was so named because it was written especially for the words of No. 162, "Crown Him With Many Crowns." Note that the melody of line 6 copies that of line 5 but is one note higher. He also composed Nos. 496, *St. George's Windsor,* and 686, a response.

367. CHRISTIAN, DOST THOU SEE THEM?

Ephesians 6: 12

St. Andrew of Crete (660-732) was born at Damascus, became a monk at Jerusalem, and later archbishop of Crete. He wrote the Great Canon for Lent, and the part appointed for the second week was very freely translated from the Greek in 1862 by John Mason Neale (1818-66), see appendix, for this hymn. The first three stanzas are all in the same form, the first half asking a question and depicting the inroads of the subtle forces of temptation, while the last half is a triumphant appeal to the Christian to be a bold victorious soldier of the cross. Some slight alterations have been made, for example: stanza 1, lines 3 and 4 were originally,

How the troops of Midian
Prowl and prowl around?

and lines 7 and 8,

Smite them by the merit
Of the holy Cross!

and stanza 2, lines 7 and 8,

Smite them by the virtue
Of the Lenten fast!

The hymn reveals the Christian's real enemy, "For we wrestle not against flesh and blood, but against principalities, against powers, against the rulers of the darkness of this world." Ephesians 6: 12.

The music was specially written for these words in 1868 by John Bacchus Dykes (1823-76), see appendix. He has followed the structure of the words by using a sober minor key for the first half of the stanza, modulating to a major key for the second half appropriate to the martial spirit of the words of this part. The name of the tune *St. Andrew of Crete,* commemorates the author of the original hymn. The change from minor to major key is not uncommon to Dykes, other examples being Nos. 129, *St. John,* and 225, *Vox Dilecti.*

368. WE'RE BOUND FOR THE LAND OF THE PURE

Genesis 2: 15

This song is that of a pilgrim who having learned of the glories of the restored Eden, unselfishly invites others to join him on his way. About one half of the hymn describes the beauties of the new earth, and the remainder is an appeal to those yet in sin. Eden remains a symbol of perfection, and its main feature, the tree of life, will be restored in God's perfect new creation (Revelation 22: 2) in the paradise of God. The word "paradise" means a park and fitly describes man's original home—"And the Lord God took the man, and put him into the garden of Eden." Genesis 2: 15. The last stanza is:—

6. March on, happy pilgrims, the land is before you,
And soon its ten thousand delights we shall prove;
Yes, soon we shall walk o'er the hills of bright glory,
And drink the pure joys of the Eden above.
We will go, we will go, we will go, we will go,
O yes, we will go to the Eden above.

The words have been attributed to the Rev. William Hunter, D.D. (1811-77) under date of 1842. He was the author of Nos. 530, "The Great Physician Now Is Near," and 662, "Let Others Seek a Home Below."

369. COME, LET US ANEW

John 17: 4

Charles Wesley (1707-88), see appendix, wrote three stanzas, each of eight lines, of this hymn which was designed for the watch night service as the old year concluded. It was first published for New Year's Day, 1750, and, like most of his hymns, quotes or paraphrases many scriptures. The incentive which he sets before the people is so to live in the forthcoming year that at its close the Lord's own statement would be appropriate to them: "I have finished the work Thou gavest Me to do." John 17: 4. Other scriptures easily recognizable are: Psalm 90: 4, 5; 2 Timothy 4: 7; Matthew 25: 21; Revelation 3: 21. The peculiar metre, now arranged as six stanzas, each of four lines of varying length, is most noticeable, showing both Wesley's remarkable fluency and his refusal to be bound by the then existing restrictions to long metre, short metre, or common metre.

370. DAY IS DONE, GONE THE SUN

Psalm 121: 3

The tune *Taps* is the United States Army Bugle Call, coming from the Pennsylvania Military College at Chester, fifteen miles south-west of Philadelphia. Soldiers added the following words:

Fading light
Dims the sight,
In the sky shines a star gleaming bright,
From afar drawing near falls the night.

The present words are a good-night blessing and are similar in thought to David's assurance, "He will not suffer thy foot to be moved: He that keepeth thee will not slumber." Psalm 121: 3.

371. I SAW ONE WEARY

Titus 2: 13

The first three stanzas of this hymn written in 1852 refer to three personalities in the early history of the Seventh-day Adventist Church. The authoress, Annie Rebekah Smith (1828-55), see appendix, was converted by Joseph Bates (1792-1872) who is referred to in the first stanza. He was a former sea captain who gave all his wealth to the promulgation of the gospel of the second advent. He always signed his letters "Yours in the blessed hope" a quotation based on the words, "Looking for that blessed hope, and the glorious appearing of the great God and our Saviour Jesus Christ." Titus 2: 13. The second stanza is a word picture of James White (1821-81), the virtual leader by pen and voice of the church in its early struggles. Facing poverty, incessant labour, fanaticism, and other hardships, his courage remained steadfast because of his firm hope in the second advent. The third stanza has often been thought to refer to John Nevins Andrews (1828-83) who was the first foreign missionary sent by Seventh-day Adventists in 1874. At the time of writing this hymn, however, he was not so well known as he was later to be. Neither could it refer to Uriah Smith, Annie's brother, who was not then a Sabbath-keeper. Annie Smith's mother stated that Annie had written her own experience, but for the sake of consistency had left masculine pronouns, and that she was quite willing for it to apply to whomsoever it fitted. Later it could well have fitted the experience of Uriah Smith who forsook a lucrative position to become a gospel minister and editor. The hymn first appeared on the front page of the *Review and Herald*, of August 19, 1852, under the title "The Blessed Hope," and it was written at Rochester, New York.

The tune *Duane Street* was composed in 1835 by George Coles (1792-1858), a Methodist minister at the Duane Street church in New York city. It is also used for No. 481, "O Solemn Thought."

372. A FEW MORE YEARS SHALL ROLL

Amos 4: 12

Horatius Bonar (1808-89), see appendix, wrote six stanzas of this hymn entitled "A Pilgrim's Song" in 1843. The last half of each stanza is really a refrain, recalling the expression in Amos 4: 12, "Prepare to meet thy God." The key word of the hymn is "few" which occurs no less than seven times in three stanzas. The two omitted stanzas are:—

2. A few more suns shall set
O'er these dark hills of time;
And we shall be where suns are not,
A far serener clime.

5. A few more Sabbaths here
Shall cheer us on our way;
And we shall reach the endless rest,
The eternal Sabbath day.

The tune named *Bonar* after the author of the words, was composed by Lowell Mason (1792-1872), see appendix.

373. PILGRIMS ON, THE DAY IS DAWNING

Hebrews 11: 13

This anonymous hymn is based on the well-known figure of the Christian being one of a group of "strangers and pilgrims on the earth" (Hebrew 11: 13), a reference to which is made also in stanza 3, line 3. The whole hymn implies a hard background with very little of the Christian joy shining through, but rather a grim determination to toil on faithfully. Notice the dark and dreary way, the anguish of life, wild storms, dangers, trials, temptations, and strife. Nevertheless, the author's eye is fixed on the prize of eternal rest in the peaceful presence of Jesus, "One receiveth the prize. . . . Every man that striveth for the mastery." 1 Corinthians 9: 24, 25. There are two omitted stanzas:—

3. Pilgrims on! though darkness cover
All earth's pathway to the tomb;
Angels o'er thy pathway hover,
'Mid the deep surrounding gloom.
Light effulgent gleams above you
From the throne of glory, where
Bright seraphic ones who love you
Witness all your grief and care!

5. Pilgrims on! the day is ending—
Life's probation day of woe;
Twilight shades e'en now are blending
With the sunbeam's faintest glow.
Soon the night of death impending,
Shall your toilsome journey end,
Hope, like starlight smiles descending
Cheers while o'er the grave you bend.

374. THERE IS A ROAD

Matthew 7: 14

Douglas Albert Raoul Aufranc (1892-), a Seventh-day Adventist doctor and dentist, used to pass frequently through the town of Thetford in Norfolk, England. For several miles before entering the town, the road was very beautiful, trees on both sides meeting overhead and giving shade. The old Roman road now little more than a footpath, ran also very close to Thetford and prompted the thought of the narrow way pointed out by our Lord just about the time when the old Roman road was being constructed in Britain nearly two thousand years ago. "Because strait is the gate, and narrow is the way, which leadeth unto life, and few there be that find it." Matthew 7: 14.

The tune *Thetford* was also composed by Dr. Aufranc and commemorates the town near which the words were inspired. He also wrote the words of Nos. 335, "Alone With Thee"; 468, "Far From All Care," and 682, "Father, I Yield to Thee My Life," and composed the tunes associated with the first two of these, namely Nos. 335, *Windy Ridge,* and 468, *Pevensey.*

375. HARK! HARK, MY SOUL!

Matthew 11: 28

Frederick William Faber (1814-63), a minister converted from the Anglican Church to the Roman Catholic, wrote seven stanzas of the hymn in 1854. It was entitled "The Pilgrims of the Night" and depicts our earthly pilgrimage as a dark night preceding the glorious eternal day in the future heavenly home. This thought is revealed in the original last lines of the last stanza which were:—

While we toil on and soothe ourselves with weeping,
Till life's long night shall break in endless love.

The sentiment of the hymn is well summed up in the scripture quotation of our second stanza, "Come unto Me, all ye that labour and are heavy laden, and I will give you rest." Matthew 11: 28. The omitted stanzas are:—

2. Darker than night life's shadows fall around us,
And, like benighted men, we miss our mark;
God hides Himself, and grace hath scarcely found us,
Ere death finds out his victims in the dark.

5. Rest comes at length; though life be long and dreary,
The day must dawn, and darksome night be past;
All journeys end in welcomes to the weary,
And heaven, the heart's true home, will come at last.

6. Cheer up, my soul! faith's moonbeams softly glisten
Upon the breast of life's most troubled sea;
And it will cheer thy drooping heart to listen
To those brave songs which angels mean for thee.

Faber also wrote Nos. 65, "There's a Wideness"; 349, "Faith of Our Fathers," and 443, "Workman of God."

The tune *Sherwin* is named after the composer William Fisk Sherwin (1826-88), see appendix. The last line of the refrain has a complete descending octave in the melody.

376. HARK! HARK, MY SOUL!

Matthew 11: 28

For comments on the words by Frederick William Faber (1814-63), see the previous hymn, No. 375.

The tune *Pilgrims* was specially written and named for these words in 1868 by the English organist and organ builder Henry Thomas Smart (1813-79). It is also known as *Vox Angelica* (= Angelic Voice). Other tunes by Smart are Nos. 113 and 487, *Regent Square;* 135 and 362, *Lancashire,* and 363, *Chebar,* reminding us of the fact that he served as organist in Blackburn, Lancashire, and also in the Presbyterian church in Regent's Square, London.

377. O HAPPY BAND OF PILGRIMS

Matthew 5: 10

Joseph, a native of Sicily, was born about the year A.D. 800. He was captured by pirates and became a slave in Crete. Later he was liberated and became a monk in Constantinople where until his death about the year 883, he wrote such a large number of hymns that he earned the title of Joseph the Hymnographer. This one of his hymns written about A.D. 840 was translated very freely by John Mason Neale (1818-66), see appendix, and appeared as eight stanzas in his "Hymns of the Eastern Church," published in 1862. The omitted stanzas are:—

3. The cross which Jesus carried
He carried as your due:
The crown that Jesus weareth
He weareth it for you.

4. The faith by which ye see Him,
The hope, in which ye yearn,
The love that through all troubles
To Him alone will turn—

5. What are they, but vaunt-couriers
To lead you to His sight?
What are they, save the effluence
Of uncreated light?

There is so little taken from the Greek hymn (as in No. 341) that it is virtually an original hymn by Neale. The words emphasize the happiness of the Christian amid all kinds of difficulties and re-echo the beatitudes which were ascriptions of blessedness or happiness, "Blessed are they which are persecuted for righteousness' sake: for theirs is the kingdom of heaven." Matthew 5: 10.

The tune *Vulpius,* written in 1609, commemorates the composer Melchoir Vulpius (1560-1616) who was a German composer of chorales, harmonizer of many hymn tunes, and editor of a German song-book which appeared in 1604.

378. WHENCE CAME THE ARMIES?

Revelation 19: 14

"And the armies which were in heaven followed Him upon white horses, clothed in fine linen, white and clean." Revelation 19: 14. The anonymous writer of this hymn identifies those described in this verse with the saints of all ages, who have not yet, of course, received their reward. However, like the Apostle John, he projects himself into the future and describes events which have not happened as though they are just taking place, e.g., "now they claim their mansion," stanza 5.

The tune *Avon,* also used for No. 124, "Alas! and Did My Saviour Bleed?" was written about 1800 by Hugh Wilson, a shoemaker of Ayrshire. It is also known as *Martyrdom* and both names commemorate the Scottish covenanters who were slain for their faith in 1679 near the Avon River, and who, as stanza 2 states, were indeed "tried soldiers of the cross" in a very literal sense.

379. THERE IS A BLESSED HOPE

Titus 2:13

The unknown author of this hymn has written three stanzas about three different topics, and then summarized them all in the fourth stanza, repeating them in reverse order. 1. The hope is the hope of heaven, "Looking for that blessed hope, and the glorious appearing of the great God and our Saviour Jesus Christ." Titus 2: 13. 2. The star is the light given by this revelation, that is, the prophecy of the deliverance from death, a "prophecy . . . as unto a light that shineth in a dark place, until the day dawn, and the day star arise in your hearts." 2 Peter 1: 19. 3. The voice is the voice of forgiveness revealed in Calvary's gift, "God is love . . . He loved us, and sent His Son to be the propitiation for our sins." 1 John 4: 8, 10.

The tune *Dennis,* also used for Nos. 432, "Blest Be the Tie," and 439, "With Willing Hearts We Tread," is an arrangement by Lowell Mason (1792-1872), see appendix, of a Swiss tune by Johann George Nägeli (1773-1836) of Zurich. He was a Swiss composer, teacher and music publisher, who reformed the teaching of music in schools. He also composed the original tune *Naomi* which is used for Nos. 322, "O, Could I Find From Day to Day," and 333, "Father, Whate'er of Earthly Bliss."

380. THERE IS SWEET REST

Hebrews 4: 9

Both words and music were written in 1878 by Franklin Edson Belden (1858-1945), see appendix, and appear in "Hymns and Tunes" 1886, and in James Edson White's "Song Anchor," 1881. The word "rest" is mentioned in three of the stanzas and implied in the second stanza, so that an apt Scripture summary could be, "There remaineth therefore a rest to the people of God." Hebrews 4: 9.

The tune *Hakes* is named after D. S. Hakes who composed five tunes in the "Church Hymnal" to Belden's words (Nos. 66, 493, 500, 613, and 629).

381. O WHO, IN SUCH A WORLD

Hebrews 12: 6

These words were written by James Montgomery (1771-1854), see appendix, in an attempt to explain in verse the perplexing problem of pain. He shows that to the Christian it is an indication to look elsewhere to a land where there is no suffering, this attitude and this hope being one the Lord has given. For we are reminded that "whom the Lord loveth He chasteneth, and scourgeth every son whom He receiveth" (Hebrews 12: 6), and that therefore our disappointments and sorrows should help us remember that we are the children of a heavenly Father who has a perfect home of happiness awaiting us.

The tune *Valentia* was arranged by George Kingsley (1811-84) of Northampton, Massachusetts, a compiler of music for young people, music teacher and organist in Boston, and later professor of music in Philadelphia. He also composed Nos. 204 and 483, *Ware,* and 458, *Elizabethtown.* The originator of the tune was Traugott Maximilian Eberwein (1775-1831) of Weimar, Germany, a violinist, and composer of operas, songs, and quartets, who became musical director for one of the German princes.

382. NEARER, MY GOD, TO THEE

Genesis 28: 10-19

Sarah Fuller Flower Adams (1805-48) wrote these words in 1840 at the request of her minister, the Rev. W. J. Fox, who was compiling a collection of hymns to be used by his own congregation of Unitarians in Finsbury, London. The fact that the authoress was a Unitarian has led to large emphasis on the non-use of the name of Christ in the hymn and has resulted in several changes.

However, the hymn is based on Jacob's experience at Bethel, where the fugitive found that although he had run away from home, he could not escape from God. "And, behold, I am with thee, and will keep thee in all places whither thou goest, and will bring thee again into this land; for I will not leave thee." Genesis 28: 15. Jacob hence found that he was indeed drawn nearer to God at Bethel which is the Hebrew word for "house of God." It is said that the title "Nearer to Thee," was inspired by the story of a martyr who was being mocked by a Roman soldier who was nailing the sufferer to a cross. "We will lift you a little nearer to your God," he jeered, only to receive the reply, "You are raising me nearer than you think."

The hymn was published in 1841 and was greatly popularized by the tune *Bethany,* composed in 1856 specifically for these words by Lowell Mason (1792-1872), see appendix. One night he lay awake and the melody came to him in the darkness, to be written down the next morning. One wonders why he did not name the tune *Bethel* which is where Jacob's experience occurred, and which is actually named in the fourth stanza.

383. O, FOR A CLOSER WALK

Genesis 5: 24

This hymn, No. 111 in "Olney Hymns," Book I, 1779, was written in 1769 by William Cowper (1731-1800), see appendix, at a time when his friend Mrs. Mary Unwin was very ill. The first two lines were written before daybreak, and the third and fourth after he fell asleep again, being "whispered to his heart in a way he had often experienced," he said. The despondent note in the first half of the hymn, typical of the poet's own up-and-down experience, is somewhat of a contrast to his title, "Walking with God." "And Enoch walked with God." Genesis 5: 24. Another of the original six stanzas reveals his unsatisfactory introspection:—

2. Where is the blessedness I knew
When first I saw the Lord?
Where is the soul-refreshing view
Of Jesus and His word?

Our stanzas 2 and 3 have been interchanged, being originally 4 and 3, so that his last three stanzas led to a mounting climax culminating in a last triumphant note as follows in the other omitted stanza:

6. So shall my walk be close with God,
Calm and serene my frame;
So purer light shall mark the road
That leads me to the Lamb.

The tune *Manoah,* also used for No. 25, "Again Our Earthly Cares We Leave," is an adaptation made by Henry Wellington Greatorex (1813-58), appearing in his "Church Music," 1851. He was born in Burton-on-Trent, Derbyshire, and emigrated to the United States in 1838 where he became organist at the Center Congregational church, Hartford, Connecticut, and later at some Protestant Episcopal churches in New York. Greatorex also composed Nos. 174, *Leighton;* 689, *Gloria Patri,* and arranged Nos. 48 and 318, *Seymour.*

384. O GOD, MINE INMOST SOUL CONVERT

1 Corinthians 15: 34

Charles Wesley (1707-88), see appendix, wrote six stanzas of a hymn entitled "An Hymn for Seriousness" of which these are the last four stanzas. The omitted ones are:—

1. Thou God of glorious majesty,
To Thee, against myself, to Thee,
A worm of earth, I cry:
An half-awakened child of man;
An heir of endless bliss, or pain;—
A sinner born to die!

2. Lo! on a narrow neck of land
'Twixt two unbounded seas I stand,
Secure, insensible:
A point of time, a moment's space,
Removes to that heavenly place,
Or shuts me up in hell.

It was published in 1749 and the second stanza suggests that it was written while on a visit to Land's End in the tip of Cornwall, when contemplating the creative power of God. Its solemn title is borne out by the expressions "impress on my thoughtful heart," "solemn weight," "dread array," "pomp," and "serious industry and fear." As with most of his hymns, Scripture is quoted or paraphrased extensively, one example being, "Awake to righteousness, and sin not." 1 Corinthians 15: 34.

The tune *Meribah* was composed in 1839 by Lowell Mason (1792-1872), see appendix, and was inspired by the words of No. 190, "When Thou My Righteous Judge Shalt Come." Again it is one of Mason's Old Testament names—the rock which Moses struck (Numbers 20: 13)—which have no association either with the words or music of the hymn.

385. MORE LOVE TO THEE

1 John 4: 17

Mrs. Elizabeth Payson Prentiss (1818-78) was passing through a time of great sorrow in 1856 which culminated in the loss of her children in an epidemic. She penned these lines after resigning herself to the fact that her deep grief was softened by the love of her Saviour. The hymn "Nearer, My God, to Thee" (No. 382) had been of great comfort to her, and she used the same metre for these words. She did not show the lines to her husband, a Presbyterian minister in New York City, until 1869 and it was first printed in that year as a leaflet and appeared in a hymn book the next year. The increase in love to Christ of which each stanza speaks, suggests a progression which is implied in the words of the verse, "Herein is our love made perfect, that we may have boldness in the day of judgment." 1 John 4: 17.

The tune was composed in 1868 by William Howard Doane (1832-1916), see appendix, and published to these words in 1870.

386. LORD, IN THE FULLNESS

Ecclesiastes 12: 1

These words were written in 1855 by Thomas Hornblower Gill (1819-1906) under the heading "Early Love" and Oliver Cromwell's statement, "How good it is to close with Christ betimes." The hymn had eight stanzas originally, those omitted being:—

1. With sin I would not make abode
While shines each golden hour;
Nor keep away from Thee, my God,
Till falls my blissful bower.

4. Why should I lend the world's poor song
These glowing lips of mine,
And keep my dull, untunéd tongue
To sing Thy songs divine?

8. I cannot, Lord, too early take
The covenant divine;
O! ne'er the happy heart may break
Whose earliest love was Thine.

The hymn throughout contrasts the vigour of youth with the languor of old age, promising also the former, and not merely the latter, to the Lord. "Remember now thy Creator in the days of thy youth, while the evil days come not, nor the years draw nigh, when thou shalt say, I have no pleasure in them." Ecclesiastes 12: 1. Gill was born in Birmingham, England, of Unitarian parents, but later he adopted the Trinitarian view. He wrote over 200 hymns, most of them with added notes, and appearing in "The Golden Chain of Praise," 1869. He also wrote No. 95, "The Glory of the Spring."

The tune by Joseph Barnby (1838-96), see appendix, is not named in his 1869 publication of "Hymns with Tunes," but a posthumous edition of 1897 names it *Holy Trinity* because it is there associated with the hymn "As Now the Sun's Declining Rays," the last stanza of which begins with the words, "To God the Father, God the Son, and God the Holy Ghost."

387. HOW CHEERING IS THE CHRISTIAN'S HOPE

Revelation 21: 4

This hymn by an anonymous author is an expression of the Christian's hope of eternal life in a land which has none of earth's sorrows. An omitted stanza is:—

4. O, how unlike the present world,
 Will be the one to come!
 Here, pain and sorrow, care and fear,
 Attend where'er we roam.

The hymn appears in the 1876 edition of "Hymns and Tunes for Those Who Keep the Commandments of God and the Faith of Jesus." Scriptures partly quoted are: "They . . . reigned with Christ," (Revelation 20: 4); "And God shall wipe away all tears from their eyes; and there shall be no more death" (Revelation 21: 4); "Neither can they die any more: for they are equal unto the angels; and are . . . the children of the resurrection" (Luke 20: 36); "Even so, come, Lord Jesus" (Revelation 22: 20); and "When He shall appear . . . we shall see Him as He is" (1 John 3: 2).

388. PURER YET AND PURER

Philippians 3: 13, 14

This hymn has been attributed to Johann Wolfgang Goethe (1749-1832), the famous German poet and philosopher, for it appears as a twelve-stanza poem under the title "Longings" in "Iphigenia in Tauris, with Original Poems," 1851. This book contains some translations from Goethe, together with original poems by Anne R. Bennet, a writer of religious verse, and she is most probably the author of these lines. Each stanza had originally four lines, those omitted being:—

5. Brighter yet and brighter,
 Virtue still perceive;
 Clearer yet and clearer,
 Know Thee and believe.

6. Christ's command obeying,
Perfect seek to be;
Earnestly desiring,
Union still with Thee.

7. Farther yet and farther,
From all evil flee;
Closer yet and closer,
Ever draw to Thee.

8. Still in heart ascending,
Up to Thee above;
And Thy truth embracing,
Hold it fast in love.

The pattern of the hymn is thus quite consistent, being composed with slight exceptions toward the end of the poem, of comparative adverbs or adjectives in lines one and three, followed by present participles in the next two odd lines. The constant desire to be better and purer and holier is similar to the constant striving of the Apostle Paul who was not content with present attainments: "Brethren, I count not myself to have apprehended: but this one thing I do, forgetting those things which are behind, and reaching forth unto those things which are before, I press toward the mark for the prize of the high calling of God in Christ Jesus." Philippians 3: 13, 14.

The music was composed in 1862 by John Bacchus Dykes (1823-76), see appendix, and named *Mary Magdalene* by him. It was specially written for the words "In the Hour of Trial," No. 327.

389. THOU ART, O CHRIST, THE LIGHT AND LIFE

1 Timothy 1: 1

Charles H. Rominger has written this personal confession of the weakness of the Christian to stand alone, and also of the glory of God's grace which gives him strength in times of doubt, and courage in times of temptation. Scriptures suggested are: "I sought the Lord, and He heard me, and delivered me from all my fears" (Psalm 34: 4); "For now we see through a glass, darkly; but then face to face" (1 Corinthians 13: 12); "For the Lord hath redeemed Jacob, and ransomed him from the hand of him that was stronger than he. Therefore they shall come and sing in the height of Zion; . . . and they shall not sorrow any more at all." Jeremiah 31: 11, 12. The hymn throughout exalts the Lord as our unique hope, the One who can answer all our fears—"Lord Jesus Christ, which is our hope." 1 Timothy 1: 1.

390. NEARER, STILL NEARER

John 6: 44

Both words and music were written by Mrs. C. H. Morris (1862-19?), a Methodist of McConnellsville, Ohio, who was converted at the age of ten years. She was a poetess and musician, and even after becoming blind in middle age, still continued her creative work by dictating her compositions, of which there are more than one thousand, to her daughter. The quiet devotional spirit of this hymn of personal experience exemplifies her own philosophy, namely that a noble and virtuous life is an essential pre-requisite for the writing of a noble poem. The hymn shows the need of a willing surrender of sin's follies under the compulsive power of a divine love, which asks for repentance; "No can can come to Me, except the Father which hath sent Me draw him: and I will raise him up at the last day." John 6: 44.

391. SHEPHERD DIVINE

Psalm 23: 1, 2, 6

This is a Seventh-day Adventist paraphrase of part of the Shepherd Psalm, for both author and composer were prominent members of this church. The words were written in 1886 by Franklin Edson Belden (1858-1945), see appendix, and the tune *Winterbourne* by Edwin Barnes (1864-1930), see appendix, and the hymn first appeared in "Hymns and Tunes," 1886, of which both men were musical editors. It is a very free paraphrase and uses only the following verses: "The Lord is my Shepherd; I shall not want. He maketh me to lie down in green pastures: He leadeth me beside the still waters." "I will dwell in the house of the Lord for ever." Psalm 23: 1, 2, 6.

Winterbourne is the prefix of the name of four Dorsetshire villages, all between thirty and forty miles from the composer's birthplace, Southampton.

392. UNSHAKEN AS THE SACRED HILLS

Psalm 125: 1, 2, 4

Isaac Watts (1674-1748), see appendix, wrote this paraphrase of the 125th psalm in 1719 and entitled it "The Saints' Trial and Safety." The third stanza is not in his version though it is a close paraphrase of the fourth verse of the psalm. The three omitted stanzas are:—

3. While tyrants are a smarting scourge,
   To drive them near to God,
   Divine compassion does allay
   The fury of the rod.

4. Deal gently, Lord, with souls sincere,
And lead them safely on
To the bright gates of Paradise,
Where Christ their Lord is gone.

5. But if we trace those crooked ways
That the old serpent drew,
The wrath that drove him first to hell,
Shall smite his fellowers, too.

The first two stanzas closely follow the thought of the words, "They that trust in the Lord shall be as Mount Zion, which cannot be removed. . . . As the mountains are round about Jerusalem, so the Lord is round about His people." Psalm 125: 1, 2.

The tune *Dundee,* used also for Nos. 84, "God Moves in a Mysterious Way," and 88, "O God of Bethel," appeared in the "Scottish Psalter" in 1615. Dundee was equivalent to the Geneva of Scotland, for it was a stronghold of the Reformation doctrine.

393. HE LEADETH ME

Psalm 23: 2

In the spring of 1862 Joseph Henry Gilmore (1834-1918), a Baptist minister, was visiting the city of Philadelphia. He was invited to address the mid-week prayer meeting and spoke there of God's leadership, using part of the Shepherd Psalm as a basis for his talk. After the meeting he continued to discuss this theme at the home of his host, deacon Wattson of Arch Street, Philadelphia. His mind was so full of the thought of God's guidance in every phase of our life, that there and then he wrote these four stanzas and passed them to his wife without comment. Without telling her husband she sent the poem to a religious periodical, *The Watchman and Reflector,* where unknown to him, it appeared in print. Three years later Gilmore was due to preach in the Baptist church at Rochester, New York, and taking up a hymn book and opening it at random he was astonished to find his own poem set to music. He did not recognize nor acknowledge his authorship of the refrain until his wife's death some years later, when he discovered his original manuscript among her papers, complete with a chorus of two lines only. The hymn is based on the words, "He leadeth me besides the still waters" (Psalm 23: 2), but also introduces the thought of "Yea, though I walk through the valley of the shadow of death, I will fear no evil." Verse 4. Gilmore was later a professor at the University of Rochester from 1868-1908.

The tune *He Leadeth Me,* otherwise *Aughton,* was composed in 1864 by William Batchelder Bradbury (1816-68), see appendix, especially for these words and was published in *The Golden Censer*. He had noticed the poem in print and named his tune from the words "leadeth me" which occur in each stanza, and four times in each chorus.

394. SAVIOUR, LIKE A SHEPHERD

Psalm 23: 2

This children's hymn appeared unsigned in 1832 in the fourth edition of "Hymns for the Young" by Dorothy Ann Thrupp (1799-1847) of London, where it has four stanzas. It was attributed in 1838 to Henry Francis Lyte (1793-1847) (see No. 50) in its second appearance in print, but all later versions have been anonymous. The first stanza derives its theme from the words, "The Lord is my Shepherd. . . . In green pastures: He leadeth me." Psalm 23: 1, 2. The omitted stanza is:—

4. Early let us seek Thy favour,
Early let us do Thy will;
Blessed Lord and only Saviour,
With Thy love our bosoms fill;
Blessed Jesus
Thou hast loved us, love us still.

The tune was composed in 1859 by William Batchelder Bradbury (1816-68), see appendix. It is here named *Shepherd* because of the title given to the Saviour in the first line of the hymn; elsewhere it is named *Bradbury* after the composer.

395. O LET ME WALK WITH THEE

Genesis 5: 24

Both the authoress and the composer of this hymn were Seventh-day Adventists. Mrs. Lillian Dale Avery-Stuttle (1855-1933) was a student at Battle Creek College, Michigan, in the late 1870s and became an editorial worker. She was a woman of deep devotion, faith, and courage, and the author of many beautiful poems and several books. One of her poems, "The Riven Veil," appeared on the front page of the *Review and Herald* in the issue dated March 16, 1933, one day before her death. Mrs. Avery-Stuttle evidently expected to be one of the glorious company who would be alive and faithful at the second advent of Jesus, and who like Enoch, would be "translated, that he should not see death." Hebrews 11: 5. "And Enoch walked with God." Genesis 5: 24. This hymn was her own favourite.

The words were set to music in 1886 by Edwin Barnes (1864-1930), see appendix, and the tune was named *Morton* to commemorate Eliza H. Morton, a former teacher at Battle Creek College.

396. THY WAY, NOT MINE

Matthew 26: 39

These words are those of a pilgrim walking along the way to the heavenly kingdom and were written by Horatius Bonar (1808-89), see appendix, as a seven stanza hymn entitled "Thy Way, Not Mine." The two omitted stanzas are:—

5. Take Thou my cup, and it
With joy or sorrow fill,
As best to Thee may seem;
Choose Thou my good and ill.

6. Choose Thou for me my friends,
My sickness or my health;
Choose Thou my cares for me,
My poverty or wealth.

The words are based on our Lord's willing acceptance of His Father's will as recorded in Matthew 26: 39: "Nevertheless not as I will, but as Thou wilt."

The tune *St. Cecilia* was composed in 1863 by the Rev. Leighton George Hayne (1836-83), composer, conductor, organist and Oxford University examiner. It was written specially for these words and named to commemorate Cecilia who is the patron saint of music. Her life was an example of these words which express perfect trust in God, for she was martyred about A.D. 225 for refusing to sacrifice to the Roman gods and for maintaining her faith in Christ as her Lord. Traditional details are that on the eve of her wedding she consecrated her virginity to God. Her husband-to-be, Valerian, embraced Christianity and was baptized, but both were martyred a few days later. Cecilia was suffocated in a hot air bath, but survived, then was so clumsily executed that she took three days to die.

397. I WILL NEVER LEAVE THEE

Hebrews 13: 5

The anonymous author has written four stanzas of comforting assurance from the standpoint of the Saviour addressing one of His followers, promising His guidance whether the days be dark or bright. While full of comfort and promise to the Christian, the words are somewhat unusual for a hymn which is sung by those who need this help, but they contain the implied thought that the singer relies on the Lord's promises and here repeats them. An omitted stanza is:—

5. Thou may'st leave My care and keeping,
Thou may'st wander far from Me;
Sorrow, then, and woe and weeping,
Mercy must mete out to thee;
To the righteous
My rich blessings all are free.

Several scriptures are quoted wholly or in part, for example: Psalm 31: 3; 23: 4; 73: 24; 91: 15; Isaiah 40: 11; Psalm 36: 8; 37: 23; Micah 7: 8; Song of Solomon 2: 4. The one chosen to summarize the hymn is, "For He hath said, I will never leave thee, nor forsake thee." Hebrews 13: 5.

The tune *Promise* has four of its twelve bars identical, namely, 1, 3, 5, and 7, and lines 3 and 4 repeat exactly lines 1 and 2.

398. JESUS, SAVIOUR, PILOT ME

Mark 4: 29

Dr. Edward Hopper (1818-88) was the pastor of the Church of the Sea and Land, in New York, and therefore had much to do with the seafaring man in his ministry. He wrote these words anonymously in 1871 in *The Sailor's Magazine,* taking the basic idea from Mark 4: 39 where Jesus stilled the storm on Galilee with the words, "Peace, be still." A separate incident recorded in Matthew 14: 24-32 concerning Jesus walking on the sea to join His disciples in their boat, is described in one of the omitted stanzas.

2. When the apostles' fragile bark
Struggled with the billows dark,
On the stormy Galilee,
Thou didst walk upon the sea;
And when they beheld Thy form,
Safe they glided through the storm.

3. Though the sea be smooth and bright,
Sparkling with the stars of night,
And my ship's path be ablaze,
With the light of halcyon days,
Still I know my need of Thee;
Jesus, Saviour, pilot me.

4. When the darkling heavens frown,
And the wrathful winds come down,
And the fierce waves, tossed on high,
Lash themselves against the sky,
Jesus, Saviour, pilot me
Over life's tempestuous sea.

The tune *Pilot* was composed in 1871 especially for these words by John Edgar Gould (1822-75), the son of a sea-captain. He was an American conductor and song publisher, and composer of several hymn tunes, one of which is No. 330, *Bera*. By the age of thirty he had a music shop on Broadway, New York City, and later he entered into partnership in a retail piano business in Philadelphia with William G. Fischer (see Nos. 518, 592, 600, 633).

399. THERE IS A SAFE AND SECRET PLACE

Psalm 91

This paraphrase of some verses of the 91st Psalm was written in 1834 by Henry Francis Lyte (1793-1847), the famous author of the hymn "Abide with Me." There were originally five stanzas, the omitted one being:—

3. The angels watch him on his way,
   And aid with friendly arm;
   And Satan roaring for his prey,
   May hate, but cannot harm.

The verses paraphrased are: "He that dwelleth in the secret place of the Most High. . . . He is my refuge." "Under His wings shalt thou trust. . . . Thou shalt not be afraid for the terror." "A thousand shall fall at thy side, and ten thousand at thy right hand; but it shall not come nigh thee." "Because thou hast made the Lord . . . thy habitation." "Because He hath set His love upon me, . . . I will set him on high. . . . He shall call upon Me, and I will answer him: I will be with him in trouble; I will deliver him, and honour him. With long life will I satisfy him." Psalm 91: 1, 2, 4, 5, 7, 9, 14-16. Lyte also wrote Nos. 16, "Praise the Lord, His Glories Show"; 50, "Abide with Me"; 252, "My Spirit on Thy Care"; 267, "Jesus, I My Cross Have Taken," and possibly 394, "Saviour, Like a Shepherd."

The tune *Communion* was composed by Stephen Jenks (1772-1856) of Connecticut, for the words of No. 124, "Alas! and Did My Saviour Bleed?" He was a lover of music, a teacher, and a composer, and also a maker of drums and tambourines.

400. O TELL ME

Song of Solomon 1: 7, 8

These words were written in 1831 by Thomas Hastings (1784-1872), see appendix, and entitled "Following the Good Shepherd." They are a paraphrase of the words, "Tell me, O thou whom my soul loveth, where thou feedest, where thou makest thy flock to rest at noon: for why should I be as one that turneth aside by the flocks of thy companions? . . . Go thy way forth by the footsteps of the flock, and feed thy kids beside the shepherds' tents." Song of Solomon 1: 7, 8.

The tune was also composed by Thomas Hastings (1784-1872), see appendix, and named *Still Water* because of its association with the Shepherd who leads "beside the still waters." Psalm 23: 2.

401. JESUS, LOVER OF MY SOUL

Jeremiah 31: 3

This well-known hymn by Charles Wesley (1707-88), see appendix, was excluded by his brother John from the hymn books for Methodists and from their supposedly final edition in 1779, though it gained a place after the death of the two brothers. It was published in 1740 in "Hymns and Sacred Poems" and was entitled "In Time of Prayer and Temptation," being born out of their struggles against opposition and lawlessness in the very early days of Methodism. John objected to Charles's very emotional and tender phrases, and particularly to the word "lover," though this idea may have been prompted by a verse of the Apocrypha, "Lord, Thou lover of souls" (Wisdom 11: 26), a similar thought being found also in Jeremiah 31: 3, "I have loved thee with an everlasting love." The hymn is noted for its simplicity and the abundant use of monosyllables, there being no less than 159 out of the 189 words of the hymn, and of the remaining 30, all but three are words of two syllables only. This same simplicity is evident in the original third stanza now omitted:—

3. Wilt Thou not regard my call?
Wilt Thou not accept my prayer?
Lo, I sink, I faint, I fall,
Lo, on Thee I cast my care.
Reach me out Thy gracious hand,
While I of Thy strength receive,
Hoping against hope I stand,
Dying, and behold, I live.

The tune *Martyn* was composed in 1834 by Simeon Butler Marsh (1798-1875) of Sherburne, New York, while riding on horseback on his circuit of singing schools, but it was written specially for the hymn, "Mary at the Saviour's Tomb." It is a simple tune, for lines 1 and 2 are repeated in lines 3 and 4, and again in lines 7 and 8, and line 6 repeats line 5. Marsh sang in a children's choir at the age of eight years, and ten years later was a singing school teacher and a choir leader.

402. JESUS, LOVER OF MY SOUL

Jeremiah 31:3

For the words, see the previous hymn, 401.

The tune *Hollingside* was composed especially for these words in 1861 by John Bacchus Dykes (1823-76), see appendix, and takes its name from Hollingside cottage and the adjoining wood near Durham. Here Dykes had his first home in the parish of St. Oswald's, while he was a minor canon in the cathedral. While the melody of lines 1, 3, and 7 is the same, the harmony of line 1 is quite different from the other two lines.

403. LEAD, KINDLY LIGHT

Psalm 112: 4

John Henry Newman (1801-90), then Anglican vicar of St. Mary's, Oxford, had travelled to the Mediterranean after a very serious illness. He was on an orange boat bound from Palermo to Marseilles in 1833 and became becalmed in the straits of Bonifacio between Sardinia and Corsica. The waiting period was a time of depression for him, and on June 16, while meditating on God's guidance, he wrote these three stanzas under the heading "Heavenly Leadings," later changed to "The Pillar of the Cloud." It was inspired by reflecting on the following verses: Psalm 112: 4: "Unto the upright there ariseth light in the darkness." Micah 7: 8: "When I sit in darkness, the Lord shall be a light unto me," and Exodus 13: 21: "And the Lord went before them by day in a pillar of cloud, to lead them the way; and by night in a pillar of fire, to give them light." Much speculation has taken place concerning the meaning of the last two lines about the "angel faces." When the author was asked what was in his mind, he admitted that he had completely forgotten. He certainly did not refer to his change from the Church of England to the Church of Rome because this did not take place until twelve years after the writing of the hymn. A full account of its writing appears in Newman's "Apologia Pro Vita Sua." It is worthy of note that the three stanzas deal with the present, the past, and the future, respectively. (1) I am far from home; (2) I was not ever thus; (3) Will lead me on.

Newman claimed that the words became so popular because of the tune *Lux Benigna,* specially written for them in August, 1865, by John Bacchus Dykes (1823-76), see appendix. It came into his mind while he was walking along the Strand, London, and was first named *St. Oswald* but later *Lux Benigna* (= kindly light) because of its association with these words. Kindly is used in the old sense of innate, or implanted.

404. MY JESUS, AS THOU WILT

Mark 14: 36

Benjamin Schmolck (1672-1737), the son of a Lutheran pastor, was a prolific writer of German hymns and religious poems. These words were written in 1704 as an eleven-stanza hymn based on Mark 14: 36, "Nevertheless not what I will, but what Thou wilt." Miss Jane Laurie Borthwick (1813-97) made a free translation from the German in 1854 and published it in her "Hymns from the Land of Luther." Our stanzas are Nos. 1, 5, and 11 of the original. She also translated No. 676, "Jesus, Still Lead On."

The tune *Jewett* was composed in 1820 by Carl Maria von Weber (1786-1826), to be played on the horns in the overture to "Der Freischutz" (= the freeshooter), his most famous opera, first produced in Berlin in 1821. It was arranged as a hymn tune in 1862 by Joseph Perry Holbrook (1822-88), an American compiler and editor. Another tune arranged from Weber's work is Nos. 48 and 318, *Seymour.*

405. THE LORD IS MY SHEPHERD

Psalm 23

This close paraphrase of the Shepherd Psalm was written in 1822 by James Montgomery (1771-1854), see appendix.

William Gawler (1750-1819) was an organist at the Asylum of Refuge for French Orphans in Lambeth, London, and in 1785 published a collection of "Psalms and Hymns," later adding other tunes for the use of the children there. The tune *Goshen* is a transposition and slight adaptation of a tune there called *St. Michel's,* which was written for girls' voices in the key of B flat, three semitones above the present setting.

406. LEAD THOU ME ON

Psalm 27: 11

These words by Harry Armstrong plead for guidance, for love, for grace, and for peace, so that the petitioner may be safely guided through the storms and temptations of life's pathway. Scripture references which express similar thoughts are:—

Stanza 1: "Teach me Thy way, O Lord, and lead me in a plain path." Psalm 27: 11.

Stanza 2: "He that loveth his brother abideth in the light." 1 John 2: 10.

Stanza 3: "But where sin abounded, grace did much more abound." Romans 5: 20.

Stanza 4: "And the peace of God, which passeth all understanding, shall keep your hearts and minds through Christ Jesus." Philippians 4: 7.

Stanza 5: "For in Him dwelleth all the fullness of the Godhead bodily." Colossians 2: 9.

The tune *Willingham* was written by Franz Abt (1819-85), a German conductor and composer of a great number of songs and part-songs. The melody has a wide range from middle C to octave F above.

407. LORD, SPEAK TO ME

Romans 14: 7

Frances Ridley Havergal (1836-79), see appendix, wrote this hymn at Winterdyne, near Bewdley, Worcestershire, on April 28, 1872, under the title, "A Prayer, 'None of Us Liveth Unto Himself.'" Romans 14: 7. It had seven stanzas, those omitted being:

4. O teach me, Lord, that I may teach
The precious things Thou dost impart;
And wing my words, that they may reach
The hidden depths of many a heart.

5. O give Thine own sweet rest to me,
That I may speak, with soothing power,
A word in season, as from Thee
To weary ones in needful hour.

6. O fill me with Thy fullness, Lord,
Until my very heart o'erflow
In kindling thought and flowing word,
Thy love to tell, Thy praise to show.

7. O use me, Lord, use even me,
Just as Thou wilt, and when, and where;
Until Thy blessed face I see,
Thy rest, Thy joy, Thy glory share.

The tune *Canonbury* is an arrangement from Nachtstücke, Opus 23, No. 4 in F, composed in 1839 by Robert Alexander Schumann (1810-56), who did not compose any hymn tunes; but several of his melodies have been arranged as such. Another example is *Schumann,* used for Nos. 461, 472 and 477. Schumann was a very able pianist until he injured his right hand permanently in 1832, after which he concentrated very successfully on composition.

408. LORD, THY CHILDREN GUIDE

Matthew 7: 14

William Walsham How (1823-97), see appendix, wrote five stanzas in 1854 of this hymn, amplifying the text found in the Sermon on the Mount—"Because strait is the gate, and narrow is the way, which leadeth unto life." Matthew 7: 14. The author mentions the roughness and the dreariness of the way, and also the temptation to a life of ease which would deter many from the better joys. The omitted stanza is: —

2. There are stony ways to tread;
   Give the strength we sorely lack:
   There are tangled paths to thread;
   Light us, lest we miss the track.
   Holy Jesus, day by day
   Lead us in the narrow way.

The tune *Rosefield* was composed by Henri Abraham Cesar Malan (1787-1864), a brilliant preacher of Geneva, who lived for some time in England. While it is a six-line tune, it is virtually one of four lines only, for lines 3 and 4 are an exact repetition of lines 1 and 2. Malan also composed *Hendon* which is used three times in "Church Hymnal," namely, for Nos. 30, "Lord, We Come Before Thee Now"; 192, "Hark! That Shout," and 273, "Take My Life and Let It Be."

409. GUIDE ME, O THOU GREAT JEHOVAH

Nehemiah 9: 19, 20

William Williams (1717-91), was studying to be a doctor when he heard Howel Harris, one of Whitefield's preachers, at an open-air meeting. He then dedicated himself to the ministry, became a Calvinistic Methodist and an itinerant preacher. There was an obvious lack of good hymns in Wales and this constituted a continual challenge to produce better ones, which this enthusiastic Welshman did with such effect that he became known as the Welsh Watts and the sweet singer of Wales. He was bilingual, writing 800 hymns in Welsh and 100 in English. This present hymn was. originally written in Welsh in 1745 and translated into English by his friend Peter Williams (1722-96). The author, however, wrote a better translation, which is used for stanzas two and three. Furthermore, he added a fourth stanza written in English:—

4. Musing on my habitation,
   Musing on my heav'nly home,
   Fills my soul with holy longing,
   Come, my Jesus, quickly come:
   Vanity is all I see,
   Lord, I long to be with Thee!

The words liken the Christian's life to the march of the Israelites through the wilderness to the Promised Land, led continually by a wise, all-powerful God, an experience ably summarized later by Nehemiah, "Yet Thou in Thy manifold mercies forsookest them not in the wilderness: the pillar of the cloud departed not from them by day, to lead them in the way; neither the pillar of fire by night, to show them light, and the way wherein they should go. Thou gavest also Thy good spirit to instruct them, and withheldest not Thy manna from their mouth, and gavest them water for their thirst." Nehemiah 9: 19, 20.

The tune *Caersalem* appeared in leaflet form in 1837 and owes its preservation to a kind deed. The composer, Robert Edwards (1797-1862), a precentor at the Bedford Street Calvinistic Methodist church, Liverpool, was ill, and the manuscript was discovered in his desk. Unknown to him, the choir practised it, and sang it as a surprise to him when he had recovered from his illness. Lines 3 and 4 are an exact repetition of lines 1 and 2.

410. LEAD THEM, MY GOD, TO THEE

Psalm 127: 3

The words of this parents' hymn echo the sentiment of the godly Hannah, who recognized in the birth of her first son, Samuel, a gift of God. "For this child I prayed; and the Lord hath given me my petition which I asked of Him." 1 Samuel 1: 27. Seeing that "children are an heritage of the Lord," (Psalm 127: 3), we can well utter the prayer that they will be led to Him. The last two stanzas reiterate the Saviour's love for children, as shown in His own words, "And whoso shall receive one such little child in My name receiveth Me" (Matthew 18: 5), and "Suffer little children to come unto Me, and forbid them not: for of such is the kingdom of God." Luke 18: 16.

The tune *Robinson* was composed by Franklin Edson Belden (1858-1945), see appendix, and appeared first in 1886 in "Hymns and Tunes."

411. SEE, ISRAEL'S GENTLE SHEPHERD

Mark 10: 13-16

The story of Jesus blessing the children is given three times, in Matthew 19: 13-15, Mark 10: 13-16, and Luke 18: 15-17, each writer giving an additional thought. Luke says merely that Jesus did not forbid the children to come to Him; Matthew says that He laid His hands on them; whereas Mark says that He took them up in His arms. "And they brought young children to Him, that He should touch them: and His disciples rebuked these that brought them. But when Jesus saw it, He was much displeased, and said unto them, Suffer the little children to come unto Me, and forbid them not: for of such is the kingdom of God. Verily I say unto you, Whosoever shall not receive the kingdom of God as a little child, he shall not enter therein. And He took them up in His arms, put His hands upon them, and blessed them." Mark 10: 13-16. Philip Doddridge (1702-51), see appendix, followed Mark's more enthusiastic description in his paraphrase of this incident, for example, "folds them in His arms." His title was "Christ's Condescending Regard to Little Children," and the five original stanzas were published posthumously in 1755. The two omitted ones are:

4. Ye little flock, with pleasure hear,
   Ye children, seek His face;
   And fly with transport to receive
   The blessings of His grace.

5. If orphans they are left behind,
   Thy guardian care we trust:
   That care shall heal our bleeding hearts,
   If weeping o'er their dust.

The tune *Evan* was composed in 1847 by William Henry Havergal (1793-1870), an Anglican clergyman, and father of Frances Ridley Havergal, see appendix. It was set to a poem by Burns, and had eight lines in common metre doubled. Lowell Mason (1792-1872), see appendix, took the first two and the last two lines and made a common metre tune from it calling it *Eva*. Havergal did not approve of this mutilation, and rewrote the tune as it now appears. Note that the last line of six syllables of the melody is exactly the same as the first six syllables of the longer first line.

412. O HAPPY HOME

Luke 19:9

The German original of this hymn was written in 1826 and published in 1833 by Carl Johann Philipp Spitta (1801-59). He was of Huguenot descent and of Pietist persuasion, being ordained to the ministry in 1828. Under the title "Salvation [is] come to this house," Luke 19: 9, he describes his own happy Christian home, where his father was a Frenchman and his mother a Jewess who had been converted to Christianity. Mrs. Sarah Laurie Borthwick Findlater (1823-1907), a sister of Jane Borthwick (see Nos. 404, 676), translated the hymn into English in 1858, and it was just as accurate a picture of her own home as it was of Spitta's. She married the Rev. Eric J. Findlater, a minister of the Free Church of Scotland at Lochearnhead. With the permission of the authoress, a revision of her translation to the present metre

11.10.11.10 was made, and this is the present version with the last stanza altered somewhat. The two omitted stanzas are:—

2. O happy home, where two in heart united,
In holy faith and blessed hope are one,
Whom death a little while alone divideth,
And cannot end the union here begun!

3. O happy home, whose little ones are given
Early to Thee in humble faith and prayer,
To Thee, their Friend, who from the heights of heaven,
Guides them, and guards with more than mother's care.

The tune *Alverstoke* was composed in 1883 by Joseph Barnby (1838-96), see appendix, specially for the words of No. 326, "Still, Still with Thee."

413. HAPPY THE HOME

John 17: 23

These words appeared in 1858 over the signature Mrs. W., but were apparently written earlier by Henry Ware, Junior (1794-1843). He was a Unitarian minister of Boston, Massachusetts, and wrote poetry merely as a means of relaxation and refreshment. This hymn expresses the love and unity in a home which exalts God as the Head, and which is therefore seen in love to one another. Such a home is a reflection of the whole family of Christians of whom Christ said, "I in them, and Thou in Me, that they may be made perfect in one; and that the world may know that Thou hast sent Me, and hast loved them, as Thou hast loved Me." John 17: 23.

The tune *St. Agnes* was composed in 1866 by John Bacchus Dykes (1823-76), see appendix. It is used also for Nos. 158, "Jesus, the Very Thought of Thee," and 209, "Come, Holy Spirit." Agnes was a young Roman girl who refused to deny her Christian faith and be married to a pagan Roman nobleman. As a result, she suffered martyrdom in A.D. 304 at the early age of 13, during the period of the Diocletian persecution.

414. MY GOD, HOW ENDLESS IS THY LOVE!

Lamentations 3: 22, 23

These words were written in 1709 by Isaac Watts (1674-1748), see appendix, under the title, "A Song for Morning or Evening." They were said by him to be a paraphrase, and while many verses in different parts of the Scriptures are suggested, the three stanzas appear to be based on Lamentations 3: 22, 23, "The Lord's mercies . . . are new every morning," and on Isaiah 45: 7, "I form the light, and create darkness."

The tune *Hursley* closely resembles a drinking song from Mozart's "Nozze di Figaro," and its similarity caused Sir Herbert Oakeley to compose *Abends* (No. 56) in an effort to displace the secular tune. It is named after the parish of Hursley, near Winchester, where John Keble was vicar. The same tune is also used for Keble's hymn, No. 321, "Sun of My Soul."

415. 'MID PLEASURES AND PALACES

John 19: 27

This poem is part of an opera, "Clari, the Maid of Milan," which was produced at the Covent Garden theatre, London, on May 8, 1823. The words were written by John Howard Payne (1791-1852), an American actor and journalist who was born in New York. He was quite a nomadic type, for after a successful first appearance as an actor in New York in 1807, he was in England by 1813, writing, and translating operettas from the French. In October, 1822, he was in Paris, well nigh penniless, disconsolate, stranded, and homesick when he wrote the words of this song, the other two stanzas of which are:—

How sweet, too, to sit 'neath a fond father's smile,
And the cares of a mother to soothe and beguile.
Let others delight 'mid new pleasures to roam,
But give me, oh, give me! the pleasures of home!

To thee I'll return, overburdened with care;
The heart's dearest face will smile on me there,
No more from that cottage again will I roam,
Be it ever so humble, there's no place like home.

Payne returned to his homeland in 1832, and was appointed as American consul to Tunis, where he died on his 61st birthday, April 1, 1852. He was buried there, but later his remains were re-interred in Oak Cemetery, Washington, and a monument was erected to his memory. This song does not really qualify as a hymn, for it neither paraphrases a Scripture truth, nor praises God, nor even mentions His name. It does describe home as a place of peace and relaxation, and in this sense it reminds of the kindly act of the Apostle John who cared tenderly for Mary the mother of Jesus after His crucifixion—"And from that hour that disciple took her into his own home." John 19: 27.

The tune *Home, Sweet Home,* was composed by Henry Rowley Bishop (1786-1855), who was knighted in 1842. He was editing a collection of national melodies and found that a Sicilian one was lacking. He therefore wrote this tune to fill the gap, and, combined with Payne's sentimental words, it made a song which achieved great popularity.

416. O PERFECT LOVE

Matthew 19: 6

One Sunday evening in 1883, in their home at Pull Wyke, Windermere, the two Blomfield sisters and some friends were singing hymns together. One of them was shortly to become Mrs. Redmayne, and her favourite tune was *Strength and Stay* by John Bacchus Dykes, see appendix, but as one of the company remarked, the words were unsuitable for a wedding. Whereupon the bride-to-be asked what was the use of having a poetess for a sister if she could not write suitable words for this favourite tune. So Dorothy Frances Blomfield (1858-1932), who later became Mrs. Gurney, repaired to the quiet of the library and returned with the words of this hymn in the short space of fifteen minutes. The company all sang it together, and it was used at her sister's wedding. An appropriate Scripture text is, "Wherefore they are no more twain, but one flesh. What therefore God hath joined together, let not man put asunder." Matthew 19: 6.

Dykes's tune has now been displaced by the present *O Perfect Love,* or *Sandringham,* by Joseph Barnby (1838-96), see appendix. Line 3 copies the melody of line 1 but is written with different harmony. This is an arrangement from an anthem specially written for the marriage of Princess Louise, sister of King George V, to the Duke of Fife on July 27, 1889.

417. I WILL EARLY SEEK THE SAVIOUR

Revelation 1: 5

This children's hymn by Mrs. L. M. B. Bateman reminds us that when Jesus was on earth He manifested love for the little ones. His life was a pattern of what ours should be, for "Christ also suffered for us, leaving us an example, that ye should follow His steps." 1 Peter 2: 21. Two illustrations are taken from the Sermon on the Mount, one, the metaphor of the narrow way, Matthew 7: 14: "Because strait is the gate, and narrow is the way, which leadeth unto life," and secondly, Matthew 7: 7, "Knock, and it shall be opened unto you." The chorus is a very free paraphrase of Revelation 1: 5: "Jesus Christ . . . that loved us, and washed us from our sins in His own blood."

The tune, unnamed, was composed by Frederick Augustus Fillmore (1856-?) of Paris, Illinois, the farmer brother of two ministers (see No. 117) of the Christian Church. He was called the farmer musician because he cared for the farm after his father died, but later he taught singing, organ, and piano, and composed songs from his farm experiences.

418. WHEN HE COMETH

Malachi 3: 17

These words were written in 1866 by William Orcutt Cushing (1823-1903), a minister of the American Christian Church who later joined the Methodist Church, serving in various New York pastorates. They are based on the Old Testament promise, "And they shall be Mine, saith the Lord of hosts, in that day when I make up My jewels." Malachi 3: 17. Cushing also wrote Nos. 550, "Beautiful Valley of Eden"; 586, "O Safe to the Rock," and 587, "Under His Wings."

The tune *Jewels* was composed by George Frederick Root (1820-95), who also composed Nos. 93 and 299 *Varina,* 620 unnamed, and 690 *Quam Dilecta.* Root was an American choir conductor, music teacher, and music publisher, who was associated with Lowell Mason (see appendix) in the Boston Academy of Music. He composed many sentimental ballads and popular Civil War songs.

419. IN OUR HEARTS CELESTIAL VOICES

Galatians 4: 6

This hymn was written during the Christmas of 1901 by Marie Corelli (1855-1924) and entitled "Children's Evening Hymn." It took about ten minutes only and satisfied her impulse to write something suitable for a child. There were nine stanzas, those omitted being:—

5. May our dreams be of Thy kingdom
Full of grace—
Where at last we hope to meet Thee,
Face to face.

6. Now the stars are shining o'er us
In the skies;
Looking like the watching angels'
Lovely eyes.

9. There, when all our prayers are ended—
Faults forgiven,
May we live with Thee for ever,
Up in heaven!

Marie Corelli was the pen-name of the daughter of the London physician Charles Mackay, and her name became famous for the many sentimental novels she wrote. While written for children the words of this hymn are suitable for any Christian, for he is a child of God who "hath sent forth the Spirit of His Son into your hearts, crying, Abba, Father." Galatians 4: 6.

The tune *Celestial Voices,* named because of these words in the first line, was composed in 1922 by Richard Francis Lloyd (1871-1943) of Liverpool.

420. JESUS, FRIEND OF LITTLE CHILDREN

2 Peter 3: 18

The words were written in 1882 by Walter John Mathams (1853-1931) at the special request of the Baptist Union. After being shipwrecked as a youth, and undergoing forced army service in Brazil, he trained for the Baptist ministry and was ordained in 1874. Later in 1900 he joined the ministry of the Church of Scotland. He was the author of many books for boys and had a very tender loving heart, especially for children. These stanzas cover more than childhood, for there is a progression of thought from childhood through youth to the end of life, the prayer being for Jesus to be the Friend through this whole period. A fitting summary is, "But grow in grace, and in the knowledge of our Lord and Saviour Jesus Christ." 2 Peter 3: 18. There are two other stanzas, now omitted:—

2. Show me what my love should cherish,
What, too, it should shun;
Lest my feet for poison flowers
Swift should run.

4. Fill me with Thy gentle meekness,
Make my heart like Thine;
Like an altar lamp, then let me
Burn and shine.

The tune *Simonside* was composed by the Seventh-day Adventist pastor, poet, and musician, Joseph Harker (1880-) after he read through the words several times and meditated about the life and character of their author. He named it to commemorate Simonside Street in Newcastle-on-Tyne, England, where he taught music for several years. He also composed No. 679, *Paraclete,* as well as many other hymns and tunes in "Advent Hymnal" and its revised edition.

421. ALL THINGS BRIGHT AND BEAUTIFUL

John 1: 3

Cecil Frances Humphreys (1818-95) who in 1850 married the Rev. William Alexander, later to become bishop of Derry, was the writer of about 200 poems and 200 hymns, most of them for children. This one was written in 1848 and appeared in her "Hymns for Little Children" based on the church catechism. She was much concerned when she overheard one of her godsons complaining about not being able to understand the catechism, so she decided to simplify the difficulties by writing hymns based on the different articles of the Apostles' Creed. This hymn amplifies the first of the twelve clauses, "I believe in God the Father Almighty, Maker of heaven and earth." Omitted stanzas are:—

3. The rich man in his castle,
The poor man at his gate;
God made them, high or lowly,
And ordered their estate.

6. The tall trees in the greenwood,
The meadows where we play,
The rushes by the water,
We gather every day.

An appropriate Scripture summary is, "All things were made by Him; and without Him was not anything made that was made." John 1: 3. Mrs. Alexander also wrote Nos. 126, "There Is a Green Hill Far Away" (article 4 of the creed); 424, "Once in Royal David's City" (article 3), and 521, "Jesus Calls Us."

The tune *Royal Oak* was adapted in 1915 by the organist Martin Fallas Shaw (1875-1958) from a seventeenth century English melody, "The Twenty-ninth of May," which was a song in honour of the restoration of Charles II to the throne on May 29, 1660. The name recalls that Charles had hidden in an oak in Boscobel, Shropshire, in 1651, after his defeat at the battle of Worcester. Shaw was one of the editors of "Songs of Praise" and in 1935 was appointed as musical director to the bishop of Chelmsford, Essex.

422. I THINK WHEN I READ THAT SWEET STORY

Matthew 19: 14, 15

Miss Jemima Thompson (1813-1906) was attending the Normal Infant School in Gray's Inn Road, London, in 1841, to learn teaching method, and heard there a Greek melody, *Salamis,* which caught her fancy and remained in her mind. She thought it would make a good hymn tune, and looked through several hymnbooks to discover suitable words but found none, as the tune is in an unusual metre. Later that same year she was journeying to Wellington, Somerset, through beautiful Taunton Vale and the melody continued to haunt her. Taking out an old envelope she wrote the first two stanzas, each of eight lines, saying of them, "A little inspiration from above, not in me." She gave it the title of "The Child's Desire," and taught it to the children in the Blagdon village school. They asked to sing it in the Sunday school, and in this way the superintendent, Jemima's father, heard it for the first time.

He sent it to the "Sunday School Teacher's Magazine" where it was first published in 1841. Jemima was always interested in missionary work and only ill-health prevented her serving overseas. She married a Congregational minister, the Rev. Samuel Luke in 1843, and later added a third stanza to her hymn to give it a missionary bias. This addition is our stanzas four and five. The omitted lines, the latter half of the original second stanza, are:—

2. . . .
In that beautiful place He has gone to prepare
For all who are washed and forgiven;
And many dear children are gathering there,
"For of such is the kingdom of heaven."

The incident described in the hymn is recorded by all three synoptic Gospel writers, one reference being: "But Jesus said, Suffer little children, and forbid them not, to come unto Me: for of such is the kingdom of heaven. And He laid His hands on them." Matthew 19: 14, 15.

The arrangements of the tune *Sweet Story* is by William Batchelder Bradbury (1816-68), see appendix, and the harmony was added in 1918 by Charles Winfred Douglas (1867-1944) of Oswego, New York, who was director of music at the Community of St. Mary, Peekskill, New York, from 1935 till his decease. He edited the "American New Hymnal" of 1916 and the "Protestant Episcopal Hymnal" of 1940.

423. I AM SO GLAD THAT OUR FATHER

Romans 5: 5, 8

Philipp Bliss (1838-76), see appendix, wrote this hymn in June, 1870, while he was staying with Major D. W. Whittle (see No. 583). It came as a direct inspiration from another hymn whose chorus was, "Oh, how I love Jesus" which he decided to reverse. He said, "Have I not been singing enough about my poor love for Jesus, and shall I not rather sing of His great love for me?" So he wrote three stanzas first of all, and the tune came to him the same night. There are three other stanzas, for example, "Jesus loves me, and I know I love Him" but they were added by some other writer. The Christian's hope is based on Christ's love for him rather than on his love for Christ, as shown in Romans 5: 5, 8: "Hope maketh not ashamed; because the love of God is shed abroad in our hearts. . . . But God commendeth His love toward us, in that, while we were yet sinners, Christ died for us." The melody was harmonized by Bliss, giving the tune *Jesus Loves Even Me*.

424. ONCE IN ROYAL DAVID'S CITY

Luke 2: 7

Mrs. Cecil Frances Alexander, née Humphreys (1818-95), wife of the bishop of Derry, wrote some of her hymns based on the Apostles' Creed in order to simplify it for the understanding of children. This hymn which appeared in her "Hymns for Little Children" in 1848, amplifies article 3 of the creed, which, referring to the Lord Jesus Christ, says, "Which was conceived by the Holy Ghost, born of the Virgin Mary." The scripture on which it is based is Luke 2: 7 stating how Mary goes to "the city of David, which is called Bethlehem" (verse 4), and "she brought forth her firstborn son, and wrapped Him in swaddling clothes, and laid Him in a manger." Verse 7. The omitted stanza is:—

6. Not in that poor lowly stable,
With the oxen standing by,
We shall see Him; but in heaven,
Set at God's right hand on high;
Where like stars His children crowned
All in white shall wait around.

Mrs. Alexander also wrote Nos. 126, "There Is a Green Hill Far Away"; 421, "All Things Bright and Beautiful," and 521, "Jesus Calls Us."

The tune *Irby* was published in 1849 especially for these words in "Christmas Carols" by Henry John Gauntlett (1805-76) who was the son of the vicar of Olney, Buckinghamshire. He possessed unusual talent, for he was an organist at the age of nine, conducted the "Messiah" at sixteen, was a lawyer at twenty, and the holder of a Mus. Doc. degree from the archbishop of Canterbury by 1843. *Irby* is named after a village in Lincolnshire, and was written first as a melody only; and harmonized in 1868 for "Hymns Ancient and Modern" where it was first named. It has virtually only four lines and not six, for lines 3 and 4 copy lines 1 and 2.

425. I WOULD BE TRUE

Philippians 4: 8

Howard Arnold Walter (1883-1918), teacher of English at the University of Tokyo, Japan, wrote these words, originally two stanzas only, on New Year's Day, 1906, entitled them "My Creed," and sent them to his mother in Connecticut. She submitted the poem to *Harper's Bazaar* and it was printed in this magazine in 1907. The third line of stanza one is very significant, "I would be strong, for there is much to suffer," for Walter suffered from a weak heart and accomplished what he did often only by sheer will-power. His words recall the Apostle Paul's injunction, "Whatsoever things are true, . . . whatsoever things are pure . . . think on these things." Philippians 4: 8. Walter was ordained to the Congregational ministry in 1910 and devoted much time to Y.M.C.A. interests.

Walter grew friendly with Joseph Yates Peek (1843-1911) of Brooklyn, New York, and in time as their friendship deepened he handed him a copy of these words. Peek thought them very valuable and worthy of preservation for posterity, and that they would be better remembered if set to music. He was a florist, however—incidentally introducing the double carnation—but not a musician even though he devoted all his spare time to music. So in 1911 he asked Grant Colfax Tullar (1869-?), a minister of the Methodist Episcopal Church, to write a tune, but forgot to bring along the words from Brooklyn to Fifth Avenue, New York City. A few days later he told Tullar that he had made a tune himself which he could not write down, nor could he sing it. However, he overcame this handicap by whistling his melody to Tullar, who jotted it down. As soon as it was played, Peek acknowledged it as Tullar's melody rather than his own and was pleased with it. Tullar's music editor, J. W. Ferman, later added the harmony, and the name *Peek* now commemorates the aspiring composer. Tullar, who started a music publishing business in 1893, also composed Nos. 123, *Nailed to the Cross,* and 545, *Face to Face.*

426. O HOLY LORD, CONTENT TO FILL

Luke 2: 52

This children's hymn was written in 1850 and published in 1851, by William Walsham How (1823-97), see appendix. The last two lines of the last stanza are almost a direct quotation of the early years of Jesus, "And Jesus increased in wisdom and stature, and in favour with God and man." Luke 2: 52. There are two other stanzas:—

3. Oh! let not this world's scorching glow
Thy Spirit's quickening dew efface,
Nor blast of sin too rudely blow,
And quench the trembling flame of grace.

4. Gather Thy lambs within Thine arm,
And gently in Thy bosom bear;
Keep them, O Lord, from hurt and harm,
And bid them rest for ever there.

The tune *Brookfield* was composed in 1855 by Thomas Bishop Southgate (1814-68), an organist in North London, and a violinist who composed mostly for piano and cello.

427. SAVIOUR, WHILE MY HEART IS TENDER

Romans 6: 16

John Burton (1803-77) the younger, of Stratford, Essex, was by trade a cooper and basket-maker, but by inclination a hymn-writer for children. He was a faithful Sunday school teacher and deacon of the church, and this is one of his hymns, entitled "Youthful Consecration," which appeared in 1850 in his "One Hundred Original Hymns for the Young." There were three stanzas each of eight lines, the omitted ones which immediately succeed the present selection, being:—

2\. . . . .
Let me do Thy will, or bear it,
I would know no will but Thine;
Should'st Thou take my life, or spare it,
I that life to Thee resign.

3\. May this solemn dedication
Never once forgotten lie;
Let it know no revocation,
Publish'd and confirmed on high.
Thine I am, O Lord, for ever,
To Thy service set apart;
Suffer me to leave Thee never,
Seal Thine image on my part.

The words reveal a complete consecration to the Lord: "Know ye not, that to whom ye yield yourselves servants to obey, his servants ye are to whom ye obey." Romans 6: 16.

The tune was composed in 1868 by Mrs. Charlotte Alington Barnard (1820-69), and is named *Brocklesbury,* after the town near Dover, Kent, where she died. Under the pen-name of "Claribel" she wrote several popular ballads, which became immediately popular both in England and in the United States.

428. HUSHED WAS THE EVENING HYMN

1 Samuel 3: 3, 4

This hymn is one of James Drummond Burns's (1823-64) original hymns for every evening of the month, and is based on the experience of the child Samuel being called by the Lord. "And ere the lamp of God went out in the temple of the Lord, where the ark of God was, and Samuel was laid down to sleep; that the Lord called Samuel: and he answered, Here am I." 1 Samuel 3: 3, 4. The words were written in 1857 after Burns had returned from a health trip to Madeira and had resumed his duties as a Presbyterian minister of the Free Church of Scotland, in Hampstead, London. The second stanza, now omitted, is:—

2. The old man, meek and mild,
The priest of Israel, slept;
His watch the temple child,
The little Levite, kept;
And what from Eli's sense was sealed,
The Lord to Hannah's son revealed.

Burns also wrote No. 315, "Still With Thee."

The tune *Samuel* was specially composed for these words in 1874 by Arthur Seymour Sullivan (1842-1900), see appendix.

429. JESUS, I WILL FOLLOW THEE

Luke 9: 61

The New Testament records instances of the Lord calling individuals and of individuals volunteering to follow before being called. Luke 9: 57-61 mentions three such without naming them. The first stanza of this hymn joins both call and response, as in the incident recorded in Mark 1: 17, 18, "And Jesus said unto them, Come ye after Me . . . and straightway they . . . followed Him." They virtually said, "Lord, I will follow Thee" (Luke 9: 61), but without the qualification and reservation that completes this verse. The second stanza calls on "the Lord . . . thy Saviour and thy Redeemer, the mighty One" (Isaiah 60: 16) to cover our weakness, and the last stanza accepts the counsel given to Joshua, "Be strong and of a good courage . . . for the Lord thy God is with thee whithersoever thou goest." Joshua 1: 9.

The tune *Glenn,* named after the authoress Grace Glenn, was composed by James Holmes Rosecrans (1844-?) of Berne, New York. After studying at Baxter's University of Music he began to compose. He lived with the Fillmores (see Nos. 117, 417) and they published his tunes. He became a preacher of the Christian Church, and professor of moral and mental sciences and Biblical literature at Carlton College, Texas.

430. JESUS, TENDER SHEPHERD, HEAR ME

John 10: 14

Miss Mary Lundie (1814-40) married the Rev. William Wallace Duncan in 1836 and in 1839 wrote this hymn for their two children, Mary and Harry. It was published two years later in her memoirs after her sudden death. The omitted third stanza was:—

3. Let my sins be all forgiven;
Bless the friends, I love so well;
Take me, when I die, to heaven,
Happy there with Thee to dwell,

a stanza which is obviously omitted from the church hymnal of a denomination that believes that death for the believer is a sleep until the second advent of Jesus. The figure is taken from Jesus' own illustration, "I am the Good Shepherd, and know My sheep, and am known of Mine." John 10: 14. Even in her short life Mrs. Duncan had already written twenty-three hymns for her children. Her younger sister Catherine (see No. 277) married Horatius Bonar, see appendix.

The tune *Shipston* is an air derived from an old Warwickshire ballad, the name commemorating a small town in the southern part of that English county. The ballad is called "Down by the Side of Bedlam City" with some of the words, "Don't you see my Billy coming?" It is the lament of a maiden for her lover Billy who was killed in the war, whom in vision she now sees in glory. The song is one of many collected by Miss Lucy Broadwood (?-1929) and is found in "English County Songs." It was first arranged as a hymn tune in 1906 by Ralph Vaughan Williams (1872-1958), who also composed No. 364, *Sine Nomine,* and arranged No. 685, *Picardy.*

431. HOW SWEET, HOW HEAVENLY

John 15: 17

"These things I command you, that ye love one another." John 15: 17. This verse and many similar statements of Scripture on the characteristic Christian virtue of love, have been expressed in poetic form here in 1792 by Joseph Swain (1761-96), a Baptist preacher of Walworth, London. He describes the true communion of saints, bound together by Christian love. Swain was of an emotional temperament, as shown also in his other hymn, No. 160, "O Thou in Whose Presence My Soul Takes Delight."

The tune *Siloam,* also used for No. 340, "By Cool Siloam's Shady Rill," was composed in 1842 by Isaac Baker Woodbury (1819-58), see appendix.

432. BLEST BE THE TIE

Philippians 2: 1, 2

John Fawcett (1740-1817) was one of Whitefield's converts who later became a Baptist minister and wrote a hymn to go with every sermon he preached. In 1765 he became pastor of the congregation at Wainsgate near Halifax, Yorkshire, and endeared himself greatly to his flock. In 1772 he received an appointment to a much more important and lucrative post in London, and although he was very devoted to and beloved by his parishioners, he decided to accept because he had a large family to support. He preached his farewell sermon but even then his people begged him to stay.

The next morning the furniture was loaded onto the removal waggons, but at the last moment the pleas of his congregation prevailed upon him and on his wife to the extent that they changed their minds, cancelled the new appointment, unpacked the furniture, and he stayed on as the minister at Wainsgate. To commemorate the depth of this true Christian feeling of love and devotion, he penned in 1772 six stanzas, the omitted ones being:—

5. This glorious hope revives
Our courage by the way;
While each in expectation lives
And longs to see the day.

6. From sorrow, toil and pain
And sin we shall be free;
And perfect love and friendship reign
Through all eternity,

and the hymn was first published in 1782. Its sentiments are those of the Apostle Paul and his converts at Philippi: "If there be therefore any consolation in Christ, if any comfort of love, if any fellowship of the Spirit, if any bowels and mercies, fulfil ye my joy, that ye be likeminded, having the same love, being of one accord, of one mind." Philippians 2: 1, 2. Fawcett also wrote No. 33, "Lord, Dismiss Us With Thy Blessing."

The hymn was originally set to *Boylston* (Nos. 205 and 502), but now to *Dennis,* an arrangement in 1845 by Lowell Mason (1792-1872), see appendix, who brought back from Europe in 1837 a Swiss tune by Hans Georg Nägeli (1773-1836) of Zurich. *Dennis* is also used for Nos. 379, "There Is a Blessed Hope," and 439, "With Willing Hearts We Tread." Nägeli also composed the original of *Naomi,* the tune for Nos. 322, "O, Could I Find from Day to Day," and 333, "Father, Whate'er of Earthly Bliss." He was a Swiss composer, teacher, and music publisher, and reformed the teaching of music in schools.

433. THE CHURCH HAS ONE FOUNDATION

1 Corinthians 3: 11

The author of this hymn, Samuel John Stone (1839-1900), when a curate at Windsor in 1866, was inspired by the stirring defence of the faith made by Bishop Gray of Cape Town, South Africa. Bishop John William Colenso (1814-83) of Natal had absorbed the higher criticism of the Old Testament, particularly of the books of Moses, and had shown very liberal views of the Scriptures and church doctrines. Bishop Gray declared him deposed from his bishopric, but Colenso's appeal to the Privy Council resulted in a decision otherwise, and he continued as Bishop of Natal until his death, continuing to hold views which attacked the inspiration of the Scriptures and denied the historicity of the Pentateuch. Stone's hymn is one of twelve, each based on an article of the Apostles' Creed, and written especially for the poorer people of his parish who recited the Creed without really understanding its meaning. The ninth article, "I believe in the Holy Catholic Church, the communion of saints," is here expounded, and reference to the Colenso controversy is seen particularly in our third stanza which was originally:

3. Though with a scornful wonder
Men see her sore opprest,
By schisms rent asunder,
By heresies distrest;
. . .

as well as in the original third stanza now omitted:—

3. The church shall never perish!
Her dear Lord to defend
To guide, sustain, and cherish,
Is with her to the end;
Though there be those that hate her,
And false sons in her pale,
Against or foe or traitor
She ever shall prevail.

Three additional stanzas were written in 1885 and one of them refers to the dissension in church circles caused by this controversy:

For Thy true Word remaineth;
No creature far or nigh,
No fiend of ill who reigneth
In hell or haunted sky;
No doubting world's derision
That holds her in despite,
Shall hold her from Thy vision,
Shall lure her from Thy light.

The hymn is truly a didactic one as intended, and many scriptures are used, one summarizing the theme being, "Other foundation can no man lay than that is laid, which is Jesus Christ." 1 Corinthians 3: 11. Stone also wrote No. 289, "Weary of Earth."

The tune *Aurelia* (= golden) was composed in 1864 by Samuel Sebastian Wesley (1810-76), grandson of Charles Wesley, see appendix, and so named because it was written especially for the words of "Jerusalem the Golden" (No. 300). However, the tune was set to Stone's words in 1872 and has been associated with it ever since. Wesley was organist at Hereford, Exeter, Winchester, and Gloucester cathedrals, and at Leeds parish church. In 1839 he received his Mus. Doc. degree from Oxford, and in 1850 became professor of organ at the Royal Academy of Music, London. *Aurelia* is used for No. 279, "Live Out Thy Life Within Me." Wesley also harmonized No. 676, *Seelenbrautigam.*

434. O GOLDEN DAY

John 10: 16

Charles Albert Dickinson (1849-1906), an American Congregational minister and Harvard graduate, wrote especially for young people. In this hymn he emphasizes the theme "One Master, Christ . . . and brethren all are we," recalling the Master's own words, "And there shall be one fold, and one shepherd." John 10: 16.

The tune *Ellacombe* is from the early 1800's and appears in a Roman Catholic hymnal in 1784, which nevertheless contains many Protestant compositions. It is also used for No. 254, "Sometimes a Light Surprises." It is easy to sing because lines 1, 3, and 7 are identical, so are lines 4 and 8, both being similar to line 2, and line 7 repeats the first six syllables of line 6.

435. O WHERE ARE KINGS

Daniel 2: 34, 35

Arthur Cleveland Coxe (1818-96), later bishop of Western New York, wrote in 1839 a ballad entitled "Chelsea" which consisted of ten stanzas each of eight lines. The first five stanzas describe King Canute of England who joined his prayer with the music that he heard from Ely Cathedral, and they draw a parallel with St. Peter's church, Chelsea, New York, situated on the Hudson River, which continued the same worship to God, even though the former worshippers of a thousand years earlier had passed away and ceased to sing. The rest of the ballad is then this hymn together with the following omitted lines:—

6\. . . .
And these that sing shall pass away;
New choirs their room shall fill!
Be sure thy children's children here
Shall hear those anthems still.

8\. Though years fling ivy over it,
Its cross peers high in air,
And reverend with majestic age,
Eternal youth is there!
. . .

9. Oh ye, that in these latter days
The citadel defend,
Perchance for you, the Saviour said
I'm with you to the end:
Stand therefore girt about, and hold
Your burning lamps in hand,
And standing, listen for your Lord,
And till He cometh—stand!

10. The gates of hell shall ne'er prevail
Against our holy home,
But oh, be wakeful sentinels,
Until the Master come!
The night is spent—but listen ye;
For on its deepest calm,
What marvel if the cry be heard,
The marriage of the Lamb!

Our last stanza suggests the dream of Daniel 2, "A stone was cut out without hands . . . became a great mountain and filled the whole earth" (Daniel 2: 34, 35), and its fulfilment in the setting up of God's everlasting kingdom (verse 44). Cox who added the extra "e" to his father's name of Cox, also wrote No. 359, "We Are Living, We Are Dwelling."

The tune *St. Anne* also used for No. 81, "O God, Our Help," was composed in 1708 by William Croft (1678-1727), organist of Westminster Abbey and of St. Anne's, Soho. He also composed No. 342, *Hanover*.

436. IN CHRIST THERE IS NO EAST OR WEST

Galatians 3: 28

John Oxenham is a pen-name adopted by William Arthur Dunkerley (1852-1941) of Manchester from Charles Kingsley's novel *"Westward Ho!"* His nephew, the Rev. Dugald Macfadyen was in charge of a pageant sponsored by the London Missionary Society which depicted the triumphs of missionary work. The exhibition was held in London in 1908 and named "The Orient in London" and Dunkerley was asked to write the libretto for the pageant of Darkness and Light. This hymn was written especially for and used in the pageant and reflects his strong crusading feelings against sectarianism. The sentiment expressed is similar to that used by the Apostle Paul in writing to the former heathen Galatians, "There is neither Jew nor Greek, there is neither bond nor free, there is neither male or female: for ye are all one in Christ Jesus." Galatians 3: 28.

The tune *St. Peter* was composed about 1836 by Alexander Robert Reinagle (1799-1877) to be used for the 118th Psalm. It is also used for Nos. 150, "How Sweet the Name," and 309, "Jerusalem, My Happy Home," and commemorates the church of St. Peter-in-the-East, Oxford, where Reinagle, of Austrian descent, was organist from 1822 to 1853.

437. LORD, HER WATCH THY CHURCH IS KEEPING

Romans 10: 14

Henry Downton (1818-85) was ordained an Anglican minister in 1843 and served as English chaplain at Geneva from 1857-73. During this period he translated several French and Swiss hymns into English, and in 1866 he was asked to write a hymn for a meeting of the Church Missionary Society. This hymn is the result and it is a compilation of many Scriptural ideas all bearing on the preaching of the gospel to every nation before the coming of the Lord, and the consequent final banishment of sin and its attendant woes. The key message of the hymn is, "How shall they believe in Him of whom they have not heard? and how shall they hear without a preacher?" Romans 10: 14.

The tune *Deerhurst,* also used for No. 237, "Jesus, Full of All Compassion," was composed in 1862 by James Langran (1835-1909), a London organist and music master at a Tottenham training college. Deerhurst is a small town near Tewkesbury, Gloucestershire, and a one-time curate there had a son who compiled the "Mitre Hymnal" which gave this name to this tune. Langran also composed No. 289, *Langran.*

438. BURIED BENEATH THE YIELDING WAVE

Colossians 2: 12

Benjamin Beddome (1717-95) was a Baptist minister for over fifty years at Bourton-on-the-Water, and wrote a new hymn for every Sunday morning. He was also the son of a Baptist minister, and in this hymn published in 1817, as in all his hymns, he embodies one central idea. This is the distinctive doctrine of baptism by immersion and he uses the definite, unequivocal word "buried" at the very beginning, quoting, "Buried with Him in baptism." Colossians 2: 12.

The tune *Azmon* is an arrangement by Lowell Mason (1792-1872), see appendix, from a tune of 1828 by Carl Gotthilf Gläser (1784-1829). The latter was a law student of Leipzig University and later became a teacher and director of music, and then a music publisher. As well as composing he also performed on the piano and violin. The name *Azmon,* an Old Testament word meaning fortress, has no associated significance.

439. WITH WILLING HEARTS WE TREAD

Romans 6: 4, 10

These words while not mentioning the word baptism were written specifically for this rite by a Baptist minister Samuel Francis Smith (1808-95) in 1843. He was also an editor of Baptist publications and the author of Nos. 454, "The Morning Light," and 510, "My Country, 'Tis of Thee." "The example of our Head" of stanza 1 refers to the baptism of Jesus Himself (Matthew 3: 15), and the words in stanza 3, "may we die to sin, and rise to life" refers to Romans 6: 4, 10, "Therefore we are buried with Him by baptism into death: that like as Christ was raised up . . . even so we also should walk in newness of life. . . . For in that He died, He died unto sin."

The tune *Dennis,* used also for Nos. 379, "There Is a Blessed Hope," and 432, "Blest Be the Tie," is an arrangement by Lowell Mason (1792-1872), see appendix, of a Swiss tune by Hans Georg Nägeli (1773-1836) of Zurich. Nägeli also composed the original of *Naomi,* the tune used for Nos. 322, "O, Could I Find from Day to Day," and 333, "Father, Whate'er of Earthly Bliss." He was a Swiss composer, teacher, and music publisher, and reformed the teaching of music in schools.

440. GO, PREACH MY GOSPEL

Mark 16: 15-17

Isaac Watts (1674-1748), see appendix, has taken the various scriptures describing the events of Ascension Day and knitted them together in a flowing paraphrase written in 1707. His title was "The Apostles' Commission; or, the Gospel Attested by Miracles." Mark 16: 15-17: "And He said unto them, Go ye into all the world, and preach the gospel to every creature. He that believeth and is baptized shall be saved; but he that believeth not shall be damned. And these signs shall follow them that believe." Matthew 28: 18-20: "All power is given unto Me. . . . Teach all nations . . . teaching them to observe all things whatsoever I have commanded you: and, lo, I am with you alway, even unto the end of the world." The omitted stanza reads:

3. Go heal the sick, go raise the dead,
Go cast out devils in My name;
Nor let My prophets be afraid
Tho' Greeks reproach, and Jews blaspheme.

The tune *Truro* is found in Thomas Williams's "Psalmodia Evangelica" of 1789, and is wrongly assigned to Charles Burney (1726-1814) who had other tunes in this book correctly to his credit. He was a composer and musical critic, and organist at Chelsea College. *Truro* has a rousing entry with its almost complete ascending scale passage of one octave, suitably broken by notes of five different time values.

441. GO, LABOUR ON

Luke 14: 16-24

Horatius Bonar (1808-89), see appendix, wrote this hymn of eight stanzas in 1836 as a special incentive to his lay helpers in Leith. It was his first hymn for adults and was entitled "The Useful Life." It was prefixed by a Greek quotation, "My soul, arise, why sleepest thou?" His inspiration came evidently from the parable of the great supper (Luke 14: 16-24), where the Lord's servants were bidden to call everyone to the feast. The final command was, "Go out into the highways and hedges, and compel them to come in" (Luke 14: 23), which is paraphrased in the latter half of the third stanza of "Church Hymnal." The omitted stanzas are:—

1. Go, labour on, spend, and be spent,
Thy joy to do the Father's will:
It is the way the Master went;
Should not the servant tread it still?

2. Go, labour on; 'tis not for nought,
Thy earthly loss is heavenly gain:
Men heed thee, love thee, praise thee not,
The Master praises; what are men?

3. Go, labour on; enough, while here,
If He shall praise thee, if He deign
Thy willing heart to mark and cheer;
No toil for Him shall be in vain.

8. Toil on, and in thy toil rejoice;
For toil comes rest, for exile home;
Soon shalt thou hear the Bridegroom's voice,
The midnight peal, Behold, I come!

The tune *Oakland* was composed in 1886 by Franklin Edson Belden (1858-1945), see appendix.

442. HOW BEAUTEOUS ARE THEIR FEET

Isaiah 52: 7-9

Isaac Watts (1674-1748), see appendix, wrote this hymn entitled, "The Blessedness of Gospel Times; or, The Revelation of Christ to Jews and Gentiles," in 1707, describing the wonderful blessings experienced by the reception of the gospel message. He has paraphrased three verses from the prophet Isaiah and intermingled with them our Lord's comments recorded in Matthew on another prophecy from Isaiah, thus: "How beautiful upon the mountains are the feet of him that bringeth good tidings, that publisheth peace; . . . that publisheth salvation; that saith unto Zion, Thy God reigneth!" Isaiah 52: 7. "But blessed are your eyes, for they see: and your ears, for they hear. For verily I say unto you, That many prophets and righteous men have desired to see those things which ye see, and have not seen them; and to hear those things which ye hear, and have not heard them." Matthew 13: 16, 17. "Thy watchmen shall lift up the voice; with the voice together shall they sing. . . . Break forth into joy, sing together, ye waste places of Jerusalem." Isaiah 52: 8, 9. The hymn was first sung after a sermon preached on these texts. It had originally six stanzas, the omitted one being:—

> 6. The Lord makes bare His arm
> Through all the earth abroad;
> Let every nation now behold
> Their Saviour and their God.

The tune *St. Thomas* is from "The Psalmody" 1770, by the music engraver Aaron Williams (1731-76), but not certainly of his composition. It has been attributed to George Frederick Handel (1685-1759) without any supporting evidence. It is a shortened form of the tune *Holborn* which appeared first in 1763 in Williams's "The Universal Psalmist." It is noteworthy that the bass has also a flowing part, with only one note the same as its preceding one. Another tune from Williams's "Psalmody" is No. 39, *Mear*.

443. WORKMAN OF GOD

John 12: 43

These words are part of a nineteen-stanza poem written in 1849 by Frederick William Faber (1814-63) and entitled "The Right Must Win." Some of the omitted stanzas are:—

> 1. Oh, it is hard to work for God,
> To rise and take His part
> Upon this battlefield of earth
> And not sometimes lose heart.

2. He hides Himself so wondrously,
As though there were no God;
He is least seen when all the powers
Of ill are most abroad.

3. Or He deserts us at the hour
The fight is all but lost;
And seems to leave us to ourselves
Just when we need Him most.

8. Ah! God is other than we think;
His ways are far above,
Far beyond reason's height, and reached
Only by childlike love.

9. The look, the fashion of God's ways
Love's lifelong study are;
She can be bold, and guess, and act,
When reason would not dare.

15. God's glory is a wondrous thing,
Most strange in all its ways,
And, of all things on earth, least like
What men agree to praise.

16. As He can endless glory weave
From what men reckon shame,
In His own world He is content
To play a losing game.

17. Muse on His justice; downcast soul!
Muse, and take better heart;
Back with thine angel to the field,
And bravely do thy part.

18. God's justice is a bed, where we
Our anxious hearts may lay,
And, weary with ourselves, may sleep
Our discontent away.

Our selection is stanzas 11, 12, 13, 14, 19. The whole hymn could be a reflection of his own experience, for he changed from an anti-Catholic to a fanatical proselytizing member of the Roman Catholic Church. See particularly his hymn, "Faith of Our Fathers," No. 349. The thought throughout the hymn is faith in God's leading even in times of darkness and of difficulty when truth is in a minority. The appeal is not to follow the example of the Pharisees, of whom it is recorded, "For they love the praise of men more than the praise of God." John 12: 43. Faber also wrote Nos. 65, "There's a Wideness," and 375 and 376, "Hark, Hark! My Soul."

The tune *Hummel* was composed in 1832 by Heinrich Christopher Zeuner (1795-1857), a German musician who emigrated to the United States in 1827 and became organist in the Park Street church in Boston, and later organist in Philadelphia.

444. HO! REAPERS OF LIFE'S HARVEST

Matthew 20: 6

Both the words and the tune *Life's Harvest* were written by Isaac Baker Woodbury (1819-58), see appendix, who has taken his inspiration from the question of the householder who "saith unto them, Why stand ye here all the day idle?" Matthew 20: 6. The tune is remarkable for the repetition in the bass part, no less than twenty C's being sounded before a change.

445. FROM GREENLAND'S ICY MOUNTAINS

Isaiah 9: 2

On the Saturday evening before Whit-Sunday, 1819, Reginald Heber (1783-1826), then vicar of Hodnet, Shropshire, was in his father-in-law's home at Wrexham. The latter, Dr. Shipley who was dean of St. Asaph and vicar of Wrexham, was to preach the following morning at a service in aid of the Society for the Propagation of the Gospel in Foreign Parts. Knowing of his son-in-law's great interest in missions, and also of his poetic ability, he asked him to write "something to sing in the morning." Heber produced the first three stanzas in a few minutes and the dean was completely satisfied. However, the author felt that it needed a concluding stanza and in twenty minutes' time he wrote the fourth. Very few changes have been made from Heber's original, a manuscript which shows his attention to detail and his meticulous care. One of his changes has not been adopted, however, namely his alteration in stanza 2 from Ceylon's to Java's because of the misplaced accent in his first effort. The words recall the vision given to the youthful Isaiah, "Whom shall I send, and who will go for us? Then said I, Here am I; send me" (Isaiah 6: 8), and also the prophetic picture the same writer gives of the result of Christ's coming to earth, "The people that walked in darkness have seen a great light: they that dwell in the land of the shadow of death, upon them hath the light shined." Isaiah 9: 2. Heber also wrote Nos. 73, "Holy, Holy, Holy"; 178, "In the Sun, and Moon, and Stars"; 340, "By Cool Siloam's Shady Rill"; 361, "The Son of God Goes Forth to War," and 476, "Bread of the World."

The tune *Missionary Hymn* was composed in 1823 and published in 1829 by Lowell Mason (1792-1872), see appendix, then a bank clerk. He had been given the stirring words by a woman in Savannah, Georgia, and in half an hour he had returned them with this tune newly written.

446. WORK, FOR THE NIGHT IS COMING

John 9: 4

Annie Louise Walker (1836-1907), to become Mrs. Coghill in 1883, wrote these lines while resident in Canada in 1854 as a young girl of eighteen years of age. She had emigrated from Staffordshire just previously, and returned to England many years later. She based her hymn on the clause in John 9: 4: "The night cometh, when no man can work," and wrote it in 7.6.7.6. double metre, the last line of the first stanza, for example, being, "Night, when man's work is done." The fourth lines were respectively:

Work 'mid the springing flowers
Rest cometh sure and soon
Work, for the daylight flies.

The authoress utterly disagreed with the reduction from six to five syllables in these lines, but the tune *Diligence,* or *Work Song,* composed in 1864 by Lowell Mason (1792-1872), see appendix, has popularized the hymn in this form. Lines 1, 3, and 7 are identical, as are also lines 4 and 8.

447. HARK! THE VOICE OF JESUS CALLING

Isaiah 6: 8

Daniel March (1816-1909) was a Presbyterian—later Congregational—minister who was invited on October 18, 1868, to preach in his own church in Philadelphia to the Christian Association. He chose for his text the missionary theme of Isaiah 6: 8, "Also I heard the voice of the Lord, saying, Whom shall I send, and who will go for Us? Then said I, Here am I; send me." He sought for a suitable hymn to sing which was appropriate to his message, but in vain, so on the impulse of the moment he sat down and wrote eight four-line stanzas inspired by the text he had chosen. Notice his reference to lay workers, who while not taking leadership, can nevertheless make a contribution to victory, as did Aaron and Hur by staying up the hands of their leader Moses (Exodus 17: 11, 12). Additions by others to the hymn are:—

If you cannot give your thousands,
You can give the widow's mite;
And the least you do for Jesus,
Will be precious in His sight.
If you cannot raise the wicked
With the judgment's dread alarms,
You can lead the little children
To the Saviour's waiting arms.

If among the older people,
You may not be apt to teach;
"Feed My lambs," said Christ our Shepherd,
Place the food within their reach.
And it may be that the children
You have led with trembling hand,
Will be found among your jewels
When you reach the better land.

The tune *Fillmore* was composed in 1886 by Franklin Edson Belden (1858-1945), see appendix. Lines 1, 3, and 7 are identical, as are also lines 4 and 8.

448. FAR AND NEAR THE FIELDS ARE TEEMING

Matthew 9:38

When our Lord was on earth and saw the great needs of the people He told His disciples to make a matter of prayer the sending forth of workers. This theme is expressed in the refrain—"Pray ye therefore the Lord of the harvest, that He will send forth labourers into His harvest." Matthew 9: 38. The first stanza refers to the preceding verse, which states that "the harvest truly is plenteous," and also to John 4: 35, which states that it is also ripe—"look on the fields; for they are white already to harvest." The period of the harvest is likened to one day in which reaping must be done in the early morning, at noontide, and even at sunset. Then in the evening of the day, the work is finished and the third stanza recalls Psalm 126: 5: "They . . . shall reap in joy."

The words were written in 1885 by J. O. Thompson, and the tune *Harvest* by J. B. O. Clemm, and copyright in 1895.

449. O ZION, HASTE

Isaiah 52: 7

Mrs. Mary Ann Faulkner Thomson (1834-1923) was a Londoner who married an American librarian, and who was a member of the Episcopal Church. In 1868 she was sitting up with one of her children who was sick with typhoid fever. She thought of the tune of the hymn, "Hark, Hark, My Soul, Angelic Songs Are Swelling" (Nos. 375, 376) which she liked very much, and had the desire to write a missionary hymn in this metre. During her vigil she succeeded in writing the words of the stanzas, but words for a refrain eluded her. However, in 1871 she completed this, taking her text from Romans 10: 15: "That preach the gospel of peace, and bring glad tidings of good things!" and also from its Old Testament counterpart, "That bringeth good tidings, that publisheth peace." Isaiah 52: 7. The two omitted stanzas are:—

2. Behold how many thousand still are lying
Bound in the darksome prison house of sin,
With none to tell them of the Savour's dying,
Or of the life He died for them to win.

3. 'Tis thine to save from peril of perdition
The souls for whom the Lord His life laid down;
Beware, lest, slothful to fulfil thy mission,
Thou lose one jewel that should deck His crown.

The tune *Tidings* was composed in 1875 by James Walch (1837-1901), an organist of Bolton, Lancashire, especially for the hymn, "Hark, Hark, My Soul." The present name is given because of the emphasis on the word tidings in the refrain, and on the idea of telling the tidings in each stanza. Walch also composed Nos. 37, *Sawley,* and 467, *St. George's, Bolton.*

450. FLING OUT THE BANNER

Psalm 60: 4

George Washington Doane (1799-1859), American Episcopal bishop of New Jersey, founded a school for girls at St. Mary's, Burlington, New Jersey, in 1837. In 1848, for a special flag-raising ceremony at this school, he wrote the words of this hymn, basing it on Psalm 60: 4, "Thou hast given a banner to them that fear Thee, that it may be displayed because of the truth." An omitted stanza is:—

3. Fling out the banner! heathen lands
Shall see from far the glorious sight;
And nations crowding to be born,
Baptize their spirits in its light.

The original last two lines of the first stanza were:—

The sun that lights its shining folds
The cross on which the Saviour died.

Doane also wrote No. 48, "Softly Now the Light of Day."

The tune *Waltham,* otherwise, *Camden,* or *Doane,* was composed for a slightly different text, "Uplift the Banner," first published in "The Hymnody" in 1872 by John Baptiste Calkin (1827-1905), Fellow of the Royal College of Organists, who also composed No. 264, *Savoy Chapel.* He was born and died in London, and was organist at the Savoy Chapel, and also professor at the Guildhall School of Music.

451. THOU WHOSE ALMIGHTY WORD

Genesis 1: 2, 3

John Marriott (1780-1825), a Church of England clergyman and rector of Church Lawford, Warwickshire, has been commemorated by his friend Sir Walter Scott, who dedicated the second canto of his long poem "Marmion" to him in these words:—

Marriott, thy harp on Isis strung,
To many a Border theme has rung.

He was extremely modest and although this hymn was written in 1813, he would not allow it to be printed in his lifetime. At length, some of his friends obtained permission to print it, and it appeared in the *Family Visitor,* a religious magazine. It was written to fit the tune to "God Save the King" (No. 506) and first printed in 1825, and quoted at a meeting of the London Missionary Society in the same year, six weeks after his death. The words are based on Genesis 1: 2, 3, "And the earth was without form, and void; and darkness was upon the face of the deep. . . . And the Spirit of God moved upon the face of the waters. And God said, Let there be light: and there was light." The lesson is then drawn of God shining the gospel light through the darkness of heathenism. The three stanzas apply in turn to the work of the Trinity—Father, Son, and Holy Ghost—all giving light, followed by the omitted stanza which summarizes them:—

4. Blessed, and holy, and
Glorious Trinity,
Wisdom, Love, Might:
Boundless as ocean's tide
Rolling in fullest pride
Thro' the world, far and wide,
Let there be light!

The hymn is now sung to the tune *Fiat Lux* (= Let there be light), composed in 1875 by John Bacchus Dykes (1823-76), see appendix, and so named because of the last words of each stanza. Note the descending passage in the melody from top E to bottom E in lines 6 and 7.

452. CHRIST FOR THE WORLD

1 Timothy 1: 15

The annual convention of the Young Men's Christian Association was held in 1869 in Cleveland, Ohio. Their motto, "Christ for the world, and the world for Christ" was formed in evergreen letters and stretched across the church. The Rev. Samuel Wolcott (1813-86), a Congregational minister of Cleveland, attended the convention and was impressed by the slogan to such an extent that on February 7, 1869, on the way home he composed this hymn as he walked along. An omitted stanza is:—

3. Christ for the world we sing;
The world to Christ we bring,
With one accord;
With us the work to share,
With us reproach to dare,
With us the cross to bear,
For Christ the Lord.

The words emphasize Christ's mission, not to His own people only, but to the whole world: "This is a faithful saying, and worthy of all acceptation, that Christ Jesus came into the world to save sinners." 1 Timothy 1: 15. Wolcott was inspired to write further hymns, ultimately more than 200, after a friend had invited him to assist in compiling a volume of hymns that same year.

The tune *Italian Hymn* was composed in 1769 by Felice de Giardini (1716-96) at the request of the Countess of Huntingdon (see No. 190) for the words "Come, Thou Almighty King" (No. 3). He was an Italian violinist who spent thirty-six years of his life in England and composed many pieces for strings.

453. THEY COME FROM THE EAST AND WEST

Luke 13: 29

Johannes Alfred Hultmann (1861-1942) was a minister of the Covenant Church, who worked both in the United States and in Sweden. He became a singing evangelist in 1897 and conducted thousands of song-evenings in Sweden and America at which the proceeds were devoted to charitable purposes. He was known as the sunshine singer, for he devoted his talent of music to the service of the Saviour. The present hymn was composed by him in Swedish, his mother tongue, and begins:—

De komma från öst and väst,
De komma från syd och nord.

When William Ambrose Spicer (1865-1952), who was secretary of the General Conference of Seventh-day Adventists from 1903-22, and president from 1922-30, visited Sweden in 1935, he heard this song being sung in Swedish and accompanied by stringed instruments. He was so delighted with it that he requested a translation of it into English so that it could be included in the "Church Hymnal" that was then being contemplated. No one volunteered, and it was not until three years later that Ellis R. Colson (1898-1967), a Seventh-day Adventist minister, heard that Pastor Spicer was still waiting for a translation. Thereupon he produced one, keeping very close to the original except for the last half of the third stanza, which described those who had died as playing on their harps in heaven already. The translation was sent to W. A. Spicer, but the translator did not know that it had been acceptable until he saw it in the new hymnal in 1941. The tune is named *Spicer* in this hymnal to commemorate the story of its inclusion. The appropriate Scripture verse is Luke 13: 29, "And they shall come from the east, and from the west, and from the north, and from the south, and shall sit down in the kingdom of God."

454. THE MORNING LIGHT

Isaiah 66: 8, 12, 18

Samuel Francis Smith (1808-95), a Harvard graduate and Baptist minister, was greatly inspired by the stirring missionary reports sent home from Burma by Adoniram Judson (1788-1850). In the words of this hymn written in 1832, he has caught the vision of the prophet Isaiah when he saw the Gentiles coming into the kingdom of God—"Who hath heard such a thing? who hath seen such things? Shall the earth be made to bring forth in one day? or shall a nation be born at once? for as soon as Zion travailed, she brought forth her children." Isaiah 66: 8. "Behold, I will extend peace to her like a river, and the glory of the Gentiles like a flowing stream." Verse 12. "It shall come, that I will gather all nations and tongues; and they shall come, and see My glory." Verse 18. The omitted stanza is:—

2. Rich dews of grace come o'er us
In many a gentle shower,
And brighter scenes before us
Are opening every hour.
Each cry to heaven going
Abundant answer brings,
And heavenly gales are blowing
With peace upon their wings.

Smith also wrote Nos. 439, "With Willing Hearts We Tread," and 510, "My Country, 'Tis of Thee."

The tune *Webb* was composed on a voyage from England to America in 1837 by George James Webb (1803-87) as a setting for a secular song beginning " 'Tis Dawn, the Lark Is Singing." It is also used for No. 354, "Stand Up! Stand Up for Jesus!" It was named *Goodwin* by Mason and Webb in their compilation of 1850 "Cantica Laudis." Webb was an organist and music teacher who emigrated from England in 1830 and assisted Lowell Mason in founding the Boston Academy of Music.

455. LORD OF THE SABBATH

Hebrews 4: 9

The anonymous author of this hymn has dilated upon the true meaning of the Sabbath, that is, a day of rest not merely from physical labour, but a day of rest for the soul, a time of freedom from sin and from the cares of this life. The double blessing mentioned in the last stanza is the blessing which was first pronounced upon the Sabbath ("God blessed the seventh day, and sanctified it," Genesis 2: 3) augmented by the second blessing of the presence of Jesus with us as we worship. "There remaineth therefore a rest to the people of God." Hebrews 4: 9.

The tune *Park Street* is probably named in commemoration of an old Puritan meeting house in Park Street, Boston. It was an arrangement made in 1820 by the Handel and Haydn Society of Boston, from an original tune composed in 1810 by Frederick Marco Antonio Venua (1788-1872), a member of the Royal Society of Musicians. The same tune is also used for No. 20, "Lord of All Being, Throned Afar."

456. ANOTHER SIX DAYS' WORK IS DONE

Exodus 20: 9, 10

Joseph Stennett (1663-1713), grandfather of Samuel Stennett (see Nos. 159, 535, 553), wrote this Sabbath hymn, which was published in 1732, as a 14-stanza poem. He was a Seventh-day Baptist pastor and ministered to his congregation in Devonshire Square, London, on Sabbaths from 1690 to his death, and on Sundays to the Sunday-keeping Baptists. Our second stanza is an addition to the poem, and the other stanzas with the two below, constitute the hymn:—

> 5. With joy, great God, Thy works we view,
> In various scenes both old and new;
> With praise, we think on mercies past,
> With hope, we future pleasures taste.
>
> 6. In holy duties let the day,
> In holy pleasure pass away;
> How sweet, a Sabbath thus to spend,
> In hope of one that ne'er shall end.

The hymn recalls the fourth commandment of the Decalogue, of which Stennett, who was also royal physician, was such a firm observer. "Six days shalt thou labour, and do all thy work: but the seventh day is the sabbath of the Lord thy God." Exodus 20: 9, 10.

The tune *Hebron* was composed in 1830 by Lowell Mason (1792-1872), see appendix, but it has no special associative significance.

457. HAIL, PEACEFUL DAY!

Genesis 2: 3

In the early days of the Seventh-day Adventist denomination there were few hymns on the Sabbath that could be sung, as they were written by devout Sunday-keepers and carried references to the first day of the week; for example, day of light, day of resurrection, first of days. Accordingly, there was a need felt by these new believers for hymns which were divorced from Sunday-keeping sentiments, the only alternative being to mutilate existing hymns (which has been done) by eliminating references to the first day of the week. Annie Rebekah Smith (1828-55), see appendix, has here supplied a new hymn, speaking of the Sabbath as it truly is, a memorial of that sacred rest of vast creation's mighty King. She mentions, too, the "holy law of love," which is a reference to the Ten Commandments, of which the Sabbath is the fourth. The third stanza, while not mentioning the Sabbath, recalls a verse which prophesies of Sabbath-keeping in the new earth. "And it shall come to pass, that . . . from one sabbath to another, shall all flesh come to worship before Me, saith the Lord." Isaiah 66: 23. An omitted stanza is:—

2. Ye saints awake, with joyful lay,
Behold its rising light, divine;
To God your grateful homage pay,
Its radiant beams around us shine.
Welcome the day He calls His own,
And fervent worship at His throne.

Slight alterations have been made in the original, which read, "Come" not "Hail, peaceful day." The hymn recalls the end of creation week when "God blessed the seventh day, and sanctified it: because that in it He had rested from all His work which God created and made." Genesis 2: 3.

The tune *Nashville* was arranged by Lowell Mason (1792-1872), see appendix.

458. HOW SWEET UPON THIS SACRED DAY

Luke 11: 2

These words were written by Eliza Lee Cabot (1787-1860), who married Professor Charles Follen in 1840. She was a Unitarian of Boston, Massachusetts, and the hymn appears under the title "Sabbath Day" in the 1831 edition of her poems. There were originally six stanzas, those omitted being as follows:—

3. With humble hope to bend the knee,
And, free from folly's leaven,
Confess that we have strayed from Thee,
Thou righteous Judge in heaven.

5. If from the bosom that is dear,
By cold unkindness driven,
The heart that knows no refuge here,
Shall find a friend in heaven;

6. Then hail thou sacred blessed day,
The best of all the seven,
When hearts unite their vows to pay
Of gratitude to heaven.

The present third stanza does not appear in Mrs. Follen's works. Notice the thought in each stanza direct, from earth to heaven, making the Sabbath day a rest in the spiritual as well as in the physical meaning of the word. The quotation is from our Lord's model prayer: "When ye pray, say, Our Father which art in heaven." Luke 11: 2

The tune *Elizabethtown* was composed by George Kingsley (1811-84) of Northampton, Massachusetts. He was a music teacher and organist in Boston, a compiler of music for young people, and later became professor of music in Philadelphia. He also composed Nos. 204 and 483 *Ware,* and arranged No. 381, *Valentia.* Both *Elizabethtown* and *Ware,* with their unusual mixture of crotchets and quavers, make a difficult rhythm for singing.

459. WELCOME, WELCOME DAY OF REST

Isaiah 58: 13

These words by an anonymous writer are a quiet devotional prayer extolling the blessings and peace of the Sabbath day. The author considers the Sabbath as a time of communion with God after the weary labour of the week, a time when praise and prayer and Bible study can be undertaken; in short, a day to be welcomed and desired: ". . . call the Sabbath a delight, the holy of the Lord, honourable." Isaiah 58: 13

The tune *Pleyel's Hymn* was adapted in 1791 by Ignace Joseph Pleyel (1757-1831), an Austrian composer who was one of Haydn's pupils in Vienna. It is taken from the slow movement of his string quartet Opus 7, No. 4, c. 1782, being an arrangement of the theme of the andante with variations. Pleyel established a piano factory in Paris in 1807, which was such a success that he devoted all his time to it and gave up musical composition.

460. HOW SWEET THE LIGHT

Exodus 31: 15

These words were written in 1821 as a Sunday evening hymn by James Edmeston (1791-1867), an architect and surveyor. The first two stanzas describe the blessed calm of the sacred day of rest when the thoughts are lifted from earth to heaven. The third stanza then likens the whole of our earthly life to the working week, and the anticipated eternal life to a restful, unending Sabbath in the presence of God. "Six days may work be done; but in the seventh is the sabbath of rest, holy to the Lord." Exodus 31: 15. Edmeston wrote over 2,000 hymns and made a practice of writing a new one and reading it for Sunday evening family worship. He also wrote Nos. 49, "Saviour, Breathe an Evening Blessing," and 87, "Lead Us, Heavenly Father."

The tune *Saxby* was composed in 1867 by an Anglican minister, Timothy Richard Matthews (1826-1910), and is named after a small town in Lincolnshire. He also wrote Nos. 103, *Margaret,* and 290, *Chenies.*

461. THIS IS THE DAY OF REST

Hosea 14: 5

John Ellerton (1826-93), vicar of Crewe Green, Cheshire, wrote this didactic hymn in 1867 in praise of Sunday, but it has been modified so as to be used as a Sabbath hymn. The illustration in the first stanza is borrowed from the Old Testament prophet Hosea —"I will be as the dew unto Israel." Hosea 14: 5. The original hymn had five stanzas, the omitted one being:—

> 1. This is the day of light,
> Let there be light today;
> O Day-spring, rise upon our night,
> And chase its gloom away.

And in 1888 Ellerton added another stanza, as follows:—

> 5. This is the day of bread,
> The Bread that Thou dost give;
> Today for us Thy feast is spread,
> That hung'ring souls may live.

These are obvious references to the first day of creation when light was created, and to the Saturday evening meeting at Troas: "Upon the first day of the week, when the disciples came together to break bread." Acts 20: 7. Our last stanza was originally, "This is the first of days," and its theme was the resurrection Sunday, as seen in the remainder of the stanza. Ellerton also wrote Nos. 34, "Saviour, Again to Thy Dear Name"; 37, "The Lord Be With Us"; 57, "The Day Thou Gavest"; 58, "Our Day of Praise Is Done," and had a part in No. 78, "God the Omnipotent."

The tune *Schumann* was arranged by Lowell Mason (1792-1872), see appendix, and George Webb (see No. 354) in an effort to raise the standard of American hymnody by taking selections from classical music and using them as hymn tunes. It appeared in their "Cantica Laudis" of 1850 under the name *White,* with credit given to Robert Schumann (1810-56), see No. 407. The same tune is also used for Nos. 472, "Jesus Invites His Saints," and 477, "We Give Thee but Thine Own." Another arrangement from Schumann is No. 407, *Canonbury.*

462. SAFELY THROUGH ANOTHER WEEK

Leviticus 23: 32

This hymn was written in 1774 by John Newton (1725-1807), see appendix, and is No. XL, Book II, of the "Olney Hymns," 1779. It had five stanzas originally, and was entitled "Saturday Evening," which was to Newton the time immediately preceding his day of rest for: "From even unto even, shall ye celebrate your sabbath." Leviticus 23: 32. Hence the original wording of our third stanza (his fourth) which began:—

4. When the morn shall bid us rise,
May we feel Thy presence near

and the fourth line of stanza 1, "On the approaching Sabbath day." The omitted stanza is:—

2. Mercies multiplied each hour,
Through the week our praise demand,
Guarded by Almighty power,
Fed and guided by His hand:
Though ungrateful we have been,
Only made returns of sin.

The tune *Sabbath* was composed in 1824 by Lowell Mason (1792-1872), see appendix, but the hymn is sung by other churches to the tune of *St. Athanasius,* No. 229.

463. O DAY OF REST AND GLADNESS

Psalm 118: 24

Christopher Wordsworth (1807-85), nephew of the famous poet William Wordsworth, and later to become the bishop of Lincoln, wrote six stanzas of this hymn in 1862. He wrote in order to inculcate the doctrines of the church, this one on the Sabbath, basing it on Psalm 118: 24: "This is the day which the Lord hath made: we will rejoice, and be glad in it." He uses several metaphors for the Sabbath, namely: a balm, a port, a garden, a fountain, a mountain, and in an omitted stanza a ladder. The omitted stanzas are:—

2. On thee at the creation
The light first had its birth;
On thee for our salvation
Christ rose from depths of earth;
On thee our Lord victorious
The Spirit sent from heaven;
And thus on thee most glorious
A triple light was given.

4. Thou art a holy ladder
Where angels go and come;
Each Sunday finds us gladder,
Nearer to heaven, our home.
A day of sweet reflection
Thou art, a day of love;
A day of resurrection
From earth to heaven above.

5. Today on weary nations
The heavenly manna falls;
To holy convocations
The silver trumpet calls,
Where gospel light is glowing
With pure and radiant beams;
And living water flowing
With soul-refreshing streams.

6. The last half of stanza three in "Church Hymnal" followed by the doxology as follows:—

To Holy Ghost be praises,
To Father and to Son;
The church her voice upraises
To Thee, blest Three in One.

The latter half of the original stanza 4 has been used with modifications, though refection, meaning eating, could have been retained, as the Sabbath is certainly a day of feeding on the Word of God, as well as reflecting on it.

The tune *Mendebras* is an arrangement of a German melody, made in 1839 by Lowell Mason (1792-1872), see appendix.

464. HAIL, HAPPY DAY!

Exodus 25: 8

These words were written by Simon Browne (1680-1732), a Congregational pastor in Old Jewry, London, (not Phoebe Brown) and speak of the Sabbath as a day when our hearts can be lifted up to God to forget the follies of earth. This kind of worship of God on the Sabbath underlies the true purpose of the tabernacle services of the Israelites: "And let them make Me a sanctuary; that I may dwell among them." Exodus 25: 8. Browne also wrote two devotional hymns with this similar thought of Christian living, namely, Nos. 204, "Come, Gracious Spirit," and 236, "Lord, at Thy Feet."

The tune *Freeport* is also used for No. 466, "Again the Day Returns."

465. WELCOME, DELIGHTFUL MORN

Psalm 80: 18

These words appear in the new selection of 1806 of John Dobell (1757-1840) of Poole, Dorset, and are there attributed to J. Hayward under the title "Sabbath morning." They refer to the day of rest as a welcome time of worship, of Bible study, and of the renewing of spiritual life. The Sabbath would be a barren day but for the Lord's blessing on the day, the spiritual presence of the King of grace, and His Spirit working upon the heart of the worshipper. In the words of the psalmist, "So will not we go back from Thee: quicken us, and we will call upon Thy name." Psalm 80: 18.

The tune *Lischer* is an arrangement by Lowell Mason (1792-1872), see appendix, about 1866, of a composition by Johann Christian Friedrich Schneider (1786-1853) of Saxony, Germany. He was a prolific composer, producing sixteen oratorios (one "The Deluge") and hundreds of songs.

466. AGAIN THE DAY RETURNS

Exodus 28: 8, 10, 11

William Mason (1725-97), the son of a vicar, was an Anglican minister born in Hull, Yorkshire, who published this hymn in 1796 in five stanzas. It was written for morning service, and reminds us that the Sabbath of the fourth commandment is also the Sabbath of creation. "Remember the sabbath day, to keep it holy . . . in it thou shalt not do any work. . . . For in six days the Lord made heaven and earth, the sea, and all that in them is, and rested the seventh day: wherefore the Lord blessed the sabbath day, and hallowed it." Exodus 20: 8, 10, 11. Mason was chaplain to King George III, and canon and precentor of York Cathedral, and wrote several poems, odes, and tragedies.

The tune *Freeport* is also used for No. 464, "Hail, Happy Day!"

467. THE DAWN OF GOD'S DEAR SABBATH

Hebrews 4: 10, 11

These words were written in 1866 by Ada Cambridge (1844-1926) of Norwich, England, as a hymn for Sunday morning, expressing the spiritual meaning of the Sabbath (as she calls Sunday) as a day of rest from sin, and a day of peace with God. This is the teaching of the writer to the Hebrews when he says, "For he that is entered into His rest, he also hath ceased from his own works, as God did from His. Let us labour therefore to enter into that rest, lest any man fall after the same example of unbelief." Hebrews 4: 10, 11. In April, 1870, Miss Cambridge married an English curate, George Frederick Cross, who was appointed rector on his wedding day, and sailed for Australia a month later. She helped her husband by being district visitor in various parishes of Victoria where he was stationed. The title of the hymn of eight stanzas is "Fourth Commandment," and it appears in the section on the Holy Communion. The omitted stanzas are:—

2. As bursts of glorious sunshine
Across a stormy sea,
Revealing to the sailors
That Port where they would be,
The calm and peaceful Haven,
The dazzling, golden shore,
The home of saints and angels,
Where sin is known no more.

3. O day when earthly sorrow
Is merged in heavenly joy,
And trial changed to blessing
That foes may not destroy—
When want is turned to fullness,
And weariness to rest,
And pain to wondrous rapture,
Upon the Saviour's breast!

7. So be it, Lord, for ever;
O may we evermore,
In Jesu's holy presence
His blessed name adore!
Upon His peaceful Sabbath,
Within His temple-walls—
Type of the stainless worship
In Sion's golden halls.

8. So that, in joy and gladness,
We reach that Home at last,
When life's short week of sorrow
And sin and strife is past;
When angel-hands have gathered
The fair, ripe fruit for Thee,
O Father, Lord, Redeemer!
Most Holy Trinity!

The hymn is one of several which were designed to be read or used at pauses in the communion service.

The tune *St. George's Bolton* was composed in 1875 by James Walch (1837-1901), and commemorates the name of one of the Bolton, Lancashire, churches at which he was organist. He also composed Nos. 37, *Sawley*, and 449, *Tidings*.

468. FAR FROM ALL CARE

Isaiah 48: 18

The tune *Pevensey* was composed by Dr. Douglas Albert Raoul Aufranc (1892-), a Seventh-day Adventist physician and dentist, after a stay at Pevensey Bay between Hastings and Eastbourne in Sussex, England. After a period of intense work and strain in the rush and bustle of the great city of London, he spent a short holiday by the sea. The peace of the quiet place, especially on the Sabbath day, contrasted vividly with the noise of the city, and the idea of the hymn was born there, although words and music were written afterwards in London. Notice the theme of the Sabbath commandment in the last three stanzas and the third line of each, suggesting the following scriptures: (2) "The remnant . . . which keep the commandments of God," Revelation 12: 17; (3) "O that thou hadst hearkened to My commandments! then had thy peace been as a river," Isaiah 48: 18; and (4) "Blessed are they do His commandments, that they may . . . enter in through the gates into the city," Revelation 22: 14.

Dr. Aufranc also wrote the words of Nos. 335, "Alone With Thee"; 374, "There Is a Road," and 682, "Father, I Yield to Thee My Life." He also composed the tunes associated with the first two of these hymns, namely, Nos. 335, *Windy Ridge*, and 374, *Thetford*.

469. WELCOME, DAY OF SWEET REPOSE!

Luke 4: 16

These words were written by Irwin Henry Evans (1862-1945), who was born in Michigan and baptized into the Seventh-day Adventist Church as a lad of twelve years. He attended Battle Creek

College and was licensed to preach in 1882 and ordained to the ministry in 1886. Five years later he was appointed president of the Michigan Conference, and until his retirement he continued in administrative work. He was president of the former Asiatic Division, of the North American Division, and of the Far Eastern Division, as well as treasurer of the General Conference of Seventh-day Adventists. He was a forceful preacher and writer as well as a capable administrator. He was chairman of the committee appointed to prepare this "Church Hymnal." His hymn emphasizes the Sabbath as beginning in Eden (Genesis 2: 2, 3) and also kept by our Lord on earth, "And, as His custom was, He went into the synagogue on the Sabbath day." Luke 4: 16.

The tune *Evans* was composed especially for these words at Glendale, California, in 1939, by Irving Arthur Steinel (1884-1945), who was also a Seventh-day Adventist. He was a church organist, and taught many years in California, after serving six years as a missionary teacher in the Philippines. He was the original accompanist for the first Voice of Prophecy quartet, and composed many songs and anthems, mostly at night while sitting up in bed. He also wrote No. 286, *Consecration Hymn.*

470. THY HOLY SABBATH, LORD

Isaiah 58: 13

The anonymous hymn writer amplifies the thought of Isaiah 58: 13 where the Sabbath is a delight even though man's secular pleasures are denied. "If thou turn away . . . from doing thy pleasure on My holy day; and call the Sabbath a delight, the holy of the Lord." Isaiah 58: 13. "The rest of the holy Sabbath unto the Lord," Exodus 16: 23, and the blessing which God put into the day at creation (Genesis 2: 3), is invoked upon the worshippers. Notice that the three aspects of worship are outlined—singing praise, hearing the Word of God, and prayer. The "endless Sabbath" of the last stanza is evidently a symbol for eternal rest from sin, and eternal worship in the presence of the eternal God.

471. THY BROKEN BODY, GRACIOUS LORD

Luke 22: 19, 20

These words by an unknown author are a very cogent summary of the ceremony and meaning of the communion service. It is noteworthy that the expression "broken body" is capable of wrong interpretation, for "a bone of Him shall not be broken." John 19: 36. The Scripture reference is therefore given from Luke's description of the last supper, where our Lord shows that the act of breaking the bread was symbolic of His sharing to the whole world the blessings of His crucifixion. "And He took bread, and gave thanks, and brake it, and gave unto them, saying, This is My body which is given for you: this do in remembrance of Me. Likewise also the cup after supper, saying, This cup is the new testament in My blood, which is shed for you." Luke 22: 19, 20. The second stanza which speaks of being "one in Thee," is in marked contrast with the jealous rivalry and its utter incompatibility with true discipleship as described in Luke 22: 24-26: "There was also a strife among them, which of them should be accounted the greatest. . . . But ye shall not be so."

The tune *Ernan,* used also for No. 60, "O Blessed Hour," was composed in 1850 by Lowell Mason (1792-1872), see appendix.

472. JESUS INVITES HIS SAINTS

1 Corinthians 10: 16, 17

Isaac Watts (1674-1748), see appendix, wrote a six-stanza hymn in 1707 entitled "Communion With Christ, and With Saints," the first two lines of which are identical with the first two lines of this hymn. The rest, however, is quite different, and is as follows:—

1. . . . .
Here pardoned rebels sit, and hold
Communion with their Lord.

2. For food He gives His flesh,
He bids us drink His blood;
Amazing favour! matchless grace
Of our descending God!

3. This holy bread and wine
Maintains our fainting breath,
By union with our loving Lord,
And interest in His death.

4. Our heavenly Father calls
Christ and His members one;
We the young children of His love,
And He the first-born Son.

5. We are but several parts
Of the same broken bread;
One body hath its several limbs,
But Jesus is the Head.

6. Let all our powers be joined,
His glorious name to raise;
Pleasure and love fill every mind,
And every voice be praise.

The meaning of the communion service is given by the Apostle Paul—"The cup of blessing which we bless, is it not the communion of the blood of Christ? The bread which we break, is it not the communion of the body of Christ? For we being many are one bread, and one body: for we are all partakers of that one bread." 1 Corinthians 10: 16, 17.

The tune, also used for Nos. 461, "This Is the Day of Rest," and 477, "We Give Thee but Thine Own," appears (as the tune *White*) in "Cantica Laudis," 1850, and is here named *Schumann* because it is thought to be taken from the works of Robert Schumann (1810-56). This collection, published in Boston in 1850, by Lowell Mason, see appendix, and George Webb, see No. 354, was designed to raise the standards of American hymnody by adapting selections from classical music. No. 407, *Canonbury* is another arrangement from Schumann.

473. ONCE IN JERUSALEM

John 13: 5-9

The rite of feet-washing is described only once in the Scriptures, in John 13: 4-17, though a reference could be made to the practice in 1 Timothy 5: 10. This hymn reminds us that Jesus instituted this ordinance of humility in order to banish evil thoughts, and incidentally to prepare the participants to partake of the Lord's Supper. "If ye know these things, happy are ye if ye do them." John 13: 17. Thomas R. Williamson, the author, also makes reference to Peter's enthusiastic response, "Not my feet only, but also my hands and my head." John 13: 9. He also refers to the New Testament practice, "Greet ye one another with an holy kiss." 1 Corinthians 16: 20, etc. Williamson, a resident of Tallmadge, Ohio, contributed poems to the *Review and Herald* between 1883 and 1893.

The tune *Alida* is an early American melody, almost entirely in the pentatonic scale (see No. 181), the exceptions being the passing notes at the end of lines 1, 3 and 7, and the last but one notes of lines 4 and 8, and a possible passing note in lines 5 and 6. It would not be out of place to play all these B's as A's, in which case the melody could well have been imported from Europe by early settlers, or from Africa by Negroes. Its name is the name of a heroine in the 1812 War, or alternatively a city of Asia Minor noted for its splendid garments. Neither appears to have any associative connection with the words.

474. ROCK OF AGES

Isaiah 42: 11

This hymn first appeared in 1776 in the *Gospel Magazine* at the end of an article by the editor, Augustus Toplady (1740-78). The article had a long and unusual title, namely, "A Remarkable Calculation Introduced Here for the Sake of the Spiritual Improvements Subjoined. Questions and Answers Relating to the National Debt." It was probably stimulated by Toplady's argument with the Wesleys concerning perfection and his effort to refute their teaching on this doctrine, for his point was to show that the number of sins committed by even a professing Christian is so enormous that he will never be able to pay the debt. Toplady calculated that the average number of sins was thousands of millions, and so he entitled his hymn, "A Living and Dying Prayer for the Holiest Believer in the World." Even such a good-living Christian has one hope only, namely that "the Lord hath laid on Him [Christ] the iniquity of us all." Isaiah 53: 6. The hymn refers to the incident at the cross, "But one of the soldiers with a spear pierced His side, and forthwith came there out blood and water," John 19: 34, and it takes its first line from Toplady's sermon on Isaiah 42: 11: "Let the inhabitants of the rock sing," where the preacher likened the rock to Christ, for He was a foundation to support, a shelter to screen, and a fortress to protect. His last stanza has been modified somewhat from his original:—

Whilst I draw this fleeting breath—
When my eye-strings break in death—
When I soar through tracts unknown—

Toplady was a Church of England preacher and curate at Blagdon, Somerset, in 1764, and a mile or two away in Burrington Combe is a memorial to him and his hymn. However, the story of his sheltering in the crevice between the limestone slabs was not current until 1850. He also wrote No. 249, "If Through Unruffled Seas."

The tune *Toplady* was composed in 1830 by Thomas Hastings (1784-1872), see appendix. The last two lines are a repetition musically of the first two lines, and line 4 copies line 3, thus making the tune quickly familiar.

475. BY CHRIST REDEEMED

1 Corinthians 11: 23-26

These words were written in 1857 especially for the service of the Lord's Supper, by George Rawson (1807-89). He was a solicitor in Leeds, Yorkshire, and a member of the Congregational church there, writing under the pen-name of "A Leeds Layman." The third line of the fourth stanza was, originally, "By one blest chain of loving rite," and stanza 2, line 2, was "Is shown in this memorial bread." This special service, while recorded in the three synoptic Gospels, is summarized in 1 Corinthians 11: 23-26, "The Lord Jesus the same night in which He was betrayed took bread: and when He had given thanks, He brake it, and said, Take, eat: this is My body, which is broken for you: this do in remembrance of Me. After the same manner also He took the cup, when He had supped, saying, This cup is the new testament in My blood: this do ye, as oft as ye drink it, in remembrance of Me. For as often as ye eat this bread, and drink this cup, ye do show the Lord's death till He come." Rawson also wrote No. 216, "Holy Spirit, Lamp of Light," which is similar in pattern to this one, namely, in having three rhyming lines followed by a fourth line common to all stanzas, with a slight modification in the fifth stanza. He assisted in the preparation of the "Leeds Hymn Book," 1853, for the Congregationalists, and "Psalms and Hymns," 1858, for the Baptists.

The tune *Nauford* was composed by Arthur Seymour Sullivan (1842-1900), see appendix. Notice the pattern of repeated notes (5 or 4) followed by a descending melody of 3 or 4 notes of the scale, also the contrary motion in the descending soprano part with the ascending bass part in the first two lines of the hymn.

476. BREAD OF THE WORLD

Matthew 26: 26-28

This hymn is one of the many written by the Anglican vicar Reginald Heber (1783-1826) for special services of the church year. It was published in 1827 in his "Hymns Adapted for the Weekly Church Services of the Year" in these two short stanzas, and entitled "Before the Sacrament." The broken bread and shed blood of our Lord are used to sustain an unusual parallel in the broken heart and shed tears of a contrite sinner, and the "love-feast" a symbol of food to the soul. The institution of this Christian ordinance is described thus, "Jesus took bread, and blessed it, and brake it. . . . And He took the cup, and gave thanks, and gave it to them, saying . . . this is My blood of the new testament, which is shed for many for the remission of sins." Matthew 26: 26-28. Heber, who was bishop of Calcutta at the time of his death, also wrote Nos. 73, "Holy, Holy, Holy"; 178, "In the Sun, and Moon, and Stars"; 340, "By Cool Siloam's Shady Rill"; 361, "The Son of God Goes Forth to War," and 445, "From Greenland's Icy Mountains."

The tune *Communion* was specially written for these words in 1938 by a Seventh-day Adventist composer, Stanley Ledington (1889-), who was born in Durham, England. He studied organ in Plymouth, and later emigrated to the United States, where he studied composition in Minneapolis and in Chicago. He was a teacher of music and art in various Seventh-day Adventist colleges, including Union College, Nebraska, for forty years. Other tunes by the same composer are Nos. 46, *For the Sabbath;* 98, *Rose of Sharon,* and 700, *Benediction.* He died in 1974.

477. WE GIVE THEE BUT THINE OWN

1 Chronicles 29: 14

This hymn, originally of six stanzas, written in 1858 and published in 1864, is an apt epitome of the self-sacrificial life of the author William Walsham How (1823-97), see appendix. The words are based on the text, "All things come of Thee, and of Thine own have we given Thee." 1 Chronicles 29: 14. The omitted stanzas are:—

4. To comfort and to bless,
To find a balm for woe,
To tend the lone and fatherless,
Is angel's work below.

5. The captive to release,
To God the lost to bring,
To teach the way of life and peace—
It is a Christlike thing.

The tune *Schumann* first appeared under the name *White* in 1850 in the publication at Boston of "Cantica Laudis" by Lowell Mason, see appendix, and George Webb (see No. 354), with credit given to Robert Schumann (1810-56). The compilers made an ambitious attempt to raise the low standard of American hymnody and choir singing by arranging classical music so as to be suitable to be sung as hymn tunes. This same tune is also used for Nos. 461, "This Is the Day of Rest," and 472, "Jesus Invites His Saints." Another arrangement from Schumann is No. 407, *Canonbury.*

478. MASTER, NO OFFERING

John 12: 3

Dr. Edwin Pond Parker (1836-1925), a Congregational minister, wrote this hymn in 1888 while he was at the Congregational Center Church, Hartford, Connecticut, a position he held from 1860 until 1912. He was also choir director of the church, and shortly after he had written the words he composed the tune also. Starting with the contrast with Mary Madgalene's costly gift—"Then took Mary a pound of ointment of spikenard, very costly, and anointed the feet of Jesus," John 12: 3—the author shows the necessity of loving service for the Master. The poem was read as the closing appeal of one of Dr. Parker's sermons.

The name of the tune *Love's Offering* was chosen by the composer to express the theme of the whole hymn. It should be observed that the hymn does not really belong to the section of offertory hymns as the offering described is not monetary at all, but rather the offering of a dedicated life to Christ in kindness, hope, mercy, and peace shown to others who are in need. Parker also arranged No. 206, *Mercy* as a hymn tune.

479. WOULD YOU WIN A SAVIOUR'S BLESSING?

Matthew 10: 8

Fanny Crosby (1820-1915), see appendix, has taken several Scripture thoughts on giving and pieced them together to form this hymn, for example: "Freely ye have received, freely give." Matthew 10: 8. "Every man according as he purposeth in his heart, so let him give; not grudgingly, or of necessity: for God loveth a cheerful giver." 2 Corinthians 9: 7. "And He saw also a certain poor widow casting in thither two mites. And He said, Of a truth I say unto you, that this poor widow hath cast in more than they all." Luke 21: 2, 3. "Great is your reward in heaven." Matthew 5: 12.

The tune *Freely Give* was composed by Theodore Edson Perkins (1831-1912), an American editor of song books and a composer of Sunday school pieces. He also composed No. 277, *Perkins.*

480. A YEAR OF PRECIOUS BLESSINGS

Ecclesiastes 12: 11

Fanny Crosby (1820-1915), see appendix, has taken a rarely used expression from Ecclesiastes 12: 11, "The words of the wise are as . . . nails fastened by the masters of assemblies, which are given from one shepherd," and applied it to God, who indeed is the Master of any assembly in His house. It is a reunion hymn, where workers review their past year's labours and look forward to ultimate victory when they can join "the angels . . . round the throne," and with them fall "before the throne . . . and worship God." Revelation 7: 11.

The tune *Anniversary* was composed in 1907 by Ira Allan Sankey (1874-1915), son of the famous singing evangelist, Ira David Sankey. He was born in Edinburgh, Scotland, and joined the music publishing business of Biglow and Main Company. He also composed some sacred songs.

481. O SOLEMN THOUGHT!

Revelation 14: 7

Roswell Fenner Cottrell (1814-92) came of French Albigensian stock and formed a group known as Cottrellites because they had left the Seventh-day Baptists, not agreeing with them in their belief in the immortality of the soul. He was interested prior to 1844 in the Millerite teachings concerning the second advent, but realized that they were not observing the true Sabbath. After the disappointment, he became acquainted with the *Review and Herald,* and in 1851 he joined the Sabbath-keeping Adventists and began to write both poetry and prose for this general paper of the church. He prepared Sabbath school lessons every week for the children in 1854. He was one time chaplain at the Battle Creek Sanitarium and president of the New York Conference. He was a powerful preacher and a forceful writer, being the author of the telling poem "It's Jewish." In this hymn, written in 1886, he emphasizes one of the distinctive doctrines of Seventh-day Adventists, the investigative judgment. Scriptures quoted in part are: "For the hour of His judgment is come," Revelation 14: 7, as well as Daniel 12: 13, Revelation 3: 5, Acts 3: 19, and Revelation 14: 1, 3. Cottrell also wrote Nos. 143, "The Wonders of Redeeming Love," and 307, "The Time Is Near."

The tune *Duane Street* was composed in 1835 by the Methodist minister George Coles (1792-1858), and commemorates the church in Duane Street, New York, where he preached the centennial sermon in 1839 on "The History and Character of Methodism." It is used also for No. 371, "I Saw One Weary."

482. THE JUDGMENT HAS SET

Matthew 12: 36

Both words and music were composed by Franklin Edson Belden (1858-1945), see appendix, and appear in "Hymns and Tunes," 1886. The heading is "Every Idle Word that Men Shall Speak, They Shall Give Account Thereof in the Day of Judgment," Matthew 12: 36, and "For the Time Is Come that Judgment Must Begin at the House of God." 1 Peter 4: 17. The investigative judgment beginning in 1844 is described, dealing first with the cases of those now dead, but soon inevitably to reach those now living. This judgment performed by an all-righteous, all-seeing Lord will be perfect, and will weigh all the evidence and motives, so that no appeal can or will be heard for those who may be found wanting.

483. ALL THINGS ARE THINE

1 Kings 8: 27

John Greenleaf Whittier (1807-92), the Quaker poet, wrote these words especially for the dedication of the Plymouth Congregational Church in St. Paul, Minnesota, in 1872. Hence the original line 4 of stanza 3 was: "In the fair garden of the West." Another slight change has been made in stanza 5, line 2, which was, "Fill with Thy love their emptiness." The hymn contains similar thoughts to some expressed in Solomon's prayer at the dedication of the Jewish temple, for example: "But will God indeed dwell on the earth? behold, the heaven and heaven of heavens cannot contain Thee; how much less this house that I have builded?" 1 Kings 8: 27. Whittier also wrote Nos. 116, "Dear Lord and Father," and 141, "We May Not Climb."

The tune *Ware,* used also for No. 204, "Come, Gracious Spirit," was composed in 1838 by George Kingsley (1811-84) of Northampton, Massachusetts. He also composed No. 458, *Elizabethtown,* and arranged No. 381, *Valentia.* He was a music teacher and organist in Boston, and professor of music in Philadelphia, and composed music for young people. Both *Ware* and *Elizabethtown* are unusual in their mixture of crochets and quavers which present a difficult rhythm for singing.

484. O BOW THINE EAR

Psalm 26: 8

John Pierpont (1785-1866), a Unitarian minister at Boston, Massachusetts, wrote these words in 1823, but they were not included in his other poems published in 1840 and therefore the hymn is listed as anonymous. The words tell of the dedication of a new place of worship to God, with a prayer that it may be a very gate of heaven for the contrite soul, and a resting place for the Spirit of God. "Lord, I have loved the habitation of Thy house, and the place where Thine honour dwelleth." Psalm 26: 8.

The tune *Samson* is from the great composer George Frederick Handel (1685-1759), and appears as part of the chorus No. 31 in the oratorio "Samson," written in 1742:

> Then round about the starry throne
> Of Him who ever rules alone.

Handel was born in Halle, Germany, but went to England on leave in 1712 and stayed permanently, becoming naturalized in 1726. He wrote numerous operas, oratorios, odes, anthems, songs, and orchestral pieces. Two other selections from his music are Nos. 100, *Christmas,* and 189, *Antioch.*

485. GREAT KING OF GLORY

Psalm 144: 12

These words are part of a hymn of six stanzas beginning "In sweet exalted strains," written in 1774 by Benjamin Francis (1734-99). He was a Welsh Baptist minister, spending forty-two years at Horsley in Gloucestershire, and he wrote this hymn for the opening of his meeting-house there. Our first stanza was his third. The reference in stanza three is to Psalm 144: 12, "That our sons . . . that our daughters may be as corner stones, polished after the similitude of a palace." Francis also revised No. 152, "Jesus, and Shall It Ever Be."

The tune *Darwall,* named after the composer, was written in 1770 by John Darwall (1731-89), vicar of Walsall, Staffordshire, to be sung to Psalm 148. He composed 150 such tunes in two parts, treble and bass, one for each of the metrical versions of the psalms. This tune was used when the new organ was opened on Whitsunday 1773 in his church. The original opening note was A the dominant and not D the tonic. It is noteworthy for a descending melody of 7 notes in lines 1 and 2, and for a rising one of 9 notes in lines 5 and 6.

486. GOD OF THE UNIVERSE

1 Kings 8: 29

This hymn for church dedication appeared first in 1841 over the signature Miss Mary O——. It invokes the presence of God on the new house of worship, that those entering there may find communion with their God, much after Solomon's prayer at the dedication of the temple at Jerusalem: "That Thine eyes may be opened toward this house night and day, even toward the place of which Thou hast said, My name shall be there: that Thou mayest hearken unto the prayer which Thy servant shall make toward this place." 1 Kings 8: 29.

The tune *Marlow* comes from the "Book of Psalmody," which was edited in 1718 by John Chetham (1699-1746), who was a schoolmaster and curate in 1739 at Skipton, Yorkshire. His book remained in use for a century and a half. *Marlow* is there written in 4/4 or common time, and has been slightly altered in melody and time to the present 3/4 time. It was set to Psalm 133 and not named in the new book of psalmody, published in 1811.

487. CHRIST IS MADE THE SURE FOUNDATION

Isaiah 28: 16

A Latin hymn of the sixth or seventh century paraphrases the description of the New Jerusalem as given in Revelation 21, and is entitled "Urbs Beata Hierusalem" (= the blessed city of Jerusalem). Dr. John Mason Neale (1816-66), see appendix, translated this hymn in 1851 and revised it in 1861, these words being four stanzas from the second part of the translation, that is, from the last five of the nine stanzas. He also translated it otherwise under the title of "Blessed City, Heavenly Salem," adding a note that the hymn was of the eighth century. It refers to the prophecy of Isaiah 28: 16: "Behold, I lay in Zion for a foundation a stone, a tried stone, a precious corner stone, a sure foundation," and to its fulfilment in the New Testament, as described in 1 Peter 2: 6, 7. The last stanza, now omitted, is a typical doxology:

> 9. Laud and honour to the Father;
> Laud and honour to the Son;
> Laud and honour to the Spirit;
> Ever three and ever one:
> Consubstantial, Co-eternal,
> While unending ages run.

The tune *Regent Square* was composed in 1867 by Henry Thomas Smart (1813-79) and is also used for No. 113, "Angels From the Realms of Glory," where it is written one tone higher in the key of C. Other tunes by Smart are Nos. 135 and 362, *Lancashire;* 363, *Chebar,* and 376, *Pilgrims.* He was an organist and organ-builder, and became blind three years before the composition of this tune. It was named to commemorate the composer's church by Dr. James Hamilton, the Presbyterian minister at St. Philip's, Regent Square, London, who edited a Presbyterian hymnbook for which this tune was specially contributed.

488. I KNOW THAT MY REDEEMER LIVES

Job 19: 25-27

These words are a paraphrase by Charles Wesley (1707-88), see appendix, of Job's magnificent expression of faith in the resurrection of the body. "For I know that my Redeemer liveth, and that He shall stand at the latter day upon the earth: and though

. . . worms destroy this body, yet in my flesh shall I see God: Whom I shall see for myself, and mine eyes shall behold, and not another." Job 19: 25-27. The original is much longer, having four stanzas each of eight lines, but the 1830 supplement to the "Wesleyan Hymn Book" and the 1875 edition have 4-line stanzas only, the omitted one being:—

3. I feel what then shall raise me up,
Th' Eternal Spirit lives in me;
This is my confidence of hope,
That God I face to face shall see.

The tune *Retreat,* also used for No. 241, "From Every Stormy Wind," was composed in 1840 by Thomas Hastings (1784-1872), see appendix.

489. ASLEEP IN JESUS!

1 Thessalonians 4: 14

In 1832 Mrs. Margaret Mackay (1802-87) visited the quiet country churchyard of the village of Pennycross, which is only two and a half miles from the busy seaport of Plymouth, Devonshire. The journey through the narrow green lanes for which Devon is still famous, the beautiful green grass in the churchyard, the lack of artificial decorations and anything unsightly, and the obvious care bestowed on the graves, all contributed to the peaceful aspect of the day. On one of the tombstones was carved the epitaph "Sleeping in Jesus," and this gave Mrs. Mackay the inspiration to write this hymn. There were originally six stanzas, those omitted being:—

4. Asleep in Jesus! Oh! for me
May such a blissful refuge be:
Securely shall my ashes lie,
And wait the summons from on high.

5. Asleep in Jesus! time nor space
Debars this precious "hiding place";
On Indian plains and Lapland snows
Believers find the same repose.

The hymn was sent to "The Amethyst," an Edinburgh annual, in 1832. Its title and the opening words of each stanza come from 1 Thessalonians 4: 14: "Them also which sleep in Jesus."

The tune *Rest* was composed in 1843 for these words by William Batchelder Bradbury (1816-68), see appendix, and so named to harmonize with the sentiment of the words.

490. HOW VAIN IS ALL BENEATH THE SKIES!

Isaiah 40: 7, 8

These words entitled "Heaven Anticipated," were written in 1828 by a Congregational minister, David Everard Ford (1797-1875). They use the language of Isaiah 40: 7, 8: "The grass withereth, the flower fadeth." The contrast is shown between our earthly hopes, which are symbolized by the passing cloud and dew and withering grass and flower, and the hope of joys to come which lie in an eternal home, free from care, from fear, and from death.

The tune *Protection* was composed by H. Abbott, who also wrote No. 252, *Day*.

491. SEE THE LEAVES AROUND US FALLING

Isaiah 64: 6

This poem is in the form of a parable of man's brief life-span drawn from the falling leaves of autumn, and based on Isaiah 64: 6, "We all do fade as a leaf." It was originally published in the *Evangelical Magazine* in 1795, with ten stanzas, entitled "The Leaf," and written by Dr. George Horne (1730-92) of Otham, Kent. The omitted stanzas are:—

2. Sons of Adam, once in Eden
Blighted when like us he fell,
Hear the lecture we are reading,
'Tis, alas, the truth we tell.

3. Virgins, much, too much, presuming
On your boasted white and red,
View us, late in beauty blooming,
Number'd now among the dead.

4. Griping misers, nightly waking,
See the end of all your care;
Fled on wings of our own making,
We have left our owners bare.

5. Sons of honour, fed on praises,
Flutt'ring high in fancied worth,
Lo! the fickle air, that raises,
Brings us down to parent earth

6. Learned sophs, in systems jaded,
Who for new ones daily call,
Cease, at length, by us persuaded,
Ev'ry leaf must have its fall!

7. Youth, though yet no losses grieve you,
Gay in health and manly grace,
Let not cloudless skies deceive you,
Summer gives to autumn place.

8. Venerable sires, grown hoary,
Hither turn th' unwilling eye,
Think, amidst your falling glory,
Autumn tells a winter nigh.

10. On the tree of life eternal,
Man, let all thy hope be staid,
Which alone, for ever vernal,
Bears a leaf that shall not fade.

Horne was a student of Hebrew and sacred literature, and wrote a commentary on the Psalms. A graduate of Oxford University, he returned as principal of Magdalen College in 1768, was appointed dean of Canterbury in 1781, and became bishop of Norwich in 1791.

The tune *Sleep* was composed by George E. Lee, who also wrote a stirring contrast in No. 541, *Jesus Is Coming Again.*

492. DARK IS THE HOUR

Revelation 14: 13

One of the doctrines of the Seventh-day Adventist Church which differs from those held generally by other Christian denominations is that of soul sleep. It is to be expected therefore that in the section of the "Church Hymnal" containing funeral hymns there would be found hymns from Seventh-day Adventist authors. This is true of the present one, entitled "Lines on the Death of William M. Smith," written by Uriah Smith (1832-1903), who was a pillar of the church for over fifty years, being secretary of the General Conference for twenty-one years, and editor of the *Review and Herald,* the general church paper, for the major part of his denominational service. He is probably best known as the author of the scholarly work "Thoughts on Daniel and the Revelation." The scripture reference quoted in the third stanza is from the apocalypse: "I heard a voice from heaven saying . . . Blessed are the dead which die in the Lord from henceforth: Yea, saith the Spirit, that they may rest." Revelation 14: 13. Uriah Smith also wrote No. 173, "O Brother, Be Faithful."

The tune *O Jesu* is so named because it was set to the hymn, "O Jesu, warum legst du mir" (O Jesus, why dost Thou leave me) in "Sammlung alter und neuer Melodien evangelischer Lieder" of 1747, by Johann Balthasar Reimann (1702-49). The tune was probably composed by this organist of Breslau, who in 1729 became organist at Hirschberg in Schleswig. The tune appeared first in the Hirschberg Gesangbuch of 1741. The "Sammlung," as its name implies, was a collection of over 350 chorales both old and new.

493. SWEET BE THY REST

Job 3: 13, 17

These words were written by Franklin Edson Belden (1858-1945), see appendix, and appear in "Hymns and Tunes," 1886. The theme recalls the description by Job of death as a sleep—"For now should I have lain still and been quiet, I should have slept: then had I been at rest. . . . There the wicked cease from troubling; and there the weary be at rest." Job 3: 13, 17.

The tune was composed by D. S. Hakes who also composed Nos. 66, 500, *Standard;* 520, 613, *My Song,* and 629—all but No. 520 being to words by Belden. This tune, like three others, remained unnamed. Hakes, in collaboration with Belden and J. E. White, brought out the "Song Anchor" in 1878, the first Sabbath school song book of Seventh-day Adventists. He also compiled "Pearly Portals for the Sabbath School," which was published in 1882 by the Pacific Press and contained 146 tunes, 90 of them original ones by Hakes. He is commemorated in the name of No. 380.

494. HE SLEEPS IN JESUS

1 Corinthians 15: 51-54

The funeral hymns of other denominations often contain references to the deceased one being in heaven, a doctrine at variance with the Biblical teaching on soul sleep. Seventh-day Adventist authors avoid this error and portray death as a sleep till the Lord returns. This hymn is by Annie Rebekah Smith (1828-55), see appendix, and was written for the *Review and Herald,* April 14, 1853, on the occasion of the death of Robert F. Harmon, brother of Ellen G. White, at Gorham, Maine, February 5, at the early age of twenty-seven. It reminds us that death is a sleep, and not the end of hope, for "We shall not all sleep, but we shall all be changed . . . at the last trump. . . . This mortal must put on immortality. . . . Death is swallowed up in victory." 1 Corinthians 15: 51-54.

The tune *Russell* was composed by another Seventh-day Adventist, Edwin Barnes (1866-1930), see appendix.

495. NOT NOW, BUT IN THE COMING YEARS

John 13: 7

This hymn of quiet confident trust was born out of the personal experience of Maxwell Newton Cornelius (1842-93), a bricklayer and contractor of Pennsylvania. His leg had been amputated when he was a young man, but in spite of this handicap he studied for the ministry and was ordained in 1871. He built up the Presbyterian church in Pasadena, California, from a membership of one hundred to one thousand in three years, soon requiring a new house of worship. Unfortunately, many of his congregation who had promised financial help failed in their businesses, and a heavy debt was left to his responsibility. Shortly after this set-back, his wife died, and at the conclusion of her funeral sermon, he quoted the words of this hymn which he had recently written just prior to 1890. The words are based on the words of Jesus recorded in John 13: 7: "What I do thou knowest not now; but thou shalt know hereafter." They were printed in a newspaper, seen by Major D. W. Whittle (see Nos. 583, 652), and cut out and carried in his Bible for some months. He added the words of the refrain and sent the whole to his friend and singing evangelist, James McGranahan (1840-1907) who composed the tune *Sometime We'll Understand,* in 1891. McGranahan studied music in Chicago under George Frederick Root, then in New York and Boston, and was a composer and a conductor. He also wrote Nos. 536, *Christ Returneth;* 568, *Shall You? Shall I?,* and 652, unnamed.

496. COME, YE THANKFUL PEOPLE

Matthew 13: 24-30

Henry Alford (1810-71), later dean of Canterbury for the last fourteen years of his life, and famous for his Greek New Testament, was vicar of Wymeswold, Leicestershire, when he wrote this hymn in 1844. He increased the number of stanzas to seven in 1867, then reduced them, and after several revisions by other hands of his text, he announced his final version of four stanzas, which appeared in his "Poetical Works," 1868. We now have substantially his original text, with the exception of lines 3 and 4 of stanza 3 which read:—

> From His field shall in that day
> All offences purge away.

The hymn is based on two different parables of our Lord, the wheat and the tares of Matthew 13: 24-30, and the seed growing secretly of Mark 4: 26-29. From the first come the expressions, "Sowed tares among the wheat," "Let both grow together until the harvest," and "Gather ye together first the tares, and bind them in bundles to burn them: but gather the wheat into my barns." From the second parable comes the verse, "First the blade, then the ear, after that the full corn in the ear." Alford also wrote No. 306, "Ten Thousand Times Ten Thousand."

The tune *St. George's, Windsor* was composed in 1858 by Sir George Job Elvey (1816-93), and commemorates St. George's Chapel, Windsor, where he was organist for forty-seven years. He believed that church music should be as stately, uplifting, and inspiring as the soaring arches and stained-glass windows of the cathedrals in which it would be rendered. His other tunes are Nos. 162 and 366, *Diademata,* and 686, a response.

497. STANDING BY A PURPOSE TRUE

Daniel 1: 8

Both words and music of this temperance hymn were written in 1873 by Philipp Bliss (1838-76), see appendix. He was a Sunday school teacher at the time in the First Congregational church in Chicago, and wrote the hymn especially for his class, getting his inspiration from Daniel's daring in opposing King Nebuchadnezzar's provision: "But Daniel purposed in his heart that he would not defile himself with the portion of the king's meat, nor with the wine which he drank." Daniel 1: 8.

498. YIELD NOT TO TEMPTATION

Romans 6:13, 14

Horatio Richmond Palmer (1834-1907), see appendix, was studying the theory of music one day in 1868. He was on an uninteresting part and ready to drop it for something more attractive when these words came to him as a sudden inspiration. He evidently yielded to the temptation nevertheless, for he laid aside his theoretical work on music and hurriedly wrote both words and music of this hymn while the idea remained with him. After submitting the manuscript to a friend for criticism, he made some slight changes in the third stanza. Since then the first line has been changed to "yielding is sin" from his original "weakness is sin." Victory is a matter of yielding to the right Master—"Neither yield ye your members as instruments of unrighteousness unto sin: but yield yourselves unto God. . . . For sin shall not have dominion over you: for ye are not under law, but under grace." Rom. 6: 13, 14.

The tune *Palmer* was first written in the key of A flat, but it is here raised one tone to B flat.

499. SOUND THE BATTLE CRY

Jeremiah 51: 11, 12

Both words and music were written in 1869 by William Fisk Sherwin (1826-88), see appendix, as a temperance hymn under the title "Christian Courage." The scripture reference is taken from Jeremiah 51: 11, 12: "Make bright the arrows; gather the shields. . . . Set up the standard upon the walls of Babylon, make the watch strong, set up the watchmen, prepare the ambushes: for the Lord hath both devised and done that which He spake against the inhabitants of Babylon." The context speaks of Babylon as wine which has made all the nations drunk and become mad (verse 7), and therefore is an apt summary of this temperance hymn.

500. RAISE THE STANDARD HIGH

Isaiah 62: 10

The words were written in 1880 by Franklin Edson Belden (1858-1945), see appendix, and appear in "Hymns and Tunes," 1886. They were inspired by the rapidly growing temperance movement throughout America, and are based on the last part of Isaiah 62: 10, "Lift up a standard for the people."

The tune *Standard* was composed in 1880 by D. S. Hakes, who also wrote Nos. 66, 493, 520, 613, and 629, all except No. 520 being to words by Belden. Of these, No. 613, *My Song,* is the only tune given a name. The metrical pattern is 5.5.7.5.5.7. rather than 10.7.10.7. as the latter obscures the rhyming scheme. Hakes collaborated with Belden and J. E. White to produce in 1878 the "Song Anchor," which was the first Sabbath school song book of Seventh-day Adventists. He also compiled "Pearly Portals for the Sabbath School" in 1882, and contributed ninety original tunes out of the 146 in this book. He is commemorated in the name of tune No. 380, *Hakes.*

501. OUT FROM THE CAMP-FIRE'S RED GLOWING

1 Thessalonians 5: 6, 7

The picture described in this temperance hymn by Arthur W. French is that of two enemies, bivouacked for the night in sight of each other's camp-fire, one being the army of the liquor traffic, the other the forces of temperance. Vigilance against subtle attacks, alertness, and cool-headedness are the qualities that will prevent the entrance of the foe. One scripture text that is applicable is, "Therefore let us not sleep, as do others; but let us watch and be sober. For they that sleep sleep in the night; and they that be drunken are drunken in the night." 1 Thessalonians 5: 6, 7.

The composer of the tune *Sleeping on Guard,* was Frank Marion Davis (1839-97), one of a musical family of Marcellus, New York, who was a choir leader, solo singer, music teacher, and song publisher. His hymn appears in "Temperance and Gospel Songs," published in 1880 by James Edson White. Davis was co-editor with White (see Nos. 230, 235) of the 160-page "Songs for Class and School," to which he contributed twenty-eight tunes and two hymns. He also composed No. 617, *Is My Name Written There?*

502. MOURN FOR THE THOUSANDS SLAIN

Proverbs 20: 1

These words were written in 1843 by Seth Collins Brace (1811-97), a Yale graduate and American Presbyterian minister who later became a Congregational minister in Connecticut. This teacher, writer, preacher, and temperance reformer was looking for some temperance hymns, and finding none, decided to write one of his own. Its title is "Temperance Hymn," and it was written for "Parish Hymns." Omitted stanzas are:—

2. Mourn for the tarnished gem
For reason's light divine,
Quenched from the soul's bright diadem,
Where God had bid it shine.

3. Mourn for the ruined soul—
Eternal life and light
Lost by the fiery, maddening bowl,
And turned to hopeless night.

The words show the deceptive and deadly nature of alcoholic liquor—"Wine is a mocker, strong drink is raging: and whosoever is deceived thereby is not wise." Proverbs 20: 1.

The tune *Boylston* was composed in 1832 by Lowell Mason (1792-1872), see appendix, and is named after a main thoroughfare of Boston, Massachusetts. It is also used for No. 205, "Come, Holy Spirit, Come."

503. O BEAUTIFUL FOR SPACIOUS SKIES

James 2: 12

In 1893, Miss Katherine Lee Bates (1859-1929) a professor of English Literature and teacher of English, made a visit to the 15,000-foot summit of Pike's Peak, Colorado, and was greatly impressed by the marvellous view of the mountains westward and the plains eastward. That evening in the town of Colorado Springs, from which the peak can be seen, she wrote the first part of this hymn recalling her experiences of the morning. "The alabaster cities" of stanza 4 is a reference to the buildings in the White City of the Columbia Exposition in Chicago. In 1895 she came across her poem in an old notebook, decided to send it for publication, and it appeared in a magazine on July 4 of that year. A paradoxical expression "thy liberty in law" in stanza 2 is an echo of the scripture verse, "So speak ye, and so do, as they that shall be judged by the law of liberty." James 2: 12.

The tune *Materna* (= motherly) was composed in 1882 by Samuel Augustus Ward (1847-1903) a composer and conductor of Newark, New Jersey. It is so named because it was written specially for the words "O mother dear, Jerusalem." It was finally set to Miss Bates's words in 1912, most probably by Dr. William Penn Brooks, president of the Massachusetts Agricultural College in Newark, New Jersey. *Materna* is also used for No. 265, "My life flows on."

504. GOD OF OUR FATHERS WHOSE ALMIGHTY HAND

Isaiah 26: 12, 13, 15

Daniel Crane Roberts (1841-1907), a Protestant Episcopal clergyman, wrote this hymn especially for the July 4 centenary celebrations in 1876 at Brandon, Vermont. Later he moved to New Hampshire, then became vicar of St. Paul's, Concord, and then State chaplain of the Army of the Republic. The hymn calls on the great Creator of the starry heavens to exercise a similar guidance over His people, protecting them from war and pestilence, and making His grace appear in their lives. Similar sentiments were expressed on behalf of the Jewish people in times of old: "Lord, Thou wilt ordain peace for us: for Thou also hast wrought all our works in us. O Lord our God, other lords beside Thee have had dominion over us: but by Thee only will we make mention of Thy name." "Thou hast increased the nation, O Lord, Thou hast increased the nation: Thou art glorified." Isa. 26:12, 13, 15.

The tune *National Hymn* was written in 1892 by the self-taught organist George William Warren (1828-1902) at the special request of Dr. J. Ireland Tucker, who wanted a suitable majestic setting to the majestic words. Its name is a fitting term for the words which commemorate American Independence Day. The last line of the melody descends a complete octave, repeating two notes only. Warren was a composer of church music and pieces for the piano, and was church organist at Albany, New York, up to 1860, at Brooklyn for the next ten years, and afterwards at St. Thomas Episcopal Church, New York.

505. GOD OF OUR FATHERS, KNOWN OF OLD

Psalm 51: 17

This poem by Rudyard Kipling (1865-1936) first appeared in the London *Times* of July 17, 1897, in honour of the diamond jubilee of Queen Victoria's accession to the throne. The next year it appeared as a hymn in an American Baptist publication. The poem gave him more trouble than anything else he wrote, for he was dissatisfied with his efforts at writing the poem promised to the *Times* for this special occasion. The newspaper editor wrote letters and then telegrams to Kipling causing him to make a final attempt. Looking through his self-rejected manuscripts, he found one, "Lest We Forget," and built his jubilee poem around this theme. Kipling himself said of his stanzas, "This is not a national hymn, and it is better to keep to the title under which I wrote it," viz., Recessional. The words in the second stanza, "The tumult and the shouting dies; The captains and the kings depart" refer to the jubilee procession of June 26, 1897; and in the third stanza, "Far called, our navies melt away; On dune and headland sinks the fire," refer to the naval review at Spithead and to the 2,500 beacon fires which were lit from Land's End to Ben Nevis. There are several Scripture references throughout the hymn, the main one which summarizes the chief intent of the poem being, "The sacrifices of God are a broken spirit: a broken and a contrite heart, O God, Thou wilt not despise." Psalm 51: 17.

The tune *Lest We Forget* was composed especially for these words by George Frederick Blanchard (1868-1926), a native of Hull, Yorkshire, who was later an organist in Weston-super-mare, Somerset. It was written in July 1898 as a baritone solo and harmonized in 1905.

506. GOD SAVE OUR GRACIOUS KING

1 Samuel 10: 24

The son of Henry Carey (c. 1687-1743), George Saville Carey, claimed in 1795 that this tune was composed by his father about the year 1740. Henry Carey was said to have sung it to celebrate the capture of Portobello on November 30, 1739, modifying older Latin words to his "God save great George our king." It was certainly sung to these words on September 28, 1745, at the Drury Lane Theatre, London, in order to counteract the news of the Jacobite victory at Prestonpans. Dr. Thomas Arne (see No. 355), the director of music at the theatre, did not know either author or composer and arranged the music so that it could be sung as a loyal toast, the king's name being mentioned to prevent the supporters of Charles from singing the same anthem, claiming him to be "our gracious king." The second stanza is unsuitable for a hymn and is omitted:—

2. O Lord our God, arise,
Scatter his enemies
And make them fall!
Confound their politics,
Frustrate their knavish tricks,
On him our hopes we fix,
O, save us all.

Henry Wadsworth Longfellow's addition in 1897 is fitting for a hymn:—

Lord, let war's tempests cease,
Fold the whole world in peace
Under Thy wings.
Make all the nations one,
All hearts beneath the sun,
Till Thou shalt reign alone,
Great King of kings.

The last four words of the two stanzas constitute a clause occurring at least three times in the Bible, for example, "And all the people shouted, and said, God save the king." 1 Samuel 10: 24. A very full discussion of the authorship of the National Anthem is found in Dr. Percy Scholes's book, *"God Save the Queen,"* published in 1954.

The tune somewhat resembles an earlier one by Dr. John (or Jan) Bull in 1619, but Carey's claims could well be true, as he was a prolific writer of ballads, notably the song "Sally in Our Alley." The same tune is used for No. 510 where it is named *America.* Carey also composed No. 337, *Carey.*

507. O GOD, BENEATH THY GUIDING HAND

Psalm 78: 3, 4

Dr. Leonard Bacon (1802-81) was born in Detroit, Michigan, but spent most of his life in New Haven, Connecticut. In that city on April 25, 1833, he delivered an address at the bi-centenary celebration in the Congregational Center church, a church to which he was appointed at the age of twenty-three and where he remained as pastor for forty-one years. For the occasion, he wrote a special commemorative hymn, the present text being the one which was revised in 1845, less one stanza which was:—

> 3. What change! through pathless wilds no more
> The fierce and naked savage roams;
> Sweet praise along the cultured shore,
> Breaks from ten thousand happy homes.

The words recall the faithful, God-fearing pilgrims who left a worthy example for their descendants to remember and to follow: "Which we have heard and known, and our fathers have told us. We will not hide them from their children, showing to the generation to come the praises of the Lord, and His strength, and His wonderful works that He hath done." Psalm 78: 3, 4. Bacon returned to Yale, where he had graduated, and while professor of divinity and lecturer there, was noted for the missionary zeal he imparted to his students.

The tune *Duke Street,* also used for No. 1 "Before Jehovah's awful throne," was composed in 1793 by John Hatton (17 ?-1793), a Presbyterian of Warrington, Lancashire. Note the almost complete octave in the ascending scale passage with which the melody opens. It was set to Addison's 19th Psalm, and its name commemorates the street in St. Helens, Windle, Lancashire, where Hatton lived for some time.

508. O CANADA!

Genesis 15: 1

Judge Adolphe Routhier of Quebec wrote the words of this patriotic poem in his native tongue, French, and it came into the possession of the St. Jean Baptiste Society, the patriotic organization of the French Canadians. In the winter of 1880 a member of this organization visited the talented musician, Calixa Lavallée, a native of Verchéres, a province of Quebec, and requested him to compose a patriotic song to Routhier's words. Although burdened with debts and sick in bed at the time, he forgot his personal troubles after reading the stirring poem, and sat down at the piano to begin to compose. Two weeks later he completed the music, which was enthusiastically received by French Canadians in particular. Many adaptations and translations of the words into English have been made, the one most generally accepted being the present version by the Hon. Robert Stanley Weir (1856-1926), recorder of Montreal, written specially for the tercentenary of Quebec in 1908. The patriotic words of the first three stanzas are followed by a prayer to

God for His protection, and for the realization of eternal verities, reminding us of God's promise to His servant Abraham, who had forsaken his native land—"After these things the word of the Lord came unto Abraham in a vision, saying, Fear not, Abram: I am thy shield, and thy exceeding great reward." Genesis 15: 1.

509. LORD, WHILE FOR ALL MANKIND WE PRAY

Psalm 85: 1

The early years of the 19th century were filled with fear in England because of the constant threat of invasion by Napoleon's armies. After this harassing time and the decline of the threat after 1815, the young Queen Victoria succeeded to the throne in 1837. These words were then written as a national hymn of prayer for England by John Reynell Wreford (1800-81), a Unitarian minister of Birmingham, who later became a teacher because of the failure of his voice. Two omitted stanzas are:—

2. Our father's sepulchres are here,
   And here our kindred dwell;
   Our children, too; how should we love
   Another land so well?

5. Here may religion, pure and mild,
   Smile on our Sabbath hours;
   And piety and virtue bless
   The home of us and ours.

The prayer for God's peace and prosperity on the land is a rewording of the psalmist's statement concerning his country, "Lord, Thou hast been favourable unto Thy land." Psalm 85: 1.

The tune *Dunfermline* first appeared in 1615 in the Scottish Psalter as one of the twelve Common Tunes to which the psalms were sung. Dunfermline, in Fifeshire, was the old capital of Scotland, and the tune has been attributed to Dean John Angus who was connected with Dunfermline Abbey at the time of the Reformation.

510. MY COUNTRY, 'TIS OF THEE

2 Corinthians 3: 17

Dr. Samuel Francis Smith (1808-95), later to become a Baptist minister, was given a German patriotic hymn (see No. 512) while yet a student. He felt inspired and impelled to write a similar hymn for his own native America to the tune which Lowell Mason (see appendix) had also given him with the German words. In half an hour these words were written and returned to Mason, and they were first sung, to the tune of the National Anthem, in the Park Street, Boston, Sunday school at the Fourth of July celebrations in 1831. The hymn is now recognized as America's national hymn. The predominating thought is that of freedom, noted in each stanza, for example:—

1. land of liberty; Let freedom ring.
2. land of the noble free.
3. Sweet freedom's song.
4. Author of liberty; freedom's holy light.

This liberty comes from a religious freedom, for "where the Spirit of the Lord is, there is liberty." 2 Corinthians 3: 17. Dr. Smith wrote about 100 hymns, many for special occasions, and two of them are included in "Church Hymnal," Nos. 439 on baptism, "With Willing Hearts We Tread," and 454 on missions, "The Morning Light." Dr. Oliver Wendell Holmes (see Nos. 20 and 144) commemorated this hymn and its author in his Class reunion poem of 1859 of the Harvard graduates of thirty years before:—

And there's a nice youngster of excellent pith—
Fate tried to conceal him by naming him Smith.
But he shouted a song for the brave and the free—
Just read on his medal, "My country, of thee!"

The tune *America* is the British National Anthem, used also by other nations. It appears in a composition by John (or Jan) Bull. See No. 506.

511. GENTLE PEACE, FROM HEAVEN DESCENDED

James 3: 17

These words by an unknown author are an illustration of the victories that peace has that are no less renowned than those of war. They are a reminder, too, of the sweet influence of the Spirit of God: "But the wisdom that is from above is first pure, then peaceable, gentle, and easy to be entreated, full of mercy and good fruits." James 3: 17.

The tune *Rathbun,* also used in 125, "In the Cross of Christ I Glory," was composed in 1849 by an organist, Ithamar Conkey (1815-67), in Norwich, Connecticut. It was named after the leading soprano, Mrs. Beriah S. Rathbun, in his choir at the Central Baptist church in Norwich, and was inspired by the words of No. 125 for which it was specially composed.

512. GOD BLESS OUR NATIVE LAND!

Deuteronomy 28: 2

This hymn is a composite one, being part of one written by William Edward Hickson (1803-70) and part of a similar but distinct hymn by John Sullivan Dwight (1812-93). The former, a boot manufacturer with a keen interest in music, wrote in 1836 what he hoped would be a new national anthem for England, and the first stanza is his composition with the exception that in line 6, the new words "And all our rights depend" have displaced his original "And Britain's rights depend." The third stanza is also of Hickson's authorship. Dwight was an American music critic who utilized a free translation made by a Harvard divinity student, Charles Timothy Brooks (1813-83), of a German patriotic hymn of 1815. The words were "Gott segne Sachsenland" (= God bless Saxony) and were the inspiration for Smith's national hymn (See No. 510). One of Brooks's stanzas was:—

> God bless our native land!
> Firm may she ever stand
> Through storm and night!
> When the wild tempests rave,
> Ruler of wind and wave,
> Father eternal, save
> Us by Thy might!

Dwight's last two lines of this additional stanza were:—

> Do Thou our country save
> By Thy great might.

The blessing of God is dependent, as of old, on the country's inhabitants' ways, customs, and laws—"And all these blessings shall come on thee, and overtake thee, if thou shalt hearken unto the voice of the Lord thy God." Deuteronomy 28: 2.

The tune *Dort* was composed in 1832 by Lowell Mason (1792-1872), see appendix, and is an abbreviated name of Dordrecht in the Netherlands, a centre of the Calvinistic faith. It is not, however, an associative name.

513. ONCE TO EVERY MAN AND NATION

Joshua 24: 15

In the year 1845 Abraham Lincoln spoke in Congress against war with Mexico, for it appeared to him to be merely an excuse for the slave-holding states of the south to gain more territory and thus extend slavery. James Russell Lowell (1819-91), poet, professor of English at Harvard, and later ambassador to Spain and then to Great Britain from 1880-85, supported this protest by writing a long poem of eighteen stanzas, each of five lines, entitled "The Present Crisis." The current controversy on slavery is well depicted in the opening stanza which ran:—

1. When a deed is done for freedom, through the broad earth's aching breast
   Runs a thrill of joy prophetic, trembling on from east to west,
   And the slave where'er he cowers, feels the soul within him climb
   To the awful verge of manhood, as the energy sublime
   Of a century burst full-blossomed on the thorny stem of time.

The poem was reduced to thirty-two lines by W. Garrett Horder (1841-1922), an English Congregational hymnologist, who put sentences together as he chose, and produced this hymn appealing to the national conscience. Note that the emphasis is on "truth," which word appears in each stanza, indeed, on standing for truth when in a minority, an action well demonstrated in Joshua's challenge to the children of Israel: "Choose you this day whom ye will serve . . . but as for me and my house, we will serve the Lord." Joshua 24: 15.

The tune *Ton-Y-Botel,* more correctly called *Ebenezer,* was composed in 1890 by Thomas John Williams (1869-1944), organist and choirmaster at Llanelly, Wales. The name means tune-in-a-bottle, from a mythical story of its discovery. The tune is actually part of an anthem called "Light in the Valley." Notice that lines 1 and 2 are repeated by lines 3 and 4, and again by lines 7 and 8, making the tune very easy to learn to sing.

514. RING OUT, WILD BELLS

Revelation 21: 5

Alfred Lord Tennyson (1809-92), the greatest of the Victorian English poets, and Poet Laureate from 1850, completed the long poem "In Memoriam" in 1849, which was a soliloquy mourning his dear friend Arthur Hallam, who died in Venice in September, 1833. This hymn is six of the eight stanzas of section 106 of this poem, which depicts the triumph of the Christian faith over injustice, falsehood, greed, and selfishness, from the parallel of the new year supplanting the old year on New Year's Eve. The two stanzas omitted from this section are:—

4. Ring out a slowly dying cause,
   And ancient forms of party strife;
   Ring in the nobler modes of life,
   With sweeter manners, purer laws.

5. Ring out the want, the care, the sin,
The faithless coldness of the times;
Ring out, ring out my mournful rimes,
But ring the fuller minstrel in.

An appropriate scripture summary could be, "Behold, I make all things new." Revelation 21: 5.

The tune *Jordan,* or *Cantate Domino* (= sing to the Lord) was composed in 1872 by Joseph Barnby (1838-96), see appendix, and was so named by another than the composer because it was written especially for the words "Sing to the Lord a Joyful Song." Another Tennyson-Barnby combination is No. 678, "Sunset and Evening Star," to the tune *Crossing the Bar.*

515. JESUS, WHERE'ER THY PEOPLE MEET

Isaiah 57: 15

These words are No. XLIV, Book II, of the "Olney Hymns," 1779, and were written by William Cowper (1731-1800), see appendix, for the special occasion when his and John Newton's prayer group moved into a larger meeting place. This is alluded to in stanza three, which was originally:—

Dear Shepherd of Thy chosen few
Thy former mercies *here* renew;

and in the omitted fifth stanza:—

5. Behold, at Thy commanding word,
We stretch the curtain and the cord; (Isaiah 54: 2)
Come Thou, and fill this wider space,
And bless us with a large increase.

The other omitted stanzas are:—

4. Here may we prove the power of prayer
To strengthen faith, and sweeten care;
To teach our faint desires to rise,
And bring all heaven before our eyes.

6. Lord, we are few, but Thou art near;
Nor short Thine arm, nor deaf Thine ear;
O rend the heavens, come quickly down,
And make a thousand hearts Thine own!

The meeting-place of God in the heart of the believer is more important than the physical building, and is so stated in the second stanza, part of which re-states Isaiah 57: 15: "I dwell . . . with him that is of a . . . humble spirit."

The tune *Malvern* was composed in 1847 by Lowell Mason (1792-1872), see appendix, but it is not an associative name.

516. SWEET THE TIME

Psalm 149: 5, 6

George Burder (1752-1832), a Calvinistic preacher who later became a Congregational pastor, wrote these words in 1779 under the title "An Hymn for Christian Company." Notice that the word "sing" occurs in each stanza, and that stanzas 2, 3, and 4 deal with the love of the Father, Son, and Spirit, respectively. An appropriate text is "Let the saints be joyful in glory: let them sing aloud upon their beds. Let the high praises of God be in their mouth." Psalm 149: 5, 6. Burder was part founder of the Religious Tract Society, the London Missionary Society, and the British and Foreign Bible Society.

The tune *Innocents* is noted as an "Ancient Litany" in the Parish Choir, a paper issued from 1846 to 1849 to promote church music. There it is set to a hymn to be sung on Innocents Day, which is the third day after Christmas. The innocents referred to are the children of Bethlehem who were slaughtered by Herod in his effort to slay Jesus, the new-born King of the Jews. The tune is similar to one composed by Joseph Smith (1800-?) of Halesowen, near Birmingham, for a song entitled "The Sun," and is said to have been given to the editor of the *Parish Choir* by the governess of the Halesowen rectory. Smith was an alto singer, who also composed tunes for Sunday school festivals.

517. THERE'S NO OTHER NAME LIKE JESUS

Acts 4: 12

Both words and music were written by Franklin Edson Belden (1858-1945), see appendix, and appear in "Hymns and Tunes," 1886, under the heading, "Neither is there salvation in any other: for there is none other name under heaven given among men, whereby we must be saved." Acts 4: 12.

518. I LOVE TO TELL THE STORY

Romans 1: 15

Miss Arabella Katherine (Kate) Hankey (1834-1911) was a devoted Sunday school and Bible class teacher of the "Clapham Sect" of evangelical Christians. The words of this hymn are from her poem "The Old, Old Story" (see No. 524) and were written in 1866. The theme recalls the devoted attitude of the Apostle Paul, who travelled the then-known world because he loved to tell the story of Jesus: "So as much as in me is, I am ready to preach the gospel." Romans 1: 15.

The tune, named *Hankey* in some hymnals, was composed in 1869 by William Gustavus Fischer (1835-1912), of Baltimore, especially for these words. Fischer, a member of the Methodist Episcopal Church, and choir leader for Moody and Sankey, added the refrain. He was a bookbinder in Philadelphia and also a piano dealer for thirty years. He became a popular song-leader, and conducted singing groups in Philadelphia as well as teaching singing and piano. He composed more than 200 gospel hymns, among them Nos. 592, *Whiter Than Snow;* 600, unnamed, and 633, *The Rock That Is Higher.*

519. HOW SHALL I FOLLOW HIM?

John 12: 26

Josiah Conder (1789-1855) was a London author, editor, and poet, and edited the first hymnbook of the Congregational Union, which contained over sixty hymns of his own composition. This hymn, written in 1824, had eleven stanzas and was entitled "Resignation and Suffering." It was based on the words, "If any man serve Me, let him follow Me." John 12: 26. In his "Hymns of Praise, Prayer and Devout Meditation" of 1856, there are ten stanzas only, those omitted from "Church Hymnal" being:—

2. Privations, sorrows, bitter scorn,
The life of toil, the mean abode,
The faithless kiss, the crown of thorn—
Are these the consecrated road?

3. 'Twas thus He suffered, though a Son,
Foreknowing, choosing, feeling all,
Until the perfect work was done,
And drunk the bitter cup of gall.

7. Yes! I would count them all but loss,
To gain the notice of Thine eye;
Flesh shrinks and trembles at the cross,
But Thou canst give the victory!

8. Thou who for Peter's faith didst pray!
Against whose blessed self were hurled
The tempter's darts; be Thou my stay:
Help me to overcome the world.

9. Thy grace can make the boastful meek,
The wavering firm, the sensual pure,
Put heavenly might upon the weak,
And make them happy who endure.

10. Oh, still that needful grace afford:
On Thee my trembling soul I cast.
Perfect Thy work within me, Lord!
And own my worthless name at last.

The tune is named after its composer William Gardiner (1770-1853), a Leicester stocking manufacturer whose hobby was to adapt tunes from his contemporary composers, Mozart, Haydn, and Beethoven, and use them as hymn-tunes in place of the inferior ones then sung. This particular tune, *Gardiner,* is sometimes known as *German,* because Gardiner said that he had found it somewhere among Beethoven's compositions. It appeared in his "Sacred Melodies," second edition, published in 1815. Gardiner also wrote No. 295, *Belmont.*

520. LIFT HIM UP

John 12:32

The theme of this hymn by May E. Warren is that the proclamation of the death of Jesus on the cross will be an attractive power to those who are groping in sin, an apt commentary therefore on our Lord's own words, "And I, if I be lifted up from the earth, will draw all men unto Me." John 12: 32. A similar statement was made also to Nicodemus (John 3: 14, 15), recalling the incident in the wilderness when: "It shall come to pass, that every one that is bitten, when he looketh upon it, shall live." Numbers 21: 8. Other references used are: John 4: 10; Matthew 11: 29; John 10: 16; Matthew 16: 24; Jeremiah 31: 3; Psalm 148: 12, 13.

The tune was composed by D. S. Hakes, who also wrote Nos. 66, 493, both unnamed; 500, *Standard;* 613, *My Song,* and 629, unnamed. He collaborated with F. E. Belden and J. E. White to produce the "Song Anchor" in 1878, the first "Sabbath School Song Book of Seventh-day Adventists." He also compiled "Pearly Portals for the Sabbath School" in 1882, and contributed ninety of the 146 tunes in that book. He is commemorated in tune No. 380, *Hakes.*

521. JESUS CALLS US

Matthew 4:18, 19

Mrs. Cecil Frances Alexander, née Humphreys (1818-95), wife of the bishop of Derry, wrote about 200 hymns and 200 poems, among them this hymn in 1852 with five stanzas. It is based on the call of the disciples—"And Jesus, walking by the sea of Galilee, saw two brethren, Simon called Peter, and Andrew his brother, casting a net into the sea: for they were fishers. And He saith unto them, Follow Me, and I will make you fishers of men." Matthew 4: 18, 19. The lesser known apostle is mentioned in the omitted stanza:—

2. As of old St. Andrew heard it
By the Galilean lake,
Turned from home, and toil, and kindred,
Leaving all for His dear sake.

Mrs. Alexander also wrote Nos. 126, "There Is a Green Hill Far Away"; 421, "All Things Bright and Beautiful"; and 424, "Once in Royal David's City."

The tune, aptly named *Galilee,* was composed specially for these words in 1874 by William Herbert Jude (1851-1922), a Baptist organist of Liverpool, and it was first published in 1887 in "Congregational Church Hymns." While the melody of line 3 copies that of line 1, half of it is harmonized completely differently.

522. NOW JUST A WORD FOR JESUS

Ezekiel 24: 19

The words by Frances Jane Crosby (1820-1915), see appendix, and the music by William Howard Doane (1832-1916), see appendix, form one of the many contributions made jointly by these two gifted Christians. The words are an inducement for Christians to testify in public of their love for their Saviour, and they were prompted by part of the verse in Ezekiel 24: 19, "Wilt thou not tell?"

523. TAKE THE NAME OF JESUS WITH YOU

Psalm 72: 19

Mrs. Lydia Baxter (1809-74), a member of the Baptist Church, was born in Petersburgh, New York, and was an invalid for many years. She took comfort, however, as expressed in this hymn, in the glorious hope held out to those who trust in Jesus. Her own home was made a strong centre of Christian influence and a rendezvous for Christian workers. These words were written in 1870 by the composer and describe Mrs. Baxter's own personal experience, for in order to strengthen her in her struggle against the pain and agony of her invalidism, she used the name of Jesus her Saviour as a defence against discouragement: "And blessed be His glorious name for ever: and let the whole world be filled with His glory." Psalm 72: 19. She also wrote No. 561, "There Is a Gate that Stands Ajar."

The tune *Precious Name* was composed in 1899 by William Howard Doane (1832-1916), see appendix.

524. TELL ME THE OLD, OLD STORY

Acts 9: 34

Miss Arabella Katherine Hankey (1834-1911), a member of the "Clapham Sect" of evangelical Christians, wrote a small booklet in verse in 1866 dealing with the life of Christ. She had suffered an illness in this year, and being weak and weary from its effects, realized that simple words and thoughts are all that we can cope with at such a time. So she wrote in simple language the story of redemption from the Garden of Eden to the manger of Bethlehem and the ministry of Jesus on earth. The book was published in 1868 under the title, "The Old, Old Story," being in two parts, the first an introductory hymn, "The Story Wanted," which is this very hymn first published in 1867; the second part is "The Story Told." The book had a very wide circulation, and was translated into several languages. Miss Hankey also wrote music for it, objecting to the present tune, which couples four-line stanzas, complete in themselves, into eight-line stanzas. Each of her stanzas uses the expression "Tell me the story." This is used also in the omitted ones:—

Tell me the story slowly
That I may take it in,
That wonderful redemption,
God's remedy for sin.

Tell me the story often,
For I forget so soon;
The early dew of morning
Has passed away at noon.

The quotation in stanza 3 follows almost the exact words of the Apostle Peter to the sick man Aeneas of Lydda: "Jesus Christ maketh thee whole." Acts 9: 34. While this text refers to physical healing, the old, old story covers spiritual healing also, as was implied in Peter's miracle, for the result was not only the restoration of an eight-year paralytic, but many "turned to the Lord" (verse 35) in that district. No. 518, "I Love to Tell the Story," is from the same poem by Miss Hankey.

The words of the hymn, newly published, were read by Major-General Russell with deep fervour and emotion at an international Y.M.C.A. convention in Montreal in 1867. Ira David Sankey (see Nos. 575, 586, 587, 673) obtained a copy of the words and sent them to William Howard Doane (1832-1916), see appendix, who had been present at the meeting. While travelling in a stage-coach on vacation in the White Mountains, he composed this tune *Evangel,* combining two stanzas into an eight-line tune, to which he added a refrain. In the hotel parlour that same evening he sang the new composition and it became very popular very soon, and is now accepted as being the natural tune for the words.

525. BAPTIZE US ANEW

Mark 1: 8-11

Both words and music were written by William Augustine Ogden (1841-97), see appendix, and recall the story of the baptism by water and by the Spirit of the Lord Jesus. The hymn prays for a fulfilment of John the Baptist's words in our lives. The scripture on which the words are based is: "I indeed have baptized you with water: but He shall baptize you with the Holy Ghost. And it came to pass in those days, that Jesus came from Nazareth of Galilee, and was baptized of John in Jordan. And straightway coming up out of the water, He saw the heavens opened, and the Spirit like a dove descending upon Him: and there came a voice from heaven, saying, Thou art My beloved Son, in whom I am well pleased." Mark 1: 8-11.

526. O, SPREAD THE TIDINGS ROUND

John 14: 16

These words were written by Francis Bottome (1823-94), an Englishman of Belper, Derbyshire, who emigrated to the United States and became a Methodist Episcopalian minister in 1850. They are based on the promise of Jesus recorded in John 14: 16, "And I will pray the Father, and He shall give you another Comforter, that He may abide with you for ever."

The tune *The Comforter Has Come,* was composed by William James Kirkpatrick (1838-1921), see appendix, and shows by the lengthening of the notes in the last line, a neat way to accommodate a tune to a seven-line poem.

527. I HEAR THE SAVIOUR SAY

1 Peter 2: 24

Mrs. Elvina Mabel Hall (1818-?) who became Mrs. Myers in 1885, was a member of the choir of the Methodist Episcopal church in Baltimore. In the spring of 1865 she jotted down the words of this hymn on the fly-leaf of a hymn-book during the prayer as she was sitting in the choir. She passed them on to the minister, the Rev. Shrick, who kept them until she should find a suitable tune. The title of the hymn is "All to Christ I Owe," and it was based on 1 Peter 2: 24, "Who His own self bare our sins." There is one omitted stanza, namely:—

4. When from my dying bed
My ransomed soul shall rise,
Then "Jesus paid it all"
Shall rend the vaulted skies.

The tune finally found for the words was one composed by John Thomas Grape (1833-?), also of Baltimore, who was taking care of the cabinet organ while the church was undergoing alterations, and who therefore had opportunity at home to play and to compose hymns. This tune was his effort to find a melody for William Batchelder Bradbury's words, "Jesus paid it all." His wife praised his composition, but his friends and choir-members thought it very commonplace. However, words and music were combined and very well received as a hymn.

528. OH, THE BEST FRIEND TO HAVE IS JESUS

Proverbs 18: 24

Peter Philip Bilhorn (1861-1936) of Mendota, Illinois, was compelled to leave school at the age of eight when his father died. Using his innate musical ability, he became an entertainer and a soloist at the age of sixteen, and performed in restaurants, taverns, and beer halls. He was converted while still a young man at meetings where G. C. Stebbins (see appendix) was the song leader, and then devoted his musical talent to gospel work. He became a music publisher in Chicago, Illinois, and was, with his brother, the producer of the first baby folding organs. He was a great friend of Seventh-day Adventists, particularly of Dr. John Harvey Kellogg, and regularly every summer used to spend a holiday at his Battle Creek sanitarium. Later he spent much time at the Glendale Sanitarium, California. He studied music under George Frederick Root (see Nos. 93, 299, 418, 620, 690), and later became a singing evangelist, working especially for the Western cowboys. Bilhorn wrote both words and music of this hymn, recalling particularly the verse, "There is a friend that sticketh closer than a brother." Proverbs 18: 24. He also wrote both words and music of No. 609, "There Comes to My Heart One Sweet Strain," to the tune *Sweet Peace.*

529. I WILL SING OF JESUS' LOVE

Psalm 59: 16

Both words and music were written in 1886 by Franklin Edson Belden (1858-1945), see appendix. They are the song of a personal experience, imitating the style of the psalmist who said, "I will sing praise to Thy name, O Thou Most High," Psalm 9: 2; "I will extol thee, O Lord; for Thou hast lifted me up," Psalm 30: 1; "I will sing of the mercies of the Lord for ever," Psalm 89: 1; "I will sing of mercy and judgment," Psalm 101: 1. The hymn is actually based on Psalm 59: 16, "I will sing of Thy power; yea, I will sing aloud of Thy mercy," and also on Ephesians 1: 7, "In whom we have redemption through His blood, the forgiveness of sins, according to the riches of His grace," under which heading it appears in "Hymns and Tunes," 1886.

530. THE GREAT PHYSICIAN NOW IS NEAR

Acts 4: 12

William Hunter (1811-77) was an Irishman of Ballymoney who emigrated to the United States while a boy of six years old. There he became a minister of the Methodist Episcopal Church in Ohio, and wrote these words in 1859. He edited religious journals and was Hebrew professor in Alleghany College. There are several other stanzas, now omitted, namely:—

2. Your many sins are now forgiven,
   O hear the voice of Jesus,
   Go on your way in peace to heaven
   And wear a crown with Jesus.

4. The children, too, both great and small,
   Who love the name of Jesus,
   May now accept the gracious call
   To work and live for Jesus.

5. Come, brethren, help me sing the praise,
   O praise the name of Jesus,
   Come, sisters, all your voices raise,
   Oh, bless the name of Jesus.

7. And when to that bright world above
   We rise to see our Jesus,
   We'll sing around the throne of love,
   His name, the name of Jesus.

While Jesus is first introduced in this hymn as the Great Physician, the emphasis is on His name, Jesus, which signifies Saviour. The words are therefore an enlargement of the Apostle Peter's declaration: "There is none other name under heaven, given among men, whereby we must be saved." Acts 4: 12. Hunter also wrote Nos. 368, "We're Bound for the Land of the Pure," and possibly 662, "Let Others Seek a Home Below."

The tune was arranged by John Hart Stockton (1813-77) of New Hope, Pennsylvania, a preacher of the Methodist Episcopal Church, musician, and composer. The last two lines of the refrain are virtually the same as each of the two halves of the stanzas. He published gospel song books in 1874 and 1875, and also wrote both words and music of No. 567, "Come, Every Soul by Sin Oppressed," to the tune *Only Trust Him.*

531. I'VE FOUND A FRIEND

Romans 8: 38, 39

James Grindlay Small (1817-88), author of many hymns and poems, was a student of Dr. Thomas Chalmers at the University of Edinburgh, and with him joined the Free Church of Scotland at the disruption of 1843. He wrote this hymn in 1863, while pastor at Bervie near Montrose, and entitled it "Jesus the Friend," publishing it three years later in his "Psalms and Sacred Songs." The last stanza recalls the triumphant reply given by the Apostle Paul to his own question, "For I am persuaded, that neither death, nor life, nor angels, nor principalities, nor powers, nor things present, nor things to come, nor height, nor depth, nor any other creature, shall be able to separate us from the love of God, which is in Christ Jesus our Lord." Romans 8: 38, 39.

The tune *Friend* was composed in 1878 at Providence, Rhode Island, during an evangelistic campaign by George Coles Stebbins (1846-1945), see appendix, and is so named because of the words to which it is sung.

532. I HAVE A FRIEND SO PRECIOUS

Matthew 11: 29

Mrs. Mary Ann Elizabeth Lancaster, née Shorey (1851-19 ?), was in attendance at church one Sunday evening in the summer of 1890 at Leytonstone, Essex, and heard a sermon on Matthew 11: 29, "Take My yoke upon you, and learn of Me; for I am meek and lowly in heart: and ye shall find rest unto your souls." The next morning, while engaged in her household duties, she was reviewing the sermon and the thoughts suggested by it, and this hymn began to form in her mind. The complete hymn, telling of dwelling, walking, talking, and working together with Jesus the Lord, was printed in December, 1890.

The tune *My Lord and I,* was composed by the American, Hubert Platt Main (1839-1925), a compiler and writer of hymns, catering for the tunes people liked to sing. He also arranged Nos. 267 and 663, *Ellesdie,* and 160, *Beloved* or *Dulcimer.*

533. ON A HILL FAR AWAY

John 3: 16

Both words and music of this hymn were composed in 1913 by George Bennard (1873-1958) of Georgetown, Ohio, while ministering at Albion, Michigan. He was the son of a publican, and while a coal-miner, joined the Salvation Army, and later became a minister in the Methodist Episcopal Church. During a real soul struggle, he was meditating on the theme of the cross and the importance it occupied in Christianity. After further study and reading of the Scripture, he saw Christ and the cross inseparably joined in the well-known verse, "For God so loved the world, that He gave His only begotten Son, that whosoever believeth in Him should not perish, but have everlasting life." John 3: 16. The title of the hymn then came into his mind, "The Old Rugged Cross," and then the melody. In vain he tried to fit words on this theme to the tune, trying on various occasions in different cities. Finally at a third attempt, freedom of composition came, and the words exalting the cross flowed freely from his mind. He sang it at the parsonage of his friends, the Rev. and Mrs. L. O. Bostwick at Pokagon, Michigan, and to his diffident question, "Will it do?" they replied that they liked it so much that they would pay for its printing. To commemorate this very popular gospel hymn, a cross twelve feet high stands just outside Reed City, Michigan, which was Bennard's last home.

534. TELL ME THE STORY OF JESUS

Matthew 20: 28

Frances Jane Crosby (1820-1915), see appendix, wrote this simple summary of the Saviour's earthly life, covering His birth, His temptation, His ministry, His crucifixion, His death, and His resurrection. The whole is effectively summed up in the Saviour's own words: "Even as the Son of man came not to be ministered unto, but to minister, and to give His life a ransom for many." Matthew 20: 28.

The tune was composed by John Robson Sweney (1837-99), see appendix.

535. 'TIS FINISHED!

John 19: 30

Dr. Samuel Stennett (1727-95), like his grandfather Joseph (see No. 456), was a prominent Seventh-day Baptist preacher and a strong supporter of religious liberty. He was pastor of the Little Wild Street church in Lincoln's Inn Fields, London. This hymn, based on the last words of Jesus on the cross, "It is finished," John

19: 30, appeared in 1787 in his friend Dr. Rippon's collection (see No. 255). It was specially written to be sung on and to commemorate Good Friday. There were six stanzas originally, and they have been altered considerably, as will be noted from the four given below. The first and the sixth correspond approximately to the first and fourth stanzas in "Church Hymnal."

2. 'Tis finished—all that Heaven decreed,
And all the ancient prophets said
Is now fulfilled, as was designed,
In Me, the Saviour of mankind.

3. 'Tis finished—Aaron now no more
Must stain his robes with purple gore;
The sacred veil is rent in twain
And Jewish rites no more remain.

4. 'Tis finished—this My dying groan
Shall sins of every kind atone:
Millions shall be redeemed from death
By this My last expiring breath.

5. 'Tis finished—Heaven is reconciled,
And all the powers of darkness spoiled;
Peace, love, and happiness again
Return, and dwell with sinful men.

Stennett also wrote Nos. 159, "Majestic Sweetness Sits Enthroned," and 553, "On Jordan's Stormy Banks."

The tune *Olden* was composed by Lowell Mason (1792-1872), see appendix.

536. IT MAY BE AT MORN

1 Thessalonians 5: 2

These words by H. L. Turner recall our Lord's injunction in Mark 13: 35 to be ready at all times, "Watch ye therefore: for ye know not when the master of the house cometh, at even, or at midnight, or at the cockcrowing, or in the morning:" although the text on which the hymn is based is "The day of the Lord so cometh as a thief in the night." 1 Thessalonians 5: 2.

The tune *Christ Returneth* was composed by James McGranahan (1840-1907), who was the singing evangelist for Major D. W. Whittle (see No. 583), as well as being a conductor and a composer. Others of his tunes are Nos. 495, *Sometime We'll Understand;* 568, *Shall You? Shall I?* and 652, unnamed.

537. CALLED TO THE FEAST

Matthew 22:11

These words by J. E. Landor are a solemn commentary on the parable of the man without a wedding garment. (Matthew 22: 1-14.) The emphasis is in the chorus: "And when the king came in to see the guests, he saw there a man which had not on a wedding garment." Matthew 22: 11. There are two other stanzas, as follows:—

Endless the sad separation then,
Bitter the cry of deluded men,
Awful that moment of anguish when
Christ the King, comes in.

Lord, grant us all, we implore Thee, grace,
So to await Thee each in his place,
That we may fear not to see Thy face
When Thou comest in.

The tune *When the King Comes In,* was specially written for these words by the Rev. Edmund Simon Lorenz (1854-?) of Dayton, Ohio, of the United Brethren Church. He also composed Nos. 643, *The Name of Jesus;* 650, *Wonderful Love of Jesus,* and 655, unnamed. He was the author of No. 650, "In Joyful High and Holy Lays," under his pen-name E. D. Mund, which is simply his Christian name elongated.

538. WHEN JESUS SHALL GATHER THE NATIONS

Luke 3: 17

These words were written by Harriet Burn M'Keever (1807-87), who was a teacher in a girls' school in Philadelphia, and also a Sunday school teacher of infants in the Protestant Episcopal Church. They appear to have been inspired by a reading of the 25th chapter of Matthew particularly, for this describes the parable of the ten virgins and their lamps, the reward to the faithful user of talents, and the expulsion of the lazy one, and the final judgment. Matthew 25: 32: "And before Him shall be gathered all nations." Matthew 25: 21: "His lord said unto him, Well done, thou good and faithful servant." Matthew 25: 30: "And cast ye the unprofitable servant into outer darkness: there shall be weeping and gnashing of teeth." Matthew 25: 7: "Then all those virgins arose, and trimmed their lamps." Matthew 25: 10: "The bridegroom came; and they that were ready went in with him to the marriage." Matthew 25: 13: "Watch therefore." The refrain is a paraphrase of Luke 3: 17: "He . . . will gather the wheat into His garner; but the chaff He will burn with fire unquenchable."

The tune *He Will Gather the Wheat,* was composed by John Robson Sweney (1837-99), see appendix.

539. IN THE GLAD TIME OF THE HARVEST

Matthew 16: 27

Both author and composer of this hymn were members of the Seventh-day Adventist Church. Lorenzo D. Santee (1845-1919), the writer of the words, was born at Hornellsville, New York, on September 19, 1845, and became a public school teacher in Kansas and Illinois. In the long summer vacation he used the school house as an evangelistic centre, and as a result was able to organize several churches. He was ordained to the gospel ministry in 1876, working mainly in Chicago and elsewhere in the Illinois Conference. He wrote many poems, fifteen of them appearing in a song book compiled by P. P. Bilhorn (see Nos. 528, 609) for another Christian denomination, and contributed verse to the *Review and Herald.* The hymn breathes the fervour of the Adventists who preached their distinctive doctrine of the millennium, which was to begin at Christ's second coming at the close of the investigative judgment. Mrs. Ellen G. White said that there were strains in this hymn that reminded her of some of the angel songs she had heard in vision. The Scripture basis is, "For the Son of man shall come in the glory of His Father, with His angels; and then He shall reward every man according to his works." Matthew 16: 27. Many other scriptures are referred to, for example: Revelation 14: 15; Revelation 20: 12, 13, 11; 1 Corinthians 15: 53; 1 Corinthians 13: 12; Revelation 21: 21; Psalm 126: 5, 6; Isaiah 35: 10; Revelation 2: 10.

The tune *When the King Shall Claim His Own,* was composed in 1886 by Edwin Barnes (1864-1930), see appendix.

540. WE KNOW NOT THE HOUR

Matthew 24: 36-42

Both words and music were written by Franklin Edson Belden (1858-1945), see appendix, and appear in "Hymns and Tunes," 1886. The heading there is a long scripture quotation selected from Matthew 24: 36, 38, 39, 42, "But of that day and hour knoweth no man, no, not the angels of heaven, but My Father only. . . . For as in the days that were before the Flood they were eating and drinking, marrying and giving in marriage, until the day that Noe entered into the ark, and knew not until the Flood came, and took them all away; so shall also the coming of the Son of man be. . . . Watch therefore: for ye know not what hour your Lord doth come." The parable of the ten virgins is also introduced in the expression in stanza three, "lamps trimmed," which comes from Matthew 25: 7.

541. LIFT UP THE TRUMPET

Matthew 24: 30

The first three stanzas of this rousing hymn by Jessie E. Strout tell of the world-wide proclamation of the second advent message, and the last two stanzas give certain signs which indicate the nearness of this event. Scripture verses implied are:—

Isaiah 58: 1: "Lift up thy voice like a trumpet."

John 14: 3: "I will come again."

Psalm 149: 5: "Let the saints be joyful in glory: let them sing aloud."

Psalm 98: 8, 9: "Let the hills be joyful together before the Lord; for He cometh."

Psalm 96: 12, 13: "Let the field be joyful, and all that is therein . . . rejoice before the Lord: for He cometh."

Matthew 24: 30: "They shall see the Son of man coming . . . with power and great glory."

Revelation: 13: 8: "The Lamb slain from the foundation of the world."

Psalm 98: 7: "Let the sea roar, and the fullness thereof."

Luke 21: 10, 11: "Nation shall rise against nation . . . and great earthquakes shall be in divers places . . . and fearful sights and great signs shall there be from heaven."

Revelation 11: 18: "And the nations were angry."

Daniel 12: 14: "The time of the end: many shall run to and fro, and knowledge shall be increased."

The tune *Jesus Is Coming Again* was composed by George E. Lee, another of whose tunes, an entirely different type, is No. 491, *Sleep*.

542. WE KNOW NOT THE TIME WHEN HE COMETH

Mark 13: 35

The uncertainty of the time of the second advent and the consequent necessity to be always ready is the theme of this hymn. It begins with an almost direct quotation from Mark 13: 35: "Ye know not when the master of the house cometh, at even, or at midnight, or at the cockcrowing, or in the morning." This is followed by the first part of this same verse, "Watch ye therefore," and Matthew 24: 44, "Therefore be ye also ready: for in such an hour as ye think not the Son of man cometh." An illustration is next taken from the parable of the virgins, when the five foolish ones said, "Our lamps are gone out." Matthew 25: 8. The hymn appears in J. E. White's "Song Anchor" of 1881, having been selected from a previous hymnal "Songs of Gratitude."

The tune *Waiting and Watching,* was composed by William Henry Pontius (1860-?) of Ohio, who became a professor in a music school in Minneapolis, Minnesota.

543. TELL IT TO EVERY KINDRED AND NATION

Revelation 14: 6

Both words and music were written in 1916 by Henry de Fluiter 1872-), who was born in Holland and emigrated to the United States, where he became a singing evangelist for the Seventh-day Adventist Church. The words look away from the dark days of Allied setbacks and retreat in World War I to the glorious day when the Prince of Peace shall put an end to war, and defeat for ever the powers of darkness. Several passages of Scripture are paraphrased; for example:—

Stanza 1. "To preach unto . . . every nation, and kindred." Revelation 14: 6. "The night is far spent, the day is at hand." Romans 13: 12.

Stanza 2. "And there shall be signs in the sun, and in the moon, and in the stars; and upon the earth distress of nations." Luke 21: 25.

Stanza 3. "Then look up, and lift up your heads." Luke 21: 28. "We have waited for Him, we will be glad and rejoice in His salvation." Isaiah 25: 9. "Blessed are those servants, whom the lord . . . shall find watching." Luke 12: 37.

Refrain: "The King of glory," Psalm 24: 7. "Worthy is the Lamb that was slain," Revelation 5: 12; "He shall reign for ever and ever." Revelation 11: 15.

The stirring march tune, *Hail Him the King of Glory,* reflects the martial spirit of the time, and is an apt vehicle for the warning message contained in the words. Another hymn and tune by the same composer is No. 38, "God Bless and Keep Thee," to the tune *Mizpah.* De Fluiter died in 1970.

544. O'ER ALL THE LAND

Luke 21: 25, 26

The tune here called, *Come, Saviour, Come,* was composed by Henry Clay Work (1832-84), of Middletown, Connecticut, for the words of his own song, "Ring the Bell, Watchman," the first stanza of which is:—

High in the belfry the old sexton stands,
Grasping the rope with his thin bony hands:
Fix'd is his gaze, as by some magic spell,
Till he hears the distant murmur, Ring, ring the bell.
Ring the bell, watchman! ring! ring! ring!
Yes! Yes! the good news is now on the wing.
Yes! Yes! they come, and with tidings to tell—
Glorious and blessed tidings, ring, ring the bell.

The song then goes on to tell of the excitement that attends some great triumph as news is brought back home. Work was the son of an abolitionist, and a strong supporter himself of this movement. He was a printer, and specialized in setting up music type. At the age of twenty-one he went to Chicago and taught himself music. His talent was increased as a result of the civil war, which spurred him to write war songs, one of his best known being "Marching Through Georgia" (1865). His war songs and temperance songs, for which he wrote both words and music, became very popular. He often set up his compositions in music type before either writing it or hearing it played beforehand. The present tune has been used in Australia for a sheep-shearers' song, "Click Go the Shears." From its original use for "Ring the Bell, Watchman," it was employed by William Claggett Gage (1842-1907), of Massachusetts, as a vehicle to proclaim an even greater day of triumph, namely, the soon coming of the Saviour, and the signs that show His coming is imminent. In this hymn, Gage first refers in general terms to the blessed hope of the glorious appearing of our Saviour Jesus Christ. Then detailed signs are given, as stated in Luke 21: 25, 26: "There shall be signs in the sun, and in the moon, and in the stars; and upon the earth distress of nations. . . . Men's hearts failing them for fear." An expression not occurring in Luke's account is taken from Matthew 24: 6 or Mark 13: 7: "Ye shall hear of wars and rumours of wars." The description in Luke then tells the parable of the fig-tree, and another expression is used in the hymn from this chapter: "When ye see these things come to pass, ye know that the kingdom of God is nigh at hand." Luke 21: 31. The refrain is in part the echo of John the revelator's words in closing the canon of Scripture: "Surely I come quickly. Amen. Even so, come, Lord Jesus." Revelation 22: 20. Gage learned printing in New Hampshire, and transferred to the *Review and Herald* at Battle Creek, Michigan, in 1867. As a temperance worker he was elected mayor of this city in 1882. He was a master printer, musician, public speaker, and also author of sixteen short answers to sixteen common objections to the Second Advent faith. He started the Gage Printing Company in Battle Creek in 1883, and later became a Seventh-day Adventist minister.

545. FACE TO FACE WITH CHRIST MY SAVIOUR

1 Corinthians 13: 12

Mrs. Frank A. (Carrie Ellis) Breck (1855-?) of Vermont, wrote verse for religious periodicals, and in all wrote about 1,500 hymns. This one uses, in part, the idea of the following scriptures:—"For now we see through a glass, darkly; but then face to face." 1 Corinthians 13: 12. "And they shall see His face." Revelation 22: 4. "And the crooked shall be made straight . . . and the glory of the Lord shall be revealed, and all flesh shall see it together." Isaiah 40: 4, 5. Mrs. Breck, who wrote most of her poems while engaged in her housework in Portland, Oregon, also wrote No. 123, "There Was One Who Was Willing."

Grant Colfax Tullar (1869-?) was staying in the home of Charles L. Mead, a minister of the Methodist Episcopal Church, in Rutherford, New Jersey, while assisting in an evangelistic campaign. At one meal there was a small quantity of jelly left, and knowing Tullar's fondness for it, Mead promised it all to him. Tullar said, "So this is all for me," and promptly the last three words registered in his mind as a theme for a gospel song. Forsaking the mundane idea of jelly, he went immediately to the piano, and began to compose words and music:—

All for me the Saviour suffered,
All for me He bled and died.

Tullar called it the jelly song, and sang it at the evangelistic meeting that evening, telling also the story of its spontaneous composition. However, he decided to revise the words, as they had been rather rapidly written. In the mail the next morning he received several poems from Mrs. Breck. One of them, "Face to Face," was in the exact metre, and has been used with this "jelly" tune ever since. Tullar received his Christian names after the current president and vice-president of the United States. He became a minister of the Methodist Episcopal Church and an evangelist. He founded a music publishing business with Isaac Meredith in 1893, and was its president for over thirty years. Tullar also composed No. 123, *Nailed to the Cross*—words also by Mrs. Breck—and No. 425, *Peek.*

546. THE COMING KING IS AT THE DOOR

Matthew 24: 33, 34

Both words and music were written by Franklin Edson Belden (1858-1945), see appendix, and appear in "Hymns and Tunes," 1886. They are based on the Lord's prophecy recorded in Matthew 24: 33, 34: "So likewise ye, when ye shall see all these things, know that it is near, even at the doors. Verily I say unto you, This generation shall not pass, till all these things be fulfilled." Other scriptures used are: "What shall be the sign of Thy coming, and of the end of the world?" Matthew 24: 3; "Ye shall hear of wars and rumours of wars. . . . For nation shall rise against nation, and kingdom against kingdom," Matthew 24: 6, 7; "This mortal shall have put on immortality." 1 Corinthians 15: 54.

547. THE GOLDEN MORNING IS FAST APPROACHING

Matthew 24: 30, 31

Both words and music of this second advent hymn were written by S. J. Graham. The following scriptures are used:

"Thou good and faithful servant . . . enter thou into the joy of thy lord," Matthew 25: 21; "And this gospel . . . shall be preached in all the world . . . unto all nations," Matthew 24: 14; "The bridegroom tarried," Matthew 25: 5; "The Son of man coming in the clouds of heaven with power and great glory. And He shall send His angels with a great sound of a trumpet, and they shall gather together His elect," Matthew 24: 30, 31; "And God shall wipe away all tears from their eyes," Revelation 21: 4; "He hath sent Me to bind up the broken-hearted," Isaiah 61: 1.

With one solitary exception, the tune *Gleams of the Golden Morning* is built on two chords and their inversions, a fact made evident by the bass part which consists of only two notes, tonic and dominant.

548. SWEET PROMISE IS GIVEN

Revelation 3: 11

Both words and music were written by Franklin Edson Belden (1858-1945), see appendix, and appear in "Hymns and Tunes," 1886. The words are based on the promise to "the church in Philadelphia," "Behold, I come quickly: hold that fast which thou hast, that no man take thy crown," Revelation 3: 11. Other scriptures used are: "Therefore let us not sleep, as do others; but let us watch and be sober," 1 Thessalonians 5: 6; "Enter thou into the joy of thy lord," Matthew 25: 21; ". . . will I grant to sit with Me in My throne," Revelation 3: 21; "The day of the Lord so cometh as a thief in the night," 1 Thessalonians 5: 2; "But of that day and hour knoweth no man," Matthew 24: 36; "Now learn a parable of the fig tree; when his branch is tender, and putteth forth leaves, ye know that summer is nigh," Matthew 24: 32; "Looking for that blessed hope, and the glorious appearing of the great God and our Saviour Jesus Christ," Titus 2: 13.

549. WATCH, YE SAINTS

Luke 21: 27

Mrs. Phoebe Palmer (1807-74), a Methodist and a close friend of Charles Fitch (see No. 338), was converted by him to the Millerite doctrine of the coming of the Lord in 1844. She wrote this hymn entitled "Jesus Comes," and it became a very popular song in early 1844 because it told in verse form of the signs of the second advent, namely: "the powers of the heavens shall be shaken," Matthew 24: 29, "Then all those virgins arose, and trimmed their lamps," Matthew 25: 7; ". . . washed their robes, and made them white in the blood of the Lamb," Revelation 7: 14; "it shall break in pieces and consume all these kingdoms," Daniel 2: 44; "But in the days of the voice of the seventh angel, when he shall begin to sound, the mystery of God should be finished," Revelation 10: 7; "And then shall they see the Son of man coming in a cloud with power and great glory," Luke 21: 27. There is one other stanza, namely:—

6. Lamb of God, Thou meek and lowly,
Judah's Lion high and holy,
Lo, Thy bride comes forth to meet Thee,
All in blood-washed robes to greet Thee.

Mrs. Palmer also wrote No. 598, "O Now I See the Crimson Wave."

The tune *Jesus Comes* was composed by William James Kirkpatrick (1838-1921), see appendix.

550. BEAUTIFUL VALLEY OF EDEN

Isaiah 51: 3

William Orcutt Cushing (1823-1903) was a minister of the Christian Church who later joined the Methodists, and who during his lifetime wrote over 300 gospel hymns. In 1875, as he was meditating, he saw in his mind's eye a vision of the heavenly country with a river in the foreground, and hills and valleys spread out in peaceful beauty on the opposite bank. He was impelled to write the words of this hymn almost as though he were describing an actual scene. As he gazed, the words "Beautiful valley of Eden" came to his lips, but when he had finished writing these lines the vision faded. They are reminiscent of the Lord's promise to restore the first perfection of Eden—"For the Lord shall comfort Zion: He will comfort all her waste places; and He will make her wilderness like Eden, and her desert like the garden of the Lord; joy and gladness shall be found therein, thanksgiving, and the voice of melody." Isaiah 51: 3. Cushing also wrote Nos. 418, "When He Cometh"; 586, "O Safe to the Rock," and 587, "Under His Wings." He attributed the beauty of the hymn largely to the peaceful melody composed by William Fisk Sherwin (1826-88), see appendix.

551. THERE'S A LAND THAT IS FAIRER THAN DAY

Isaiah 35: 10

Joseph Philbrick Webster (1819-75) of New Hampshire, was a musician of a very sensitive nature, subject to fits of depression in which he would completely ignore even his best friends. One day in 1867 he was in this kind of mood as he came to the place of business of Sanford Fillmore Bennett (1836-98) in the town of Elkhorn, Wisconsin. Bennett had been an editor and a teacher in Eden, New York, but after the Civil War became the proprietor of a drug store in this town. On entering, Webster turned his back on his friend and did not utter even one word of greeting. Having known him for about six years, and realizing that he was in one of his strange moods, Bennett asked what was the matter. "No matter," was the reply, "it will be all right by and by." The answer started a train of thought in Bennett's mind as he thought of the spiritual truth in the statement, and he said, "The sweet by and by! Would not that make a good hymn?" Immediately he set to work and quickly penned three stanzas and a refrain. He handed the words to Webster, who brightened up at once, caught the inspiration of the moment, and sat down and wrote the melody. Calling for a violin, he played this melody and then wrote the harmony of "Sweet By and By." In the short space of half an hour they and two other friends who had come in, were singing the hymn as it is now published. The second stanza especially recalls Isaiah 35: 10: "And the ransomed of the Lord shall return, and come to Zion with songs and everlasting joy upon their heads: they shall obtain joy and gladness, and sorrow and sighing shall flee away."

552. I WILL SING YOU A SONG

Revelation 21: 18

In 1865, Philip Phillips (1834-95) had been reading John Bunyan's "Pilgrim's Progress" and had been very much impressed by the description of Christian and Hopeful entering the gate of the celestial city. He thought that there was material here for a good hymn so he sent the following extract to Mrs. Ellen M. Huntingdon Gates (1836-1920), who was a didactic poetess and hymn-writer of Torrington, Connecticut.

"Now I saw in my dream that these two men went in at the gate; and lo! as they entered, they were transfigured; and they had raiment put on that shone like gold. There were also that met them with harps and crowns, and gave them to them; the harps to praise withal, the crowns in token of honour. Then I heard in my dream that all the bells in the City rang again for joy, and that it was said unto them, 'Enter ye into the joy of our Lord! . . . Now just as the gates were opened to let in the men I looked in after them, and behold the City shone like the sun; the streets also were paved with gold: and in them walked many men with crowns on their heads, palms in their hands, and golden harps, to sing praises withal. There were also of them that had wings, and they answered one another without intermission, saying, 'Holy, holy, holy, is the Lord!' And after that they shut up the gates; which when I had seen I wished myself among them." A description of the holy city is given in the last two chapters of the Bible, part of it in Revelation 21: 18, "And the building of the wall of it was of jasper: and the city was pure gold, like unto clear glass." Phillips's request for a suitable hymn was answered by Mrs. Gates sending the words of this hymn. He re-read the extract from Bunyan, went to the organ, and composed the tune *Home of the Soul,* under the inspiration of the words. Phillips, who was born in Jamestown, New York, was a gospel singer known as the singing pilgrim, as he peddled music from place to place, playing his songs on a melodeon. He composed melodies which were harmonized by others, chiefly by Silas Jones Vail (see No. 561) or by Hubert Platt Main (see Nos. 160, 267, 532, 663). Two others of his tunes are Nos. 561, unnamed, and 576, *Stand Like the Brave.*

553. ON JORDAN'S STORMY BANKS

Revelation 15: 2, 3

These words were written in 1787 by Dr. Samuel Stennett (1727-95), the son and grandson of a Seventh-day Baptist minister, whose example and profession he also followed. He wrote seven stanzas under the title "The Promised Land," those omitted being:—

2. O the transporting rapt'rous scene
   That rises to my sight!
   Sweet fields, arrayed in living green,
   And rivers of delight.

3. There generous fruits that never fail,
   On trees immortal grow:
   There rocks, and hills, and brooks, and vales,
   With milk and honey flow.

5. No chilling winds, or poisonous breath,
   Can reach that healthful shore:
   Sickness and sorrow, pain and death,
   Are felt and feared no more.

This figure of crossing the swelling, stormy river of Jordan before death and entering the heavenly Canaan to enjoy eternal life is not however strictly Biblical. It is an extension of the parallel with the Israelites who came to the Jordan in Joshua's time when it was truly a time of flood (Joshua 3: 15), but the Lord caused the waters to cease so that they passed over into Canaan's land. Another occasion associated with the Jordan and with death and eternal life concerns the translation of the prophet Elijah, who, however, was crossing in the other direction from Jericho eastward. Again a miracle was performed, for Elijah smote the waters with his mantle and he and Elisha went over on dry ground (2 Kings 2: 8). In neither case was there the struggle against Jordan's waves, and we owe this figure to John Bunyan's usage in "Pilgrim's Progress," where he describes Christian reaching the end of his journey, and all the trumpets sounding for him on the other side as he makes his triumphal crossing of the watery barrier. The refrain quotes the language of Revelation 15: 2, 3 concerning the victorious Christians who "stand on the sea of glass . . . and . . . sing the song of Moses the servant of God, and the song of the Lamb." Samuel Stennett also wrote Nos. 159, "Majestic Sweetness Sits Enthroned," and 535, " 'Tis Finished."

The tune, unnamed, was composed by Tullius Clinton O'Kane (1830-1912) of Ohio, who was a travelling salesman for organs and song books from 1867, a public school principal in Cincinnati, Ohio, for seven years, and a professor of mathematics in the Wesleyan University of Delaware, Ohio.

554. THERE IS A LAND OF CORN AND WINE

Deuteronomy 33: 28

Edgar Page Stites (1837-19 ?), a prominent business man of Cape May, New Jersey, dropped his surname to acquire a pseudonym. In this hymn, written in 1876, the words have been altered here and there from the original, making our hymn in the future tense instead of in the past. The first two stanzas and refrain were first completed, and then the author was so overcome by his emotions that he wept. One week later the last two stanzas were completed under great emotional strain with prayer and weeping. The scripture heading given by the author was Deuteronomy 33: 28, "A land of corn and wine," hence his words, "This is heaven's borderland" where we now have, in stanza 2, "In that celestial, happy land." The original refrain was:—

O Beulah land, sweet Beulah land,
As on thy highest mount I stand
I look away across the sea
Where mansions are prepared for me,
And view the shining glory shore
My heaven, my home for evermore.

The tune *Beulah Land* was composed by John Robson Sweney (1837-99), see appendix, and the hymn was first sung at a large gathering of Methodist believers at Ocean Grove, New Jersey.

555. SHALL WE GATHER AT THE RIVER?

Revelation 22: 1

One very hot summer day in 1864, a Baptist minister, Robert Lowry (1826-99), see appendix, sat at the window of his study in Brooklyn, New York. At the time a fierce epidemic was raging, and his heart was touched at the sight of so many mourners in the streets who had laid loved ones to rest. The following question came into his mind as he was meditating, "At the parting of the river of death, shall we meet again at the river of life?" He was doubtless influenced by the revelator's description: "And He showed me a pure river of water of life, clear as crystal, proceeding out of the throne of God and of the Lamb." Revelation 22: 1. Lowry moved over to his organ and composed both words and music of this hymn spontaneously. Omitted stanzas with slight alterations are:—

At the smiling of the river,
Mirror of the Saviour's face (or, Rippling with)
Saints whom death will never sever,
Lift their songs of saving grace.

And one largely unused:—

On the bosom of the river,
Where the Saviour king we own,
We shall meet and sorrow never,
'Neath the glory of the throne.

556. ANGEL VOICES SWEETLY SINGING

Revelation 21: 1, 4

Horatius Bonar (1808-89), see appendix, the greatest of the Scottish hymn writers, published this hymn of twelve stanzas in 1861 in the "Quarterly Journal of Prophecy," of which he was the editor. He has based it on the description of the New Jerusalem and quotes in each stanza and in the refrain the motto of his family, "Heaven at Last." "And I saw a new heaven and a new earth. . . . And God shall wipe away all tears from their eyes." Revelation 21: 1, 4.

The tune *Heaven at Last,* was composed by William James Kirkpatrick (1838-1921), see appendix.

557. SHALL WE MEET BEYOND THE RIVER?

Romans 8: 18

Horace Lorenzo Hastings (1831-?) began to write hymns and to preach sermons at the age of seventeen years. He was a minister of the Adventist Christian Church (see No. 180) and wrote fourteen stanzas (each of eight lines) of this hymn in New York city in 1858. It shows his belief in the soon coming of the Lord and looks forward to the joys of the celestial city. The glories there far outweigh the stormy trials experienced here on earth, "For I reckon that the sufferings of this present time are not worthy to be compared with the glory which shall be revealed in us." Romans 8: 18. The present selection is from the first half of original stanzas 1, 4, 11, and 9. Other lines omitted are:—

Where the music of the ransomed
Rolls its harmony around,
And creation swells the chorus
With its sweet melodious sound?
Shall we meet many a loved one
That was torn from our embrace?
Shall we listen to their voices
And behold them face to face?

Several tunes were fitted to the words, but Hastings liked best the present one composed in 1866 by Elihu S. Rice, who was secretary and chorister of the Baptist Sunday school at Logansport. He was a hardware store clerk who later became a preacher. His manuscript was sent to Robert Lowry, see appendix, who was the editor of the musical department of a Sunday school paper in Philadelphia, and it was published in 1866.

558. IN THE LAND OF FADELESS DAY

Revelation 21: 16

John R. Clements (1868-?), an Irishman who was taken to the United States in infancy, was a grocer who was interested in the Christian Endeavour movement. Here he has taken statements from the last two chapters of the Bible for this hymn on the New Jerusalem, making very little paraphrase but using as far as possible the actual words of scripture, for example:—

Stanza 1—Revelation 21: 16: "And the city lieth foursquare."
Revelation 21: 25: "There shall be no night there."
Revelation 21: 1: "For the first heaven and the first earth were passed away."

Stanza 2—Revelation 21: 21: "And the twelve gates were twelve pearls; every several gate was of one pearl: and the street of the city was pure gold."

Stanza 3—Revelation 21: 25: "And the gates of it shall not be shut at all by day."
Revelation 22: 1: "A pure river of water of life, clear as crystal."

Stanza 4—Revelation 21: 23: "And the city had no need of the sun . . . to shine in it . . . and the Lamb is the light thereof."

Refrain—Revelation 21: 4: "And God shall wipe away all tears . . . there shall be no more death . . . neither shall there be any more pain."

The tune *No Night There* was composed by Hart Pease Danks (1834-1903) of New Haven, Connecticut. Although a carpenter he composed over 1,000 songs of popular taste, one of them being No. 7, the unnamed tune to "The Lord in Zion Reigneth." He was a boy soprano, and later a singer and conductor of Chicago. He made a speciality of composing sacred music.

559. PASS ME NOT, O GENTLE SAVIOUR

Luke 18: 35-43

This hymn is one of the several hymns of Fanny Crosby (1820-1915), see appendix, which were set to music by William Howard Doane (1832-1916), see appendix. Miss Crosby was visiting one of New York's prisons in 1868, and during her address to the convicts appealed to them to accept Christ as their Saviour. She was interrupted by one prisoner who exclaimed, "Good Lord, don't pass me by." Doane first suggested the title, "Pass Me Not, O Gentle Saviour," and Miss Crosby worked on it until she had made it a real prayer from the heart. Being blind herself, she could understand the experience of the blind in their world of darkness. The incident recalled is that of the blind beggar outside Jericho who heard the sound of a multitude passing by. Asking what was the cause, he received the reply "that Jesus of Nazareth passeth by." Luke 18: 37. Then he cried out anxiously and would not be silenced until he was brought into the Saviour's presence. The authoress has brought out the lesson from the sight given to the blind man that our spiritual blindness can likewise be cured and vision restored by the grace of God.

560. I'VE WANDERED FAR AWAY FROM GOD

Luke 15: 18

Both words and music were written by William James Kirkpatrick (1838-1921), see appendix, and arose because of his burden for a young man's soul. He was the song leader of a camp-meeting at Rawlinsville, Pennsylvania, in 1902, and had used one soloist frequently. This singer had a wonderful voice and used it very expressively and emotionally, but Kirkpatrick knew that this was merely outward form, for the singer was by no means a Christian. He longed for this talented voice to be wholeheartedly dedicated to the cause of Christ, and he prayed in his own private devotions that the soloist would be convicted of his own need of a Saviour. He thought of the prodigal son who said, "I will arise and go to my father, and will say unto him, Father, I have sinned against heaven, and before thee," Luke 15: 18, and while still in prayer, the words of the refrain formed themselves in his mind. Concluding his prayer, he committed the words to paper, and then the words of the stanzas followed in quick succession. He soon composed a suitable tune, and believed that this song was God's answer to his prayer for the young singer. In the evening he handed the manuscript to the soloist, who rendered it with his customary fervour and interpretation. But the song also reached his own heart and caused him to surrender his life to God. "And he arose, and came to his father." Verse 20.

561. THERE IS A GATE THAT STANDS AJAR

Revelation 21: 25

Mrs. Lydia Baxter (1809-74) of Petersburgh, New York, was an enthusiastic member of the Baptist Church. She married Colonel John Baxter and moved to New York city, making her home and her sick-room a centre where Christians were welcomed. She was for many years an invalid, but this affliction evidently drew her near to the Saviour as revealed in this hymn written by her in 1872, concerning the cross and the crown, and also in her other, No. 523, "Take the Name of Jesus With You." The words of this hymn are based on the verse, "The gates of it shall not be shut at all by day: for there shall be no night there." Revelation 21: 25. It is said that the words were stimulated by Mrs. Baxter's hearing of a wayward girl who came back home to find that the door had been left unlocked all the time, with the expectation, hope and prayer that she would return.

The melody was composed by Philip Phillips (1834-95), a gospel singer known as the singing pilgrim from his practice of peddling music around the countryside and singing it to his accompanment on a small melodeon. He also wrote Nos. 552, *Home of the Soul,* and 576, *Stand Like the Brave.* The melody was then arranged and harmonized by Silas Jones Vail (1818-83) of Brooklyn, New York, whose hobby was the writing of hymn tunes. It will be observed that with the exception of the C sharp accidental in the refrain, the melody is in the pentatonic scale (see No. 181).

562. O WEARY SOUL THE GATE IS NEAR

John 10: 9

James Rowe (1866-19 ?) was born in England, emigrated to the United States in 1890, and began hymn writing about six years later. This is one of his thousands of hymns and is partly based on the parable of our Lord recorded in John 10: 1-10 where He likens Himself to a door through which a man shall be saved by entering. "I am the door: by Me if any man enter in, he shall be saved, and shall go in and out, and find pasture." John 10: 9.

Like most of his other hymns, this one was set to music to the tune *Just Outside the Door,* by Benton D. Ackley (1872-1958) of Spring Hill, Pennsylvania, who was organist in several churches in New York and Philadelphia, and also pianist for the evangelist Billy Sunday. Ackley was a Methodist minister and music editor who composed over 3,000 gospel songs.

563. SOFTLY AND TENDERLY

Matthew 11: 28

Will Lamartine Thompson (1847-1909) was born in East Liverpool, Ohio, and showed an early talent for musical composition. After study at the Boston Conservatorium of Music he produced a popular song which swept the United States, followed by two others which had almost equal success. In 1887, however, he decided to turn his talent from composing secular songs to writing gospel songs, and set up his own firm for publishing hymn books. The present hymn, both words and music, are by Thompson, and it was used extensively in Europe and America in the Moody-Sankey revival campaigns. The words are an enlargement of the pleading words of the Saviour to those who are weighed down and weary with the burden of sin, "Come unto Me, all ye that labour and are heavy laden, and I will give you rest." Matthew 11: 28.

564. WHILE JESUS WHISPERS TO YOU

Matthew 11: 28

Will Ellsworth Witter (1854-?) of Wyoming Valley, New York, had been reading the biography of Philipp Bliss (see appendix), and his songs were running through his mind. He was so impressed that he prayed God that he, too, might be inspired to write such helpful hymns that would convert sinners. Two of his pupils were wayward, and his heart was burdened for them. One summer day in 1877, he was in the field haymaking when his thoughts crystallized into the words of this hymn. They seemed to sing themselves into his brain, so he hurriedly left the hayfield, rushed upstairs into his brother's bedroom, and while on his knees, wrote these words which are a reminder of the Saviour's invitation, "Come unto Me, all ye that labour and are heavy laden, and I will give you rest." Matthew 11: 28. Witter later entered the Baptist ministry in 1884.

The tune *Come, Sinner, Come!* was composed in 1878 by Horatio Richmond Palmer (1834-1907), see appendix. Lines 1 and 3 are identical, as are also lines 5 and 7. The even lines alternate, 2 and 6 being the same, and 4 and 8.

565. CHRIST IS KNOCKING AT MY SAD HEART

Revelation 3: 20

Both words and music of this hymn were written by Horatio Richmond Palmer (1834-1907), see appendix. The words are based on the thought expressed in the text, "Behold, I stand at the door, and knock: if any man hear My voice, and open the door, I will come in to him." Rev. 3: 20.

566. THERE'S A STRANGER AT THE DOOR

Revelation 3: 20

The words of this hymn by Jonathan Bush Atchinson (1840-1882), an American Methodist preacher, are an amplification of the invitation and promise given in Revelation 3: 20, "Behold, I stand at the door, and knock: if any man hear My voice, and open the door, I will come in to him, and will sup with him, and he with Me."

The tune *Let Him In* was composed by Edwin Othello Excell (1851-1921) of Ohio, a Methodist song composer. He was a brick-layer who studied music in his spare time, and sang at his work. The Georgia evangelist, Sam P. Jones, heard him sing and invited him to become his choir conductor, from which beginning he formed an association of twenty years as a gospel singer. Excell was also associated as a singer with Dwight L. Moody's evangelistic campaigns, and also published some hymn books. He composed Nos. 591, *My Father Knows,* and both words and music of No. 638, "I Have a Song I Love to Sing," to an unnamed tune.

567. COME, EVERY SOUL BY SIN OPPRESSED

Isaiah 1: 18

Boths words and music of this hymn were written by John Hart Stockton (1813-77) of New Hope, Pennsylvania, a Methodist Episcopal preacher, musician, and composer, who published gospel song books in 1874 and 1875. The message of the hymn is the simple one of forgiveness to those who trust God: "Come now, and let us reason together, saith the Lord: though your sins be as scarlet, they shall be as white as snow." Isaiah 1: 18. Stockton also arranged the music for No. 530, "The Great Physician Now Is Near." It will be noted that the melody is in the pentatonic scale (see No. 181). Ira David Sankey (1840-1908) (see Nos. 575, 586, 587, 673) found the hymn in his scrapbook, liked it, and altered the refrain from the original "Come to Jesus," to the present "Only trust Him," and published it in this form in 1873.

568. SOMEONE WILL ENTER THE PEARLY GATE

Revelation 21: 21

The original words from which this hymn was taken were written by Mary E. Inman of Evart, Michigan, and first published in the *Review and Herald* of September 14, 1886. The poem was entitled "Some One" and consisted of four stanzas as follows:—

1. Some one will enter the gates of pearl
By and by;
Some one will walk the streets of gold,
The city's beauties will behold,
And taste those pleasures all untold:
Shall you? shall I?

2. Some one a crown of life will have
By and by;
Some one the glorious King will see,
From toils and pains of earth be free,
And evermore with Christ will be:
Shall you? shall I?

3. Some one will be with anguish filled
By and by;
Some one before the Judge will quail,
To gain eternal life will fail,
Among the lost will weep and wail;
Shall you? shall I?

4. Some one will shout the victory
By and by;
Some one will join the angel band:
Some one be found at God's right hand;
Some one with overcomers stand:
Shall you? shall I?

Miss Inman contributed poems regularly to the *Review and Herald,* the general church paper of Seventh-day Adventists, fourteen of them from Evart, Michigan, between 1886 and 1892, and one from Grand Rapids, Michigan, in 1893. The poem was modified by G.M.J. (could this be James McGranahan, the composer of the tune?) to the present eight-line hymn which is a personal appeal to the singer to identify himself with those who will finally be saved in God's eternal kingdom. The repeated questions would be just as euphonious in the form "Will you? Shall I?" and more in accordance with modern practice, but usage has accustomed the present version with two "shalls." Scriptures referred to in the hymn are: "Every several gate was of one pearl: and the street of the city was pure gold." Revelation 21: 21. "Be thou faithful . . . and I will give thee a crown." Revelation 2: 10. "And there shall be no more . . . sorrow." Revelation 21: 4. "And they shall reign for ever and ever." Revelation 22: 5. "And the door was shut. . . . But he answered and said, Verily I say unto you, I know you not." Matthew 25: 10, 12.

The tune *Shall You? Shall I?* was composed by James McGranahan (1840-1907), a singing evangelist for Major D. W. Whittle (see No. 583). He studied music in Chicago under George Frederick Root (See Nos. 93, 299, 418, 620, 690), in New York and in Boston, and was also a conductor and composer. He composed Nos. 495, *Sometime We'll Understand;* 536, *Christ Returneth,* and 652, unnamed.

569. JESUS IS TENDERLY CALLING

Matthew 11: 28

These words were written by Frances Jane Crosby (1820-1915), see appendix, and were based evidently on the appeal of Jesus as recorded in Matthew 11: 28, "Come unto Me, all ye that labour and are heavy laden, and I will give you rest."

The tune was composed by George Coles Stebbins (1846-1945), see appendix, while he was in Great Britain on an evangelistic campaign visit with Moody and Sankey in the years 1883-85.

570. O TENDER AND SWEET WAS THE FATHER'S VOICE

John 7: 37

In the year 1878 in Springfield, Massachusetts, a minister gave a testimony concerning one of his sons, a Yale student, and the dramatic experience he had had in surrendering to the Lord. The son was attending one of D. L. Moody's evangelistic meetings and a stranger sitting next to him urged him to become a Christian. Finding a partial response, he even walked home with him, and before parting, prayed that the Lord would enable the young man to make his decision for Christ that night. Approaching the house along the driveway the son suddenly stopped, drew a line across the gravel with his walking stick, and said to himself, "I must decide tonight. If I cross the line, my life is for Christ; if I go around it, I will live for the world." For half an hour the inward struggle raged until finally he cried, "O God, help me to decide aright." Then, the wrestling over, he leaped across the line, rushed into his father, and told him he had decided to be a Christian. This story, related by the father, impressed the whole congregation and was printed the next morning in the newspaper. Mrs. N. K. Bradford of Palmer, Massachusetts, read the incident and sat down and penned the words of this hymn. Its title was "Over the Line," and it was based on John 7: 37, "Let Him come unto Me." She sent the poem to the editor of the newspaper, E. H. Phelps, who set it to music.

The present tune *Over the Line* was composed in 1895 by Franklin Edson Belden (1858-1945), see appendix.

571. WHOSOEVER HEARETH

Revelation 22: 17

In Chicago in 1869, Henry Moorhouse, the boy preacher, conducted a series of meetings in Moody's church. For seven successive evenings he used the same text, John 3: 16, "God so loved the world." Philipp Bliss (1838-76), see appendix, was in attendance and, greatly impressed by the clear exposition of the gospel, was inspired to write both words and music of this hymn. He uses the language of Revelation 22: 17, "And the Spirit and the bride say, Come. And let him that heareth say, Come. . . . And whosoever will, let him take the water of life freely," words which give added weight to those in John 3: 16, "Whosoever believeth in Him should not perish, but have everlasting life."

572. JESUS, THE LOVING SHEPHERD

John 10: 11-16

Both words and music of this hymn were written by William Augustine Ogden (1841-97), see appendix, and here Jesus is depicted as the Shepherd of the sheep. This illustration is taken from our Lord's own parable recorded in John 10. "I am the good shepherd: the good shepherd giveth his life for the sheep," verse 11; "My sheep hear My voice," verse 27; "the wolf catcheth them, and scattereth the sheep," verse 12; "there shall be one fold, and one shepherd," verse 16.

573. ALL TO JESUS I SURRENDER

1 Thessalonians 5: 23

These words were written in 1896 by Judson W. Van de Venter (1855-1939) of Dundee, Michigan, who wrote over 100 hymns. He was an art teacher who had visited European art galleries for further study of his speciality. While singing in the choir one day in Sharon, Pennsylvania, he felt an urge to become an evangelist. He followed his inclination and worked with the evangelist W. S. Weeden, the composer of the tune, touring both the United States and England. This hymn, one of their several joint compositions, has come into popularity because of its frequent use in the Torrey-Alexander missions. An omitted stanza, the fourth, is:—

4. All to Jesus I surrender,
   Lord I give myself to Thee,
   Fill me with Thy love and power,
   Let Thy blessing fall on me.

An appropriate scripture passage giving the idea of full surrender is, "And the very God of peace sanctify you wholly; and I pray God your whole spirit and soul and body be preserved blameless unto the coming of our Lord Jesus Christ." 1 Thessalonians 5: 23.

The tune *I Surrender All* repeats lines 1 and 2 to provide lines 3 and 4. In the refrain there are two similar descending passages of five notes in the melody, reaching a climax in a descent of a complete octave in the last two lines.

574. SING THEM OVER AGAIN TO ME

John 6: 68

Philipp Bliss (1838-76), see appendix, wrote both words and music of this hymn in 1874. The words are an echo of the words of Jesus to His disciples: "The words that I speak unto you, they are spirit, and they are life," John 6: 63; and also of the Apostle Peter's reply, "Thou hast the words of eternal life," John 6: 68.

All but four of the chords in the tune *Wonderful Words of Life* are either based on the tonic or dominant or their inversions.

575. I HAVE A SAVIOUR

James 5: 16

The words of this prayer of intercession, reminding of James 5: 16, "Pray one for another," were written by Samuel O'Malley Cluff. He was an Irish clergyman who later left the Church of England and became a member of the Plymouth Brethren. The words were printed in leaflet form and a copy found its way in Ireland into the hands of Ira David Sankey (1840-1908) in 1874. An omitted stanza is:—

4. I have a peace; it is calm as a river,
A peace that the friends of this world never knew;
My Saviour alone is its Author and Giver,
And O could I know it was given to you!

Sankey set the words to music of his own composition, this being the second hymn that he wrote. He joined the Methodist Episcopal church at the age of fifteen years, and became a choir leader and Sunday school superintendent. He joined Dwight Lyman Moody (1837-99) as solo singer in their revival campaigns. He also composed Nos. 586, *Hiding in Thee;* 587, unnamed, and 673, *The Ninety and Nine.*

576. O CHRISTIAN, AWAKE!

Ephesians 6: 14-17

Miss Frances Jane Crosby (1820-1915), see appendix, has here expanded into a hymn the injunction of the Apostle Paul to take "the shield of faith . . . and take the helmet of salvation, and the sword of the Spirit. . . . Stand therefore" (Ephesians 6: 16, 17, 14), as well as his parallel counsel: "It is high time to awake. . . . Let us put on the armour of light." Romans 13: 11, 12.

The tune *Stand Like the Brave,* is a joint effort by Philip Phillips (1834-95) and William Batchelder Bradbury (1816-68), see appendix. Phillips was a gospel singer known as the singing pilgrim because of his peddling of songs from place to place, and singing them to his own accompaniment on a melodeon. He also composed the melodies of Nos. 552, *Home of the Soul,* and 561, unnamed, to the words "There Is a Gate that Stands Ajar."

577. THE LORD IS MY LIGHT

Psalm 27: 1

James Nicholson, an American Methodist minister, has taken as the basis of this hymn the triumphant expression of David, "The Lord is my light and my salvation; whom shall I fear? the Lord is the strength of my life." Psalm 27: 1. Clouds by day and darkness by night cannot extinguish the light of faith, and human weakness is covered by divine strength. Nicholson also wrote No. 592, "Lord Jesus, I Long to Be Perfectly Whole."

The tune was composed by Dr. J. W. Bischoff (1849-1909), the blind organist and choir director for thirty-five years of a Congregational church in Washington, D.C., who also revised the tune of No. 35, "God Be With You."

578. BLESSED LORD, HOW MUCH I NEED THEE!

John 15: 5

Both words and music of this hymn were written in 1886 by Franklin Edson Belden (1858-1945), see appendix, and were based on John 15: 5, "Without Me ye can do nothing." The words also contain the counsel given by the True Witness to the Laodicean church: "Thou art wretched, and miserable, and poor, and blind, and naked. I counsel thee to buy . . . white raiment, that thou mayest be clothed." Revelation 3: 17, 18.

579. WE'LL BUILD ON THE ROCK

Matthew 7: 24-26

Both words and music of this hymn were written in 1886 by Franklin Edson Belden (1858-1945), see appendix. The words are based on the concluding part of the Sermon on the Mount: "Whosoever heareth these sayings of Mine, and doeth them, I will liken him unto a wise man, which built his house upon a rock: and the rain descended, and the floods came, and the winds blew, and beat upon that house; and it fell not: for it was founded upon a rock." Matthew 7: 24, 25. It also uses: "A foolish man, which built his house upon the sand." Matthew 7: 26. And "For other foundation can no man lay than that is laid, which is Jesus Christ." 1 Corinthians 3: 11.

580. HAVE I NEED OF AUGHT, O SAVIOUR!

Psalm 73: 25

These words, published by Corie F. Davis in 1881, are an amplification of the psalmist's expression of trust in God: "Whom have I in heaven but Thee? and there is none upon earth that I desire beside Thee." Psalm 73: 25. The contrast is then made between the friendship of the Saviour on the one hand and earthly blessings on the other, such as the love of friends, good health, financial assets. In the fourth stanza there is an echo of the Apostle Paul's similar declaration, "Yea doubtless, and I count all things but loss for the excellency of the knowledge of Christ Jesus my Lord." Philippians 3: 8. There were originally six stanzas, those omitted being:—

3. Who, like Thee, can soothe and cheer me
When in grief and tears?
Who, like Thee, can soothe my passions,
Quiet all my fears?

6. All my heart in this life needeth,
Find I, Lord, in Thee;
All my heart in heaven asketh
Is, my Saviour, Thee!

The tune *Only Thee* was composed by Dr. William Oscar Perkins (1831-1902) who also contributed No. 602, an unnamed tune for the words "Jesus, Thou Hast Promised." Perkins was a music teacher, lecturer, and choral conductor, having studied music in Boston and in Europe, receiving the degree of Mus. Doc. in 1879. Over sixty of his musical works have been published.

581. MY HOPE IS BUILT ON NOTHING LESS

Matthew 7: 24-27

Edward Mote (1797-1874) was a cabinet-maker who was converted at the age of sixteen during his apprenticeship. He used to make a daily journey from his home in Southwark in the city of London to engage in his business. As he went to work he had an idea of writing a hymn on the gracious experience of a Christian. Walking up Holborn Hill in 1834 he conceived the words of the refrain, evidently taking them from the last part of the Sermon on the Mount, which describes two men, one who "built his house upon a rock" and the other, "A foolish man, which built his house upon the sand." Matthew 7: 24-27. Later in the same day he completed the four stanzas and sang the complete hymn at a friend's house the following Sunday. Finding them to be acceptable, he wrote two more stanzas at home the next Sunday and had the hymn printed. His title for the hymn was "The Immutable Basis of a Sinner's Hope." Our first stanza is a selection from Mote's second and first stanzas, the other halves of which are:—

1. Nor earth, nor hell, my soul can move,
   I rest upon unchanging love.
   . . .

2. . . .
   Midst all the hell I feel within.
   On His completed work I lean;

His fifth stanza was:—

5. I trust His righteous character,
   His counsel, promise, and His power;
   His honour and His name's at stake
   To save me from the burning lake.

Our last stanza has the words "When He shall come with trumpet sound," which have displaced the original "When I shall launch in worlds unseen." Mote later became a Baptist clergyman and ministered at Horsham, Sussex, for twenty-six years.

The tune, *The Solid Rock,* was composed in 1863 by William Batchelder Bradbury (1816-68), see appendix. The music for the stanzas consists of two identical halves in all four parts.

582. WHEN WE WALK WITH THE LORD

Hebrews 5:9

At one of Dwight Lyman Moody's evangelistic meetings a young man stood up and gave his testimony in the words, "I am going to trust, and I am going to obey." Daniel Brink Towner (1850-1919) of Rome, Pennsylvania, the soloist at the meeting, jotted down the words and sent them with the story of the incident to James H. Sammis (1846-1919), a Presbyterian minister. He wrote the words of the chorus first, then added the stanzas and sent them to Towner. The delights of a present, successful Christian experience described in the five stanzas amplify the statement concerning our Lord Jesus Christ, who "became the author of eternal salvation unto all them that obey Him." Hebrews 5:9. Sammis was born in Brooklyn, New York, and become a business man in Logansport, Indiana, giving this up to become the secretary of the Y.M.C.A. Later, in 1909, he was a teacher in the Bible Institute of Los Angeles.

The tune *Trust and Obey,* was composed by Towner, who studied music under George Frederick Root and others, and joined Dwight Lyman Moody as soloist and musical director in 1885, later becoming director of music at the Moody Bible Institute in Chicago from 1893 until his death in 1919. He received the honorary degree of Mus. D. from the university of Tennessee in 1900, and was on the faculty of the Los Angeles Bible Institute in his later years. He wrote over 100 gospel songs, one of them being the tune of No. 589, "Anywhere With Jesus."

583. DYING WITH JESUS, BY DEATH RECKONED MINE

Isaiah 27: 3

Major Daniel Webster Whittle (1840-1901) lost his right arm in the American Civil War, but later became a soldier of the cross, preaching in evangelistic campaigns with James McGranahan (see Nos. 495, 536, 568, 652) as song leader and soloist. At the Chicago World's Fair he was impressed by the remark made by his friend Henry Varley, "I do not like the hymn 'I Need Thee Every Hour' very well, because I need Him every moment." (See No. 258.) This prompted a line of thought which resulted in the writing of these words with the expression "moment by moment" occurring once in each stanza and three times in the refrain. Whittle brought the manuscript to Ira David Sankey (see Nos. 575, 586, 587, 673) saying that he would give his copyright of both words and music if he would print 500 copies for him for distribution to his friends. This constant care of the Lord for His people every moment is mentioned in Isaiah's parable of the vineyard, "I the Lord do keep it; I will water it every moment; lest any hurt it, I will keep it night and day." Isaiah 27: 3. Under his nom-de-plume of El Nathan, Whittle also wrote No. 652, "There Shall Be Showers of Blessing."

The tune *Moment by Moment* was composed by his daughter Mary, or May, Whittle, later the wife of Will R. Moody, son of Dwight Lyman Moody.

584. WILL YOUR ANCHOR HOLD?

Hebrews 6: 19

These words were written by Priscilla Jane Owens (1829-99), a teacher and a Sunday school teacher of Baltimore. The Christian's anchor is the hope he has in the promises of God: "Which hope we have as an anchor of the soul, both sure and steadfast." Hebrews 6: 19. She also wrote Nos. 637, "We Have Heard a Joyful Sound," and 655, "Give Me the Bible," and other hymns for children's services.

The tune *We Have an Anchor* was composed by William James Kirkpatrick (1838-1921), see appendix.

585. THE LORD'S OUR ROCK

Isaiah 25: 4

The words of this hymn were written by the Rev. Vernon J. Charlesworth (1839- ?), the headmaster of Charles Haddon Spurgeon's (see No. 40) orphanage. They recall various scriptures, namely: "For thou hast been . . . a refuge from the storm, a shadow from the heat," Isaiah 25: 4; "And a man shall be as an hiding place from the wind, and a covert from the tempest . . . as the shadow of a great rock in a weary land," Isaiah 32: 2; "The floods have lifted up, O Lord. . . . The Lord . . . is mightier than the noise of many waters." Psalm 93: 3, 4. Charlesworth also edited and altered No. 208, "Lord, I Hear of Showers of Blessing."

The tune *A Shelter in the Time of Storm* was composed by Franklin Edson Belden (1858-1945), see appendix.

586. O SAFE TO THE ROCK

Psalm 61: 2, 3

William Orcutt Cushing (1823-1903) of Massachusetts was requested by Ira David Sankey (1840-1908) to send something new to help him in his gospel work of singing sacred solos at evangelistic revival meetings. Cushing accepted this request as a call from God, and prayed that the Lord would give him something that would glorify Him. He later said that this hymn, written in 1876 in Moravia, New York, was the outgrowth of many tears, heart-conflicts and soul-yearnings, of which the world could know nothing. The history of many spiritual battles was behind it. Note the constant reference to Christ as the Rock, four times in three stanzas, and in the refrain also, and one reference to Him as the Refuge. The inspiration comes from the psalmist's own experience: "From the end of the earth will I cry unto Thee, when my heart is overwhelmed: lead me to the rock that is higher than I. For Thou hast been a shelter for me, and a strong tower from the enemy." Psalm 61: 2, 3. Cushing was a minister of the American Christian Church, who later joined the Methodists. He also wrote Nos. 418, "When He Cometh"; 550, "Beautiful Valley of Eden," and 587, "Under His Wings."

The tune *Hiding in Thee* was composed by Ira David Sankey (1840-1908), the well-known musical evangelist and song-leader associated with Dwight Lyman Moody (1837-99). Sankey, a member of the Methodist Episcopal Church from the age of fifteen years, also composed Nos. 575, 587, both unnamed, and 673, *The Ninety and Nine.*

587. UNDER HIS WINGS

Psalm 91: 4

William Orcutt Cushing (1823-1903) has developed the thought of Psalm 91: 4: "Under His wings shalt thou trust," in this hymn. Other expressions from the same psalm occur in this hymn, namely: "shall abide under the shadow of the Almighty" (verse 1); "He is my refuge" (verse 2); "There shall no evil befall thee" (verse 10); "Because He hath set His love upon me." Verse 14. Cushing was a minister of the American Christian Church, who later joined the Methodists. He also wrote Nos. 418, "When He Cometh"; 550, "Beautiful Valley of Eden," and 586, "O Safe to the Rock."

The tune, unnamed, was composed in or about 1899 by the singing evangelist Ira David Sankey (1840-1908), this being one of his last compositions. He joined the Methodist Episcopal Church as a lad of fifteen years of age, and became associated as solo singer with the evangelist Dwight Lyman Moody (1837-99) in many campaigns. He also composed Nos. 575, unnamed; 586, *Hiding in Thee,* and 673, *The Ninety and Nine.*

588. 'TIS SO SWEET TO TRUST IN JESUS

1 Peter 3: 5

Louisa M. R. Stead (1871-1917) was born in Dover, England, and emigrated to the United States in 1871. She wished to do missionary work overseas, but was rejected for China because of her poor health. Later she married, but after a few years, while on summer holidays, she witnessed her husband lose his life in a gallant attempt at rescuing a boy who was struggling against the undertow of a Long Island beach. She was left with her four-year-old girl without adequate financial support. On one occasion she was reduced to such impoverished circumstances that there was no food left in the house. Her prayer for the Lord to provide was answered miraculously when she found a basket of groceries and money the next morning. The experience led her to write the words of this hymn, the four stanzas of which speak of trust in each of their first lines, and this word occurs twice in the refrain. It is a word frequently found in the Scriptures, often in the Psalms, but the text listed as a title is 1 Peter 3: 5 because the writer of the hymn was a woman: "The holy women also, who trusted in God." The words are a response to the invitation of Psalm 62: 8, "Trust in Him at all times; ye people, pour out your heart before Him." Mrs. Stead later fulfilled her earlier desire, for she re-married in 1900, and with her husband, a Methodist missionary, served in Southern Rhodesia until her death at Umtali in 1917.

The tune, unnamed, was composed in 1882 by William James Kirkpatrick (1838-1921), see appendix.

589. ANYWHERE WITH JESUS

Proverbs 3: 23-26

These words were written in 1886 by Jessie H. Brown (1861-1921), who in 1896 married John E. Pounds of the Central Christian Church in Indianapolis. She was born in Hiram, a suburb of Cleveland, Ohio, and began writing for weeklies while a young girl of fifteen years. The editor later referred to some of her verse as being very suitable for use as hymns. There are two other stanzas, namely:—

2. Anywhere with Jesus I need fear no ill,
Though temptations gather round my pathway still;
He Himself was tempted that He might help me,
Anywhere with Jesus I may victor be.

4. Anywhere with Jesus over land and sea,
Telling souls in darkness of salvation free;
Ready as He summons me to go or stay,
Anywhere with Jesus when He points the way.

The hymn is an apt commentary on the following scripture: "Then shalt thou walk in thy way safely, and thy foot shall not stumble. When thou liest down, thou shalt not be afraid: yea, thou shalt lie down, and thy sleep shall be sweet. Be not afraid of sudden fear, neither of the desolation of the wicked, when it cometh. For the Lord shall be thy confidence, and shall keep thy foot from being taken." Proverbs 3: 23-26.

The tune, unnamed, was composed by Daniel Brink Towner (1850-1909) of Rome, Pennsylvania, a bass singer as a boy, and then a vocal teacher. He was soloist and musical director for Dwight Lyman Moody's evangelistic campaigns from 1885, and director of music at the Moody Bible Institute, Chicago, from 1893. He received the Mus. D. degree from the university of Tennessee in 1900, and later was on the faculty of the Los Angeles Bible Institute for ten years. He also wrote over 400 gospel songs, one of them being No. 582, *Trust and Obey*.

590. JUST WHEN I NEED HIM

Matthew 14: 27

William Charles Poole (1875-1949), a Methodist minister of Maryland, in this hymn written in 1908, depicts in the first three stanzas three different characteristics of the Lord Jesus. He is present, He is faithful, and He is powerful. There are of course countless other characteristics of the Lord, so the last stanza summarizes and describes Jesus as our all: "But Christ is all, and in all." Colossians 3: 11. The refrain emphasizes the sympathetic, encouraging nature of the Friend of friends, recalling the thought of two scriptures: "Now our Lord Jesus Christ Himself . . . comfort your hearts," 2 Thessalonians 2: 16, 17; and "Jesus spake unto them, saying, Be of good cheer," Matthew 14: 27. As a boy, Poole composed verse, and during his life as a preacher, wrote many religious articles, over 500 gospel hymns, and sacred poetry. He was prominent in the temperance cause and was superintendent of the Delaware Anti-Saloon League at one time.

The tune, unnamed, was composed in 1908 by Charles Homer Gabriel (1856-1932), who also composed Nos. 631, *Higher Ground,* and both words and music of 641, "When All My Labours and Trials Are O'er," to *Glory Song.*

591. I KNOW MY HEAVENLY FATHER

Psalm 103: 14

Sarepta Myrenda Irish (1838-1900) was born in Albion, Pennsylvania, and while still a girl spent many hours writing verses. She married James Henry, a school teacher, on March 7, 1861, and to this union were born twin boys who died in infancy in February, 1862, a son Alfred in the spring of 1865, a daughter Mary, a second son Arthur in 1867, and a third a few years later. But in May, 1871, the young husband passed away suddenly, leaving the young widow and her four young children penniless. Three months later her youngest child also passed away. Mrs. Henry began to write poems and magazine articles, and then to teach in the same job performed by her late husband, continuing to write poems (for which she received prizes), articles, and books, to support her growing family. Then from 1874 she felt a great burden to organize a temperance campaign against the sordid saloons and prevalent drunkenness that were so patent in her day. She became the national evangelist for the Woman's Christian Temperance Union, and spent twenty years travelling and lecturing across the United States of America. Illness sometimes manifested itself, causing her to cancel some of her engagements, and early in 1895 she collapsed from a heart attack and had to rest and resign herself to future years of invalidism. However, in August, 1896, she entered the Battle Creek Sanitarium for treatment from Dr. John Harvey Kellogg, who confirmed that she had an incurable heart condition from which she had suffered for eight years. The quiet atmosphere of this Sabbath-keeping institution impressed her, and contemplation of the Scriptures during this restful period convinced her, too, that she should forsake her lifelong Methodist connection and keep the Sabbath. Before the end of the year she was baptized and became a member of the Seventh-day Adventist Church, from then on becoming a regular contributor to the church paper, the *Review and Herald.* A short time afterwards, early in 1897, she was anointed, and special prayer was made for her healing. She was immediately cured, and Dr. Kellogg's subsequent medical examination revealed no cardiac weakness whatever. With this new lease of life, Mrs. Henry set about to disarm the great prejudice then existing against Seventh-day Adventists, and sought to divorce the Sunday legislation agitation from the Woman's Christian Temperance Union. Her active life was suddenly brought to a close by an attack of pneumonia, and she passed away on January 16, 1900. Further details of her inspiring leadership are to be found in the biography by her granddaughter, Margaret Rossiter White, entitled "Whirlwind of the Lord," published by the Review and Herald, 1953. The words of Mrs. Henry's hymn express her father's faith—he was a godly Methodist pioneer minister—and her own faith. She was willing to trust her heavenly Father in every little detail of life, in times of sorrow and bereavement, in times of physical sickness, and in the last hour when one must descend into the valley of the shadow. It is fittingly summarized in Psalm 103: 14: "For He knoweth our frame; He remembereth that we are dust."

The tune, *My Father Knows,* was composed by Edwin Othello Excell (1851-1921) of Ohio, one of the singers in the evangelistic campaigns of Dwight Lyman Moody. He was a Methodist song composer, and choir conductor for the evangelist Sam P. Jones, as well as being an ardent prohibitionist, like the authoress of the hymn. He also composed Nos. 566, *Let Him In,* and words and music of 638, "I Have a Song I Love to Sing."

592. LORD JESUS, I LONG TO BE PERFECTLY WHOLE

Psalm 51: 7

James Nicholson, an American Methodist minister, wrote these words under the title of "Holiness Desired." The inspiration for them comes from David's penitential prayer of Psalm 51, the refrain of the hymn using the latter part of verse 7, "Wash me, and I shall be whiter than snow." Two other expressions, "Create in me a clean heart," verse 10, and "The sacrifices of God are a broken spirit," verse 17, are found in stanzas 4 and 2 respectively. Nicholson also wrote No. 577, "The Lord Is My Light."

The tune *Whiter Than Snow,* was composed by William Gustavus Fischer (1835-1912) of Philadelphia, a member of the Methodist Episcopal Church, who at one time was the leader of the choir for the Moody-Sankey evangelistic meetings. He had been a bookbinder and piano dealer, and became a composer, writing more than 200 gospel songs. He also composed Nos. 518, 600, both unnamed, and 633, *The Rock That Is Higher.*

593. LOOK UPON JESUS, SINLESS IS HE

Isaiah 1: 18

Both words and music were written in 1899 by Franklin Edson Belden (1858-1945), see appendix, and the hymn first appeared in "Christ in Song," which he compiled and published. It is a simple, clear presentation of the doctrines of reconciliation, justification, sanctification, and glorification (see stanza 4), and is an enlargement of "Though your sins be as scarlet, they shall be as white as snow." Isaiah 1: 18.

594. I AM THINE, O LORD

Hebrews 10: 22

Miss Frances Jane Crosby (1820-1915), see appendix, composed this hymn of personal devotion in 1875, while on her knees, an attitude which is mentioned in stanza 3, "when I kneel in prayer." Its title is "Holiness Desired," and it is a song of consecration based on the text, "Let us draw near with a true heart." Hebrews 10: 22. It was written in Doane's home in Cincinnati, Ohio.

The tune *Draw Me Nearer,* was furnished by William Howard Doane (1832-1915), see appendix, another one of the numerous gospel hymns originating from those two dedicated Christians.

595. JESUS, KEEP ME NEAR THE CROSS

Galatians 6: 14

The tune *Near the Cross,* was composed first, in the year 1869, by William Howard Doane (1832-1915), see appendix. He played it over to his friend, Miss Frances Jane Crosby (1820-1915), see appendix, requesting her to compose some words for it. She tried, but had no inspiration whatever until she remembered that she had omitted her usual practice of praying before attempting to write a hymn. She knelt in prayer and then very quickly dictated these words to her assistant, also in the year 1869. They amplify the boast of the Apostle Paul, "But God forbid that I should glory, save in the cross of our Lord Jesus Christ." Galatians 6: 14.

596. TAKE THE WORLD, BUT GIVE ME JESUS

Ephesians 3: 18, 19

These words were written by Miss Frances Jane Crosby (1820-1915), see appendix, the theme being, "The world is crucified unto me, and I unto the world." Galatians 6: 14. The refrain is a partial paraphrase of Ephesian 3: 18, 19—"the breadth, and length, and depth, and height; and to know the love of Christ."

The tune was composed by John Robson Sweney (1837-99), see appendix.

597. I WOULD BE, DEAR SAVIOUR, WHOLLY THINE

Exodus 32: 29

Both words and music were composed in 1886 by Franklin Edson Belden (1858-1945), see appendix. The scripture on which the hymn is based is, "Consecrate yourselves today to the Lord . . . that He may bestow upon you a blessing," Exodus 32: 29, and it appears under the title "Wholly Thine" in "Hymns and Tunes," 1886.

598. O NOW I SEE THE CRIMSON WAVE

Zechariah 13: 1

Mrs. Phoebe Palmer (1807-74), a Methodist believer of Boston, Massachusetts, later of New York, was a friend of Charles Fitch (see No. 338), and was converted to the Millerite doctrine of the second advent by him. She wrote these words, using the figure of Zechariah 13: 1: "There shall be a fountain opened . . . for sin and for uncleanness," in which sinners may wash their robes and make "them white in the blood of the Lamb." Revelation 7: 14. She also wrote No. 549, "Watch, Ye Saints."

The tune *The Cleansing Wave* was composed by her namesake, Phoebe Palmer, who became Mrs. Joseph Fairchild Knapp (1839-1908). She was an organist in St. John's Methodist church in New York City, and also composed No. 608, an unnamed tune set to "Blessed Assurance, Jesus Is Mine!"

599. FATHER, WE COME TO THEE

Psalm 46: 1

The words were written in 1880 by Franklin Edson Belden (1858-1945), see appendix, and appear in "Hymns and Tunes," 1886. The verse which inspired them is Psalm 46: 1, "God is our refuge and strength, a very present help in trouble," although in "Christ in Song (Revised)," 1908, Belden placed the following text at the head of the hymn: "Behold, we come unto Thee; for Thou art the Lord our God." Jeremiah 3: 22.

The tune, also in the same hymnal, to these words, was composed in 1880 by W. J. Bostwick, who is commemorated by some caustic lines in the *Australasian Union Conference Record* of May 14, 1906, written by E. C. Chapman, an American, then the manager of the Avondale Press. The critical but doubtless factual poem is as follows:—

HOW BOSTWICK WENT TO RUIN

Among the force of workers
Who laboured in the cause,
Back early in the eighties,
An able man there was,
Who, skilled in art of printing,
And bright in other lines,
Arose to point of influence
While working on the *Signs*.
He wrote that piece of music
"Father, we come to Thee,"
He taught upon the Sabbath
And longed his Lord to see.
He was most neat and careful
About his work and dress,
Excelled in teaching music,
And strove to do his best.

But Bostwick used his pepper,
And meats well-seasoned too,
Until he got dyspepsia,
As many people do;
From day to day the sorrows
Of heartburn grew apace
Until his nose got rosy
While pallid was his face.
He went to find a tonic,
And took down not a few.
Till grog had gained a victim,
And ruined Bostwick, too;
For when he took to drinking,
And many glasses bought,
He begged, and stole, and borrowed,
And died a drunken sot.

Thus Bostwick's hopes have perished,
A downward course he ran,
Who might have been a power,
Revealing Christ to man.
We trust his fate may teach us
Our living to conform
To all the light that's given
Concerning health reform.
Let's circulate the journals
Which teach the better way,
And with *Good Health* established,
We'll work and watch and pray.

E. C. CHAPMAN.

600. I AM COMING TO THE CROSS

Philippians 3: 8

The words of this hymn were written in Brooklyn in 1870 by a Methodist Episcopal clergyman and evangelist, William McDonald (1820-1901) of Belmont, Maine, and published in 1871. He was prominent in the National Holiness movement and editor of the Boston Christian Witness, and produced these words because he needed a hymn "to aid seekers of heart purity while at the altar." They took only a few minutes to compose, and came into McDonald's mind as he was meditating in his study. They are based on Philippians 3: 8: "Yea doubtless, and I count all things but loss for the excellency of the knowledge of Christ Jesus." An omitted stanza, the fourth, is:—

4. In Thy promises I trust,
Now I feel the blood applied:
I am prostrate in the dust,
I with Christ am crucified.

The tune was composed by William Gustavus Fischer (1835-1912), a bookbinder of Philadelphia, piano dealer, and composer, and at one time choir leader for Moody and Sankey's evangelistic campaign. He also composed Nos. 518, unnamed; 592, *Whiter Than Snow,* and 633, *The Rock That Is Higher.*

601. BE SILENT, BE SILENT

Habakkuk 2: 20

The words were written by Frances Jane Crosby (1820-1915), see appendix, based on Habakkuk 2: 20: "But the Lord is in His holy temple: let all the earth keep silence before Him."

The tune *Tread Softly* was composed by William Howard Doane (1832-1915), see appendix, one of many composed by him for the blind authoress.

602. JESUS, THOU HAST PROMISED

Matthew 18: 20

Eden Reeder Latta (1839-?) of Indiana was a friend of William Augustine Ogden, see appendix, and wrote over 600 gospel hymns. This one is based on our Lord's promise recorded in Matthew 18: 20, "For where two or three are gathered together in My name, there am I in the midst of them." There is also a hint of the experience of the two disciples who walked to Emmaus on the resurrection day, to whom the Lord revealed Himself: "He took bread, and blessed it. . . . And their eyes were opened, and they knew Him." Luke 24: 30, 31. The last sentence of the hymn recalls

Proverbs 4: 18, "But the path of the just is as the shining light, that shineth more and more."

Dr. William Oscar Perkins (1831-1902), who composed the tune, also wrote No. 580, *Only Thee.* He was a composer, choir conductor, lecturer and writer on music, and music teacher. He received the degree of Mus. Doc. in 1879, and later taught and composed music in New York, 1882-86, in London, 1886-94, and finally in Boston, Massachusetts.

603. TAKE TIME TO BE HOLY

1 Peter 1: 16

A wealthy Englishman and son of a Sunderland shipowner, William Dunn Longstaff (1822-94), heard a sermon by a returned missionary from China, Dr. Griffith John, on the text, "Be ye holy; for I am holy" 1 Peter 1: 16, and as a result wrote the words of this hymn in 1882. The verse is a quotation from Leviticus 11: 44 where it appears as a description of a future event, rather than as an imperative command. Longstaff showed his poem to the Moody-Sankey evangelistic team when they visited the north of England, and Sankey passed it on to Stebbins.

Eight years later, George Coles Stebbins (1846-1945), see appendix, was leading the music in an evangelistic revival in India. The subject of holiness was mentioned, and Stebbins recalled Longstaff's poem, which he had kept among his papers. He searched for it and having found it, set the words to this tune, *Holiness,* in the spring of 1890.

604. LORD, FOR TOMORROW AND ITS NEEDS

Proverbs 27: 1

These words expressing the very practical truth of consistent Christian living "today," were written in 1877 over the signature S. M. X., a sister of Notre Dame. They were printed in 1880 with other verses for the students of the Liverpool, England, training college, and identified later as the work of Sybil F. Partridge (1856-1917). There were nine stanzas originally, each of four lines, those omitted being:—

6. Let me with Thee, my own true Life,
In spirit stay;
Stay Thou with me, my only Strength,
Just for today.

7. And if today my tide of life
Shall ebb away,
Let me Thy sacraments receive,
Sweet Lord, today.

8. Let me in purgatorial fires
Brief space delay:
Oh! let me, if today I die,
Go Home today.

The emphasis throughout the hymn on "today" reminds us against putting off our good deeds until tomorrow. A daily, day by day contact with God is His desire for us. The wise man said, "Boast not thyself of tomorrow; for thou knowest not what a day may bring forth." Proverbs 27: 1.

The tune *Vincent* was composed in 1893 for this hymn by Horatio Richmond Palmer (1834-1907), see appendix, and commemorates Bishop Vincent who was the founder of the Chautauqua literary and scientific movement (see Nos. 51, 218).

605. I NEED THEE, PRECIOUS JESUS

1 Peter 2: 7

These words were written in 1855 by an Anglican clergyman, Frederick Whitfield (1829-1904) of Threapwood, Shropshire, and later incumbent of Kirkby-Ravensworth, Yorkshire. There were six stanzas each of eight lines under the title "The Need of Jesus," and they were based on the text, "Unto you therefore which believe He is precious." 1 Peter 2: 7. Our selection is stanza 2, 3b, 5b, and 6, and the omitted lines are:—

3. I need Thee, precious Jesus!
I need a friend like Thee,
A friend to soothe and sympathize,
A friend to care for me:
. . .

4. I need Thee, precious Jesus!
For I am very blind;
A weak and foolish wanderer,
With a dark and evil mind:
I need the light of Jesus
To tread the thorny road,
To guide me safe to glory,
Where I shall see my God.

5. I need Thee, precious Jesus!
I need Thee, day by day,
To fill me with Thy fullness,
To lead me on my way.
. . .

together with the first stanza which the author wished to have retained:—

1. I need Thee, precious Jesus!
For I am full of sin;
My soul is dark and guilty,
My heart is dead within:
I need the cleansing fountain,
Where I can always flee:
The blood of Christ most precious,
The sinner's perfect plea.

Whitfield is also the author of No. 171, "There Is a Name I Love to Hear."

The tune *Rutherford* is so called because it is the one usually associated with Samuel Rutherford's hymn "The Sands of Time Are Sinking." Rutherford (1600-61) was a great scholar, preacher, and reformer, who was imprisoned for his religious principles and martyred for his faith. The composer of the tune was Chretien d'Urhan (1788-1845), a noted violinist, and it was written in 1834 for a French hymn. It was later arranged in its present form by Edward Francis Rimbault (1816-76) of Soho, London, who also composed No. 310, *Happy Day*. He was one of the founders of the Music Antiquarian Society in 1840, and took a great interest in editing old church music.

606. I COME TO THE GARDEN ALONE

John 20: 15-17

It has been objected that this hymn is a sentimental nature hymn with no reverence in it, but the circumstances of its writing show that it refers to the Garden of Gethsemane and the resurrection of Jesus. In March, 1912, C. Austin Miles (1868-1946) of Lakehurst, New Jersey, was sitting in the dark room where he kept his photographic equipment, and where incidentally his organ stayed. He took his Bible, which fell open at his favourite chapter, John 20, which he re-read. Then gazing at the light blue wall opposite him, he seemed to see the story enacted before him in his mind's eye. There were Peter and John and Mary Magdalene coming to the tomb, and then there was Mary Magdalene alone, talking with the "gardener," who revealed Himself as the risen Lord. Miles came to himself with muscles tense, gripping his Bible, and immediately under the inspiration of his vision, wrote the poem as quickly as he could. "The first day of the week cometh Mary Magdalene early, when it was yet dark. . . . She supposing Him to be the gardener, saith unto Him. . . . Jesus saith unto her, Mary . . . I ascend unto My Father . . . and to My God." John 20: 1, 15-17.

In the evening of the same day he composed the tune *In the Garden* for the words he had written earlier.

607. THERE'S SUNSHINE IN MY SOUL TODAY

2 Corinthians 4:6

Affliction does not always bring sorrow or repining, as is well demonstrated in this hymn written by Eliza Edmunds Hewitt (1851-1920) of Philadelphia, a personal friend of Fanny Crosby, and a Sunday-school worker for the Presbyterian Church. She suffered with spinal trouble for many years, then improved slowly, and while still convalescent, began writing, and composed more than two thousand hymns. Here she speaks of joyous things only, sunshine, music, springtime, and gladness, which come because of a satisfying Christian experience and the presence of Jesus in the life. The hymn is an excellent illustration of the text, "For God, who commanded the light to shine out of darkness, hath shined in our hearts, to give the light of the knowledge of the glory of God in the face of Jesus Christ." 2 Corinthians 4: 6. She also wrote No. 626, "I Am Thinking Today of That Beautiful Land."

The tune was composed by John Robson Sweney (1837-99), see appendix, who was a former chorister of Mrs. Hewitt's church.

608. BLESSED ASSURANCE, JESUS IS MINE!

1 John 3:2

The tune of this hymn was in use before the words, being composed in 1873 by Mrs. Joseph Fairchild Knapp (nee Phoebe Palmer) (1839-1908), a singer and organist of St. John's Methodist church, New York City. She visited Frances Jane Crosby (1820-1915), see appendix, and played the tune over to her. Finding that it pleased the blind authoress very much indeed, Mrs. Knapp asked her to write words for it. She played it the second time and noticed that Miss Crosby was kneeling in prayer. After the third playing, Fanny Crosby began dictating rapidly the words of the hymn we now have. The theme of the refrain re-echoes the words of the psalmist, "I will sing unto the Lord as long as I live: I will sing praise to my God while I have my being." Psalm 104: 33. The scripture on which it is based, however, is 1 John 3: 2, "Beloved, now are we the sons of God." Mrs. Knapp also composed No. 598, *The Cleansing Wave.*

609. THERE COMES TO MY HEART ONE SWEET STRAIN

John 14: 27

Peter Philip Bilhorn (1861-1936) of Mendota, Illinois, was compelled to leave school at the age of eight when his father died. Using his innate musical ability he became an entertainer and a soloist at the age of sixteen, and performed in restaurants, taverns, and beer halls. He was converted while still a young man at meetings where G. C. Stebbins (see appendix) was the song leader, and then devoted his musical talent to gospel work. He became a music publisher in Chicago, Illinois, and was, with his brother, the producer of the first baby folding organs. He was a great friend of Seventh-day Adventists, particularly of Dr. John Harvey Kellogg, and regularly every summer used to spend a holiday at his Battle Creek sanitarium. Later he spent much time at the Glendale Sanitarium, California. He studied music under George Frederick Root (see Nos. 93, 299, 418, 620, 690), and later became a singing evangelist, working especially for the Western cowboys. Bilhorn was in conversation with a friend who asked the composer to write a song to suit his voice. On inquiring as to what type of song, the reply came, "Oh, any sweet piece." Whereupon Bilhorn changed the spelling of the last word in his mind and composed the theme *Sweet Peace* that same evening. The following year, while travelling by train with Major D. W. Whittle (see Nos. 583, 652), Bilhorn wrote the words which suggest the following scriptures: "Peace I leave with you, My peace I give unto you," John 14: 27; "Having made peace through the blood of His cross, by Him to reconcile all things," Colossians 1: 20; "For other foundation can no man lay than that is laid, which is Jesus Christ," 1 Corinthians 3: 11; and "The peace of God, which passeth all understanding, shall keep your hearts and minds through Christ Jesus," Philippians 4: 7. Bilhorn also wrote both words and music of No. 528, "Oh, the Best Friend to Have Is Jesus."

610. FAR AWAY IN THE DEPTHS OF MY SPIRIT

John 14: 27

In August, 1889, W. D. Cornell, evangelist, poet, and fluent preacher, was present at the Methodist camp-meeting near West Bend, Wisconsin. Deeply devotional meetings had been conducted in the tent, and he remained seated there jotting down the thoughts that had been passing through his mind. Still lost in meditation, he got up and went out, unwittingly dropping the paper on which he had just written these words. An hour later, the song leader, W. George Cooper (1840-1927), came in, found the stanzas, made some alterations and completed the hymn. Then he sat down at the organ and composed the tune *Wonderful Peace* for it. The word "peace" occurs five times in the five stanzas, and three times in the refrain, and recalls the Saviour's promise to His disciples at a time of great stress: "Peace I leave with you, My peace I give unto you. . . . Let not your heart be troubled, neither let it be afraid." John 14: 27.

611. WHAT A FELLOWSHIP, WHAT A JOY DIVINE

Deuteronomy 33: 27

Professor Anthony Johnson Showalter (1858-1924) was a composer, publisher, and singing teacher of Rockingham County, Virginia. He studied under George Frederick Root (see Nos. 93, 299, 418, 620, 690) and others in Chicago, and also overseas in France, England, and Germany. One night in 1887 he returned to his temporary lodging-place in Hartselle, Alabama, to find two letters awaiting him from former pupils in South Carolina. Strangely enough, each letter stated that the writer had lost his wife on the same day. In his reply, Showalter quoted Deuteronomy 33: 27, the blessing of Moses to the children of Israel: "The eternal God is thy refuge, and underneath are the everlasting arms." Then thinking of others who might also be troubled, he wrote the words of the refrain, and sent them to the prolific hymn-writer Elisha Albright Hoffman (1839-1929), in Lebanon, Pennsylvania. Hoffman, a minister of the Evangelical Association, wrote the three stanzas and returned them to Showalter, who then set stanzas and refrain to the tune *Leaning on the Everlasting Arms.* Hoffman came from a musical family, who used to spend their morning worship in singing hymns. He also wrote words and music of No. 644, "Christ Has for Sin Atonement Made," to the tune *What a Wonderful Saviour.*

612. THERE IS SUNLIGHT ON THE HILLTOP

Psalm 9: 1

This hymn, entitled "The Blessed Hope," was written by Mrs. M. T. Haughey, and is really a short poem contrasting the light that shines on hill, sea, and meadow, with the greater light that shines in her heart, much after the manner of Paul's analogy in 2

Corinthians 4: 6: "For God, who commanded the light to shine out of darkness, hath shined in our hearts, to give the light of the knowledge of the glory of God in the face of Jesus Christ." Like David, Mrs. Haughey is fully committed: "I will praise thee, O Lord, with my whole heart." Psalm 9: 1. Another illustration is taken from Isaiah 52: 2, "Shake thyself from the dust . . . O captive daughter," and this figure is continued in Isaiah 61: 10, "I will greatly rejoice in the Lord, my soul shall be joyful in my God; for He hath clothed me with the garments of salvation, He hath covered me with the robe of righteousness." Complete dedication mentioned in the third stanza recalls Matthew 22: 37, "Thou shalt love the Lord thy God with all thy heart, and with all thy soul, and with all thy mind." The lamp of love, mentioned in the third stanza, reminds of Matthew 5: 16, "Let your light so shine before men, that they may . . . glorify your Father which is in heaven." The last halves of the second and third stanzas are identical, and describe the future home of glory: "For the glory of God did lighten it, and the Lamb is the light thereof." Revelation 21: 23. Both words and music were first published by permission of John Quincey Adams Haughey.

613. O JESUS, MY REDEEMER

Psalm 118: 14

These words were written by Franklin Edson Belden (1858-1945), see appendix, and appear in "Hymns and Tunes," 1886. They are based on Psalm 118: 14, "The Lord is my strength and song, and is become my salvation." The last stanza catches some of the thought of the succeeding verse, "The voice of rejoicing and salvation is in the tabernacles of the righteous." Verse 15.

The tune *My Song,* was composed by D. S. Hakes, who also wrote Nos. 66, 493, 500, *Standard;* 520 and 629, all of them except No. 520 being to words by Belden. Hakes's tunes are mostly unnamed.

614. MY FATHER IS RICH IN HOUSES AND LANDS

Romans 8: 17

The theme of this hymn by Hattie Eugenia Peck Buel (1834-1910) of Cazenovia, New York, is that of a poor orphan who has been adopted into a rich family. Even though the riches do not yet appear, the rich Son of the family voluntarily endured the humiliating experience of extreme poverty in order to identify Himself with His adopted brethren. The refrain uses the thought of Romans 8: 17, "And if children, then heirs; heirs of God, and joint-heirs with Christ," who after all, is "King of kings, and Lord of lords," Revelation 19: 16. In 1878, Mrs. Buel had attended church at Thousand Island Park, New York, and while walking home meditated on the joy of being a child of a king. She sat down and wrote these words, not intending them as a hymn, and sent them to the *Northern Christian Advocate,* Syracuse, as a poem.

They were seen in this magazine by the Rev. John B. Sumner, and he composed the tune *A Child of the King* in the autumn of 1878 without Mrs. Buel's knowledge. A few months later she heard the hymn sung by a soloist in the Manlins Methodist church, New York.

615. SAFE IN THE ARMS OF JESUS

Deuteronomy 33: 27

This is another hymn by the partnership of Frances Jane Crosby (1820-1915) for the words, and William Howard Doane (1832-1915) for the music. For both, see appendix. In this case, the tune was composed first and proved to be a very popular melody. Doane wrote it on April 30, 1868, on a train journey while on a business trip, and later in 1870 requested Fanny Crosby to write a suitable hymn to the tune, as he wished to use it at a Sunday school convention in Ohio. He suggested the words of the first line to be "Safe in the arms of Jesus." Miss Crosby said that they were very appropriate, being spoken by the music, and after half an hour in an adjoining room, she returned with the complete hymn. They are a Christian enlargement of the Old Testament text: "Underneath are the everlasting arms," Deuteronomy 33: 27, and also of Isaiah 40: 11: "He shall gather the lambs with His arm, and carry them in His bosom."

Another story, not quite in harmony with the foregoing, says that on the previous day Fanny Crosby heard some drunken brawlers arguing in the street. The altercation led inevitably to fighting, and frightened a little child, who clung to her mother. Taking her up, the mother comforted her little girl by telling her she was safe in mother's arms. The incident thus gave a setting for the authoress to write on the parallel topic of "Safe in the arms of Jesus," One whose love is greater than a mother's. This hymn was Fanny Crosby's favourite of her more than 8,000 hymns. It will be noticed that the music of the refrain is identical with the music for the first half of the hymn.

616. THE HOME WHERE CHANGES NEVER COME

1 Corinthians 10: 10

W. H. Bellamy has written of the sorrows and trials of earth, reminding us that Christ suffered them also, and that therefore He will not forget us. Our part is to have patience and not to complain. A fitting summary of his poetic counsel could be found in 1 Corinthians 10: 10: "Neither murmur ye, as some of them also murmured." Other scriptures mentioned are: "There shall be no more . . . sorrow, nor . . . pain," Revelation 21: 4; "And the soldiers platted a crown of thorns, and put it on His head," John 19: 2; "But if we hope for that we see not, then do we with patience wait for it," Romans 8: 25; and "Let us labour therefore to enter into that rest, lest any man fall after the same example of unbelief," Hebrews 4: 11.

The tune *Wait, and Murmur Not,* was composed by William James Kirkpatrick (1838-1921), see appendix.

617. LORD, I CARE NOT FOR RICHES

Luke 10: 20

These words were written by Mrs. Mary Ann Kidder, née Pepper (1820-1905), a Baptist believer of Boston, Massachusetts, who spent more than half her life in New York City, and who wrote about 1,000 hymns. These words are based on Luke 10: 20: "Rejoice, because your names are written in heaven," a theme which is emphasized in the refrain. The promise in Isaiah 1: 18 is quoted almost word for word in the second stanza: "Though your sins be as scarlet, they shall be as white as snow." In one hymnal, the last line of the third stanza reads, "Yes, my name's written there," with a similar alteration in the last two refrains.

The tune *Is My Name Written There?* was composed at Burr Oak, Michigan, in July, 1876, by Frank Marion Davis (1839-97) of Marcellus, New York, who also composed No. 501, *Sleeping On Guard.* He was co-editor in 1881 with James Edson White (see Nos. 230, 235) of the 160-page "Songs for Class and School," to which he contributed twenty-eight tunes and two hymns. Though coming from a musical family, he alone followed this profession, and became a piano teacher, solo singer, choir leader, and publisher of songs for Sunday school and on temperance.

618. SITTING AT THE FEET OF JESUS

Luke 10: 39

This hymn is based on the incident recorded in Luke 10: 38-42, which describes the visit of Jesus to the home in Bethany where lived His friends Lazarus, Mary and Martha. Martha, whose chief interest was the comfort of her Guest, felt that her sister Mary was not taking her share of the work, and tried to enlist the Master's support in commanding Mary to help. Mary had lived a very chequered life up to this, and had been lifted from the depths of sin through forgiveness. She was consequently much more interested in spiritual than in material things, and "sat at Jesus' feet, and heard His word." Luke 10: 39. The gospel writer Luke also records in great detail Mary's anointing of Jesus, and gives inspiration for the expression "weep and pray" in the second stanza: "She hath washed My feet with tears," Luke 7: 44; and also for the words, "I lay my sins and sorrows" as Mary did: "Her sins, which are many, are forgiven," Luke 7: 47. The experience of Mary Magdalene is here used in this hymn as a type of the sincere, repentant Christian, who, by sitting as she did at the feet of the Master, will gain grace and righteousness from the Saviour.

The tune *Humility* is virtually only a four-line piece of music, for lines 3 and 4 repeat the first two lines, and the last two lines imitate lines 5 and 6, each with the exception of the final chord.

619. WATCHMAN, BLOW THE GOSPEL TRUMPET

Ezekiel 33: 2-5

These words were written by Dr. H. L. Gilmour, who flourished about 1894, and emphasize the responsibility of every Christian in general, and every minister in particular. Ezekiel's figure of a watchman is borrowed: "If the people of the land take a man of their coasts, and set him for their watchman: If when he seeth the sword come upon the land, he blow the trumpet, and warn the people . . . he that taketh warning shall deliver his soul." Ezekiel 33: 2, 3, 5. Other scriptures used are: "The Lord hath anointed me to preach good tidings . . . to proclaim liberty to the captives," Isaiah 61: 1; "Come; for all things are now ready," Luke 14: 17; "Go out into the highways and hedges," Luke 14: 23; and "Come unto Me, all ye that labour and are heavy laden, and I will give you rest," Matthew 11: 28.

The tune, unnamed, was composed by William James Kirkpatrick (1838-1921), see appendix.

620. O WHERE ARE THE REAPERS?

Joel 3: 13

These words were written by the American Eben Eugene Rexford (1848-1916), a flower-culture specialist who started writing for the press at the early age of fourteen. They are based on the following scriptures: "Put ye in the sickle, for the harvest is ripe,"

Joel 3: 13; "In the time of harvest I will say to the reapers, Gather ye together first the tares . . . but gather the wheat into my barn," Matthew 13: 30; "Go ye therefore into the highways, and as many as ye shall find, bid to the marriage," Matthew 22: 9; and "The harvest truly is plenteous, but the labourers are few; pray ye therefore the Lord of the harvest," Matthew 9: 37, 38. Rexford first wrote, "O we are the reapers," which was acceptable to G. F. Root and I. D. Sankey, but D. L. Moody asked for the present revision to "O where are" so as to avoid the implication that there were no other soul-winners except the Moody-Sankey team. Rexford became the editor of a farm journal in Wisconsin, and used his poetic talent in writing verse to fill empty spaces in the journal. He also wrote No. 658, "They Brought Their Gifts to Jesus," but is probably best remembered for his sentimental song, "Silver Threads Among the Gold."

The tune, unnamed, was composed by George Frederick Root (1820-95), an American choir conductor, music teacher, and music publisher, who associated with Lowell Mason (see appendix) in the Boston Academy of Music. He also composed Nos. 93 and 299, *Varina;* 418, *Jewels,* and 690, *Quam Dilecta.*

621. SOWING IN THE MORNING

Psalm 126: 6

These words were written by Knowles Shaw (1834-78) of Venice, Ohio, who while still an infant moved with his parents to Indiana. At the age of twelve years, his father died and bequeathed to him his violin. Soon he was earning more by playing at dances and concerts than he was by working on the farm. Consequently he became an entertainer, singer and musician for a living. He dedicated his talent to the Lord, and conducted revival meetings from 1859 onwards and became a singing evangelist and itinerant preacher. He lost his life—the only fatality—in a railway accident near McKinney, after returning to Columbus, Mississippi, from an evangelistic mission in Dallas, Texas. The hymn is based on the following scriptures: "In the morning sow thy seed, and in the evening withhold not thine hand," Ecclesiastes 11: 6; "He that observeth the wind shall not sow; and he that regardeth the clouds shall not reap," Ecclesiastes 11: 4; "He that goeth forth and weepeth, bearing precious seed, shall doubtless come again with rejoicing, bringing his sheaves with him," Psalm 126: 6; and "The harvest is the end of the world; and the reapers are the angels." Matthew 13: 39.

The tune, *Bringing in the Sheaves,* was composed by George A. Minor, who followed the fashion current in his day of repeating the words of the theme several times and then adding the last line of the stanza to make a refrain.

622. ONE MORE DAY'S WORK

John 9: 4

Miss Anna Bartlett Warner (1820-1915) was a deeply religious woman, who wrote several novels and stories, using the pen-name Amy Lothrop. She used to compose a fresh hymn every month for use in her Sunday school in West Point, New York, this hymn written in 1869 being one of them, and No. 29, "We Would See Jesus," being another. While the opening lines and the refrain strike a note of gloom, the hymn is really a happy one, emphasizing the pleasure of service for Christ, and the desire to enter more fully into working for Him. An apt scripture summary is found in our Lord's own words, "I must work the works of Him that sent Me, while it is day." John 9: 4.

The tune was composed by Robert Lowry (1826-99), see appendix.

623. RESCUE THE PERISHING

Luke 14: 23

In the summer of 1869 Frances Jane Crosby (1820-1915), see appendix, visited a mission in one of the worst slum districts of the Bowery in New York City. Here she heard of the needs of the perishing souls who were dying without hope and without God in the world. Her sympathies were aroused for these neglected people, and as a result these words were written. The hymn emphasizes the command, "Go out into the highways and hedges, and compel them to come in." Luke 14: 23. She had appealed to any young man who had turned away from his mother's teaching to speak to her after the service. One did, and while riding home, these lines formed in her mind and she dictated them to a friend before retiring that night. The next morning she sent the stanzas to her friend William Howard Doane (1832-1915), see appendix, in Cincinnati. He had asked for a hymn on this topic, so he then composed this tune, which is sometimes called *Rescue,* because of the associated words.

624. THROW OUT THE LIFE LINE

Jude 23

In 1886 the Rev. Edward S. Ufford (1851-1930) was living on the Massachusetts coast at Westwood, near Boston. One day while walking along the beach at low tide he came across the wreck of a ship held fast in the sand. He tried to imagine what had happened before the ship had been dashed to pieces in the gale, and visualized a sinking sailor clinging to a spar and drifting out of reach. The spiritual lesson inspired him to write these four stanzas in fifteen minutes, and also to compose a melody for them. The struggling seaman depicted in the hymn reminds one of David's illustration of his own metaphorical sinking, "Save me, O God; for the waters are come in unto my soul. I sink in deep mire, where there is no standing: I am come into deep waters, where the floods overflow me." Psalm 69: 1, 2. The real import of the words is, however, better found in a verse which speaks of a different environment, "And others save with fear, pulling them out of the fire." Jude 23.

In 1889, George Coles Stebbins (1846-1945), see appendix, obtained the hymn, and made a few changes in the music to bring it to its present form.

625. HARK! 'TIS THE SHEPHERD'S VOICE I HEAR

John 10:16

The words of this hymn were written by Alexcenah Thomas, and tell the story of Jesus the Shepherd seeking the lost sheep, and of the obligation on these who are found to follow His example and to search for others who are likewise lost. Scriptures used are: "I am the Good Shepherd," John 10: 11; "If he lose one of them, doth not [he] leave the ninety and nine in the wilderness, and go after that which is lost?" Luke 15: 4; "And other sheep I have, which are not of this fold: them also I must bring, and they shall hear My voice," John 10: 16; "My sheep wandered through all the mountains, and upon every high hill," Ezekiel 34: 6; and "Go ye into all the world, and preach," Mark 16: 15.

The tune *Bring Them In* was composed by William Augustine Ogden (1841-97), see appendix.

626. I AM THINKING TODAY OF THAT BEAUTIFUL LAND

Daniel 12:3

Mrs. Eliza Edmunds Hewitt (1851-1920), a Presbyterian Sunday school worker of Philadelphia, suffered from a spinal disease which constantly gave her pain. Out of her affliction she wrote many hymns, but kept no record of their origin. This one seems to be based on Daniel 12: 3: "They that turn many to righteousness as the stars for ever and ever," for there is no Bible text speaking of stars in a crown except Revelation 12: 1, which does not refer to individual soul-winners at all. Each stanza reiterates the theme, that of leading someone to the eternal kingdom, using in the first stanza the metaphor "stars in my crown," in the next stanza the expression "winner of souls," and in the last stanza "living gems."

Mrs. Hewitt also wrote No. 607, "There Is Sunshine in My Soul Today."

Her poems attracted the attention of John Robson Sweney (1837-99), see appendix, who was a chorister in her church, and both of these hymns were set to tunes of his composition, this one to *Will There Be Any Stars?*

627. HE THAT GOETH FORTH

Psalm 126: 6

In 1836, Thomas Hastings (1784-1872), see appendix, wrote two stanzas, each of eight lines, of this hymn which urges to mission service. Its opening is almost identical with the first sentence of Psalm 126: 6, "He that goeth forth and weepeth, bearing precious seed, shall doubtless come again with rejoicing, bringing his sheaves with him." The words of Jesus at Samaria are also paraphrased: "Lift up your eyes, and look on the fields; for they are white already to harvest." John 4: 35.

The tune *Stockwell,* also used for No. 207, "Let Thy Spirit, Blessed Saviour," was composed in 1847 by Darius Eliot Jones (1815-81) of New York. He edited a hymn-book, was a conductor of church music, and later studied for the Congregational ministry, being ordained in 1858.

628. BRIGHTLY BEAMS OUR FATHER'S MERCY

Matthew 5: 14, 16

One wild stormy night with no stars to be seen and the waves running mountains high, a steamer on Lake Erie was endeavouring to put into the harbour of Cleveland, Ohio. There was a tall lighthouse to guide the ships, and in addition a number of smaller lights just above sea-level to act as an extra safeguard and to show the main channel. On this particular night these lower lights were extinguished, and the ship crashed onto the rocks, losing nearly everyone on board. Dwight Lyman Moody, the renowned evangelist, related this story in 1874 and drew the spiritual lesson, and Philipp Bliss (1838-76), see appendix, who was in the congregation, composed both words and the accompanying tune, *Lower Lights.* Moody's words were, "Brethren, the Master will take care of the great lighthouse; let the lower lights be burning." So while Jesus claimed Himself, "saying, I am the light of the world," John 8: 12, it is not a contradiction to read that He required His followers to be lesser lights reflecting His own glory. "Ye are the light of the world. . . . Let your light so shine before men, that they may see your good works, and glorify your Father which is in heaven." Matthew 5: 14, 16.

629. IF ANY LITTLE WORD OF MINE

Galatians 6: 2

These words were arranged in 1908 by Franklin Edson Belden (1858-1945), see appendix, and appear in "Christ in Song" under the heading, "Bear ye one another's burdens." Galatians 6: 2. The original author was a Manchester jeweller, Robert Walmsley (1831-1905), a Congregational Sunday school worker. The words were published in his "Sacred Songs for Children of All Ages," 1900, which consisted of forty-four Whit week festival hymns. To the present twelve lines plus refrain there is one other stanza, namely:—

3. Then many a burden shall be eased
Because I help to bear it,
And many a care be lighter made
Because I try to share it;
And many a grief shall fly away
When my bright song shall bid it;
And Christ, the Lord of love, shall say,
" 'Twas unto Me ye did it!"

The tune was composed by D. S. Hakes, who also wrote Nos. 66, 493, 500, *Standard;* 520 and 613, *My Song,* all of them except No. 520 being tunes to Belden's words.

630. SOME DAY THE SILVER CORD WILL BREAK

Ephesians 2: 8

At a Methodist camp-meeting at Poughkeepsie in 1891, Dr. Howard Crosby (not related to Fanny Crosby) spoke on the subject of grace, and described the glowing colours and the glory of the changing sunset. However, Frances Jane Crosby (1820-1915), see appendix, who was virtually blind from birth, was unable to share his vision and said, "I cannot see the sunset, but some day I shall see my Saviour face to face." Later that week Dr. Crosby died suddenly, and this event caused Fanny Crosby to wonder what her first impression of heaven would be. She realized then that her first vision would be her Saviour's face. A few days later, L. H. Biglow asked her to write a hymn on the subject of the prayer-meeting, and after retiring for an hour, and re-assembling her thoughts of the past few days, she returned with four stanzas which she gave to Mr. Biglow, who put them away and evidently forgot all about them. The fourth stanza was:—

4. Some day; till then I'll watch and wait,
My lamp all trimmed and burning bright,
That when my Saviour opes the gate,
My soul to Him may take its flight.

Fanny Crosby, in speaking of death, had said, "The same grace that teaches us how to live, will teach us how to die." Her hymn is based on the statement, "For by grace are ye saved through faith; and that not of yourselves: it is the gift of God." Ephesians 2: 8. The mention of the silver cord in the opening line is a reference to Solomon's euphemistic description of death in Ecclesiastes 12: 6, 7, "Or ever the silver cord be loosed, or the golden bowl be broken. . . . Then shall the dust return to the earth as it was." The hymn was made public in 1893 at a summer convention in Northfield, Massachusetts, when Miss Crosby recited it after giving a short address at Ira David Sankey's (see Nos. 575, 586, 587, 673) request.

Four or five weeks later he cut the poem out of a newspaper, gave it to George Coles Stebbins (1846-1945), see appendix, who composed and sang the music, *Saved by Grace,* for it at Newport, Rhode Island, at one of Moody's evangelistic meetings.

631. I'M PRESSING ON THE UPWARD WAY

Philippians 3: 14

The words were written by Johnson Oatman, Jr. (1856-1930), a Methodist minister of Lumberton, New Jersey, and were based on the Apostle Paul's ideal: "I press toward the mark for the prize of the high calling of God in Christ Jesus." Philippians 3: 14. The author draws the picture of a climber who seeks to leave the lowlands of this world and scale the peaks which give a vision of the glory land. This hymn and No. 275, "Deeper Yet," are two of the 5,000 hymns written by Oatman, whose songs preached the gospel message far more widely and effectively than his pulpit sermons.

The tune *Higher Ground* was composed by Charles Homer Gabriel (1856-1932), who also composed No. 590, unnamed, and both words and music of No. 641, "When All My Labours and Trials Are O'er," to the tune, *Glory Song.*

632. CLOSER TO THEE, MY FATHER, DRAW ME

Jeremiah 30: 21

These words by Mrs. E. W. Chapman, a writer of sacred poetry, describe the compelling power of the Trinity, for the stanzas speak in turn of Father, Saviour or Son, and Spirit. They recall the verses of Hosea 11: 4; "I drew them with cords of a man, with bands of love," and Jeremiah 31: 3: "I have loved thee with an everlasting love: therefore with lovingkindness have I drawn thee," and also "I will cause him to draw near, and he shall approach unto Me," Jeremiah 30: 21.

The tune was composed by John Harrison Tenney (1840- ?) of Rowley, Massachusetts, who was a teacher in Battle Creek College, Michigan, in its early days. In its structure, note that the melody of line 3 imitates that of line 1, but is written one semitone lower. Tenney composed music to two other of Mrs. Chapman's poems, "Look to the Lighthouse" and "Trust in Jesus." He was a deacon in the Congregational church at Linebrook, Massachusetts, became a Seventh-day Adventist, but left this church with J. H. Kellogg.

Because of delicate health, he developed an early interest in music in order to compensate for his inability to take part in games. In association with others he took part in editing thirty song books.

633. O SOMETIMES THE SHADOWS ARE DEEP

Psalm 61: 2

Erastus Johnson (1826-1909) of Maine, was a teacher, farmer, and man of many parts, with a strong religious bias throughout his long life. He was present at the Y.M.C.A. convention in Carlisle, Pennsylvania, in 1873, at which was announced the failure of several banks. The resulting gloom among the delegates who had lost considerable sums of money, was the atmosphere which stimulated Johnson to write these words. He took part of a verse from the Psalms and applied it fittingly to a Christian's varied experience: "From the end of the earth will I cry unto Thee, when my heart is overwhelmed: lead me to the Rock that is higher than I." Psalm 61: 2. The author has expanded the expression "when my heart is overwhelmed," to include sorrow and weariness; and uses figures familiar to a pilgrim, a rough path, a long day, a steep climb. Then the refrain quotes the last part of the verse, where the Lord is likened to a strong rock that provides protection and rest, even though financial disaster and its accompanying evils threaten.

The tune *The Rock That Is Higher* was composed by William Gustavus Fischer (1835-1912), a member of the Methodist Episcopal church, who also composed Nos. 518, 592, *Whiter Than Snow,* and 600, two of these being unnamed tunes. He was a bookbinder of Philadelphia, piano dealer, and composer of more than 200 gospel songs. At one time he was choir leader for Moody and Sankey in their evangelistic campaign.

634. ONE THING I OF THE LORD DESIRE

Psalm 51: 10

These words were written in 1887 by Walter Chalmers Smith (1824-1908) while a minister of the Free Church of Scotland in Edinburgh. He was later moderator of the Free Church. They are based on King David's plea: "Create in me a clean heart, O God." Psalm 51: 10. The refrain paraphrases the words of verse 2 of the psalm, "Wash me throughly from mine iniquity."

635. REDEEMED! HOW I LOVE TO PROCLAIM IT!

Lamentations 3: 58

The words were written by Frances Jane Crosby (1820-1915), see appendix, and based on Lamentations 3: 58, "O Lord, Thou hast pleaded the causes of my soul; Thou hast redeemed my life." There are many other scriptures quoted, however, for example: "Thou . . . hast redeemed us to God by Thy blood," Revelation 5: 9; "My presence shall go with thee," Exodus 33: 14; "And my tongue shall speak of Thy righteousness and of Thy praise all the day long," Psalm 35: 28; "Thine eyes shall see the King in His beauty," Isaiah 33: 17; "God my maker, who giveth songs in the night," Job 35: 10; and "The Spirits of just men made perfect," Hebrews 12: 23.

The tune was composed in 1882 by William James Kirkpatrick (1838-1921), see appendix.

636. O WHO IS THIS THAT COMETH?

Isaiah 63: 1-5

These words were written by the Rev. R. W. Todd, and are a paraphrase of the prophet Isaiah's picture of Christ dying for our salvation alone. "Who is this that cometh from Edom, with dyed garments from Bozrah? this that is glorious in His apparel, travelling in the greatness of His strength? I that speak in righteousness, mighty to save. Wherefore art Thou red in thine apparel, and Thy garments like him that treadeth in the winefat? I have trodden the winepress alone; and of the people there was none with Me . . . the year of My redeemed is come . . . therefore Mine own arm brought salvation unto Me." Isaiah 63: 1-5.

637. WE HAVE HEARD A JOYFUL SOUND

Psalm 96: 2

These words were written by Miss Priscilla Jane Owens (1829-99), a public school teacher, especially for the anniversary of her Sunday school in Baltimore. One slight change has been made from the original in stanza 2, line 6, which was identical with the same line in the fourth stanza, but now reads, "Echo back, ye ocean caves." The hymn is based on Psalm 96: 2: "Show forth His salvation from day to day." Miss Owens also wrote Nos. 584, "Will Your Anchor Hold?" and 655, "Give Me the Bible."

The tune *Jesus Saves,* was composed in 1882 by William James Kirkpatrick (1838-1921), see appendix.

638. I HAVE A SONG I LOVE TO SING

Psalm 130: 7

Edwin Othello Excell (1851-1921) of Stark County, Ohio, was a bricklayer's apprentice, who at the age of twenty-two became a Sunday school worker, where he discovered and developed a talent for writing hymns for children. He was also a sweet and powerful singer, who was invited by the Georgia evangelist, Sam P. Jones, who heard him singing at his work, to be his choir conductor. He associated with Dwight Lyman Moody and with Gipsy Smith in some of their evangelistic campaigns, and edited forty different hymn-books. His words for this hymn, written in 1884, echo the thought of Psalm 130: 7: "With Him is plenteous redemption."

Excell also composed the tune for these words, and also Nos. 566, *Let Him In,* and 591, *My Father Knows.*

639. THE HOMELAND!

Revelation 21: 1, 4

These words were written in 1855 by the Rev. Hugh Reginald Haweis (1838-1901), although they have also been attributed to William Lindsay Alexander. Haweis was an author and a skilled violinist, and for his last thirty-five years minister of St. James, Marylebone. The hymn is based on the description of the new earth given in Revelation 21: 1, 4: "I saw a new heaven and a new earth. . . . And God shall wipe away all tears from their eyes; and there shall be no more death, neither sorrow, nor crying, neither shall there be any more pain."

The tune was composed in 1903 by George Coles Stebbins (1846-1945), see appendix.

640. COME, WE THAT LOVE THE LORD

1 Peter 1: 8

Isaac Watts (1674-1748), see appendix, wrote a ten-stanza hymn in 1707 entitled "Heavenly Joy on Earth," of which we have here stanzas 1, 3, 9, and 10. The omitted stanzas are:—

2. The sorrows of the mind,
Be banished from this place,
Religion never was designed
To make our pleasures less.

4. The God that rules on high
And thunders when He please,
That rides upon the stormy sky,
And manages the seas.

5. This awful God is ours,
Our Father, and our love:
He shall send down His heavenly powers
To carry us above.

6. There shall we see His face,
And never, never sin;
There, from the rivers of His grace,
Drink endless pleasures in.

7. Yes, and before we rise
To that immortal state,
The thoughts of such amazing bliss
Should constant joy create.

8. Children of grace have found
Glory begun below:
Celestial fruit on earthly ground
From faith and hope may grow.

The theme and the title are an amplification of the Apostle Peter's similar thought: "Though now ye see Him not, yet believing, ye rejoice with joy unspeakable and full of glory." 1 Peter 1: 8.

The tune *Marching to Zion,* was composed in 1867 by Robert Lowry (1826-99), see appendix, who added the words of the refrain to Watts's lines.

641. WHEN ALL MY LABOURS AND TRIALS ARE O'ER

1 Peter 5: 1

Both words and music were written in 1900 by Charles Homer Gabriel (1856-1932) in the space of one single evening, and were inspired by the slogan "Glory," which Ed Card, the superintendent of the Sunshine Rescue Mission in St. Louis, Missouri, used frequently during the meetings. He used the word also in his prayers, earnestly and convincingly, and would invariably end with the clause, "And that will be glory for me." His reverent use of this expression earned him the nickname of "Old Glory Face," a term which was used endearingly. The future bliss of the saints is likewise described by the apostle Peter, who looked forward to being "also a partaker of the glory that shall be revealed." 1 Peter 5: 1.

He also composed Nos. 590, an unnamed tune, and 631, *Higher Ground.*

642. JUST OVER THE MOUNTAINS

Revelation 21

Charles P. Whitford (1843-1931) of Vermont, was the son of prominent Millerites who became First-day Adventists. He joined that church in 1866, but after working at the Battle Creek Health Reform Institute, joined the Seventh-day Adventists in 1867. He was a singing evangelist in many tent efforts and also a Bible worker, and after ill-health forced him into premature retirement in Florida, wrote tracts and articles for the press. He edited "Songs for Service in Church and Home" in 1905, which contains eighteen poems or arrangements and four melodies of his own composition. The words of this hymn are a picture of the New Jerusalem as it appears to a pilgrim nearing the end of his journey. The land promised is an antitype of God's literal promise to the Israelites emerging from Egypt: "To the land which the Lord will give you, according as He hath promised." Exodus 12: 25. The "homeland of eternal rest" is a reminder of Hebrews 9: 15: "They which are called might receive the promise of eternal inheritance," a land and "a city which hath foundations, whose builder and maker is God." Hebrews 11: 10. The second stanza draws on the vision given to John of the New Jerusalem recorded in Revelation 21: "And I John saw the holy city, New Jerusalem" (verse 2); "And he carried me away in the spirit to a great and high mountain, and showed me that great city, the holy Jerusalem" (verse 10); "And the street of the city was pure gold" (verse 21); "And the building of the wall of it was of jasper" (verse 18). This same chapter furnishes the idea of the refrain: "And her light was like unto a stone most precious" (verse 11); "And the gates of it shall not be shut at all by day" (verse 25).

The tune, *We Are Nearing Home,* was composed by John Robson Sweney (1837-99), see appendix.

643. THE NAME OF JESUS IS SO SWEET

Hebrews 13: 8

These words by the Rev. W. C. Martin describe the comfort that Jesus brings to the Christian, and the refrain reiterates the well-known verse, "Jesus Christ the same yesterday, and today, and for ever." Hebrews 13: 8. Other scripture phrases or ideas used are: "That worthy name," James 2: 7; "Perfect love casteth out fear," 1 John 4: 18; and "O magnify the Lord with me, and let us exalt His name together. I sought the Lord, and He heard me, and delivered me from all my fears." Psalm 34: 3, 4.

The tune, *The Name of Jesus,* was composed especially for these words by the Rev. Edmund Simon Lorenz (1854- ?) of Dayton, Ohio, of the United Brethren Church. He received a B.D. from Yale, and studied in Leipzig before becoming a minister and college president. When his health failed, he developed his hobby for music, and founded a publishing house for sacred music. He also composed Nos. 537, *When the King Comes In;* 650, *Wonderful Love of Jesus,* and 655, unnamed, and wrote the words of No. 650, "In Joyful High and Holy Lays," under the pseudonym of E. D. Mund, his Christian name re-written.

644. CHRIST HAS FOR SIN ATONEMENT MADE

Isaiah 9: 6

Both words and music were written in 1891 by Elisha Albright Hoffman (1839-1929) of Orwigsburg, Pennsylvania, and based on the verse: "And His name shall be called Wonderful." Isaiah 9: 6. Hoffman was a prolific writer, writing tunes for others' verses, and verses for others' tunes. He made his home in Lebanon, Pennsylvania, and was a minister of the Evangelical Association, like his father before him. As a boy, his morning worship in the family consisted of singing hymns. He also wrote the words of No. 611, "What a Fellowship, What a Joy Divine."

645. PRAISE HIM! PRAISE HIM!

Psalm 146: 2

These words were written in 1869 by Miss Frances Jane Crosby (1820-1915), see appendix, and were inspired by the psalmist's outburst of praise, "While I live will I praise the Lord: I will sing praises unto my God while I have any being." Psalm 146: 2.

Some alterations have been made, as the original was without a refrain, the last part of stanza one being:—

O ye saints that dwell on the mountain of Zion,
Praise Him! praise Him ever in joyful song.

So, too, the last halves of the other two stanzas were:—

2. . . . .
Loving Saviour, meekly enduring sorrow,
Crowned with thorns that cruelly pierced His brow;
Once for us rejected, despised, and forsaken,
Prince of Glory, He is triumphant now.

3. . . .
Death is vanquished! Tell it with joy, ye faithful,
Where is now thy victory, boasting grave?
Jesus lives! No longer thy portals are cheerless;
Jesus lives, the mighty and strong to save.

The tune was composed by Chester G. Allen (1812-77), who also wrote No. 21, *Lebanon*. He was a teacher of singing in New York, and also conducted singing at conventions.

646. THIS IS MY FATHER'S WORLD

Psalm 24: 1

Maltbie Davenport Babcock (1858-1901) was a powerful Presbyterian preacher of the United States of America, and wrote several long poems. These words are an extract from a 16-stanza poem entitled "Thoughts for Everyday Living," written in 1901 and published posthumously. Babcock was a great lover of nature, and composed this poem while outdoors meditating on God's goodness. A fitting scripture summary would be: "The earth is the Lord's, and the fullness thereof." Psalm 24: 1. His intense interest in God's created works may be seen in several of the omitted stanzas which follow:—

1. This is my Father's world.
On the day of its wondrous birth
The stars of light in phalanx bright
Sang out in heavenly mirth.

6. This is my Father's world.
From His eternal throne,
He watch doth keep when I'm asleep,
And I am not alone.

7. This is my Father's world.
Dreaming I see His face,
I ope my eyes and in glad surprise
Cry, "The Lord is in this place."

8. This is my Father's world.
I walk a desert lone.
In a bush ablaze to my wandering gaze
God makes His glory known.

9. This is my Father's world.
Among the mountains drear,
'Mid rending rock and earthquake shock,
The still, small voice I hear.

10. This is my Father's world.
From the shining courts above,
The Beloved One, His only Son,
Came—a pledge of deathless love.

11. This is my Father's world.
Now closer to heaven bound,
For dear to God is the earth Christ trod,
No place but is holy ground.

12. This is my Father's world.
His love hath filled my breast,
I am reconciled, I am His child,
My soul has found His rest.

13. This is my Father's world.
A wanderer I may roam.
Whate'er my lot, it matters not
My heart is still at home.

15. This is my Father's world.
The battle is not done;
Jesus who died shall be satisfied,
And earth and heaven be one.

The tune *Terra Beata* (= blessed land) was composed in 1915 by Franklin Lawrence Sheppard, a Baltimore business man and prominent layman of the Presbyterian Church. He had an idea that the melody was a subconscious survival of an air that his mother had taught him, so in his song book he designated it merely as a traditional English melody.

647. TO GOD BE THE GLORY

Psalm 126: 2

Frances Jane Crosby (1820-1915), see appendix, wrote this hymn in 1875 under the title of "Praise for Redemption." There are many scripture texts that speak of the "great things" that God has done, one well-known one being Psalm 126: 2, "The Lord hath done great things," which is repeated in the next verse of the same psalm. Otherwise, the hymn is not a paraphrase of any particular scripture. However, two other psalm references are indicated, namely, Psalm 85: 6: "Thy people . . . rejoice in Thee" and Psalm 96: 8: "Give unto the Lord the glory due unto His name."

The tune was composed by William Howard Doane (1832-1916), see appendix, a friend of the authoress, who wrote many other tunes for her words.

648. MY GLORIOUS VICTOR

Exodus 21: 2-6

In Old Testament times, a slave was bound for a period of six years, after which time he was to be set free. If, however, he found conditions so much to his liking in the household, and loved his master so much that he did not wish to avail himself of his freedom, then he was to undergo a ceremony which declared him the perpetual slave of his master. The latter, in the presence of the judges, bored the lobe of his ear as a token of his willing life-long service. (Exodus 21: 2-6.) Handley Carr Glyn Moule (1841-1920), recalling this custom, wrote this Christian interpretation of it in 1890, in "Hymns of Consecration and Faith," showing his willing service for his Master. Moule was later bishop of Durham; he also wrote No. 336, "Come In, O Come!"

The tune *Staincliffe* was composed in 1875 by Richard William Dixon (1810-80), an amateur composer of Newcastle-on-Tyne, Northumberland, England.

649. WAKE THE SONG

Isaiah 51: 3

This hymn, both words and music, was composed by William Fisk Sherwin (1826-88), see appendix, as a temperance anniversary song. This gives point to the reference in stanza two to "banners" and "the festal day," and to the title of the tune, *Anniversary Song*. The happy nature of the hymn, with its adoration and praise to Father, Son, and Spirit (note this reference to the Trinity in stanza three), looks forward to the restoration of all things in a renewed "Eden . . . joy and gladness shall be found therein, thanksgiving, and the voice of melody." Isaiah 51: 3.

650. IN JOYFUL HIGH AND HOLY LAYS

2 Samuel 1: 26

The theme of this hymn by E. D. Mund, otherwise Edmund Simon Lorenz (1854- ?), is the wonderful love of Jesus, a phrase which ends each stanza and occurs twice in the refrain. The expression is used in the Scriptures of the deep affection that existed between the two men David and Jonathan, which is described in the former's lament over the latter's untimely death: "Thy love to me was wonderful." 2 Samuel 1: 26. This is symbolic of the greater love that Jesus had for His brethren, exceeding even that of Jonathan's. The last two stanzas are a series of vivid contrasts, many of them using Scriptural figures, as follows: "He maketh the storm a calm," Psalm 107: 29; "When I sit in darkness, the Lord shall be a light unto me," Micah 7: 8; "Take balm for her pain," Jeremiah 51: 8; "It is sown in weakness; it is raised in power," 1 Corinthians 15: 43; "Who is a God like unto Thee, that pardoneth iniquity," Micah 7: 18; "When men are cast down, then Thou shalt say, There is lifting up," Job 22: 29; and "That God may be all in all," 1 Corinthians 15: 28. Lorenz elongated his first Christian name, Edmund, for this pseudonym E. D. Mund.

The tune, *Wonderful Love of Jesus,* was composed specially for his own words by the Rev. Edmund Simon Lorenz (1854- ?) of Dayton, Ohio, a minister of the United Brethren Church. He received a B.D. from Yale, studied in Leipzig, and became a minister and college president. When his health failed, he developed his hobby of music, and founded a firm of sacred music publishers. He also composed Nos. 537, *When the King Comes In;* 643, *The Name of Jesus;* and 655, unnamed.

651. A WONDERFUL SAVIOUR IS JESUS MY LORD

Isaiah 32: 2

Frances Jane Crosby (1820-1915), see appendix, has gathered several scriptures together in this hymn to describe our wonderful Saviour: "And His name shall be called Wonderful," Isaiah 9: 6; "He is at my right hand, I shall not be moved," Psalm 16: 8; "As thy days, so shall thy strength be," Deuteronomy 33: 25; "And a man shall be as an hiding place from the wind, and a covert from the tempest; as rivers of water in a dry place, as the shadow of a great rock in a weary land," Isaiah 32: 2; and "I will put thee in a clift of the rock, and will cover thee with My hand," Exodus 33: 22.

The tune *He Hideth My Soul,* was composed specially for these words by William James Kirkpatrick (1838-1921), see appendix.

652. THERE SHALL BE SHOWERS OF BLESSING

Ezekiel 34: 26

El Nathan was the nom-de-plume of Major Daniel Webster Whittle (1840-1901), who wrote No. 583, "Dying with Jesus, by Death Reckoned Mine." From being a soldier in the American Civil War, where he lost his right arm, he became a soldier of the cross, conducting evangelistic campaigns with James McGranahan as his song leader. This hymn is based on God's promise to Israel through the prophet Ezekiel: "And I will make them and the places round about My hill a blessing; and I will cause the shower to come down in his season; there shall be showers of blessing." Ezekiel 34: 26. The experience of Elijah on Mount Carmel is recalled in the second stanza: "There is a sound of abundance of rain," 1 Kings 18: 41, and given a spiritual meaning—the bestowing of the abundant blessing of God.

The tune was composed by James McGranahan (1840-1907), who was Whittle's song leader and musician. He studied under George Frederick Root (see Nos. 93, 299, 418, 620, 690) in Chicago, and later in New York and Boston, and was a composer as well as a conductor. He also composed Nos. 495, *Sometime We'll Understand;* 536, *Christ Returneth;* and 568, *Shall You? Shall I?*

653. DON'T FORGET THE SABBATH

Exodus 20: 8-11

These words were written by Frances Jane Crosby (1820-1915), see appendix. They use the following scriptures in order: Exodus 20: 11: "The Lord blessed the Sabbath day"; Exodus 20: 9, 10: "Six days shalt thou labour, and do all thy work: but the seventh day is the Sabbath of the Lord thy God: in it thou shalt not do any work"; Exodus 20: 8: "Remember the Sabbath day, to keep it holy"; John 14: 6: "Jesus saith unto him, I am the way"; Revelation 21: 6: "I will give unto him that is athirst of the fountain of the water of life freely"; Isaiah 58: 13: "Call the Sabbath a delight"; Ephesians 3: 17: "That Christ may dwell in your hearts by faith."

The tune was composed by William Batchelder Bradbury (1816-68), see appendix.

654. HOLY DAY, JEHOVAH'S REST

Genesis 2: 3

Both words and music were written by Franklin Edson Belden (1858-1945), see appendix. The basic scripture is Genesis 2: 3:

"And God blessed the seventh day, and sanctified it: because that in it He had rested from all His work which God created and made." The hymn appears as No. 1313 in "Hymns and Tunes," 1886, and reflects the arguments that were so necessary at that time to show the binding claims of the Sabbath day, this Sabbath truth having been so long neglected, and rising to great prominence with the rise of the Seventh-day Adventists after 1844. A less combative version is No. 242 in "Hymns and Tunes," which has the same two stanzas to begin with, and then proceeds as follows:—

3. While we praise our Maker's name,
We His faithful promise claim;
Meet with us, dear Lord, we pray,
Thine we are, and Thine this day.

4. Let Thy Spirit on us shine,
Help us keep Thy law divine;
Day by day so shall we be
Shining lights, O Lord, for Thee.

655. GIVE ME THE BIBLE

Psalm 119: 105

These words were written by Miss Priscilla Jane Owens (1822-99), a public school and Sunday school teacher in Baltimore, Maryland. They are based on Psalm 119: 105: "Thy word is a lamp unto my feet, and a light unto my path." The expression in the first stanza, "Jesus came to seek and save the lost," is almost identical with Luke 19: 10: "For the Son of man is come to seek and to save that which was lost"; and the refrain "in the narrow way," is a reminder of the words of Jesus in His sermon on the mount, "Because strait is the gate, and narrow is the way." Matthew 7: 14. Miss Owens also wrote Nos. 584, "Will Your Anchor Hold?" and 637, "We Have Heard a Joyful Sound."

The tune was composed by the Rev. Edmund Simon Lorenz 1854- ?) of Dayton, Ohio, of the United Brethren Church, who also composed Nos. 537, *When the King Comes In;* 643, *The Name of Jesus;* and 650, *Wonderful Love of Jesus,* and wrote the words of this last hymn, "In Joyful High and Holy Lays," under his pen-name of E. D. Mund, his own first name elongated. Lorenz received a B.D. from Yale, and then studied overseas at Leipzig before becoming a minister of the United Brethren Church. He became a college president, and when his health failed, pursued his hobby of music, and founded a publishing firm which concentrated on sacred music.

656. A GLORY IN THE WORD

2 Corinthians 3: 18

John Campbell's "Comprehensive Hymnbook," 1837, contained 1,000 hymns, many of them by Isaac Watts and Charles Wesley as altered by George Whitefield. From this collection, these words by an anonymous author describe the effect of the Word of God on the sinner's life when he uses it as a book which is divinely inspired. First we are reminded that: "Your iniquities have separated between you and your God, and your sins have hid His face from you." Isaiah 59: 2. This results in "having the understanding darkened . . . because of the blindness of their heart." Ephesians 4: 18. The change is wrought by the Spirit of God, "For ye were sometimes darkness, but now are ye light in the Lord. . . . For the fruit of the Spirit is in all goodness and righteousness and truth." Ephesians 5: 8, 9; "But we all, with open face beholding as in a glass the glory of the Lord, are changed into the same image from glory to glory." 2 Corinthians 3: 18. The change is a continual one, being a growth in holiness and love. "May grow up into Him in all things." Ephesians 4: 15.

The tune *Ortonville,* also used for No. 159, "Majestic Sweetness Sits Enthroned," was composed in 1837 by Thomas Hastings (1784-1872), see appendix.

657. ON THE SHORE BEYOND THE SEA

Acts 16: 9

Both the words and the tune, *Missionary's Farewell,* of this hymn were written by the Rev. Isaiah Baltzell (1832-93) of Frederick City, Maryland. His parents were Lutherans, but he joined the United Brethren Church, followed later by his parents. In 1850 he was ordained to the ministry, serving in several pastorates in Maryland and in Pennsylvania. With Edmund Simon Lorenz (see Nos. 537, 643, 650, 655), he edited twelve books of sacred songs. This missionary hymn suggests the vision given to the great missionary, the Apostle Paul, when he heard the Macedonian call, "Come over . . . and help us." Acts 16: 9. His response was to go "with a straight course," verse 11, by ship to its chief city, which was, of course, a foreign country to the Tarsus-born Jew. The refrain echoes the Lord's call to Isaiah: "Whom shall I send, and who will go for Us? Then said I, Here am I; send me." Isaiah 6: 8. The second stanza likens the heathen world to the vineyard in the parable of Matthew 20, when at the third hour, the sixth, the ninth, and even the eleventh hour, the lord of the vineyard "found others standing idle." Matthew 20: 6. The last stanza emphasizes the claims of the Lord above even family relationships, as stated by Him: "He that loveth father or mother more than Me is not worthy of Me: and he that loveth son or daughter more than Me is not worthy of Me." Matthew 10: 37.

658. THEY BROUGHT THEIR GIFTS TO JESUS

Proverbs 23: 26

These words are a kind of parable leading up to the application in the refrain, which is a commentary on Proverbs 23: 26: "My son, give Me thine heart." The hymn was written by Eben Eugene Rexford (1848-1916), an American writer who was also a specialist in flower culture. He contributed many stories and poems to magazines and edited a farm journal in Wisconsin. He also wrote No. 620, "O Where Are the Reapers?" He is perhaps best remembered for his song, "Silver Threads Among the Gold." He used his poetic talent in writing verse as space fillers in magazines and journals.

The tune *Something for Jesus* was composed by Joseph Garrison.

659. I'M BUT A STRANGER HERE

Hebrews 11: 9, 10

These words were written in 1835 by Thomas Rawson Taylor (1807-35) of Bradford, Yorkshire, during his last illness, which resulted in death at an early age. He had been a Congregational minister for a brief period from 1830 to 1833, but retired because of ill health, and took up the teaching of the classics. Then, evidently anticipating his early demise, he wrote four stanzas concerning his strong hope of a better land. The omitted one is:—

4. Therefore I murmur not,
Heaven is my home:
Whate'er my earthly lot,
Heaven is my home:
And I shall surely stand,
There at my Lord's right hand;
Heaven is my fatherland,
Heaven is my home.

The hymn reiterates the same hope of Abraham who "sojourned in the land of promise, as in a strange country. . . . For he looked for a city which hath foundations, whose builder and maker is God." Hebrews 11: 9, 10. The words were written to the tune of the old Scottish melody *Robin Adair*.

The tune *Oak* was composed in 1854 by Lowell Mason (1792-1872), see appendix.

660. HOW TEDIOUS AND TASTELESS THE HOURS

Psalm 73: 25

These words were written in 1779 by John Newton (1725-1807), see appendix, while associated with William Cowper (1731-1800), see appendix, at Olney, Buckinghamshire, and appear as No. XLVI in "Olney Hymns," 1779. The title is "Fellowship with Christ," with the scripture, "None upon earth that I desire beside Thee," Psalm 73: 25, and the hymn indicates the change in Newton's own life after becoming a preacher of the gospel.

The tune *Contrast,* also used for Nos. 199, "We Speak of the Realms," and 200, "I Long to Behold Him," is attributed to Lewis Edson (1784-1820), and derives its name, which was given probably in 1802, from the contrast in certain words of this hymn, for example, December-May, prison-palace. It is taken from an early American melody belonging to a secular song of about 1772, entitled "Farewell, Ye Green Fields and Sweet Groves." Edson, a blacksmith of Massachusetts and of Connecticut, conducted singing schools, and was himself a well-known singer.

661. OUT ON AN OCEAN ALL BOUNDLESS WE RIDE

Hebrews 10: 34

These words were written prior to the year 1844 by a Millerite Adventist, and speak of the hope of the soon coming of Christ. They are listed as anonymous in "Hymns and Tunes," 1886, but Franklin Edson Belden in his "Christ in Song" of 1908, attributes them to William Fairfield Warren (1833-1929) of Williamsburg, Massachusetts. He was a Methodist Episcopal minister and professor of systematic theology in Bremen, Germany. At Boston he helped to organize the university and carried the responsibility of president from 1873 to 1903. Line 5 of the first stanza has been incorrectly repeated in many hymnals as "we've rode" instead of the grammatically correct "we rode." The words liken the Christian to a sailor on a stormy sea making for the quiet harbour of heaven, his eternal home. They present the contrast between earth's stormy experience and heaven's pleasant prospect, much after the experience described in Hebrews 10: 34: "Knowing in yourselves that ye have in heaven a better and an enduring substance."

The tune *Homeward Bound,* also anonymous, is ascribed in "Christ in Song" to John William Dadmun (1819-90), a Methodist minister of Massachusetts, but elsewhere to C. S. Harrington. Lines 1, 3, and 7 are identical, so are lines 2, 4, and 8, and also lines 5 and 6.

662. LET OTHERS SEEK A HOME BELOW

John 14: 2

These words are the last two stanzas of a five-stanza poem by the Rev. William Hunter, D.D. (1811-77), who went to the United States as a lad of six, joined the Methodist Church, and became a professor of Hebrew and Biblical Literature. The omitted stanzas are:—

1. My heavenly home is bright and fair:
Nor pain nor death can enter there;
Its glittering towers the sun outshine;
That heavenly mansion shall be mine.

Refrain: I'm going home, I'm going home,
I'm going home to die no more.
To die no more, to die no more,
I'm going home to die no more.

2. My Father's house is built on high,
Far, far above the starry sky.
When from this earthly prison free,
That heavenly mansion mine shall be.

3. While here, a stranger far from home,
Affliction's waves may round me foam;
Although, like Lazarus, sick and poor,
My heavenly mansion is secure.

The fourth stanza is our first two stanzas minus "We'll be gathered home" and with "o'erflow" for "o'erthrow." The fifth stanza is our stanza three and four with "All nature sink and cease to be" for the last line. The words reflect the Millerite Adventist teaching, and show the lively hope those believers had of the Lord's appearing. The signs of the stars falling (1833) and the sun and moon being darkened (1780) were to them but recent events: "The sun shall be darkened, and the moon shall not give her light, and the stars of heaven shall fall." Mark 13: 24, 25. The theme of the whole hymn is obviously repeated in each of the last lines, "In my Father's house are many mansions." John 14: 2. The refrain is identical with the refrain of a similar Advent song written by Mrs. Elizabeth Mills (see No. 199) and published in the 1881 edition of "Song Anchor," a Sabbath school song book for Seventh-day Adventists:—

O land of rest for thee I sigh,
When will the moment come
When I shall lay my armour by
And dwell in peace at home.

The original words of the refrain were: "We'll wait till Jesus comes," and so appear in the hymnals of 1861, 1869, and 1872.

Hunter also wrote Nos. 368, "We're Bound for the Land of the Pure," and 530, "The Great Physician Now Is Near."

The tune *Land of Rest* was composed by Dr. William Miller (1801-78) and arranged in 1859 by William James Kirkpatrick (1838-1921), see appendix.

663. GRACIOUS FATHER, GUARD THY CHILDREN

Jude 24

These words by an anonymous Adventist reflect the spirit of the early believers as they sought to live godly lives in the daily expectation of the coming of the Lord. Various scriptures are quoted in part, as follows: Jude 24: "Unto Him that is able to keep you from falling"; Psalm 119: 105: "Thy word is a lamp unto my feet, and a light unto my path"; 1 Corinthians 1: 7: "Waiting for the coming of our Lord Jesus Christ"; Colossians 3: 24: "Ye shall receive the reward"; James 1: 27: "To keep himself unspotted from the world"; Psalm 60: 4: "Thou hast given a banner to them that fear Thee, that it may be displayed because of the truth"; Leviticus 25: 10: "It shall be a jubilee unto you; and ye shall return every man unto his possession"; Romans 8: 2: "Christ Jesus hath made me free from the law of sin and death"; and John 8: 36: "If the Son therefore shall make you free, ye shall be free indeed."

The tune *Ellesdie,* also used for No. 267, "Jesus, I My Cross Have Taken," was arranged in 1873 by Hubert Platt Main (1839-1926) from an original tune which probably came from Wolfgang Amadeus Mozart (1756-91), the famous Viennese composer and musical genius. Nos. 161 and 190, *Ariel,* are also an arrangement from a tune by this same composer. Main, a composer and musical editor, also arranged No. 160, *Beloved* or *Dulcimer,* and composed No. 532, *My Lord and I.*

664. LONG UPON THE MOUNTAINS

Ezekiel 34: 12

Annie Rebekah Smith (1828-55), see appendix, wrote this hymn to describe the experience of the early Seventh-day Adventist believers, and to encourage their hearts by the hope of the second coming of the great Shepherd to gather His flock. It appeared in the *Review and Herald* of December 9, 1851, with the heading, "So Will I Seek Out My Sheep, and Will Deliver Them Out of All Places Where They Have Been Scattered in the Dark and Cloudy

Day." Ezekiel 34: 12. The hymn was sung at the first General Conference, May 20, 1863, held at Battle Creek, Michigan.

The tune *St. Asaph* was published in 1872 and named *Thanksgiving* because of the recovery from typhoid fever of Edward VII, who was then Prince of Wales. The composer was William Samuel Bambridge (1843-1923) of New Zealand, who came to England as a lad of six and became music master at Marlborough College for forty-seven years. The tune was actually written for Baring-Gould's hymn, "Through the Night of Doubt and Sorrow." In 1874 the name was changed to *St. Asaph,* the name of a town in North Wales.

665. HOW FAR FROM HOME?

Isaiah 21: 11, 12

These words were written in 1853 by Annie Rebekah Smith (1828-55), see appendix, and appear in the *Review and Herald* of November 29 of that year. They make use of the ideas in the following scriptures:—

Stanza 1. "Watchman, what of the night? The watchman said, The morning cometh." Isaiah 21: 11, 12.

Stanza 2. "I press toward the mark for the prize." Philippians 3: 14.

Stanza 3. "There shall be signs in the sun, . . . and upon the earth . . . the sea and the waves," Luke 21: 25; "The whole creation groaneth," Romans 8: 22; "With the trump of God." 1 Thessalonians 4: 16.

Stanza 4. "They which came out of great tribulation," Revelation 7: 14; "And God shall wipe away all tears from their eyes." Revelation 7: 17.

There were five stanzas originally, the omitted one, the fourth, being:—

4. How far from home? ah, then, I cried
To God, who marks each plaintive sigh:
A still, small voice, within, replied,
Not far from home am I!
Then weep no more, though round thy way
Afflictions rise, and doubt and fear,
While myriad voices sweetly say,
The pilgrim's home is near.

The tune *How Far From Home?* is from an anonymous American song, " 'Tis Midnight Hour," the words of the first stanza of which are:—

'Tis midnight hour, the moon shines bright,
The dewdrops blaze beneath her ray,
The twinkling stars their trembling light
Like beauty's eyes display.
Then sleep no more, though round thy heart
Some tender dream may idly play,
For midnight song, with magic art,
Shall chase that dream away.

Note the similarity of line five between "sleep no more" and Annie Smith's words in each of her stanzas, "weep no more."

666. I'M A PILGRIM

Hebrews 11: 13

Mary Stanley Bunce (1810-83), daughter of a Congregational minister at Beaufort, South Carolina, married Charles E. Dana in 1835, but was widowed in 1839. She married Professor Robert D. Shindler of Shelby College, Kentucky, in 1848, and later moved to Texas. She was an early Adventist believer following the preaching of William Miller, joining several different denominations in her search for truth. She wrote these words in 1841 in the expectation of the Advent two or three years later, and here takes the thought of Hebrews 11: 13: " . . . confessed that they were strangers and pilgrims on the earth," applying it to the Adventist believers who were frequently ridiculed for their faith in the heavenly city soon to appear. Note that the rhyme in the stanza is only between lines three and four. Mrs. Dana also wrote No. 232, "Flee as a Bird."

The tune *I'm a Pilgrim* is an old Italian air *Buono Notte* (= good-night).

667. AWAKE, MY SOUL, IN JOYFUL LAYS

Isaiah 63: 7

Samuel Medley (1738-99) was a Baptist minister at Watford, Herts., and then for twenty-seven years at Liverpool, after having served in the Royal Navy, and he used to write hymns to summarize his sermons. This one of nine stanzas appeared in 1785 and is based on Isaiah 63: 7: "I will mention the lovingkindness of the Lord." The omitted stanzas according to Medley's 1789 version are:—

3. When I was Satan's easy prey,
And deep in debt and bondage lay,
He paid His life for my discharge,
His lovingkindness is so large.

5. When earthly friends forsake me quite,
And I have neither skill nor might,
He's sure my helper to appear,
His lovingkindness is so near.

6. Often I feel my sinful heart
Prone from my Jesus to depart,
And though I oft have Him forgot,
His lovingkindness changes not.

7. So, when I pass death's gloomy vale,
And life, and mortal powers shall fail—
O may my last expiring breath
His lovingkindness sing in death!

8. Then shall I mount and soar away
To the bright world of endless day;
There shall I sing, with sweet surprise,
His lovingkindness in the skies.

9. There, with their golden harps, I'll join,
And with their anthems mingle mine;
And loudly sound on ev'ry chord,
The lovingkindness of the Lord.

Stanzas 4 and 5 in "Church Hymnal" do not appear in the 1789 edition of his "Hymns." The hymn was written while he was visiting a Baptist friend in London. Asking the daughter of the house to bring paper and ink, he retired to his room and shortly afterwards returned with the hymn completed. Medley also wrote No. 161, "O Could I Speak the Matchless Worth."

The tune *Loving-kindness* has been attributed to William Caldwell of Tennessee, and appears in his collection "Union Harmony," 1837, but also earlier in the "Christian Lyre," 1831, by Joshua Leavitt, who was a pastor in Connecticut, a militant reformer against slavery and intemperance, and an associate of Charles G. Finney. Caldwell collected hymns and tunes for their evangelistic revival meetings, and published them in monthly parts, Volume I of the "Christian Lyre" appearing in April, 1831, and Volume II in October, followed by a supplement. This effort to utilize popular songs and tunes of like character met opposition from Mason and Hastings, see appendix.

668. RISE, MY SOUL, AND STRETCH THY WINGS

Ephesians 2: 6

Robert Seagrave (1693-1759) of Twyford, Lincolnshire, was a minister who, having failed to reform the clergy of the Church of

England, followed the Wesleys and Whitefield, and became an intimate friend of the latter. He wrote this hymn for his own congregation in 1742, one year after leaving the Anglican Church, and published it with fifty original hymns in his "Christian Worship." There were four stanzas, entitled "The Pilgrim's Song," and they give a good description of how the hope of heaven helped the early Methodists to endure the sorrows of earth. The omitted stanza is:—

> 3. Fly me riches, fly me cares,
> Whilst I that coast explore;
> Flatt'ring world, with all thy snares,
> Solicit me no more.
> Pilgrims fix not here their home;
> Strangers tarry but a night,
> When the last dear morn is come,
> They'll rise to joyful light.

The sentiment of the words is that of the Apostle Paul, who said that Christ "hath raised us up together, and made us sit together in heavenly places in Christ Jesus." Ephesians 2: 6.

The tune *Amsterdam* is attributed to Dr. James Nares (1715-83), who also wrote No. 32, *Nares*. He was an organist at York Minster and at the Chapel Royal, Windsor, and was a trainer of boys' choirs. He received the degree of Doctor of Music from Cambridge University in 1756, and published treatises on singing and on the playing of the organ and the harpsicord.

669. HOW SWEET ARE THE TIDINGS

Titus 2: 13

This anonymous hymn of the early Adventists contrasts the loneliness, sorrow, and death of this earthly life with the glorious hope of the soon coming of Jesus. Various Scripture phrases are used, for example: Luke 8: 1: "The glad tidings of the kingdom of God"; 1 Peter 2: 11: "As strangers and pilgrims"; Titus 2: 13: "The glorious appearing of the great God and our Saviour Jesus Christ"; Revelation: 22: 20: "Surely I come quickly"; 1 Corinthians 15: 25: "For He must reign"; Ezekiel 37: 12: "I will open your graves, and cause you to come up"; Revelation 20: 13: "And the sea gave up the dead which were in it"; Luke 13: 29: "And they shall come from the east, and from the west, and from the north, and from the south"; Revelation 19: 4: "Saying, Amen; Alleluia"; and 1 Peter 5: 4: "Ye shall receive a crown of glory."

The tune *He's Coming* is taken almost unchanged from a marching song, "Bonny Eloise, the Belle of the Mohawk Vale," which was a popular song of the army bands of both North and South in the American civil war. It was composed in 1858 by John Roger Thomas to words by George W. Elliott, beginning:—

O sweet is the vale where the Mohawk gently glides
On its clear winding way to the sea.

It became the song of the year. Thomas was a Welshman, an opera singer, and a prolific composer, and produced many successful secular song tunes.

670. FATHER, I STRETCH MY HANDS

Psalm 88: 9

Charles Wesley (1707-88), see appendix, wrote these stanzas in 1741 under the heading "A Prayer for Faith." He has asked Peter's question, "Lord, to whom shall we go?" John 6: 68; and has used the psalmist's expression, "I have stretched out my hands unto Thee," Psalm 88: 9; and also the ascription of Paul to the Lord Jesus in Hebrews 12: 2: "Jesus the author . . . of our faith." There were originally six stanzas, the second, now omitted, being:—

2. What did Thine only Son endure
Before I drew my breath;
What pain, what labour, to secure
My soul from endless death.

Our sixth stanza is an addition, using the words of the chorus tune to which the hymn is now sung.

The tune *I Do Believe* is an early American melody also named *Camp-meeting,* usually sung to the words

I will believe, I do believe
That Jesus died for me,

and often used as a camp-meeting chorus.

671. LOOK FOR THE WAYMARKS

Daniel 2: 31-44

Both words and music were written by Franklin Edson Belden (1858-1945), see appendix, and appear in "Hymns and Tunes," 1886. Four scriptures are listed at the head of the hymn, namely: Deuteronomy 29: 29: "The secret things belong unto the Lord our God: but those things which are revealed belong unto us and to our children for ever"; Amos 3: 7: "Surely the Lord God will do nothing, but He revealeth His secret unto His servants the prophets"; 2 Peter 1: 21: "For the prophecy came not in old time by the will of man: but holy men of God spake as they were moved by the Holy Ghost"; Daniel 2: 28: "There is a God in heaven that revealeth secrets, and maketh known to the king Nebuchadnezzar what shall be in the latter days." The hymn is an exposition of Nebuchadnezzar's dream and Daniel's interpretation of it (Daniel 2: 31-44), giving a brief history of the Assyrian (Babylonian), Persian, Greek, and Roman empires, followed by a divided Europe, and finally by Christ's everlasting kingdom. Following the hymn in "Hymns and Tunes" is a short explanation of the prophecy, giving further point to the name of the tune, *Look for the Waymarks.*

672. A GREAT AND MIGHTY WONDER

Luke 2: 14

St. Germanus (634-734) was the author of this hymn based on the song of the angels to the shepherds at the birth of Jesus, "Glory to God in the highest, and on earth peace, goodwill toward men." Luke 2: 14. It was translated in 1862 by John Mason Neale (1818-66), see appendix, from part of a long Greek poem on the wonder-working image of Edessa, with a note attributing it to St. Anatolius of Constantinople, who lived about A.D. 458. There were six stanzas, those omitted being:—

3. And we with them triumphant
Repeat the hymn again:
To God on high be glory
And peace on earth to men.

4. While thus they sing your Monarch,
Those bright angelic bands,
Rejoice, ye vales and mountains!
Ye oceans, clap your hands!

6. And idol forms shall perish,
And error shall decay,
And Christ shall wield His sceptre,
Our Lord and God for aye.

The melody is an old Rhineland folk-song which was first published in 1599 in the *"Alte Katholische Geistliche Kirchengesang"* to the words *"Es ist ein ros' entsprungen"* (= A rose has bloomed), one of the many songs to the Virgin Mary. It is essentially a musical phrase of two lines sung three times over, with a different phrase of one line between the second and third repetition. It was harmonized in 1609 by the German musician Michael Praetorius (1571-1621), said to be the most prolific composer of his time. His real name was Schulz, and in 1604 he was appointed organist to the Duke of Brunswick, and later musical director. He composed a large number of sacred and secular songs and wrote a treatise on musical instruments.

673. THERE WERE NINETY AND NINE

Luke 15: 3-7

Elizabeth Cecilia Douglass Clephane (1830-69), daughter of the sheriff of Fife, wrote these words, published in 1868 in "The Children's Hour," as a poem based on the parable of the lost sheep (Luke 15: 3-7). The parallel scripture is Matthew 18: 12, 13: "If a man have an hundred sheep, and one of them be gone astray, doth he not leave the ninety and nine, and goeth into the mountains, and seeketh that which is gone astray? And if so be that he find it, verily I say unto you, he rejoiceth more of that sheep, than of the ninety and nine which went not astray." The poem appeared in 1874 in the *Christian Age,* where it caught the attention of Ira David Sankey (1840-1908), who was travelling by train with his colleague Dwight Lyman Moody, from Glasgow to Edinburgh, Scotland. Sankey read it to the evangelist, who did not appear to show much interest, but nevertheless he cut it out and kept it in his pocket. At Moody's second evangelistic meeting in the capital city the topic was "The Good Shepherd." Moody had spoken, followed by Horatius Bonar (see appendix), and then Moody asked Sankey to sing a solo appropriate to the address to close the service. Sankey thought immediately of the Shepherd Psalm, but that was not suitable as a solo, and suddenly he seemed to hear a voice, "Sing the hymn you found on the train." So with a silent prayer for divine help he placed the newspaper clipping on the organ and struck the chord of A flat. Then he began playing and singing, composing the music note by note as he went along. After the second stanza he had it well remembered and it was easy to complete the hymn. Later Sankey said that it was the most intense period of his life. Miss Clephane also wrote No. 280, "Beneath the Cross of Jesus," and Sankey composed Nos. 575, unnamed, 586, *Hiding in Thee,* and 587, unnamed. He became a member of the Methodist Episcopal Church at the age of fifteen years, and showed a great interest in Sunday school work and in the Young Men's Christian Association. Sankey became Moody's solo singer in their evangelistic campaigns.

The tune *The Ninety and Nine* remains as it was spontaneously composed in the meeting in 1874.

674. IN HEAVENLY LOVE ABIDING

Psalm 23: 4

Anna Laetitia Waring (1823-1910) was a profound Hebrew scholar, studying this language in order to be able to read the Psalms in their original tongue. She based this hymn on the general tenor of the 23rd Psalm, and it was published in 1850 under the title of "Safety in God," with the accompanying text, "I will fear no evil: for Thou art with me." Psalm 23: 4. The second and third stanzas particularly are a fairly close paraphrase of the Shepherd Psalm. Miss Waring, a Quaker who later joined the Church of England, also wrote Nos. 82, "Beneath Thy Wing," and 332, "My Heart is Resting."

The tune *Abiding* was composed by Jakob Ludwig Felix Mendelssohn-Bartholdy (1809-47) of Hamburg, Germany, the noted composer of oratorios, cantatas, and orchestral and piano music. He also composed Nos. 111, *Mendelssohn;* 257, *Trust;* 687, unnamed, and 692, *Birmingham,* and arranged No. 217, *Munich.*

675. WHEN WILT THOU SAVE THE PEOPLE?

Psalm 28: 9

This so-called national hymn was written by Ebenezer Elliott (1781-1849), the corn-law rhymer of Sheffield, Yorkshire, and appeared in his "More Verse and Prose," 1850, during the agitation for the repeal of the corn laws. He wrote verse for the local newspaper, and in this particular poem, inveighs against the current unjust use of power, against unchristian oppression, and against prevalent vice. It may well have been inspired by the thought of Psalm 28: 9: "Save Thy people, and bless Thine inheritance: feed them also, and lift them up for ever." The last part of the first stanza recalls the prophetic word: "Surely the people is grass. The grass withereth, the flower fadeth." Isaiah 40: 7, 8.

The tune *Kendal* was composed in 1906 by Arthur Somervell (1863-1937), and is named after the large town in the English Lake District near his birthplace, Windemere. He was a professor at the Royal College of Music in London in 1894, and later inspector of music in schools, being knighted in 1929.

676. JESUS, STILL LEAD ON

Psalm 48: 14

Count Nicholas Ludwig von Zinzendorf (1700-60), was a wealthy nobleman, son of a minister of state in Saxony. He established a home for Moravians who had been expelled, and reorganized the Moravian Society, becoming their bishop in 1737. He was banished from Saxony, became a missionary and a prolific hymn-writer, and later was a friend of John Wesley (see No. 330), influencing him to use hymns in public worship. This present hymn is a composite one, and four stanzas appeared in 1778 as a combination of two of his former hymns, one being the 1721

"Seelenbräutigam," from which he took three stanzas, the other being *"Glanz der Ewigkeit,"* which provides our stanza two. The omitted stanza is:—

3. When we seek relief
From a long-felt grief;
When oppressed by new temptations,
Lord, increase and perfect patience;
Show us that bright shore
Where we weep no more.

The words seeking God's continual direction are a reminder of the psalmist's complete trust in God. "He will be our guide even unto death." Psalm 48: 14. The hymn was freely translated from the German in 1846 by Jane Laurie Borthwick (1813-97) and revised by her in 1854. She also translated No. 404, "My Jesus, as Thou Wilt." Zinzendorf also wrote Nos. 62, "Eternal Depth of Love Divine," and 330, "O Thou to Whose All-Searching Sight."

The melody was composed in 1697 by Adam Drese (1620-1701), a Pietist musician who burned all his opera and secular compositions after being converted. Pietism was a movement in Germany similar to Methodism in England, in that it emphasized practical religion in a then arid Lutheranism. The tune is named *Seelenbräutigam* (= souls of the bridegroom) after the first word of Drese's (and incidentally Zinzendorf's) hymn, which was sung to this tune. Lines 5 and 6 repeat lines 1 and 2, and the longer middle lines are similar in that the melody of line 4 is an interval of a third below line 3. The harmony was supplied by Samuel Sebastian Wesley (1810-76), the famous cathedral organist, and grandson of Charles Wesley. He served at Hereford, Exeter, Winchester, and Gloucester cathedrals, and at Leeds parish church. He received the Mus. Doc. degree from Oxford in 1839, and was appointed as professor of organ at the London Royal Academy of Music in 1850. He also composed Nos. 279 and 433, *Aurelia.*

677. MASTER, THE TEMPEST IS RAGING

Mark 4: 37-41

Miss Mary Ann Baker, a member of the Baptist Church in America, had undergone a severe bereavement. Her father and mother had died, and now in 1874 her brother had contracted the same disease that had proved fatal to them. He had travelled south to a warmer climate to try to restore his health, but word came to Miss Baker that he, too, had succumbed. Bitter thoughts arose in her heart, and she became rebellious against God's dealings in her life. However, on further thought her stormy feelings were stilled much as the literal tempest on Galilee was stilled by the Master: "And the wind ceased, and there was a great calm."

Mark 4: 39. About that time in 1874, Dr. Horatio Richmond Palmer (1834-1907), see appendix, asked her to prepare several songs on the subject of the current Sunday school lessons. This hymn on the theme of Christ's stilling the tempest, and its spiritual application, was the result. The appropriate scripture is found in Mark 4: 37-41, with parallel versions in Matthew 8: 24-27 and Luke 8: 23-25.

The tune *Peace, Be Still!* was composed in 1874 by Horatio Richmond Palmer (1834-1907), see appendix.

678. SUNSET AND EVENING STAR

Revelation 22: 4

Alfred Lord Tennyson (1809-92) succeeded William Wordsworth as Poet Laureate of England in 1850, and became a peer in 1884. When eighty years of age, in October, 1889, he was travelling on the Isle of Wight from Aldworth to Farringford and was thinking about the "moaning of the bar," or the noise of the tide on the sand. After dinner, he had written this lyric, saying that it came in a moment. The Pilot of the poem he defined as "that Divine and Unseen who is always guiding us." Tennyson did not regard the poem as a hymn, for he said that a good hymn was the most difficult thing in the world to write, for it had to include both the commonplace and the poetical. "As soon as you cease to be commonplace and use an expression out of the common, it ceases to be a hymn." In spite of this, his words are often used as a hymn at funeral and memorial services. Tennyson asked his son to be sure to include "Crossing the Bar" at the end of all editions of his poems. The poet's wish to meet his Pilot face to face after death is the cry of all mankind, and such a promise is made to all of God's servants, for "they shall see His face." Revelation 22: 4. Tennyson also wrote No. 514, "Ring Out, Wild Bells."

The tune *Crossing the Bar* was composed specially for these words in 1893 by Joseph Barnby (1838-96), see appendix, whose tune, No. 514, *Jordan,* is set to words by Tennyson also. The last line but one is notable for a rise of a seventh, followed by a stately descending passage of nine successive notes of the scale.

679. BREATHE ON ME, BREATH OF GOD

Job 33: 4

Dr. Edwin Hatch (1835-89), born of Nonconformist parents, became a Church of England minister in the East End of London, and later Professor of Classics at Trinity College, Toronto, Canada. Then he became rector of a high school in Quebec, and in 1867 returned from Canada to be vice-principal of St. Mary's Hall, Oxford, and Reader in Ecclesiastical History for four years before his death. A deeply religious and profound scholar, he wrote these words in 1878 as an ordination hymn, and they first appeared in a hymnbook in 1886. The title of the original was "Between Doubt and Prayer," and it forms a commentary on Job 33: 4: "The spirit of God hath made me, and the breath of the Almighty hath given me life." A slight change has been made in stanza 3, line 2, which was originally "Blend all my soul with Thine." The fourth stanza has also been changed in the second line from "So shall I never die" to "constant be," making better theology and also better rhyme.

The hymn is a subjective one for quiet meditation, and this stimulated the composition of the tune, *Paraclete*. Joseph Harker (1880-) loved the words, and built the tune to suit them in 1914, naming the tune after the Greek word for the Comforter, the Holy Ghost. Pastor J. Harker, a Seventh-day Adventist minister and musician and composer, also wrote No. 420, *Simonside*.

680. ANCIENT OF DAYS

Psalm 105: 39

William Croswell Doane (1832-1913), son of George Washington Doane (see Nos. 48, 450), also became bishop of Albany in the Protestant Episcopal Church, as did his father before him. He wrote this hymn in 1886 for the celebration of the 200th anniversary of the granting of the charter of the city of Albany, New York, giving thanks to God for His blessings of prosperity and peace. The expression "Ancient of Days" is taken from Daniel 7: 9, which describes a glorious scene around the throne. The first stanza tells of His continuing gift of light and life. The next three stanzas then speak of the work of the three persons of the Godhead—the Father who leads, the Son who gives peace, and the Holy Ghost who gives power. The fifth stanza to the triune God expresses praise for His goodness and love. Several scriptures are used with a symbolic anti-typical meaning, for example, in stanza 2: "He spread a cloud for a covering; and fire to give light in the night." Psalm 105: 39.

The tune *Ancient of Days* was composed in the same year, 1886, especially for the anniversary hymn, by John Albert Jeffrey (1851-?), who was bishop Doane's organist in the Episcopal cathedral at Albany. He gave it the name *Albany,* where he was then resident.

681. THERE IS A PLACE OF QUIET REST

Psalm 130: 5

In 1903, two of the nieces of Cleland Boyd McAfee (1866-1944), professor of philosophy at the Theological Seminary, Chicago, had died suddenly of diphtheria, and the whole family, though broken in spirit, still trusted in God. McAfee had been in the habit of writing a special hymn, both words and music, for the quarterly communion service of his Presbyterian church, and the circumstances of this bereavement evoked the thought that there was peace and comfort near to the heart of God. He composed these words under the title "The Heart of God," and also the tune *Near to the Heart of God,* and his church choir rehearsed it and then sang it on the Saturday night outside his elder brother's home, where the rest of the family were in quarantine. The hymn was preserved by another brother, also a minister, who used it in his congregation in the Presbyterian church, Berkeley, California. The idea of waiting for God is a very common one in the Bible, a typical text being: "I wait for the Lord, my soul doth wait." Psalm 130: 5.

682. FATHER, I YIELD TO THEE MY LIFE

Romans 6: 19

The words of this hymn were written by Dr. Douglas Albert Raoul Aufranc (1892-), a Seventh-day Adventist doctor and dentist resident in London. They were written at a time of his life when he was rather sad and unhappy. Friends had disappointed him and failed him, and life seemed to hold very little that was satisfying. Hence the reference to "sordid pleasures, sin and strife" of stanza one, and "foes and friends who ever fail" of stanza two, and "earth's fleeting pleasures" of stanza four. The hymn was written rather quickly, but has brought much comfort and blessing to the discouraged and the dying, especially the triumphant climax of the last stanza. The complete consecration described is that spoken of by the Apostle Paul: "Now yield your members servants to righteousness unto holiness." Romans 6: 19. Dr. Aufranc also wrote the words of Nos. 335, "Alone with Thee"; 374, "There Is a Road"; and 468, "Far From All Care," together with their accompanying tunes: 335, *Windy Ridge;* 374, *Thetford,* and 468, *Pevensey.*

The melody *The Promised Land,* was composed in 1840 by Miss M. Durham, and harmony is provided in a minor key.

683. PRAISE GOD, FROM WHOM ALL BLESSINGS FLOW

Psalm 148: 1, 2

Dr. Thomas Ken (1637-1711), bishop of Bath and Wells, wrote Morning Hymn (No. 44), Midnight Hymn, and Evening Hymn (No. 53), for the boys of Winchester School in 1674. At the end of each of these three hymns he placed this doxology as a concluding stanza. The Psalms are full of praise, a fitting text for this doxology being Psalm 148: 1, 2: "Praise ye the Lord. Praise ye the Lord from the heavens: praise Him in the heights. Praise ye Him, all His angels: praise ye Him, all His hosts."

The tune, *Old Hundredth,* also used for No. 13, "All People That On Earth Do Dwell," has been associated with Psalm 100 for nearly four centuries, and is probably by Louis Bourgeois (1510-c. 1561). He was appointed by John Calvin in Geneva to provide musical settings for the metrical psalms. He added harmonies, to Calvin's disapproval, altered secular melodies, and adapted German psalm tunes, and his work resulted in a tremendous stimulation of congregational singing in Geneva. The earliest known version of the tune is in a Huguenot Psalter compiled by Guillaume Franc of Rouen (died 1570), and published in Geneva in 1551 where it is set to Psalm 134. The prefix "Old" refers to the version of 1562, by Sternhold and Hopkins, of metrical psalms, this particular tune being set, of course, to Psalm 100. The New Version was by Tate and Brady in 1696.

684. O THOU WHO HEAREST EVERY HEARTFELT PRAYER

Psalm 65: 2

These words by Frederick Arthur Jackson (1867-1942) ask God to prepare the hearers for a Sabbath day rich in blessing: "O Thou that hearest prayer, unto Thee shall all flesh come." Psalm 65: 2.

The tune *Morecambe* was published in 1870 by Frederic Cook Atkinson (1841-96) especially for the words "Abide with Me" (No. 50). He was assistant organist at Norwich cathedral, and later for many years in Bradford, Yorkshire. Morecambe is a town in Lancashire, noted for the music festival held there. The same tune, raised one tone to the key of C, is used for No. 336, "Come In, O Come!"

685. LET ALL MORTAL FLESH KEEP SILENCE

Habakkuk 2: 20

In the Greek Orthodox churches at Easter time, the liturgy of St. James is sung at Holy Communion and it is preceded by a prayer. Gerard Moultrie (1828-95), an Anglican clergyman of Rugby, Warwickshire, who made a speciality of treating topics untouched by other hymn-writers, such as early Greek, Latin, and German hymns, translated this prayer from the Greek in 1864. It is really part of a four-stanza hymn, the omitted lines being:—

2. King of kings, yet born of Mary,
As of old on earth He stood,
Lord of lords, in human vesture—
In the body and the blood—
He will give to all the faithful
His own self for heavenly food.

3. Rank on rank the host of heaven
Spreads its vanguard on the way,
As the Light of light descendeth
From the realms of endless day,
That the powers of hell may vanish
As the darkness clears away.

4. At His feet the six-winged seraphs,
Cherubim with sleepless eye,
Veil their faces to the Presence,
As with ceaseless voice they cry,
Alleluia, Alleluia,
Alleluia! Lord most high.

Our stanza echoes the thought of Habakkuk 2: 20: "But the Lord is in His holy temple: let all the earth keep silence before Him."

The melody *Picardy* is a 17th century French carol, or possibly earlier, coming from that northern district of France, but is first found in print in *"Chansons Popularies des Provinces de France,"* 1860. It was harmonized by Ralph Vaughan Williams (1872-1958), a specialist in English country folksongs. He received the degree of Mus. Doc. from Cambridge University in 1901, and the Order of Merit in 1935 for his services to music. He also harmonized No. 364, *Sine Nomine,* and No. 430, *Shipston.*

686. LORD, HAVE MERCY

1 Kings 8: 58

John Calvin (1509-64), who was much averse to having the Scriptures distorted or paraphrased, wrote the Ten Commandments in metrical form, and had the words "Lord, have mercy" sung after the repetition of each commandment. Then followed the prayer for strength to keep the command of the Lord, after the manner of King Solomon's prayer: "That He may incline our hearts unto Him, to walk in all His ways, and keep His commandments." 1 Kings 8: 58.

Sir George Job Elvey (1816-93), organist of St. George's Chapel, Windsor, for forty-seven years, and knighted in 1871, wrote this setting of the music for this prayer. He also composed Nos. 162 and 366, *Diademata,* and 496, *St. George's, Windsor.*

687. ALMIGHTY FATHER

Isaiah 30: 18

This short two-line phrase incorporates the thought of the last part of Isaiah 30: 18: "Blessed are all they that wait for Him."

The tune is an arrangement from Jakob Ludwig Felix Mendelssohn-Bartholdy (1809-47) of Hamburg, the famous composer of oratorios, orchestral and piano music. It appears in his oratorio "Elijah," where the prophet pleads on Mount Carmel, and this oratorio was composed in 1846 in Leipzig, Germany. Mendelssohn also composed Nos. 674, *Abiding;* 692, *Birmingham,* and the originals of the two arrangements in 111, *Mendelssohn,* and 257, *Trust.*

688. HEAR OUR PRAYER, O LORD

Psalm 116: 1, 2

The words are a partial paraphrase of Psalm 116: 1, 2: "I love the Lord, because He hath heard my voice and my supplications. Because He hath inclined His ear unto me, therefore will I call upon Him as long as I live."

The musical setting is taken from a publication of 1903, by George Whelpton (1847-1930), which contained other responses and a hymn for dismissal. The composer was born in Redbourne, Hertfordshire, and emigrated as a boy of four years to the United States, where he later served in the American army. He also worked as a pharmacist and as an editor, and was a choir director in Buffalo for over twenty years.

689. GLORY BE TO THE FATHER

Ephesians 3: 21

This lesser doxology, as it is called, was first introduced in the second century of the Christian era, linking the Psalms and the New Testament teaching on the deity of Christ. The second clause was added three or four centuries later. The nearest scripture equivalent is found in Ephesians 3: 21: "Unto Him be glory in the church by Christ Jesus throughout all ages, world without end. Amen."

The musical setting, *Gloria Patri* (= glory to the Father), is taken from Henry Wellington Greatorex's (1811-58) Collection of Church Music, 1851. He was born in Burton-on-Trent, Derbyshire, and emigrated to the United States in 1838, where he became organist at the Center Congregational church, Hartford, Connecticut. Later, he served as organist in various New York Protestant Episcopal churches. He also arranged Nos. 25 and 383, *Manoah;* 48, *Seymour,* and 174, *Leighton.*

690. THE LORD IS IN HIS HOLY TEMPLE

Habakkuk 2: 20

The words (see Nos. 699 and 703) are a direct quotation and repetition from Habakkuk 2: 20: "But the Lord is in His holy temple: let all the earth keep silence before Him."

The tune *Quam Dilecta* (= how delightful) is by George Frederick Root (1820-95), who also composed Nos. 93 and 299, *Varina;* 418, *Jewels,* and 620, unnamed. He was an American choir conductor, music teacher, and music publisher, and associated with Lowell Mason, see appendix, in the Boston Academy of Music.

691. LET THE WORDS OF MY MOUTH

Psalm 19: 14

These words are used by Jewish worshippers as a response to silent prayer in the synagogue service. They are almost an exact quotation (meditation is not in the plural) from Psalm 19: 14: "Let the words of my mouth, and the meditation of my heart, be acceptable in thy sight, O Lord, my strength, and my redeemer."

The tune *In Corde Meo* (= in my heart) is taken from the "Sacred Quartets," 1862, of Adolph Baumbach (1830-80), who emigrated from Germany to the United States, where he became a piano and organ teacher.

692. CAST THY BURDEN UPON THE LORD

Psalm 55: 22

This response is a collection of quotations from the Psalms, namely: "Cast thy burden upon the Lord, and He shall sustain thee: He shall never suffer the righteous to be moved," Psalm 55: 22; "He is at my right hand, I shall not be moved," Psalm 16: 8; "For Thy mercy is great unto the heavens," Psalm 57: 10; and "Yea, let none that wait on Thee be ashamed." Psalm 25: 3.

The tune *Birmingham,* a modification of No. 217, *Munich,* was composed by Jakob Ludwig Felix Mendelssohn-Bartholdy (1809-47) of Hamburg, Germany, and is taken from the oratorio "Elijah," which was first performed at Birmingham, England, on August 26, 1846. This famous composer of oratorios, cantatas, and orchestral and piano music, also wrote Nos. 111, *Mendelssohn;* 257, *Trust;* 674, *Abiding,* and 687, unnamed.

693. O PRAISE THE LORD, ALL YE NATIONS

Psalm 117

This response is a complete, exact, unabridged quotation of the shortest chapter in the Bible, Psalm 117. An Amen is added.

The tune *Laetatus Sum* (= I was glad) is a chant by Joseph Barnby (1838-96), see appendix.

694. LORD, KEEP US SAFE THIS NIGHT

Psalm 34: 7

The words, also set to a different tune in No. 696, *Vesper,* ask for a fulfilment of the promise of Psalm 34: 7: "The angel of the Lord encampeth around about them that fear Him, and delivereth them." They are the third stanza of a hymn by John Leland (1754-1841), and appeared in 1792 in "Philomela, or A Selection of Spiritual Songs." The omitted stanzas are:—

1. The day is past and gone,
The evening shades appear,
O may I ever keep in mind,
The night of death draws near.

2. I lay my garments by,
Upon my bed to rest;
So death will soon remove me hence,
And leave my soul undressed.

4. And when I early rise,
To view th'unwearied sun,
May I set out to win the prize
And after glory run.

5. Then when my days are past,
And I from time remove,
Lord, may I in Thy bosom rest,
The bosom of Thy love.

Leland was a Baptist minister of Grafton, Massachusetts, who in an active life preached 8,000 sermons, wrote 30 pamphlets, and baptized over 1,500 persons. He is commemorated for his work on the first amendment to the United States constitution guaranteeing freedom of religion, by the Leland-Madison Park at Orange, Virginia, a town in which he ministered for fourteen years.

The tune, arranged from Ludwig van Beethoven (1770-1827), one of the greatest composers of orchestral and pianoforte works, is wrongly attributed to his variation on the Sonata Appassionata, Opus 57.

695. THE LORD BLESS YOU AND KEEP YOU

Numbers 6: 24-26

These words are a slight modification of the blessing of Moses, which in the Authorized Version reads: "The Lord bless thee, and keep thee: the Lord make His face shine upon thee, and be gracious unto thee: the Lord lift up His countenance upon thee, and give thee peace." Numbers 6: 24-26.

The tune *Choral Blessing* was composed in 1900 by Peter Christian Lutkin (1858-1931), and dedicated: "To my friend William Smedley." Lutkin also wrote No. 128, *Lanier*. He was an organist at various Protestant Episcopal churches in America, music editor of the "Methodist Hymnal," and founder and dean of the school of music at North Western University, where the Lutkin Hall of music perpetuates his memory.

696. LORD, KEEP US SAFE THIS NIGHT

Psalm 34: 7

The words are a prayer requesting the fulfilment of the promise of Psalm 34: 7: "The angel of the Lord encampeth round about them that fear Him, and delivereth them." The same words are set to a different tune in No. 694, and are there commented on in full.

The tune *Vesper Hymn* was composed in 1938 by Edgar Halstead (1885-) especially for a choir which he conducted in Manchester, England. The tune previously sung to these same words (No. 694) had become hackneyed through constant use, and a new tune supplied freshness. The first two phrases, each of six syllables, are combined into one phrase of twelve syllables, converting an ordinary short metre tune into the unusual 12.8.6. Another tune by the same composer and organist is No. 96, *Snowdon*. He died in 1969.

697. WITH PRAISE, O GOD, WE WORSHIP THEE

Psalm 95: 6

Leroy Edwin Froom (1890-), a minister of the Seventh-day Adventist Church, was the pioneer in 1927 of the *Ministry* magazine, a journal for ministers. He is also the author of the four volumes of *"Prophetic Faith of Our Fathers,"* which presents the Seventh-day Adventist Church in its true historical position as the repository of truths belonging to the early Christian church. He was a member of the committee which produced this denominational hymnal, and wrote many gospel songs, both words and music, always, however, in the unusual method of writing the music first. This brief response of prayer and praise recalls several scriptures, for example: "O come, let us worship and bow down: let us kneel before the Lord our maker," Psalm 95: 6; "For this God is our God for ever and ever: He will be our guide even unto death," Psalm 48: 14; and "In all thy ways acknowledge Him, and He shall direct thy paths." Proverbs 3: 6.

The tune *Response* was composed in 1939 by Leroy Edwin Froom, and another of his compositions is No. 702, *Benediction,* to his words, "Dismiss Us, Lord, With Blessing." Froom died in 1974.

698. THE SHADOWS LENGTHEN

Jeremiah 6: 4

This four-line stanza is really one of five lines, for four of the lines are of ten syllables each, all rhyming—abide, Guide, betide, hide—and the fifth is a separate five-syllable line. The Scripture verses suggested are: Jeremiah 6: 4: "For the shadows of the evening are stretched out"; Luke 24: 29: "Abide with us"; James 2: 23: "He was called the Friend of God"; Psalm 48: 14: "He will be our Guide"; Exodus 33: 22: "I will put thee in a clift of the rock"; and Isaiah 26: 3: "Thou wilt keep him in perfect peace."

The music *Vesper* by Walter A. Parkyn, is written to emphasize the metre of 10.10.10.10.5, for the last five chords are almost a plagal cadence suggesting an Amen.

699. THE LORD IS IN HIS HOLY TEMPLE

Habakkuk 2: 20

The words are a direct quotation from Habakkuk 2: 20 (see Nos. 690, 703).

The musical setting *Pontiac* was composed in the town of this name in Michigan in 1934 by Pastor Donald Frederick Haynes (1907-), where he was conducting a public mission effort, and where he used the musical sentence as a theme song. He graduated from Atlantic Union College, from the Seventh-day Adventist Theological Seminary, and from the George Peabody College for teachers, and has been a Seventh-day Adventist minister in New York, Washington, North Carolina, Colorado, and elsewhere, and has also composed over 200 hymns as well as many other arrangements of hymns. Haynes died in 1975.

700. LORD, BLESS THY WORD TO EVERY HEART
Psalm 119: 133

This benediction is a denominational one, for the writer of the words, Pearl Waggoner Howard (daughter of Jessie Fremont Waggoner Moser of No. 286), is a well-known Seventh-day Adventist authoress, while the composer, Stanley Ledington (1889-), was a teacher for forty years in Seventh-day Adventist academies and colleges. He was born in Durham, England, and studied organ in Plymouth and composition in Minneapolis, receiving the Mus. Bac. degree from the Sherwood Music School in Chicago. He has written a number of anthems, and also Nos. 46, *For the Sabbath;* 98, *Rose of Sharon,* and 476, *Communion.*

The words can be summarized by the psalmist's prayer, "Order my steps in Thy word," Psalm 119: 133, and the title of the tune *Benediction* shows the intention of having them used as a closing prayer. Mrs. Howard died in 1969 and Ledington in 1974.

701. HOLY SPIRIT, FAITHFUL GUIDE
John 16: 13

This short stanza is a summary of the vital work of the Spirit of God—to lead us into truth that will finally bring us into the eternal kingdom of truth. Our Lord plainly stated that this was the function of the Holy Spirit: "When He, the Spirit of truth, is come, He will guide you." John 16: 13; and "He shall give you another Comforter, that He may abide with you." John 14: 16.

The tune *Holy Spirit* was composed in 1939 by Paul O. Campbell.

702. DISMISS US, LORD, WITH BLESSING
Psalm 28: 7, 9

The tune *Benediction* was composed in 1934 by Leroy Edwin Froom (1890-), a minister of the Seventh-day Adventist Church, and author of the *"Prophetic Faith of Our Fathers."* He was conscious of the lack of a suitable closing item for the choir or for the congregation, and according to his undeviating custom, composed the tune first of all.

He then wrote the words appropriate to the tune, words which in part recall the psalmist's cry: "With my song will I praise Him. . . . Save Thy people, and bless Thine inheritance," Psalm 28: 7, 9. Froom also wrote both words and music of No. 697, "With Praise, O God, We Worship Thee," to *Response.* Froom died in 1974.

703. THE LORD IS IN HIS HOLY TEMPLE

Habakkuk 2: 20

The words are a direct quotation from Habakkuk 2: 20 (see Nos. 690, 699).

The musical setting was composed by Karl Pomeroy Harrington (1861-1953), an organist, musical editor, and choir director of the Methodist Church in the United States of America. He also wrote No. 106, *Christmas Song. Invocation Sentence* was written in 1903 for the chapel service of the University of Maine, where Harrington was a teacher, in order to produce a reverent atmosphere, and when the composer played the first two chords, quiet was obtained immediately.

Biographical Appendix

of authors and composers from whose works seven or more selections have been included in "Church Hymnal"

JOSEPH BARNBY (1838-96) was born on August 12, 1838, at York, England, and as a boy of seven years was singing in the choir in York Minster, and at the age of twelve was an organist. At the age of sixteen he became a pupil at the Royal Academy of Music where Arthur Seymour Sullivan was a fellow student. In 1863 he became church organist at St. Andrew's, Wells Street, London, and four years later started a choir, Barnby's choir, which developed into the Royal Choral Society, and of which he was the conductor until his death. He was organist at several London churches, particularly at St. Anne's, Soho, where he established the annual performance of Bach's Passion Music. In 1875 he was appointed director of music at Eton College and continued there until 1892, when he became Principal of the Guildhall School of Music. For his services to church music he was knighted in 1892. He was a splendid choirmaster, and did much to popularize good sacred music, being musical adviser to Novello's music firm. He wrote nearly 250 hymn tunes, as well as anthems, part songs, vocal solos, and an oratorio "Rebekah," and edited five hymnbooks. He died in London on January 28, 1896, and was buried at Norwood. His tunes are:—

43	*Laudes Domini*	6.6.6.6.6.6.
52	*Merrial*	6.5.6.5.
262	*Cloisters*	11.11.11.5.
350	*St. Chrysostom*	8.8.8.8.8.8.
365	*Sarum*	10.10.10.4.
386	*Holy Trinity*	8.6.8.6. (C.M.)
412	*Alverstoke*	11.10.11.10.
416	*O Perfect Love*	11.10.11.10.
514	*Jordan*	8.8.8.8.8.8.8.8. (L.M.D.)
678	*Crossing the Bar*	Irregular
693	*Laetatus Sum*	Chant

EDWIN BARNES (1864-1930) was born in Shirley, a suburb of Southampton, England, on March 15, 1864. Although he had not travelled more than twenty miles from home in his first seventeen years, he accepted an invitation from Dr. John Harvey Kellogg in 1881 to go to the United States to Battle Creek, Michigan, where he became organist for the Seventh-day Adventist church there. He continued his musical studies and made five visits to Europe to improve his knowledge of voice, of piano, and of organ. He was a thorough teacher, and as well as being head of the music department at Battle Creek College for nearly twenty years, he raised the cultural standards of the city by bringing noted singers and musicians to assist in oratorios held there. In 1903 he directed the chorus at the dedication of the new Battle Creek Sanitarium, which replaced the one that had been destroyed by fire the previous year. Barnes formed an Amateur Music Club and instituted an annual May festival of music at Battle Creek. He also operated the Battle Creek Conservatory of Music, where piano, organ, voice, and violin were taught, but this closed in June, 1926, because of his ill-health. He served as organist in the First Congregational church in Battle Creek as well as choir director, holding these positions for a continuous period of more than thirty years. Not only was he a teacher of piano, organ, and voice, but he directed choral societies and orchestras, and on occasion directed the visiting New York Symphony Orchestra, and the Chicago orchestra. In 1920, Hillsdale College, Michigan, conferred on him the honorary degree of Doctor of Music because of his outstanding service in this field. He composed many hymn tunes and organ pieces, and with Franklin Edson Belden and James Edson White selected the hymns for the first official hymnbook of Seventh-day Adventists, "Hymns and Tunes," which was published in 1886. He was one of the two musical editors of this work and contributed to it twenty original tunes and one arrangement. Some of his hymn tunes were named after English towns, commemorating the country of his birth, some even after towns in his home county of Hampshire. He died at Battle Creek, Michigan, on April 11, 1930. His contributions to "Church Hymnal" are:—

6	*Southampton*	12.10.12.10.
144	*York*	8.8.8.8. (L.M.)
216	*Salisbury*	7.7.7.5.
293	*Heber*	8.8.8.8. (L.M.)
391	*Winterbourne*	8.8.8.8. (L.M.)
395	*Morton*	8.8.8.8.8.8.
494	*Russell*	8.8.8.8. (L.M.)
539	*When the King Shall Claim His Own*	8.7.8.7.8.7.8.7.

FRANKLIN EDSON BELDEN (1858-1945) was born at Battle Creek, Michigan, on March 21, 1858, the son of Albert Belden and Sarah Harmon, the latter being the elder sister of Ellen G. White. He received most of his education in the Seventh-day Adventist College, which was established there in 1874. About the year 1876 he went with his parents and the James Whites (his uncle and aunt) to California and began composing music there. Because of bronchial trouble he moved to Colorado where, in 1881, he married a girl with musical talent. To this union was born a daughter, Linnie Belden, who has supplied these biographical details of her father. Belden returned to Battle Creek in the early '80's to connect with the publishing work of the Seventh-day Adventists, and published song books for this growing denomination. With Edwin Barnes he was music editor for their first official hymnbook, "Hymns and Tunes," 1886, and with his cousin James Edson White, he brought out "Joyful Greetings for the Sabbath School," also in 1886. In 1895, he produced "Gospel Song Sheaf" and "Christ in Song" and also other books of patriotic music. He became manager of the Review and Herald Publishing Company, and continued at Battle Creek until about 1910, when he began to write songs for Billy Sunday, which were included in his book "Songs for the King's Business." Unfortunately, his later years were marred by a misunderstanding with the Seventh-day Adventist Church over royalties that he maintained should have gone directly to missionary work as he had intended, rather than into the publishing house, which was an organization of the church. However, all his papers and manuscripts were donated to the theological seminary of the church after his death. Belden showed his musical genius by frequently writing a song while listening to a sermon, taking the text as the theme. Often he and Mrs. Belden, who were choir members, would sing the newly composed hymn for the congregation at the conclusion of the sermon in place of the final hymn. The book "Christ in Song" contains many of these hymns and tunes, the original manuscripts of which were usually given to the preacher. In the present "Church Hymnal" he has sixteen complete hymns with tunes, seven words only, and six tunes only—a grand total of forty-five, the largest individual contribution of all. They are:—

31	"Eternal Father, God of Love"	
	Mason	8.8.8.8. (L.M.)
183	"Let Every Lamp Be Burning Bright"	
	Diligence	8.7.8.7. Refrain
191	"He's Coming Once Again"	
	Verdi	6.6.8.6.6.6.8.6. (S.M.D.)
380	"There Is Sweet Rest"	
	Hakes	9.7.9.7.
482	"The Judgment Has Set"	
	Unnamed	11.8.9.7. Refrain
517	"There's No Other Name Like Jesus"	
	Unnamed	8.7.8.7. Refrain
529	"I Will Sing of Jesus' Love"	
	Unnamed	7.7.7.7. Refrain
540	"We Know Not the Hour"	
	Unnamed	12.12.12.6. Refrain

546	"The Coming King Is at the Door"	
	Even at the Door	8.8.8.6. Refrain
548	"Sweet Promise Is Given"	
	Hold Fast Till I Come	10.11.10.11. Refrain
578	"Blessed Lord, How Much I Need Thee"	
	Unnamed	8.7.8.7. Refrain
579	"We'll Build on the Rock"	
	Unnamed	9.8.9.7. Refrain
593	"Look Upon Jesus, Sinless Is He"	
	Cover with His Life	9.9.9.9. Refrain
597	"I Would Be, Dear Saviour, Wholly Thine"	
	Wholly Thine	9.6.9.5. Refrain
654	"Holy Day, Jehovah's Rest"	
	Unnamed	7.7.7.7. Refrain
671	"Look for the Waymarks"	
	Look for the Waymarks	10.10.10.10. Refrain
66	"Like As a Father"	
391	"Shepherd Divine"	
493	"Sweet Be Thy Rest"	
500	"Raise the Standard High"	
599	"Father, We Come to Thee"	
613	"O Jesus, My Redeemer"	
629	"If Any Little Word of Mine"	
29	*Unnamed*	11.10.11.10.
410	*Robinson*	6.4.6.4.6.6.6.4.
441	*Oakland*	8.8.8.8. (L.M.)
447	*Fillmore*	8.7.8.7.8.7.8.7.
570	*Over the Line*	10.7.10.6. Refrain
585	*A Shelter in the Time of Storm*	L.M. Refrain

PHILIPP BLISS (1838-76) was born in Clearfield County, Pennsylvania, on July 9, 1838, and christened Philipp with two p's. He disliked the final p, and when older separated it so that it appeared as though it stood for the initial letter of a second Christian name. As a boy of ten years of age, he heard the piano for the first time and stood entranced, as he had previously only heard the flute. He recognized the instrument because he had heard it described by his mother, and the music appealed to a hidden talent in his heart. He attended a singing school conducted by William Batchelder Bradbury, and later became a music teacher touring the countryside. A turning point in his life came in 1864 when he sent to the music publishing firm of Root and Cady a secular song, "Lora Vale," which he had composed, requesting a flute instead of payment if the song was published. With the flute came an invitation to come to Chicago, where he joined G. F. Root's firm and with him conducted musical institutes and conventions. He and his wife sang gospel duets together, and by 1870 he was director of music at the First Congregational Church in Chicago, and Sunday-school superintendent the next year, although he had been a Methodist earlier. Music bubbled up within this handsome, genial baritone, and he was always on the alert for stories or incidents that would inspire hymns. Many of his gospel songs were written to stories told by Dwight L. Moody in his sermons. His gospel songs were sung and popularized in England in 1874 by Ira D. Sankey, and in that same year Bliss joined Major D. W. Whittle as a singing evangelist. On Sankey's return from England, he and Bliss collaborated to issue a joint song-book, "Gospel Hymns and Sacred Songs," which became amazingly popular and started a flood of other gospel hymn collections of inferior value. His prolific output came to an untimely end on December 29, 1876, when the train in which he was travelling back to Chicago, plunged through a weak bridge at Ashtabula, Ohio. The carriages caught fire, but the composer escaped, only to lose his life as he returned to the burning wreck in a vain effort to save his wife. In his baggage, his friends found an unfinished hymn, which was almost prophetic, namely:—

> I know not what awaits me,
> God kindly veils my eyes.

In Rome, Pennsylvania, Philipp Bliss is commemorated by a monument, recalling him particularly as the author and composer of the hymn "Hold the Fort."

Bliss wrote both words and music of:—

228 "Almost Persuaded"
Almost 9.9.6.6.6.4.

423 "I Am So Glad that Our Father"
Jesus Loves Even Me 10.10.10.10. Refrain

497 "Standing by a Purpose True"
Daniel 7.5.7.6. Refrain

571 "Whosoever Heareth"
Whosoever Will 10.11.11.7. Refrain

574 "Sing Them Over Again to Me"
Wonderful Words of Life 8.6.8.6.6.6. Refrain

628 "Brightly Beams Our Father's Mercy"
Lower Lights 8.7.8.7. Refrain

and the tune for
313 *It Is Well* 11.8.11.9.

HORATIUS BONAR (1808-89) was born on December 19, 1808, at Edinburgh, Scotland. He was educated at the High School in this city and at the University, where he came under the influence of Dr. Thomas Chalmers and Edward Irving. The former inspired him to become a minister of the gospel, and the latter to study the prophecies of the Bible. Bonar completed his theological studies and began his ministerial duties in St. John's, Leith, in 1833, one of the slum areas of this part of Edinburgh. There he began to write hymns in order to interest the children, one beneficial result being a great interest in the Sunday school, which flourished as the children and youth sang Bonar's words to popular tunes. Adults preferred psalm singing, which indeed was the only permitted method among the Presbyterians, the psalter being the only hymn-book, according to ecclesiastical law. Bonar was ordained a minister of the Church of Scotland in 1838, and was transferred to the Kelso parish church. At the Disruption in 1843 he took an active part with and followed his teacher Chalmers into the Free Church of Scotland, remaining at Kelso. In 1853 he received the degree of Doctor of Divinity from the University of Aberdeen, and in 1856 visited Egypt and Palestine. He returned from Kelso to Edinburgh in 1866 to the Chalmers Memorial Church, where he ministered for another twenty-one years. He was appointed Moderator of the General Assembly of the Free Church of Scotland in 1883, and died July 31, 1889. His pen was active throughout a busy life of prayer and piety. He wrote about 600 hymns and sixty translations of the Psalms, and also hundreds of tracts. His hymns are simple and subjective but most appealing, doubtless because of his effort to fill them with, as he said, the love and light of Christ. During the revival of 1873-74 he wrote especially for the gospel singer Ira David Sankey. Bonar was a devout student of prophecy, and for many years edited the *Quarterly Journal of Prophecy,* which began in 1848 and to which he regularly contributed a hymn. He believed also in the imminent return of the Lord Jesus Christ, this being a major interest, and evident also in many of his hymns. All of his hymns were written casually and were not revised or polished, as he considered that they were of little importance. He gave instructions that no memoir of himself should be written:—

> My name and my place and my tomb all forgotten,
> The brief race of time well and patiently run,
> So let me pass away, peacefully, silently,
> Only remembered by what I have done.

His hymns in "Church Hymnal" are the eleven following:—

67 "O Love of God"
174 "Come, Lord, and Tarry Not"
177 "The Church Has Waited Long"
225, 226 "I Heard the Voice of Jesus Say"
270 "Give Thou Thy Youth to God"
278 "I Lay My Sins on Jesus"
334 "Calm Me, My God"
372 "A Few More Years Shall Roll"
396 "Thy Way, Not Mine"
441 "Go, Labour On"
556 "Angel Voices Sweetly Singing"

WILLIAM BATCHELDER BRADBURY (1816-68) was born at York, Maine, on October 6, 1816, of musical parents whose poverty precluded them from giving their son an early training in music. His talent was apparent, however, for as a boy of fourteen he played a variety of instruments, although up to that time he had not seen a piano or organ. He went to Boston and studied under Lowell Mason, who encouraged him to make music composition his life-work. He became a teacher of singing in Maine, and specialized in composing songs for Sunday schools. He was organist in the Baptist Church and directed musical festivals and singing classes, later becoming director of music at the Baptist Tabernacle in New York City. In 1847 he made a visit to England and to Germany to study music methods and on his return to the United States he joined Lowell Mason, George Frederick Root and Thomas Hastings in organizing musical conventions that revolutionized American hymnody. Bradbury was a pioneer in publishing music for Sunday schools and did his best to exclude the unworthy secular tunes which then abounded. His own compositions are not at all first class, but they served their purpose in saving hymns from falling into a very cheap category, virtually being a compromise between high-brow music and popular street songs. In one of his singing schools Philipp Bliss was a student and received encouragement from Bradbury just as the latter had from Mason. Bradbury was also the one who suggested to Fanny Crosby that she turn her poetic gift to the writing of hymns. In later life he became a piano maker with his brother. He composed the cantata "Esther," and published sixty hymnbooks. Bradbury died at Montclair, New Jersey, on January 7, 1868. His tunes selected for "Church Hymnal" are:—

4	*Harvey's Chant*	8.6.8.6. (C.M.)
41, 253	*Zephyr*	8.8.8.8. (L.M.)
121	*Olive's Brow*	L.M.
180	*Dawning*	8.7.8.7.8.7.8.7.
208	*Even Me*	8.7.8.7. Refrain
222	*Woodworth*	L.M. (8.8.8.8.)
234	*Aletta*	7.7.7.7.
316	*Sweet Hour*	L.M. Doubled
317	*Brown*	C.M. (8.6.8.6.)
393	*He Leadeth Me*	L.M. Refrain
394	*Shepherd*	8.7.8.7.8.7.8.7.
422	*Sweet Story*	Irregular
489	*Rest (Bradbury)*	L.M.
576	*Stand Like the Brave*	11.11.11.11. Refrain
581	*The Solid Rock*	L.M. Refrain
653	*Unnamed*	12.13.13.13. Refrain

WILLIAM COWPER (1731-1800) was born at Berkhampstead, Hertfordshire, on November 26, 1731, and pronounced his name Cooper, as indeed it used to be spelled by his forebears. One notable forebear was his great-grandfather's great-grandfather, who was Lord Mayor of London in the mid-sixteenth century. Cowper's mother died when he was six years old, and this upset his already highly strung sensitive nature, which was further worsened by bullying at the boarding school at Markyate to which he was then sent. He was further educated at Westminster School, and then in a solicitor's office to train for the legal profession. His father died in 1756, whereupon his friends arranged for him to become a clerk in the House of Lords, but he had a complete nervous breakdown when he learned that he had to appear in person for an examination for this post, and as a result spent the next eighteen months in an asylum. His youth was plagued by mental attacks, and several times he attempted suicide during these periods of mental instability, until he found some measure of relief and comfort in the home of the Rev. Morley Unwin at Huntingdon in 1765. Unfortunately, this friend died two years later following an accident, but Mrs. Unwin cared for him like a mother, and with her he moved to the small town of Olney in Buckinghamshire. Here he associated with John Newton, the converted slave-captain, until the latter's transfer to London in 1779. Together they conducted revival meetings in the town, and compiled the "Olney Hymns" published in 1779, which contained sixty-eight by Cowper and 280 by Newton. Apart from this lasting contribution to posterity, Cowper became a leading English poet, and turned his talent to the writing of common everyday things. He wrote of nature, of daily life, even of humdrum things, expressing common sentiments in excellent verse, and giving voice to the growing humanitarian movement. He spent much time on a translation of Homer, and on his greatest work, "The Task," which extolled simple piety and natural pleasures. Other poems now well remembered today are, for example, "John Gilpin," and "The Loss of the Royal George." After Mrs. Unwin's death in 1797, Cowper's mental powers declined and his interest in life waned until he died at East Dereham, Norfolk, on April 25, 1800. His poems in "Church Hymnal" are:—

84 "God Moves in a Mysterious Way"
163 "There Is a Fountain"
248 " 'Tis My Happiness Below"
254 "Sometimes a Light Surprises"
298 "Hark, My Soul! It is the Lord"
383 "O, For a Closer Walk!"
515 "Jesus, Where'er Thy People Meet"

FRANCES JANE CROSBY (1820-1915), was born at Southeast, Putman County, New York State, on March 24, 1820, but at the age of only six weeks she lost her eyesight because of the ignorant application of a mustard poultice to her eyes. Her father died soon afterwards, but these difficulties did not affect her happy disposition. While still of tender years, about eight, she wrote:—

Oh, what a happy soul am I!
Although I cannot see,
I am resolved that in this world
Contented I will be;
How many blessings I enjoy
That other people don't!
To weep and sigh because I'm blind
I cannot, and I won't!

One of her advantages was that she was able to write undisturbed by outside distractions, though she evidently possessed a gift for rhyming and had an acute memory. In 1835 she was sent to the New York Institute for the Blind, where she later became one of the teachers, and where she met and married in 1858 a blind musician, Alexander van Alstyne. Their only child died in infancy, and Fanny's husband died in 1883. She wrote popular verse and secular songs with great success until about the year 1864, when William Batchelder Bradbury suggested that she devote her talent to writing Christian songs. From that time she never wrote another secular song, but diverted all her energy to gospel songs, praying before their composition. She contracted with one publishing firm to supply three hymns a week for a year, and even apart from this, wrote copiously. She used a bewildering array of over 200 pen-names and in her lifetime wrote more than 8,000 hymns. She died peacefully at Bridgeport, Connecticut, on February 12, 1915. Her poems in "Church Hymnal" are:—

7 "The Lord in Zion Reigneth"
259 "All the Way My Saviour Leads Me"
*324 "'Tis the Blessed Hour of Prayer"
479 "Would You Win a Saviour's Blessing?"
480 "A Year of Precious Blessings"
*522 "Now Just a Word for Jesus"
534 "Tell Me the Story of Jesus"
*559 "Pass Me Not, O Gentle Saviour"
569 "Jesus Is Tenderly Calling"
576 "O Christian Awake"
*594 "I Am Thine, O Lord"
*595 "Jesus, Keep Me Near the Cross"
596 "Take the World, but Give Me Jesus"
*601 "Be Silent, Be Silent"
608 "Blessed Assurance, Jesus Is Mine"
*615 "Safe In the Arms of Jesus"

*623	"Rescue the Perishing"
630	"Some Day the Silver Cord Will Break"
635	"Redeemed! How I Love to Proclaim It!"
645	"Praise Him! Praise Him!"
*647	"To God Be the Glory"
651	"A Wonderful Saviour Is Jesus My Lord"
653	"Don't Forget the Sabbath"

*Tunes by William Howard Doane.

WILLIAM HOWARD DOANE (1832-1916) was born at Preston, Connecticut, and became a manufacturer of woodworking machinery in Cincinnati, Ohio. He was, however, very musically minded and used this talent in church work in that city. He was a Baptist Sunday school superintendent for a number of years, and acted as choir conductor of the Norwich, Connecticut, Harmonic Society. His chief contribution to fame was the composition of over 2,000 hymn tunes which he began writing at the age of thirty, many of them being to words by his friend Fanny Crosby. He also published over thirty collections of music for Sunday school use, and composed cantatas and anthems. He worked with the evangelists Dwight Lyman Moody and Ira David Sankey, writing gospel songs for their missions. In 1875, Denison University, Ohio, conferred on him the degree of Mus. Doc. He died in Cincinnati in 1916 at the advanced age of eighty-four. His tunes, many of them unnamed, are:—

*324	——	13.12.13.7.6. Refrain
385	——	6.4.6.4.6.6.6.4.
*522	——	7.6.7.6. Refrain
523	——	8.7.8.7. Refrain
524	*Evangel*	7.6.7.6.7.6.7.6. Refrain
*559	*Pass Me Not*	8.5.8.5. Refrain
*954	*Draw Me Nearer*	10.7.10.7. Refrain
*595	*Near the Cross*	7.6.7.6. Refrain
*601	*Tread Softly*	6.5.6.5. Refrain
*615	*Refuge*	7.6.7.6.7.6.7.6 Refrain
*623	*Rescue*	6.5.10.6.5.10. Refrain
*647	*To God Be the Glory*	11.11.11.11. Refrain

*Words by Fanny Crosby.

PHILIP DODDRIDGE (1702-51) was born in London on June 26, 1702, a weak and sickly child, the twentieth in the family. His mother was the daughter of a Lutheran minister who had fled from Bohemia to England because of religious persecution, and she brought him up in the non-conformist faith. His father was the son of a Church of England clergyman who had resigned his living rather than subscribe to the Act of Uniformity, which required obedience to the Anglican prayer book in its entirety. Doddridge was orphaned while still a child, and was cared for by friends. He showed signs of academic ability and religious devotion and was therefore offered an education to train for the Anglican ministry. However, the University statutes were unacceptable to his inbred and cultivated Independent—or Congregational—theological principles, so he was forced to decline the offer, and instead trained at Kibworth in Leicestershire for the ministry of the Independent Church. In 1723 he completed the course and succeeded his teacher Jennings at Kibworth. Six years later he was chosen to conduct a new academy being established at Market Harborough, but he was transferred in the same year to Northampton. He was appointed to the Castle Hill church and directed the theological seminary for twenty-two years, training many other young men for the Congregational ministry, the main subjects being philosophy and theology. In 1736 he received the degree of Doctor of Divinity from the University of Aberdeen. His health was never very good, and in September, 1751, he was persuaded to make a journey to Lisbon to find a cure, but he died there of tuberculosis on October 26, 1751. He was a co-founder of the hospital in Northampton, and to his memory in that town there stands the Doddridge Memorial Chapel. In his day the congregation was mostly unable to read or write, and hymns were "lined out" or read out line by line for the people to sing a line at a time. Doddridge took advantage of this deficiency by composing hymns based on the subject of his sermon, and having them read and sung as the closing hymn, thus impressing the lesson on his hearers. Most of his nearly 400 hymns were of this type, and were based on his sincere, practical sermons. In the "Church Hymnal" his contributions are:—

21 "My Gracious Lord, I Own Thy Right"
64 "How Gentle God's Commands"
88 "O God of Bethel"
175 "Awake, Ye Saints"
310 "O Happy Day! That Fixed My Choice"
351 "Ye Servants of the Lord"
355 "Awake, My Soul!"
411 "See, Israel's Gentle Shepherd"

JOHN BACCHUS DYKES (1823-76) was born at Hull, Yorkshire, on March 10, 1823, receiving his middle name from his maternal grandfather. In his early years he showed great musical ability, being able to play by ear anything he heard, and when he was only ten years old he played the organ in his father's church. While at St. Catherine's College, Cambridge, he took a part in founding the University Musical Society, becoming its conductor, and contributed humorous verse and melodies to it. In 1847 he was ordained, and turned his talent then to sacred music. In 1849 he was moved to Durham, where he remained in the service of the church until his death, being minor canon, precentor in the Cathedral, director of the Cathedral choir, and vicar of St. Oswald's. In 1856 he began writing a succession of hymn tunes that used good harmonies so that they were suitable for singing by the different parts of his choirs. He composed over 300 tunes for the revitalized Anglican Church, which was then ready to follow the movement for congregational hymn-singing started by Watts and Wesley. Dykes was able to write music at any time and in any place, no matter what distractions there were, and his musical abilities were recognized by the Mus. Doc. degree granted in 1861 by Durham University. His later years were marred by differences with his bishop due to Dykes's high church practices, but his real worth was appreciated by a generous memorial fund that reached over £10,000 for the support of his family. He died at Ticehurst, Sussex, on January 22, 1876. His tunes, all of them named for some good and specific purpose, and which appear in "Church Hymnal" are:—

18, 166 *Beatitudo*	C.M. (8.6.8.6.)
26 *Pax Dei*	10.10.10.10.
73 *Nicaea*	11.12.12.10.
86 *Dominus Regit Me*	8.7.8.7.
127 *St. Drostane*	L.M. (8.8.8.8.)
129 *St. John*	6.6.6.4.8.8.4.
158, 209, 413 *St. Agnes*	C.M.
214 *St. Cuthbert*	8.6.8.4.
225 *Vox Dilecti*	C.M.D. (8.6.8.6.8.6.8.6.)
298 *St. Bees*	7.7.7.7.
306 *Alford*	7.6.8.6.7.6.8.6.
325 *Almsgiving*	8.8.8.4.
367 *St. Andrew of Crete*	6.5.6.5.6.5.6.5.
388 *Mary Magdalene*	6.5.6.5.6.5.6.5.
402 *Hollingside*	7.7.7.7.7.7.7.7.
403 *Lux Benigna*	10.4.10.4.10.10.
451 *Fiat Lux*	6.6.4.6.6.6.4.

THOMAS HASTINGS (1784-1872) was born in Washington, Connecticut, on October 15, 1784. At the age of two years he moved to Clinton, New York, where his natural musical talent became evident, for at the age of eighteen he was leading the village choir. He taught music in 1806, and from 1816 onwards devoted his whole time thereto. With Solomon Warriner he published "Musica Sacra" and the "Utica Collection" of original tunes. He settled in Utica, New York, in 1823, and started a religious journal, the *Western Recorder*, which he used to propagate his special views on church music in order to attempt to rescue it from the low level to which it had sunk. His "Union Minstrel" appeared in 1830, and in the next year with Lowell Mason he published "Spiritual

Songs for Social Worship," mainly to offset and counteract the influence of Joshua Leavitt's gospel hymns (see No. 667). His attempts to raise the standard of church music led to his being called to New York in 1832 to put his theories into practice, and he served as choirmaster for twelve churches there. With W. B. Bradbury he published many books on music and on hymns through the following twenty years, generally of high standard, and with Lowell Mason and Bradbury he edited a psalmody collection. The University of New York conferred on him the degree of Doctor of Music in 1858. He composed about 1,000 original tunes and wrote 600 hymns, many of them for tunes already in use with words whose metres did not really correspond. He died in New York on May 15, 1872. His hymns and tunes in "Church Hymnal" are:—

Hymns:—

302 "Hail to the Brightness"
400 "O, Tell Me, Thou Life and Delight of My Soul"
627 "He that Goeth Forth"

Tunes:—

159, 656	*Ortonville*	C.M. (8.6.8.6.)
184	*Zion*	8.7.8.7.4.7.
241, 488	*Retreat*	L.M. (8.8.8.8.)
400	*Still Water*	11.10.11.10.
474	*Toplady*	7.7.7.7.7.7.

FRANCES RIDLEY HAVERGAL (1836-79) was born at Astley, Worcestershire, on December 14, 1836, the youngest child of an Anglican rector, William Henry Havergal (see No. 411). She moved to Worcester in 1845 when her father was appointed canon of the cathedral there. She began to write verse at the age of seven, and later learned many languages both ancient and modern. She was a brilliant pianist and very fond of singing, but sang only sacred songs. At the age of fourteen she committed her soul to God her Saviour, and "earth and heaven seemed brighter from that moment." Four years later she was confirmed as a member of the Anglican Church. Miss Havergal was a deeply religious and devout Christian with an intense personal connection with the Lord Jesus Christ. She was very familiar with the Scriptures, and used their language extensively and almost subconsciously in her hymns. She enjoyed piecing together what she called "a bit of Bible mosaic," and had learned by heart much of the Scriptures, so that her mind was saturated with them, and the sacred words and phrases came to be part of her vocabulary. In a preface to a short collection of her hymns she claimed that almost every line had been taken from the Bible or could be proved therefrom. Of her hymns she wrote, "Writing is praying with me, for I never seem to write even a verse by myself, and I feel like a little child writing. You know a child would look up after every sentence and say, 'And what shall I say next?' This is just what I do. I ask that at every line He would give me, not merely thoughts and power, but also every word, even the very rhymes. Very often I have a most distinct and happy consciousness of direct answers." Miss Havergal died at Oystermouth, Glamorganshire, while on holiday on June 3, 1879. Her poems in "Church Hymnal" are:—

164 "O Saviour, Precious Saviour"
196 "Thou Art Coming, O My Saviour"
230 "I Gave My Life for Thee"
256 "I Am Trusting Thee"
273 "Take My Life, and Let it Be"
279 "Live Out Thy Life Within Me"
407 "Lord, Speak to Me"

WILLIAM WALSHAM HOW (1823-97) was born at Shrewsbury, Shropshire, on December 13, 1823, and educated at the famous Public School there and afterwards at Wadham College, Oxford. He became a curate at Kidderminster in 1845, was ordained in 1946, and returned to Shropshire, serving in various districts as curate, rector, rural dean, and canon. In 1879 he was appointed bishop of Bedford, a diocese which then included the slum area of East London. There he practised his motto: "Feed with the Word, feed with life," and he revived the spiritual life of his churches by his kindly, sympathetic ministry. He appealed so much to his flock that he was variously known as the children's bishop, the poor man's bishop, and the omnibus bishop. He declined promotion to the much more lucrative bishopric of Durham, but did transfer in 1888 to become bishop of Wakefield. How wrote many poems, sermons, and other prose, sixty hymns, and was joint editor with his friend John Ellerton (see No. 34 *et al.*) of "Church Hymns," which was issued by the Society for the Promotion of Christian Knowledge in 1871, and which was more popular to Anglicans with low-church leanings than their own "Hymns Ancient and Modern." How died on August 10, 1897, while on holiday in Leenane, County Mayo, Ireland. His hymns selected for "Church Hymnal" are:—

5 "God's Free Mercy Streameth"
133 "On Wings of Living Light"
217 "O Word of God Incarnate"
231 "O Jesus, Thou Art Standing"
364, 365 "For All the Saints"
408 "Lord, Thy Children Guide"
426 "O Holy Lord, Content to Fill"
477 "We Give Thee But Thine Own"

WILLIAM JAMES KIRKPATRICK (1838-1921) was born in Ireland on February 27, 1838, and while still a child emigrated with his parents to the United States, where they settled in Duncannon, Pennsylvania. He worked as a carpenter, but his chief interest was music and he learned to play the violin, 'cello, flute, and fife. He joined the Methodist Episcopal Church at the age of seventeen, and thereafter devoted his life to sacred music. In the American Civil War he served in 1861-62 with the 91st regiment of Pennsylvania Volunteers as principal musician and fife major. For the remainder of the war he was a shipbuilder, and for twelve years thereafter he continued in his trade and worked for a furniture manufacturer in Philadelphia. He had always been interested in Sunday-school work, and in 1859 had edited some camp-meeting songs. He became an organist and musical director in 1865 in Philadelphia, and in 1878 forsook his carpentry and became a writer of gospel songs and editor of sacred music. With John Robson Sweney he compiled nearly fifty song books, and then another forty more of his own. He died on September 29, 1921, in Germantown, Philadelphia, while composing the following words which were found at his feet written in pencil on a piece of paper:

> Just as Thou wilt, Lord, this is my cry:
> Just as Thou wilt, to live or to die.
> I am Thy servant; Thou knowest best:
> Just as Thou wilt, Lord, labour or rest.
> Just as Thou wilt, Lord—which shall it be,
> Life everlasting is waiting for me,
>
> Or shall I tarry here at Thy feet?
> Just as Thou wilt, Lord, whate'er is meet.

Kirkpatrick wrote the words of—

560 "I've Wandered Far Away from God"

and the following tunes, some unnamed:—

275	*Deeper Yet*	6.6.6.6. Refrain
526	*The Comforter Has Come*	6.6.6.6.6.6.6.
549	*Jesus Comes*	L.M. Refrain
556	*Heaven at Last*	8.8.8.5. Refrain
560	*Lord, I'm Coming Home*	8.5.8.5. Refrain
584	*We Have an Anchor*	10.9.10.9. Refrain
588	———	8.7.8.7. Refrain
616	*Wait, and Murmur Not*	L.M. Refrain
619	———	8.7.8.7. Refrain
635	———	9.8.9.8. Refrain
637	*Jesus Saves*	7.6.7.6.7.7.7.6.
651	*He Hideth My Soul*	11.8.11.8. Refrain

ROBERT LOWRY (1826-99) was born in Philadelphia, Pennsylvania, on March 12, 1826. As a child he loved music, and although untrained in musical composition he had natural talent for composing hymn tunes. He attended the Lewisburg University in Pennsylvania and graduated in 1854, and then entered the Baptist ministry, serving in various pastorates in New York, Brooklyn, West Chester, Lewisburg, and later in Plainfield, New Jersey. He actually preferred preaching to hymn-writing and did not begin the latter until he was forty years of age, when the music publishing firm of Biglow and Main asked him to prepare a Sunday school hymnbook. In this he was most successful, for he was the editor of many hymnbooks and Sunday school song books, for example, "Bright Jewels," "Pure Gold," and others, thereby encouraging the gospel song movement in the United States. In New Jersey he was the president of the Baptist Sunday School Union, and in 1872 published a collection of original songs for them. He became professor of rhetoric and literature at Lewisburg, and in 1875 received the degree of Doctor of Divinity from that university. He was appointed chancellor in 1876, which office he held till 1882 in this institution, which is now known as Bucknell University. Lowry died at Plainfield, New Jersey, in 1899. His hymns and tunes in "Church Hymnal" are:—

Hymns:—

265 "My Life Flows On"
555 "Shall We Gather at the River?"
640 "We're Marching to Zion"—chorus only.

Tunes:—

258	*Need*	6.4.6.4. Refrain
259	*Lowry*	8.7.8.7.8.7.8.7.
283	*Something for Jesus*	6.4.6.4.6.6.6.4.
555	———	8.7.8.7. Refrain
622	———	7.6.5.5.6.4.6. Refrain
640	*Marching to Zion*	S.M. Refrain

LOWELL MASON (1792-1872) was born at Medfield, Massachusetts, on January 8, 1792, of a musical father and grandfather. He began work first as a weaver of straw hats, then as a bank clerk in Savannah, Georgia, from 1812. His spare time was devoted to musical activities, for he was organist for and directed the choir of the Presbyterian church, wrote music, and compiled his first collection of psalm tunes in 1820. This latter was published in 1822 by the Handel and Haydn Society of Boston, and its great financial success finally induced Mason to leave Savannah and to settle in Boston in 1827. He became president of the Handel and Haydn Society, and with G. J. Webb (see 354 *et al.*) he founded the Boston Academy of Music in 1832 for the purpose of instructing children as well as adults in music. With W. B. Bradbury and Thomas Hastings he began singing conventions for music teachers and classes for teachers, raising the musical standards of the country by propaganda and by lectures. He agitated for universal musical education in the public schools, and pioneered this work among children, demonstrating it successfully by organizing concerts and festivals conducted by the children themselves. This musical appreciation among the children led to a great interest in music in the next generation. His enthusiasm for music led him to learn to play every type of musical instrument available. He wrote hymn tunes partly to divorce congregations from the prevailing custom of singing only psalms, and they proved very popular to most denominations. Many of his tunes were secular song tunes from Europe which he had gathered on a visit to Germany to study methods of teaching. In 1855 Mason received the degree of Doctor of Music from New York University. This enthusiastic teacher and pioneer of church music died at Orange, New Jersey, on August 11, 1872. Selections in "Church Hymnal" number thirty-eight different tunes, their names often having no associated significance. They were chosen at random, many of them from the Old Testament, others from town or village names in his native New England, others from overseas towns. Note the absence of refrains, which had not come into vogue in his day.

60, 471 *Ernan*	L.M. (8.8.8.8.)
83, 338 *Uxbridge*	L.M.
137 *Ward*	L.M.
140 *Rockingham New*	L.M.
154 *Migdol*	L.M.
161, 190 *Ariel*	8.8.6.8.8.6.
163 *Fountain*	C.M.D. (8.6.8.6.8.6.8.6.)
175 *Zerah*	CM. (8.6.8.6.)
185 *Rodman*	11.10.11.10.
189 *Antioch*	C.M.
205, 502 *Boylston*	S.M. (6.6.8.6.)
220 *Hamburg*	L.M.
227 *Hartel*	L.M.
233 *Downs*	C.M.
246 *Olivet (Harlan)*	6.6.4.6.6.6.4.
249 *Selvin*	S.M.
251 *Herbert*	C.M.
269 *Mount Vernon*	8.7.8.7.
302 *Wesley*	11.10.11.10.
307 *Anvern*	L.M.
322, 333 *Naomi*	C.M.
323 *Henley*	11.10.11.10.
358 *Laban*	S.M.
372 *Bonar*	S.M.D. (6.6.8.6.6.6.8.6.)

379, 432, 439	*Dennis*	S.M.
382	*Bethany*	6.4.6.4.6.6.6.4.
384	*Meribah*	8.8.6.8.8.6.
438	*Azmon*	C.M.
445	*Missionary Hymn (Heber)*	7.6.7.6.7.6.7.6.
446	*Work Song*	7.6.7.5.7.6.7.5.
456	*Hebron*	L.M.
457	*Nashville*	8.8.8.8.8.8.
462	*Sabbath*	7.7.7.7.7.7.7.7.
463	*Mendebras*	7.6.7.6.7.6.7.6.
512	*Dort*	6.6.4.6.6.6.4.
515	*Malvern*	L.M.
535	*Olden*	L.M.
659	*Oak*	6.4.6.4.6.6.6.4.

HAROLD AMADEUS MILLER (1891-1966) was born at Tonawanda, New York, on November 14, 1891. In early childhood his parents were Seventh-day Adventists, but due to many activities occurring on Friday evenings in which their two older sons were involved, they gradually drifted away from the church. Miller's father was a musician and piano teacher, who had also instructed Harold, who showed a marked interest in and a talent for music. In fact, during his father's absence for study in Vienna, Austria, Harold, then sixteen years old, carried on teaching Miller senior's piano pupils. The family moved to Syracuse, New York, to re-establish connections with the Seventh-day Adventist Church, and the Miller boys here became acquainted with students from the South Lancaster Academy, Massachusetts (now Atlantic Union College). It was here that Harold Miller read of Mozart's dislike for his middle name Gottlieb, and of his decision to change it to Amadeus, which is the Latin form of the original German, meaning God-loved. Seeing that he himself was named Harold Gottlieb, and disliking this second name (that of an uncle), Miller decided to follow Mozart's lead, and henceforth became H. A. instead of H. G. Miller. He attended the Academy, where he was later baptized, and joined the Seventh-day Adventist Church at Syracuse. He was soon invited to become head of the music department at Mount Vernon Academy, where he remained for thirteen years from 1916 to 1929. Then he served as music teacher, choir leader, and music director, in Washington Missionary College, Maryland (now Columbia Union College), in Southern Junior College, Tennessee, in Union College, Nebraska, in Pacific Union College, California, and in Southern Missionary College, Tennessee, totalling thirty-seven years of musical service in Seventh-day Adventist educational institutions. His tunes were dedicated to teachers, to students, and to friends who were interested in his compositions, and were written solely as a contribution to the work and progress of the church he loved and served. He passed to rest on December 6, 1966. Of his more than 200 published hymns and songs, the following ten tunes are included in "Church Hymnal":—

23	*Preston*	8.7.8.7.8.7.8.7.
28	*Rogers*	8.8.8.8. (L.M.)
59	*Vesper*	8.6.8.6. (C.M.)
79	*Schroeder*	8.8.8.8.
80	*Massachusetts*	8.8.8.8.
147	*Collegedale*	8.6.8.6.
170	*Jenkins*	6.6.8.6.6.6.8.6.
215	*Wirak*	7.7.7.7.
236	*Branson*	8.6.8.6.
240	*Woods*	8.8.8.8.

JAMES MONTGOMERY (1771-1854) was born at Irvine, Ayrshire, on November 4, 1771, of Irish parents who belonged to the Moravian faith. They went to the West Indies as missionaries, and sent James, then a boy of seven years, to the Fulneck Seminary near Leeds, Yorkshire, to train for the ministry. He devoted more attention to poetry, which was forbidden at the school, than to his studies, and on the death of his parents, left school and found work as a shop-assistant. He went to London to try to eke out a living by selling his poems, but was unsuccessful, and in 1792 he became assistant printer of the *Sheffield Register.* Two years later, the owner-editor of this paper, Robert Gales, fled the country to avoid prosecution because of the radical views he had published, and Montgomery took over the business, remaining as editor for thirty-one years. He changed its name to the *Sheffield Iris,* but, he, too, got into trouble with the authorities for his articles, and suffered terms of imprisonment in 1795 and 1796. Montgomery was a devout member of the Church of England, and a strong supporter of the British and Foreign Bible Society, and of foreign missions. He possessed childlike simplicity and strong faith in God, and denounced vigorously the slave traffic then prevalent, influenced doubtless by the fact that his parents had worked for the West Indian slaves. He wrote many secular poems which in his own estimation—and confirmed by posterity—were of less value than his 400 hymns. His paraphrases of the psalms and his hymns show his wide knowledge of the Scriptures. Next to Watts and Wesley he was an outstanding contributor to English hymnody. He died in Sheffield on April 30, 1854, and is honoured by a stained-glass window in the Parish Church there. His hymns are:—

113 "Angels from the Realms of Glory"
122 "Go to Dark Gethsemane"
153 "Come, Let Us Sing the Song of Songs"
253 "The Tempter to My Soul Hath Said"

257 "Call Jehovah Thy Salvation"
319 "Prayer Is the Soul's Sincere Desire"
327 "In the Hour of Trial"
347 "Work While It Is Today"
381 "O Who, in Such a World as This"
405 "The Lord Is My Shepherd"

JOHN MASON NEALE (1818-66) was born in London, England, on January 24, 1818, and educated at Sherborne Grammar School, Dorset, and Trinity College, Cambridge. He showed a marked talent for writing sacred poetry, carrying off prizes eleven times at the University. He was expert at linguistics also, and during his lifetime had a working knowledge of twenty languages. He used both of these talents to good effect in his pioneer work of translating Greek and Latin hymns of the early church, and making of their irregular metres excellent poems in English. Neale was ordained in 1841, but his strong leaning toward high church practices, coupled, too, with his poor health, led him into a life of comparative obscurity. Though interested in the Oxford Movement, which resulted in many Anglican clergymen joining the Church of Rome, he remained in the Church of England. From 1846 until his death he was warden of Sackville College, East Grinstead, Surrey, virtually an old men's home, a position which earned him a mere pittance, but which nevertheless did give him opportunity to use his classical scholarship. His efforts to help the poor, the orphans, and the unfortunate, were misunderstood, but his poetic and linguistic talent was recognized and rewarded by the honorary degree of Doctor of Divinity granted by Harvard University. Neale was a very humble man, claiming no rights for his hymns, but making them freely available to any who wished to use them, considering them as an offering to the work of God. While the substance of his hymns was provided in the originals, quite often his translations are completely new creations, and always show his original poetic talent. Neale died at East Grinstead, Surrey, on August 6, 1866. His hymns selected in "Church Hymnal" are:—

15 "All Glory, Laud and Honor"
109 "O Come, O Come, Immanuel"
135 "The Day of Resurrection"
136 "Come, Ye Faithful"
202 "O What Their Joy Must Be"
300 "Jerusalem the Golden"
341 "Art Thou Weary?"
367 "Christian, Dost Thou See Them?"
377 "O Happy Band of Pilgrims"
487 "Christ Is Made the Sure Foundation"
672 "A Great and Mighty Wonder"

JOHN NEWTON (1725-1807) was born in London on July 24, 1725, his father, who was rarely at home, being a ship's captain, and his mother a sincere Christian woman, a Dissenter, who taught him to pray, and who intended to dedicate him to the ministry. However, she died just before he was seven years old, and four years later, on his eleventh birthday, he went to sea on his father's ship and made five voyages to the Mediterranean. In 1744 he was impressed as a midshipman on a man-of-war, but he deserted, was recaptured, and demoted. He was transferred to a West African trading ship and engaged in the slave trade on this coast, an occupation which in his day was not incompatible with religion. Although Newton wished for a more humane profession, he nevertheless became the captain of a slave ship, but he fell on hard times and bound himself to an unscrupulous slave dealer, and in miserable conditions virtually served as a slave himself. He was providentially found by the captain of another ship who was under direction from Newton's father, and with him he returned to England by a circuitous route, although the ship was almost wrecked on its voyage. Throughout his chequered career, Newton's conscience was never completely stifled, possibly due to a large extent to his devoted Christian wife, Mary Catlett, whom he married in 1750. His recovery from a malignant fever in Africa, the "white man's grave," his reading of Thomas a Kempis's book on "The Imitation of Christ," and his deliverance from a terrible storm at sea in 1748, were all potent factors in bringing him back to Christ. He forsook the sea in 1755 and settled in Liverpool, becoming a tide-surveyor there, and his conversion was strengthened and established by his contact with Wesley and Whitefield. He decided to study for the ministry and finally, in 1764, was ordained and appointed as curate at Olney, Buckinghamshire. There he was joined by the poet William Cowper, and they conducted a series of revival meetings in the town. Together they published the "Olney Hymns" in 1779, Newton contributing 280 of them and Cowper sixty-eight. These hymns were designed to promote faith and to comfort sincere Christians, and consisted of 141 hymns on Bible texts, 100 occasional hymns, and 107 miscellaneous ones. In 1779 Newton transferred to St. Mary Woolnoth, in Lombard Street,. London, where he remained until his death on December 21, 1807. His dying words were, "My memory is nearly gone, but I remember two things—that I am a great sinner, and that Jesus Christ is a great Saviour." His epitaph, composed by himself, in St. Mary Woolnoth, where he is buried, reads: "John Newton, clerk, once an infidel and libertine; a servant of slaves in Africa; was by the rich mercy of our Lord and Saviour Jesus Christ, preserved, restored, pardoned, and appointed to preach the faith he had long laboured to destroy, near sixteen years at Olney in Bucks, and twenty-seven years in this church."

"Church Hymnal" contains seven hymns by Newton, as follows:—

25 "Again Our Earthly Cares We Leave"
150 "How Sweet the Name"
295 "Amazing Grace"
304 "Glorious Things of Thee Are Spoken"
318 "Come, My Soul"
462 "Safely Through Another Week"
660 "How Tedious and Tasteless the Hours"

WILLIAM AUGUSTINE OGDEN (1841-97) was born in Franklin County, Ohio, on October 10, 1841, and moved with his parents to Indiana in 1847. As a child he showed much musical talent, and while engaged in the American Civil War he organized a male choir. After hostilities ceased he resumed his musical studies under Thomas Hastings and Lowell Mason in Boston. In 1870 he published his "Silver Song," which was tremendously successful, selling half a million copies. His "New Silver Song for Sunday School," published in 1872 at Toledo, Ohio, contains ninety-eight tunes and nine hymns by Ogden. He became a teacher of music and conducted large choirs at various conventions both in the United States and Canada. He moved to Toledo, Ohio, in 1881, and six years later was appointed superintendent of music in the public schools, which position he held until his death on October 14, 1897. He published eighteen song books, some in conjunction with other musicians, composed two oratorios—"Josiah" and "The Birth of Christ"—and also two cantatas. His hymns and tunes selected in "Church Hymnal" are:—

Hymn:

345 "Working, O Christ, With Thee"

Tune:

625	*Bring Them In*	8.8.8.8. Refrain

Hymns and Tunes:

344	"Anywhere, Dear Saviour"	
	Anywhere, Dear Saviour	6.5.6.6.7.7.10.
525	"Baptize Us Anew"	
	Baptize Us Anew	5.5.6.5. Refrain
572	"Jesus, the Loving Shepherd"	
	Lovingly, Tenderly Calling	7.6.7.6.7.6.7.6. Refrain

HORATIO RICHMOND PALMER (1834-1907) was born at Sherburne, New York, in 1834, and at the early age of seventeen became a church organist. He showed great musical ability and in 1857 was appointed director of the Rushford Academy of Music in New York. In 1861 he transferred to Chicago, but returned to New York in 1874. The University of Chicago conferred on him the degree of Doctor of Music in 1880. In 1884 he directed the Church Choral Union, which considerably improved church music and had a membership of 4,000 singers. Three years later he became dean of the summer school of music at Chautauqua (see Nos. 51, 218) in the Finger Lakes region of New York State, and directed the choir there for the next fourteen years. Palmer was the author of several works on the theory of music as well as being composer, lecturer on music, and music publisher, and his choral collections proved to be very popular and good sellers. He studied music overseas both at Berlin and at Florence. He died at Yonkers, New York, in 1907. His contributions to "Church Hymnal" are:—

Words:

498	"Yield Not to Temptation"	
565	"Christ Is Knocking at My Sad Heart"	

Tunes:

498	*Palmer*	6.5.6.5.6.5.6.5. Refrain
564	*Come, Sinner, Come!*	7.4.7.4.7.4.7.4.
565	*Shall I Let Him In?*	8.5.9.6.8.8.9.6.
604	*Vincent*	8.4.8.4.8.4.8.4.
677	*Peace, Be Still!*	8.7.9.7.8.6.10.7. Refrain

WILLIAM FISK SHERWIN (1826-88) was born in 1826 and as a young man joined the Baptist Church. He studied under Lowell Mason and became a teacher of vocal music. He was particularly interested in the development and growth of Sunday schools, and composed many hymn tunes for use in developing these schools. He was an outstanding choral group leader, genial and enthusiastic, and these qualities led him to be chosen by the Chautauqua Literary and Scientific Society (see Nos. 51, 218) as their organizer, music director, and chorus director for their annual gatherings at Lake Chautauqua in the Finger Lakes District of New York State. Sherwin died in 1888. His hymns in "Church Hymnal" are:—

Words:

499	"Sound the Battle Cry"	
649	"Wake the Song"	

Tunes:

51	*Chautauqua*	7.7.7.7.4. Refrain
218	*Bread of Life*	6.4.6.4.6.4.6.4.
375	*Sherwin*	11.10.11.10. Refrain
499	*Battle Cry*	5.5.5.3.5.5.5.4. Refrain
550	———	8.6.8.6. Refrain
649	*Anniversary Song*	8.8.8.7.8.8.8.7. Refrain

ANNIE REBEKAH SMITH (1828-55), only daughter of Samuel and Rebekah Spalding Smith, was born at West Wilton, New Hampshire, on March 16, 1828. She joined the Baptist Church in 1838, and became a follower of William Miller, but after the disappointment of October, 1844, lost interest in the teaching on the second advent of Christ. She trained to become a school teacher, later specializing in painting, and in 1851, while in her profession in Charlestown, Massachusetts, received a letter from her mother inviting her to attend a meeting conducted by Joseph Bates in Somerville, two miles away. She decided to go merely to please her mother, and dreamed that she did go, that she arrived late, seated herself near the door, and heard a sermon on the 2,300 days of Daniel 8: 14. On the evening of the actual meeting she started in good time but missed her way, and the dream was then fulfilled in every detail. The preacher, Bates, who was then a Sabbath-keeper, had also had a complementary dream which was realized that evening also. In three weeks Annie had decided to keep the seventh-day Sabbath, and she thereupon devoted her poetic talent to writing for the Seventh-day Adventist church paper, the *Review and Herald.* Her first effort, "Fear Not, Little Flock," appeared in the issue of September 16, 1851 (now hymn No. 664), and led to her being invited in 1852 to join the editorial staff, then at Saratoga Springs, New York. She refused at first because of her poor health and weak eyes, but after being urged, accepted, and then her eye affliction was healed through special prayer. She did proof-reading, copy-editing, and became assistant editor, refusing other much more remunerative positions offered to her in the teaching profession. She contracted tuberculosis and died at Wilton on July 26, 1855, after less than four years' service to the church. In this brief period, she wrote numerous hymns which made a permanent impression on the early believers and brought encouragement to those who laid the foundation of the church which was later to be named Seventh-day Adventist. Annie Smith's book, "Home Here, and Home in Heaven," 1855, contains twenty-five hymns as well as miscellaneous poems, and sixteen other poems were published after her death in a book issued by her mother. Two days before her death she composed her last lines, as follows:—

"Oh, shed not a tear o'er the spot where I sleep,
For the living and not for the dead ye may weep;
Why mourn for the weary who sweetly repose,
Free in the grave from life's burden of woes?
I long now to rest in the lone, quiet tomb,
For the footsteps of Jesus have lightened its gloom;
I die in the hope of soon meeting again
The friends that I love, with Him ever to reign."

The distinctive doctrines of the second advent, with its hope of heaven, will be noted in most of her present contributions.

247 "Toil on a Little Longer"
251 "I Ask Not, Lord, For Less"
268 "Blessed Jesus, Meek and Lowly"
312 "Weeping Endures But For a Night"
314 "When Darkness Gathers"
371 "I Saw One Weary"
457 "Hail, Peaceful Day"
494 "He Sleeps in Jesus"
664 "Long Upon the Mountains"
665 "How Far From Home?"

GEORGE COLES STEBBINS (1846-1945) was born on a farm in East Carlton, Orleans County, New York, on February 26, 1846. At the age of thirteen he decided to become a professional musician, and the next year he attended a singing school. He moved to Chicago in 1868 and was a clerk in a music store. The next year he was selling song books in Chicago and finding outlets for his musical gift. He became director of music at the First Baptist church there in 1870, and in 1874 was the choir director of the Clarendon Street Baptist church in Boston under its pastor, Dr. A. J. Gordon. There he met Dwight Lyman Moody and joined the Moody-Sankey evangelistic team as a singer in 1876, remaining with them until 1900. Stebbins accompanied the evangelists in three overseas campaigns, one of them in Great Britain from 1883-85, where he composed many of his tunes. He was an intimate friend also of Fanny Crosby, and composed tunes for many of her poems, e.g., Nos. 569 and 630. He produced for Moody's campaigns a large number of gospel song books in collaboration with Ira David Sankey and James McGranahan, deliberately using his talent for writing music in the service of the gospel of Jesus Christ. He distinguished between a church hymn and a gospel song by defining the former as invoking God, the latter as inviting man. He died a few months short of his hundredth birthday, on October 6, 1945. From his 1,500 tunes, the "Church Hymnal" uses:—

49	*Evening Prayer*	8.7.8.7.
272	*Stebbins*	9.9.9.9.
531	*Friend*	8.7.8.7.8.7.8.7.
569	———	10.8.10.7. Refrain
603	———	6.5.6.5.6.5.6.5.
624	———	10.10.10.11. Refrain
630	*Saved by Grace*	8.8.8.8. Refrain
639	———	7.6.7.6.7.6.7.6.

ARTHUR SEYMOUR SULLIVAN (1842-1900) was born at Lambeth, London, on May 13, 1842, his father being an Irish bandmaster and teacher of music. He inherited a talent for music, and by the time he was eight years old he could play every wind instrument in his father's band. In 1854 he was a chorister at the Chapel Royal and he won a scholarship at the Royal Academy of Music in 1856, taking first place above Joseph Barnby. This enabled him to study music on the Continent, so he spent over two years in the conservatorium at Leipzig. His voice had now broken so he studied piano, theory, composition, orchestration, and conducting, returning to London in 1861. He was church organist at St. Michael's, Chester Square, London, and a teacher of music devoting much of his time to composition. In 1867 he became professor of composition at the Royal Academy, and was appointed musical editor of "Church Hymns," composing most of his hymn-tunes during the period 1867 to 1874. He was principal from 1876-82 of the National Training School of Music, which later became the Royal College of Music. For his services to music he received the honorary degree of Mus. Doc. from Cambridge in 1876 and from Oxford in 1879, and a knighthood from the Queen in 1883. He is well remembered for his association with W. S. Gilbert and the light music of the Savoy operas, but he composed excellent oratorios, overtures, anthems, secular songs, and church and choral music. He died in Westminster, London, on November 22, 1900, and was buried in St. Paul's Cathedral. His tunes in "Church Hymnal" are:—

19	*Angel Voices*	8.5.8.5.8.4.3.
95	*Noel*	8.6.8.6.8.6.8.6. (C.M.D.)
136	*St. Kevin*	7.6.7.6.7.6.7.6.
263	*Courage, Brother*	8.7.8.7.8.7.8.7.
284	*Leominster*	6.6.8.6.6.6.8.6. (S.M.D.)
319	*Audite Audientes Me*	8.6.8.6.8.6.8.6.
345	*St. Edmund*	6.4.6.4.6.6.6.4.
360	*St. Gertrude*	6.5.6.5.6.5.6.5. Refrain
428	*Samuel*	6.6.6.6.8.8.
475	*Nauford*	8.8.8.4.

JOHN ROBSON SWENEY (1837-99) was born at West Chester, Pennsylvania, in 1837, and became a prominent member of the Methodist church there. While still a boy he showed his musical ability by composing a piece of music, and by the time he was twenty-two years old he was teaching music. In the American Civil War he led a military band, and after being discharged, joined the Pennsylvania Military Academy in Chester, Pennsylvania, as professor of music. He received the degrees of Mus. Bac. and Mus. Doc. from this institution. In 1871 he turned his attention to writing sacred music, and thenceforth concentrated his talent on composing hymn-tunes. He was a pianist and a violinist, and also a song leader in the Sunday school, and a choir leader. He was responsible for editing over sixty hymnbooks and gospel song books, collaborating with William James Kirkpatrick in publishing many of them. Sweney died on April 10, 1899. "Church Hymnal" contains eight of his tunes, each having a refrain, namely:—

212	*Sweney*	8.7.8.7. Refrain
534	———	8.7.8.7.8.7.8.7. Refrain
538	*He Will Gather the Wheat*	9.8.9.8. Refrain
554	*Beulah Land*	8.8.8.8. Refrain
596	———	8.7.8.7. Refrain
607	———	8.6.8.6. Refrain
626	*Will There Be Any Stars?*	12.9.12.9. Refrain
642	*We Are Nearing Home!*	11.11.11.11. Refrain

ISAAC WATTS (1674-1748) was born in Southampton, England, on July 17, 1674, to a family of Huguenot ancestry who had been persecuted for their religious convictions. He followed the Nonconformist practices of his parents, and was therefore denied an education in the University, which would prepare him for the ministry of the Anglican Church only. Watts was an inveterate versifier from childhood, and at the age of eighteen he complained to his father, a deacon in the Independent congregation, of the poor hymns that were sung. It was the custom then to "line out" the psalms for the people to sing line by line, as a large majority were illiterate. His father sarcastically suggested that young Isaac write better ones, and the son took the father at his word, preparing for the next Sunday a hymn based on Revelation 5: 6-10, beginning:—

> Behold the glories of the Lamb
> Amidst His Father's throne,
> Prepare new honours for His name
> And songs as yet unknown.

He kept this up week by week for two whole years, bringing satisfaction to the congregation at Southampton, and starting a revolution in hymn-singing throughout the world. He had already spent two years, 1690-1692, in a Nonconformist academy in Stoke Newington, London, studying to become a minister of the gospel. He became a private tutor in 1696 in the family of Sir John Hartopp in London, assistant pastor of the Mark Lane congregation of Independents in London in 1698, and sole pastor in 1700. From his birth he was never in robust health, and as an adult he was only five feet tall and of unprepossessing appearance. A fever in 1712 incapacitated him physically, but did not affect his very acute mind. After this illness, he entered the home of his friend Sir Thomas Abney at Stoke Newington, and lived there the life of a semi-invalid for the remaining thirty-six years of his life. In 1728 he was honoured by the University of Edinburgh with the degree of Doctor of Divinity. Watts wrote about 600 hymns, which were well received by Anglicans as well as by Dissenters, and their popularity helped to ease the friction between these two religious groups. He paraphrased all the 150 psalms of David in "The Psalms of David Imitated, 1719," departing from the actual wording and rewriting them from a Christian, instead of from a Jewish standpoint. For example, he modified the Old Testament references to sacrificial bullocks to the New Testament sacrifice of Christ; the singing in Zion to the ascension of Christ; and the promises of material blessings on the Israelites to the blessings of grace and the glories of eternal life to the believers. So he turned David's imprecatory psalms against his enemies into hatred against sin and against Satan its author. Without doubt he was one of the greatest British hymn writers, and pioneered a new mode of religious expression, and his "Hymns and Spiritual Songs, 1707," was the first real hymnbook of the English language. He died on November 25, 1748, and was buried in Bunhill Fields, London. A memorial bust stands to his honour in the Poet's Corner in Westminster Abbey. His hymns in "Church Hymnal" are as follows, nearly all of them written in short, common, or long metre, due probably to the lack of tunes in other metres available at that time, and also doubtless to the fact that his hymns were a sufficient innovation in themselves to psalm-singing congregations:—

1 "Before Jehovah's Awful Throne"
2 "From All That Dwell Below the Skies"
4 "With Reverence Let the Saints Appear"
11 "The Lord Jehovah Reigns"
14 "Praise Ye the Lord"
24 "How Pleasant, How Divinely Fair"
39 "Lord, in the Morning"
46 "Sweet Is the Work, My God"
69 "High in the Heavens"
72 "Early, My God, Without Delay"
81 "O God, Our Help"
89 "God Is the Refuge"
93 "I Sing the Mighty Power"
118, 119, 120 "When I Survey the Wondrous Cross"
124 "Alas! and Did My Saviour Bleed?"
140 "My Blest Redeemer"
172 "Come, Sound His Praise"
179 "He Reigns! the Lord, the Saviour, Reigns!"
189 "Joy to the World"
209 "Come, Holy Spirit"
240 "Show Pity, Lord"
242 " 'Tis by the Faith of Joys"
299 "There Is a Land of Pure Delight"
356 "Am I a Soldier of the Cross?"
392 "Unshaken as the Sacred Hills"
414 "My God, How Endless Is Thy Love!"
440 "Go, Preach My Gospel"
442 "How Beauteous Are Their Feet"
472 "Jesus Invites His Saints"
640 "Come, We That Love the Lord"

CHARLES WESLEY (1707-88) was born at Epworth, Lincolnshire, on December 18, 1707, the youngest of the family of eighteen children of an Anglican country parson. He went to Westminster School, London, where his older brother John already was, and was captain of the school in 1726. He proceeded to Christ Church College, Oxford, gaining his degree in 1729. While at the University, he and his brother John and George Whitefield and a few others founded the "Holy Club," which adopted methodical study, prayer, fasting, and devotional habits, attended communion service regularly, and devoted itself to philanthropic works. The strict rules and regular methods of the club members for prayer and devotion later gave the name Methodist to the adherents of the Wesley brothers. Charles was ordained a minister of the Church of England, and in 1735 he went to Georgia as secretary to the governor, General Oglethorpe. On the voyage over the Atlantic during a terrible storm, when the mast broke and the mainsail split, he was greatly impressed by the quiet Christian confidence of a party of twenty-six Moravian immigrants, travelling from Germany to Savannah, and realized that he himself lacked much in his spiritual life. He returned from Georgia in 1736 a failure, and in England two years later came under the influence of another Moravian, Peter Bŏhler. On Whit Sunday, May 21, 1738, Charles was truly converted (see No. 155). He was an itinerant preacher in England, Scotland, and Wales until 1749, when he married Sally Gwynne and settled in Bristol in the west of England. He disapproved of his brother John's ordination of Wesleyan preachers, and maintained his connection with the Church of England until his death. "I have lived," he said, "and I die in the communion of the Church of England, and I will be buried in the yard of my parish church." He died on Marcn 29, 1788, and was buried, not in City Road, but in the churchyard of St. Marylebone, North London. Wesley had a gift for poetry, and wrote verse continually, his letters and his love letters being in rhyme. Even on his death-bed he dictated a hymn beginning—"In age and feebleness extreme." He was a most prolific hymn writer, being credited with over 6,500 hymns, most of them long ones! Many of them are personal, showing great depth of feeling, and they appealed to the spiritually starved people who, under Wesley's preaching, found renewed life, hope, and faith in the Scriptures. Charles's son Samuel (1766-1837) was a noted composer with High Church leanings, especially musically, and Samuel's son, Samuel Sebastian (1810-76), was a noted cathedral organist. Wesley's hymns in "Church Hymnal" are:—

18 "O For a Heart to Praise My God"
47 "Forth in Thy Name"
68 "Jesus, Lord, We Look to Thee"
80 "Holy as Thou, O Lord"
83 "God of My Life"
111 "Hark! the Herald Angels Sing"
131 "Hail the Day That Sees Him Rise"
132 "Our Lord Is Risen"
134 "Christ the Lord Is Risen Today"
142 "Love Divine"
148 "O Love Divine, How Sweet Thou Art!"
151 "O Love Divine, What Hast Thou Done!"

155 "O For a Thousand Tongues"
169 "Thou Hidden Source"
176 "Lo! He Comes"
200 "I Long to Behold Him"
233 "Jesus, to Thee I Now Can Fly"
234 "Depth of Mercy!"
243 "Come, O Thou Traveller"
250 "When, My Saviour, Shall I Be"
292 "O How Happy Are They"
293 "Awake! Jerusalem, Awake!
342 "Ye Servants of God"
366 "Soldiers of Christ, Arise"
369 "Come, Let Us Anew"
384 "O God, Mine Inmost Soul Convert"
401, 402 "Jesus, Lover of My Soul"
670 "Father, I Stretch My Hands"

CATHERINE WINKWORTH (1827-78) was born at Ely Place, Holborn, London, on September 13, 1827, and lived first near Manchester, and then later in life at Clifton, Bristol. She was very gifted intellectually without being proud or aloof, rather she showed genuine culture and refinement. She had an intimate knowledge of the German language, and understood the religious feelings of these people. Not only so, but she was able to convey this sentiment in her translations of German hymns, and these works proved to be devotional classics. They were entitled *"Lyra Germanica,"* the first series being published in 1855 and proving so popular that it ran into twenty-three editions, and the second series, appearing in 1858, went into twelve editions. Miss Winkworth also wrote "Christian Singers of Germany" in 1869, and also the "Chorale Book for England" in 1863, the latter being a collection of good chorale tunes from Germany. She died suddenly at Monnetier in Savoy, France, on July 1, 1878. Her translations in "Church Hymnal" are:—

12 "Praise to the Lord"
27 "Blessed Jesus, at Thy Word"
55 "Now God Be With Us"
90 "Now Thank We All Our God"
110 "All My Heart This Night Rejoices"
197 "Wake, Awake, for Night Is Flying"
294 "Lift Up Your Hands"

ISAAC BAKER WOODBURY (1819-58) was born in Beverley, Massachusetts, and at the age of thirteen went to Boston in order to study music, which was the dominant factor in his life. He learned to be a blacksmith, but, after teaching himself music, devoted his time to playing, editing, and composing music. He learned the violin, and promoted singing in schools and in choirs. When nineteen years old, he went for a year's study of music to London and Paris, the first of his many visits to Europe. He founded a musical association in Vermont and directed singing schools and composed many popular secular songs. In 1849 he settled in New York and became a music teacher, and edited *The Musical Review* and *The Musical Pioneer*. With collaborators he compiled in 1842 the Boston Musical Education Society's "Collection of Church Music," and in 1845, "The Choral." Another of his publications was "The New Lute of Zion," in which he expressed his ideals on music as follows: "The music is designed not for the fastidious and scientific musicians whose highest delight, and perhaps sole worship is music as an art, but for those who love to worship God in the simple song of praise." Woodbury was never in very good health and made frequent journeys seeking a cure. On one of these to the southern states of America he died at Columbia, South Carolina, in 1858, at the very early age of thirty-nine. He has one hymn with its tune, and five other different tunes in "Church Hymnal," namely:—

Words:

444 "Ho! Reapers of Life's Harvest"

Tunes:

24	*Burton*	8.8.8.8. (L.M.)
173	*Faithful*	11.8.11.8.11.8.11.8.
243	*Selena*	8.8.8.8.8.8.
339	*Chopin*	8.6.8.6. (C.M.)
340, 431	*Siloam*	8.6.8.6.
444	*Life's Harvest*	7.6.7.6.7.6.7.6.

Scriptural Index

Index of Composers and Arrangers of Tunes

Index of Tunes

Index of Authors, Arrangers, and Translators

Index of First Lines

Supplementary Index of First Lines

which are not first lines in Church Hymnal